# Rural Development in India

(PAST, PRESENT AND FUTURE)

CHALLENGE IN THE CRISIS

# Rural Development in India

## (PAST, PRESENT AND FUTURE)
## CHALLENGE IN THE CRISIS

VASANT DESAI

Himalaya Publishing House
ISO 9001:2015 CERTIFIED

Second Revised Edition : 2005
Reprint : 2007, 2009, 2010, 2012, 2013, 2015, 2018
Reprint : 2020
Reprint : 2024

Published by : Mrs. Meena Pandey
for **HIMALAYA PUBLISHING HOUSE PVT. LTD.,**
"Ramdoot", Dr. Bhalerao Marg, Girgaon, Mumbai - 400 004.
**Phone:** 022-23860170, 23863863; **Fax:** 022-23877178
**E-mail:** himpub@bharatmail.co.in; **Website:** www.himpub.com

Branch Offices :

New Delhi : "Pooja Apartments", 4-B, Murari Lal Street, Ansari Road, Darya Ganj, New Delhi - 110 002. Phone: 011-23270392, 23278631; Fax: 011-23256286

Nagpur : Kundanlal Chandak Industrial Estate, Ghat Road, Nagpur - 440 018. Phone: 0712-2721215, 2721216

Bengaluru : Plot No. 91-33, 2nd Main Road, Seshadripuram, Behind Nataraja Theatre, Bengaluru - 560 020. Phone: 080-41138821; Mobile: 09379847017, 09379847005

Hyderabad : No. 3-4-184, Lingampally, Besides Raghavendra Swamy Matham, Kachiguda, Hyderabad - 500 027. Phone: 040-27560041, 27550139

Chennai : No. 34/44, Motilal Street, T. Nagar, Chennai - 600 017. Mobile: 09380460419

Pune : "Laksha" Apartment, First Floor, No. 527, Mehunpura, Shaniwarpeth (Near Prabhat Theatre), Pune - 411 030. Phone: 020-24496323, 24496333; Mobile: 09370579333

Cuttack : Plot No. 5F-755/4, Sector-9, CDA Markat Nagar, Cuttack - 753 014, Odisha. Mobile: 09338746007

Kolkata : 3, S.M. Bose Road, Near Gate No. 5, Agarpara Railway Station, North 24 Parganas, West Bengal - 700 109. Mobile: 09674536325

Printed at : Geetanjali Press Pvt. Ltd., Nagpur. On behalf of HPH.

# || Shradhanjali ||

***"nā jayate mriyate vā kadāchin***
***nāyam bhūtvā bhavita vā na bhūyah***
***ajo nityah sāsvoto yam purano***
***na hanyate hanyamane sarire"***

*"For the soul there is neither birth nor death at any time.*
*He has not come into being, does not come into being*
*& will not come into being.*
*He is unborn, eternal, ever existing and primeval.*
*He is not slain when the body is slain."*

To my parents
**Late Ranganath Balwantrao Mutalik Desai**
(August 16, 1909 - August 23, 2006)

a true *karmayogi* in words and deeds,
a progressive farmer and visionary
&
**Late Laxmidevi Ranganath Mutalik Desai**
(June 19, 1914 - January 14, 2000)

a fond mother, an embodiment of humility

whose inspiration lead to the study of
**Rural Development**
in all its aspects.

In one lifetime,
you did enough to inspire generations

People who never met you, or saw you,
are still awed by the generosity of your spirit.

And your vision will help us see far beyond tomorrow.

You gave us so much,
that no one can ever take your place in our hearts.

*Oh. Mother Earth!*

*Yours hills, snowclad mountains, forests,*

*In all shapes and formations*

*Bring happiness to us.*

*I bow to you*

*With all my might, I shall save*

*Your cultivable fertile and nourishing black and red*

*Soils which are strong and resistant,*

*And protected by our ancestors,*

*From getting weak by destruction and degradation*

***(Atharva Veda, Kand-123.)***

(Sukt-I, Mantra-II)

"India is destined to emerge as a major powerhouse of the evolving global economy and in the process also get rid of the chronic poverty, ignorance and disease which still affect large sections of our society."

***– Dr. A.P.J. Abdul Kalam***

"The real India lives in the villages. Unless we are able to uplift the tribals and the backward classes, India faces a dark future."

***– Swami Vivekanand***

"Our aims must be to restore to the villages the power to meet their own requirement."

***– Rabindranath Tagore***

'I shall work for an India in which the poorest shall feel that it is their county in whose making they have an effective voice, an India in which there shall be no high class and low class of people, an India in which all communities shall live in perfect harmony'.

*– Mahatma Gandhi*

**RURAL DEVELOPMENT MISSION STATEMENT**

- Rural development comprises a wide range of activities. Its needs and potential vary greatly from village to village.
- Rural development is essential for combating poverty and improve the standard of living of the people.
- Rural sector activities which provide a source of livelihood to more than 73 per cent of the population, significantly influence the level and pattern of economic development. As such, rural development needs a special recognition by the state.
- Agriculture is the main economic activity. It can be improved through resource development, technological innovation, establishment of up-stream and down-stream linkage industries and general upgrading of the various agricultural support services.
- Integrated development of rural industries is a key input of rural development
- Rural development needs the application of new and innovative modern technology and transparent marketing techniques.
- Rural development needs rural participation, rural awareness, rural urge to grow and prosper and sustain development by playing a catalyst role in the rural society.
- Rural developments success depends on planning, project design and a careful identification of the various target groups in the community and an equally careful assessment of the capacity of local institutions to act as implementing agencies.
- To be effective, it is important that rural development management be decentralised through greater delegation of authority and accountability be given to the local grass root levels.

**CREDO OF RURAL DEVELOPMENT**

Go to the peasant people
Live among the peasant people
Plan with the peasant people
Work with the peasant people
Start with what the peasant. people know
Build on what the peasant people have
Bring in new awareness introduce innovative technology.
Teach marketing strategy. Educate the rural people provide rural infrastructure.
Build skills. Foster rural entrepreneurship improve the quality of work. Build a base of rural wealth motivate to change and growth.
Teach by showing, learn by doing
Not a showcase but a pattern
Not odds and ends but a system
Not piecemeal but integrated approach
Not to conform but to transform
Not relief but release

# RURAL DEVELOPMENT

"The real India lives in the villages. Unless we are able to uplift the tribals and the backward classes, India faces a dark future."

***Swami Vivekananda***

"Go from village to village, do good to humanity and to the world at large."

***Swami Vivekananda***

"If the village perishes, India will perish, too. It will be no more India. Her own mission in the world will get lost. The revival of the village is possible only when it is no more exploited."

***Mahatma Gandhi***

".....the ambition of the greatest man of our generation has been to wipe every tear from every eye. That may be beyond us, but as long as there are tears and suffering, so long our task will not be over...."

***Jawaharlal Nehru***

"The Panchayat shall have all the authority and jurisdiction required. Since there will be no system of punishments in the accepted sense, the Panchayat will be the legislature, judiciary and executive combined to operate for its year of office..... Here, there is perfect democracy based upon individual freedom. The individual is the architect of his own government."

***Mahatma Gandhi***

# NEW RULES

Indian agriculture has witnessed an overall trajectory of growth in three distinct phases.

Yet there are other critical problems. Public investment in agriculture has been almost stagnant for the past decade. With the inability of the government to continue the scale of subsidies, the cost of Indian farm products keeps increasing remorselessly.

Indian farmers, on their part, are grappling with problems of declining soil fertility and water salinity, the rise of complex pest pathologies that affect existing wheat and rice varieties, and a host of other biotic and genomic troubles.

Confronted by multiple crises, Indian agriculture must grow larger and better. First to feed — the 200 million Indians and to accelerate the process of rural development.

The Rural Infrastructure Fund has become a vehicle to finance the official irrigation plan. It must revive to power the Indian farmer and his organisations to diversify, trade and improve his income. All of that will now be WTO-compatible. After Doha, the main challenge is at home. The road map abroad is no longer hazy.

Land and water development groups, local infrastructure projects in road or communication sectors, products developed in R&D institutions, training for production with improved techniques and market development schemes by local and community groups are necessities today. Drainage, soil shaping, contour management, improvement and management of lower-level canals, desilting of tanks, raising embankments, fish culture, market development, controlled grazing and related activities have to grow. Policy reforms required for the replication of such projects on a required scale include lending through a weather or project cycle and financial institution designing structures for community collateral of viable projects.

**Other Voices**

- Buffer stocks are not a cost-effective way of ensuring against food scarcity. Trading is a more efficient way to do that. We find many countries holding far in excess of their requirements. Costs of storage and holding stocks are tremendously high.

  *World Bank adviser **Vijay Vyas,** May 1986*

- The prospects for Indian agriculture can be bright or not bright depending on what you do... We have not had a vision for our agriculture as a major source of economic strength. We have looked upon it as means of feeding the urban population. Whenever we talk of employment we say the agricultural sector should look after itself. Whenever it comes to income it goes somewhere else. This dichotomy must end.

  *ICAR director-general **M.S. Swaminathan,** January 1989*

# INTERESTING INDIA

- India has 2.4% of the world's land, but support 16% of the global population.
- Total geographic area: 329 million hectares.
- Forest cover: 76.5 million hectares or 23.4%.
- Waste lands, which can be re-forested: 7.5 million hectares.
- India has the world's largest rice cultivated area.
- India is the world's 6th largest electricity generating country.
- India also consumes 4% of the total electricity generated.
- World Wildlife Fund, WWF-India is the world's largest wildlife conversation organisation.
- Sunderbans is the world's largest estuarine mangrove forest as well the largest river delta, created by the Ganga and Brahmaputra. Rising sea levels have already begun to erode the Sunderbans.
- Himalayas, the world's youngest mountains are also known as the Water Towers of Asia as they have the largest concentration of glaciers outside the Polar caps.
- It is estimated that changes to the Himalayan glacier ecosystem could reduce India's freshwater availability by as much as 30%.
- Symbolically India is represented by the elephant.

# PREFACE

The development of rural areas and the rural people has been primary concern in the economic planning and development process of the country. It is now realized that to emerge as a strong and modern nation and to secure its rightful place in the comity of nations, sustainable development in rural areas, is an essential prerequisite.

Rural development and Poverty reduction are topmost on India's development agenda. They are interlinked, inter-connected and are the two sides of a same coin. To fulfil these goals, the poor (rural poor) must find new and better opportunities for their livelihood.

Provision of basic social services, such as health care, water and sanitation, and education must also be expanded and improved. Economic growth must enable the poor to engage in the process and benefit from it without devouring the natural resource endowments on which the prospects of our future generations depend.

An effective legal framework for the accountability of public institutions and a capacity of citizens to assert their legal rights are minimum requirements for the sustainability of the rural development goals. Public institutions must have the capacity to deliver appropriate services and assist people in identifying their needs and priorities.

Poor governance, corruption, and lack of accountability forestall development. Legal and institutional reforms will help create conditions for active citizenship so the poor have access to information to enable them to understand and secure their rights.

By increasing accountability, public institutions will become more transparent in their operations, enabling citizens to understand how resources are used and decisions made, and providing clearer avenues for grievance resolution. Active citizenship implies a legal framework that enables citizens to effectively articulate their views.

While the rural development goals are universal, no single approach is likely to be effective everywhere. However, the goal can only be achieved and sustained when the policies, laws, and institutions implicated in this effort are also aligned to meet this challenge.

The majority of the rural poor are landless agricultural labourers and small farmers with large families, limited human resources and little access to credit. Poverty is more prevalent among females than males and among ethnic and minority groups, tribals and dalits.

Although economic growth can reduce poverty by generating employment and incomes. but it is to be supplemented by human development. This means a proper balance between the economic and social agendas. It means ensuring adequate nutrition, health care and education. It means investing in social capital and creating the right policy environment for those investments.

Rural development, over the years, has emerged as "a strategy designed to improve the economic and social life of a specific group of people — the rural poor. It involves extending the benefits of development to the poorest among those who seek a livelihood in the natural areas, This group includes small and marginal farmers, tenants. landless labourers and rural artisans etc." The objectives of rural development encompass improved productivities, increased employment, higher incomes for target groups as well as a minimum acceptable levels of food, clothing, shelter, education and health. Growth with social justice is the objective of Indian economic planning. But the compulsions of the economic situation, as they unfolded themselves over the years, charaterised by a high rate of population growth and less than commensurate increase in food production, adverse weather etc. made pursuit of the growth aspect more imperative than the social justice aspect of development programmes.

The removal of poverty remains a central concern of planning in India. The stress continues to be on complementary strategies, increasing employment, meeting basic needs, reduction in the inequalities in income and wealth, and raising the productivity of the poor – all integrated with human development. Consistent with this objective, the Ninth Plan's development strategy and the pattern of growth emerging from it are expected as lead to a reduction in absolute poverty at a faster rate than in the past. The plan envisaged an expanded coverage under the various anti-poverty programmes. Taking into account the highly comfortable position of food stocks with the public sector, it may be possible to expand the employment oriented anti-poverty programmes at a still faster pace, than envisaged in the plan document. Every effort will be made to plug various loopholes in the operation of anti-poverty programmes and to integrate these and various sectoral and area development programmes into a comprehensive design of integrated development of each area. The plan pays special attention to the problems faced by the more vulnerable sections of our society, such as the scheduled castes, the scheduled tribes, women and children. It recognises that, in a situation in which poverty is pervasive, the perception of needs and priorities must not be a merely "male" perception but must take into account explicity the special needs and problems of women.

Of course, these are all intricately linked. Poverty reduction cannot occur without infrastructure development — the provision of roads, electricity, water and sanitation, transportation and communication. Nor can it occur without improvement in health, education, job creation and livelihood outcomes, which in turn depend substantially on the quality of infrastructure. So, if poverty reduction is the overarching goal of the country development agenda, then infrastructure and human development along with livelihood opportunities must form the core of the poverty reduction strategy.

The thrust has been laid on faster agricultural growth, agricultural diversification, push towards agro-processing and the encouragement of rural-based industries.

In a multi-pronged attack on rural poverty and rural development, the emphasis should be on the importance of constituting a decentralised planning authority and setting up machinery at the district level to formulate an integrated district/block/village development plans which would combine both the development and beneficiary aspects, with the shared objective of amelioration of poverty. More importantly, stress on rural development is an integrated manner. The need of the hour is that rural development programme must be devised to synchronise with self-reliance and self-respect. The plans of action should be re-oriented to operate their own programme and ensure rural development on an ongoing basis. I firmly believe that the only way to make real progress is to help rural people learn how to develop themselves. The development of rural areas/people can't be solved with give aways or government programmes.

**Organisation of the Book**

The Book "Rural Development in India — Past, Present and Future" consists of fourty-two chapters grouped into eight sections — Rural India, Rural Development, Present Rural Development Programmes, Approach to Rural Development, Financing Rural Development, Rural Management, Future of Rural Development and case studies. And, select bibliography is presented in section nine. While past Rural Development are discussed in section two, Planning and other related issues are clubbed with finance.

The analysis, information discussion and charts and graphics provide a new insight to the students of rural development, rural economists as well as the lay reader interested in rural development.

**Acknowledgement**

My debt to those who have helped me in one way or other is heavy indeed. While I take this opportunity to thank all of them — they are too numerous to be mentioned in a brief preface, I would like to acknowledge my deep sense of gratitude to Dr. Narendra Kumar for his ungrudging help at all stages.

I am grateful to all those who helped me in the completion of this study. I would also like to acknowledge my deep sense of gratitude to the veteran rural economists for their guidance. Thanks are also due to Shri K.N. Pandey, Professor M.A. Gidwani, Mr. Nilaver, Mrs. Phalguni Ravi and Mr. M.V. Desai for their suggestions for effecting a number of stylistic improvements.

While I owe a debt of gratitude to a large number of friends and well-wishers, the opinions expressed in this book are entirely mine and I alone take the responsibility for shortcomings, if any. I also express my sincere thanks to my publishers, Himalaya Publishing House Pvt. Ltd., Mumbai, and their efficient editorial staff who helped in publishing this book in a record time.

**— Vasant Desai**

# CONTENTS


Preface

1. Introduction 1

**SECTION ONE : RURAL INDIA 11**

2. Socio Economic Structure of Rural India 13
3. Rural Poverty 26

**SECTION TWO : RURAL DEVELOPMENT 45**

4. Meaning and Content of Rural Development 47
5. Rural Development: An Overview 59
6. Early Attempts at Rural Development 71
7. National Programmes of Rural Development 77
8. Community Development Programme 87
9. Employment Guarantee Scheme 92
10. Issues in Rural Development 96

**SECTION THREE : PRESENT RURAL DEVELOPMENT PROGRAMMES 113**

11. Wage Employment Programmes 117
12. Self-Employment and Entrepreneurship Development 136
13. Special Area Development Programmes 169
14. Rural Housing Programmes 177
15. National Social Assistance Programme 185
16. Rural Water Supply Programme 188
17. Rural Sanitation 196

**SECTION FOUR : APPROACH TO RURAL DEVELOPMENT 203**

18. Agriculture and Rural Development 205
19. Imperatives for Wise Water Magement 222
20. Energy Management 234
21. Modern Agricultural Technology 242
22. Social Forestry 257
23. Rural Industrialisation 269
24. Land Reforms and Rural Development 294

| | | |
|---|---|---|
| | **SECTION FIVE : FINANCING RURAL DEVELOPMENT** | **313** |
| 25. | Credit Needs of the Rural Poor | 315 |
| 26. | The National Bank for Agriculture and Rural Development | 327 |
| 27. | Techniques of Lending to Agriculture | 340 |
| 28. | Area and Project Approach to Bank Lending | 351 |
| 29. | Decentralised Credit Planning | 362 |
| 30. | District Credit Plans | 365 |
| 31. | Block Level Planning | 379 |
| 32. | 20-Point Programme and Rural Development | 388 |
| | **SECTION SIX: RURAL MANAGEMENT** | **403** |
| 33. | Agencies for Rural Development | 405 |
| 34. | Role of Voluntary Agencies | 430 |
| 35. | Vikas Volunteer Vahini | 437 |
| 36. | Council for Advancement of People's Action and Rural Technology | 449 |
| 37. | Rural Management | 460 |
| 38. | Training for Rural People | 471 |
| 39. | Panchayats for Rural Development | 494 |
| | **SECTION SEVEN : FUTURE OF RURAL DEVELOPMENT** | **525** |
| 40. | Future of Rural Development | 527 |
| 41. | Rural Development in the 21st Century | 552 |
| | **SECTION EIGHT: EXPERIMENT IN RURAL DEVELOPMENT** | **575** |
| 42. | Case Studies | 578 |
| | Annexure - I | 603 |
| | **SECTION NINE : SELECT BIBLIOGRAPHY** | **609** |
| | Books | 609 |
| | Reports | 615 |

*Seventy-six per cent of our people live in the villages. India is poor because the villages of India are poor. India will be rich if the villages of India are rich. Therefore, the basic problem is to remove the poverty from the Indian villages.*

— *Jawaharlal Nehru*

*I would say that if the village perishes, India will perish too. India will no more be India. Her own mission in the world will get lost.*

— *Mahatma Gandhi*

*I ask you (youngmen) to go to the villages and busy yourselves there, not as their masters or benefactors, but as their humble servants. Let them know what to do and how to change their modes of living from your daily conduct and way of living. Only feeling will be of no use just like steam, which by itself is of no account unless it is kept under proper control when it becomes a mighty force. I ask you to go forth as messengers of God, carrying balm for the wounded soul of India.*

— *Mahatma Gandhi*

# Chapter 1

# INTRODUCTION

## In Perspective

During the last six decades, the country's inward-looking and public sector driven industrialisation strategy let to rates of growth and rural development far more modest than expected. Indeed, in the post independence period, the country has made notable social and economic achievements among them, the eradication of famine, the reduction in population growth and the creation of a large pool of technical and scientific talent. However, rural poverty and rural development is still a far cry.

All is not bleak, there are some bright spots which have become role models to rural development and human resource development. The strategies are indigenous and centered around the local needs. It encompasses people, environment, health, education, social habits, participation etc. Here the future is bright. What is more, these people have achieved this sustainable development through hard work and with little government help.

In this background, the future of rural development in India is sustainable and feasible. The need of the hour is to create the right atmosphere in rural areas. In this regard rural India can give its long battle to reduce poverty and rural development a new impetus.

## What is Rural Development?

Development as a concept when applied in the specific context of rural India acquires a new meaning as rural development. Fundamentally, development of rural area means not only the aggregate development of the area but also development of the people living in rural areas. The objectives of development include sustained increase in per capita output and incomes, expansion of productive employment and greater equity in the distribution of the benefits of growth, Rural development, over the years, has emerged as "a strategy designed to improve the economic, social and cultural life of a specific group of people living in rural areas." The objectives of rural development are multi-directional as well as multi-dimensional. It aims at increased employment, higher productivity, higher income as well as minimum acceptable levels of food, clothing, shelter, education, health and building up of a sound value system which is in keeping with the high cultural heritage of the country. Thus rural development means all aspects of human development. Rural development must constitute a major part of development strategy if a larger segment of those in greatest need to benefit.

## Why Rural Development?

For centuries, the village socio-economic fabric has undergone a sea change. Besides, over 31 crore of rural people do not have adequate income, employment opportunities, fall short of demand, coupled with illiteracy, ignorance, land under cultivation is not only diminishing but also gets further fragmented, ecology degraded, infrastructural facilities do not match with the growth of rural population. In addition, rural population is unorganised. The apathy of the villages is accentuated by the social and deep-rooted caste hierarchy. The village level politics has further deteriorated with the dilution of the spiritual value systems. To lift the people from these moorings, integrated rural development is the only answer. Though man cannot overcome all the limitations his environment imposes upon him, he can always attempt to modify it to suit his convenience. In this matter of gradual adaptation, man has brought about many changes. In this direction, rural development is the core of development and is a continuous process.

## Rural Development Prescriptions

In order to alleviate the lot of the rural poor, comprising the small and marginal farmers, landless labourers, rural artisans, women, tribals etc., the government — the centre as well as state — operates various programmes since the First Plan. Broadly speaking, these schemes are either beneficiary-oriented or directed towards infrastructure building. The former benefit the individuals and their families directly, while the later are directed towards infrastructure strengthening activities that have an indirect, long-term impact on the rural population. In addition, there are some time-bound programmes limited to small geographic areas. In a way, these programmes are economic-oriented, and as such touches only one aspect of rural development, improving income generation of the beneficiaries. The dilemma will still be there; how to make life better for rural poor without encouraging the migration to urban areas and still improving their chances of work and livelihood.

As it stands sociological, psychological and cultural aspects as well as organisational and managerial skills are not given due attention in regard to rural development.

Jawaharlal Nehru aptly observed that *"The real change comes, of course, from within the village, from the very people living in the village and is not imposed from outside. It is a process of self-development and self-reliance. The outsider can only help a little, give some guidance and push here and there. That little help may, of course, be of the greatest importance or it can light a flame which shed its light over very much wider areas. But the test of success is how far the people of a village shoulder their burdens and have developed a spirit of self-reliance and mutual co-operation."*"

The main issues of rural development are rising poverty, growing population, inadequate infrastructure, negation of basic amenities, ill-health, fragmentation of land, continued exploitation of rural poor, illiteracy, ignorance, deep-rooted apathy, debased value systems, under employment, rampant unemployment, lack of direction and motivation, social pressures and compulsions, social evils, destruction of eco-system, blind urban imitation, lack of awareness, lack of organised efforts etc. The process of development should start with eradication of deprivations on one end and on the other greater involvement in higher production without affecting the eco-system and fuller development of human resources in rural areas.

*Harvesting water for sustainable development*

## Strategy

In order to catalyze development in rural areas, top priority has been accorded to Rural Development, not only in terms of allocations of funds and resources but also through introduction of new programmes and restructuring of the existing ones. There has been a paradigm shift in the policy of rural development, in terms of which the rural poor are treated as resource, whose ideas and experiences form an integral part of the development strategy. The strategy of Rural Development broadly includes.

- Bridging the rural-urban divide — In order to ensure equitable distribution of resources for rapid development in rural areas, the allocation of funds for rural development programmes has been enhanced from one plan to another.
- Making rural people the arbiter of their own destiny — For the development to be in consonance with the people's wishes and aspirations, the emphasis has been shifted towards participation of people in development process through Panchayati Raj Institutions and Self-Help Groups etc.
- Creation of enabling environment for better economic opportunities and growth — Providing connectivity to all unconnected habitations through Pradhan Mantri Gram Sadak Yojana and development of village infrastructure through works undertaken under Sampoorna Grameen Rozgar Yojana.
- Providing avenues of dignified living through provision of shelter, water and clean environment.
- Social mobilization of rural poor for economic upliftment through Swarnjayanti Gram Swarojgar Yojana.
- Ensuring food security and employment to the rural poor through Sampoorna Grameen Rozgar Yojana.

- Restoring lost/depleted productivity of the land through watershed development programmes.

## The Process

The government have relied on two approaches to develop rural areas since independence the first based on the anticipation that the effect of aggregate rural growth spread to all group in society that result in real growth and the second that specific rural development programmes are experimented with some success. However, in recent years, the government's strategy is on its emphasis on providing the conditions for accelerated and sustained labour intensive growth, while expanding investment in human capital development. The process of development is to be integrated, sustainable and pervasive.

## Overview

Rural development is the main pillar of the nation's development. The reasons for this are obvious. Inspite of rapid urbanisation, a large section of our population still lives in the villages. Secondly, rural India has lagged behind in development because of many historical factors. In order to correct the developmental imbalances and to accord due priority to development in rural areas Ministry of Rural Development is implementing a number of programmes aimed at sustainable holistic development in rural areas. The thrust of these programmes is on all-round economic and social transformation in rural areas, through a multi-pronged strategy, aiming in the process, to reach out to most disadvantaged sections of the society. In order to catalyse development in rural areas, during the last three years, top priority has been accorded to rural development, not only in terms of allocations of additional funds and resources but also through introduction of new programmes and restructuring of existing ones.

To ensure adequate budgetary support for sustainable development in rural areas, the allocations for rural development have been increased substantially. The budgetary outlay for Rural Development Programme has been Rs. 3,01,069 crore in the 11th plan (2007-12) as against Rs. 1,21,928 crore in the 10th plan (2002-07) Rs. 74,686 crore in the 9th plan (1997-2002) and Rs. 34,425 crore in the Eight plan (1992-97).

**Table 1**

**PLAN OUTLAY TO RURAL DEVELOPMENT : BY HEADS OF DEVELOPMENT** *(Rs. in crore)*

| *Plan* | *Period* | *Agriculture* | *Irrigation* | *Rural Development* |
|---|---|---|---|---|
| Third | 1961-66 | 1,088.9 | 666.7 | — |
| Fourth | 1969-74 | 2,320.4 | 1,354.1 | — |
| Fifth | 1974-79 | 4,864.9 | 3,876.5 | — |
| Sixth | 1980-85 | 5695.1 | 12.160.0 | 5,363.7 |
| Seventh | 1985-90 | 12,792.6 | 16,589.9 | 15,246.5 |
| Eighth | 1992-97 | 22,467.2 | 32,525.3 | 34,425.4 |
| Ninth | 1997-2002 | 42,462.0 | 55,420.0 | 74,686.0 |
| Tenth | 2002-2007 | 58,933.0 | 1,03,315.0 | 1,21,928.0 |
| Eleventh | 2007-2012 | 1,36,381.0 | 2,10,326.0 | 3,01,069.0 |

*Source :* Economic Survey, 2007-2008.

In the last few years, there has also been a paradigm shift in the strategy for rural development with focus on decentralisation through speedy and effective devolution of financial and administrative powers to the Panchayati Raj Institutions. A strategic pro poor policy in terms of which the rural poor are treated as a resource rather than as a burden, whose ideas and experience are now an integral part of the development strategy. As such, the emphasis has shifted towards participation of people through Panchayati Raj Institutions (PRIs) and Self Help Groups (SHGs) in the planning, formulation and execution of the programmes.

Panchayati Raj Institutions constitute the core of decentralised developmental planning and its implementation. Under most of the rural development programmes a crucial role to PRIs in the programme implementation has been assigned. The Ministry is also vigorously pursuing with the State Governments for expeditious devolution of requisite administrative and financial powers to PRIs as envisaged under 73rd Amendment Act. In All India Panchayat Adhyakshas Sammelan held in April, 2002, a 'National Declaration' resolving that the State Governments will ensure the implementation of Provisions of Constitution (73rd Amendment) Act, 1992 and the Provisions of Panchayats (Extension to Scheduled Areas) Act, 1996 by December, 31, 2002 was adopted by consensus. As a result of the persistent efforts made by the government significant gains in the area of devolution of administrative and financial powers by the States to PRIs have been noticed. Barring a few States, Panchayat elections have also been held in most of the States during the last two years. On 25th December, 2002, under drinking water sector, a new initiative 'Swajal Dhara' empowering the Panchayats to formulate, implement, operate and maintain drinking water projects has been launched. In order to further involve PRIs in the development process, a new initiative 'Hariyali' has been launched by Hon'ble Prime Minister on 27th January, 2003. Hariyali has been launched to strengthen and involves Panchayati Raj Institutions in the implementation of Watershed Development Programmes namely IWDP, DPAP and DDP. Under this initiative, the Gram Panchayats would execute watershed projects with technical support from the Block Panchayat/Zilla Panchayat who would act as Project Implementation Agency (PIA) for all watershed projects in a particular block.

Land is a critically important national resource. Its efficient management is vital for economic growth and development of rural areas. Concerted efforts are being made through Area Development Programmes of Department of Land Resources such as Integrated Wastelands Development Programme, Drought Prone Areas Programme and Desert Development Programme to regenerate and rejuvenate wastelands and degraded lands. All the Area Development Programmes are being implemented through the watershed development approach. Some of the major achievements and initiatives in this regard are – three-fold increase in budget provision for Wasteland Development Programme.

## Conclusion

The present living conditions of the rural people calls for rural development on a war-footing, No doubt, the issues and problems are many and also complicated. These have to be either solved or overcome, so that the rural sector can effectively contribute to the accelerated development of the economy. The task calls for planned and committed effort by the government and other agencies with the fullest participation of the rural people *i.e.,* the beneficiaries.

The problems of rural development is a complex one. It calls for a sincere attempt without any political jargon attached. The future development of rural development largely depends upon how much momentum the country can impart to the management of various stages of development and motivate rural people within the confines of an individual and collective development process. The aim of rural development, therefore, be the overall development of humanity and enrichment of rural cultural heritage. In short, there is a need for integrated development of not only rural people, but also of villages. What is more important is that the living standards (social, economic and cultural) of rural people are raised for harmonious growth. So that all people in rural India live in harmony, peace and contentment. Each one is assured of nutritious meal, adequate clothes, clean house in a clean environment, basic education, employment throughout the year, all weather roads, adequate supply of drinking water, avenues for cultural progress without any distinction of caste or creed.

**Box 1**

**NURTURING THE ECOSYSTEM**

The proposed dredging of the Palk Straits is a marine disaster but the debate revolves around whether or not it is the Ram Setu. The cold desert of Ladakh is facing unprecedented heat. Our rivers are being turned into sewers, with sludge, human waste and industrial effluents replacing clean water. Uncontrolled loggins is denuding our forests but the authorities turn a blind eye because they receive their share of the illegal booty. Virgin lands in Orissa and Bihar are being turned over to MNC's for mining with no thought to the ecological toll. Tigers are dying, lions are vanishing, elephants are being killed, Bundelkhand faces a drought yet again and the only things the Indians want to talk about is development and progress. When will we realise that the developed lifestyle is a choice that is simply not sustainable ?

As a culture, we perfected the art of minimal consumption and maximum harmony with nature a good two thousand years ago. Right after we created the world's first planned cities with indoor plumbing and drainage in the Indus Valley civilisation. But today all we hanker after are the amenities deemed essential by the developed world. Air conditioners, refrigerators, and conspicuous luxury. We follow suit blindly. In a tropical country we emulate countries that lie in the temperate zone and build huge buildings of glass. And then put in air conditioning. We discard traditional wisdom like earthenware pots to cool water and use refrigerators that promise to deplete our already damaged ozone layer. Being confronted with the reality of climate change does not spark of a national debate on environment protection. We are more excited about the carbon credits market. Essentially we will adopt only enough green technology to allow corporations and business houses to sell the carbon they are not thus emitting to first world companies and citizens. So basically, the developed world continues to consume resources at a rate disproportionate to their population, and a selected few in the third world countries like India become carbon dollar millionaires. Meanwhile, the Sunderbans keep getting eroded, un-seasonal rains spark another round of farmer suicides, and chemicals keep leaching into the soil. And yes, we keep offering to dismantle ships and manufacture other toxic industrial products in India that the developed world is outsourcing because they do not want to contaminate their environment. And we do it because we place development over environment. We have some of the most stringent environmental laws in India. And probably the worst implementation record. Zero implementation is the correct assessment. As citizens we have the right to protest against the ecological callousness of our elected representatives. As parents we have the obligation to preserve the environment for our descendents. But we are being blinded by money and comfort. Refusing to realise that the consequences of our ecological ignorance are frighteningly close at hand. As for our aspirations towards the American lifestyle, it works out to approximately 4% of the earth's inhabitants consuming 25% of the global resources. You do the math and decide whether you can afford to sit back in your complacency. Nurturing the ecosystem is the foremast task of rural people. It is the core objective of rural development.

The need of the hour is to provide basic infrastructure, adequate water, right education, improved health facilities, consultancy, technical awareness, conservation of land environment and ecology, planned cultivation, social forestry, irrigation facilities, check dams, adequate credit, right market for their produce, right price and basic skills in agriculture, non-agricultural activities and rural industries.

To make rural development a reality, all new initiatives to the rural economy for not just back-end support but also for development and growth, making for a unique self-sustaining business model. Rural development initiative, or social forestry programme, one has to begin engaging farmers, women and rural people long before it came in vogue and benefits began to be seen, seizing credit along the way for transforming villages (rural areas) into pulsating economic communities and vibrant rural environment.

The basic approach advocated in the study is that the development agencies are not substitute for the decision-making of the rural people. They are basically there to improve the environment of the decision-making of the rural people. The development strategies are impregnant with the actions which facilitate the decision-making of the rural people which are consistent with their upliftment. The overall framework could be somewhat is as indicated below:

**NATIONAL POLICY FOR RURAL DEVELOPMENT**

*Government agencies in charge of the activities concerning rural people*

1. Provide legal framework for undertaking activities.
2. Evolve identity relevant technologies.
3. Provide extension input.
4. Administer subsidy programme.
5. Run special programmes for generating employment for the people whose main working asset is manual labour.

*Financial Institutions*

1. Supply credit for pursuing the activities.

*Input Suppliers*

1. Supply inputs and services for pursuing the activities.

*Marketing Agencies*

1. Purchase product of the rural producers.
2. Offer post-harvest technological assistance to the farm sector

**RURAL DECISION-MAKER**

1. Makes decision regarding the type of activity and level of activity.
2. Borrows for investment and working capital.
3. Purchases inputs and services for implementing the first decision.
4. Supplies farm products to the market and utilities services for post-harvest activities.

## Annexure I

# THE PROBLEM

Poverty has many dimensions. In addition to low income (living on less than $1 a day), illiteracy, ill health, gender inequality, and environmental degradation are all aspects of being poor. This is reflected in the Millennium Development Goals, the international community's unprecedented agreement on the goals for reducing poverty (box 1.) The multidimensional nature of poverty is also reflected in the World Bank's two-pronged strategy for development-investing in people and improving the investment climate. That five of the eight goals and one of the two prongs of the strategy for development concern health and education signals how central human development is to human welfare.

### Box 2
### THE EIGHT MILLENNIUM DEVELOPMENT GOALS

With starting points in 1990 each goal is to be reached by 2015:

1. **Eradicate extreme poverty and hunger**

   Halve the proportion of people living on less than one dollar a day.

   Halve the proportion of people who suffer from hunger.

2. **Achieve universal primary education**

   Ensure that boys and girls alike complete primary schooling.

3. **Promote gender equality and empower women**

   Eliminate gender disparity at all levels of education.

4. **Reduce child mortality**

   Reduce by two-thirds the under-five mortality rate.

5. **Improve maternal health**

   Reduce by three-quarters the maternal mortality ratio.

6. **Combat HIV/AIDS, malaria, and other diseases**

   Reverse the spread of HIV/AIDS.

7. **Ensure environmental sustainability**

   Integrate sustainable development into country policies and reverse loss of environmental resources.

   Halve the proportion of people without access to potable water.

8. **Develop a global partnership for development**

   Raise official development assistance.

   Expand market access.

Three points about the Millennium Development Goals: First, to be enduring, success in reaching the goals must be based on systemwide reforms to support progress. Second, focusing on these outcomes does not imply focusing on education and health services alone. Health and education outcomes depend on too many other factors for that to work—everything from parents' knowledge and behaviour, to the ease and safety of reaching a health clinic or school, or the technology available for producing outcomes. Third, in countries that have already achieved universal primary completion or low infant and maternal mortality rates, the spirit of the Millennium Development Goals—time-bound, outcome-based targets to focus strategies—remains important.

But progress in human development has lagged behind that in reducing income poverty (figure 1). The world as a whole is on track to achieve the first goal—reducing by half the proportion of people living on less than $1 a day—thanks mainly to rapid economic growth in India and China, where many of the world's poor live. But the world is off track in reaching the goals for primary education, gender equality, and child mortality.

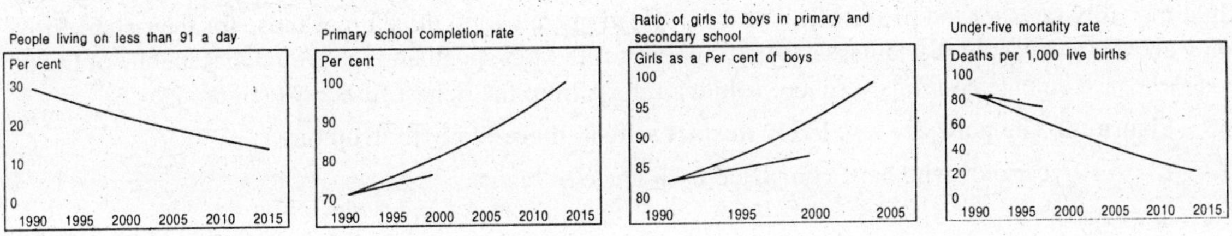


*Fig. 1. Progress in human development off track*

To reach all of these goals, economic growth is essential. But it will not be enough. The projected growth in per capita GDP will by itself enable five of the world's six developing regions to reach the goal for reducing income poverty (table 1). But that growth will enable only two of the regions to achieve the primary enrollment goal and none of them to reach the child mortality goal. If the economic growth projected for Africa doubles, the region will reach the income poverty goal—but still fall short of the health and education goals. In Uganda, despite average annual per capita GDP growth of 3.9 percent in the past decade, child mortality is stagnating—and only partly due to the AIDS epidemic.

**Table 1**

**ECONOMIC GROWTH ALONE IS NOT ENOUGH TO REACH ALL THE MILLENNIUM DEVELOPMENT GOALS**

| | | *People living on less than $1 a day* | | *Primary school completion rate* | | *Under-five mortality* | |
|---|---|---|---|---|---|---|---|
| | *Annual average GDP per capita growth 2000-2015* (per cent per year)* | *Target (per cent)* | *2015 growth alone (per cent)* | *Target (per cent)* | *2015 growth alone (per cent)* | *Target (per 1,000 births)* | *2015 growth alone (per 1,000 births)* |
| East Asia | 5.4 | 14 | 4 | 100 | 100 | 19 | 26 |
| Europe and Central Asia | 3.6 | 1 | 1 | 100 | 100 | 15 | 26 |
| Latin American and the Caribbean | 1.8 | 8 | 8 | 100 | 95 | 17 | 30 |
| Middle East and North Africa | 1.4 | 1 | 1 | 100 | 96 | 25 | 41 |
| South Asia | 3.8 | 22 | 15 | 100 | 99 | 43 | 69 |
| Africa | 1.2 | 24 | 35 | 100 | 56 | 59 | 151 |

* GDP Growth projections from World Bank (2003a).

*Note:* Elasticity assumed between growth and poverty is—1.5, primary completion rate is 0.52 under-five mortality is –0.48.

*Sources:* World Bank (2003a), Devarajan (2002).

Because growth alone will not be enough to reach the goals, the international community has committed itself—in a series of recent meetings in Monterrey, Doha, and Johannesburg—to greater resource transfers by developed countries and better policies and institutions in developing countries. The level of resource transfers is difficult to calculate precisely. Some estimates are converging around a figure of $40 billion to $60 billion a year in additional foreign aid—so long as the money is accompanied by policy and institutional reforms to enhance the productivity of domestic and external resources.

Focusing on the human development goals, this Report describes the reforms in services needed to achieve them. Ensuring basic health and education outcomes is the responsibility of the state (box 2). But many governments are falling short on their obligation, especially to poor people. In Armenia and Cambodia, child mortality rates for the poorest fifth of the population are two to three times those for the richest fifth. Only about 60 percent of the adolescents in the poorest fifth of the population in the Arab Republic of Egypt and Peru have completed primary school, while all those from the richest fifth have (figure 2).

**Figure : 2 The poor are less likely to start school, more likely to drop out**

15- to 19-year olds who have completed each grade or higher.

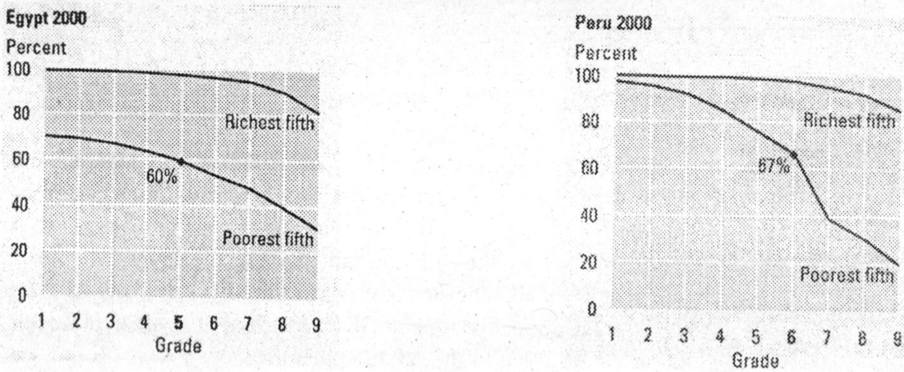


*Fig. 2.*

*Note :* The grade number boldfaced denotes the end of the primary cycle (grade 5 for Egypt and India; grade 6 for Niger and Peru)

*Source :* Analysis of Demographic and Health Survey Data.

**Box 3**

**SERVICES—A PUBLIC RESPONSIBILITY**

By financing, providing, or regulating the services that contribute to health and education outcomes, governments around the world demonstrate their responsibility for the health and education of their people. Why? First, these services are replete with market failures—with externalities, as when an infected child spreads a disease to play-mates or a farmer benefits from a neighbour's ability to read. So the private sector, left to its devices, will not achieve the level of health and education that society desires, Second, basic health and basic education are considered fundamental human rights. The Universal Declaration of Human Rights asserts an individual's right to "a standard of living adequate for the health and well-being of himself and of his family, including...medical care...[and a right to education that is]...free, atleast in the elementary and fundamental stages." No matter how daunting the problems of delivery may be the public sector cannot walk away from health and education. The challenge is to see how the government—in collaboration with the private sector, communities, and outside partners—can meet this fundamental responsibility.

To meet this responsibility, governments and citizens need to make the services that contribute to health and education—water, sanitation, energy, transport, health, and education—work for poor people. Too often, these services are failing. Sometimes, they are failing everybody—except the rich, who can opt out of the of the public system. But at other times, they are clearly failing poor people.

❑ ❑ ❑

# SECTION ONE

# RURAL INDIA

## ANATOMY OF RURAL INDIA

## TWO INDIAS

| *Privileged* | *Underprivileged* |
|---|---|
| Urban | Rural |
| Well-fed | Undernourished/hungry |
| Drainage/Water/Sanitation | Poor Sanitation |
| Hospitals/Communication } Well | Inadequate water supply, irrigation facilities<br>Inadequate Hospitals, Schools Roads etc. |
| Housing/Education } Developed | Poor housing, Poor education |
| High Credit Facility | Low credit facilities |
| Higher Literacy | Higher illiteracy |
| Market Oriented | Inadequate market facility |
| English Speaking | Non-English speaking |
| Doctors/Engineers/Accountants | Less qualified/little or no<br>Inadequate — |
| MBAs/Computermen/Businessmen | Income earning skill, Non-Professionals |
| High Skilled | Unskilled/Traditional Landless |
| Employed in the organised sector | Unemployed/under employed/seasonal employment |
| Technically Advanced | Untouched by technology |
| Good counselling | Low/inadequate counselling |
| IT, Communication sectors have opened up ample opportunities | Seasonally employed in the unorganised sector |
| Plenty of Employment opportunities | Restricted employment opportunities in Agriculture |
| High in awareness | Low in awareness |
| Tax payers | No tax payers |
| '5-Star' culture | Squalor. Traditional Culture |

*Note :* Anybody who enjoys full-time employment even in the unorganised sector is, in a real sense, privileged.

## HUMAN RIGHTS FOR ALL

**Article 1.** All human beings are born free and equal in dignity and rights. They are endowed with reason and conscience and should act towards one another in a spirit of brotherhood.

**Article 23.** (1) Everyone has the right to work, to free choice of employment, to just and favourable conditions of work and to protection against unemployment.. (2) Everyone, without any discrimination, has the right to equal pay for equal work. (3) Everyone who works has the right to just and favourable remuneration ensuring for himself and his family an existence worthy of human dignity, and supplemented, if necessary, by other means of social protection. (4) Everyone has the right to form and to join trade unions for the protection of his interests.

**Article 25.** (1) Everyone has the right to a standard of living adequate for the health and well-being of himself and of his family, including food, clothing, housing and medical care and necessary social services, and the right to security in the event of unemployment, sickness, disability, widowhood, old age or other lack of livelihood in circumstances beyond his control. (2) Motherhood and childhood are entitled to special care and assistance. All children, whether born in or out of wedlock, shall enjoy the same social protection.

**Article 26.** (1) Everyone has the right to education. Education shall be free, at least in the elementary and fundamental stages. Elementary education shall be compulsory. Technical and professional education shall be made generally available and higher education shall be equally accessible to all on the basis of merit. (2) Education shall be directed to the full development of the human personality and to the strengthening of respect for human rights and fundamental freedoms. It shall promote understanding, tolerance and friendship among all nations, racial or religious groups, and shall further the activities of the United Nations for the maintenance of peace. (3) Parents have a prior right to chose the kind of education that shall be given to their children.

## Times are exciting.
## Villages are progressing.
## Eyes are twinkling.
## You've never had
## a better time to shine brighter.

From one end to another, India's tiny corners have taken big steps forward. Many villages resemble small towns, and many towns resemble small cities. With television, cell phones and internet, rural India isn't lagging too far behind. On the highway of progress, this is the moment to grow even faster. So go ahead, diversify into value-added agriculture and agro-processing, and gain from these excellent times. Build your dreams, spread the enthusiasm and make India stronger and shine even brighter.

***Highlights:***

- Higher rural tele-density
- Community involvement in elementary education
- Greater penetration of TV and radio in villages
- Greater village road connectivity.

*"Bridging the rural-urban divide- In order to ensure rapid development in rural areas, the budgetary support for implementing the various rural development schemes have been increased many folds over the years."*

# Chapter 2

# SOCIO ECONOMIC STRUCTURE OF RURAL INDIA

## Introduction

For a better understanding of rural economics, particularly in the context of advancement of agriculture and rural development, it is quite necessary to understand the structure of rural society. In fact, rural environment provides a deep insight into the present-day problems facing rural areas in India. Though Indian economy has shown some signs of improvement in some sectors in the post-independence period, a large section of rural people is still ignorant and live in poor conditions. The picture of rural India is still gloomy. It is proposed to provide a broad framework of rural India so that it may draw the attention of the authorities to the need for integrated rural development.

## India — A Land of Villages

India is a land of villages and her economy continues even today to be mainly rural. The village is also an important unit in the organisation of Indian social life. Here, one comes across the typical Hindu way of life. It is natural that in a land of such overwhelming rural population. the village community should exercise by far the greatest influence upon the social, economic and political life of the country.

An average village consists of a few hundred acres of land, supporting about fifty to two hundred rural families. On approaching an Indian village, we find that it is a cluster of mudhouses and thatched huts, narrow, uneven and winding streets running between rows of houses, thatched or roofed with tiles made perhaps by the local potter. Moreover, a low standard of living, an inadequate and ill-balanced diet, meagre and rough clothing, insanitary housing, the prevalence of disease, dirt and squalor, and, above all, ignorance and illiteracy are the characteristic features of an Indian village. In this connection, B.H. Baden-Powell says, "...The term (village) does not refer merely to a street or group of buildings—as in England of today; it includes both the cluster of houses and surrounding lands cultivated. Such a group has always a local name and known limits."

A village is an important unit conditioned by nature and tradition. More often than not the causative factors behind this population settlement, such as topography, easy accessibility, security of shelter, fertility of land, proximity of water, etc., either singly or jointly, appear to be missing. Presently, the availability of land appears to be the only important factor behind continued village settlement.

A village is not usually an architect's delight, In certain regions—for example, Kerala—it is difficult to realise where one village ends and the other begins. In many States, however, the village shows a cluster formation. It is necessary to walk a few kilometres from the village to reach a town, a health centre, a repairs centre, a market place, a bus stand or the railway station. The village is distinguished by a multitude of hamlets, *pucca* built houses being few and far between. There are no paved streets, no public latrines (only very few private latrines), no regular or storm-water drains. Occasionally, there is a community well and very few private wells. The source of water in many cases is more than a couple of kilometres away and is probably a brook, a river or a tank. The water is often brackish.

The hamlets are usually unfit for human habitation and lack conveniences like electricity. The household is generally unorganised because there is very little to organise. There is no furniture; household utensils are few and earthenware is often used for the storage of water, food, etc. Clothing is generally limited to what is worn on the body. Quilts and *dhurries* are a luxury. Fuel consists mostly of cowdung or cheap firewood. There is no problem of lighting as the village people retire by dusk. very few hamlets can boast of even hurricane lanterns; a majority can afford only improvised lamps. There is no problem of storage, for there is very little to store. Household animals and human beings live in very close proximity. A few own a cow, a buffalo or a pair of bullocks. Some have a sheep some poultry, but limited in number. Hygiene is hardly a conscious habit.

## Village in India

The village in India holds a unique place, both in the social and economic spheres. In the past, a village was a homogeneous, closely-knit and self-sufficient unit. Community feeling and the tradition of co-operation in the small villages has been aptly described by the poet, Rabindranath Tagore. Dwelling on the bonds of kinship in the villages, he said: "To establish a personal relationship between man and man has been India's constant endeavour. One has to retain contact even with distant relatives; filial ties are not loosened when children come of age; and our ties of kinship include neighbours and many others in the village, irrespective of caste or circumstance. There are relationships with teacher and priest, guest and mendicant, landlord and tenant—not ties prescribed by the scriptures, but those of the heart. such is our nature. We accept relationship of utility only after we have sanctified them by a kinship of the heart."

The village communities, wrote Sir Charles Metcalfe, were "little republics, having nearly everything they can want within themselves, and almost independent of any foreign relations. They seem to last where nothing else lasts."

Although each epoch of India history had its own share of social changes, the epochs seldom encompassed the whole society. The caste system and the joint family helped to maintain the solidarity of village community life, though inner conflicts continued to smoulder in society.

It is high time that we started paying attention to this basic problem to the minimum rural settlement that should form the basis for the planning and implementation of all programmes of integrated rural development. The problem is not only to determine the size of such a minimum unit but to devise ways and means of bringing such minimum units existence by grouping clusters of villages and providing them with the necessary social and economic services and the with resources which link them into new viable villages. In this way, the necessary transport facilities may be established between the villages composing any given cluster so that each cluster of villages constituting a new village may function as one integrated unit.

> "The poor often don't get the water they need so desperately. This lack of access to water has much to do with governance and the way water is managed"
>
> Tadao China, ADB President

> Today, the vision an integrated, prosperous, poverty-free and peaceful Asia is no longer a dream, but an achievable goal

> Infrastructure is critical for realizing sustained economic growth, and has strong positive linkages with other sectors

> "People are so much better performed about health and Nutrition. Now there is more knowledge so it is easier to work in local community"
>
> Fahrinawati, a midwife at Kurau

> "Our goal is to serve the people and alleviate poverty among our farmers"

*A Warli village*

## Rural People

There were 212.6 million people living in rural areas in 1901, half of them in active employment. In 2001 rural population has increased to 721.1 million. Although the ratio of rural population has declined from 89.2 percent to 71.2 percent during the century it has adversely affected the poor very hard. On the other hand the density of population has increased, land under agriculture has diminished, affected the forests and exodus to urban areas accelerated agricultural labour continued to be exploited. The gap between the rich and the poor further widened.

**Table 1**

**GROWTH OF POPULATION**

*(in million)*

| *Year* | *Total* | *Rural* | *% share* | *Urban* | *% share* |
|---|---|---|---|---|---|
| 1901 | 238.4 | 212.6 | 89.2 | 25.8 | 10.8 |
| 1911 | 252.1 | 226.2 | 89.7 | 25.9 | 10.3 |
| 1921 | 251.3 | 223.2 | 88.8 | 28.1 | 11.2 |
| 1931 | 278.9 | 245.5 | 88.0 | 33.4 | 12.0 |
| 1941 | 318.6 | 274.5 | 86.2 | 44.1 | 13.9 |
| 1951 | 361.1 | 298.7 | 82.7 | 62.4 | 17.3 |
| 1961 | 439.2 | 360.3 | 82.0 | 78.9 | 18.0 |
| 1971 | 546.2 | 439.1 | 80.1 | 109.1 | 19.9 |
| 1981* | 683.3 | 523.8 | 76.7 | 159.5 | 23.3 |
| 1991@ | 846.4 | 628.7 | 74.3 | 217.6 | 25.7 |
| 2001** | 1028.7 | 721.1 | 71.2 | 291.3 | 28.8 |
| 2010*** | 1234.9 | 740.9 | 60.0 | 494.0 | 40.0 |

* Includes projected population of Assam where 1981 census was not conducted.

@ Includes projected population of J & K where 1991 census was not conducted.

** Projected 2010 urban population projected to rise to 42%.

*** Projected.

*Source :* Registrar General of India, Ministry of Home Affairs.

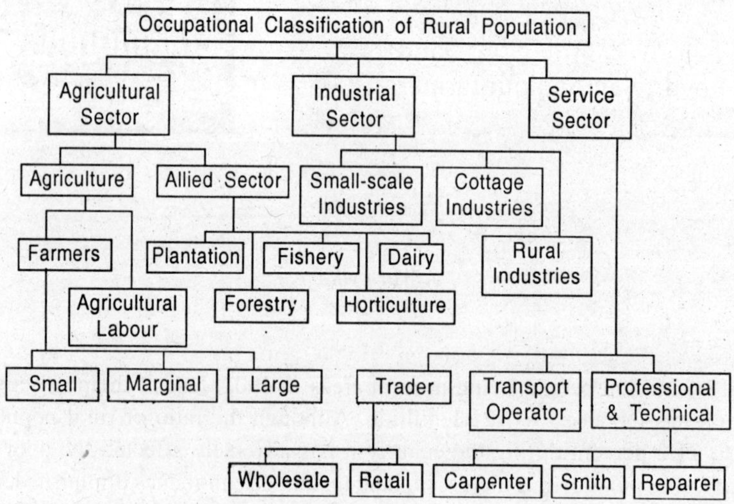


*Fig. 1. Occupational classification of rural population*

**Box 1**
**RURAL INFRASTRUCTURE**

In the context of the need for stepping up agricultural growth rate to 4.5 per cent in the Ninth Five Year plan, the importance of rural infrastructure in sectors like irrigation, roads, bridges, etc. needs no emphasis. Good infrastructure is essential for better productivity of capital and labour. In addition, it also helps check the migration of rural population to urban areas. In our country where more than 60 per cent of the population lives in rural areas and nearly two-third of the work force derives their livelihood from agriculture, the rural infrastructure assumes crucial importance. However, one of the basic limitations to create adequate infrastructure is lack of resources. Difficult financial position of the state governments, mainly responsible for development and maintenance of rural infrastructure, has been a cause of concern, with many well-intentioned infrastructure projects found languishing for want of resources. This apart, it was found that the commercial banks who were assigned the role of channeling atleast 18 per cent of their total lending to agriculture were not able to fulfil their commitment. It was, therefore, considered desirable to create a fund out of the shortfall in commercial banks lending for agriculture by the name of Rural Infrastructure Development Fund (RIDF) to be managed and operated by the National Bank.

## Agriculture

*Fig. 2 Agriculture*

Despite some industrialisation, India remained primarily an agricultural economy at the beginning of the century. The share of the factory industries in total national income barely exceeded 6 per cent in normal year; the primary sector, that is, agriculture contributed 60 per cent or more of the total income, and two-thirds of total people employed were in the agricultural sector.

The total area irrigated in 1900-01 was 32.58 million acres and the total area cropped stood at 220.35 million acres. Eighty five per cent of the cropped area was for food crops with remaining devoted to oil seeds and fibre crops. Today, the gross irrigated area stands at 68 million hectares and the area under various crops at 186.4 million hectares. The product pattern has more or less remained unchanged in the last 100 years.

Agriculture provides subsistence to over two-thirds of its workforce directly or indirectly dependent on agriculture and generates about 28 percent of its GDF and over 15 percent of its exports. Thus agriculture and the related activities dominate the rural economy.

## Rural Activities

Broadly, rural activities are grouped into three sectors *viz* agriculture and allied activities, village industries, rural artisans and service sector.

**Table 2**

**PAST AND PRESENT MACRO-SCENARIO ON EMPLOYMENT AND UNEMPLOYMENT (CDS BASIS)**

| | *(Million)* | | | *Growth per annum (%)* | |
|---|---|---|---|---|---|
| | 1983 | 1993-34 | 1999-2000 | 1983 to 1993-94 | 1993-94 to 1999-2000 |
| **All India** | | | | | |
| Population | 718.20 | 894.01 | 1003.97 | 2.00 | 1.95 |
| Labour Force | 261.33 | 335.97 | 363.33 | 2.43 | 1.31 |
| Workforce | 239.57 | 315.84 | 336.75 | 2.70 | 1.07 |
| Unemployment rate (%) | (8.30) | (5.99) | (7.32) | | |
| No. of unemployed | 21.76 | 20.13 | 26.58 | –0.08 | 4.74 |
| **Rural** | | | | | |
| Population | 546.61 | 658.83 | 727.50 | 1.79 | 1.67 |
| Labour Force | 204.18 | 255.38 | 270.39 | 2.15 | 0.96 |
| Workforce | 187.92 | 241.04 | 250.89 | 2.40 | 0.67 |
| Unemployment rate (%) | (7.96) | (5.61) | (7.21) | | |
| No. of unemployed | 16.26 | 14.34 | 19.50 | –1.19 | 5.26 |
| **Urban** | | | | | |
| Population | 171.59 | 234.98 | 276.47 | 3.04 | 2.74 |
| Labour Force | 57.15 | 80.60 | 92.95 | 3.33 | 2.40 |
| Workforce | 51.64 | 74.80 | 85.84 | 3.59 | 2.32 |
| Unemployment rate (%) | (9.64) | (7.19) | (7.65) | | |
| No. of unemployed | 5.51 | 5.80 | 7.11 | 0.49 | 3.45 |

*Source :* Planning Commission.

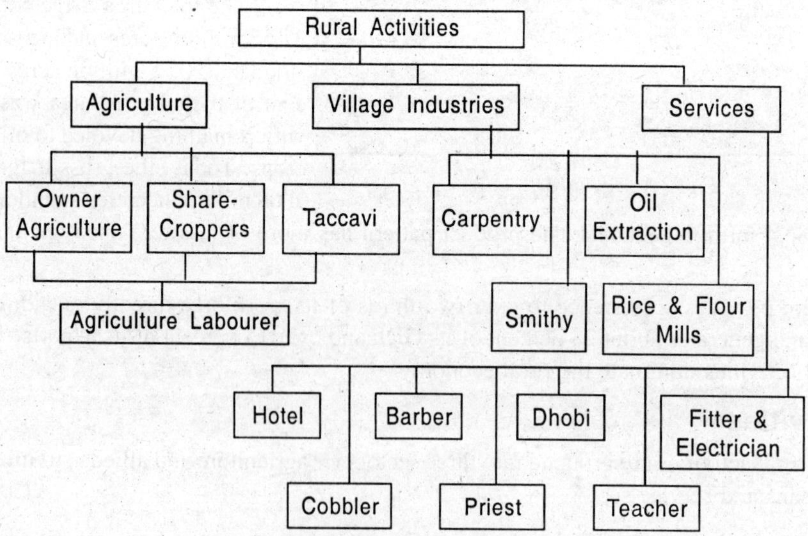


*Fig. 3. Rural Activities*

A free flow of goods and services reduces the element of market apportionment. It becomes possible to set up the needed focal points and roadside centres for remote villages to provide marketing services both for input supplies and output sales and procurement. All these factors, put together, *i.e.*, improvement of knowledge and education, demonstration between effect, easy availability of essential inputs, easy access to the produce market and, above all. Interaction the village communities and the urban-based extension services as well as the socio-cultural, economic and political organisations, provide strong stimuli to the growth and development in the agricultural and rural sector.

*Fig. 4. RIDF - Wai Tank Project — Yavatmal, Maharashtra*

The provision of electricity for agricultural purpose and household consumption acts as a catalytic agent of development. The very presence of an electric motor at the farm gives it a new configuration and changes the farmer's whole outlook. Similarly, the availability of electricity in villager's homes changes the perceived status and the outlook of the farming/rural families altogether. They become more responsive to new ideas and develop and urge to progress, which is a great motivating force for improving their farm efficiency and living standards. With the presence of the approach roads it becomes easy to install and maintain the electricity infrastructure in the village and the later subsequent defaults can be corrected easily and promptly. Roads and electricity have a great interaction effect on the growth and development of agriculture, ameliorating the living conditions in the villages.

The third important element of the rural infrastructure is the provision of school level education. This also promotes rural and urban cultural interactions and improves the human capital in the villages a great deal. These three factors put together, *i.e.* roads, electricity and education enhance the mobility of the rural populations, and lend dynamism to their outlook. These factors, interacting together, encourage consciously conceived out-migration. Access to education, demonstration effect and mobility created an insatiable urge in the village youngsters to move out for better incomes. While out of the country, they absorb different values, develop work habits which are highly productive, and also accumulate financial resources. When they return to their farms and villages, they are different personalities who work in a more productive and progressive manner. These three elements of rural infrastructure, *i.e.* roads, electricity and education, have a direct impact on agricultural growth and rural development by improving and enhancing human capital, social and economic mobility and inter-community interactions for a healthy social, cultural and economic environment, both at the farm level and in the rural households. There are, no doubt, other important elements of socio-economic infrastructure, such as provision of health services marketing services, banking, post and telegraphic services, playgrounds, community halls.

**Table 3**

**RURAL URBAN DICHOTOMY**

| S.No. | Item (1) | Unit (2) | Rural areas (3) | Urban areas (4) |
|---|---|---|---|---|
| 1. | Population | Per cent | 70.7 | 29.3 |
| 2. | Number of Households | Nos.in 000s | 96,867 | 28,906 |
| 3. | Population per household | Number | 5.8 | 5.5 |
| 4. | Dependency Ratio | | | |
| | (i) 0-14 years | Per cent | 40.5 | 36.5 |
| | (ii) above 60 | Per cent | 6.9 | 5.4 |
| 5. | Infant Mortality | Per 1000 live births | 114 | 65 |
| 6. | Sanitation | Per cent | 0.7 | 28.4 |
| 7. | Per capita Monthly Private Consumption Expenditure on | | | |
| | (i) Education | Rupees | 0.26 | 1.36 |
| | (ii) Health | Rupees | 1.02 | 1.40 |
| | (iii) Private Tutor | Rupees | 0.01 | 0.13 |
| 8. | Literacy | Per cent | 29.7 | 57.4 |
| 9. | Schools with one teacher as a percentage of total school | Per cent | 35.1 | 5.8 |
| 10. | Schools conducted in the open space | Number | 39,000 | 1,124 |
| 11. | Schools conducted in thatched huts | Number | 46,457 | 1,262 |
| 12. | Schools conducted in kutcha and mud buildings | Number | 97,744 | 3,608 |
| 13. | Primary schools according to shortage of rooms | Number | 3,17,228 | 27,000 |
| 14. | Primary schools with urinals and latrines | Per cent | 10.10 | 55.9 |
| 15. | Primary schools with drinking water | Per cent | 37.7 | 67.7 |
| 16. | Primary schools with Black Boards | Per cent | 5.85 | 78.1 |
| 17. | School with mats/furniture | Per cent | 35.7 | 18.3 |
| 18. | Hospitals | Number | 1,945 | 5,424 |
| 19. | Share of Hospitals | Per cent | 26.4 | 74.6 |
| | Number of Hospital Beds | Number | 69,008 | 4,45,981 |
| | Share of Hospital Beds | Per cent | 13.4 | 86.6 |
| 20. | Share of Dispensaries | Per cent | 58.5 | 41.5 |
| 21. | Potabale Water Supply | Per cent | 56.2 | 72.9 |
| 22. | Villages with Taps | Per cent | 5 | 67 |
| 23. | Villages with all-weather Roads | Per cent | 30.0 | 100.1 |
| 24. | Villages Electrified | Per cent | 64.0 | 100.0 |
| 25. | Rural Households Electrified | Per cent | 21.0 | |
| 26. | Share of Agriculture in consumption of electricity | Per cent | 16.9 | |
| 27. | Electricity distributed to households | Per cent | 6.5 | 56.0 |
| 28. | Houses without latrines as a percentage of total houses | Per cent | 92.4 | 33.0 |
| 29. | Houses with Source of Drinking water supply with the Tap as a percentage of total household | Per cent | 4.7 | 67.0 |
| 30. | Housing Shortage | Lakhs | 223 | 69 |

**Table 3 (Contd.)**

| | (1) | (2) | (3) | (4) |
|---|---|---|---|---|
| 31. | Number of Operational Holdings | | | |
| | (i) Marginal | Nos. in 00s | 5,05,252 | — |
| | (ii) Percentage share of Total | Per cent | 56.5 | — |
| | (iii) Small | Nos in 00s | 1,60,779 | — |
| | Percentage share of Total | Per cent | 18.0 | — |
| | (iv) Semi-medium | Nos. in 00s | 1,25,071 | — |
| | Percentage share of Total | Per cent | 14.0 | — |
| | (v) Medium | Nos.in 00s | 80,884 | — |
| | Percentage share of Total | Per cent | 9.1 | |
| | (vi) Large | Nos. in 00s | 21,554 | |
| | Percentage share of Total | Per cent | 2.4 | |
| | Total | Nos. in 00s | 8,93,530 | |
| | | | 100.0 | |
| 32. | Average size of Operational Holding | | | |
| | (i) Marginal | Hectares | 0.39 | |
| | (ii) Small | Hectares | 1.43 | |
| | (iii) Semi-medium | Hectares | 2.76 | |
| | (iv) Medium | Hectares | 5.97 | |
| | (v) Large | Hectares | 17.22 | |
| 33. | Assets and Debts | | | |
| | (i) Average value of total assets | Rupees | 36,090 | 40,573 |
| | (ii) Assets less than Rs. 10,000/- | Per cent | 39.0 | 45.0 |
| | (iii) Land | Per cent | 62.1 | 32.4 |
| | (iv) Building | Per cent | 20.7 | 35.7 |
| | (v) Households in debts | Per cent | 20.0 | 17.0 |
| | (vi) Average debt per indebted household | Rupees | 3,311 | 5,930 |
| | (vii) Debt owned to institutions | Per cent | 61.2 | 59.9 |
| 34. | Banking | | | |
| | (i) Bank Offices | Per cent | 55.6 | 44.4 |
| | (ii) Bank Offices per lakh of population | Number | 5.6 | 11.0 |
| | (iii) Bank Deposits | Per cent | 13.8 | 86.2 |
| | (iv) Per capita Deposits | Rupees | 221 | 4,464 |
| | (v) Bank Advances | Per cent | 13.6 | 86.4 |
| | (vi) Per capita Advances | Rupees | 140 | 2,950 |
| 35. | Post Offices | Number | 1,29,394 | 15,325 |
| 36. | Post Offices per lakh of population | Number | 25 | 10 |
| 37. | Per capita income (1970-71) | Rupees | 440 | 1,201 |
| 38. | Per capita income (at current prices) | Rupees | 710 | 3,650 |
| 39. | Number of poor | Million | 232.2 | 50.5 |
| 40. | Population below poverty line | Per cent | 28.3 | 25.7 |

## Rural Infrastructure

Most of the village population in India are small and are dispersed over the countryside. This makes it financially and administratively difficult to provide the required amenities and the development infrastructure to all these populations. Usually, the remote villages suffer the most. They often have poorer soils and lack irrigation facilities. Their poverty calls for urgent and utmost attention, but being comparatively difficult locations, they receive the scantiest consideration. The lack of easy approach to these villages is the major reason for their being left out of the mainstream of development. In most of the agro-climatically homogeneous regions, villages which have asphalted approach roads have always experienced higher growth and development, compared to those which do not have any such approach roads. Similarly, if we examine the road development per square kilometer area in different states vis-a-vis the agricultural growth rate experienced in these states, we will find a high degree of correlation between these two variables. In fact, when we think of the rural infrastructure to support dynamic socio-economic superstructures, the village approach roads assume primary importance. One major factor which has made a singular contribution to the agricultural/rural development of Punjab and Haryana, is the priority given to the village approach roads. All the villages are approachable through the asphalt roads. Not only that, villages have circular roads around, making the asphalt road accessible to every village household. This reduces the communication gap between the villages and the urban-based socio-economic, cultural and political centres of activity. Education leading to a bilateral flow of knowledge and understanding, makes demonstration effects more visible.

**Table 4**

**BASIC AMENITIES IN VILLAGES**

*(Percentages of village having a particular amenity located within a specified distance by State.)*

| | *Facility* | *All-India* | *Minimum* | *Maximum* |
|---|---|---|---|---|
| **A.** | **Within 2 Km** | | | |
| 1. | Metalled Road | 45.8 | 22.2 Meghalaya | 98.3 Kerala |
| 2. | Bus Stop | 40.3 | 17.3 Nagaland | 98.0 Kerala |
| 3. | Post Office | 53.2 | 18.6 Meghalaya | 99.7 Kerala |
| 4. | Primary School | 90.1 | 81.3 Rajasthan | 99.7 Kerala |
| 5. | Middle School | 43.8 | 39.4 Nagaland | 98.6 Kerala |
| 6. | High School | 20.9 | 20.2 Gujarat | 96.7 Kerala |
| 7. | Dispensary | 24.6 | 8.7 Meghalaya | 90.6 Kerala |
| 8. | Health Centre | 12.0 | 5.6 Rajasthan | 46.7 Kerala |
| 9. | Daily Market | 14.8 | 7.4 Maharashtra | 56.1 Kerala |
| 10. | Hat | 26.8 | 13.4 Gujarat | 51.8 Kerala |
| 11. | F.P. Shop for Grocery | 35.1 | 10.2 Nagaland | 98.8 Kerala |

**Table 4 (Contd)**

| | | | | |
|---|---|---|---|---|
| **B.** | **Within 5 Km.** | | | |
| 12. | Railway Station | 18.3 | — | 33.2 |
| | | | Sikkim | Punjab |
| 13 | Hospital | 35.5 | 9.1 | 78.4 |
| | | | Meghalaya | Kerala |
| 14. | Fertiliser Depot | 43.9 | 6.8 | 93.2 |
| | | | Nagaland | Kerala |
| 15. | Seeds Store | 40.3 | 6.5 | 64.9 |
| | | | Nagaland | Kerala |
| 16. | Agri. Pump Repair | 18.8 | 2.9 | 64.9 |
| | | | Meghalaya | Kerala |
| 17. | Storages & Warehousing | 20.7 | 3.3 | 66.5 |
| | | | Sikkim | Nagaland |
| 18. | Veterinary dispensary | 45.2 | 17.2 | 81.5 |
| | | | Rajasthan | Karala |
| 19. | Credit Co-operative | 60.8 | 7.2 | 95.9 |
| | | | Nagaland | Kerala |
| 20. | Bank | 39.9 | 6.9 | 96.1 |
| | | | Nagaland | Kerala |
| **C.** | **General** | | | |
| 21. | Electrical | 33.4 | 4.7 | 99.8 |
| | | | Meghalaya | Haryana |
| 22. | Village with Drinking Water | 92.6 | 75.3 | 99.4 |
| | | | Sikkim | Punjab |

*Source: Economic and Political Weekly, 6.4.1985.*

Any scheme of economic programme aimed at eradicating poverty — in rural as well as urban areas — has to be multi-pronged. The package scheme should make available all resources in adequate quantities as well as of good quality. This apart, the rural poor has to be trained in skills and introduced to modern technology. Further, they should be assured of a good market and a better return for their product.

## Conclusion

The picture of rural India as it emerges from the facts gives above is quite gloomy. The situation would have been even worse but for the measures adopted by successive governments since Independence to improve the rural economy and, to some extent, its structure.

Foodgrains production has increased from 52 million tonnes in 1951-52 to 212 million tonnes in 2001-2002. Production of commercial crops like cotton, jute and sugarcane, fruits and vegetables has also increased significantly. However, in regard to pulses and oilseeds, particularly the former, success has eluded us till now. The pathetic dependence on food air and foodrains imports has been successfully overcome. Had it not for the massive increase of 508 million in population during this period, per capital availability of foodgrains would have gone up substantially. This, however, does not mean every person would have been well fed since we cannot assume that everyone would have had adequate purchasing power to buy the needed food. But had the population grown more slowly, landlessness and unemployment would have been definitely less, and to that extent, earning of the poor would have been higher.

Since the beginning of planning, the range and rate of change have increased tremendously and as a result, the rural communities are also experiencing unprecedented changes. As a result, the social structure and social organisation of the village are also affected. The democratisation of the polity, abolition of discrimination of various kinds, attempt to reduce the abysmal economic inequality by reducing the extent of concentration of wealth, increasing facilities of health, education, recreation, all these have a differential impact on different segments of rural population and as a result, the traditional stable relationship and institutional arrangements among the various rural groups are undergoing radical transformations.

Inspite of our planned development, efforts involving deployment of huge resources in financial, material and human terms during the last three and a half decades spread over seven five year plans, the standard of living of the rural people has not changed significantly.

As regards planning, there is growing evidence that investments in the public sector have not only sustained but also enriched the private enterprise; that the income distribution has increasingly been tilted in favour of the organised sector of the economy as against unorganised sector; that the bureaucracy, the professional groups, the rural elite and the politicians have improved their share in the national cake at the cost of agriculture and weaker sections of the population; and that inter-personal income and wealth disparities have increased so sharply over the last four decades in India. The ruling Congress party proved to be a vehicle of maintaining the status quo rather than serve as an instrument of social change and transformation. The administrative system that India inherited from the British was obviously unsuited to the task of initiating a process of rapid social and economic change that the country required urgently after independence.

Finally, the growth model and development strategy that were adopted, relegated agriculture and rural development to a back seat in the mistaken belief that sufficient linkages existed between the urban and rural sectors of the economy and that the development of the top sector would automatically inject growth impulses into the other sectors. The belief was based on the analogy of Western experience in the nineteenth century, which was simply inapplicable to the Indian situation.

Seventy per cent of the people in India live in over 5,87,226 villages. According to the available data, over 30 per cent of rural people aggregating 29.65 crores live below the proverbial poverty line. On the basis of empirical studies, except Punjab, the average income of rural people in all States fall below the poverty line. Poverty is not only noticed in income but also in living conditions too. Thus rural poverty has become multi-dimensional in character. Poverty is not only of income but also of health, literacy, character, culture, housing, clothing etc. In short, more than 40 crores of rural people are existing in an hostile and unhygienic environment.

## FOOD FOR THOUGHT

**Despite India's economy growing at a heartening rate of over eight per cent, it still continues to have alarming number of malnourished children.**

**Here is a glance at the country's woeful record:**

- Indian with 46 per cent malnourished children, is among the most malnourished countries in the world.
- Bangladesh has the highest number of malnourished children in the world.
- A World Bank report had estimates that India could lose about 2.5 billion US dollars in productivity every year because of malnourishment.
- India's malnourishment rate has consistently remained on the higher side even though it has fallen among poor nations of Sub-Saharan Africa.
- In states like Bihar and Orissa, upto 60 per cent of children fall in the category of low nutrition, whereas in Punjab and Kerala, the rate is 25-30 per cent.

## SURGING AHEDA FOR IMPLEMENTATION OF PEOPLE'S PLAN

- Human Development Index and Human Poverty Index development for the first time, directly capturing the process of human development at the State level in India by covering nearly 70 distinct social indicators of the various aspects of quality of life and well-beling of the people.
- All States are assisted for bringing out State Human Development Reports to benchmark the status and progress of human development at the district level and recommend policy planning interventions.
- Monitorable targets explicitly specified to be achieved by 2007 for the first time covering economic, social and environmental dimensions of human development which among others the following:
  - (a) All children to complete 5 years of schooling.
  - (b) Reduction in Infant Mortality Rate to 45 per 1000 live births.
  - (c) All villages to have sustained accesss to potable drinking water.
- 163 priority agenda and thrust areas identified to give special push for the implementation of monitorable largets.
- Pradhan Mantri Gramodaya Yojana (PMGY) introduced and Rs. 13,700 crore allocated as Additional Central Ass-istance to all the States in order to achieve the objective of sustainable human development at the village level.
- 15% of allocated PMGY funds earmarked to be spent specifically by all States for nutrition and another 15% for mid-day meal scheme.
- Rs. 394 crore allocated as Additional Central Assistance for 51 backward districts covering all Atates and Union Territories for Nutrition Programme of Adolescent Girls.
- Approval given in principle to PURA - a programme for Providing Urban Services to Rural Areas, to approximately 40,000 villages 10 4130 clusters.

**"The poor ofter don't get the water they need so desperately. This lack of access to water has much to do with governance and the way water is managed"**

**Tadao China, ADB President**

**Today, the vision an integrated, prosperous, poverty-free and peaceful Asia is no longer a dream, but an achievable goal**

**Infrastructure is critical for realizing sustained economic growth, and has strong positive linkages with other sectors**

**"People are so mush better performed about health and Nutrition. Now there is more knowledge so it easier to work in local community"**

**Fahrinawati, a midwife at Kurau**

**"Our goal is to serve the people and alleviate poverty among our farmers"**

*"Under **Bharat Nirman**, developmental works are undertaken in the areas of irrigation, road, rural housing, rural water supply, rural electrification and rural telecommunication connectivity. Specific targets are to be achieved under each of these goals so that there is accountability in the progress of this initiative. Bharat Nirman is viewed as an effort to unlock rural India's growth potential and to be a key for ushering a new era. It is also expected that Bharat Nirman will lead to considerable rural assets creation along with the National Rural Employment Guarantee Act. Bharat Nirman however is a collective agenda in which every Indian has a role either as a user or as a partner."*

# Chapter 3
# RURAL POVERTY

## Introduction

The phenomenon of poverty does not only affect the individual (poor) but is productive of danger to nations. The Philadelphia Charter has postulated that "Poverty anywhere constitutes a danger to prosperity everywhere."

Poverty is proverbial and universal. It is relative term and it is understood in relation to prosperity. Poverty and prosperity are comparative concepts. Hence from time immemorial, the poor have co-existed with the rich in India as well as throughout the world. Adam Smith says "Man is rich or poor according to the degree in which he can offered to enjoy the necessaries, the conveniences, and the amusements of life." The word degree is not equal in all periods and in all places. What is more, even among poor, there are again poor in the higher bracket and poor in lower bracket. We have discussed the concept of poverty and assessed the causes of rural poverty in India in this chapter. The discussion is in fact a forerunner of the varied measures of integrated rural development.

## What is Poverty?

Poverty is deprivation. Such deprivation has four essential features. First, it is deprivation of the basic necessities of life food, clothing and housing, from which, according to me, all other accompanying deprivations flow, educational and intellectual deprivation, cultural and moral deprivations, what anthropologists have come to call the culture of poverty. Second, deprivation means being deprived of what one is entitled to. Everyone is entitled, has right, to a decent standard of living, and deprivation negates this entitlement and right. Third,there are various degrees of deprivation which we in this country have covered by inventing such terms as the poorest of the poor, the very poor and the poor.

- Poverty is a mind set, accompanied by low morale, low expectation, low resourcefulness, low ability.

- Low levels of education and health support underpin and sustain the mind set of poverty
- Social structures perpetuate poverty

Poverty is a multi-faceted concept. Various authorities have defined it in relative terms. Townsend has said: "Poverty must be regarded as a general form of relative deprivation which is the effect of the maldistribution of resources. That section of the population whose resources are so depressed from the mean as to be deprived of enjoying the benefits and participating in the activities which are customary in that society can be said to be in poverty." This is to the same thing as saying that the poor are the 10 percent or 20 percent in every society with the least resources.

Martinrein observes: "Three broad concepts of poverty can be identified. Poverty can be defined as subsistence, inequality and externality. Subsistence is concerned with the minimum provision needed to maintain health and working capacity. Inequality is concerned with the relative position of the income groups to each other. The concept of poverty must be seen in the context of society as a whole. To understand the poor we must study the affluent. Externality is concerned with the social consequence of poverty for the rest of the rather than in terms of the needs poor."

According to Gillin and Gillin: "Poverty is that condition in which a person, either because of inadequate income or unwise expenditure, does not maintain a scale of living to provide for his physical and

**Box 1**
**POVERTY IS CANCER NOT FLU**

What is critical for human progress is poverty of opportunity, not poverty of income. Poverty of income is often the result, poverty of opportunity is often the cause. Poverty of opportunity is an multidimensional concept, embracing lack of education and health, lack of economic assets, social exclusion, and political marginalisation. It is time to say a final farewell to single-dimensional measures of income poverty (like the World Bank's measure of $ 1 a day), and to adopt a multidimensional concept, however inadequate its measurement may be in the initial stages. Let us honestly recognize that poverty is not merely a flu, it is more like a cancer. We cannot leave intact the model of development that produces persistent poverty and wistfully hopes that we can take care of poverty downstream through limited income transfers or discrete poverty reduction programmes. If the poor lack education, if they lack critical assets (particularly land) if they lack credit since the formal credit institutions refuse to bank on them, if they are socially, excluded and politically marginalised, then a few technocratic programmers downstream are not the real answer. The real answer lies in changing the very model of development, from traditional economic growth to human development, where human capabilities are built up and human opportunities enlarged, where people become the real agents and beneficiaries of economic growth rather than remain an abstract residual of inhuman development processes.

Such human development models rely on certain core strategies for the elimination of poverty—in particular basic education for all, land reforms, credit to the poor, equitable growth, women's empowerment, and good governance. This is the main lesson from the experience of several countries which have substantially reduced poverty over the last two decades, including Malaysia, China, Republic of Korea, and Colombia.

These experiences show the these countries restructured their models of development to generate pro-poor growth. Poverty was treated as a fundamental problem, requiring basic changes in the economic system, not mere cosmetic tinkering.

(Source : Mahbub ul Haq in UNDP 1998.)

mental efficiency and to function usually according to the standards of the society of those things which are requisite for an individual to maintain himself and those dependent upon him for health and vigour."

Combining the two aspects of production and resources utilisation, poverty of defined as "a kind of organisation of production where the mass of the people, constituting the main productive resource of the economy vices they need because the non-human resources required to activate them are owned by a few who use it for the production of goods and services they need, because the non-human resources required to activate them are owned by a few who use it for the production of goods and services they require." Mahatma Gandhi considered poverty was the curse of God. He wrote: "Poverty was the curse of God. It deprived you of everything: food, clothing, shelter, your self-respect, your humanity, even your soul. In poverty, you suffered not only hunger, nakedness, the cruelty of cold and heat, the blind fury of Nature's wild elements; you also suffered from humiliation, loss of human dignity. You were driven to acknowledge defeat and overwhelmed by distress and despair. You were compelled to take to crime or beggary for a morsel of bread, women having to sell their own souls to keep their bodies or those of their wives and children, to keep the wolf from the door, to put an end to their pangs of hunger or thirst." Sri Aurobindo, however looked at it from the point of view of an organised society. He said: "The acceptance of poverty is noble and beneficial in a class or an individual, but it becomes fatal and pauperizes the life of its richness and expansion if it is perversely organised into a general or national ideal. Poverty is no more a necessity of social life than disease of the natural body; false habits of life and an ignorance of our true organisation are in both cases the peccant causes of an avoidable disorder."

Poverty was earlier a quantitative measure of economic deprivation. But, now the emphasis is equally on lack of opportunities, access to resources and other human development parameters. Even today, at the turn of the century, a quarter of the world's population lives a miserable life of absolute poverty as measured by the one dollar per day international norm. If the definition of poverty were expanded to incorporate the human development parameters, world poverty level would touch 60 per cent.

In India, the Net Poverty Line measures the amount of money required to replenish the energy equivalent of 2,400 k cal per day in urban areas (2,100 in rural). This is about half a kg of rice, which translate as Rs 7-8/day/person. With this very, very low cut off, 26 per cent Indians fall below the poverty line (BPL). Internationally, two dollars/day/person is poverty and one dollar/day/person is chronic poverty. If you apply these yardsticks, 70 per cent of our people will qualify as poor and the BPL 26 per cent will qualify as worse than chronically poor. *The UN has estimated that 70 per cent of the world's poor are women.*

## The Why of Poverty

The basic cause is that small number in the country own the assets- land, houses, stocks and shares and deposits in the banks (both in 'black and white') while the majority of people are assetless. Incomes which enable one to buy what is needed and liked in food, clothing, housing (and cultural goods), are earned through working in wage employment and self-employment, or as return—rent, interest, profit—on the property one owns.

## The Environment of Poverty

Poverty has been one of the factors affecting economic growth. Even the varied strategies adopted through proved beneficial turned out to be suicidal for the harmonious growth of mankind.

As a result, there is a decline in value system and followed by severe side effects affecting the social fabric. Income poverty is only one aspect of the community. Poverty means deprivation or denials. These are classified into four categories:

(*i*) Deprivation of the basic necessities of life—food, clothing and housing.

(*ii*) Deprivation of values (cultural poverty)—educational, intellectual, cultural and moral.

*(iii)* Deprivation of a decent standard of living, right to work and right to live in peace.

*(iv)* Deprivation of entitlements because of concentration with a few. Poverty is a phenomenon induced by inequality broadly. Poverty is classified as follows:

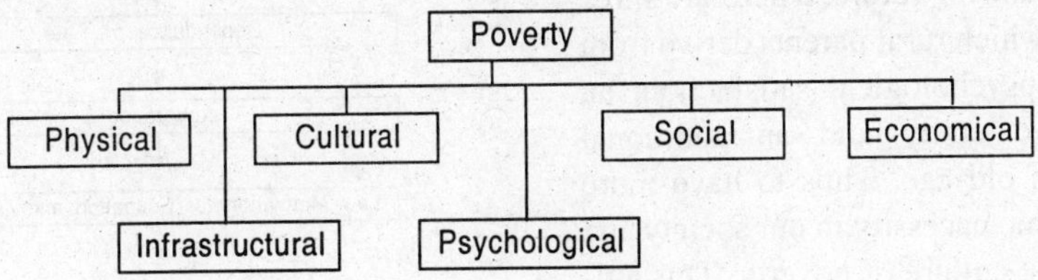


*Fig. 1. Types of Environment*

The environment of poverty is conditioned by malnutrition which increases vulnerability to decease as well as reduces learning ability. Malnutrition adversely effects fuller mental development, physical growth, productivity, the span of working years, all of which significantly influence the economic potential of men and women. Lack of education increases ignorance and reduces the scope for self-improvement and also ignorance of means-to prevent sickness. It also effects the norms and value system. Illiteracy and fertility is a vicious combination. Poor housing, with lack of basic amenities provide for poor physical environment which results in high incidence of water-borne and air-borne diseases. On the other hand, continuous learning environment, which *inter alia* develops ignorance about food sources, diet, food preparation, storage, etc. Poor health also reduces one's ability to absorb food. The net result of malnutrition, illiteracy, poor housing and poor health is reduced production of basic goods and low incomes. This also results in low skills, lower productivity and lower income. Poverty affect the quality and quantity, of human capital, which is the end and means of economic growth.

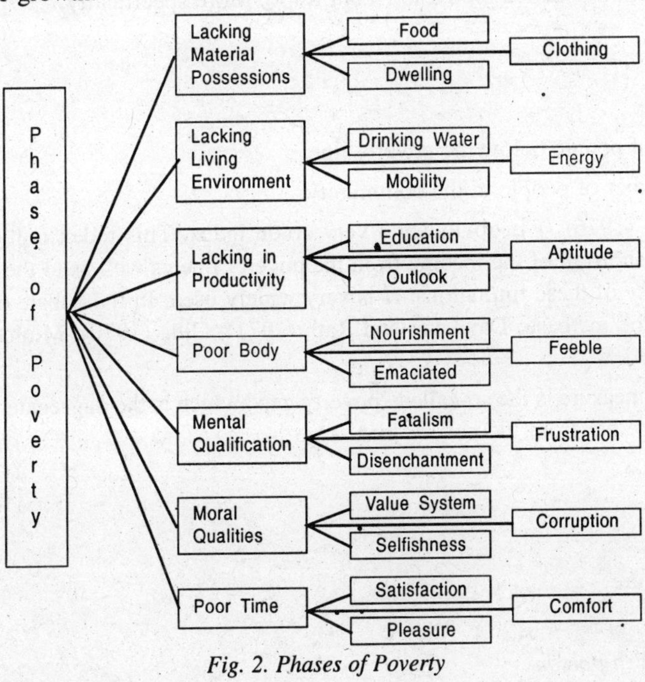


*Fig. 2. Phases of Poverty*

## The Culture of Poverty

The culture of poverty is associated with a sense of resignation, fatalism, a low motivation for education and change, inadequate preparation for an occupation and no plan for future. There are three types of satisfaction which rural parents derive from additional child—a psychological satisfaction, an additional productive entity and an additional source of security in old age. Thus to have more children is an economic necessity in our society and it is a reflection of the culture of poverty. This attitude has also let to strong son preference in India and discrimination against women. Males have an easier accessibility to educational facilities than females do. There is positive evidence to conclude that the health status of women declined over the last thirty years. Such attitude reveals the poverty of culture and thus a vicious circle is created. It is only socio-economic change that can break this vicious circle. The best way to bring about this socio-economic change is to provide educational and gainful employment opportunities.

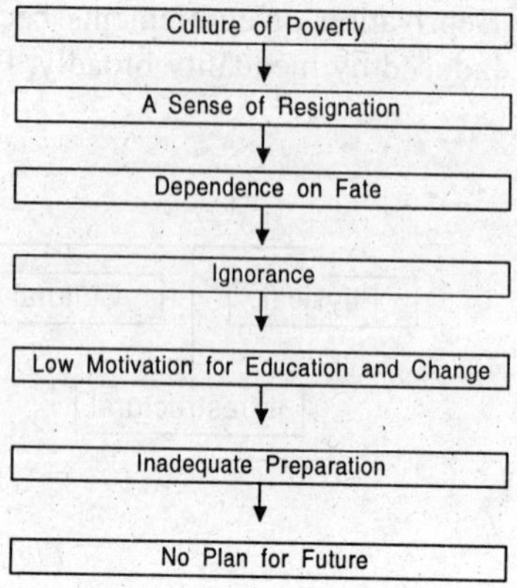


*Fig. 3 : Culture of Poverty*

## Measurement of Poverty

The measurement of poverty involves two distinct problems, namely:

*(i)* The specification of "poverty line" ; and

*(ii)* Determination of the index of poverty.

In India, most of the studies on poverty regard the proportion of people below the poverty line as the index of poverty. This ratio is called the Head Count Ratio. More specifically,

$H = \frac{q}{n}$, where

H = Poverty Index

q = The number of people below the poverty line.

n = The total number of people in the community.

According to Sen (1976) *H* is obviously a very crude index. This index is highly insensitive to the extent of the aggregate shortfall of the income from the poverty line as well as to the distribution of income amongst the poor. Inspite of these limitations, *H* is very widely used. In the debate on whether or not rural poverty in India is on the increase, Dandekar and Rath (1971), Ojha (1970), Minhas (1970) and Bardhan (1971) have used this index.

Another common measure is the so-called "poverty gap" which is the aggregate shortfall of the income of all the poor taken together from the poverty line. That is,

$$I = \frac{i=1}{qz}$$

where gi = Z ~ yi

In the above measure,

z = Poverty line

Yi-Income of the i'*th person*

q = number of poor people

The above ratio gives us the percentage of their mean shortfall from the poetry level. This measure is totally insensitive to the number of people living below the poverty line. Thus, while the head-count ratio (*H*) is completely insensitive to the extent of the poverty shortfall per person, the income-gap ratio (*I*) is completely insensitive to the index of poverty. But (*H*) and (*I*) is completely insensitive to the numbers involved. According to Sen (1976) has suggested a measure which is sensitive to the gaps in the incomes of the poor. His measure is: P = H (I + (1 – I) G)

where,

$$H = \frac{q}{n} = \text{Head-count ratio}$$

$$I = \frac{i - 1\ gi}{qz} = \text{Income gap ratio}$$

and *G* is the Gini coefficient of the income distribution of the poor.

The index lies in between zero and unity. If P = 0, this index shows that every one has an income greater than z, and if P=1 everyone has zero income. In practice of course, P will never take these two extreme values.

Referring to the problem of poverty, A. K. Sen says that the usual procedure is to identify some level of income which is required for the recommended balanced diet, and to consider those falling below that level as poor. He has added two more criteria:

(*i*) We should be concerned not merely with the number of people living below the poverty line but also with the amounts by which the incomes of the poor fall short of the specified poverty level; and

(*ii*) The bigger the shortfall from the poverty level, the greater should be the weight per unit of that shortfall in the poverty measure.

On this basis, Sen develops his P measure of poverty as:

$$P = \frac{2}{(q + 1)\ xy\ {*}i = 1}\ i = q$$

Where

n is the population size.

y in the income of ith individual arranged in the ascending order of magnitude.

Y is the minimum acceptable level of income or the poverty line.

q is the number of people at or below the poverty line.

**Box 2**

**POVERTY MEASUREMENT**

Three different measures of poverty—the headcount index (H), the poverty gap index (PG), and the squared poverty gap index (SPG)—which belong to the general class of poverty measures introduced by Foster, Greer and Thorbecke (1984) are now widely used to capture alternative dimensions of poverty corresponding to its incidence, depth, and severity respectively. H, is given by the proportion of the population whose per-capita consumption or income level (measured standard of living) is below the poverty line whose real value is fixed over time. H measures the incidence of poverty. However, H has its limitation because it does not give an indication of how the poor population is distributed along the consumption or income spectrum below the poverty line. The other two measures provide such information. The PG, is the average distance below the poverty line in the population (counting the non-poor as having zero poverty line. The PG captures the depth of poverty. The last measure SPG, which measures the severity of poverty among the poor, is based on the individual poverty gaps raised to a power of 2.

## Rural Poverty

Poverty in general connotes deficiency or insufficiency of acceptable material needs of the people. It can cover a range from extreme want of necessities resulting in debility due to malnutrition to falling short of having comfortable means, which may conceptually be categorised as absolute and relative. Poverty also encompasses other vital component of life like, straits etc. As a matter of fact, poverty in India is treated as an absolute phenomenon. The needs have often been expressed in terms of a basket of food items satisfying certain desirable calorie requirements. The minimum income or consumption expenditure which enables one to attain this basket, is known as poverty line. This is just one of the method of measuring poverty. In fact, poverty of character exists among the rich and vice versa. But, in reality, great difference of opinion on finding either the energy norms or the monetary equivalent of it due to the regional and demographic variation in the population of India.

The Planning Commission in India has adopted the following definition for poverty "In the Sixth Plan (1980-85) a daily intake of 2,400 calories per capita in rural areas and 2,000 in urban areas, corresponding to a consumption expenditure or Rs.65 per capita per month in rural areas and Rs.75 per capita per month in urban areas, has been adopted to define the poverty line.

**Table 1**

**CHANGES IN RURAL POVERTY BY AGRO-CLIMATIC REGION**

| *Region* | *Headcount 1987-88* | *Headcount 1972-73* | *Per cent change* |
|---|---|---|---|
| **I. Smallest percentage reduction in poverty 1972-73 and 1987-88** | | | |
| Haryana eastern | 18.6 | 16.0 | +16.5 |
| UP southern | 50.2 | 44.5 | +12.7 |
| UP eastern | 42.7 | 41.6 | +2.6 |
| J&K Jhelum valley | 13.4 | 13.1 | +2.4 |
| Bihar central | 51.9 | 52.9 | –1.9 |
| Rajasthan western | 28.3 | 29.1 | –2.6 |
| Rajasthan north eastern | 29.2 | 30.1 | –3.1 |
| Karnataka inland southern | 31.9 | 33.5 | –4.8 |
| Bihar northern | 53.0 | 56.3 | –5.9 |
| TN northern | 52.9 | 56.3 | –6.0 |
| **II. Largest percentage reduction in poverty 1973-74 and 1987-88** | | | |
| Gujarat Saurashtra | 16.9 | 30.2 | –44.2 |
| Maharashtra inland western | 30.2 | 54.3 | –44.3 |
| Kerala southern | 26.7 | 48.9 | –45.5 |
| Maharashtra coastal | 29.2 | 61.6 | –52.6 |
| Gujarat eastern | 33.4 | 71.5 | –53.3 |
| AP inland northern | 21.5 | 46.9 | –54.2 |
| WB Himalaya | 26.5 | 61.0 | –56.5 |
| AP coastal | 17.0 | 39.8 | –57.2 |
| Karnataka coastal and ghats | 10.7 | 39.6 | –73.1 |
| UP Himalayan | 8.4 | 42.1 | –80.1 |

## Who are the Poor?

Factors such as population density, ecological conditions and the availability of irrigation and transport account for some of these differences among India's states and even within them. Other conditions affecting the rural poor—gender, literacy, land ownership, employment status, and caste — create a more consistent pattern. Thus an illiterate rural woman, a member of a scheduled tribe or caste, a person living in a landless household or dependent on wage earning, all face a significantly higher than average risk of poverty. According to the NCAER survey, the incidence of poverty was

- 52 per cent for the landless as a whole,
- 68 per cent for landless wage-earners,
- 50 and 51 per cent for the roughly 206 million members of scheduled castes and tribes, respectively,
- 45 per cent for households in which all members were illiterates compared to 27 per cent for households where both male and female adult read and write.

*Source:* Dreze and Srinivasan (1996).

## Poverty in India

- 300 million people live below the poverty line in India.
- Of which, 200 million are hungry.
- World's largest population of poor.
- Official anti-poverty schemes have had marginal impact.
- Trickle down linkages weak in Indian economy.

## Why the Problem Persists

- The population has grown crossing 105 crores.
- Inadequate resource to deal with the problem.
- Government sponsored anti-poverty schemes too small, too thinly spread out.
- Asset creation programmes hijacked by middle men.
- Faulty design mislocates root cause of poverty in income and wealth factors

## Impact of Government Schemes

- Eliminates famine, but not poverty.
- Creates psychology of dependence and helplessness.
- Food for work programmes dislocate families, children suffer most.
- Encourages massive corruption.

**Box 3**
**WHO IS POOR ?**

**Evidence from village studies in UP and Bihar**
A typical "poor" household, according to villagers, is one at the low end of the caste hierarchy (most often a member of the Scheduled Castes (SCs) or Scheduled Tribes (STs). While the SC and ST households are usually grouped in a separate hamlet at the edge of the village, a few of these families occupy a homestead plot in the village which belongs to their upper castes employer. Landlessness in terms of lack of access to fertile, well-watered agricultural land was mentioned as a cause and charateristic of poverty in every village. Lack of a homestead plot was said to be particularly grave, since the homeless are often forced to enter into an attached labour agreement with a wealthy household in order to secure a place to live. Attached labourers usually receive a small plot of land (homestead and/or agricultural) and other benefits from their patron, such as access to credit and food during lean periods. In the worst case the attached laborer is further bound to his patron through chronic indebtedness. Debt bondage though illegal in India, can still be found, is called upon to do so, usually at a wage that is no more than half the rate for unattached casual labour. When not working for the patron, the attached labourer must work for other employers on a casual basis. Even those who have homestead land are used for collection of forest products.

Particularly in areas with high tribal populations, the very poor were often used for collection of firewood or fodder for their livelihood. The women and children of these households are often the primary collectors of these products. Contributing in this way to household subsistence deprives these children of educational opportunities that would equip them to break the cycle of poverty. In addition to endangering their lives, collection and sale of forest products adds significantly to the "double burden" of domestic and external responsibilities that all but the wealthiest women must bear. Widows or the abandoned wives of migrant labourers are particularly vulnerable. Particularly if they have small children to support, these women were invariably placed among the "poorest" by interviewers in all the study villages.

(*Source.* Klozel *et. al.* forthcoming.)

## Causes of Rural Poverty in India

Poverty has many faces. And its causes vary from one thinker to another, and from one environment to another. Henry and George hold that the main cause of poverty is the personal ownership of large area of land. Karl Marx is of the opinion that "Poverty is the exploitation of the labourer by the capitalist." Malthus, on the other hand, enunciated that the rapid growth of population was the main cause of poverty. Has arithmetic progression, while population increases in geometric progression." However, poverty is the result of multiple causes. Economic, political, geographical, social and cultural factors, individually or collectively, contribute to poverty.

Among the important economic factors, the steady growth of population and the prevalent inheritance laws have resulted in the fragmentation of land. Moreover, the economically non-viable farmers sell their land to big landlords and or traders or urban dwellers and become agricultural labourers themselves; they have some partial employment. Low productivity coupled with some vices push a large number of people into poverty. The birth rate among the poor is also higher. Ignorance is a contributory factor. For example, Family Planning Workers' in an Indian village demonstrated the use of condoms by unrolling them on a bamboo pole and holding aloft the pole for all to see. With reassuring nods from everyone, the workers left the village with enough stocks of condoms. But when they returned some months later, they were surprised to observe groups of pregnant woman, who complained about the ineffectiveness of the new technology. The women insisted they had followed the instructions to the letter. And when the family planning worker visited their homes, they found the condoms gathering dust in corners, that the condoms had been duly unfurled on bamboo poles and were gathering dust. The poor, because they are poor, often resort to robbery, etc. In short, there is a decline in the value system. Exploitation by the affluent also functions. In other words, poverty strikes the poor, physically, materially, socially and culturally.

In rural areas, land is the principal productive asset. But land is very unevenly distributed.

The problem of poverty has been aggravated by the steady increase in population and the consequent rise in unemployment. By and large, the lower income groups tend to have larger families. This fact, to some extent, accounts for the low consumption and high unemployment among the poor. Moreover, they suffer from social disabilities. Most of them belong to scheduled castes/tribes and other backward classes. They are illiterate and are engaged mostly in unskilled occupations, in which the wages are very low.

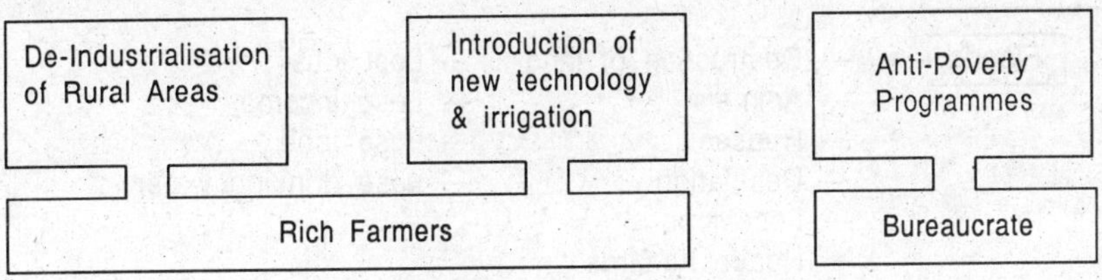


Rural Population Rising at 2.5%
Rural Employment at 0.5%
Rural Real Income at 0.8%

*Fig. 4. Causes of Rural Poverty*

Most significantly, the perpetuation of rural poverty is ensured by the double strategy of deindustrialising the rural area and pumping into agriculture resources which fall into the hands of rich farmers. To make matters worse, the bureaucrats pocket a large proportion of the funds allocated under the so-called anti-poverty programme.

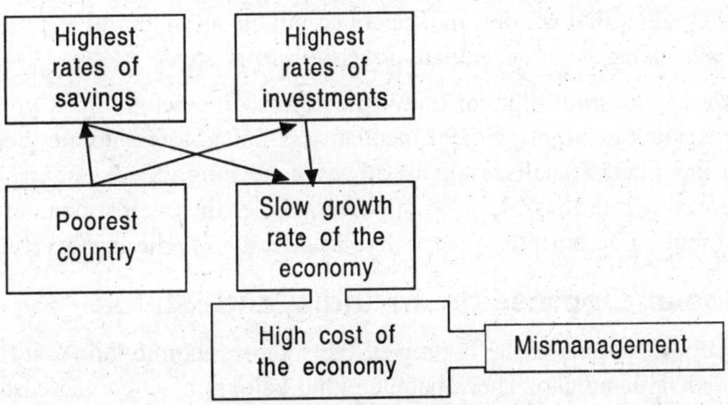


*Fig. 5. Growth Process*

The rural poor are caught in another vicious circle. Whatever little improvement occurs in their income or assets in one year is washed away in the next. In a drought year, the incomes of the agriculturists fall all along the line except the incomes of those who have assured irrigation. Drought affects both the rich and the poor farmers. In fact, during the drought period, the crisis overtakes everyone and ultimately affects industry. All these developments push the poor further down the line. They lose jobs they lose incomes; and they cannot buy food.

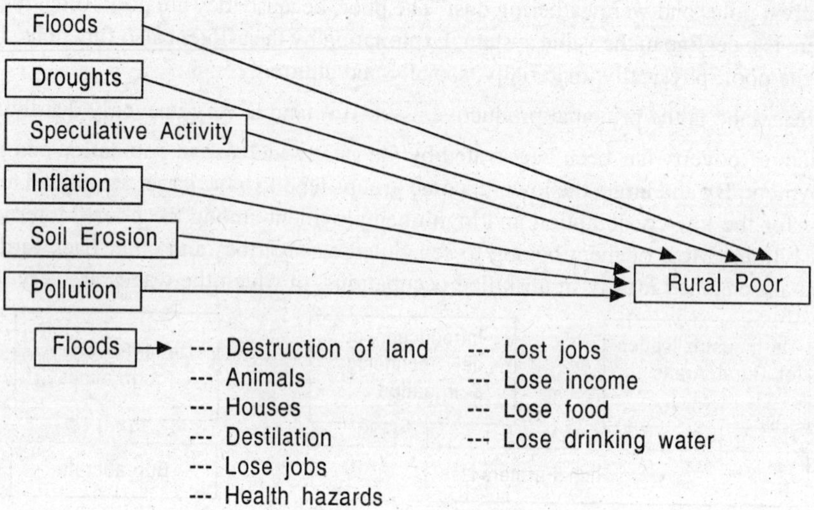


*Fig. 6. Vicious Circle of Poverty*

And when floods come, there is the destruction of other assets. Lands are washed away. Cattle disappear. Houses collapse. The poor are uprooted in the process. They lose jobs. Health hazards for them become serious.

According to a recent study, the causes of poverty are abject poverty (having meagre means of livelihood), unemployment (agriculture provides about 175-190 days of work in the year), lack of employment opportunities outside agriculture, depressed wages (in the case of increase in the labour force in rural areas), political disputes (wranglings over land, women, family feuds or status), inefficiency, caste systems and illiteracy. The inadequacy of civil amenities, inefficient communication facilities, problems of transport and non-availability of safe drinking water accentuate poverty in rural areas.

The causes of poverty are multi-dimensional—they are social, economical, political, managerial, organisational, cultural, psychological, etc. Social inequality is linked to economic inequality—- each being the cause and effect of the other. Socialist slogans, however meaningful, are only useful means of winning the votes of the ignorant, illiterate masses, to be in power. Under the biggest democracy in the world, vast numbers of people continue to be born in poverty, live in poverty and die in poverty.

## Poverty Plus Social Oppression in India and States

- About one-fifth of Indians at the bottom of the socio-economic ladder suffer a double injustice: poverty plus social handicap. These people either belong to scheduled castes or scheduled tribes (SC or ST).
- Exploitation of man by man is pervasive in Indian society. But because of social discrimination, the scheduled castes and scheduled tribes have suffered from it in the most intense and inhuman form.
- The traditional economy, society and culture of the tribals inevitably tend to disintegrate in the face of the inexorable penetration of the so-called civilised world. What do the tribals gain as a result? Their 'gains' are—
  - — Loss of proprietorship of their ancestral lands to civilised outsiders, *i.e.* moneylenders, merchants, professionals, rich farmers and all sorts of upstarts:

— Bonded slavery, mysteriously mounting debts, exploitation through miserable wages; and
— Insult and humiliation at the hands of petty government officials.

- But even while continuing to be deeply shocked and indignant about the still continuing discrimination and oppression, it would be better if we maintain a broad, historical perspective and recognise the significant changes that have taken place since independence. There is no other developed country where similar changes have been effected for the benefit of its advantaged groups.

A little over half of the operational land-holding belong to marginal farmers with a size of holding of less than I hectare. Another nearly one-fifth of the holding belong to small farmers with a size of holding between and 2 hectares. These two small groups share 70 per cent of the farm holding in the country. Among the rural poor, mention should be made of Harijans and tribals. Both of them are landless.

Wide inter-State disparities are visible in the poverty ratios between rural and urban areas as also in the rates of decline of poverty. Among major States, Orissa, Bihar, West Bengal and Tamil Nadu had more than 50 percent of their population below the poverty line in 1983. By 1999-2000, while Tamil Nadu and West Bengal had reduced their poverty ratios by nearly half, Orissa and Bihar continued to be the two poorest States with poverty ratios of 47 and 43 percent respectively. In 1999-2000, 20 States and Union Territories had poverty ratios which were less than the national average. Among other States, Jammu and Kashmir, Haryana, Gujarat, Punjab, Andhra Pradesh, Maharashtra and Karnataka also succeeded in significantly reducing the incidence of poverty.

If poverty which has assumed such alarming dimensions is to be eliminated in this country, the policy of the government should primarily be to increase the productivity in agriculture and village industries. The second priority should be to help the poor in rural areas to earn more income through gainful and productivity activity.

The Tenth Plan had a similar approach. It set out the principal objectives as follows:

*(i)* the removal of unemployment and significant under-employment;

*(ii)* an appreciable rise in the standard of living of the poorest sections of the population;

*(iii)* provisions by the State of some of the basic needs of the people in these income groups like clean drinking water, adult literacy elementary education, health care, rural roads, rural housing for the landless and minimum services for the urban slums.

## Poverty, the Result of Sub-normal Access to Resources

The economic health of a household enterprise depends on its access to resources, both internal and external. Inter-household variations in income levels can be explained mainly in terms of their varying accessibility to resources. Absolute poverty is thus the result of a subnormal accessibility to resources. Resources available for use to a household may be sub-normal when:

- all resources are quantitatively inadequate;
- there is an imbalance between resources, with one (or more) acting as a constraint and one (or more) being under-utilised;
- one (or more) resource is inferior in quality, and therefore, acts as a constraint on the fuller utilisation of other resources.

For example, a landless labour household has only labour as its resource. To be productive, it relies on complementary resources from other households. If the collective access to resources in the community is insufficient to generate enough demand for labour to support the minimum level of living among landless labour households, the community's access to resources would be sub-normal, though this would not be true for all individual households. In some cases, all resources may be quantitatively inadequate to yield and income above the poverty line. The more common occurrence is one of imbalance where restricted availability of one or more critical resource (*e.g.*, labour) are under-utilised. The imbalance may also be potential; for instance, lack of knowledge or information may prevent a fuller utilisation of other resources and hence lead to a low income.

Poverty is that condition in which there is a shortage of articles and facilities to satisfy the basic needs of human life. Such condition may occur because of one's own undisciplined way of life, neglect of one's duties and responsibilities and squandering of the wealth in one's possession. It may also occur on account of natural calamities like floods, famines or of human frailties leading to destruction of crops, dwelling as well as minimum infrastructure. So poverty continues to persist.

**ANATOMY OF RURAL POVERTY IN INDIA**

| | *Type of Poverty* | *Extent of Rural Poverty* |
|---|---|---|
| 1. | Income | 80 per cent of the rural population earn less than Rs 6,500 per household per year. The average income of rural household was only Rs 4,550 per annum in 1988-89. |
| 2. | Marginal and Small Farming | Over 50 per cent of India's cultivator household cover only 9 per cent of cultivated area. the average size of operational holding is only 0.41 hectare and its irrigated component is only 0.08. Their income level is not different from that of agricultural labourers. The 65 per cent of rural families who together operate 9 per cent or less of the total land in India and own even a lower percentage of total assets are essentially deprived section who require some other form of income to survive throughout the year. |
| 3. | Agricultural Labourers | The population of agricultural labourers without any land is growing at an annual average inspite of migration. There were 7.50 crore agricultural lab-ourers in 2001. And, over 65 per cent of agricultural labourers are landless. |
| 4. | Rural Wages | The real wages of the agricultural labourers appears to have remained more or less stagnant, though the money wages have increased marginally, female and child labourers are not only paid less but are also exploited. |
| 5. | Problem Villages | As on 1-4-1985, there were 1,61,428 problem villages in India. The criteria for problem villages include:<br>*(a)* Those which do not have an assured source of drinking water within a reasonable distance, say 1.6 km.<br>*(b)* Those where the sources of water supply are endemic to water-borne disease like cholera, guinea worms, etc., and<br>*(c)* Those where the available water suffers from excess of salinity, iron of fluorides or other toxic elements hazardous to health.<br>During four years of the 7th plan, 1,34,776 villages have been covered. |
| 6. | Electricity in Rural India | Though 75 per cent of the villages were electrified as at end March 1988 only 10 per cent of rural household had access to electricity. Frequent breakdown in power supply affected agricultural operations quite adversely. It means that still over 90 per cent rural households do not have any access to electricity. |
| 7. | Roads | 3,30,282 villages (53.5 per cent) are not connected by all weather roads. Good-roads are the necessary prerequisite for improving the quality of life and eco-nomic conditions in rural India. |
| 8. | Illiteracy | According to the 1981 census, 36.75 crores of rural people are illiterate, accounting for 70 per cent of the rural population. What is more 59 per cent of males and 82 per cent of females are illiterate. Of which, 29 crores of adults are illiterate. Literacy is of supreme importance for health |

| | | |
|---|---|---|
| 9. | Rural Population | 52.55 crores or 76.69 per cent of the total population are living in rural areas. The rural death rate is nearly 70 per cent higher than the urban death rate and the death rate in the age group of 0-4 years are very high at 127 per 1000. |
| 10. | Malnutrition *** | Adequate nutrition is essential for good health and productivity. Malnutrition and under-nutrition afflicts 84 per cent of rural population of all strata reducing their energy and motivation, undermining their performance in every walk of life. It also reduces considerably their resistance to disease. According to the 1981 census, there are 11,18,948 disabled people in rural areas. |
| 11. | Housing 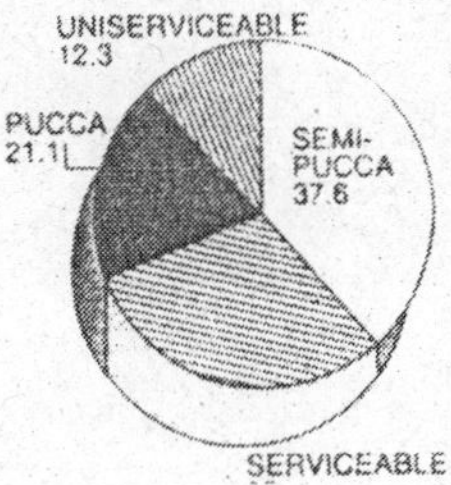  | The housing problem is further aggravated by the increase in population at the rate of 2.5 per cent per annum. But the problem of housing goes beyond just meeting the backlog and future demand. The type-wise classification of the current household stock also leaves much to be desired. In 1981, for instance, the rural areas hold only 21.1 per cent house in the *pucca* category, and about 12.3 per cent in the unserviceable *kutcha* category. In the urban areas, *pucca* houses accounted for nearly 6.5 per cent of the total and *kutcha* constructions for 11 per cent, the remainder being in the *semi-pucca* category. A large segment of rural population continue to live in unhygienic environment. 61.6 per cent of the total number of rural houses are built with poor material. 10.3 per cent are built with grass, leaves, reeds etc., 42 per cent by mud and 7.3 per cent with unburnt bricks. Housing shortage in rural India is expected to rise from 16.1 million units in 1981 to 22.3 million units by 1990 and 30 million units by 2000 A.D. Sanitation is quite negligible. 92.4 per cent of rural houses have no latrine facilities. |
| 12. | Unemployment | Over 16.02 million rural people are unemployed and about 23.55 million are under-employed. In addition over 30.39 million non-workers in rural India can work effectively, provided appropriate work opportunities are made available to them. This includes a large segment of women. |
| 13. | Financial Institutions | There are 1,27,123 post offices 31,094 commercial bank branches and 88,000 primary agricultural credit societies in rural India. These, however, cover only one-third of the rural population and villages in rural India. |
| 14. | Poverty Line | Even according to the existing measurement of poverty, over 55 per cent of the rural people (over 27.50 crores) live below the poverty line. If a composite view is considered, more than 75 per cent of the people continue to live below the poverty line in rural India. Poverty in rural India is manifested in a multi-directional way. The dimension of rural poverty is deep rooted as well as spreading. In absolute terms, on the present reckoning, people living below the poverty line may increase to 437.50 million by 2000 A.D. |

## POVERTY LINE—DIFFERENT ESTIMATES

**I. Planning Commission**

(at 1960-61 Prices)

Rs.20 per month-bare minimum level of living.

**II. P.K. Bardhan**

(at 1960-61 Prices)

Rs.15 per month for rural and

Rs.18 per month for urban areas on this basis, in 1968-69, 54 per cent of rural and 41 per cent of urban population was below poverty line.

**III. V.M. Dandekar and Nilkanth Rath**

(at 1960-61 Prices)

Rs.15 per month for rural and

Rs.22.50 per month for urban areas, on this basis, 40 per cent of the rural population and 50 per cent of the urban population was below poverty line.

**IV. National Sample Survey**

In 1973-74, about 46 per cent of the total population was below poverty line.

**V. Planning Commission**

In 1977-78, 48 per cent of rural and 41 per cent of urban population was below poverty line.

**VI. I.Z. Bhatty**

About 70 per cent of rural population was below poverty line.

**VII. Dr. P.V. Sukhatme**

About 15 per cent in rural 25 per cent in urban areas are below poverty line on the basis of minimum calories requirements varying between 2,100 to 2,400 calories.

**III. Planning Commission**

(at 1984-85 prices)

The per capita monthly expenditure at the poverty line has been estimated to be Rs. 107 in rural areas and Rs. 122 in urban areas. On the basis of NSS consumer expenditure distribution 38th round, 1983, 39.9 per cent of rural and 27.7 per cent of urban population was below poverty line.

*Note :* The above estimates partly differs due to different reference years.

The Planning Commission has been estimating the incidence of poverty at the national and state level using the methodology contained in the report of the Expert Group on Estimation of Proportion and Number of Poor (Lakdawala Committee) and applying it to consumption expenditure data from the large sample surveys on consumer expenditure conducted by the National Sample Survey Organisation (NSSO) at an interval of approximately five years. The latest available large sample survey data on consumer expenditure are for the 55th Round covering the period July 1999 to June 2000.

In the earlier Surveys, the NSSO estimated monthly consumption expenditure on the basis of responses using a 30-day recall period for all food and non-food items. In the 55th Round, the consumption expenditure on clothing, footwear, medical (institutional) and durable goods were collected using a 365-day recall period. In the case of all other non-food items, the 30-day recall period was used as earlier. The data on consumption expenditure on food items were collected using two different reference periods of last 30-days and last 7-days from the same households.

**Table 2**
**ESTIMATES OF INCIDENCE OF POVERTY IN INDIA**

| Year | *Poverty ratio (%)* | | | *Number of poor (million)* | | |
|---|---|---|---|---|---|---|
| | *Rural* | *Urban* | *Combined* | *Rural* | *Urban* | *Combined* |
| 1973-74 | 56.4 | 49.0 | 54.9 | 261.3 | 60.0 | 321.3 |
| 1977-78 | 53.1 | 45.2 | 51.3 | 264.3 | 64.6 | 328.9 |
| 1983 | 45.7 | 40.8 | 44.5 | 252.0 | 70.9 | 322.9 |
| 1987-88 | 39.1 | 38.2 | 38.9 | 231.9 | 75.2 | 307.1 |
| 1993-94 | 37.3 | 32.4 | 36.0 | 244.0 | 76.3 | 320.3 |
| 1999-00 | 27.1 | 23.6 | 26.1 | 193.2 | 67.1 | 260.3 |
| 2007* | 21.1 | 15.1 | 19.3 | 170.5 | 49.6 | 220.1 |

* Poverty projection for 2007.

*Source:* Tenth Five Year Plan, Vol. I. Planning Commission.

No generally acceptable yardstick has so far been evolved to measure poverty, with the result that the prevailing poverty line is an engima. The imprecise nature of this line enables the framing of hypotheses to suit the socio-political compulsions. The prevalent methodologies are only expressions in monetary terms of consumption at a precise level. This does not include in monetary terms of consumption at a precise level. This does not include other basic needs like clothing, housing, medicine and education. On this basis, the cut off point of poverty will be Rs. 180 per capita per month in rural areas and Rs.210 in urban areas, at the 1988-89 prices as against Rs.107 and Rs.122 at the 1984-85 prices. Average size of family to consist of five persons, the poverty line per annum is pitched in monetary terms at Rs. 10,800 and Rs 12,600 for the rural and urban scenarios. Accordingly, 70 per cent of rural and 50 per cent of urban population are living below the poverty line. In absolute terms about 505 million in rural and 95 million in urban areas are living in poverty in 1989, inspite of Nine Five Year Plans and the achievements in the last 56 years since independence.

**Table 3**
**TRENDS IN RURAL POVERTY LINE**

| *Years* | *Monthly Per Capita Rs.* | *Poverty line Rs.* | *Population below the Poverty line (persons in millions)* |
|---|---|---|---|
| 1960-61 | 20 | 1,200 | 172 |
| 1977-78 | 65 | 3,500 | 245 |
| 1984-85 | 107 | 6,400 | 271 |
| 1988-89 | 180 | 10,800 | 441 |
| 1998-99 | 320 | 19,200 | 500 |
| 1999-20 | 340 | 20,400 | 505 |

(*) For a family of five persons per annum.

## The Remedical Measures

Is there a way out of this morass- a morass where inequality results in poverty and poverty accentuates inequality?

Yes, there is a way out, but it is hard and almost an impossible one.

The hard nature of the solution lies in the fact that we, who are the beneficiaries of this unequal and unjust system, should accept the fact that our system is unequal and unjust, and not try to cover it up by calling the system a national system, and hoodwink both ourselves and the poor majority by speaking of our being on a path of accelerated economic growth, which high technology and modernisation brings, as a result of which poverty will decline and disappear (Even in this verbiage there is no reference to the root cause of poverty, inequalities, in our society). Our system is not a national system : It is a system which serves the wealthy minority, and the power groups comprising and spawned by them. We are not in an economy which is growing in an accelerated way; we are accelerating the growth of those sectors which serve those who have the purchasing power. And high tech and modernisation are instruments of this lopsided growth which will further accentuate inequalities. Will we recognise these hard facts, because without such recognition, we cannot rid our society of poverty.

**'Our system is not a national system :** It is a system which serves the wealthy minority and the power groups comprising and spawned by them. We are not in an economy which is growing in an accelerated way, we are accelerating the growth of those sectors which serve those who have the purchasing power. And high tech and modernisation are instruments of this lopisded growth which will further accentuate inequalities'.

## Conclusion

Perceptions of poverty are wide and varied. Peter Townsend in his well known treatise "The Poor and the Poorest" observes that people are deprived of conditions of life which ordinarily define membership of society, and that if they lack or are denied resources to obtain access to these conditions of life and thereby fulfil membership to obtain access to these conditions of life and thereby fulfil membership of society, they are in poverty. And Streeten has observed that the poverty norm moves up with the average income because the desire to belong is an almost biological basic need and is expressed as a desire to live at a basic standard that is regarded by society as decent.

In India, poverty line is the most austerely defined in the world in terms of nutritional parameteres. The growing population has added to poverty and lack of employment opportunities. Yet around 20 crore are hungry. We have so many schemes but no concerted effort. Let me tell you that with globalisation, and the liberalisation of imports, the problem of food security will worsen. Our approach to the poor should not be that we want to feed them but that we must enable them to feed themselves with dignity. Self-help groups or, perhaps, agricultural coperatives are the answer. Again the people should plan the family, educate themselves and lead a life of self-help.

Decentralisation is the key to food security. Arming panchayati raj institutions with legal, financial, technological and managerial resources will help.

Over the years, inspite of a number of poverty alleviation programmes in India, the number of poor has increased. Inflation and growing unemployment and under-employment has made the life of the poor more miserable and pathetic.

**Table 4**

**INDIA'S GLOBAL POSITION ON HUMAN AND GENDER DEVELOPMENT**

| *Country* | *HDI Rank* | *GDP per capita (PPP US$) minus HDI rank* | | *GDI Rank* | | *HDI rank minus GDI rank* | *Life Expectancy at Birth (years)* | *Combined GER (Primary, Secondary & Tertiary education)* | *Physicians per one lakh people* | *Infants with low birth weight (%)* |
|---|---|---|---|---|---|---|---|---|---|---|
| | *2000* | *2005* | *2005* | *2000* | *2005* | *2005* | *2005* | *2005* | *2000-04* | *1998-05* |
| Norway | 1 | 2 | 1 | 2 | 3 | –1 | 79.8 | 99.2 | 313 | 5 |
| Australia | 5 | 3 | 13 | 1 | 2 | 1 | 80.9 | 113 | 247 | 7 |
| Sri Lanka | 89 | 99 | 07 | 70 | 89 | –1 | 71.6 | 62.7 | 55 | 22 |
| China | 96 | 81 | 05 | 77 | 73 | 1 | 72.5 | 69.1 | 106 | 4 |
| Indonesia | 110 | 107 | 06 | 91 | 94 | 1 | 69.7 | 68.2 | 13 | 9 |
| India | 124 | 128 | –11 | 105 | 113 | 0 | 63.7 | 63.8 | 60 | 30 |
| Pakistan | 138 | 136 | -8 | 120 | 125 | –7 | 64.6 | 40 | 74 | 19 |
| Bangladesh | 145 | 140 | 0 | 121 | 121 | 1 | 63.1 | 56 | 26 | 36 |
| Nepal | 142 | 142 | 08 | 119 | 128 | –4 | 62.6 | 58.1 | 21 | 21 |
| Mozambique | 170 | 172 | –16 | 144 | 150 | –1 | 42.8 | 52.9 | 3 | 15 |
| Niger | 172 | 174 | –1 | 146 | 155 | –1 | 55.8 | 22.7 | 2 | 13 |

*Source :* UNDP Human Development Reports 2002 and 2007.

❑ ❑ ❑

# SECTION TWO

# RURAL DEVELOPMENT

Rural development has a long history in India. In a broad sense, even the passing of the India Co-operative Societies Act in 1904 can be taken as a rural development measure. Legislation regarding tenancy right and rents. consolidation of land-holdings, regulation of money-lending and marketing of agricultural products can as well be stated as rural development measures.

But in the era of planned economic development, the concept of rural development has undergone a sea change. It now means measures such as increasing employment opportunities, production, productivity and similar other measures to bring about economic and social change in the rural areas, especially for the benefit of poorer section.

Rural development, over the years, has emerged as "a strategy designed to improve the economic and social life of a specific group of people—the rural poor. It involves extending the benefits of development to the poorest among those who seek a livelihood in the rural areas. This group includes small and marginal farmers. tenants, landless labourers and rural artisans etc." The objectives of rural development encompass improved productivities increased employment, higher incomes for target groups as well as a minimum acceptable levels of food, clothing, shelter, education and health. Growth with social justice is the objective of Indian economic planning. But the compulsions of the economic situation, as they unfolded themselves over the years, characterised by a high rate of population growth and less than commensurate increase in food production, adverse weather, etc., made pursuit of the growth aspect more imperative than the social justice aspect of development programmes.

The removal of poverty remains a central concern of planning in India. The stress continues to be on complementary strategies increasing employment, meeting basic needs, reduction in the inequalities in income and wealth, and raising the productivity of the poor—all integrated with human development.

With this concept of Rural Development in view, the initial attempts at rural development were to set up an admininstrative infrastructure which would devise and implement development programmes. The Community Development (CD) Programme initiated in 1952 and the setting up of the Panchayati Raj Institutions were the first measures undertaken with the objective of co-ordinated rural development, stimulating voluntary community effort for self-betterment. The National Extension Service was launched alongside the C.D. Project. "The Service was intended to give scientific and technical help to the village people so that they could improve their lives. While the stress on agricultural scheme remained, the work programme in N.E.S blocks was less than in the Community Development Blocks... The two programmes were, however, complementary." But these could not achieve their main objective of self-reliance in village communities and the social overheads provided under them did not improve the income generating capacities of the rural poor. The emphasis has been on employment and poverty alleviation.

In order to ensure that the fruits of economic reforms are shared by all sections of society, five elements of social and economic infrastructure, critical to the quality of life in rural areas, were identified. These are health, education, drinking water, housing and roads. To impart greater momentum to the efforts in these sectors, the Government launched the Pradhan Mantri Gramodaya Yojana (PMGY) The Ministry of Rural Development has been entrusted with the responsibility of implementing the drinking water, housing and roads component of PMGY.

There is a close link between rural connectivity and growth, be it in the area of trade, employment, education or healthcare. The Pradhan Mantri Gram Sadak Yojana (PMGSY) launched on 25th December, 2000 seeks to provide all-weather roads to all unconnected rural habitations with a population of more than 500 persons in the next seven years. A well conceived programme have been devised and an allocation or Rs. 2,500 crore has been made in the Budget 2000-2001 for this programme. The primary focus of the Pradhan Mantri Gram Sadak Yojana will be on construction of new roads. The programme also aims to upgrade, to specifications, existing roads in rural areas so as to achieve connectivity through all weather roads. It has been estimated that an investment of Rs 10 lakhs will bring 165 persons above the poverty line.

## SUSTAINABLE POVERTY ALLEVIATION

- The right way to remove poverty.
- The growth of population to be checked.
- Pay adequate attention to farm and non-farm employment.
- Focus on land reforms.
- We also need to take the focus away from wheat and rice to jowar. This could be the answer to our food needs.
- Create high profit agro-businesses on large scale to provide sustainable basis for poverty removal.
- Utilise part of the surplus to provide quality education and health care for men, children and women.
- Advantages of agro-business route.
- Large employment potential, high incomes, encourages non-dependence.
- Keeps families together, exposes village poor to modern technology and management.
- Establish a National Nutrition Trust with about 20 million tonnes of foodgrains at its disposal.
- Promote local good banks.
- Need for political commitment backed by professional and scientific expertise.
- If poverty alleviation schemes are to be sustained, they must derive from profitable economic activity.
- Subsidies, grants aid and largesse perpetuate the mind set of poverty.
- Poverty alleviation schemes must address the core problem of education and dignified employment for the very poor.

"Whenever you are in doubt... apply the following test. Recall the face of the poorest and the weakest man whom you may have seen, and ask yourself, if the step you contemplate is going to be of any use to him. Will he gain anything by it? Will it restore him to a control over his own life and destiny?.... then you will find your doubt and your self melting away." —*M.K. Gandhi*

*"Making rural people the arbiter of their own destiny & to provide for economic upliftment by self employment—For the development to be in consonance with the people's wishes and aspirations, emphasis is put on participation of people as also social mobilization of rural poor through Self-Help Groups and Panchayati Raj Institutions."*

# Chapter 4

# MEANING AND CONTENT OF RURAL DEVELOPMENT

## Introduction

Development of rural areas has been the avowed objective of planning in India. Poverty alleviation and welfare of the people, basically involves increased production and more importantly equal distribution and creating productive employment opportunities to rural people both in the farm and non-farm sectors.

With the opening of their economy, rural people have come under the urban influence and fallen victims to some of its ills. Over the years, the rural scene has seen a sea change. Under the circumstance, the concept of rural development acquires a significant meaning. More importantly the content of rural development should touch the life of all rural people. The process of development covers rural environment, rural poor and other weaker sections of the rural society.

The Tenth Plan has declared the development of rural and farm sector as one of the main objectives of the Plan and are channelising consciously physical, financial and human resources into rural development. However, rural development is fast becoming a fashionable catchword not only with government and political leaders but also with the corporate sector. The emphasis in this context is on finding what are called "approaches that work" for rural development and upliftment of the poor without disturbing property and social relations and by applications of business management methods and sophisticated technologies. The conventional philanthropic attitude of helping the poor is no longer regard as adequate. A more comprehensive approach is gaining ground in influential circles among socially and economically powerful interest groups. Recently, participants from 51 countries and several international organisations discussed their "approaches" in Delhi. The total cost of the exposition the organisers estimated to be 6,20,000 dollars (or Rs. 9.30 crores) The final achievement was the outline of a 'book' of the assembly which will be supported by an information system which, the organisers proudly claimed, included 'a computer data base'. All very sophisticated indeed very modern and very managerial. How exactly the exposition and its sponsors would be able to help uplift the rural poor in India is anybody's guess. In the backdrop of these varied interests, it is quite pertinent to analyse critically and discuss the issues in rural development in relation to rural India.

## Rural Development

The Rural Development Sector Policy Paper of the World Bank observed that "Rural development is a strategy designed to improve the economic and social life of a specific group of people—the rural poor. It involves extending the benefits of development to the poorest among those who seek a livelihood the benefits of development to the poorest among those who seek a livelihood in the rural areas. The group includes small-scale farmers, tenants and the landless." Again a World Bank publications defines rural development as "improving the living standards of the masses of the low-income population residing in rural areas making the process of rural development self-sustaining."

The World Bank definition of rural development is based inherently on an operational approach constrained by the practicalities of allocating loan resources over a wide spectrum of countries, ensuring maximum economic returns to them. In a seminar on approaches to rural development in Asia, discussions were centred around a definition of "rural development as a process which leads to a continuous rise in the capacity of the rural people to control their environment accompanied by a wider distribution of benefits resulting from such control." this definition is composed of three important elements:

(1) Rural development should be viewed as a process of raising the capacity of the rural people to control their environment. Environment does not mean only agriculture or economic development. It includes all aspects of rural life—social, economic, cultural and political;

(2) Rural development as a process should continuously raise the capacity of the rural people to influence their total environment, enabling them to become initiators and controllers of change in their environment rather than being merely the passive objects of external manipulation and control; and

(3) Rural development must result in a wider distribution of benefits accruing from technical developments and the participation of weaker sections of the rural population in the process of development.

G. Parthasarathy opines that "The critical element in the rural development is improvement of living standards of the poor through opportunities for better utilisation of their physical and human resources; in the absence of this, utilisation of rural resources has no functional significance. Making the process of rural development self-sustaining not only implies the mobilisation of capital and use of technology for the benefit of the poor but their active involvement in the building up of institutions as well as in functioning of these." Michael Todaro views that "Rural development encompasses (1) improvement in levels of living, including employment, education, health and nutrition, housing and a variety of social services; (2) decreasing inequality in the distribution of rural incomes and in rural-urban balances in incomes and economic opportunities; and (3) the capacity of the rural sector to sustain and accelerate the pace of these improvement."

Rural development in the ultimate analysis involves the provision of opportunities for the optimum utilisation of the human resources in rural areas. Human resource development in its turn can take place only on the foundation of adequate nutrition and work opportunities. It is, therefore, necessary to base rural development programmes with the primary aim of providing opportunities for the human population to achieve optimum expression of their physical and mental potential. Such programme should have the following four major components:

*(a)* Economic emancipation of the family with particular attention to provision of adequate employment opportunities to women who are largely engaged at present in unpaid and underpaid jobs, often characterised by physical drudgery;

(*b*) Education of children and adults;

(*c*) Provision of minimum needs, such as safe drinking water supply, health care, rural communication, etc and,

(*d*) Promotion of a small family norm through social and health education.

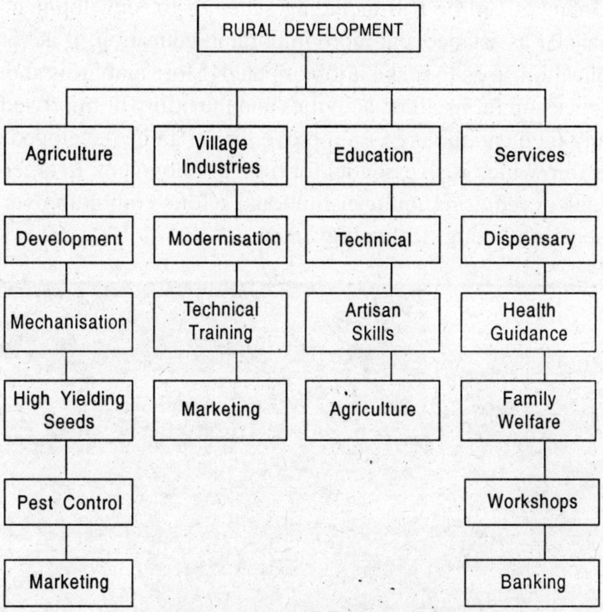


*Fig. 1. Components of Rural Development*

Rural development has been accorded a priority by the government and rightly so. The emphasis placed on rural development is not new. Even prior to Independence, Gandhiji had succinctly pointed out the importance of developing villages, if India is to develop as a whole. No doubt, substantial efforts were made in the past to develop rural areas and yet the rural poor continue to live in abject poverty. Independence and the Five Year Plans have fetched little benefits to them and meant little change in their age-old ways of living.The major shortcoming of the efforts made to develop village was that they were piece-meal in nature and did not take into account the kaleidoseopic difficulties of rural areas varying in pattern from region to region. Rural development is not an easy job as not only economic problems are involved but also the social and psychological issues are inter-mingled with stagnant agriculture and lack of allied activities. The caste problem is again a major issue as about 23.6 per cent of the rural population (15.64 crores) comprises scheduled castes/tribes. Consequently, inertia and indifference have taken deep roots giving rise to suspicion and the lack of urge to develop.

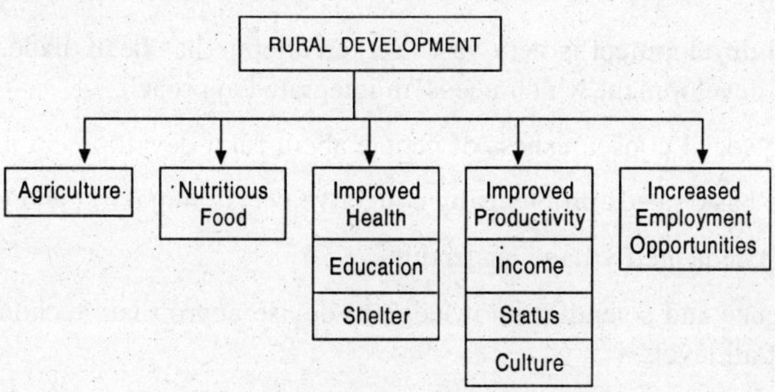


*Fig. 2. Phases of Rural Development*

## Multi-faceted Problem

The efforts made in the past to overcome rural backwardness were generally confined to single problem and single institution. If effective strategy for rural development is to formulated, rural problems will have to be studied in all its aspects comprising socio-economic and psychological issues. Only then, can package programme of rural development can be had including schemes for development of agriculture and allied activities, rural crafts, financial assistance and more important, education. It is very essential to change the present system of rural education so as to make it job oriented. More emphasis should be placed on teaching improved agricultural practices on farms allied activities and the utility of improved tools, both in agriculture and cottage industries. Only then can the urge to improve the lot an be developed in rural areas. It will also help to develop new leadership which is so essential for rural development. In other words rural development is a multi-dimensional problem requiring multi-institutional efforts combining various disciplines like education, finance, management, marketing, technology, etc.

*Fig. 3.*

## Scope of Rural Development

The scope of rural development is very vast. Yet, an attempt has been made here to indicate some of the broad areas of rural development which needs an integrated approach.

(1) Developing social consciousness of people about rural development and it lasting benefits.

(2) Solving the basic needs problems by collective decision making and collective action.

(3) Building up dedicated village leadership.

(4) Use of science and scientific knowledge to devise appropriate technology for improving productivity at all levels.

(5) Development of agriculture and allied sectors.

(6) Improved water management by building tanks, small dams on the nullas and building canals etc.

(7) Creating new employment opportunities by subsidiary occupations.

(8) Developing cottage and village industries based on local resources.

(9) Developing non-farming skills to promote and sustain service sector.

(10) Developing an efficient delivery system, leading to easy supply of inputs, credit and good outlet for their products.

## Aims of Rural Development

Rural development aims at ensuring that the fruits of economic development reach the villages, and the common man. Broadly the aims are :

- **Bridging the rural-urban divide:** To ensure rapid and time bound development, budgetary support for implementing the various rural development schemes has increased manifold in recent years.
- **Guaranteeing wage employment and ensuring food security:** This is sought to be achieved through the National Rural Employment Guarantee Act.
- **Making rural people the arbiters of their own destiny and to provide for their economic uplift by self-employment:** For the development to be in consonance with the people's wishes and aspirations, emphasis is put on participation of people as also social mobilization of rural poor through Self-Help Groups and Panchayati Raj Institutions.
- **Creating rural infrastructure for better economic opportunities and growth:** Connectivity is provided to all unconnected habitations through Pradhan Mantri Gram Sadak Yojana (PMGSY). Village level infrastructure is also created through works undertaken under wage employment schemes.
- **Ensuring dignified living:** The Ministry provides shelter, water and clean environment through schemes for rural housing, drinking water and sanitation.
- **Restoring lost or depleted productivity of the land for better livelihood opportunities:** This is done through integrated watershed development programmes and initiating effective land reform measures for providing land to the landless rural poor.

## A Strategy for Rural Development

Rural development is a strategy designed to improve the economic and social life of a specific group of people—the rural poor. It involves extending the benefits of development to the poorest among those who seek a livelihood in the rural areas. A strategy for rural development must recognise three points. Firstly, the rate of transfer of people out of low productivity agriculture and related activities into more rewarding pursuits has been slow; and, given the relative size of the modern sector in most developing countries, it will remain slow. Secondly the mass of the people in the rural areas of developing countries face varying degrees of poverty; their position is likely to get worse if population expands at unprecedented rates while limitations continue to be imposed by available resources, technology, and institutions and organisations. Thirdly, rural areas have labour, land and at least some capital which, if mobilised, could reduce poverty and improve the quality of life.

Rural development recognise, however, that improved food supplies and nutrition, together with basic services such as health and education cannot only directly improve the physical well-being and quality of life of the rural poor, but can also indirectly enhance their productivity and their ability to contribute to the national economy. It is concerned with the modernisation and monetisation of rural society and with its transition from traditional isolation to integration with the national economy.

A strategy for rural development aimed at raising growth rates and distributing the fruits of growth more fairly implies greater interaction between the modern and traditional sectors especially in the form of increased trade in farm produce and in technical inputs and services.

A programme of rural development must embrace a wide range and mix of activities, including projects to raise agriculture output, to improve health and education, to expand communications and to improve housing. The mix of activities will vary with the requirements of a region and the priorities assigned to components within a programme at particular times and at particular stages of development. The programme may be based on a series of sequential projects—first health, then education, then agricultural development. In sum rural development programmes or projects area intended to provide a sustained increase in the rural poor in a given area. In some instances, this may require emphasis on indirectly productive operations. But, in the main, the focus is on activities which either raise income directly, or at least provide the potential to be more productive.

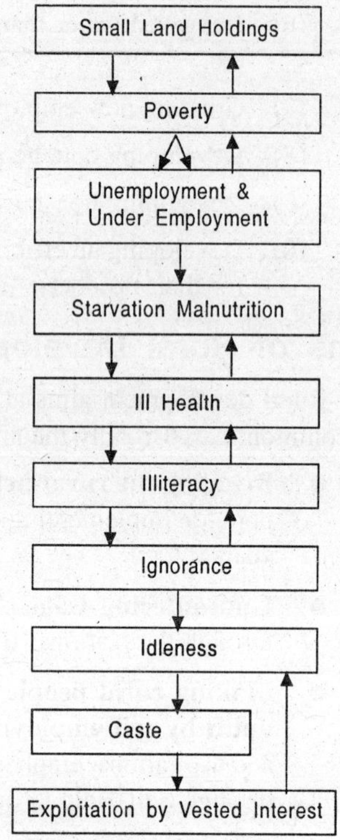


*Fig. 4. Barriers to Socio-economic Development in Rural Development*

## The Policy Framework

A strong commitment to rural development policies at the national level is required for effective implementation of the varied programmes. Rural development can be achieved once there is firm commitment. During the first three plans, the emphasis was on overall growth. In the Fourth Plan, however, some awareness arose regarding the very low levels of consumption of the poor, and so some schemes were drawn up for the development of the backward areas and the weaker sections. In the Fifth Plan, removal of poverty was one of the major consideration in the formulation of development programmes. A determined attack on this problem was the main theme of the development effort during the plan period.

*(i)* Improving productivity and thereby income of the rural poor;

*(ii)* Ensuring enlarged employment opportunities at a faster pace;

*(iii)* Removal of unemployment and significant reduction in under employment;

*(iv)* An appreciable rise in the standard of living of the poorest sections of the population; and

*(v)* Provision by the state of some of the basic needs of the people like clean drinking water, elementary education, health care, rural roads, etc.

Table 1 summarises the policy on rural development pursued in each of the plans.

**Table 1**

**PLAN POLICES ON RURAL DEVELOPMENT**

| | *Plan* | *Policy* |
|---|---|---|
| I. | (1951-56) | Community development as method and National Extension Service as the agency. |
| II. | (1956-61) | Co-operative Farming; Local participation |
| III. | (1961-66) | Panchayati raj, three-tier model of democratic decentralisation. |
| IV. | (1969-74) | Special clientele-based and area-based programmes. |

| | | |
|---|---|---|
| V. | (1974-79) | Introduces the concept of 'minimum needs'. |
| VI. | (1980-85) | Emphasis on strengthening the socio-economic infrastructure in rural areas, alleviating rural poverty and reducing regional disparities. Integrated Rural Development Programme. |
| VII. | (1985-90) | Emphasis on creating new employment opportunities, special programmes for income generation through asset endowments, land reforms, participation of people at grass-roots level. |
| VIII. | 1992-1997 | Ensuring the basic needs of the rural poor. |
| IX. | 1997-2002 | Emphasis in creating new infrastructure in rural areas. |
| X. | 2002-2007 | Providing new wage earning avenues to the rural poor. |
| XI. | 2007-2012 | Bharat Nirman. |

Agriculture and allied activities like animal husbandry, dairying, forestry, fishery, etc. and cottage and small scale industries offer considerable scope for labour absorption and income generation for the poverty stricken rural masses with relatively low but quick result-producing investments. Increased production in rural areas will lead to higher purchasing power in the hands of the millions of the rural people which, in turn will create more effective demand both for agriculture and industrial commodities.

Realising the pivotal role that agriculture can play in the overall economic development of the country and elimination of poverty, this sector has been assigned high priority in the current Five Year Plan. The main thrust of the strategy is to expand employment opportunities by bringing more areas under irrigation and by developing cropping patterns and improved cultural practices which optimise the use of land, water and labour resources. The allied programme of animal husbandry, dairying, forestry and fisheries are also being intensified to maximise employment opportunities and to supplement income of rural poor. After agriculture, household and small scale industries producing consumer goods for mass consumption hold out the greatest potential for employment. This is a sector which had received inadequate attention in the earlier plans.

## Importance of Rural Development

Rural development is necessary not only because an overwhelming majority of the population lives in villages but also because the development of rural activities is essential to accelerate the pace of overall economic development of the country. Rural development has assumed greater importance in India today than in the earlier period in the process of development of the country. There is much evidence to show that public interest in rural development is growing rapidly. Reaching the benefits of development to India's 5,75,000 villages and improving the living standards of the rural people, particularly of those living below the poverty line, have been the avowed goals of India's Five Year Plans and the 20-Point Programme. More and more effort has been directed in the successive plans to improve the rural economy. The government has initiated a number of programmes to solve the chronic problem of villages in India. Even then, the percentage of people living below the poverty line in rural areas has been steadily increasing from year to year.

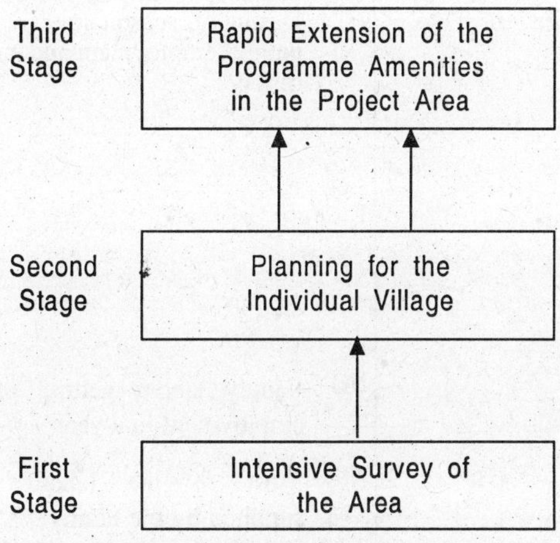


*Fig. 5. Stages of Development*

In any discussion of rural development there are three stages:

First : the presentation of the true facts.

Second : the process of reasoning, and,

Third : the conclusions that can widely be drawn from the facts and reasoning.

Further, rural development steer around agriculture and allied activities, rural industries and forestry, which are the mainstay of the much needed sunshine to the rural areas. One of the important structural requirements for success of our development plans are the quality of management and a suitable organisation. The importance of matured management overrides all other factors having a bearing on accelerated economic growth. The managerial component of the task of improving the living standards of our rural poor is even more complex and far more gigantic. The key to success must surely lie in building up teams of trusted, dedicated and motivated people.

**Table 2**

**STAGES IN THE EVOLUTION OF RURAL DEVELOPMENT AND THEIR CHARACTERISTICS**

| | *Characteristics* | *Single Enterprise (subsistence)* | *Diversified* | *Specialised* |
|---|---|---|---|---|
| 1. | Pattern of Enterprise | One/few crops of one dominant variety/activity-rearing of livestock-Non descript breeds | Crop+Animal Husbandry | One dominant enterprise *i.e.*, cash crops or highly specialised animal breeds. |
| 2. | Principal Purpose of Production | Domestic consumption (No gap between produced/consumed form of consumption, sometimes inverse relation with price) | Domestic Consumption and market; sheep husbandry is highly market-oriented. The nature of product/product mix and the type of market differs from the highly specialised one. | Serving the market: form of product and type of market is quite different from earlier stages. |
| 3. | Employment Pattern | Seasonal-precarious: *(i)* During off season no gainful employment and lack of food. | Balanced/Stabilised | Somewhat seasonal: But high level of employment. Per unit of land/other production unit employment higher. Changes in the roles and proportions of family and hired labour in total employment in the farm. Fall in the marginal significance of the family labour wage as a source of income. |
| | | *(ii)* Family labour getting part employment in a year. | Family Labour getting stable employment. | |
| | | *(iii)* Most of the labour is supplied by the family. | | |
| | | *(iv)* Specialised and yet unskilled less efficient labour/ workforce. Specialised for the enterprise non-specialised for activity. One labourer does all type of jobs. | | |

| | | | | |
|---|---|---|---|---|
| 4. | Income Levels | Low | Medium | High |
| 5. | Stability of income flows | Low because of natural forces—leading to starvation-precarious position of the family. | High | Low (because of market forces) but no starvation. Farm business income has no direct impact on the standard of life of the farmer. |
| 6. | Internal Saving | Low/nil/negative | Low | High |
| 7. | Percentage Share of Family Income in the Value of Total Output | High | In between | Low |
| 8. | Risk-bearing Capacity | Negative | Fairly good | High |
| 9. | Level and pattern of Capital Investment: Absolute and Relative | Low/absolute as well as per unit of labour, therefore more labour per unit of land and also per unit of capital (Land value is low and animals are cheaper). | Medium | |
| 10. | Productivity per unit of land/labour | Low | Medium | High |
| 11. | Farmer's knowledge regarding agriculture | Low and specialised (New openings restricted). Sources of knowledge is father and family. | Medium and Diversified | High and specialised: Sources of knowledge are institutionalised (Radio, News medium, TV, formal education). |
| 12. | Need and nature of dependence on supporting system | Non-partial (Partial either because sub-port is not available or there is nothing to make use for). | Partial | Full. The role/involvement of the supporting system in the farm business is very essential. The farmer is able to easily indicate the need for such support. |

*Source :* This table is adopted on the basis of the Table quoted by Ronam Weitz, in his book *From Peasant to Farmer* p. 20, published by Columbia University Press, 1971.

*Note :* At the single enterprise subsistence level, the family labour gets an exclusively large share in total employment. The labour is specialised so far as enterprise is concerned. As regards activity, the same labour does all types of jobs from preparing the field to harvesting and threshing. There is some division between male, female and child labour. The nature of works schedule also is such where a single labour unit can take up one operation (land tilling threshing, etc.) after another because there is only one type of crop or crops of similar agronomic characteristics.

In the case of diversified pattern, labour becomes less specialised as two enterprises are taken up simultaneously. However, in certain cases, there is a natural division of labour between male and female member in the family. For instance, by and large, dairying is looked after by the female labour.

At the highly specialised level, labour becomes specialised, more particularly activity/operation – wise, and is highly efficient because of experiment of division of labour and the work tool/capital that is employed per unit of labour.

For some further discussion on some of the variables shown in the Table, refer to Ronam Weitz, in his book *From Peasant to a Farmer,* pp. 20, published by Columbia University Press, 1971.

## Problems of Rural Settlement

The problems of rural settlement are the outcome of physical, economic and cultural aspects of the region and the settlement site. These are:

*(a)* *(i)* Unplanned villages with narrow, crooked and inadequately drained streets;

*(ii)* Problem of floods during the rainy season;

*(iii)* Outbreak of fire in the village and death toll in the summer season due to heat-waves and due to cold waves in the winter respectively, and epidemics such as influenza, typhoid, cholera, smallpox and measles during monsoon and other seasons;

*(iv)* Lack of open spaces for playground and grazing;

*(v)* Lack of drinking water and bathing grounds for the common people;

*(vi)* Changing courses of rivers and the ever-present problems of embankment erosion.

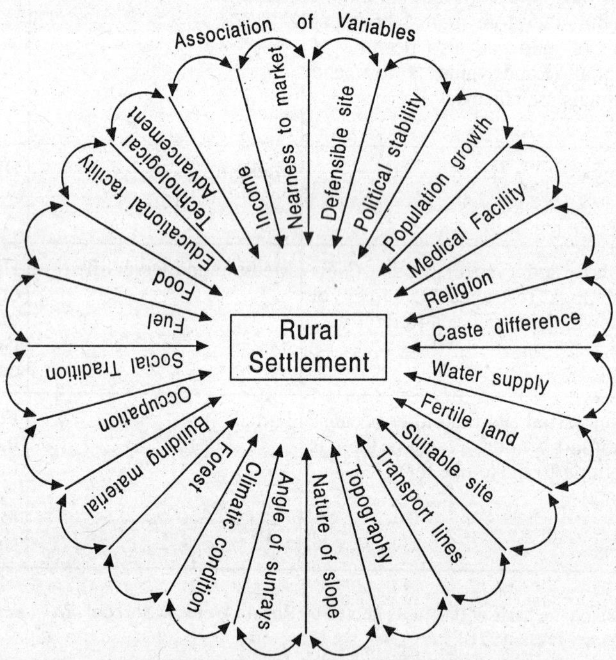


*Fig. 6. Ecological Balance of Rural Settlements*

*(b)* *(i)* Lack of building materials, particularly for the poor;

*(ii)* Old structure in a dilapidated condition and smaller rudimentary huts presenting a very pitiable sight;

*(iii)* No arrangement for septic tanks either for a family or for the whole community;

*(iv)* Lack of space for storing grains and keeping animals as a result of which animals and human beings share the common living space;

*(v)* Lack of several necessary items, *e.g.,* electricity and medical and educational facilities;

*(vi)* Lack of roads, railways and other lines of communication;

*(vii)* Fragmented holdings and small plots, which call for consolidation;

*(viii)* Non-availability of rural credit and guidance for house improvement are not available;

*(ix)* Lack of marketing facilities in the neigbhourhood.

*(c)* *(i)* Fear of thieves and dacoits;

*(ii)* Caste barriers and untouchability in most villages;

*(iii)* Development of rural slums because of congested houses, over-crowding and insanitary conditions;

*(iv)* Lack of recreation, *e.g.,* cinema, community hall, theatre and other forms of cultural activity;

*(v)* Lack of a cremation ground for the human dead and animals;

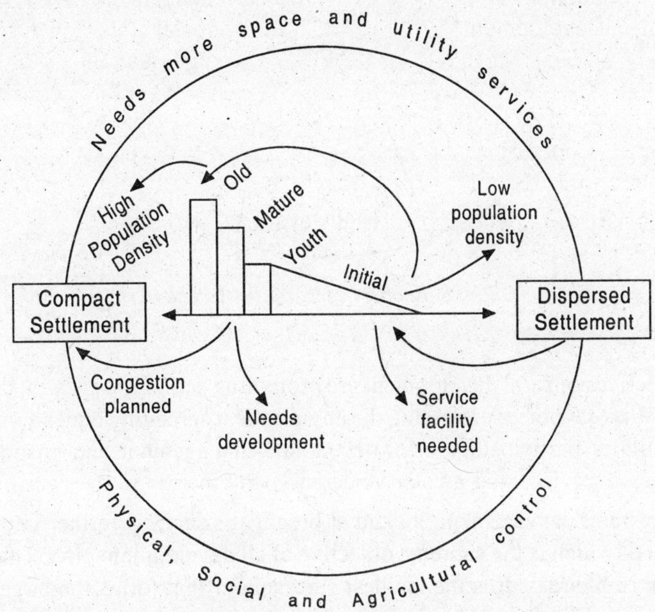


*Fig. 7. Cycle of Rural Settlements*

*(vi)* Non-availability of designs for better homes using indigenous materials;

*(vii)* Absence of demonstration of better construction methods and simple, inexpensive improvements in houses.

Ecological conditions favour the formation of concentric rings of similar persons in the traditional caste-oriented village. Sectoral growth and location of rural settlement and lower-order places on either side of transportation routes are favourable conditions of settlement.

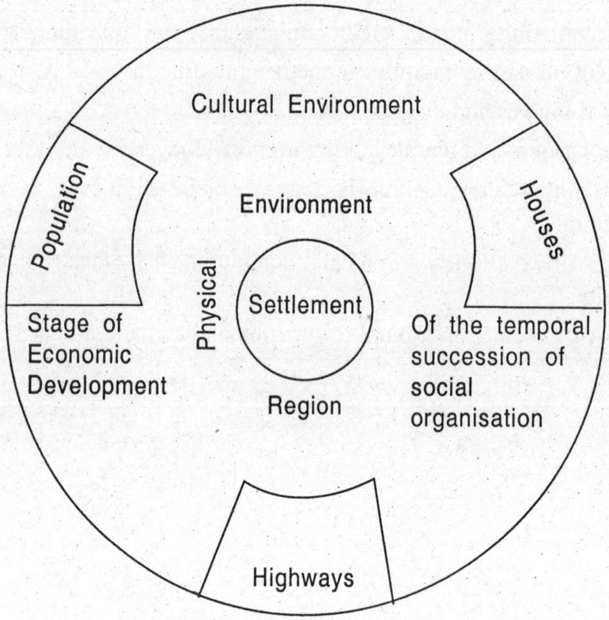


*Fig. 8. Ecology of Rural Settlements*

## Conclusion

The strategic objectives of rural development are promoting economic growth, developing human resources, improving the status of women; protecting the environment spreading education, and good governance. Good governance facilitates participatory macro-economic management and ensure that the rural people have better access to basic services and greater voice and participation in the decisions affecting them.

The importance of rural development, looked at broadly as such, is further intensified by the fact that poverty, the eradication of which is the supreme objective of all development efforts has the widest incidence, and in fact its source in rural areas. It is the landless rural labour that forms the largest reservoir of poverty in the country, and is the source of urban poverty too. Industrialisation can, to an extent reduce the incidence of poverty, specially urban poverty, but to have this effect, industrialisation not only has to be labour-intensive, but perhaps more importantly, mass based. The latter characteristic, namely, the mass-base, can be acquired by production of goods and services of mass consumption, sustained by steady increase of the purchasing power of masses, resulting from additional employment created by the labour intensity of the industries concerned. Indeed, it is only such mass-base that can ensure continued expansion of industries leading to a level of industrialisation commensurate with the size and population of the country. Industrialisation based on elite consumption, on the other hand, has limited potential. The narrowness of the base restricts its growth. It can create only islands of affluence in the surrounding sea of poverty.

In the ultimate analysis, therefore, it is rural development in the broad sense of the term that holds the key to all economic progress, industrial or agrarian, urban or rural. There is no basic conflict between rural and urban interests, between industry, heavy or light, and agriculture. The conflict is really between the elite and the masses and this conflict exists as much in urban areas between the urban elite and the urban poor, as in the rural areas between the rural elite and the rural masses.

❑ ❑ ❑

*'Let us not be satisfied with just giving money. Money is not enough, money can be got, but they need your hearts to love them. So, spread your love everywhere you go.'*

— *Mother Teresa*

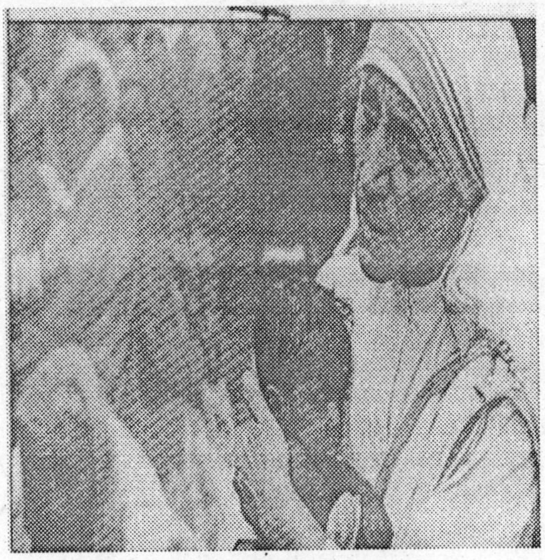

# Chapter 5

# RURAL DEVELOPMENT: AN OVERVIEW

## Introduction

India is a land of villages. A vast majority of its people depend for their livelihood on farm and non-farm activities. Many of them do not have any means of earning. Further they do not have access to necessary food, shelter, drinking water and sanitation facilities, resulting in poverty and suffering. Ensuring opportunities to enable them to cross over poverty on a sustainable basis is a formidable challenge. Since independence, it has been the task of the Government to fight poverty and inequality in the vast rural areas and to provide a dignified life to the rural people.

In the post-independence period, the government (both centre and state) is engaged in bringing about rapid and sustainable development and socio-economic transformation in rural India. It has an integrated perspective towards improving the quality of life of rural poor and ensuring equity and effective people's participation. The responsibilities of the state covers almost whole spectrum of rural life.

The state interventions aim at:

- providing sustainable income through self employment programmes, *viz.*, Sampoorna Grameen Rozgar Yojana (SGRY), Development of Women and Children in Rural Areas, Supply of Improved Toolkits to Rural Artisans (SITRA) and Swarnjayanti Gram Swarozgar Yojana (SGSY)
- opening up of avenues for supplemental income earning opportunities through wage employment programmes, *viz.*, SGSY, Pradhan Mantri Gram Sadak Yojana (PMGSY), Employment Assurance Scheme (EAS) and Million Wells Scheme (MWS);
- promoting decentralisation of power and nurturing local self governance through Panchayati Raj Institutions;

- augmenting housing stock to provide shelter to the poor – Indira Awaas Yojana (IAY);
- creating access to safe drinking water and acceptable sanitation facilities to all rural inhabitants – Rural Water Supply and Sanitation Programme;
- securing social assistance to the poor through National Social Assistance Programme (NSAP);
- raising durable and quality community assets such as school buildings and road connectivity through the National Rural Roads Development Agency (NRRDA) to extend support to the PMGSY;
- harmonizing land relations through land reforms towards an egalitarian social structure;
- enhancing and releasing the full potential of natural resources, especially that of wastelands and degraded lands through area development programmes and watershed development and in the process help in raising farm incomes and to restore ecological balance –'Drought Prone Areas Programme (DPAP), Desert Development Programme (DDP), Integrated Wastelands Development Projects (IWDP);
- enlarging participation of Voluntary Organisations through Council for Advancement of People's Action and Rural Technology (CAPART) for community development.

In ancient period, villages were governed by their own assemblies. What is more, villages were self reliant and attached great importance to agriculture. This is also because of slow communication, undeveloped transport system. The population was little, more of virgin land.

Over the years a sea change has taken place in socio-economical and political spheres. For centuries India came under foreign rule. More importantly, the industrial revolution in the early 19th century destroyed the rural industry, which eventually converted India into a captive market for factory made goods. This destroyed the village industries, service sector and enhanced unemployment. With the opening up of the village economy with better roads rails a continuous exodus of rural people commenced. This is like brain drain from the country. The spread of formal education made the rural educates to prefer easy urban jobs than rural jobs. Today, a large proportion of rural people live in thatched houses with mudwalls under most unsanitary conditions. Today, rural areas are promising market for consumer goods, agricultural inputs and as well as luxury items. At the same, there is no assured market for their goods. Rural India continues to be neglected.

The progress of the varied programmes in operation are not up to the expected level due to certain constrains like agroclimatic conditions, migratory character of the rural people, lack of knowledge of the rural people about the programmes being implemented and supervision on the part of officers or officials. The employment opportunities should be created for local physical resources for their optimum utilization and programmes should be implemented without any intervention from local politicians, rich farmers and other vested interests.

*Fig. 1. A Well Constructed under Million Wells Scheme: Keelaiyur, Tamil Nadu*

As a result, in spite of several efforts for promoting rural development through a number of programmes, planning monetary and fiscal policies, the conditions of the rural poor have remained by and large static and the number of rural poor is alarmingly large. What is more, with the steady rise in rural population and prevalent social customs, ignorance, illiteracy, the number is multiplying at a faster rate. In addition, crime and social disorder has been spreading at a faster rate afflicting the social fabric of rural India. The worst affected are the rural poor. This lays stress that rural development programmes are to be revamped, restructured, planned at the micro-level and implemented, with professional efficiency. The need of the hour is a sound organisation and efficient management.

Finally, the success of the various agencies depends upon the persons who are responsible for implementing them. They must have sufficient experience and possess a high level of mobilised competence. Team spirit and collective work are essential. There must be channels of free communication in all directions. Decentralisation policy must be adopted. Rules and procedures must be made flexible for getting better results from the implementation of the programmes. A programme should have an inbuilt organisation, planned approach and professional implementation.

Inspite of over five decades of planning and the all round economic development, the incidence of rural poverty continues unabated. The number of rural people living below poverty line is estimated to be over 31 crores. Over the years, the number of rural people living below the poverty line has increased marginally since the beginning of the planned era. The main resource of livelihood in rural India is land. Rural poverty is associated with the ownership patterns of land. Data on ownership of land resources reveal that 12.3 per cent of the rural population owned no land, 58.6 per cent owned less than one hectare and 28.0 per cent owned land between 1 to 2 hectares. What is more, 58.6 per cent of marginal farmers owned only 11.2 per cent (19.50 million hectares) of operated area (165.34 million hectares). The average size of an operational land holding was less than 0.35 hectares. The 20 per cent small farmers owned about 13.8 per cent of operated land with average operated holding of 1.43 hectares. The moot point is that, whether these agricultural holdings sustaining the bulk of the rural population is a viable unit. if not, what is the alternative possible.

Since the structure of land ownership had failed to meet the ends of social justice, ceilings were imposed on larger holdings and the surplus land was sought to be distributed among small and marginal farmers. The emerging agricultural structure has perpetuated inequality of resources. The qualitative changes taking place in the mode of operation, irrigation, commercialisation, introduction of new technology, have worsened the position of the rural poor. More and more people depend on regular employment opportunities and earnings through the competitive market framework. More people and less employment opportunities forced people to accept low wages and or bonded labour. These institutions and technological changes increased the disparities among the rural poor. Rural poverty spread to other vital areas of normal life and ruined, the normal environment. Now rural poverty is multi-dimensional in character.

A number of rural development programmes have been experimented in the post-independence period. In the fifties, the Government embarked on the path of rural reconstruction with the Community Development Programme. It was conceived as a people's programme to harness local resources and energy of the masses for socio-economic uplift of all people living in rural areas. The state was to play the role of a catalytic agent trying to nurture the efforts of the people with technical, material and financial support. However, the expected response has allegedly failed to materialise owing to impersonal approach on the part of officials at the block levels, political hold of well-to-do in blocks and the inequitous agrarian structure which was a great handicap in bringing about a sense of equality and participation among rural masses. One further reason for its failure was the rapid expansion of the programme to cover the entire country in the face of resource constraint particularly that of trained manpower, organisational and managerial capability and resources.

In the sixties, the emphasis shifted from egalitarian development programmes towards adoption of programmes which offered scope for improving agricultural productivity. It was believed that by raising the size of agricultural output, the benefits would trickle down to the poor. With the application of newly found high-yielding varieties of seeds in the farms and intensive agricultural development programme began the period of green revolution in selected areas. The agricultural production rose substantially. While the output rose with more efficient employment of resources, the programme led to sharpening of social and regional disparities. Further, after initial impact of new varieties of seeds, the stagnation set in.

In the seventies, the theory of 'trickle-down' was questioned. Quick sample surveys conducted by the governmental agencies confirmed that the rural development programmes had so far not made any direct impact on poverty. These surveys in addition to highlighting the growing disparities between various sections of the population also helped in identifying the vulnerable groups of the rural population. The small and marginal farmers, agricultural labourers and the artisans were the most affected sections. With these experiences of the past, it was realised that the growth and distribution thereof could not be seen in isolation and therefore the goals of output growth and equitable distribution had to be pursued simultaneously.

The programmes have promoted subsidiary occupations such as dairy, poultry, piggery, goat rearing, fishery, sheep rearing, sericulture, etc. among small and marginal farmers. It has also helped these groups by supplying water through state-owned tubewells to their farms and through lift irrigation schemes. The programmes encouraged small farmers and agricultural labourers to participate in the above-mentioned activities, and thus helped to supplement their agricultural income with income from these subsidiary occupations.

With the failures of earlier schemes and a limited success of the recent schemes, it was realised that something very radically different had to be done to alleviate poverty and augment the income-earning capacities of the rural poor. In view of this, the Government embarked on the programme of Integrated Rural Development Programme (IRDP). The programme aims at raising income and employment opportunities through agricultural, animal husbandry (dairy) practices, village crafts or services. It intends to serve the landless, marginal farmers, rural unemployeds, poor rural artisans and craftsmen, scheduled castes and scheduled tribes through technical and financial support measures.

The Government has laid a great deal of emphasis in the Seventh Plan on IRDP and has proposed to gear up the development machinery at all levels so that the benefits from the programme ultimately converge and lead to direct and tangible improvements in the income and consumption of the households below the poverty line. IRDP is thus one of the most ambitious and perhaps the most debated programme of rural development undertaken so far. Principally, it continues to be a poverty alleviation programme rather than a development process.

Various studies on the impact of the rural development or anti-poverty programme implementation have highlighted a number of short-comings. However, a few of the weaknesses in its implementation are summarised here:

The majority of the beneficiaries were not eligible for assistance under the programme. Targets are fixed without realistically understanding the magnitude of poverty in a specific region resulting in benefits being liberally passed on to well-off sections. The programme has not helped in raising the income of those families who were below poverty line to the desired level. The large scale financing under a scheme in an area restricts work availability and creates a problem of marketing. The study also notes that the targets for employment creation under the IRDP are unrealistic.

In a massive anti-poverty programme like IRDP, both formulation and implementation have to be flawless. In fact, monetised development does not mean only pumping money into the economy but entails that supportive facilities are to be provided for its optimal absorption. This involves also public participation in a measure which is conducive not only to their own ultimate benefit, but to the smooth implementation of the programme. For this, an awareness has to be created among the public, and this could be achieved only by closer and direct relationship with the beneficiaries.

There is no involvement of financing agencies in the process of identification of beneficiaries and therefore, there was a general feeling that the programme was thrust upon them for financing more as a political weapon. The quality of lending has been observed to be much below the standard in as much as that in financing milch animals no proper care was taken regarding their milk yield, breed, availability of fodder, etc. The administrative pattern of subsidy has resulted in unscrupulous elements taking advantage of subsidy rather than the real purpose of improving the standard of rural people *i.e.* the target groups. Cases of pocketing of subsidy by the bureaucratic local politicians and farmers are quite large.

It seems that the target group approach puts all the rural poor in one category without bothering about their potential viability or their capacity to run enterprises independently. It offers self-employment in small enterprises to all the poor including the poorest ones. This uniform approach does not seem to be acceptable on two grounds. Firstly, all the households are not equally viable as some are potentially viable while others are not. For example, a small farmer with 2 or 4 hectares of land can be a viable unit using his access to the credit market, while a farmer with one acre cannot do so as he has no access to the credit market. This is because they do not have the required risk bearing capacity or the enterprising attitude. There is no need to offer self-employment to these poor. The target group approach, however, does not consider this aspect and offers an asset even to these households. In other words, a major weak point of the approach is that it emphasizes self-employment too much and in the process attempts to offer the same kind of solution to all the poor. The staff of the development administration, co-operative and banking staff should function more independently without any interference from the rich who have established political clout and control over the panchayat and co-operative societies. It is absolutely essential that the planning component of this strategy is strengthened substantially. These programmes should not only be properly integrated with other programmes but these should themselves be planned systematically and implemented professionally.

It must be accepted that all the poor do not need self-employment. Self-employment and wage employment should be provided to the poor on the basis of their suitability and acceptability. But, the vested interest representing the Indian reaction is the force obstruction such genuine, social reforms for the society and its people. Naturally, class struggle for development in India is very likely to be bitter and more severe in the years to come, unless the evil forces are put under check or erased. These institutions are supposed to treat all the deserving rural public alike and render instant guidance in all the spheres. Such uniform and unbiased treatment from such rich institutes will boost the morale of the rural poor and nullify the evil forces of the rural rich. A psychological treatment to the poor giving them the impressions that government support is stand-by for their welfare, gives them greater enthusiasm to work hard. Similarly, liquor, tobacco, which are injurious to health should be banned. Rural people should be freed from these social evils by enforcing a complete ban on them.

The existing rural development programme should be revamped, well planned and implemented so as to uplift the rural poor on one hand and develop the rural environment on the other hand. There existed potentialities for increasing income and employment through agro-based enterprises amongst the rural poor. The various reasons for the slow pace of rural development programmes, inter alia, include lack of follow-up programme, irregular and inadequate supply and lack of honesty and sincerity of the agencies, etc. Industrial units should be established to provide regular employment to the unemployed and under-employed; loan procedure should be simplified and loans should be given on need basis and agro-service centres should be established to meet the increasing needs of repairs and services of farm machinery.

It is said, Dreams Never Die — I believe it

But the Dreamer can die dreaming?

The picture of rural poverty and rural development as it emerges from the discussion in the foregoing pages is quite disquieting and gloomy. Rural India is still haunted by poverty, hunger, unemployment, under-employment, social tension, insecurity and helplessness. The situation would have been even worse but for the various measures adopted by successive plans since Independence to improve the rural economy.

Foodgrains production has increased from 52 million tonnes in 1951-52 to 212 million tonnes in 2000-2001. Indian agriculture has displayed a remarkable resilience despite erratic and uneven rainfall in the last quarter of the 20th century.

In recent years, agricultural production strategy continued to lay emphasis on acceleration of foodgrains production through expansion in irrigation, increased use of fertilizers and high yielding varieties of seeds, improved agricultural implements and machinery, implementation of dry land farming and desert development programme. Production of commercial crops like cotton, jute and sugarcane, fruits and vegetables has also increased significantly. However, in regard to pulses and oilseeds, success has eluded us till today. The pathetic dependence on food aid and foodgrains imports has been successfully overcome. However, per capita net availability of foodgrains per day has increased marginally from 395 grams per day in 1951 to 685 grams in 2001. In fact, it is quite stationary in recent years. For a vast number of poor people, pulses constitute the principle source of protein, which, in fact, has declined from 75 grams in 1951 to 53.5 grams in 2001. This therefore, should be viewed with great concern. The poverty and pulses has been quite critical in the post-Independence period.

According to an important study, foodgrains move easily from a surplus rural area to far away cities, but rather tardily to a deficit rural area just nearby, because these nearby areas are usually too poor to attract food supplies. In respect of per capita daily calorie supply as per cent tage of requirement, had fallen in Indian while most of the countries have showed improvement.

Infant mortality has come down from around 225 to 250 in the late 1940s to 70 in 2001 and death rate from 27.4 to 8.5. Life expectancy has gone up from 32 to a little over 65 years. Birth rate has also declined, though not to the extent necessary to check excessive growth in population. In the result, the country has to shoulder the growing problem of the old, invalid and the neglected in coming years.

School enrolment of children in the age group 6-11 has increased significantly. Currently the primary school enrolments equal or exceed the estimated number of boys in these school going ages; two-thirds of the girls in the age group are also in schools. Achievements in rural areas are lower than in urban areas.

The literacy rate has gone up from 12.6 per cent in 1951 to 60 per cent in 2003, but the number of illiterates has also gone up at the same time. While for all age groups, the literacy rates in rural India was 35.5 per cent, 45 per cent for males and 20 per cent for females and as for age group above 35, the rate was lower at 23.2 per cent – 38 per cent for males and 8.6 per cent for females. Compared to urban centres, a large number of families in rural India are illiterate as well as ignorant. Poverty of education still persists. Poverty, illiteracy and ignorance persists in rural India.

Out of the total 66.4 million houses in rural India, two-thirds are made by grass and mud. 72.9 per cent of rural people depend upon wells for drinking water. 91.7 per cent of rural households depend upon kerosene for lighting. And, 92.4 per cent do not have latrines. Poverty of poor environment and poor infrastructure persists. The condition of rural infrastructure in India ranges from sub-standard to terrible.

There were still over 410 million non-workers in rural India. With the continued fragmentation of land, a large number of farmers are driven into the agricultural labour force. Of which, a good number migrate to urban areas in search of new pastures. Poverty of land to the landless continues to haunt the rural areas.

Population below poverty line in rural India, has stood at 40 per cent. The percentage of population below poverty line vary widely from 69 per cent in Orissa to 11.9 per cent in Punjab. About one-fifth of India is at the bottom of the socio-economic ladder which suffer from poverty and social handicap. Because of social discrimination, the scheduled castes and scheduled tribes continue to suffer in the most intense and inhuman form.

Rural poverty is multi-directional. Half of the rural population are poor in food consumption, poor in health, live in mud houses, illiterate, ignorant, suppressed as well as exploited by the well-to-do kinsmen. Unemployment is rampant, per capita income is lowest. So also per capita consumption. What is more, people below the poverty line in rural areas are multiplying at a higher rate, inspite of higher infant mortality and death rate. Optimism is clearly lacking in rural India.

Although our objectives announced from time to time during the planned era, are laudable, they have made little impact on the rural society. What has happened is that the inequality in rural India has widened further. Our conspicuous failures are in our efforts to reduce poverty and unemployment.Though a large number of special schemes have been launched for the benefit of the weaker sections, particularly to agricultural labourers, small farmers and scheduled castes and scheduled tribes, have hardly made any appreciable impact on the magnitude of poverty and unemployment. Industrial development since Independence, though remarkable by any token, has not been able to generate commensurate employment necessary to absorb the surplus labour from rural areas and reduce the dependence of the labour force on agriculture.

Thus, judged by critical, social and economic indicators, our progress during the last five decades is far from satisfactory. What went wrong? Did the country follow wrong policies of rural development? Was our administrative machinery inadequate or inefficient to implement various programmes of rural development and ensure social justice? Whether our urban approach to solve the rural problems was inadequate or biased? Was our planning defective? Was our approach about abolition of poverty and unemployment hollow and utopian? Or our leadership did not mean what they said? Did the rich in rural areas corner the bulk of benefits of rural development and even of the schemes specifically meant for the weaker sections? Whether the strategy of creating economic assets in the hands of the rural families is more desirable than creating wage employment on a massive scale? These are difficult questions to answer, but they must be answered.

Rural poverty may not be eradicated completely, but efforts should be made to reduce the incidence to a bare minimum. This is an uphill task, which calls for a pragmatic approach to rural development. The rural development programmes implemented through plans have only touched the surface. It calls for a micro-planning approach to find solutions to the multi-dimensional problems of rural India.

What we need is new ideas, not merely new investment or new technology. We need new ideas to turn around the elephantine public sector that is always falling flat on its face, new ideas to make good use of the Rs. 1,50,000 crores worth of deposits in the banking system without fuelling inflation, new ideas to utilise funds from Indians abroad, and above all, new ideas to snatch planning out of the clutches of bureaucrats, who are always happy pushing files, adding a note here and another minute, but making sure at the same time that nothing really changes. Development means change and a system that abhors change can hardly cope with the problems that development always brings in its wake.

Each successive Plan has seen a progressive increase in the ranks of unemployed and relative poverty. What is more important, the various developmental activities with a total public sector plan expenditure of Rs. 2,00,037 crores could not make any dent on these crucial problems. The assumptions at the beginning of the planning era that the gains from the overall growth of the economy will percolate downwards to the poor through market forces in terms of employment, increased wages and/or lowering of prices has been belied. The benefits got filtered away to the urban and the privileged sections of the society. What has been reaching the rural poor has been a mere trickle. Inspite of this little success, the process of rural development is quite meaningful. It has, at best restricted the downward momentum to some extent.

## A Strategy for Rural Development

The term 'strategy' means the dynamic process by which a programme is aligned with the organisational structure to meet the demands of the environment. The concept has, of course, been extensively applied to corporate management. However, as far as rural development is concerned, strategy means approach adapted for the distribution of benefits of public programmes. One of the crucial thing is that, the strategy must be so designed that the desired results are created through the programmes.

**Table 1**

**RURAL DEVELOPMENT STRATEGIES: EVOLUTION**

| | *Approach* | *Emphasis* |
|---|---|---|
| *(i)* | Rural reconstruction | Village centred movement based on principles of voluntary effort. |
| *(ii)* | Community development | Rural development based on ideas of motivation. |
| *(iii)* | Target sector | Intensive development of a selected sector or sectors of activity with emphasis on concentrating in areas of comparative advantage. |
| *(iv)* | Target groups | Growth with social justice for the weaker sections of population. |
| *(v)* | Growth centres | Spatial planning and development. |
| *(vi)* | Backward area development | Reduction of regional imbalances in development. |
| *(vii)* | Minimum needs | Equalisation of social consumption. |
| *(viii)* | Area planning with full employment | Rural development in an area frame with the removal of unemployment and poverty as an important aim. |

Rural development is a strategy designed to improve the economic and social life of a specific group of people – the rural poor. It involves extending the benefits of development to the poorest among those who seek a livelihood in rural areas. A strategy for rural development must recognise three points. Firstly, the rate of transfer of people out of low productivity agriculture and related activities into more rewarding pursuits has been slow; and, given the relative size of the modern sector in most developing countries, it will remain slow. Secondly, the mass of the people in the rural areas face varying degrees of poverty; their position is likely to get worse if population grows at unprecedented rates while limitations continue to be imposed by available resources, technology, and institutions and organisations. Thirdly, rural areas have labour, land and at least some capital which, if mobilised, could reduce poverty and improve the quality of life.

Rural development recognizes, however, that improved food supplies and nutrition, together with basic services such as health and education, cannot only directly improve the physical well-being and quality of life of the rural poor, but can also indirectly enhance their productivity and their ability to contribute to the national economy. It is concerned with the modernisation and monetisation of rural society, and with its transition from traditional isolation to integration with the national economy.

A strategy for rural development aimed at raising growth rates and distributing the fruits of growth more fairly implies greater interaction between the modern and traditional sectors especially in the form of increased trade in farm produce and in technical inputs and services.

The objectives of development include sustained increases in per capita output and incomes, expansion of productive employment and greater equity in the distribution of the benefits of growth. In other words, it means that people should have adequate income to improve their living standards on a continuing basis. This inter alia means they should be employed and their productivity should improve. This implies reducing poverty and human misery by increasing the productivity of the poor and providing them greater access to goods and services. Rural development must constitute a major part of a development strategy if rural poor are to benefit.

A programme of rural development must embrace a wide range and mix of activities, including projects to raise agricultural output, to improve health and education, to expand communications and to improve housing. It also includes improvement of the rural infrastructure and rural environment. Villages should be connected with all-weather roads, ensured with safe drinking water throughout the year, proper sanitation, facilities for treatment of diseases as well as inculcating healthy habits, education including adult education to increase their sense of awareness of better living and good life. Education will also improve their communication capabilities and improve their ability to utilise the programme services and benefit thereby.

The strategy suffers from the fact that its main thrust does not get reflected in the actual implementation of the plan. The programme of poverty alleviation as initiated in the block is not capable of solving the problem of poverty in the foreseeable future. The integrated strategy is not being practised at all, and the efforts at the grass-root level are being channelised only towards the target group approach which is inadequate in eradicating the rural poverty. Lack of people's participation and training to the beneficiaries are the other strategic shortcomings in the programme. An examination and analysis of the implementation of the varied rural development programmes lay emphasis on the weak organisational structure, lack of appropriate planning at the village level, lack of concern, lack of managerial competence, lack of motivation. These aspects are summarised as follows:

(1) The planning models adopted are mainly macro-dynamic in character and are not suited to the rural environment in India.

(2) Similarly, the rural development programmes general as well as specific, lacked political will followed by inept and inefficient administration, wrong priorities. As a result, they benefitted the already better off.

(3) In absence of structural transformation, the effect of the varied programmes failed to percolate to the rural areas and in particular the rural poor inspite of laudable objectives.

(4) The programme priorities were to pull poor people above the poverty line, there was lack of adequate concern for the priorities and productivity.

(5) Although the rural development programmes were all viable, their implementation lacked concern. The inefficiency and delay in implementation of varied programmes led to wastages of scarce resources.

(6) There was lack of adequate investment in human resources in rural areas. Technical and vocational skills and elementary education to rural population is not properly given. People's education acts like a foundation for rapid growth.

(7) Economic growth in rural India has been followed by rising disparities in individual and regional assets. As a result, the gap between the rich and the poor continues to widen. There has been rising unemployment, under-employment, exploitation and increasing poverty in rural areas. In the wake of this, there is an increase in usurping tendency in rural areas.

(8) The introduction of new technology like irrigation, fertilizers, better seeds, tractors, oil engine, etc., helped the already rich and/or big farmers rather than the small and marginal farmers, agricultural labourers and/or rural artisans.

(9) The delayed and unsuccessful implementation of land reform policy has brought imbalances in the land ownership. This lead to the increasing disparities among the farmers in rural areas. Although the land reforms aimed at helping the tenants and the landless labourers, strengthened the economic base of the rural elite and owner cultivator.

(10) In absence of creating awareness of rural development among the rural poor, the benefits of these varied programmes experimented since the commencement of the First Plan, have, by and large, not reached the target groups.

(11) Awareness as well as socio-economic improvement is related with literary movement. Education helps every citizen, particularly the rural poor to acquire knowledge and skills which would enable them to be a productive and creative member of society.

(12) Family welfare and family planning programmes, literary improvement, involvement of women programmes are to be integrated with other rural development programmes, particularly, community participation must be recognised.

**Table 2**

**PHYSICAL PERFORMANCE OF SPECIAL EMPLOYMENT AND POVERTY ALLEVIATION PROGRAMMES**

*(in million)*

| | *Programmes* | *2000-01* | | *2001-02* | | *2002-03* | |
|---|---|---|---|---|---|---|---|
| | | *Target* | *Achievement* | *Target* | *Achievement* | *Target* | *Achievement* |
| **A.** | **Programmes in rural areas** | | | | | | |
| 1. | JGSY – mandays of employment generated £ | – | 260.29 | – | 262.42 | | 201.47+ |
| 2. | EAS – mandays of employment generated £ | 259.45 | 218.39 | 339.19 | 260.55 | | 209.83+ |
| 3. | SGSY – Total Swarozgaris assisted | – | 1.01 | – | 0.94 | | 0.37+ |
| 4. | IAY – Dwelling units | 1.24 | 1.17 | 1.29 | 1.17 | 1.31 | 0.82> |
| 5. | ARWSP – Habitation/villages | 0.08 | 0.07 | 0.05 | 0.02 | 0.06 | 0.03** |
| 6. | CRSP – (No. of Sanitary latrines) | 1.26 | 0.62 | – | 0.05 | – | – |
| 7. | NSAP – | | | | | | |
| | *(a)* NOAPS – Beneficiaries ££ | 5.58 | 5.15 | 5.06 | 5.43 | – | – |
| | *(b)* NFBS – Beneficiaries ££ | 0.21 | 0.2 | 0.16 | 0.16 | – | – |
| | *(c)* NMBS – Beneficiaries* | 1.82 | 1.45 | – | – | – | – |

| | | | | | | | |
|---|---|---|---|---|---|---|---|
| **B.** | **Programmes in urban areas** | | | | | | |
| 1. | PMRY – (i) Micro-enterprises @ | 0.22 | 0.19 | 0.22 | $0.15^P$ | 0.22 | 0.04 |
| | (ii) Employment generated $ | 0.30 | 0.28 | 0.30 | $0.23^P$ | 0.30 | 0.06 |
| 2. | SJSRY$$ of which | | | | | | |
| I | USEP – | | | | | | |
| | *(i)* Beneficiaries | – | 0.10 | – | 0.08 | – | 0.06** |
| | *(ii)* Persons trained | – | 0.09 | – | 0.11 | – | 0.08** |
| II | UWEP – mandays of employment generated | – | 15.87 | – | 3.63 | – | 5.74** |
| 3. | Beneficiaries covered under community structure component | – | 28.73^ | – | 29.59^ | – | 29.90^** |
| 4. | Beneficiaries assisted under DWCUA | – | 0.007 | – | 0.18 | – | 0.014** |

*Notes :*

– : Targets are not fixed.

P : Provn. Figs.

@ : Cases disbursed. For 2002-03, achievement is up to November, 2002.

$ : Estimated @ 1.5 per case disbursed loan. For 2002-03, achievement is up to November, 2002.

$$ : Swarna Jayanti Shakari Rozgar Yojana came into operation from December, 1997.

^ : Cumulative information since it is a continuous process.

+ : Up to December, 2002.

> : Up to December 31, 2002.

** : Up to January, 2003.

£ : JGSY & EAS merged into Sampoorna Grameen Rozgar Yojana (SGRY) w.e.f. 25-9-2001.

££ : Transferred to States w.e.f. 2002-03.

* : Transferred to Ministry of Health and Family Welfare w.e.f. 2001-02.

*Source :* Planning Commission and other concerned Departments.

## Conclusion

Rural development is a part of the same process of economic and social change. A number of rural development programmes have been formulated by the Government and the industry, voluntary agencies, etc. to improve the living standards of the rural poor as well as bringing back the past glory to the village economy. Banks have been implementing them by providing necessary financial assistance. There are multi-discipline institutions for rural development. What is wanting at the present moment is the co-ordinated and sustained effort. What is more, it is necessary to bridge the gaps of inequalities in rural areas. This could be attempted by well organised service co-operatives to give support to farming and other farm and non-farm activities in the rural environment.

Towards this end, the corporate sector, banks and other financial institutions should invest sizeable portion of their profits towards increasing basic infrastructure like schools, hospitals, health centres and take up the onerous task of propagating family planning, planned parenthood and motivating rural people to achieve a higher living standard. Rural development is a human development programme and, therefore, it should be above party politics. The motto should be to help with all the might the down-trodden irrespective of caste, creed, sex, etc.

Rural development should be looked upon not merely as ameliorating the socio-economic conditions of the rural people but also as motivating rural people to take up the integrated development of rural areas. In this direction, the process of development should originate at the individual level then linking it to family and then to a group of families and the village. It should develop from bottom to top. The people's active participation will bring in a sea-change in the scale and scope of operation. The results are in terms of change rather than the sum of crores of rupees spent on a project without bringing any benefit to the concerned people. The experiments in rural development have remained more or less at the top. It is, therefore, necessary that emphasis should be laid on 'Planning' from the bottom and that the exclusive reliance, so far placed on the 'pyramid structure' approach, be given up.

Awakening and awareness brings about a significant change in the outlook of the rural poor – both men and women – and in their general economic and social standing. They will become bolder, self-reliant and capable of handling the varied socio-economic and cultural problems that confront them in the development process.

Rural development is a continuous process. It will continue to receive the attention of the intellectuals to sharpen the focus or evaluating the performance of a programme or formulating and implementing a new programme. As such, rural development should find its rightful place in the deliberations and studies. There is a greater need for vocational training to a large section of people. More importantly their lost confidence is to be restored, so that they can meet the challenges with courage. The structure, organisation, component of rural area may change significantly, but the process of development will continue.

In the ultimate analysis, the desire for development, the direction this process takes and the momentum it gathers, depends upon the will of the people. Various institutions for rural development can help in harnessing the energies of the people, especially of the rural people as well as the student community and in providing institutional and organisational channels for their efforts. The environment in the country today is conducive for concerted action in improving rural environment and rebuild rural civilisation.

❑ ❑ ❑

## Chapter 6

# EARLY ATTEMPTS AT RURAL DEVELOPMENT

## Introduction

A few of the early attempts at rural development in India are enumerated in this chapter.

## Sriniketan Experiment

In India, Sriniketan experiment in the beginning of this century was considered to be the first attempt in rural development. Sri Rabindranath Tagore, a visionary and poet had brought a sea change in the environs surrounding Sriniketan in West Bengal. The programme aimed at socio-economic as well as moral rehabilitation of rural community. As part of the rural development programme, monkeys and malaria was eradicated in first phase. Later on, new strategy of agriculture, new breeds of cows, poultry and village crafts were introduced. Doors of education were opened to village children, adults. In addition, villagers were educated in the use of new agricultural implements by way of demonstrations.

The experiment was quite successful in a small area and in a few villages. The level of economy looked up and the standard of living of people improved. New awakening and confidence arose among the villagers. The experiment, however, could not be carried out for want of continued professional guidance and trained personnel. Over and above, the government machinery tried to work in a mechanical routine.

Inspite of innumerable handicaps, Tagore's ideas and influence inspired and penetrated every corner of Sriniketan. He constantly urged that "our practical achievements, our clean milk, our fresh eggs, our flourishing co-operatives, were all useful means, but still only means towards the achievement of much greater end." He urged to draw up all resources, in music, song, drama and dance, at Santiniketan, so as to enrich lives and to increase delight in every kind of artistic expression, until the cultivators could produce a richness and a wealth of cultural life, and rejuvenation of those ancient art forms that still survived, but so tenuously around the village.

## Martandum Experiment

Martandum was a densely populated market place in Kerala state then (South Travancore), for the surrounding 40 villages within a radius of 5 kms. The people were poor. The land was worn out. There were a few cottage industries. The quality of produce was poor. Wages were low. Water problem was chronic. Large number of families were indebted. Interest rates were as high as 300 per cent per annum, *i.e.* on a loan of Rs.1000/-, interest of Rs.300/- to be paid per year. Mr. Spender Hatch studied the problems and initiated a five pronged rural reconstruction programme in 1921.

The philosophy of rural reconstruction was peoples' own programme. The personnel were only to help them achieve the programmes.

The philosophy of rural reconstruction principles were:

(1) The programme of rural reconstruction was peoples' own programme. The personal were only to help them achieve the programmes.

(2) Help the people to help themselves upwards on all sides of life comprising spirit, mind, body, economic, social and cultural.

(3) People of all communities were to be included.

(4) It is the poor who require help more and, therefore, reach the poorest.

(5) Implement a comprehensive programme, and as such attention was devoted to the development of poultry keeping, bee-keeping, and other cottage industries like mats and basket making, palmyra, sugar, hand-women cloth, etc.

(6) Spirituality should be the basis of every programme.

(7) Simplicity should be the key-note of the programme. Unless the whole rural reconstruction movement remained simple it would cost too much and perforce would stop short of benefits to millions of rural people.

(8) Honorary unpaid service help make an efficient and highly productive extension service.

(9) Close co-operation between the rural people and the government officials is a must.

(10) Emphasis was laid on training of workers.

Miss Ouwerkerk in her study, about the developing village in India has aptly observed that "It has evoked in them enthusiasm, a desire to improve, a spirit of co-operation and a new self-respect. This new spirit among the people makes it possible to work out a comprehensive programme of rural reconstruction." Since the programme was on a small scale its success to short lived. However, it emphasised the need for a comprehensive programme for rural reconstruction.

## The Gurgaon Experiment

Mr. Brayne was posted as Deputy Commissioner of Gurgaon district in 1920. He was moved at the uncertainty of rainfall, abject poverty, filthy dwellings, ill-health, ignorance, illiteracy of the rural people. With a view to improve the living conditions of the rural people living in Gurgaon district, he evolved a new technique of village development called the "Gurgaon Scheme." This was, in other words, the practical application of the principle that the central figures, *viz.,* the villager himself must be made to take greater interest in himself and in his village before any results can be achieved; and the government agencies should do more to combine and co-ordinate their activities in order to assist, help and guide him. The Gurgaon scheme claimed to deal with the whole life and the activity of the peasant and his family and to present a complete remedy from the terrible conditions in which he lived.

| DEVELOPMENT WORK UNDER THE GURGAON SCHEME | |
|---|---|
| Institutional | School—Health Association—Women's Institution. |
| Sanitation | Latrine, Urinals, Drinking water. |
| Agricultural Development | Model farms—improved seeds and implements—preventive measures—co-operative farming. |
| Education | School Teacher as the centre of activity. |
| Co-operation | Co-operation in all activities. |
| Social Reforms | Prohibition of child marriages—Education of girls—thrift—reducing litigation, combating indebtedness. |

According to Mr. Brayne, "Our object in Gurgaon has been to jerk the villager out of his old groove, convince him that improvement is possible, and kill his fatalism by demonstrating that both climate, disease and pests can be successfully fought. He must be laughed out of his uneconomic and unhealthy customs, and taught better ways of living and farming. Further the secrets of our success were to deal with the whole of village life, to take the whole district as the field of operations and to deluge the areas with every form of propaganda and publicity that we could devise of adopt or afford. Uplift is a mass movement, a combined assault, and no area, no part of the life and no method of attack can be neglected."

The developmental work was taken up under Gurgaon scheme under these sub-heads:

(a) **Institutional Work Comprised in the Setting Up of:** *(i)* School of Rural Economy to train guides for the rural uplift. The school managed a farm of 51 acres on long lease for the purpose of providing practical training to the students. The curriculum of the studies including scouting, co-operation, practical agriculture, first aid, infant welfare, public health, domestic hygiene and sanitation, village hygiene and sanitation, stock breeding and elementary veterinary training. The students were expected to qualify in the examination in first-aid and co-operation and special test in all the other subjects. Those who qualified in this test were appointed as village guides. The village guides were entrusted with these duties: *(a)* development of co-operation, *(b)* public health work, collecting list for, preparing people for vaccinators' visit, *(c)* cleaning of villages by digging of manure pits, putting in of windows, ventilators, etc., in the houses; *(d)* agriculture demonstration and sale of improved ploughs and other implements, improved seeds, Persian wheel, etc. *(ii)* Domestic School of Economics to uplift village women. The curriculum of studies in the domestic school included reading and writing up to primary standard, in the case of illiterate women, and some instructions in sewing, knitting and making clothes, embroidery work, toy making, cooking, hygiene, sanitation, first aid and child welfare, etc. *(iii)* Health Association to promote public health; and *(iv)* Women's Institute to manage the ladies' garden in Gurgaon and also to organise games, and magic lantern shows for the women and first-aid classes.

(b) **Rural Sanitation Work:** With a view to improve living conditions in the villages by using manure pits as latrines, and preserving sweepings, rubbish and dung in properly dug pits. Efforts were also initiated to fight epidemics like small-pox, plague and cholera.

(c) **Agricultural Development Programme:** The programme was launched to exhort farmers to set up model farms, use improved seeds, adopt Gurgaon plough and other improved implements; use preventive measures against crop pests, killing of field rats and monkeys, and drawing out other harmful insects by keeping lanterns in the fields. The programme also emphasised on the consolidation of fragmented land holdings on co-operative basis. The principal objective of this programme aimed at increasing yield per hectare, so that the farmer gets a fair return on his efforts.

(d) **Education:** Under the scheme, the school teacher was made the centre of all development activities in the village. Mr. Brayne emphatically stated "The village school teacher with his school library, his night school and his scouts must be the centre of uplift and culture and he must be so trained that he can solve all the simple problems of the villager, whether they are agriculture, social or moral or relate to public health."

(e) **Co-operation:** Co-operation was given special thrust as the cornerstone of reconstruction of rural areas. Everyone will extend whole-heatedly co-operation in the development of the village economy.

(f) **Social Reforms:** Mr. Brayne had also realised that any process of economic development should run concurrent with speedy social reforms, social reforms were aimed at: *(i)* prohibition of child marriages, *(ii)* education of girls in the mixed schools, *(iii)* abolition of purdah, *(iv)* curtailment of ceremonial expenditure, *(v)* introduction of marriage registers by which litigation in family disputes is very much lessened, *(vi)* propaganda against injurious litigation, and *(vii)* combating indebtedness.

The Gurgaon scheme may be described as a judicious combination of the villagers' own efforts with the activities of the nation building departments. It marked a definite departure in the technique of village improvement. The programme at Gurgaon awakened the people and the government to the vital problem of village reconstruction.

Sir M.L. Darling aptly commented: "Pits were dug in thousands. Hissar bulls and Gurgaon plough bought in thousands and Persian wheels put up in scores. Villages were cleaned, and recleaned, multitudes attended the annual Palwal fair, large sums were raised for high schools and many girls went to school with boys. Activity was unprecedented, and a few who took part in it could resist its contagion... But unfortunately after seven months all is changed, and the optimistic estimate is that among the peasant themselves no more than one-third of the activity remains."

Mr. Brayne himself realized that "Good work, excellent work is going on all over the Punjab. You can travel all day and find nothing that offend either eye or nose. Village after village and zail after zail have been turned into models of new life. Marvellous changes have been made and there is a feeling of life and movement in the air. Have we found the incentive then? Will this work last and spread? Alas, no! This work is not being done by villagers determined to live a better life but by villagers determined to please their district officers. A good enough motive in its way but not the motive we are looking for. There is no permanence about this kind of work. What if the district officer's attention is diverted elsewhere, or he wants something different done, or in a different series of villages?"

## Baroda Experiment

The first rural reconstruction centre was set up in 1932 and the work commenced in a group of villages round Kosamba (in Navsari District). The basic idea underlying the rural reconstruction experiment in rural areas around Baroda were: "The single outstanding fact in the agricultural economy of India is that owing to seasonal and other conditions, work on the land is possible only during a portion of the year. Millions of people are, thus, unemployed over periods of the year ranging from two to three months in the highly irrigated areas to as much as eight to nine months in the dry tracts. This long interval of enforced idleness and dreary waiting between crop and crop leads to evil, economic and moral, which it is unnecessary to describe to those who know village life in India–the squalour and rivalries, and factions and the litigation which has been described as "our second greatest industry." No lasting improvement can be achieved in the conditions of rural life unless all sides of it are attacked at the same time; the many sides of it are all so closely interconnected."

The centre aimed at: *(i)* effecting an improvement in all aspects of rural life *i.e.* changing the outlook of the agriculturists, the problem being "the development of the desire for a higher standard of living," *(ii)* to undertake intensive work to release this aim, *(iii)* to develop best type of village leadership; and to undertake the following programmes:

*(a)* *Economic Programme* consisted of *(i)* development of subsidiary occupations like kitchen-gardening, weaving, poultry farming, sericulture, bee-keeping, etc., *(ii)* farm improvements in cotton and other crops, *(iii)* co-operative society to inculcate thrift; and *(iv)* the village panchayats to provide for sanitation, village roads and drinking water supply.

*(b)* *Education and Moral Programmes* included adult education; development of community sense and of a feeling of solidarity in the village; propaganda against evils like early marriages and unreasonable customs connected with social observances; the proper use of village libraries; the scout movement and other educative work through lantern lectures; in short, making village life full and interesting. The village school should be the centre of all such activities.

The programme of rural reconstruction was to be part of a wider programme for bringing about a rapid increase in standard of living. Increased agriculture production lay at the root of all development. Therefore the programme was progressively expanded to cover measures such as provision of irrigation facilities; conservation of soil; production of nucleus seed; their multiplication and distribution; education in agriculture and supplementary occupations.

From the commencement it was recognised that efforts to increase agriculture production could not succeed unless they were supplemented by programmes for ensuring to villages minimum amenities needed by them.

**CENTRE'S PROGRAMME OF RURAL RECONSTRUCTION**

| | | |
|---|---|---|
| Changing the outlook | Farm Improvement<br>Subsidiary<br>Occupations | Adult Education<br>Feeling of Solidarity<br>Removal of Ignorance |
| Village Leadership | Co-operative Society<br>Village Panchayat | Education |

## Rural Reconstruction

The programme laid thrust on the following points: Firstly there should be a comprehensive programme of improvements carefully organised for improving all aspects of rural life. Secondly, increased agricultural production holds the key to the success of the movement. Programmes for this purpose to cover all areas should be worked out from year to year and there should be an efficient organisation for supplies and services and credit. Third, the block team should work unitedly and with a single aim and its activities co-ordinated. The best non-official leadership should be enlisted for the programme. Fourth, the agency in the village through which to assist every family should be the panchayat and co-operative, the village school and library should be the centre for most activities. The Baroda experiment was a great success.

| Stages | Baroda Programme of Rural Development |
|---|---|
| 1st | Comprehensive Programmes |
| 2nd | Increased Agricultural Production |
| 3rd | United Working |
| 4th | Non-Official Leadership |
| 5th | Village panchayat as a co-ordinator |

## Bombay Experiment

An intensive scheme for rural reconstruction was launched by the then Bombay government with a view to carry on the Mahatma Gandhiji's programme of Sarvodaya. This is first rural reconstruction scheme, sponsored by the government in the pre-independence era for the development of backward rural economy.

Gandhiji wrote in the *Harijan* in 1942. "My idea of village swaraj is that it is a complete republic, independent of its neighbours for its own vital wants, and yet inter-dependent for many others in which dependence is a necessity. Thus, every village's first concern will be to grow its own food crops and cotton for its cloth. It should have a reserve for its cattle, recreation and play ground for adults and children. The village will maintain a village theatre, school and public hall. It will have its own water works ensuring clean water supply. This can be done through controlled wells or tanks... As far as possible every activity will be conducted on the co-operative basis... The government of the village will be conducted by the Pan- chayat... Here there is perfect democracy based upon individual freedom."

This schemes is largely based on Gandhiji's idea of Sarvodaya, Gandhiji was visibly moved by the ignorance, disease and poverty of rural people and dreamt of village reconstruction that would fire the imagination of village people and lead them through self-help to insure ample good for all, adequate health protection and medical services, free education, local self-government, self-employment through village industries.

The main thrust was to inculcate among the villagers the spirit of self-help and mutual co-operation. The sanchalak was responsible for organising reconstruction.

❑ ❑ ❑

Chapter 7

# NATIONAL PROGRAMMES OF RURAL DEVELOPMENT

## Introduction

The task of accelerating growth with greater social justice cannot be accomplished without a fuller utilisation of resources and opportunities in order to improve the quality of life of the have-nots in its totality. The well-conceived policies and programmes of rural development are to be matched by a high sense of commitment for village betterment.

The Community Development Programme adopted a systematic integrated approach to rural development with an hierarchy of village level workers and block level workers drawn from various fields to enrich rural life. Agriculture, animal husbandry, public health, women's development, rural industries etc., found special niche in the framework cast for this purpose. 5000 National Extension Service Blocks were created under the Community Development Programme by the end of the Second Five Year Plan. During the Third Five Year Plan the momentum was maintained through a series of developmental schemes though allocations under the NES programme tapered. This was succeeded by the Small Farmers' Development Agencies followed by Marginal Farmers' Development Agencies, Crash Schemes for Rural Employment, Food for Work Programme, Drought Prone Areas Programme and Desert Development Programmes in the early seventies. The contents of all these programmes were to strengthen the rural base of the economy specifically the primary sector, comprising agriculture, animal husbandry etc. and employment through labour intensive works that would create the infrastructure of roads and other community assets for the benefit of the rural people.

## Milestones

Keeping in view the need for introduction of new innovative technologies and ensuring science and technology inputs in rural development programmes in appropriate forms, the government has constituted a

Science and Technology Advisory Committee in the Department of Rural Development. Among other things, the terms of reference of the Committee is to analyse the existing scientific and technological contents of rural development so as to identify the lacunae and deficiencies in the conceptual framework, approaches, strategy and knowledge base of the programme, and provide necessary correctives.

The scope of CAPART has been widened. Close links with other government departments and science and technology agencies are to be established to ensure better co-ordination. These include Department of Science and Technology, Council for Scientific and Industrial Research, Indian Council for Agricultural Research, Department of Non-Conventional Energy Sources, National Wastelands Development Board, Khadi and Village Industries Commission and Department of Electronics.

Based on the National Seminar on Poverty Alleviation Programmes organised to ascertain the views of academicians, experts and specialists in the field of rural development and representatives from the central and state governments, the strategy for poverty alleviation was reviewed. An assessment of the impact of the existing programmes and improvements required to upgrade the quality of life in rural areas was undertaken and the guidelines of the programmes modified to the extent feasible.

A massive training programme for increasing the capabilities of rural development functionaries has been planned to cover all the personnel in a period of two years. An intensive programme to train the trainers for taking up increasing responsibilities has been launched.

A detailed study of the existing wholesale market facilities for fruits and vegetables in cities with a view to assessing the projected needs for the next 15 years and planning for their development has been initiated for the whole country.

The Rural Development Department co-sponsored the Seminar on Agricultural in 2000, in commemoration of the Nehru centenary celebrations.

The scheme for organisation of beneficiaries through voluntary organisations was reviewed and enlarged to include special components for training social animators and social organisers with a view to increase people's participation in development programmes.

Rural housing has been brought under the Department of Rural Development. A new apex bank—National Housing Bank (NHB) has been established to provide finance as well as necessary assistance to accelerate the process of building houses for the houseless in rural as well as urban areas.

A major process of consultation with the grassroot level elected representatives of the Panchayats was started with the Panchayati Raj Sammelan of the Northern and Western States in Delhi in January 1989 with similar consultations to follow in the other regions. This would mark an important step in strengthening the process of democratic decentralisation of authority and planning.

A draft for Rs. 15 crores was presented to Life Insurance Corporation as premium under the Group Insurance Scheme for the beneficiaries of Integrated Rural Development Programme. The scheme was introduced throughout the country from 1st April 1988. The objectives of the insurance scheme is to ensure that the dependents of an IRDP beneficiary do not slip below the poverty line on the death of the beneficiary. The insurance benefit is Rs. 3000. Further, the assets created under IRDP loan will remain with the family and the enterprise continued. The insurance benefit will be doubled in the case of death by accident.

## General Appraisal

Although the national rural development programmes are recasted and renamed from time to time to suit the ruling government, the basic thrust remains to be infrastructure development, income generation, employment, socio-economic upliftment. New awareness is to provide urban facilities in rural areas (PURA). Which is against the cultural ethos of rural India. The best course of action is to organise rural people and empower them to develop their areas.

## Annexure A

# PROGRAMMES FOR RURAL DEVELOPMENT

The problem of rural development in India is multidimensional and complex and its crux is removal of abject poverty and ignorance. With this end in view, a number of rural development programmes have been devised. These programmes can broadly be classified under five categories, viz (I) Programmes where banks play a major role, (II) Government sponsored programme, (III) Labs to land programmes, (IV) Social welfare programmes and (V) Insurance schemes.

## I. PROGRAMMES WHERE BANKS PLAY A MAJOR ROLE

- ***Integrated Rural Development Programme (IRDP)***

  IRDP is a multisectoral, multilevel and multisectional approach integrating the efforts of all development age-ncies including banks for upliftment of people below poverty line. Various programmes like Small Farmers' 'Development Agency (SFDA), Marginal Farmers and Agricultural Labourers' Development Progr-amme (MFALDP), and Command Area Development Programme (CADP) which were in operation tending to particular sector, purpose, area prior to IRDP were integrated to form IRDP which was introduced in 2,000 community development blocks in April 1978. From 2nd October 1980, it was extended to all the 5,004 blocks of the country.

  The target group is small/marginal farmers, agricultural labourers and village artisans and others below poverty line (annual income below Rs. 6,400). However, since the aim of the IRDP is to help the poorest of the poor persons with annual income of less than Rs. 4,800 are given priority.

  The scheme is implemented with the help of District Rural Development Agency (DRDA) who assists in identification of beneficiaries and preparation of suitable schemes for the area. The purpose of the scheme is to create productive assets and cover minor irrigation, dairy, poultry, fisheries, etc.

  The scale of finance is restricted to unit cost. A central subsidy ranging from 25 to 50 per cent is available, which is treated as margin. Interest is charged at the rate of 10 per cent per annum.

- ***Self Employment for Educated Unemployed Youth (SEEUY)***

  Launched on 15th August 1983 the scheme intends to provide employment to educated unemployed youth.

  The scheme covers all persons aged between 18 to 35 years with minimum 10th Standard education or ITI trained education, at centres with population of less than 10 lakhs. The family income should be less than Rs. 10,000 per annum.

  The scheme is especially aimed at three sectors *viz*., industry, service and business with a maximum loan component of Rs. 35,000, Rs. 25,000 and Rs. 10,000 respectively, and nil margin up to loan amount of Rs. 25,000. Interest rate ranges from 10 per cent per annum to 13.5 per cent per annum. Central subsidy up to 25 per cent is available which is kept in fixed deposit in the name of the borrower, to be adjusted after 75 per cent of the loan is recovered. The target is 2.5 lakh beneficiaries per year. Minimum 30 per cent of the beneficiaries should be scheduled castes and scheduled tribes.

- ***Self Employment Programme for the Urban Poor (SEPUP)***

  SEPUP was introduced on 15th August 1986 in all metropolitan urban and semi-urban centres with a population of over 10,000 and cities not covered by the IRDP. An applicant under this scheme should be permanent resident of the place for the preceding three years. having his/her name in ration card, whose family income does not exceed Rs. 7,200 per annum. The RBI directive of 2nd November 1988 has excluded the income of children below 14 years while calculating the family income.

  One beneficiary for every 300 population is selected and a maximum loan of Rs. 5,000 per family with 10 per cent per annum interest and nil margin is given. A central subsidy of 15 per cent is available. Project cost should not exceed Rs. 5,000. More than one member from a family can be financed, subject to the minimum loan amount.

- ***Differential Rate of Interest (DRI)***

  The scheme was introduced in March 1972. A target of one per cent of the aggregate advances of the previous year is fixed for lending to economically weaker sections of the society under the scheme, 40 per cent of which should go to scheduled castes and scheduled tribes. Two-third of the advances should be issued through rural/semi-urban branches.

Family income should not exceed Rs. 7,200 per annum is urban/semi-urban areas and Rs. 6,400 per annum in rural areas where their land holding should be within one acre of irrigated and 2.5 acres of unirrigated land. Land holding criterion, however does not apply to SCs/STs.

Maximum loan amount eligible is Rs. 5,000 for term loan and Rs. 1,500 for working capital. Indigent students pursuing higher education who do not get scholarship can avail assistance under the scheme up to a loan amount Rs. 25,000, provided family income criterion is satisfied. Orphanages, women's homes, institutions for the handicapped can also avail assistance under the scheme for production saleable goods. While the income does not apply to such institutions loan amount per member should be adhered to.
A very low interest rate of 4 per cent per annum is charged. Margin is nil. No subsidy is available Recipient of subsidy under any scheme is not eligible. DRI/IRDP/SEPUP are mutually exclusive.

- ***Service Area Approach (SAA)***
  The shortcomings observed in lead bank schemes prompted the planners to think of an intensive area approach to rural development and SAA evolved in 1988. Under the new SAA each branch will be allotted 15-20, villages, which will be assessed by the branch manager, after a survey of the villages. These branch plans will be aggregated is block plans and incorporated in the district plan by the lead bank.
- ***Special Foodgrain Production Programme (SEPP)***
  Introduced in April 1988, the programme aims to help reach the foodgrains target of 166 million tonnes for 1988-89 and 175 million tonnes for 1989-90.

  As many as 169 potential districts in 14 states have been identified for immediate and concerted action, covering five major crops, viz, rice, wheat, maize, gram and arhar.

  By efficient planning and better management of critical inputs and transfer of technology, the programme aims at increasing the per hectare yield for achieving the proposed additional production.

## II. GOVERNMENT SPONSORED SCHEMES

The various schemes of the government could be further grouped as schemes for employment, area development and others.

### (A) Employment Schemes

- ***Crash Scheme of Rural Development (CSRD)***
  It was started in April 1971. The duration of the scheme was three years. The important objects of the scheme were direct generation of employment on an average continuously over a working season of 10 months through essentially labour intensive projects aimed to production of assets or works of a durable nature. Totally unemployed persons are given preference.
- ***Pilot Intensive Rural Employment Project (PIREP)***
  This was implemented during 1972 to 1976 in 15 blocks situated in various parts of the country with different economic and ecological conditions. It was an action-cum-pilot study project on the characteristics of employment in the particular selected areas.
- ***Food For Work Programme (FFWP)***
  Conceived in 1976-77, the basic objective of the programme was to create additional employment in rural areas through utilisation of surplus foodgrains available in the buffer stock for payment as wages and to create thereby durable community assets. Besides being successful in achieving its basic objectives, the programme resulted in many other benefits to the rural poor, like price stabilisation of foodgrains, ensuring minimum wages to the worker and improving their nutritional standards.
- ***National Rural Employment Programme (NREP)***
  In 1980-81, FFWP was reviewed and restructured as NREP, as a number of shortcomings were noticed in the implementation of FFWP. The expenditure for the programme is shared by central and state governments. The basic objectives of the scheme remain the same as FFWP. Wages are paid in part as foodgrains and in part cash.

- ***Rural Landless Employment Guarantee Programme (RLEGP)***
  Launched in 1983, the programme aims to improve and expand employment opportunities for rural landless, with a view to providing guarantee of employment to at least one member of every landless labour household up to 100 days in a year. The programme is fully funded by the central government. The landless labourers particularly schedule castes/scheduled tribes are given preference.

  The types of works undertaken under FFWP/NREP/RLEGP are construction of rural link roads, land development, minor irrigation projects, social forestry, construction of schools, dispensaries, etc. The NREP and RLEGP are proposed to be merged.

- ***Training of Rural Youth for Self Employment (TRYSEM)***
  Introduced on 15th August 1979 the scheme imparts through training necessary skills and technical knowledge to rural youth in the age group to 18 to 35 years, enabling them to take up gainful avocation. The objective is to train two lakh youth per year, at an average of 40 persons per block.

  Trainees are given financial assistance during training and a tool kit costing Rs. 250. Loans can be obtained thereafter to take up the trade in which they are trained.

- ***Scheme of Preparing Ex-servicemen for Self Employment (PEXSEM)***
  The scheme was launched in 1983. Under the scheme, to encourage retiring/retired defence personnel to settle down in rural areas close to their homes training and financial assistance are given to them to take up self employment.

  Apart from conveyance allowance. (Rs.1000) and training fee (Rs. 50 per month), the trainee is given a stipend of Rs. 250 per month as boarding and lodging expenses. Subsidy on project coats as well as interest subsidy is available.

## (B) Area Development Schemes

Specific schemes were introduced taking into account the peculiarities, climatic conditions of the areas. Some of them are:

- ***Intensive Agriculture District Programme (IADP)***
  In order to solve the food crisis during January 1959, the Government of India invited a team of foreign experts in agricultural production to study India's food production problem and to recommend ways and means to increase production on an emergency basis. Sponsored by the Ford Foundation, the main recommendation of this team was IADP.

  The recommendation was given a concrete shape by another team which visited India is October 1959 and a ten-point pilot programme was evolved. The ten-points were adequate and readily accessible farm supplies, farm credit, an intensive education programme, simple individual farm plans, stronger village institutions, assured prices for the produce, reliable marketing facilities, rural public works, evaluation and analysis and a coordinated approach.

  The ultimate aim was to improve the farmers' lot in the areas selected for the purpose and creation of a sound agricultural base for overall economic development and social uplift.

- ***Intensive Agricultural Area Programme (IAAP)***
  The scheme was for intensive development of important crops such as wheat, paddy, millets, cotton, sugarcane, etc. About 20-25 per cent of the cultivated area of the country was selected for intensive agricultural development.

  The scheme advocated higher adoption of modern technology and use of fertilisers, improved seeds, etc in order to achieve progressive increase in the production of main crops in the selected areas.

- ***Desert Development Programme (DDP)***
  The scheme was formulated to control the desert development conditions and to provide suitable condition for raising the levels of production and employment potential in the area.

The areas found in hot and cold arid zones showing signs of desert development were covered.

The aim was sought to be achieved through groundwater development and utilisation, construction of water storage structures, afforestation with special emphasis on shelter belt plantation, grassland development and sand dune stabilisation, rural electrification of tubewells/pumpsets and development of hortic-ulture/agriculture/animal husbandry.

- ***Drought–Prone Areas Programme (DPAP)***
  The basic concept of the DPAP is optional utilisation of available land, water and human resources, which calls for a detailed analysis of resource endowment of the area. Based on the criteria of level and periodicity of rainfall, intensity and past occurrence of drought and proportion of irrigated area to the total cultivated area, the area is chosen for implementation of the programme. Dry farming technology *i.e* choice of appropriate variety of crops, salvage of irrigation water for supplementary irrigation and intercropping are taken into account. Pasture development is also given importance.

- ***Command Area Development Programme (CADP)***
  Experience showed that irrigation potentials already created could not be optimally utilised for want of on-the-farm infrastructure. For utilisation of available water most productively, the command areas should be fully prepared to receive the supplies.

  The National Commission on Agriculture, therefore, recommended that an irrigation project should include all engineering works from the source of supply to the outlets and drains, all engineering works in the command area including land levelling, shaping, construction of water courses, field channels, field drains and roads and other items pertaining to agriculture, animal husbandry, forestry, etc.

  The Government of India advised setting up of Command Area Development Authorities by the state governments for achieving these objectives.

- ***Tribal Area Development Programme (TADP)***
  The scheme is aimed at overall development of tribal area and to foster the economic development of the tribal population so as to bring these backward areas on par with the developed areas of the state. Increased agricultural production and development of forest resources gained importance. For provision of credit and marketing, Large Sized Adivasi Multi–purpose Societies (LAMPS) were formed. Protective legislation to free the tribals from bondage of indebtedness was introduced.

- ***Hill Area Development Programme (HAPD)***
  In order to evolve a suitable pattern of development in hilly backward areas and to remove regional disparities, this programme was introduced. Integrated development of agriculture and allied activities, land development by way of terracing, soil conservation, minor irrigation, etc., were adopted. The farmers, gardeners and the like were trained on the use of technological developments to maximise output of agricultural horticultural and animal production.

## (C) Other Schemes

- ***Minimum Needs Programme***
  Introduced in 1974, the aim of the programme was to improve the quality of life in rural areas through provision of facilities for education, sanitation, potable water, rural roads, electricity and environmental improvement. Domestic cooking energy and public distribution are recent additions to the programme.

- ***Rural Industries Scheme***
  A centrally sponsored scheme for rural industries projects was taken up in 1962-1963, with the object of evolving techniques for establishing viable industrial units in rural areas for using local raw materials and talent. It also aimed at reducing imbalances in regional development and providing gainful employment opportunities in rural areas. The District Industries Centre and the Khadi and Village Industries Commission work actively to promote rural industries, such as, handicrafts, handlooms and powerlooms, coir, silk etc. Other industries like processing of cereals and pulses, oil, cane, gur and khandsari, non-edible oils and soap, beekeeping, handmade paper, pottery, gobar gas etc. are also encouraged.

- ***Rural Electrification Scheme***
This scheme reflects the socio-economic priorities of the government and calls for 100 per cent electrification of all villages and optimal exploitation of minor irrigation potential with special accent on the areas inhabited by the weaker sections of the society. With a view to achieving this objective. Rural Electrification Corporation (REC) was formed. So far 100 per cent electrification has been achieved in eight states. By the end of Eighth Plan, all villages in other states are expected to be electrified by the REC under the scheme.

- ***Massive Agriculture Production Programme (MAPP) or Massive National Programme of Assistance to Small and Marginal Farmers (PASMA)***
A higher man to land ratio, low fertility status of land and poor acreage yield led to the evolution of an agricultural production programme for the benefit of small and marginal farmers. The scheme was launched in 1983-1984. Subsidised schemes for strengthening minor irrigation and water management, land development and purchase of fertiliser and quality seeds are formulated. The subsidy is shared by the central and state governments.

- ***Twenty Point Programme (TPP)***
The new TPP-1986 aims at eradication of poverty, creation of fuller employment, fair distribution of essential commodities and environmental improvement.

  Out of the 20 points, 14 points have been earmarked for bank assistance. They are attack on rural poverty, strategy for rainfed agriculture, better use of irrigation water, bigger harvests, enforcement of land reforms, special programmes for rural labour, health for all, justice to SCs/STs, equality for women, housing for poor, improvement of slums, new strategy for forestry, concern for the consumer and energy for the villages.

- ***Biogas Programme***
The scarcity of power resources led planners to search for alternative sources of non-conventional energy. Biogas programme emerged out of this search. Started in early 70s the programme sought to use feed materials like cowdung, night soil, agricultural waste, etc., for production of gas which could be used for domestic as well as irrigation purposes. Apart from providing energy, the digested slurry provides good manure. The government subsidises the cost of the project.

## III. LABS TO LAND PROGRAMMES

To boost production, adoption of modern techniques is important. The breakthrough achieved in research projects is required to be imparted and put in use for effective results. Realising this, many programmes were introduced to increase agricultural production and to devel'opment animal husbandry. Details are:

### (A) Agricultural Production

- ***High Yielding Variety Programmes (HYVP)***
Launched in the kharif season of 1966-67, this has resulted in substantial increase in foodgrains. The programme advocated balanced use of fertiliser, plant protection measures, identification of suitable varieties for different areas through minikit programmes, timely planting; and raising of nurseries. Wheat, rice, jowar, maize and bajra are the crops included in this programme.

- ***National Seeds Project (NSP)***
The NSP was started in 1977. The Central Seed Commission and Central Certification Board advise an seed varieties, purity and germination standards. The government notifies varieties of various crops for regulating the quality of their seeds.

- ***Multiple Cropping Programme (MCP)***
The scheme of National Demonstration and Multiple Cropping was introduced with the aim of maximising production per unit of land by taking 3-4 crop rotations in a year, by demonstrating to the farmers the production potential of every unit of area of land using high yield variety and adopting multiple cropping pattern. Despite the low intensity of irrigation in certain areas and longer duration varieties with the introduction of short duration varieties and all improved practices this programme has gained special significance to small farmers who have greater labour resources to work on a unit of land.

- ***Pulses Programmes***
  For increasing pulse production, programmes like Intensive Pulse Development Programme and Special Moong Production Programme etc., were introduced.

## (B) Allied Activities

Next to agriculture, animal husbandry and allied programmes have the largest employment potential. They provide subsidiary occupations and other gainful employment at the location itself and make better utilisation of female and child labour. Further these programmes have a large in-built potential for generating indirect employment and ancillary activities like manufacture of livestock feed, fabrication of dairy and poultry equipment and animal based industries like leather manufacturing, wool knitting, etc., get a boost:

- ***Dairy Development Programmes (DDP)***
  Intensive Cattle Development Project and Fodder Development Programme were formulated for increasing milk production. Intensive Cattle Development Project was started in 1964-65 in milk shed areas. It is a comprehensive project paying attention to all aspects of cattle development, like provision of adequate breeding facilities, quick growing fodder crops and subsidised rearing of selected progeny.
  Fodder development programme aimed at achieving quick transfer of technology in all aspects of fodder production, conservation and utilisation. The approach was to promote fodder production as an integral part of crop production so that a mixed farming system was promoted.
  The Dairy Development Programmes culminated in Operation Flood I & II schemes, with the aid of the World Bank. Amul experiment in Gujarat is a living model of this programme and cooperative approach.
- ***Other Programmes***
  Special Livestock Production Programme aimed at improving goat and sheep rearing, piggery and poultry development. Scientific poultry breeding programmes were taken up. Apart from these, pisciculture and sericulture were also developed.

# IV. SOCIAL WELFARE PROGRAMME

Being a social welfare state, the government is keenly aware of its obligation to promote social welfare. Many schemes which were evolved in this direction are listed below:

- ***Community Development Programme (CDP)***
  Launched in 1952, the programme aimed at providing suitable infrastructure for extension work. The basic objective of the movement was to secure the full development of material and human resources of rural areas and to develop local leadership and self governing institutions. Community development was sought to be achieved with the active participation and initiative of the people. Trained workers act as catalytic agents to motivate people and impart knowledge and techniques to the villagers. It has helped people to become more aware of their needs and responsibilities with effect from 1st April 1969, CDP has been the responsibility of the state governments.
- ***Applied Nutrition Programme (ANP)***
  The scheme aims at improving the nutritional standards of people, particularly mothers and children in rural areas. It imparts knowledge on hygienic preparation of foods that retain their nutritional value and demonstrates improved techniques of cooking and feeding. The concept of ANP has been enlarged to include minimum services like immunisation, health care services, environmental sanitation, supply of potable water, etc. The programme is implemented by the state governments with the help of UNICEF, WHO and FAO.
- ***Educational Programmes***
  Rural Functional Literacy Programme (RFLP) and National Adult Education Programme (NAEP) are the two important programmes. RFLP's contribution to education is primarily in the area of training, which is provided in all functional areas of agriculture and allied activities, including technical trade such as maintenance of tractors, pumpsets, etc. Training is also provided in preventive health care. Suitable persons are selected for the purpose and trained free of cost.

  NAEP implies a comprehensive proof of community uplift through community action. Therefore, it comprises literacy with emphasis on health, recreation and home life of adults. Besides class room lectures for the target group, literacy is spread through reading rooms and mahila mandals.

- ***Development Of Women and Children in Rural Area (DOWCRA)***
  The scheme focuses attention on the women members of the families of IRDP target groups and provides supporting services needed to enable them to take up income generating activities. Female literacy, child care facilities while the mothers are at work, provision of working conveniences and suitable appliances, etc., draw attention under the scheme. A one time grant contribution of Rs.15,000 per group as revolving fund to be utilised for income generating activities, training demonstration and child care facilities is available, which is shared equally by the central/state governments and the UNICEF.

## V. INSURANCE SCHEMES

Credit insurance, crop insurance and life insurance are the main schemes under this category:

- ***Credit Insurance***
  The Deposit Insurance and Credit Guarantee Corporation of India offers a measure of protection to banks and other financial institutions which extend credit to borrowers of small means and to small scale industries. The insurance premia for limits up to Rs. 25,000 is borne by the credit institutions. Various priority sector advances are covered under the scheme.

- ***Crop Insurance***
  The Comprehensive Crop Insurance Scheme, introduced on 1st April 1985, is an area based credit linked voluntary scheme, covering wheat, paddy, millet, oil seeds and pulses.
  All farmers availing crop loans for these crops from co-operative credit societies, RRBs and commercial banks are eligible for insurance coverage under the scheme.

  Barring a few states, other states had implemented the scheme. The scheme was kept voluntary to make it more popular and beneficial to the farmers so that they evince interest in the scheme on their own.
  The mounting losses under the scheme led the government to suspend the scheme in January 1988 and the states were advised not to notify any crop for kharif 1988.

  However, it has been reintroduced from the coming rabi season by limiting the sum insured per farmer to Rs. 10,000 irrespective of the amount of loan taken and also reducing the insurance coverage from 160 per cent to 100 per cent of the loan amount. A high level committee is set up to conduct an indepth study and critically review the functioning of the scheme.

- ***Life Insurance***
  The organised workforce in India were provided a good measure of social security by various schemes such as Employees' State Insurance Scheme (1948), Employees' Provident Fund Scheme (1952), Family Pension Scheme, Deposit-linked Life Insurance Scheme, Gratuity, etc. However, only 10 per cent of the total work-force in the country is organised. There was thus a felt need for low-cost social welfare schemes, especially for workers below the poverty line and agricultural labourers, who could not bear any part of the cost of a social welfare scheme.

  A pioneering scheme was first introduced by the Gujarat Government, by which all landless agricultural labourers between the ages of 18 and 60 were covered for a sum assured of Rs. 1,000 with the cost entirely borne by the Gujarat Government.

  Inspired by this, was born the world's largest group insurance scheme, know as the Landless Agriculture Labourers' Group Insurance (LALGI) Scheme. Introduced in August 1987, the scheme covers all landless agricultural labourers between the ages of 18 and 60 for a sum assured of Rs. 1,000, at a premium of Rs. 10 per head per annum, which is borne by the central government. Approximately, over three crore landless labourers are covered under the scheme. The scheme is to be run as a pilot measure for three years after which it will be reviewed.

- ***Insurance for IRDP Loanees***
  A similar scheme for IRDP loanees, who are granted loan on or after 1st April 1988 has been launched on that date. The scheme provides life cover for Rs. 3,000 for natural death and Rs. 6,000 for death by accident. The loanee should be aged between 18 and 60. Approximately 40 lakh beneficiaries are covered by the scheme. The cost is borne by the central government.

- ***Social Security Fund***

  In the latest Union Budget, a social security fund with a corpus or Rs. 100 crores has been created. The fund is to be utilised towards payment of 50 per cent cost of group schemes for groups of workers sustaining themselves on a day-to-day basis. So far, handloom weavers and rickshaw pullers/drivers are covered under the scheme.

  Apart from these, a number of low cost group insurance schemes to cover productive rural assets are in operation. The cost, however, is borne by the beneficiaries, either individually or through their associations.

  Almost each and every aspect of rural development is thus sought to be covered by specific schemes. And yet, the impact on rural development is not notable. Multiplicy in programmes and implementing agencies is probably the bane for the effective development. Consolidation of the various programmes could perhaps be a solution for their effective implementation.

❑ ❑ ❑

# Chapter 8

# COMMUNITY DEVELOPMENT PROGRAMME

## Introduction

During the first quarter of the present century, it was realised that if the poverty of India's teeming millions is to be removed, more attention had to be given to rural areas where 80 per cent of Indian population are living. Therefore, several experiments in rural reconstruction were undertaken by official and non-official agencies which proved the beneficial effects of intensive area projects in which activities in various fields of development were closely integrated.

The rural development programmes, introduced in the First Plan aimed at initiating and directing a process of change with a view to transform the social and economic life of villages. The desired change in social life and the production process of the agrarian economy was sought to be achieved by initiating various progressive schemes of socio-economic development programmes. The necessary instrument for the implementation of this programme came which is known as Panchayati Raj System. Community Development Programme was the result of this right experiment.

Community development has been defined as "a movement designed to promote better living for the whole community with the active participation and on the initiative of the community."

Essentially, community development was looked upon as an integrated approach to local development as a part of the bigger scheme of planned national development. As a process, it involved a sequential and inter-dependent progression of changes — economic, social, political and psychological. It was tended to assume the character of a movement because the programme it signified emanated from an egalitarian ideology.

Shri V.T. Krishnamachari, while reviewing the objectives of the Community Development Programme and the National Extension Service Programme, touched the following points:

(1) Leading rural population from chronic under-development to full employment.

(2) Leading rural population from chronic agricultural under-production to full production by scientific knowledge.

(3) The largest possible extension of the principles of co-operation by making rural families creditworthy.

(4) Increased community efforts for the benefit of the community as a whole, such as village roads, tanks, wells, schools, community centre, children's park, etc.

In short, the aim of Community Development Programme is not merely to provide ample food, clothing and shelter, health and sanitation facilities in villages, but more important than the immediate material improvement is the change in outlook of the people, instilling in them an ambition for a richer and fuller life and developing the capacities of an individual so that he can master matters for himself.

## The Essence of the Programme

The change in rural life has been thought to be brought about by concerted efforts and an integrated approach making an assault on all facets of rural life through a single multi-purpose agency viz. C.D. Projects. The programme vividly recognises:

*(a)* Triple Tenets of Faith:
- (1) muscles can do it;
- (2) muscles can be trained to do it, and
- (3) conditions can be created to do it.

*(b)* Triple Character of Rights:
- (1) Right to live;
- (2) Right to earn; and
- (3) Right to receive what is earned.

*(c)* Triple Rules of Business:
- (1) evaluation;
- (2) integration; and
- (3) standardisation.

Thus, the central theme of C.D. Programme is to change the rural man from tradition to modernity and to make him worthy of his existence.

## Contents of the Programme

The principal idea behind the community development programme is to change the basic attitude of the rural-folk from tradition to modernity. To accomplish this objective, community development embraces all those programmes that touch the very existence of human living *e.g.* agriculture and related matters, irrigation, communication, education, health, supplementary employment, housing, training, and social welfare activities. According to the Planning Commission there are three major activities involved in these programmes:

*(i)* an increase in production and employment in the agricultural sector.

*(ii)* the application of the principles of self-reliance and co-operation on an extensive scale for which a variety of institutions have been set-up, such as the provision for free education, free medical aid, sanitation and public health measures etc.

*(iii)* maximum utilisation of available manpower resources.

# ORGANISATION AND ADMINISTRATIVE SET-UP

The organisation and administration of the programme at various levels is carried out thus:

**At the Centre:** Under the Ministry of Agriculture and Irrigation the Department of Rural Development is now in overall charge of the programme.

**At the State Level:** The actual execution of the programme is the responsibility of the State Governments.

**At the District Level:** The statutory Zilla Parishads are responsible for the implementation of the programme in the districts. These are assisted by Block Development Officers.

**At the Block Level:** The Panchayat Samiti is in the charge of the programme.

**At the Village Level:** There are Village Level Workers or the Gram Sewaks and Gram Sevikas who act as multi-purpose men and women and are in charge of multi-purpose extension work in about 10 villages. The panchayat is in overall control of the programme and is helped by associate organisations.

Under the Programme, the unit of operation is the development block which represents on an average 100 villages with a population of about 100,000 persons spread over an area of 150 to 170 square miles. This programme has three broad features:

(1) The Village Unit,

(2) Mandi Unit, and

(3) Development Block.

## Implementation of the Programme

The Community Development Programme was launched on 2nd October, 1952, with 55 pilot projects on an experimental basis. The programme is implemented in units of blocks, each block covers an area of about 400-500 sq. kms. with about 100 villages and a population of about 1 lakh. There are presently 5,026 CD blocks, covering a population of about 47 crores spread over all the 6 lakh villages in the country. In order to meet the demand of the villages for the extension of resources, a less intensive scheme called the National Extension Service (NES) was created from October 2, 1963. In both the CD and the NES, the work of agricultural extension was a common factor, but in the former it was more intensive.

Initially, the pattern of three stages of development of a block was introduced. The NES represented the first or the preparatory stage that created conditions for transition to a more intensive second stage of development. The final stage was known as the post-intensive phase. The pattern was revised in 1959 on the recommendations of the Balwantrai Mehta Committee. The old pattern was substituted by a two-stage pattern. A CD block enters the first stage of intensive development for five years. On the completion of this stage, the block enters the second stage for another 5 years with a relatively reduced budget provision. By the time, a block completes the second stage, it becomes a permanent unit of planning and development and establishes channel for developmental expenditure.

## Resources of the Programme

Finances for the Community Development Programme are drawn both from the people and the government. The CD programme being essentially a people's programme, prescribes, a qualifying scale of voluntary contribution from the people in the form of labour as well as money. The balance of expenditure in a block is met by the State, the expenses are shared between the Central Government and the State Governments. State governments are free to provide resources for the programme from within their State Plans according to the priority accorded to the programmes by them. The Central Government's assistance to the States takes the form either of loans or of annual lumpsum grants.

From the above account of the programme, the following three conclusions about the genesis of this programme, can be derived. *Firstly,* the programme aims at an overall change in the life pattern of hitherto semi-stagnant rural economy. *Secondly,* the programme rests for its success on a voluntary contribution from the people, who are largely to be its beneficiaries. *Finally,* the financial obligation of the programme is also shared between the people and the Government.

## Evaluation of the CD Programme

Commenting on the programme, Prof. Toynbee described it as "one of the most beneficent revolutions in the peasantry's life that have been known, so far, to the history." The U.N. Technical Mission headed by Shri M.J. Coldwel praised the programme, "as one of the major experiments of the twentieth century, the results of which are of world-wide interest, and which represents an effort of unprecedented magnitude to establish a progressive system of agriculture in a land of impoverished soil and a more democratic social structure in a hierarchical society."

## A Critical Review of the Working of Programme

The success or otherwise of the CD programme in India has provoked extreme opinions; one of which sees in it a sovereign remedy for all rural ills while the other is contained in the remark that through it only the CD department has developed continuously and not the community. The experience shows that the community development programme has largely failed to live to its ideal. The underlying philosophy of the programme was that it was to stress and make obligatory for the people to participate in the programme, in the form of their voluntary contribution of labour and money. The State was visualised mainly as a channel to direct people's resources. This is how the programme came to be known as the people's programme. However, the basic character of the programme was soon lost, and it acquired the status of any other programme organised and directed by the State. The long sights of the programme directors were fixed on achieving the stipulated targets rather than evoking people's co-operation. After a period of two and a half decades or so, the programme stands discredited, in spite of the fact that the entire country has been covered by it. People's initiative and participation had always been lacking, the Government has also lost interest in the programme.

## Causes of Failure

The causes of the failure of the community development programme are as follows:

*(a)* Uneven distribution of the benefits of the programme.

*(b)* Absence of clearly defined priorities in the programme.

*(c)* Failure to evoke popular response.

*(d)* Unqualified personnel.

*(e)* Lack of functional responsibility.

*(f)* *Ritualism:* A spirit of ritualism permeated the block programmes and inauguration, opening or foundation stone laying became the be-all and end-all at all block activities. The Project Officers were purposely emphasising the welfare aspect of the programmes so that they could show to the visiting dignitaries some tangible result of their efforts. But the creation of these welfare activities only kindled the dissatisfaction with the economic condition of the people.

## General Appraisal

A general appraisal of the working of programme in the country indicates that, in spite of various difficulties and problems, it has proved a valuable asset to general economic and social development. The programme became catchy enough to spread fast and wide so that it created demands which far outstripped the available supplies and services. It awakened consciousness in the people and made them articulate for needs which they had not felt before. With the network of a co-ordinated structure of extension teams, co-operatives, farmers' associations, youth clubs and other voluntary organisations, it has helped the tradition bound village communities to shed-off dogmas and overcome resistance to change and has thus made its own impact on people's attitudes and motivations. It has made people pragmatic and rational. By the very process of stimulating aspirations for planned development, the programme has led to the establishment of new statutory local government institutions and the strengthening of the existing ones.

❑ ❑ ❑

# Chapter 9

# EMPLOYMENT GUARANTEE SCHEME

## Introduction

The Employment Guarantee Scheme operated in Maharashtra is significant instrument of planned rural development. It has two important bearings — one is the immediate reality in which the rural poor (unemployed as well as under-employed) are able to capitalise their labour and earn wages to improve their living standards, the other is the consequence it can produce to generate a process of local resource development eventually strengthening the self-employment opportunities and enterprise of the people.

"While the population is increasing at a very rapid rate, food production is lagging behind our requirements. The problem of rural unemployment and under-employment which is a chronic characteristic of our economy needs to be immediately tackled as it is causing an adverse effect on agricultural production. The Employment Guarantee Scheme, therefore, has assumed vital importance not only for the state of Maharashtra but for the country as a whole, considering the grave danger that rural unemployment poses to the national economy. The national importance of the scheme is also highlighted by the fact that it attempts to protect the interest of the largest and the weakest section of society *i.e.,* landless labourers."

## The Concept

The elimination of poverty by providing gainful employment to the most disadvantaged section of community should be an integral part of any programme of economic development. In Maharashtra, therefore as early as in 1965, a pilot scheme for an integrated area development in Tasgaon block was undertaken to test the possibility of providing productive employment and opportunities for increased incomes for the rural poor, particularly, the agricultural labourers and the small and marginal farmers. Further more, since 1969, a pilot scheme for giving a guarantee of employment was also undertaken on a village basis in selected blocks. The lessons from these pilot schemes have been utilised in formulation of a more comprehensive scheme called the Employment Guarantee Scheme of Maharashtra which was introduced throughout the state with effect from the year 1972-73, as a part of the 15-point programme for economic development. The state government has given the statutory support to the guarantee of employment through the Employment Guarantee Act 1977, which has been brought into force from 26-1-1979.

A fundamental premise of Employment Guarantee Scheme, launched in May 1972, with statutory status in January 1979 is:

(a) Gainful and productive employment, gainful to the individual and productive to the economy, in approved works to all unskilled persons in rural areas who need work and are prepared to do manual work but cannot find it either on farm or allied operations in the area or on the normal plan/non-plan works implemented by the government departments, the zilla parishads, the panchayat samities and the gram panchayats.

(b) Only productive works which results in the creation of durable community assets. The works relating to minor irrigation, soil conservation, land development, road development in hilly and inaccessible areas, plantation of trees along canal and roadside are some illustrations of such productive works.

(c) Works having the cost of unskilled element of more than 60 per cent of the total cost are permitted and have to be invariably executed departmentally (and not through any contractor) by various implementing agencies of the government and zilla parishads.

The Employment Guarantee Scheme has assumed vital importance not only for Maharashtra but for the country as a whole, considering the grave danger that rural unemployment poses to the national economy. The national importance of the scheme is also highlighted by the fact that it attempts to protect the interests of the largest and the weakest section of society, that is, landless labour. Under the Act every adult person in rural areas has acquired the right to work *i.e.* the right to get guaranteed employment for doing unskilled manual work.

## Aims and Objectives of the Scheme

The aim of the Employment Guarantee Scheme is to provide gainful and productive employment gainful to the individual and productive to the economy on approved works to all unskilled persons in the rural areas including the areas of 'C' class Municipal Councils, who need work and are prepared to do manual labour but cannot find it on their own. The participant has no choice of work or the area of work. The guarantee is given at the district level, but operationally work is provided at the panchayat samiti level. The operation of the scheme has been so designed as to ensure that labour is deployed to the extent possible on existing construction activities in the area and care is taken to see that the Employment Guarantee Scheme does not adversely affect agricultural operations and production and that the scheme is not to be activated where work is available on plan or non-plan works in progress. In fact, the scheme is residual in the sense that full provision for plan and non-plan scheme should be made and expenditure on any work should not be incurred from Employment Guarantee Scheme funds unless the budget provision is fully exhausted. Work is to be provided under the scheme within 15 days of receipt of a notice of demand for work. A fundamental objective of the scheme is that the works undertaken should result in the production of durable community assets and that wages paid to the workers should be linked with the quality of work output.

## Salient Features

(i) Guarantee of unskilled employment is provided to all persons residing in the rural areas. Now under the Maharashtra Employment Guarantee Act statutory base has been given for this guarantee.

(ii) The persons demanding work have no choice of work. The guarantee is to provide work anywhere in the district, though operationally work is normally provided within the panchayat samiti area.

(iii) Work is to be provided to any person demanding employment within 15 days of such demand. The work to be provided should normally last for atleast 30 days so as to avoid frequent shift of the labour from one work to another.

(iv) Only productive works are permitted under the scheme. The major types of works which have been taken up under the scheme are labour intensive components of major and medium irrigation projects, minor irrigation, percolation and storage tanks, soil conservation and land development works, anti-water logging and water draining, drains and distributor canals, field channels and afforestation works. Where such productive works are not available road works are taken up.

(v) Only such works of which the cost of unskilled component is more than 60 per cent of the total cost are permitted under the scheme.

(vi) The works are invariably executed departmentally and, therefore, there is no intermediary between the government and the labour. Only exception is made when skilled items of the tank works are to be executed in the interest of the speedy completion of work. Such works can be executed through piece workers on conditions that the local labour should be used and they should be paid wages according to the schedule of rates prescribed by the government.

(vii) The wages are linked to the quality and quantity of the output of work by the labourer.

(viii) The wages prescribed for the Employment Guarantee Scheme are so designed that an average person working diligently for 7 hours should earn a total wage equal to the minimum wage for agricultural labour in the lowest zone in the state. This will ensure that the operation of the scheme does not affect agricultural operations and at the same time the agricultural labour is assured of the minimum wage.

(ix) A blue print of works which can be taken up under the scheme is kept ready for each panchayat samiti so that there is practically no time lag between the registration of the actual demand for work and starting of the work. In order to enable the authorities responsible for implementation of the scheme to plan for the operation of the scheme, a manpower budget is being prepared in each panchayat samiti.

The main improvements brought about by the Employment Guarantee Act 1977 are:

(i) Payment of unemployment allowance to any adult person in the rural area who has registered for work under the Act and who is not provided with employment within 15 days of asking for it.

(ii) Ex-gratia payment up to Rs.5000/- in case of death or disablement of workers, and

(iii) Powers of Collector to direct the village panchayat to take up work from the Village Employment Fund in case it is not expedient for the state government to provide employment immediately on any other work.

## Gains from Employment Guarantee Scheme

The most important gain is the breaking down of the caste barrier since all rural workers work together on a project irrespective of caste or religious affiliations. Besides, multiplier effects of investments on Employment Guarantee Scheme works are important since it has provided permanent employment creation and increased agricultural production though various irrigation and soil conservation works. This has also helped in introducing new remunerative crops.

• With urbanites contributing a profession tax at stipulated slabs, accrual under Employment Guarantee Scheme from this relatively affluent section of the community is estimated to be around Rs. 60 crores. With growing income in cities, more resources can be tapped from urban dwellers, and this way the objective of transferring surplus income from haves in cities to have-nots in villages is achieved, thus paving the way for a more egalitarian order in the society. Indirectly urban savings with their inflationary overtones are siphoned off for the betterment of underprivileged sections residing in rural Maharashtra.

Employment Guarantee Scheme has acted as a lever for enforcing minimum wages for farm labour in the countryside. Landless labourers are rid from the ill-effects of bonded conditions under which they had to suffer the tyranny of village overlords and bigwigs in the rural interior. Lakhs of farm labourers have heaved a sigh of relief with Employment Guarantee Scheme coming to their rescue and giving them a ray of hope for breathing a fresh air of freedom and generating a fervour for creative existence in the otherwise dull surroundings of pedantic and humdrum rural environment.

❑ ❑ ❑

*To sum up, plainly but crisply, as voiced by a child in a poem:*

*"So friends, let's make an effort to make the environment spic and span because at last the sufferer would be man!"*

# Chapter 10

# ISSUES IN RURAL DEVELOPMENT

## Introduction

The experiences of government programmes, voluntary agencies, industry and the financial intermediaries, particularly banks, in the task of rural development bring into light some problems and issues. In fact, these hurdles have been responsible for none-too-impressive performance of rural development. Although, some programmes have resulted into significant progress but have also resulted into inequality and given birth to a neo-rich culture on the basis of western culture in Indian way. As a result, poor in rural India continue to multiply and remain poor. Even though, rural development programmes should be taken up with enthusiasm there should be no illusions about the inherent difficulties and complexities of rural development.

## Issues

The issues in rural development are basically related to growing population, diminishing land holdings, degradation of natural resources, exodus of labour, slow spread of education, widening disparity between haves and have nots, faulty programmes, non-responsive governance, inadequate rural orientation and misuse of funds.

This apart, rural participation in rural development is minimal. The sense of pride and the psychological adaptation to rural way of life are difficult to inculcate. Many factors have occurred to destroy them. As a result of such forces acting on rural life, the flow of rural-urban migration has changed from a trickle to a torrent. The village economy, at the farmers' and agricultural labour families' level, is based on urban monetary support from migrant population; the agriculturists and big cultivators depend upon government subsidy and financial (and political) patronage and support. This relationship is very complicated and very much politicised. But unless this aspect of the problem of rural transformation is adequately and appropriately tackled, the life-force to rural population will fail to circulate in a natural and healthy manner. Unless this is taken care of in time and remedied suitably, the village life will meet its thrombosis, and, without rural culture, India will become a soulless country. In this gigantic task of saving the country, political withdrawal from rural life and creation of a harmonious and self-sustaining rural economy must proceed along with responsive personnel who should emerge from the villages themselves for village administration (rather than occupying the seats in Delhi's central complex); the village administration should be primarily the responsibility of the villagers, the rural youth as well as of the village elders, not of the personnel imported or deputed from outside.

**Table 1**
**ISSUES IN RURAL DEVELOPMENT**

| *S. No.* | *Issues* | *Impact* | *What is to be done* |
|---|---|---|---|
| 1. | Pressure of Population | Increased pressure on land. Higher dependency on agriculture. Swelling of the ranks of agricultural labourers. Destruction of ecology. Rise in unemployment and under-employment. | The growth should be brought down to 1 per cent. One child policy to be strictly adhered to. |
| 2. | Land Holdings | Land holding size has shrunk significantly. Small and marginal farmers increased from 69.7% in 70-71 to 74.5% in 1980-81 and it may rise to about 80% by 1990-91 and 86% by 2001 A.D. | To be consolidated into viable units or co-operative farming practiced effecting change in the law of inheritance. Alternatively, corporate farming to be practiced. |
| 3. | Education | Because of illiteracy and ignorance exploitation is rampant. Limited use of modern technology; limited participation in the development programmes. | To be increased many fold. Along with formal education, vocational education should be given preference in rural areas. |
| 4. | Deterioration in value systems | Affecting the society in multidirectional way and restricting the growth of the economy. Instead affecting the social fabric adversely | Value systems to be enriched by setting example at the highest level and intellectuals should lead the people on right path. |
| 5. | Agriculture | The Green Revolution had its side affects in environmental pollution, silting etc., low yields in spite of higher utilisation of inputs. Too much dependence on urban industries. | Productivity should be increased both in dry land and irrigated areas. Policies should be framed to benefit the smaller strata of rural people. |
| 6. | Infrastructure | Inadequate and imbalanced. Wherever infrastructures are developed, people are more influenced by city life. | Minimum needs of rural areas should be created by the rural people with the assistance of the governments. |
| 7. | Employment | A large section of agricultural labour, women, marginal and small farmers, rural artisans are affected. They invariably live below the poverty line. Employment opportunities are diminishing year after year. | Employment opportunities in non-farm sectors to be created. To do this, market avenues are to be established. If need be, protection and subsidy should be provided to goods manufactured in rural areas. Rural industrialisation holds the key to rural development. |

**Box 1**

## ACCESS TO BASIC SERVICES – A LONG WAY TO GO

- 52% of Indian households live in pucca houses; only 21% have the shelter of a concrete roof.
- 60% of the households do not have a source of drinking water within the premises.
- 64% of the households lack basic sanitation facilities.
- 50% of the households continue to depend on fuelwood as a cooking fuel.
- Aganist 88% of the urban households, only 44% of the rural households have access to electricity.
- 35% of Indians are still illiterate.

*Source :* Census of India (2001)

## Rural Population

During the ten decades, rural population rose by 515 million from 210 million in 1901 to 725 million in 2001. The growth was highest at 105 million in 1991-2001 decade as against 95 million in the previous decade. The level of rural population is likely to be around 835 million in 2011 and 950 million in 2021. It means that about 225 million more people within the age group of 20 will be added during the next two decades. On the present reckoning, the population below poverty line in rural areas is expected to be around 425 million in 2021 A.D. as against 275 million in 1981. Growth of rural population will, therefore, have to be checked drastically so that the impact of rural development becomes meaningful and effective.

## Structure

The causes of rural poverty are structural in nature. They do not stem from what its people have done or not done, but from the social and economic relations that prevail in rural India. The National Commission on Agriculture (1976) has pinpointed the need for reordering of the agricultural structure for the establishment of a prosperous and egalitarian rural society. On the one hand, only 13 per cent of farmers own over 55 per cent of land and 55 per cent own only 12 per cent of cultivated land. Small and medium cultivators account for over 87 per cent of total cultivators. A far more important structural hurdle is the excessive and growing fragmentation of landholdings. Consolidation operation should be given high priority in irrigated areas and in the command areas of irrigation projects. On the social front, caste barriers have to be removed if the benefits of development is to reach all sections of people.

An analysis of the rural economic structure indicates that agriculture—the mainstay of the rural population—is declining. Per capita land availability has come down from 0.95 hectares in 1947 to 0.47 hectares in 1987 and is projected to slide further to 0.33 hectares by 2000 A.D. The share of agriculture in the GDP also has fallen from 59 per cent in 1951 to 54.2 per cent in 1961, to 45.24 per cent in 1973-74 and further to 33.8 per cent in 1986-87. At the same time the share of the workers in agriculture did not decline. It remained at 79.4 per cent in 1961, 82.51 in 1971 and 80.98 per cent in 1981. This would mean a growing marginalisation of the rural population depending on agriculture.

Thus agriculture is ceasing to be viable for a growing proportion of the rural population. *Employment opportunities within this sector are on the decline.* The rural labour force has been increasing at an ever growing rate from 9 million in the First Plan to nearly 40 million in the Seventh Plan.

## Water

India receives 4,000 billion cubic metres (BCM) of water every year through precipitation, of which 1,869 BCM is estimated as the maximum availability per year. Due to severe limitation imposed by topographic, physiography, and interstate issues, etc. Around 1,122 BCM is currently estimated as the maximum utilisable resource. Moreover, since most of it is concentrated in the southwest monsoon (from June to September) and falls unevenly (from as low as 100 mm in western Rajasthan to as high as 9,000 mm in Meghalaya), the availability of water varies enormously in different river basins. The present per capita water availability in India is about 1,250 $m^3$, which puts India in the category of 'water-stressed' countries. By 2050 this is projected to fall further to 750 $m^3$.

Different economic sectors are going to demand increasing quantities of water. For example, according to Rao (1997), the water demand of the domestic sector rose from 25 BCM in 1990 to 35 BCM in 2000, while that of irrigation rose from 460 BCM in 1990 to 630 BCM in 2000.

Studies by the IWMI (International Water Management Institute) have shown that much of western and peninsular India will suffer from acute scarcity in the coming 25 years. Conflicts around water will intensify at the local, meso, and regional levels. Agriculture will progressively lose its share of irrigation water to industrial and municipal uses.

Groundwater depletion threatens agricultural sustainability and rural livelihoods. Besides, it places the resource out of the reach of the poor, who are unable to afford higher costs of extraction. An effective policy framework for groundwater management has not evolved as yet. The National Water Policy of 1987 was revised to reflect major international and national developments and culminated in the Water Policy of 2002. Some of the thrust areas of the National Water Policy are the emphasis on participation among users, improving water quality, emphasis on rehabilitation and resettlement in large-scale irrigation projects, the need for an integrated approach within the water sector, revamping institutional mechanisms, and improving the sustainability of water projects.

Given India's federal structure, the National Water Policy remains a mere statement of intent in the absence of state-level programmes. Only some state governments have drafted water policies in the past five years. Some states have tried to raise prices in irrigation, and some incentives have been built in for state governments to rationalise water tariffs. Some states have put in place measures to encourage the formation of water users associations to take over functions in operation and maintenance of irrigation schemes.

There has been a renewed emphasis in recent years on rejuvenating aquifers through rainwater harvesting and watershed protection measures. While these efforts play an important role in augmenting the supply of groundwater resources, there remains an important challenge of carrying out these activities on a large enough scale to make a significant difference. At the same time, to be effective, they will need to be supported by demand-side management measures.

There is also a need to develop policies that allow an integrated view of the management of water and power resources. In the Indian context, the practice of supplying power at low, flat rates encourages farmers to pump water indiscriminately. Besides, the unreliability of power supplies encourages farmers to pump water whenever it is available. The cheap availability of power for pumping groundwater for irrigation is also an issue affecting the financial health of the state electricity boards.

Aggravating the effect of lower levels of water resources is the poor quality of water. Water quality measures in BOD (biochemical oxygen demand) shows an upward trend in the period 1992-2001. (BOD refers to the amount of oxygen required by microorganisms to degrade organic pollutants. A higher level of BOD signifies a higher level of organic pollution load. The acceptable level of BOD for drinking quality surface water before treatment is 3 mg/litre.) Out of the monitoring stations along India's rivers extending over a total riverine length of about 45,000 km, 14 per cent shows high pollution (BOD greater than 6 mg/litre) and 19 per cent shows moderate pollution (BOD 3-6 mg/litre).

On the other hand, the MPN count (most probable number — a count of the bacterial coliform population in water) as revealed by the CPCB published reports shows a fluctuating trend. A major reason for the stress on water resources is the rising shortfall in the provision of basic municipal services including water supply, sanitation, and solid waste management.

**Box 2**

**WATER MANAGEMENT: IMPROVING CO-ORDINATION**

Perhaps in no sector is the challenge of integration as important as in water, which is dealt with by a number of ministries. The Ministry of Water Resources deals with the development of surface and ground water resources and inter-basin transfers of waters. The Ministry of Environment and Forests deals with water quality and environment matters, largely through its pollution monitoring network that operates through the Central Pollution Control Board. Water is also a subject of the Ministry of Power (for electricity generation). The Ministry of Rural Development implements rural drinking water schemes. Urban drinking water and sanitation are the prerogative of the Ministry of Urban Development and Poverty Alleviation.

While the above ministries deal with water specifically, it is also the interest of other ministries, such as the Ministry of Agriculture (for irrigation), the Ministry of Health and Family Welfare (for health impacts associated with water), and the Inland Waterways Authority of India (for navigation). Overall planning of water is the concern of the Ministry of Finance and the Planning Commission.

The fragmented approach to water management is seen not just across ministries but also within the Ministry of Water Resources. Within this nodal ministry, there are three separate technical organisations.

The Central Water Commission has as its mandate the development of surface water. The Central Ground Water Board concerns itself with the development and monitoring of ground water resources. The National Water Development Agency was created in 1982 to examine the subject of inter-basin transfers and to prepare feasibility reports.

Needless to say, the fragmented approach to water management highlighted above creates a false dichotomy across (1) sectors or uses and (2) source (surface and ground water). Overcoming this fragmentation will be necessary as water becomes scarce and needs to be diverted from one use sector to another.

**Box 3**

**THE 'UTTAM URJA' MODEL**

The Uttam Urja project has been implemented by TERI to provide energy services through entrepreneurs to rural areas in parts of Rajasthan and Uttaranchal. The main task has been to develop an energy service network incorporating local NGOs, dealers, and retailers. The 'household lighting packages' is sold through local enterprises under the brand name Uttam Urja. The customer pays a basic upfront cost and then the equated instalments for a specified period, after which the ownership of the device is transferred to him. During this period, major maintenance costs such as battery and printed circuit board replacement are borne by the service provider.

Initial experiences in the application of this approach in rural India led the project implementers to believe that for large scale dissemination of renewable energy technologies (RETS) the focus would have to be on new product development, reducing the cost of systems, better after-sales service, and affordable finance options. For example, consumer surveys conducted at the beginning of the project had indicated a market for a larger domestic lighting system (DLS),a system not eligible for subsidy, to power televisions and other domestic appliances. In order to meet this demand, the project team developed and produced a large DLS (50 Wp).

Local assembly of all systems was undertaken in Bikaner and Rishikesh, which reduced the cost of systems considerably. In addition to the cost factor, local assembly reduced the delivery time of systems considerably and promoted efficient after-sales service. During this period, a system of dealer incentives was created. TERI also initiated tie-ups with banks in Bikaner and Rishikesh for financing the systems through banks and self-help groups. Loan recovery is close to 100 per cent. Payments can be made quarterly or biannually depending on the convenience of the customers. The objective of this approach is to free the consumer from problems of high upfront costs, maintenance, replacement, etc. which have so far been responsible for limited penetration and impact of RETS in rural areas.

*Source: INSTEP with business opportunity, Issue 1, December 2001, New Delhi : TERI*

## Education

Development is not just the economic and material development of a country, but also the development of the individual personality and of perception, awareness and compassion. Human capital is created and human input in production is significantly improved by spending on education. There is a very strong case for education and training of farmers. Fortunately, in this sea of ignorance education is a lighthouse. The State of Kerala is a model of human development. Its literacy rate is 100 per cent; its infant mortality rate (56 per thousand live births) is one of the lowest among Indian states; its life expectancy (57) correspondingly high and its birth rate (25.9) among the lowest in India. The key of course, is education. The commitment has been towards mass education, including female education. It ought to serve as an example to the rest of the country. Agricultural education should become much more business oriented. It should produce trained people who would be ready to undertake agricultural enterprises, both on-farm and off-farm. The need for good agricultural scientists and extension workers is also not to be ignored. But, if this task is to be performed by agricultural universities, much more investment and better management of agricultural education system than obtaining at present are required.

**Box 4**

**A NEW ALLIANCE FOR THE FORESTRY SECTOR**

The Srinivasan Services Trust (SST), an organisation initiated by Sundaram Clayton Ltd and TVS Motor Company, has recently facilitated sustainable forest management in Tamil Nadu – a pioneering attempt that could serve as a model for other corporates. SST'S community development activities have been integrated with the ongoing afforestation and regeneration efforts of the Tamil Nadu Forest Department (TNFD) in Tamil Nadu. With the technical advice and guidance of TERI, SST became part of two major programmes of TNFD, the TAP (Tamil Nadu Afforestation Project) and the Ecodevelopment Project, since 1999. The SST'S involvement has brought about several significant innovations such as the following:

*Fig. 1 New Alliance for the forestry sector*

- Providing professional expertise in developmental interventions to strengthen the initiatives of the TNFD for JFM.
- Creating partnership with various ongoing government rural development schemes/projects on poverty alleviation and environmental conservation for mobilising resources.
- Liaising with local administration to execute development works.
- Adoption, reconstruction, and maintenance of existing infrastructure.

SST's interventions in the programme have given concrete shape to the concept of sustainable forest development, which is about creating a balancing among the ecological, social, and economic benefits of the area. This experiment has provided a breakthrough that can be replicated or further experimented with on an extended scale all over the country.

*Source : Corporate in a Green Voyage:* Partnership between the Forest Department and TVS-SST in Tamil Nadu, 23 pp: TERI, 2002.

## Forests and Biodiversity

Forests are ecological systems and provide a wide array of ecological and economic services. They provide the poor with fuel for their hearths and the affluent a view of nature in repose; they help farmers, in unseen ways, by regulating the flow of water and preventing the washing away of soil; and they store genetic wealth for future generations. Forests are a renewable resource : to use them sustainably, we cannot take out from forests more than what is added.

In a country as diverse as India, with a complex society, the forests face a range of pressures. It is difficult to quantify these pressures, leave alone trace their impacts. A listing of some of these pressures follows.

## Outright Plunder

This usually goes unnoticed at the national level. One example of this is popularly known as the Bastar scam. Between 1992 and 1996, a nexus of government officials, politicians, and timber merchants conspired to strip the Bastar district of a significant amount of timber.

## Diversion of Land to Other Uses

It has been estimated that the Forest Conservation Act of 1980 reduced diversion of land from 1,50,000 hectares to 16,000 hectares annually by 1997. However, in the subsequent four years, the diversion of land has risen to 95,500 hectares.

## Increased Demand for Industrial Wood

This was estimated to be about 58 million cubic metres in 2000.

## Subsistence Needs of Villagers

29 per cent of villages in India are estimated to be living in or near forests. Villagers depend on the forests for fuelwood and fodder. With forests being effectively 'open access' resources, fuelwood and fodder extraction often reduce the vegetative cover.

Ecological conservation also aims to protect different ecosystems. Mangrove forests are among the most productive and biodiverse wetlands on earth. Mangrove cover in the country has declined by 5 per cent from 1997. The continuing degradation and depletion of this vital resource reduces not only terrestrial and aquatic production and wildlife habitats, but also the environmental stability of coastal forests that afford protection to inland agricultural crops and villages.

In recent years there has been a shift in the approach to managing forests and biodiversity. Management has sought to include people and ecological concerns. For example, joint forest management guidelines were revised in February 2000 and again in December 2002 to strengthen the institutional mechanism. The corporate sector is also coming forward to assist in the management of forests in India.

*Fig. 2. The rural areas lack access to renewable sources of energy, Solar, for instance*

## Productivity

In agriculture, with the prospect of zero per cent growth in land availability, increasing production would be possible only if there is a greater investment in irrigation and other agricultural inputs. Agriculture, therefore, has become a demanding sector. It demands increasing investments but these investments do not yield adequate returns because they are not effective. For example, because of the defective water conveyance system tailenders do not get water and because of waterlogging at some pockets, it is estimated that 25 per cent of the area under some crops are damaged substantially. The NCA has observed that Indian agriculture has to be put on the high road to development as a robust and dynamic system. The central objective is to enable the vast mass of cultivators (particularly medium and small) whose production potential are being wasted today, to combine in full measure their manpower with modern technology so that the whole agrarian economy rises rapidly to ever higher levels.

What is more important is, therefore, not how much is invested, but how well invested. One of the reasons for less adequate return from investment is the failure in the maintenance of assets. Replacement of maintenance has been neglected and therefore it has become necessary to prepare a "maintenance plan" as complementary to the "development plan". Also, there has been in recent years heavy expenditure on non-development items which needs to be curbed. In the present context, agricultural plans, both horizontal and vertical, have to be prepared crop-wise for each village, block, district and state and be implemented with the co-operation of farmers, agricultural labourers, etc. Unless and until people's active participation is not forthcoming, disparity will continue and at the cost of the poor men, the rich, the political workers, contractors, moneylenders, traders and other middlemen will go on deriving ample benefit, thus widening the disparity between the haves and the have-nots in rural areas. Another important point is that, instead of spending money on welfare measures, the same may be earmarked for productive purposes, which will go a long way in developing primary sector in rural India.

## Technology

Productive efficiency of the rural poor improves their income level. The labour efficiency increase, if associated with wage increase, also improves their income status. The improvement in living conditions, health and sanitation, environment, technology, increases their real income. This indirectly helps in income redistribution in favour of the rural poor. The total redistribution will increase if the direct income transfers to the rural poor in various forms are taken into account. But the indirect transfer has got a better status since the rural poor becomes active partners in development.

Developments in science and technology can be fruitfully utilised for the development of the rural poor through increase in productive efficiency of investment resources as well as that of the rural labour, conservation of resources used by them, improvement in their living conditions, health and sanitation. There is need, however, to improve the efficiency of the information delivery system for better dissemination of knowledge and technology. There exist immense possibilities of improving the productivity of investments already made to a substantial extent through marginal increase in investments and better organisational capabilities. If, adopted, this will help in income redistribution in favour of the rural poor.

More importantly, there is a need to introduce technologies which are simple and which can be adapted to varied conditions existing in different rural communities by the simple rural people without much education. It should benefit a large number of people, and flexible and adaptable to the changing needs of the community. At the same time it must be as inexpensive as possible without depending on high cost energy sources. The technologies should be such as would promote autonomous, economic and social development relying on local skills and resources.

**Table 2**

**DYNAMICS OF THE TECHNOLOGY DIFFUSION PROCESS**

| *Characteristics* | *Major Stages of the Life Cycle* | | |
|---|---|---|---|
| | *Introduction* | *Growth* | *Maturity* |
| 1. Innovation aspects | — More advanced and sophisticated product than existing one | — Mature product with very few refinements | — Both product and process stable |
| | — Rapid, frequent and major changes in products. | — Rapid, frequent and major process changes | — Technology readily available and transferred to developing countries. |
| | — Product change stimulated by pressure groups and user needs | — Process changes stimulated by rising volume | — Technology development is systematic. |
| | — Technology closely held by the innovating firm | — Monopoly of technology decreases as a result of diffusion and licensing | — Technological substitution gets under way |
| | — Technology development is uncoordinated | — Technology development segmental | |
| 2. Production aspects | — Non-standard and diversified product line, often including custom designs | — At least one standard design to have significant production volume | — Standardised product and production process. |
| | — Flexible and inefficient short-run production | — Mass-production introduced, although techniques may differ | — Efficient mass-production runs |
| | — Small-scale plant located near user or source of technology | — Large general-purpose plants with specialised sections | — Large-scale, highly specialised plants |
| | — Inputs are limited to generally available materials | — Specialised materials may be developed | — Special materials needed |
| | — Use of general-purpose equipment, requiring highly skilled labour | — Some subprocesses automated, creating "islands of automation" requiring semi-skilled labour | — Specialised equipment mostly automatic |

| | | | |
|---|---|---|---|
| 3. Economic aspects | — Low investment due to use of conventional equipment<br>— Innovating firm leads with others entering the field to capitalise on success.<br>— Very low demand due to uncertainty<br>— "Sellers' market" and low price elasticity | — High investment due to increased volume and specialised equipment<br>— Large number of firms with many casualties and mergers<br>— Demand increases with product performance and standardisation<br>— "Balanced market" and growing price elasticity | — Very high investment in automation and economies of scale.<br>— Number of firms decline with lower margins.<br>— Very high demand and product differentiation<br>— "Buyer's market" and lower price |
| 4. Management aspects | — Overall strategy is "product performance maximisation"<br>— High scientific and engineering skills essential<br>— Very little competition<br>— Market creation very critical | — Overall strategy is "sales maximisation"<br>— High financial and production management skills essential<br>— High competition due to emulators<br>— Protection against imitation very critical | — Overall strategy is "cost minimisation".<br>— High marketing, distribution and cost management skills essential<br>— Very high competition<br>— Maintaining market share very critical |
| 5. Socio-political aspects | — Technological substitution for a previous function or activity<br>— Socio-political implications unclear<br>— Environmental impacts unknown<br>— Governmental involvement normally absent<br>— Socio-cultural compatibility assured superficially | — Institutional modifications for growing rate of substitution<br>— Socio-political reactions observable<br>— Environmental impacts surface<br>— Some involvement by government<br>— Societal values are modified | — Technology becomes pervasive in society.<br>— Socio-political implications become critical<br>— Environmental impact assessment is critical<br>— Major concern regarding governmental regulations.<br>Significant effect on value system |

**Table 3**

**CHANGING PERSPECTIVE OF TECHNOLOGY THROUGH THE HISTORY OF INDUSTRIALISATION**

| *Factors* | *Technological changes occurring over time* | | | |
|---|---|---|---|---|
| *Relation with industrialisation* | *Non-industrialised situation* | *Industrialising situation* | *Semi-industrialised situation* | *Industrialised situation* |
| Type of society | Hunting and gathering | Mining and farming | Processing and manufacturing | Recycling and synthesizing |
| Preoccupation of society | Survival needs satisfaction | Basic needs satisfaction | Achievement needs satisfaction | Self-actualisation needs satisfaction |
| Major role of technology | Increasing muscle power | Reducing drudgery | Large-scale production | Increasing brain power |
| Predominant type of hardware technologies | Hand tools | Equipment and device | Machines and factories | Automation and robotics |

| Basic source of software technologies | Instinct and common sense | Common sense and experience | Education and training | Modelling and simulation |
|---|---|---|---|---|
| Understanding the importance of technology | None | Essential tool for producing food and shelter | Essential tool for increasing productivity | Master key for development |
| Choice of technologies | No choice | Very little choice | Some choice | Varied choice |
| Time perspective in the development of technologies | None | Immediate future | Short-range future | Long-range future |
| Market aspect in the development of technologies | None | Localised concentration | Internal consumption-oriented | International market-oriented. |

## Employment

The entire rural development programme should be employment-oriented. The main areas of employment potential being crop production, irrigation, animal husbandry, fisheries and forestry programmes. And, at least 30-40 per cent of the rural labour force should be provided employment in the non-agricultural rural sector. In order to provide gainful employment to the labour force, the west has suggested a two-pronged strategy consisting of *(i)* maximisation of employment potential in the various agricultural programmes, and *(ii)* full exploitation of the employment potential in non-agricultural rural activities. Towards this, manufacturing of consumer products be decentralised and packaging, processing, marketing and trade be developed in the rural sector. The main objective is to create maximum employment opportunities to the rural educated and uneducated labour force, so that they will continue to live in rural environment with assured standard of living.

## Rural Unemployment

Unemployment and under-employment persists in rural India. It is one of the key issues of rural development.

Unemployment is an evil from which all countries including the developed countries are suffering. Unemployment and under-employment constitute the principal reason behind the poverty of rural masses. In the words of Robert McNamara, "unemployment is not only robbing men of minimal means to make their way but leaving their pride broken and their ambition atrophied."

In India, there are three types of unemployment in rural areas. Firstly, there is disguised unemployment. Family farms are overmanned as no alternative employment opportunities are available. An unnecessarily large number of persons work on the farms and labour of many persons is not required. It can be dispensed with without affecting the output. In other words, marginal productivity of labour is zero. Such unemployment is estimated to be between 20 to 25 per cent of the labour force in agriculture.

Secondly, there is seasonal unemployment arising from the fact that agricultural operations are not undertaken during a part of the year. Agriculturists do not find enough work to keep them occupied throughout the year. No seasonal unemployment exists in areas under double cropping. In view of a small percentage of cropped area under double cropping, seasonal unemployment is quite large in India.

Thirdly, there is chronic unemployment which is very similar to open unemployment found in cities. In this case, the villagers do not get any work throughout the year.

## Causes of Rural Unemployment

The problem of unemployment in the rural sector is rather serious and what is more important is that the problem of under-employment in the rural sector remains as intractable as that of unemployment. It is an anomally that in many parts of the country, during the busy agricultural season, shortages of labour are frequently reported, while over the greater part of the year, they are engaged in allied activities without continuous employment.

We may observe that unemployment and under-employment in rural areas has been due to:

(1) The rapid growth in population;
(2) The non-availability of subsidiary occupations in the rural areas;
(3) The inadequate development of non-agricultural sector from the employment point of view;
(4) Small holdings which keep the cultivators and landless labourers busy only for a part-time. This is accentuated by the unevenness in distribution of holdings;
(5) The decay of the cottage industries;
(6) Unremunerative nature of the agricultural economy due to rural indebtedness, typical pattern of village life, illiteracy etc.;
(7) Seasonal nature of agriculture operations causing idleness among the agriculturists;
(8) Scarcity of capital characterised by poor overheads and equipments and inadequacy of working capital;
(9) Unwillingness of the villagers to move out and leave the pastoral surroundings to take up employment elsewhere;
(10) Existence of the joint family system which is an unofficial agency for providing relief to the unemployed;
(11) Prevalence of self-employment on a large scale;
(12) Lack of occupational mobility due to social institutions, particularly the caste system;
(13) Rudimentary structure, limited horizons and lack of aspirations which enable the farmers to be satisfied with a very low level of income; and
(14) Allotment of lesser resources to agriculture as a proportion of the total in every plan, beginning with Second Plan till the Fifth Plan.

## Frustrated Rural Youth

The socio-psychological features of the rural youth have undergone a significant change in the last two decades. *The rural youth of today are more frustrated than were their precedessors. Their frustration is a result of non-fulfilment of their growing expectations of an improvement in the quality of life.* At the same time, they are being strongly influenced by the ripples of socio-cultural changes emanating from the urban areas. The cinema has contributed substantially to bringing about this change.

This and the growing exposure to modern lifestyle have strongly influenced the average rural youth's personal habits such as smoking, hair style, manner of dress, etc. They have also influenced his ambitions, expectations and even provided him heroes to follow. He is also exposed to certain new social behavioural mannerisms such as indulging in alcohol, group vandalism and agitation. *Naturally, for the frustrated youth perception and foresight are blurred.* There are two important elements that clash in his psycho-process. Ambition which is a characteristic of the youth meets unemployment face to face. The latter undermines hope. Youth find it difficult to gain competence if there is little for them to do. After all competence can be gained only with some work opportunity. Thus it is in a way a cause-and-effect cycle in which the youth often find themselves trapped.

## Motivation

Rural people, particularly those on subsistence living should be motivated to work hard, live in a clean environment, maintain good health, keep away from the vices, practice family planning and have a small family. This will go a long way in improving the rural environment as well as improving the socio-economic conditions of the poor. Motivation of people is a great task and this could transform the village community quite considerably. In fact, value reorientation should be the forerunner of rural development. As Gandhiji said, "The poorest shall feel that it is their country, in whose making they have an effective voice, in which there will be no high class or low class of people."

## Finance

The banker participates in the process of rural development through the instrument of credit. Whatever, therefore, affects credit—its demand, availability, utilisation, effectiveness and recovery—becomes relevant to the bankers. The factors affecting all these aspects, though interlinked, vary in various ways and are determined by a variety of factors. Demand for credit, for instance, is governed basically by the worthwhile activities that the farmer can take up, the need for credit for undertaking such activities, the farmer's own conviction about the need for such credit and also by the farmer's credit absorbing capacity. It is supported by the state's policy regarding development projects, grant of subsidy provision of extension services etc. The strategy should be to promote positive factors and reduce the impact of negative factors, if these cannot be altogether eliminated.

Finance is the core of development, commercial banks have mobilised deposits in rural areas. The central government and state governments spend crores annually. If this amount is given to banks, they can create credit and finance the rural development projects throughout the country without any wastage. And, at the same time create an atmosphere for building up enormous assets in rural areas. In order to achieve desired result the financial institutions serving in rural areas should provide package finance and guide the borrower from one stage to another. It means a need for selfless leadership and timely finance along with other key inputs will accelerate the process of rural development.

## Organisation

What rural development needs most at present is organisation. We have to develop a suitable organisational set-up which can tackle effectively the various issues involved in rural development. It has to be a professional approach and not mere ideology. Again, it would take quite some time to start the development process as instantaneous changes cannot be had in the outlook, habits, ways of living, ideology, beliefs, suspicions and customs of the rural folks. It should not be forgotten that rural development means understanding the rural people in the first instance. Therefore, the know-how of villagers should not be derided. Actually, it should be the starting point for rural development. The process of rural development is learning, both by villagers as well as those concerned with rural development. Flexibility in approach would be very essential if rural development is to succeed. Based on experience, suitable changes will have to be made in the strategy. If such changes are not made on time, the process would generate indifference and even contempt among villagers.

## Local Leadership

A component of rural development is peoples' participation in the planning process and execution thereof. This aspect of village work needs to be emphasised even at the risk of repetition. Non-participant civic and political culture has been a feature of traditional Indian society which has slowed the growth of local self-government. There is a danger that the rural people could get accustomed to outsiders providing help and solutions to problems without any role on their part which is an essential element in development process. Industry's rural development projects will have to be geared to avoid this dependence. Agencies of change which are external to the village community have to make a deliberate effort to build up local initiative and participation. Involving beneficiaries in organising the programme can lead to a more relevant service and improved benefits for the intended groups. Changes and adaptations may thus be incorporated in the programme. Involvement may arise out of the direct participation of beneficiaries in planning and implementation. A local organisation — voluntary agency or panchayat — may participate in the programme on behalf of the beneficiaries provided the programmes are well understood and appreciated by the rural people.

The influence of committed community agencies has been demonstrated in several fields. The panchayat could not emerge as a model of an effective local organisation representing the interests of the poor. The State agencies are to formulate and support policies while panchayats are to serve as a potential instruments for effective delivery of programmes and services.

Decentralisation and delegation of powers and functions are a crying need along with a simplification of procedure, specially at the grassroot level. In keeping with the true nature of rural development, decision making and implementation personnel must be multi-disciplinary and multi-sectoral. At the same time they must be wedded into a team so that each member supplements and strengthens the others. A free flow of communication from top to down and *vice versa* is essential so that the policy making and the implementation process remain continually integrated. Furthermore, the changes released by developmental programmes since the fifties call for better qualified personnel in the rural development hierarchy. This demands an enlarged input of training of the personnel concerned.

## Community Spirit

Allocation of responsibilities at various levels of rural development hierarchy must be well defined and clear cut and the authority must be commensurate with responsibility. Accountability must be made precise at each level and, what is more, must be enforced. No less vital is the need for developmental functionaries to mobilise the local populace and specific interest groups and enlist their participation in programmes.

There is a need for creating a community spirit in the village and a sense of belonging in spite of economic or social differences. Motivation, education, skills and organisation of the rural poor constitute the essential conditions for giving success to the frontal attack that is now being made on rural poverty. Panchayats and Gram Sabhas have to play a key role in rural development. Only then the fruits of development via science and technology can be availed of for better life.

## Model of Development

It has been pointed out repeatedly by sociologists that local conditions vary so widely in India, that each model has to be suitably adapted. There are differences not only in physical conditions, but also in the attitudes of people based on diehard traditions. In the present context, there shall be as many models as the number of villages in India. Each village's requirement differ from one another. However, for a normal village, development of agriculture through improved seeds, fertilisers, lift irrigation and land development, social forestry, etc., village crafts, health, nutrition, sanitation, etc. models have to be integrated for integrated rural development as well as human development of the village. In formulating a model of rural development, care should be taken about the availability of supportive infrastructure and the market economics.

Block level planning will have to be given full support in order to ensure that development of agriculture takes place and rural activities receives the necessary fillip. For this purpose the government officials incharge of various development departments would need to supply data, on village-wise basis to the bank managers in respect of their service areas. Further, many departments would also have to formulate programmes for strengthening the infrastructure and linkage support for various activities so that viability of the rural activities proposed to be financed by banks will improve.

**Box 5**
**AN APPROACH TO SUSTAINABLE DEVELOPMENT**

The biggest challenge facing India's environmental management, as in the case of several other countries, is the fragmented approach to environmental issues. Environmental considerations continue to be extraneous to decision making on social and economic issues, thereby leading to decisions that are useful in the short run but counterproductive in the long run. India's environment is managed through a plethora of legislation and fragmented policies spread over several ministries in the Central and State governments. Despite the felt need for integrating various institutions towards a common approach to environment management, little by way of concrete action has happened. Many state governments continue to not give adequate importance to their environmental commitments, either due to lack of sensitivity or scarcity of financial, human, and technical resources.

The Government of India's recent initiative to prepare a comprehensive National Environmental Policy is a welcome and long overdue step towards addressing some of these considerations. The objective of the proposed policy is to harmonise the needs of development and the environment. The government's efforts towards preparing a national strategy for sustainable development is another significant step towards operationalising the principles of sustainable development at different levels of governments. These initiatives are also a positive step towards fulfilling India's international environmental commitments. The ultimate importance of these initiatives will of course depend on how these translate into substantive action.

## Training

The question of training people to provide the leadership and skills required for the tasks of development, acquired some urgency in the face of the magnitude of the task. There are government agencies like the National Institute of Rural Development, Hyderabad, and Administrative Staff Colleges in the States which provide training to officials employed in rural development work. Absence of personnel trained in the combination of skills, which is required at the village level, has been the first problem faced by organisations involved in village development.

In this field, industry and financial institutions could break new ground in several ways. Besides providing training to the people employed in the rural development projects, they can also assist in devising adequate course material for training. More important, however, would be provision of career opportunities to those who may want to enter the field of rural development. It has been noticed in programmes of government, as well as the experience of voluntary agencies that postings of staff for short duration create problems in social acceptability and, therefore, affect the success of extension agent. Industrial organisations and banks will have to ensure continuity of personnel by providing incentives which would make rural development projects as attractive, if not more, as assignments in the production or commercial fields.

A trained farmer, led by a good leader as gram sevak, are essential prerequisites for maintenance of quality as to efficiency in agricultural operation and higher productivity. To meet the new challenges, the farmer has to receive education and training in improving his skills. Although the value of education as an instrument of agricultural development is recognised, the question is one of what type of education? There has to be of course, elementary education co-related as far as possible with agriculture and allied activities. Training arrangements for the masses of tiny cultivators, tenants, share croppers and agricultural labourers as well as rural artisans and craftsmen in the use of improved tools, implements and machinery like tractors, oil engines, etc. All along, the farmers have to be trained in family planning, hygiene, sanitation, etc. In the forest areas, particularly, tribals are to be educated in re-afforestation and its gains. What is most needed is that every member in the community, should think more in terms of society and the country. Efforts be also directed in building national character and integrity. Social values have to be raised to improve the living conditions in the rural areas. Towards this end, rural training programmes will have to be reoriented. Education and training should make continuous endeavours to improve — to improve themselves, to improve the effectiveness of their team and to improve the quality of life of the village, so that it can serve the purpose in the best manner possible.

The programme has undoubtedly initiated a trend and a philosophy. Its experience shows up the need for a radical change in the educational system in the rural areas. Vocational training should become an integral part of the school curriculum and should enable the pupils to acquire a broad technical background so that they can branch off into a vocation at any stage.

The national development policy no longer relies on wage employment as a permanent solution to the problem of rural unemployment. The new thrust is on discovering avenues of self-employment, particularly in the non-farm sector. It may also mean a shift in the occupation of the rural population towards the tertiary and secondary sectors. This calls for a complete re-thinking on the educational policy and strategy. Rural IITs, rural training cells and training-cum-production centres should gain popularity. Skill development for gainful self-employment should become the ethos of the educational system.

Finally, we need to move away from a piecemeal approach to NRM to one that allows a greater consideration of cross-sectoral concerns and inter-ministerial involvement *(Box 6)*. This is where pricing of water, power, and other agricultural inputs needs consideration along with pricing of agricultural products. This also implies that the intrinsic role of natural resources and the environment in development and welfare has to be woven into the overall strategy of every sector and cannot only be the responsibility of MoEF. Better co-ordination is needed also in the organisational set-up at various levels: from the Centre down to the village and watersheds. The 10th Plan notes that while lack of financial resources may be an important cause of persisting environmental problems, the more important factors relate to inadequacy of emphasis and poor governance. It is heartening to note that the Plan explicitly recognises the interlinked nature of economic growth, social development, and natural resource management. It also sets the following monitorable targets that mirror the United Nations' Millennium Development Goals. A set of time bound and measurable goals and targets were agreed to at the United Nations Millennium Summit (2000) for combating poverty, hunger, disease, illiteracy, environmental degradation and discrimination against women:

- Reduction of poverty ratio by 5 per cent by 2007 and by 15 per cent by 2012.
- Providing gainful and high-quality employment at least to addition to the labour force over the 10th Plan period.
- All children in school by 2003; all children to complete five years of schooling by 2007.
- Reduction in gender gaps in literacy and wage rates by at least 50 per cent by 2007.
- Reduction in the decadal rate of population growth between 2001 and 2011 to 16.2 per cent.
- Increase in literacy rates to 75 per cent within the Plan period.
- Reduction of infant mortality rate (IMR) to 45 per 1,000 live births by 2007 and to 28 by 2012.
- Reduction of maternal mortality ratio (MMR) to 2 per 1,000 live births by 2007 and to 1 by 2012.
- Increase in forest and tree cover to 25 per cent by 2007 and 33 per cent by 2012.
- All villages to have sustained access to potable drinking water within the Plan period.
- Cleaning of all major polluted rivers by 2007 and other notified stretches by 2012.

## Conclusion

In short, rural development should aim at improving the rural environment and also the lot of the weaker sections of the rural community. It should break the age-old inertia and motivate the people. Secondly, the involvement of female population in the rural development process has to be kept in mind. Social workers with devotion and dedication to their job would therefore be very essential if the village women are to be convinced about the importance of adopting a new way of life like family planning, child care and hygiene.

Another important ingredient of village development is not only to impart improved knowhow but also to ensure that it is assimilated by the villagers and implemented effectively. For this, follow-up is necessary to understand the difficulties in both assimilation as well as implementation so that corrective measures can be taken in time. The local priest, teacher and post master can be effectively drawn into the process as they wield a lot of influence on the village population. No change comes without pangs and it would be the organisers who would have to bear the majority of these pangs in the form of patience and determination to the job.

**Box 6**

A dynamic and flexible organisation with a global vision and a local focus, TERI is the largest developing-country institution working to move human society towards finding innovative solutions to make the world a better place to live in. Setting off with its main focus on documentation and information dissemination activities in 1974, TERI moved to research activities in the fields of energy, environment, and sustainable development in 1982. The genesis of these activities lay in TERI's firm belief that efficient utilisation of energy, sustainable use of natural resources, large-scale adoption of renewable energy technologies, and reduction of all forms of waste would move the process of development towards the goal of sustainability.

With a staff strength of over 500, drawn from multidisciplinary and highly specialised fields, the diverse activities in TERI range from formulating local and national-level strategies to suggested global solutions. Driven by such global vision and local concerns, TERI has established regional centres in Bangalore, Panaji (Goa), Guwahati and Kolkata and has a presence in Japan and Malaysia. It has also set up affiliate institutes in Washington and London.

TERI's emphasis on training, capacity building, and education led to the setting up of the TERI School of Advanced Studies in 1999 – an evolving research university offering doctoral programmes in bioresources, biotechnology, energy, environment, and regulatory and policy studies.

TERI hosts the annual Delhi Sustainable Development Summit, which is swiftly emerging as a major forum for the convergence of globally renowned leaders and thinkers concerned with issues of sustainability.

❑ ❑ ❑

# SECTION THREE

# PRESENT RURAL DEVELOPMENT PROGRAMMES

**Rural Development Programmes In Operation**

| Sr. No. | Programme | Launched on | Remarks |
|---|---|---|---|
| 1. | Jawahar Gram Samridhi Yojana (JGSY) | 01.04.1999 | Restructuring of JRY, NREP and RLEGP. |
| 2. | Pradhan Mantri Gram Sadak Yojana (PMGSY) | 25.12.2000 | |
| 3. | Indira Awaas Yojana (IAY) | 1985-86 | |
| 4. | Pradhan Mantri Gramodaya Yojana (Gramin Awaas) (PMGY) | 2000-2001 | |
| 5. | Samapra Awaas Yojana (SAY) | 1999-2000 | |
| 6. | Swarnjayanti Gram Swarozgar Yojana (SGSY) | 01-04-1999 | Restructuring of IRDP, TRYSEM DWCRA, GKY, MWC, SITRA. |
| 7. | Employment Assurance Scheme (EAS) | 02-10-1993 | Merged with SGRY |
| 8. | National Social Assistance Programme (NSAP) | 15-08-1995 | The programme has three components *viz.*, NOAPS, NFBS & NMBS |
| 9. | Sampoorna Grameen Rozgar Yojana (SGRY) | 25-09-2001 | Restructuring of IGSY and EAS Merged with NREGS with effect from 01-04-2008. |
| 10. | Annapurna | 01-04-2000 | |
| 11. | Drought Prone Areas Programme | 1973-74 | |
| 12. | Desert Development Programme (DDP) | 1977-78 | From 1995-96 the coverage has been extended to a few districts. |
| 13. | Integrated Wastelands Development Programme (IWDP) | 01-04-1995 | |
| 14. | Accelerated Rural Water Supply Programme (ARWSP) | 1972-73 | |
| 15. | Centrally sponsored Rural Sanitation Programme (CRSP) | 1986<br>01-04-1999 | Restructed programme. |
| 16. | Land Reforms<br>*(i)* Distribution of land<br>*(ii)* Consolidation of Holdings<br>*(iii)* Prevention of Alienation and Restoration of Alienated Tribal Lands | | |
| 17. | Panchayati Raj | 1946-1992 | 2,27,698 Village Panchayat<br>5,906 Intermediate Panchayats<br>474 district Panchayats |
| 18. | Empowerment of Women | | |
| 19. | National Rural Employment Guarantee scheme (NREGS) | 07-09-2005<br>02-02-2006 | * NREGS was notified<br>* Launched in 200 districts<br>* Extended to additional 130 districts in 2007-08<br>* Cover all rural areas from 01-04-08. |
| 20. | Provision of Urban Amenities in Rural Areas (PURA) | 15-08-2003 | Achieving balanced social-economic development. |

## APPROVED OUTLAYS IN RESPECT OF PLAN SCHEMES OF THE DEPARTMENT OF RURAL DEVELOPMENT

*(Rs. in crores)*

| Sl. No. | Name of the Department | Approved Outlay | | |
|---|---|---|---|---|
| | | 2006-2007 | 2007-2008 | 2008-2009 |
| 1 | 2 | 3 | 4 | 5 |
| 1. | Department of Rural Development | 24025.62 | 27500.00 | 31500.00 |
| 2. | Department of Land Resources | 1418.00 | 1500.00 | 2400.00 |
| 3. | Department of Drinking Water Supply | 6000.00 | 7560.00 | 8500.00 |
| | **Total:** | 31443.62 | 36560.00 | 42400.00 |

### DEPARTMENT OF RURAL DEVELOPMENT *Plan*

*(Rs. in crores)*

| Sl. No. | Name of the Scheme | Approved Outlay | | |
|---|---|---|---|---|
| | | 2006-2007 | 2007-2008 | 2008-2009 |
| 1 | 2 | 3 | 4 | 5 |
| 1 | Sampoorna Gramin Rozgar Yojana | 3000 | 2800.00 | — |
| 2 | National Rural Employment Guarantee Scheme | 11300 | 12000.00 | 16000.00 |
| 3 | Swarnajayanti Gram Swarozgar Yojana | 1200 | 1800.00 | 2150.00 |
| 4 | DRDA Administration | 220 | 212.00 | 250.00 |
| 5 | Rural Housing | 2920 | 4040.00 | 5400.00 |
| 6 | Pradhan Mantri Gram Sadak Yojana | 5225.62 | 6500.00 | 7530.00 |
| 7 | Grants to National Instituted of Rural Dev. | 12.00 | 10.00 | 15.00 |
| 8 | Assistance to C.A.P.A.R.T | 70.00 | 60.00 | 50.00 |
| 9 | PURA | 10.00 | 10.00 | 30.00 |
| 10 | Management support to RD Programmes and Strengthening District Planning Process | 68.00 | 68.00 | 75.00 |
| | **Total: Plan** | **24025.62** | **27500.00** | **31500.00** |

### DEPARTMENT OF LAND RESOURCES *Plan*

*(Rs. in crores)*

| Sl. No. | Name of the Scheme | Approved Outlay | | |
|---|---|---|---|---|
| | | 2006-2007 | 2007-2008 | 2008-2009 |
| 1 | 2 | 3 | 4 | 5 |
| 1 | Integrated Watershed Management Programme | | | |
| | (a) Programme Component | 1115.00 | 1114.54 | 1825.00 |
| | (b) EAP Component | 80.00 | 86.46 | 50.00 |
| | **Total- (IWMP)** | **1195.00** | **1201.00** | **1875.00** |
| 2 | National Programme for Comprehensive Land Resource Management | 150.00 | 145.00 | 473.00 |
| 3 | Professional Support, Capacity Building, M&E, IEC, TDET etc. | 20.00 | 99.00 | — |
| 4 | Others | 3.00 | 5.00 | — |
| 5 | Bio-fuel | 50.00 | 50.00 | 50.00 |
| 6 | National Rehabilitation & Resettlement Policy | — | — | 2.00 |
| | **Total-Land Resouces** | **1418.00** | **1500.00** | **2400.00** |

### DEPARTMENT OF DRINKING WATER SUPPLY

*(Rs. in crores)*

| Sl. No. | Name of the Scheme | Approved Outlay | | |
|---|---|---|---|---|
| | | 2006-2007 | 2007-2008 | 2008-2009 |
| 1 | Rural Water Supply Programme | 5200.00 | 6500.00 | 7300.00 |
| 2 | Rural Sanitation Programme | 800.00 | 1060.00 | 1200.00 |
| 3 | Total : Drinking Water Supply | 6000.00 | 7560.00 | 8500.00 |

## MAJOR POVERTY ALLEVIATION AND EMPLOYMENT GENERATION PROGRAMMES

- **Pradhan Mantri Gram Sadak Yojana (PMGSY)**

The PMGSY was launched on December 25,2000 as a 100 per cent centrally sponsored scheme with the primary objective of providing all-weather connectivity to the eligible unconnected habitations in the rural areas. The programme is funded mainly from the accruals of diesel cess in the Central Road Fund. In addition, support of the multilateral funding agencies and the domestic financial institutions is being obtained to meet the financial requirements of the programme. Up to December, 2007, about 1,42,750 kilometre-long roadworks have been completed with a cumulative expenditure of Rs. 27,382.24 crore.

- **Indira Awaas Yojana (IAY)**

This scheme aims at providing dwelling units, free of cost, to the poor families of the Scheduled Castes, Scheduled Tribes, freed bonded labourers and also the non-SC/ST persons below the poverty line in rural areas. The scheme is funded on a cost sharing basis of 75:25 between the Centre and the States. During the current financial year, Rs. 4,032.70 crore have been earmarked for release to DRDAs under Indira Awaas Yojana (IAY) for construction of 21.27 lakh houses. As per the information received from the State Governments, 9.39 lakh houses have been constructed up to November, 2007.

- **Swarnjayanti Gram Swarozgar Yojana (SGSY)**

The Swamijayanti Gram Swarozar Yojana (SGSY) was launched in April 1999 after restructuring the integrated Rural Development Programme(IRDP) and allied programmes. It is the only Self Employment Programme currently being implemented for the rural poor. The objective of the SGSY is to bring the assisted swarozaris above the poverty line by providing them income generating assets through bank credit and Government subsidy. The scheme is being implemented on cost sharing basis of 75.25 between the Centre and States. Up to December 2007, 27.37 lakh self-help groups (SHGs) have been formed and 93.21 lakh swarozgaris have been assisted with a total outlay of Rs. 19,340.32 crore.

- **Sampoorna Grameen Rozgar Yojana (SGRY)**

The Sampoorna Grameen Rozgar Yojana (SGRY) was launched on September 25, 2001. The objective of the programme is to provide additional wage employment in the rural areas as also food security, alongside creation of durable community, social and economic infrastructure in the rural areas. In 2007-08 up to December 31, 2007, the number of person-days of employment generated under SGRY was 11.60 crore, while the Centre's contributions in terms of cash and foodgrain component up to December 31, 2007, were Rs. 1,142.27 crore and 9.55 lakh tonnes, respectively. Under the special component, about 0.55 lakh tonnes of foodgrain have been released to calamity hit States in the current year up to December 2007. SGRY programme in 330 districts has already been subsumed in National Rural Employment Guarantee Scheme (NREGS) (200 districts in first phase during the year 2006-07 and 130 additional districts in second phase during 2007-08). SGRY programme will be entirely subsumed in NREGS with effect from April 1, 2008.

- **Swarna Jayanti Shahari Rozgar Yojana (SJSRY)**

In December 1997, the Urban Self-Employment Programme (USEP) and the Urban Wage Employment Programme (UWMP), which are the two special components of the Swarna Jayanti Shahari Rozgar Yojana, were substituted for various programmes operated earlier for urban poverty alleviation. The fund allocation for the scheme was Rs. 344 crore during 2007-08 and Rs. 256.41 crore has been realised upto December 4, 2007. During 2007-08, under USEP, 0.44 lakh urban poor were assisted to set up micro/group enterprise and 0.60 lakh urban poor were imparted skill training up to end of November 2007. Under UWEP, the mandays of employment generated was 6.77 lakh up to end of November 2007. Cumulative coverage of beneficiaries under the Community Structure Component was 358.13 lakh up to end of November 2007.

- **DPAP, DDP and IWDP**

Drought Prone Areas Programme (DPAP) was launched in 1973-74 to tackle the special problems faced by areas constantly affected by severe drought conditions. While Desert Development Programme (DDP) was launched in 1977-78 to mitigate the adverse effects of desertification, the Integrated Wasteland Development Programme (IWDP) has been under implementation of all three programmes has been shifted from sectoral to watershed basis from April 1995. So far, in 2006-07 up to January 31, 2007, 3,076 new projects covering 15.38 lakh ha. 2,270 new projects covering 11.35 lakh ha. and 463 new projects covering 21.08 lakh ha. have been sanctioned under DPAP, DDP and IWDP, respectively.

- **Valmiki Ambedkar Awaas Yojana (VAMBAY)**

VAMBAY, launched in December 2001, facilitates construction of dwelling units for slum dwellers, and provides a healthy and enabling environment through community toilets under Nirmal Bharat Abhiyan, a component of the scheme. The Central Government provides a subsidy of 50 per cent, with the balance provided by the State Governments/Union Territories. Cumulatively, up to March 2006, Rs. 936.63 crore had been released as Central subsidy for the construction/upgradation of 4,58,630 dwelling units and 65,331 toilet seats. For 2006-07, Central allocation of Rs. 75 crore has been made for meeting the committed liabilities for on-going projects. VAMBAY has been subsumed in Integrated Housing and Slum Development Programme (IHSDP) launched along with Jawaharlal Nehru Urban Renewal Mission (JNNURM) on Dec. 3, 2005.

- **Jawaharlal Nehru National Urban Renewal Mission (JNNURM)**

JNNURM, which is for a seven years period from 2005-06, has two main components—Basic Services to the Urban Poor (BSUP) Programme and Integrated Housing and Slum Development Programme (IHSDP). BSUP was launched to assist cities and towns in taking up housing and infrastructural facilities for the urban poor in 63 selected cities in the country. IHSDP for taking up housing and slum upgradation programmes in non-BSUP cities was launched along with BSUP in December 2005. The allocation for JNNURM in 2006-07 (BE) is Rs. 4,900 crore.

- **National Rural Employment Guarantee Scheme (NREGS)**

With the NREG Act being passed in September, 2005, the NREGS was implemented from February 2, 2006 in 200 identified districts of the country with the objective of providing 100 days of guaranteed unskilled wage employment to each rural household opting for it. The ongoing programmes of SGRY and National Food for Work Programme (NFEWP) have been subsumed under NREGS in these districts. NREGS will cover all districts of the country within five years. The NREGS, a demand-driven scheme, has its focus on works relating to water conservation, drought proofing (including afforestation/tree plantation), land development, flood-control/protection (including drainage in waterlogged areas) and rural connectivity in terms of all-weather roads. Of the Rs. 11,300 crore allocated for NREGS in 2006-07 (BE), Rs. 6,714.98 crore was released up to January 31, 2007 have been expanded to 330 districts in the second phase. The remaining 266 districts have been notified on September 28, 2007 where the scheme will come into effect from April 1, 2008. As against the employment demanded by 2.61 crore rural households, 2.57 households have been provided wage employment during 2007-08. A budget allocation of Rs. 12,000 crore (including NER component) was made for 2007-08 and Rs. 10,501.02 crore has been released till 30.01.2008.

- **Bharat Nirman**

This programme, which was launched in 2005-06 for building infrastructure and basic amenities in rural areas, has six components, *viz.* rural housing, irrigation potential, drinking water, rural roads, electrification and rural telephony. Bharat Nirman has received a budgetary outlay of Rs. 24,603 crore in 2007-08 as against Rs. 18,696 crore (including NER component) in 2006-07.

- **Mid-day Meal Scheme**

This Scheme, which was launched in August 1995, is intended to give boost to universalization of primary education by increasing enrollment, relention and attendance while contributing to the nutrition of students in primary classes. The allocation has been enhanced to Rs.7,324 crore in 2007-08 from Rs. 5,348 crore in 2006-07.

- **Rajiv Gandhi National Drinking Water Mission**

This programme was introduced as one of the five Societal Missions in 1986 and was called the National Drinking Water Mission. It was renamed as Rajiv Gandhi National Drinking Water Mission in 1991. Allocation of funds has been increased from Rs. 4,680 crore in 2006-07 to Rs. 5,850 crore in 2007-08.

- **National Rural Health Mission**

The National Rural Health Mission was launched on April 12, 2005, to provide accessible, affordable and accountable quality health services to the poorest households in the remotest rural regions. Allocation increased to Rs. 9,947 crore in 2007-08 from Rs. 8,207 crore in the previous year.

- **Jawaharlal Nehru National Renewal Mission (JNNURM)**

JNNURM, which is for a seven-year period from 2005-06, has two main components—Basic Services to the Urban Poor (BSUP) Programme and Integrated Housing & Slum Development Programme (IHSDP). BSUP was launched to assist cities and towns in taking up housing and infrastructural facilities for the urban poor in 63 selected cities in the country. IHSDP, which was launched simultaneously with BSUP in December 2005, is taking up housing and slum upgradation programmes in non-BSUP cities. A budgetary provision of Rs. 4,987 crore has been made in 2007-08 as against Rs. 4,595 crore in 2006-07.

*"Guaranteeing wage employment and ensuring food security—This is sought to be achieved through the National Rural Employment Guarantee Act and Sampoorna Grameen Rozgar Yojana."*

## Chapter 11

# WAGE EMPLOYMENT PROGRAMMES

### Introduction

The high incidence of poverty in rural India is directly related to prevalence of unemployment and under-employment on a large scale. A majority of the rural population is landless and sustains entirely on wage employment. While the self-employment programmes are intended to remove poverty on a sustainable basis there is need to take care of the wage employment needs of the rural poor. The rural workforce continues to suffer due to excessive seasonality of employment lack of wage employment opportunities and low wage rates. Migration of labour, discrimination between wages paid to men and women distressed child labour etc. are therefore, common features of rural areas.

Efforts to provide wage employment as a short run strategy for alleviation for rural poverty has been a major component of development planning in India. The major programmes under implementation in this direction are the Jawahar Rozgar Yojana (JRY), Employment Assurance Scheme (EAS). The Million Wells Scheme (MWS) is also one such programme which helps the beneficiary to acquire an asset for his/her sustained self-employment on land-based activities.

## JAWAHAR ROZGAR YOJANA/JAWAHAR GRAM SAMRIDHI YOJANA (JGSY)

### Introduction

The Jawahar Rozgar Yojana (JRY) was started in April, 1989 by merging the on-going National Rural Employment Programme (NREP) and Rural Landless Employment Guarantee Programme (RLEGP) into a single rural employment programme.

The government restructured JRY and EAS and launched a new programme Jawahar Gram Samridhi Yojana (JGSY) to develop rural infrastructure at the village level in a planned manner. This programme has come into effect from 1st April 1999.

## Objectives

The main objective of JRY is generation of additional gainful employment for the unemployed and under–employed persons, both men and women in rural areas. The secondary objective of the Yojana is creation of durable community and social assets. The Yojana has been designed to arrest the seasonality of wage employment and provide a positive impact on the prevailing wage rates in rural areas. It also contributes to improvement in the quality of life of the rural poor by providing supplementary source of income through wage employment and by creating community and social assets.

## Main Features of JGSY

- The main emphasis of Jawahar Gram Samridhi Yojana (JGSY) is to create rural infrastructure at the village level.
- Implementation of the Jawahar Gram Samridhi Yojana entirely by the Village Panchayat.
- Direct release of funds to the Village Panchayats by District Rural Development Agencies (DRDAs)/Zilla Parishads (ZPs).
- Village Panchayats is the sole authority for preparation of Annual Action Plan and its implementation with the approval of Gram Sabha.
- Empowerment to the Gram Sabha for approval of schemes/works.
- Village Panchayats can execute works/schemes up to Rs. 50,000/- without technical/administrative approval. However, Gram Sabha's approval is a must.
- 22.5% of JGS funds have been earmarked for individual beneficiary schemes for SCs/STs.
- 3 per cent of annual allocation would be utilized for creation of barrier free infrastructure for the disabled.
- Wages under JGSY will either be the minimum wages notified by the States or higher wages fixed by States through the prescribed procedure.
- Panchayats can suitably relax 60:40 wage-material ratio for building up demand driven rural infrastructure.
- 15 per cent of funds can be spent on maintenance of assets.
- Social Audit by the Gram Sabha.
- Village level monitoring & vigilance committee to oversee and supervise the works/schemes undertaken.
- DRDA/ZP is responsible for overall guidance, coordination, supervision, monitoring and periodical reporting.

## Works to be Taken Up

All works that result in the creation of durable productive community assets can be taken up by the village panchayat under the programme as per the felt need of the area/people. Care has been taken to build up of demand driven infrastructure with sustainable low-cost technology.

## Target Group and Special Safeguards for Certain Sections

The JRY/JGSY is targeted to benefit people living below the poverty line in rural areas. Preference, however, is given to the Scheduled Castes, the Scheduled Tribes and freed bonded labourers. At least 30% of employment is to be provided to women under the Yojana. 22.5% of funds have to be to spent on individual beneficiary schemes for the direct benefit of SCs/STs.

**Following works should be given priority:**

- Infrastructure for SCs/STs habitations.
- Infrastructure support for JGSY.
- Community infrastructure for education and health; and
- Other social, economic and physical infrastructure.

**The following works will not be allowed to be taken up:**

- Building for religious purposes such as temple, mosque, gurudwara, church etc.
- Monuments, memorium, statue, idols, arch gate/welcome gate.
- Bridges.
- Building for higher secondary schools.
- Building for colleges.
- Desiltation of tanks.
- Black topping of roads.

*Fig. 1. Creating assets for community under JRY for additional gainful employment*

## Implementing Agencies

JRY is implemented in a decentralised fashion by the Panchayati raj institutions. The major share of funds are utilized at the village level by the Gram Panchayats. At the district level the responsibility of co-ordination, guidance and monitoring is vested with the DRDAs/ZPs, Intermediate Panchayats/ Village Panchayats in a district in the ratio of 15:15:70.

The resources allocated to DRDA/ZP, intermediate panchayats and gram panchayats are to be spent within the geographical boundaries of each unit. These funds cannot be diverted under any circumstances except where two or more intermediate level panchayats/gram panchayats decide to pool the resources together to take up a work for their common benefit.

*Fig. 2. Durable assets are created under Jawahar Gram Samridhi Yojana*

## Financial and Physical Performance Under JRY/JGSY

Since its inception in 1989-90 up to November 2001 the Yojana has been able to generate a total 73,576.53 lakh mandays of employment. The expenditure during this period was Rs. 30,395.62 crores. The year-wise financial and physical performance under JRY/JGSY since 1989-90 is given in Table-1

**Table 1** *(Rs. in crores)*

| *Year* | *Total Funds Available* | *Funds Utilised* | *Percentage Utilisation* |
|---|---|---|---|
| 1992-93 | 3594.63 | 2709.59 | 75.38 |
| 1993-94 | 4767.63 | 3878.71 | 81.36 |
| 1994-95 | 5418.22 | 4268.33 | 78.78 |
| 1995-96 | 5791.90 | 4466.91 | 77.12 |
| 1996-97 | 2583.38 | 2163.98 | 83.77 |
| 1997-98 | 2872.03 | 2451.65 | 82.82 |
| 1998-99 | 2222.16 | 1243.71 | 55.97 |
| 1999-2000 | 2795.88 | 2035.27 | 72.80 |
| 2000-2001 | 1703.67 | 711.35 | 41.75 |

Among the positive aspects highlighted in the Evaluation Report are that nearly 82.16% of available funds were spent of community development projects; construction of rural link roads received the highest priority; average wages paid per manday of the unskilled workers were more or less on the lines of minimum wages prescribed under the Act; the wage and non-wage component of the expenditure was 52.84:47.16; by and large, payment of wages to workers was made either on a daily basis or weekly basis; muster rolls were maintained; of the total assets created, 76.11% were found to be in good/satisfactory condition; the share of SCs/STs in generation of employment was satisfactory; roughly, 11 mandays of employment were created during the reference period; family members of the workers also received employment during the last 30 days preceding the date of survey and 76.96% of the assets were created by Village Panchayat.

The evaluation, however has highlighted some inadequacies. More than 50% of elected panchayat heads were not imparted training for implementation of JRY works. The share of women in employment generation was less than the prescribed 30%. 49.97% of the works could not be completed on account of shortage of funds. Some discrepancies were observed between payment of wages to male and female workers. The use of locally available material in various works undertaken by Panchayats was not appreciable.

## Earmarking of Resources

There is no sectoral earmarking of resources under JGSY, except the following:

*(a)* 22.5% of the annual allocation must be spent on individual beneficiary scheme for SCs/STs as per JGSY guidelines. Diversion of funds meant for SCs/STs to other works is not permitted.

*(b)* 3% of annual allocation would be utilized for creation of barrier free infrastructure for the disabled. In case, funds are not utilized under this head, the village panchayat may utilize the funds for other works under JGSY.

*(c)* The State Government are provided an amount of Rs. 10.00 lakh or 1% of the annual allocation, whichever is less, to meet the training expenses of officials/non-officials (elected Panchayat functionaries) involved in the implementation of JGSY provided that at least 75% of this must be spent on the training of non-officials (Panchayat functionaries). The funds for the purpose have been released to the States of Orissa, Assam, Himachal Pradesh, Punjab, West Bengal, Madhya Pradesh, Uttar Pradesh, Goa, Tamil Nadu, Andhra Pradesh and Tripura during the current year. The remaining States UTs. have been asked to submit a proposal in this regard.

## New Initiatives and Looking to the Future

JGSY is implemented by the village panchayats with active participation of people. The programme, therefore, empowers the village panchayats and the people. The programme also contributes significantly in creating social and community assets and economic infrastructures at the village level. In order that the panchayat have reasonable autonomy in implementation of the programme and have freedom from bureaucratic control in approval and technical scrutiny of the works and at the same time become effective in development of the basic infrastructures at the village level, steps are being taken to restructure and entrust the implementation of JRY entirely to the Village Panchayats.

# EMPLOYMENT ASSURANCE SCHEME

## Introduction

The Employment Assurance Scheme (EAS) was introduced w.e.f 2nd October, 1993 in the rural areas of 1778 blocks of 2.61 districts in which the Revamped Public Distribution System (RPDS) was in operation. The blocks selected were in the drought prone areas, desert areas, tribal areas and hill areas.

## Expansion of EAS

During 1994-95, EAS was extended to 409 blocks under DPAD/DDP and Modified Area Development Approach (MADA) blocks having larger concentration of tribal population. In March, 1995 the scheme was further extended to 256 blocks (233 flood prone blocks in the States of Uttar Pradesh, Bihar and Assam, and 23 blocks of Jammu and Kashmir in view of the special conditions prevailing there). The Intensified Jawahar

Rozgar Yojana (IJRY) was merged with EAS w.e.f. 1.1.1996. Consequently, 722 non-EAS blocks in 120 IJRY districts were also covered under EAS. On universalisation, the remaining blocks were covered under the scheme in two phases *i.e* 1,123 blocks in 1996-97 and 1,121 blocks in 1997-98. At present, the scheme is being implemented in all the 5448 rural blocks of the country.

## Objectives

The primary objective of the Employment Assurance Scheme is to provide gainful employment during lean agricultural season in manual work to all able bodied adults in rural areas who are in need and desirous of work, but cannot find it. The secondary objective is the creation of economic infrastructure and community assets for sustained employment and development.

## Salient Features

- The scheme is operative in all the rural blocks of the country.
- It is demand driven scheme with no fixed earmarking of annual funds for any district or block.
- Expenditure is shared between the Centre and the States on 80:20 basis.
- The Central assistance under the scheme is directly released block-wise to DRDA/ZPs based on the demand for wage employment and expenditure.
- All adult rural poor normally residing in the villages are covered.
- A maximum of 2 adults per family are provided the assurance of up to 100 days of employment. New works will not be opened under this scheme if employment potential is available through plan and non-plan works already in progress and the assurance could be fulfilled by utilising the same.
- Works should be labour intensive which result in the creation of durable productive assets.
- As an individual beneficiary oriented scheme, on the land of BPL families, horticulture development is a permitted activity.
- Implementing agencies are Block Development Officers, District Officers of various line Departments and PRIs at all three levels. The desirous workers have to get themselves registered with village level workers or Gram Panchayats and are issued a family card.
- When about 10 workers demand work, new projects can be started by the block level officer for providing employment.
- The State Level Coordination Committee the Rural Development Programmes is responsible for the overall supervision, guidance and monitoring of EAS.

## Block-wise Entitlement of Funds under EAS

As per the present classification of block into 'A', 'B' and 'C' categories, the central share of each instalment to the block is Rs.40 lakhs, Rs.30 lakhs and Rs.20 lakhs respectively. The State share is Rs 10 lakhs, Rs. 7.50 lakhs and Rs. 5 lakhs respectively.The shelf of projects for new works to be taken up in each of the categories should not exceed 150% of the funds expected by a block in two instalments.

The classification of the block into 'A', 'B' and 'C' categories was made earlier on the basis of the criteria of backwardness and size of the population. These were mostly blocks in hilly, tribal, drought prone and desert areas. These criteria were followed up to the merger of IJRY with EAS. As per this criteria blocks with population above 1,96,287 were put in 'A' category; block with population between 1,96,287 and 65,585 were put in 'B' category and blocks with population below 65,585 were put in 'C' category. Consequent upon universalisation of EAS all the remaining blocks have been put in 'C' category for the purpose of determining the entitlement of funds by each.

*Fig. 3. Getting Connected: A bridge constructed under EAS*

## Financial and Physical Performance under EAS

Since inception of EAS in 1993-94 to December 2000, a total of 745.24 lakh mandays of employment have been generated by utilising Rs. 650.16 crores.

The year-wise financial and physical performance under EAS since 1993-94 is given below in Table 2.

## Number of Persons Registered under EAS

A total of 4.12 crore persons have been registered under EAS in various States/UTs since inception of the scheme up to November, 1998.

**Table 2**
**FINANCIAL & PHYSICAL PERFORMANCE**

*(Rs. in crores)*

| *Year* | *Central release* | *State release* | *Total funds available including OB* | *Total utilisation* | *% utilisation* | *Wage days generated (In lakhs)* |
|---|---|---|---|---|---|---|
| 1993-94 | 439.10 | 109.66 | 548.76 | 183.75 | 33.48 | 494.74 |
| 1994-95 | 1128.52 | 281.73 | 1775.26 (365.01) | 1235.45 | 69.59 | 2739.56 |
| 1995-96 | 1705.69 | 425.94 | 2671.45 (539.81) | 1720.61 | 64.61 | 3465.27 |
| 1996-97 | 1939.59 | 484.19 | 3383.34 (959.54) | 2160.41 | 63.85 | 4030.02 |
| 1997-98 | 1968.72 | 491.75 | 3425.88 (964.84) | 2307.95 | 67.37 | 3816.77 |
| 1998-99 | 1988.45 | 496.68 | 3357.80 (872.66) | 2882.18 | 85.84 | 4279.36 |
| 1999-2000 | 1736.42 | 593.11 | 2329.53 (581.14) | 2182.60 | 74.99 | 2786.17 |
| 2000-2001-31.12.2000 | 722.00 | 171.26 | 1554.37 (661.11) | 650.16 | 41.83 | 745.24 |

## Evaluation

The Programme Evaluation Organisation (PEO) Wing of Planning Commission is in the process of evaluating the programme.

## Some Recently Introduced Changes in EAS

- Panchayati Raj Institutions of all three levels have been included as implementing agencies.
- The shell of Projects would be prepared based on suggestions of Gram Sabhas and Panchayats as well as from other sources like line departments, people's representatives etc. as per felt needs of the people.
- Registration of wage-seekers would be done in Gram Panchayats and work-site etc.
- The implementing agencies have been permitted to utilise one person from among the beneficiaries group as animator/leader/facilitator in maintenance of muster roll payment of wages, monitoring of quality of works etc. Such person will be eligible to receive wages applicable to unskilled labourers.
- The States have been requested to evolve and publish "Rural Standard Schedule of Rates" as has already been done by some States to eliminate the role of contractors is EAS works.
- To make the implementation of the programme more transparent instruction have been issued to all the states to exhibit prominently the details of funds received, works sanctioned, estimated cost, quantity of material used, workers engaged and wage rates etc, in the Panchayat Office/work site. The accounts of the Gram Panchayats are open for scrutiny by the Gram Sabha.
- To avoid multiplicity of Committees and as per the recommendation of the Standing Committee of Parliament a decision has been taken to merge District and Block level EAS Committees with the existing Vigilance and Monitoring Committees.
- In case of Karbi-Anglong and North Kachar hill districts of Assam the Principal Secretaries of the respective Autonomous Hill Councils have been declared as Implementing Agencies of EAS in place of the Deputy Commissioners.

## PRADHAN MANTRI GRAM SADAK YOJANA (PMGSY)

Rural road connectivity is not only a key component of Rural Development in India, it is also recognised as an effective Poverty Reduction Programme. Notwithstanding the efforts made, over the years, at the State and Central levels, through different programmes, even after five decades of Independence, about 40% of India's village do not have proper road connectivity.

Keeping in view the fact that rural roads are vital to economic growth and to measures for poverty alleviation in the villages, Government's resolve to provide total rural connectivity was indicated in the address of the Hon'ble President to the joint sitting of Parliament on 25th October, 1999, when a programme of construction of all-weather roads in the rural areas was announced.

The Rural Roads Programme as a component of the Pradhan Mantri Gramodaya Yojana (PMGY) was announced by the Finance Minister in his Budget Speech, 2000-2001.

The Department of Rural Development had in January, 2000, set up a National Rural Roads Development Committee under the chairmanship of Shri Nitin Gadkari to assess the magnitude of the task, the volume of funds required and to suggest implementation strategies as also suitable agencies for the same. The Committee submitted its Report in May, 2000. The gist of its recommendations are enclosed at Annexure-V.

In April, 2000, the Union Cabinet decided that 50% of the diesel cess would be set apart for rural roads and made available to the Ministry of Rural Development. In December, 2000, Parliament enacted legislation imposing diesel cess and earmarking 50% of the cess to the development of rural roads.

In his Address to the Nation on 15th August, 2000, the Prime Minister stated:

"For the first time since Independence, the Central Government has devised a well conceived and time-bound programme for rural roads. This hundred percent centrally sponsored scheme, which is called the "Prime Minister's Rural Roads Scheme", aims to connect within the next three years, every village that has a population of more than one thousand, through good all-weather roads. By 2007, every village with a population more than five hundred will be similarly connected."

*Fig. 4. Availability of Roads Ensures Prosperity*

This Ministry, accordingly, drew up a programme, the Pradhan Mantri Gram Sadak Yojana (PMGSY) which envisages an investment of about Rs. 60,000 crores to achieve the objectives outlined by the Prime Minister. Since the diesel cess to be collected over the next seven years is far less than the requirement, it is proposed to utilize the cess receipts to leverage further funds, both from the market as well as from External Funding Agencies. The Scheme also provides for a projectised approach and tight monitoring of the performance by the States. The details of the allocations made to the States/Union Territories for Rural Roads for 2000-2001 by the Planning Commission are at Annexure-VI.

*Fig. 5. Rural Roads for Accelerated Socio-Economic*

The Pradhan Mantri Gram Sadak Yojana was launched by the Honb'le Prime Minister on 25th December 2000. Guidelines of the programme have been issued to all the States/UTs on 15th December, 2000. The primary focus of the programme is on construction of new roads. It is proposed to connect about 1 lakh villages in the next seven years. Besides, upgradation (to prescribed standards) about 5 lakh kilometers of existing roads will be taken up under the Programme, so as to achieve connectivity through a good all-weather roads.

The key elements of the Pradhan Mantri Gram Sadak Yojana are as follows:

- Preparation of Master Plans-District Rural Roads Plans to be generated, based on block-level Plans;
- Project Implementation Units to be formed to ensure professional and timely completion;
- Execution on a Project Mode;
- Ensuring Standard Specifications, including adequate cross-drainage works;
- Time-bound Execution – completion in 9-12 months; Penalty clauses for time overruns; No escalation permitted;
- Strict Quality Control – independent monitors to inspect works.

The Programme further envisages —

- Ready availability of land for the roads;
- Maintenance of the roads by Panchayati Raj Institutions;
- Encouraging use of locally available materials for construction of roads;
- Planting of trees on either side of the roads.

Proposals have been received from several States/UTs and others are expected shortly. Proposals worth about Rs. 658 crores have been approved by the end of January 2001. It is expected that the entire allocation of Rs. 2,500 crores available for this year, will be released to the States well before the end of the financial Year.

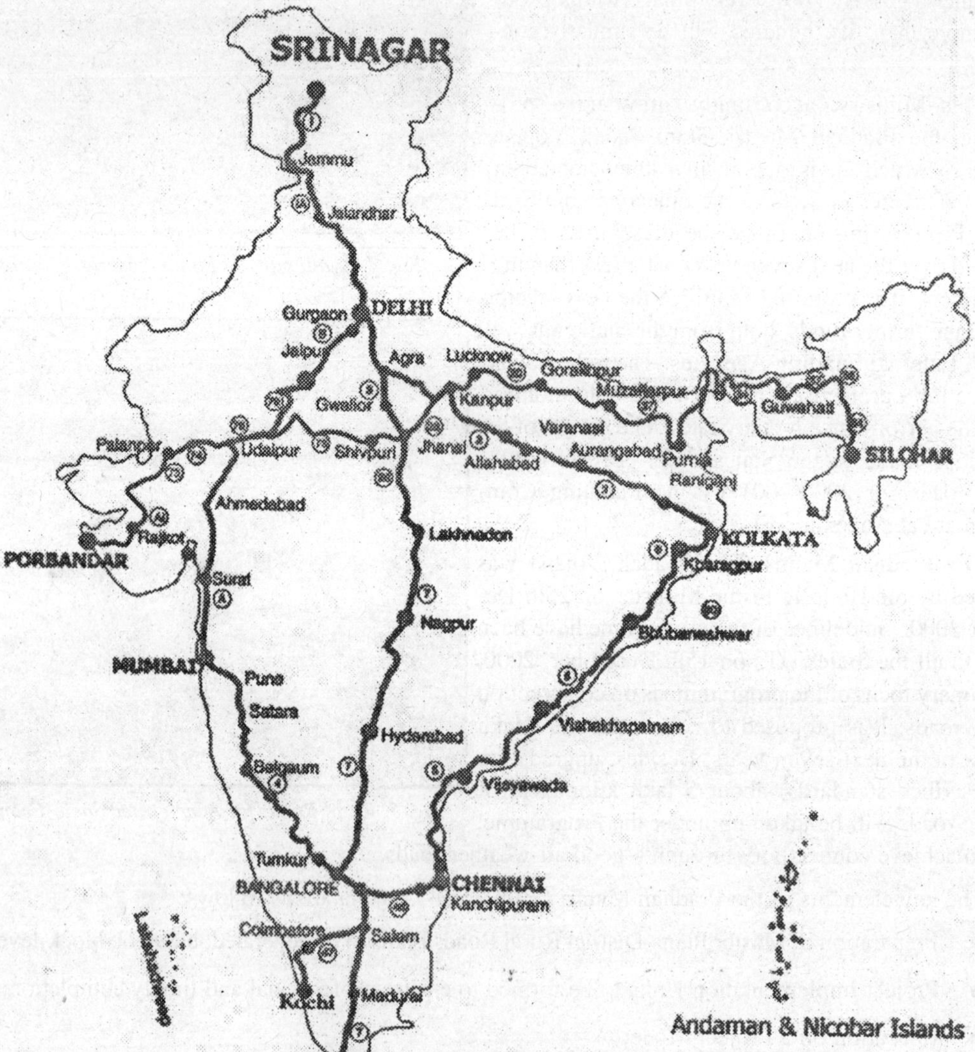


*Fig. 6.*

In the heart of India, life is changing. There are better roads, wider highways, and new railway lines. Linking distant villages, connecting remote corners, and uniting you with urban India. In fact, the entire spectrum of infrastructure from telecom to power is improving. Catalysing business, transport and trade. Bringing you more opportunities, fresh markets, and newer customers. So go ahead, gain from these excellent times. Build your dreams, spread the enthusiasm, and make India stronger and shine even brighter.

# MILLION WELLS SCHEME

## Introduction

Million Wells Scheme (MWS) was launched as a sub-scheme of National Rural Employment Programme (NREP) and Rural Landless Employment Guarantee Programme (RLEGP) during 1988-89. It continued as a sub-scheme of Jawahar Rozgar Yojana from April 1989 to 31.12.95. From 1.1.96 MWS is an independent scheme.

## Objectives

The objective of the scheme is to provide open irrigation wells free of cost to poor, small and marginal farmers who are below the poverty line and freed bonded labourers.

## Target Group

Up to 1992-93, the target group for MWS comprised of small and marginal farmers belonging to SCs/STs and freed bonded labourers. From 1993-94 onwards, MWS has been extended to include poor small and marginal farmers belonging to non-SC/ST category as well, who are below the poverty line and are listed in the IRDP register of the village. The financial assistance provided to SC/ST poor, small and marginal farmers under MWS, however, must not be less than two-thirds of the total funds utilised under the scheme in any year.

## Allocation of Funds

The MWS is a centrally sponsored scheme. Funds under the scheme are shared between the Centre and the States on 80:20 basis. State-wise allocation is arrived at on the basis of the proportion of rural poor in a State to the total rural poor in the country. State Governments fix the district-wise allocation and physical targets keeping in view the size of the unirrigated land in a district, potential for well irrigation and need for improvements of land held by the rural poor.

*Fig. 7. Harvesting of water through a stop dam*

## Works to be Taken up under MWS

MWS is primarily intended to provide open wells. Tube wells and bore wells are not to be taken up under this scheme. However, where wells are not feasible due to geological factors, funds under the scheme could be utilised for other works of minor irrigation like irrigation tanks, water harvesting structures and also for the development of lands belonging to the target group. The fund cannot be diversed for any other purpose.

Each well/irrigation source constructed under MWS has to be located in the holding of the beneficiary and an entry to that effect should be made in the revenue records.

The beneficiaries themselves undertake the construction of wells through their own labour and by hiring local labour for which they are paid. Engagement of contractors is strictly prohibited under the scheme.

## Cost/Area Norms

The cost/area norms in regard to works under MWS is decided by a committee comprising of Chief Secretary/Secretary (Rural Development), Secretary (Planning), Secretary (Irrigation) and Chief Engineer Minor Irrigation of the State.

## Implementing/Executive Agency

At the district level DRDA/ZP is the implementing agency of the scheme. But the beneficiaries themselves execute the construction of wells under MWS through their own labour for which they area paid or by hiring local labour. In no case the work should be entrusted to contractors.

**Table 3**

*(Rs in crores)*

| *S.No.* | *Year* | *Allocation* | *Funds Utilised* | *No. of Wells Constructed* |
|---|---|---|---|---|
| 1. | 1988-89 | 271.40 | 132.99 | 50345 |
| 2. | 1989-90 | 0 | 108.16 | 87634 |
| 3. | 1990-91 | 524.63 | 279.74 | 56433 |
| 4. | 1991-92 | 524.63 | 495.19 | 122328 |
| 5. | 1992-93 | 605.33 | 534.05 | 180995 |
| 6. | 1993-94 | 954.37 | 639.74 | 151673 |
| 7. | 1994-95 | 1049.61 | 776.18 | 158780 |
| 8. | 1995-96 | 559.07 | 538.29 | 142685 |
| 9. | 1996-97 | 559.07 | 502.33 | 108897 |
| 10. | 1997-98 | 559.07 | 495.61 | 103499 |
| | Sub-total | 5607.18 | 4502.28 | 1213269 |
| 11. | 1998-99 (Up to Nov. 1998) | 561.10 | 225.89 | 49821 |
| | Grand Total | **6168.28** | 4728.17 | 1263090 |

## Performance under Million Wells Scheme

Since inception of the scheme in 1988-89 till 1997-98 a total of 12.63,090 wells have been constructed under MWS with an expenditure of Rs. 4,728.17 crores. The total number of beneficiaries 12,63,090. The year-wise resources allocated, utilised and wells constructed since inception under MWS is given in Table 3.

## Monitoring and Supervision

The DRDA/ZP is also responsible for monitoring and supervision of the scheme in the district. The state level monitoring is the responsibility of the State Level Co-ordination Committee of the State. At the State level, Secretary, Rural Development is the modal agency for implementation of the scheme.

## Recently introduced changes in MWS

Some recently introduced changes in MWS are as follows:

- Strict compliance to ensure 2/3rd of MWS expenditure for the benefit of SCs/ STs;
- Providing lifting device to the beneficiaries wherever needed under IRDP/SC/ST Finance Corporations etc;
- Educating beneficiaries in improved farm practices through agricultural extension programmes;
- Active involvement of the Panchayati Raj Institutions in planning and selection of MWS beneficiaries. The village panchayat has to select the beneficiaries which have to be then approved by the DRDA/ZPs;
- Reservation of 3% allocation for the year for disabled persons. This reservation would be horizontal reservation *i.e.* disabled persons belonging to SCs/STs and others would fall in their respective categories;
- Fixation of district-wise physical and financial targets from 1997-98 onwards which was not done earlier;
- Priority to given to MWS beneficiaries under the horticulture development component of Employment Assurance Scheme.

# SAMPOORNA GRAMEEN ROZGAR YOJANA (SGRY)

The new programme was launched on 25th September, 2001 by merging the on-going schemes of JGSY and EAS with an annual outlay of Rs. 10,000 crore to provide additional wage employment in the rural areas.

## Objectives

The objectives of the Programme are to provide additional wage employment in the rural areas as also food security, alongside the creation of durable community, social and economic infrastructure in the rural areas. The programme is self-targetting in nature with special emphasis to provide Wage Employment to women, scheduled castes, scheduled tribes and parents of children withdrawn from hazardous occupations. The salient features of SGRY are:

- The Sampoorna Grameen Rozgar Yojana (SGRY) a Centrally Sponsored Scheme (CSS) is being implemented with the total outlay of Rs. 10,000 crores.
- Under the Scheme, 50 lakh tonnes of foodgrains amounting to about Rs. 5,000 crore (at economic cost) is being provided every year, free of cost, to the State Governments and Union Territory Administrations.
- Rs. 5,000 crore has been kept to meet the cash component of wages and material cost.
- The cost of the cash component of the Programme is shared by the Centre and State in the ratio of 75:25.
- The payment of foodgrains is to be made by the Ministry of Rural Development to the Food Corporation of India (FCI) directly.
- About 100 crore mandays of employment are envisaged to be generated every year in the rural areas through the SGRY.
- Every worker seeking employment under the SGRY will be provided minimum 5 kgs. of foodgrains (in kind) per manday as part of wages.
- The balance of wages will be paid in cash so that they are assured of the notified minimum wages.

- The State Governments and UT Administrations will be free to calculate the cost of foodgrains (paid as part of wages) at either BPL rates or APL rates or anywhere between these two rates.
- Panchayati Raj Institutions (PRIs) can take up works as per the felt need of the areas.

The scheme envisages employment generation of 100 crore mandays annually. Under the scheme, 50 lakh tonnes of foodgrains amounting to about Rs. 5,000 crore (at economic cost) is being provided every year, free of cost, to the State Government and Union Territory Administrations. Rs. 5,000 crore has been kept in meet cash component of wages and material cost. Every worker seeking employment under the SGRY is provided minimum 5 kg, of foodgrains (in kind) as part of the wages. The balance of the wages is paid in cash.

SGRY is the one scheme whose implementation is 100% through the three tiers of Panchayati Raj Institutions, Each level of the Panchayats is independently responsible for the implementation of the Programme. It has been ensured that at least a minimum of Rs. 25,000 and foodgrains of an equal value goes to every Gram Panchayat every year under SGRY. For the first time so much of the resources have been put at the disposal of PRIs. 5% of the resources under SGRY have been reserved for distress areas. A special component of SGRY has been created which is a relief measure for calamity affected areas for ensuring food security. 10% of the foodgrains have been reserved under the special component of the SGRY to meet emergency arising out of natural calamities.

## Strategy

The scheme is exclusively implemented by the Panchayat Raj Institutions as one of the integrated scheme. The programme resources are shared by all the three tiers *viz.*, District Panchayat, Intermediate Panchayat and the Village Panchayat in the proportion of 20:30:50. Each level of Panchayat is an independent unit for formulation of Action Plan and executing the scheme. The details of activities/works taken up by the PRIs are as under:

(i) **District Panchayats-** 20% of the resources are reserved at the District level and are to be utilized by the District Panchayats/DRDAs preferably in the areas suffering from endemic labour exodus/areas of distress as per the Annual Action Plan approved by the District Panchayats/DRDAs.

(ii) **Intermediate Level Panchayats-** 30% of the resources are allocated among the Intermediate Level Panchayats. While allocating the resources, equal weightage is to be given to the proportion of SC/ST population and of rural population of the respective Intermediate Level Panchayat areas to those of the Districts. The works will be taken as per their own Annual Action Plan approved by the Intermediate Level Panchayats. However, while selecting the works, to be taken up, preference will be given to the areas, which are backward, calamity prone or face migration of labour.

(iii) **Village Panchayats-** 50% of the resources are allocated among the Village Panchayat for generation of supplementary wage employment and creation of demand driven community village infrastructure, which includes also durable assets to enable the rural poor to increase opportunities for sustained employment.

## Works to be Taken Up

The works to be taken up must be labour intensive, leading to the creation of additional wage employment, durable assets and infrastructure, namely, water conservation and water harvesting; drought proofing, including afforestation and tree plantation; irrigation canals, including micro and minor irrigation works; renovation of traditional water bodies, including de-silting of tanks; land development; flood-control and protection works, including drainage in waterlogged areas; rural connectivity to provide all-weather access. While taking up the works, emphasis should be given on labour intensive works. Purely material oriented works are not to be taken up. It should be ensured that sustainable and cost effective works are taken up under the Programme.

The works taken up should be in a manner that they are capable of giving a boost to the rural economy besides creating additional employment opportunity as well.

## Conclusion

SGRY is fully planned and implemented by the Panchayati Raj Institutions (PRIs) in economy as a whole. The success of this programme fairly depends upon the quality of delivery mechanism, which finally rests with the implementing agencies i.e., the PRIs. The SGRY has an economic aspect as well. Our goals are not merely generation of additional mandays and provide food security to the rural poor but at the same time channelising its vast potential in nation building exercise through the development of human resource and economic infrastructure which may transform the rural face and give boost to the nation's economy. SGRY programme is entirely merged in National Rural Employment Scheme (NREGS) with effect from 01-04-2008.

## National Rural Employment Guarantee Scheme (NREGS)

The National Rural Employment Guarantee Act aims at enhancing the livelihood security of the people in rural areas by providing guaranteed wage employment through works that develop the livelihood resource base of that area so that in that process of employment generation durable assets are built up. The Act was enacted in September 2005. It was notified in 200 districts of 27 States on February 02, 2006, and was extended to 130 additional districts in 2007-08. All the remaining rural areas have been notified with effect from April 1, 2008.

## Significance of NREGA

The significance of NREGA lies in the fact that it operates at many levels. It creates a social safety net for the vulnerable by providing a fall-back employment source, when other employment alternatives are scarce or inadequate. It adds a dimension of equity to the process of growth. It creates a right-based framework for wage employment programmes, by conferring legal entitlements and the right to demand employment upon the workers and makes the Government accountable for providing employment in a time bound manner. By prioritizing natural resource management, and emphasizing the creation of durable assets it holds the potential of becoming a growth engine for sustainable development of an agriculture based economy. Finally, its operational design built around strong decentralization and lateral accountability to local community offers a new way of doing business and a model of governance reform anchored on the principles of transparency and grass root democracy. In this way, the potential of NREGA spans a range from basic wage security and recharging rural economy to a transformative empowerment process of democracy.

**SALIENT FEATURES OF THE ACT**

### *Right based framework*

- Adult members of a rural household who are willing to do unskilled manual work may apply for registration to the local Gram Panchayat, in writing, or orally..
- The Gram Panchayat after due verification will issue a Job Card. The Job Card will bear the photograph of all adult members of the household and is free of cost.
- A Job Card holding household may submit a written application for employment to the Gram Panchayat, stating the time and duration for which work is sought.

### Time bound guarantee

- The Gram Panchayat will issue a dated receipt of the written application for employment, against which the guarantee of providing employment within 15 days operates. If employment is not provided within 15 days, daily unemployment allowance, in cash has to be paid. Liability of Payment of unemployment allowance is of the Sates.
- Work should ordinarily be provided within 5 km radius of the village or else extra wages of 10% are payable.
- Wages are to be paid according to minimum wages. Disbursement of wages has to be done on weekly basis and not beyond a fortnight.

### Women empowerment

- At least one-third of persons to whom work is allotted work have to be women.

### Work site facilities

- Work site facilities such as creche, drinking water and shade have to be provided.

### Decentralised planning

- The shelf of projects has to be prepared by Gram Sabha. At least 50% of works have to be allotted to Gram Panchayats for execution.
- Panchayat Raj Institutions [PRIs] have a principal role in planning and implementation.

### Labour intensive works

- A 60:40 wage and material ratio has to be maintained. Contractors and use of labour displacing machinery is prohibited.

### Public accountability

- Social Audit has to be done by the Gram Sabha.
- Grievance redressal mechanisms have to be put in place for ensuring a responsive implementation process.

### Transparency

- All accounts and records relating to the Scheme are to be made available to any person desirous of obtaining a copy of such records, on demand and after paying a specified fee.

### Permissible works:

- Water conservation
- Drought proofing (including plantation and afforestation)
- Irrigation canals
- Minor irrigation, horticulture and land development on the land of SC/ST/-BPL/IAY and land reform beneficiaries
- Renovation of traditional water bodies
- Flood protection
- Land development
- Rural connectivity
- Any other work that may be notified by the Central Government in consultation with the State Government.

## Funding

**The Central Government bears the cost on the following items:**

- The entire cost of wages of unskilled manual workers.
- Seventy five percent of the cost of material and wages of skilled and semi-skilled workers.
- Administrative expenses as may be determined by the central government, which will include *inter alia*, the salary and the allowances of the Programme Officer and his supporting staff and work-site facilities.
- Expenses of the National Employment Guarantee Council.

**NREGA Statistics National Overview**
**(FY 2007-08) Upto Mid-January-2008**

1. Employment demanded by households: 2.75 crore
2. Employment provided to households: 2.72 crore
3. Person-days (in crore)

| | | |
|---|---|---|
| * Total | : | 96.03 |
| * SCs | : | 25.90 [26.97%] |
| * STs | : | 29.40 [30.62%] |
| * Women | : | 41.52 [43.23%] |
| * Others | : | 40.73 [42.41%] |

4. Total available fund [including OB]: Rs. 16,059.94 crore.
5. Total Central Release : 10,307.70 crore
6. Total State Release : 1,109.80 crore
7. Expenditure: 9,833.95 crore
8. Total works taken up: 13.11 lakhs
   * Works completed : 4.09 lakhs
   * Works in progress : 9.02 lakhs
9. Works break up:
   * Water conservation and water harvesting 3.63 lakhs [27.69%]
   * Renovation of traditional water bodies: 1.02 lakhs [7.76%]
   * Provision of irrigation facility: 1.86 lakhs [14.16%]
   * Micro irrigation works: 0.58 lakhs [4.42%]
   * Drought proofing: 1.16 lakhs [8.84%]
   * Flood control and protection: 0.31 Lakhs [2.35%]
   * Rural connectivity: 2.22 [16.92%]
   * Land development: 1.89 lakhs [14.42%]

## Out-comes so far

Two years of implementation of NREGA vindicates the self-targeting, demand-based nature of the programme. It is also evident that the nature of employment is seasonal and that the duration of employment sought varies according to the prevailing opportunities of employment offered under local agricultural practices and other alternative forms of employment and all job card holding families do not necessarily request for the full 100 days of employment.

The success of the NREGS depend mainly on the greater and efficient functions of the Panchayats, quality of planning, quality of works, maintenance of authentic muster rolls, transparency in works, strict monitoring, free public access to all information, strict field verification, minimum administrative interference, minimum expenses on administrative expenses, regular training and knowledge network. More importantly, no political and bureaucratic interference in the implementation of the NREG scheme in its present form and content.

*Fig. 7. Generating wage employment under SGRY*

## Deficiencies

According to the Comptroller and Auditor General (CAG), barely 3.2 per cent of the 50 million registered households could set the full 100 days employment under the scheme. The average employment provided was just 18 days. The main deficiency was the lack of adequate administrative and technical manpower at the block and gram panchayat levels. The lack of manpower adversely affected the preparation of plans, scrutiny, approval, monitoring and measurement of works and maintenance of the stipulated records at the block and GP level. Another deficiency is malpractices, which range from inflated measurement to workers not being on rolls to work given to contractors against the rules. In many states technical staff has not been appointed to manage the scheme. In some cases states have not received the money needed from the centre.

## Panchayats have a major role

The NREGS has many features that make it different from other rural employment schemes of the government. Firstly, it is set up under an act of Parliament, the National Rural Employment Guarantee Act (NREGA) 2005. This gives it the status of a law, and it cannot be dismantled, except by Parliament. Its main USP is that under it any family that applies for work will be entitled to a total of 100 days of unskilled agricultural work at specified minimum wages for any of its adult members. Furthermore, every family that wants work will first have to register with the local gram panchayat, which will then issue it a job card, a booklet which is a kind of identity card with photos of all adult members and would also record the work given and the wages earned by the members of that family.

A job card holding family must then apply for employment, and must be given employment within 15 days of the application for a minimum period of 14 days. This would be paid by the Central government. If it is not given the work it has to be paid a daily unemployment allowance to be paid by the state government. The panchayats are to be involved in a major way by seeing to it that at least half the work is given by them and not by government departments like irrigation, PWD, agriculture or forestry. Thus while the scheme is funded by the Centre, the states and the panchayats share in its implementation.

The panchayats are to have a major role in planning and deciding upon the work needed under the NREGA. Each district has to prepare a shelf of permissible projects from water conservation, drought proofing (including plantation and afforestation), irrigation works, renovation of traditional water bodies, land development, flood protection and rural connectivity. Thus a crucial aspect of the NREGA is building up agricultural asset to increase productivity besides providing employment.

## HOW THE FLAGSHIP SCHEMES HAVE DONE

Several well-intentioned programmes are bogged down by poor implementation and widespread corruption.

| *SCHEME* | *STATUS* | *REMARK* |
|---|---|---|
| **National Rural Employment Guarantee Scheme** | Average employment generated last year was just 18 days against the promised 100 days, says a CAG audit report. | NREGS has become platform for corruption. Diversion of funds, fudging of data to show payments for work not done, etc., are rampant. |
| **Jawaharlal Nehru Urban Renewal Mission** | Over 370 projects valued at Rs.31,300 crore have been approved and 51 cities have formally committed themselves to implementing the reform agenda. | Rampant corruption and lack of transparency in allocating funds are hampering this programme |
| **Bharat Nirman** | Approved rural infrastructure projects are running over two years behind schedule. With respect to irrigation and roads, only 20 per cent of targets have been achieved | Systematic problems plague implementation of the programme. Delays are causing massive cost overruns |
| **National Rural Health Mission** | A total amount of 10,223 crore (approximately) has been spent during the first year | There is no administrative control. No attention has been paid to monitoring the quality of medical care given to rural people |

*Infrastructure: Dogged by troubles*

*Education: Expectations not met*

❑ ❑ ❑

## Chapter 12

# SELF-EMPLOYMENT AND ENTREPRENEURSHIP DEVELOPMENT

## Introduction

Economic development of any region is an outcome of purposeful human activity. Men assume various roles in the development process, namely, as organizer of human capital, natural material resources, worker and consumer. He stands at the centre of the whole process of economic development. According to Schumpeter, economic development consists of "employing resources in a different way" in doing a new combination of means of production. The entrepreneur locates ideas and puts them into effect in the process of economic development.

In the rural setting, self-employment and entrepreneurial development has been an important component of rural development. It not only supplements agriculture, the mainstay of the rural economy, but also channelises the rural energy into a creative mould. In particular, this will go a long way in empowering women and the poor alike. Further, it creates employment opportunities, income generation and wealth creation. Thus, it is a unique tool of rural development.

The need of the hour is to channelise the energies in a proper direction. Focus should be placed on organisation, education, imbibing skills, awareness comparing and in stilling self-confidence among the rural people.

## Entrepreneurial Growth

Entrepreneurship growth is slow in India and women's entrepreneurship a still slower and negligible due to the discouraging social factors, such as unfavourable family background, lack of education, dual role of women, lack of aptitudes and training, absence of individualistic spirit, lack of freedom to choose a job according to ability, influence of sex, caste, kinship, custom and family burden etc. All these retarding causes are due to the unfavourable socio-economic conditions and tradition-bound society.

**Box 1**
**THE SECOND-MOST ENTREPRENEURIAL NATION**

It's simple really. Entrepreneurship equals ideas.

The long-suffering British have a joke about Indians. Why don't Indians do well in football, it goes. The punchline: Well, you show them a corner and they put down a shop. Most humour is a reflection of reality and this joke is probably a fallout of the growing number of Indian shopkeepers in England, particularly London. However, Indians in India, the consensus went, weren't cut out to be entrepreneurs. Sociologist Max Weber blamed India's caste system for this, arguing that it restricted each caste to its traditional occupation. Inspired by Weber, social psychologist David McClelland said Indians had religious values that didn't promote achievement motivation, the desire to achieve for its own sake. Weber also offered a corollary that stated that Jains and Parsis made good businessmen because they have certain religious values that were the equivalent of the protestant work ethic. That things have changed since the days of Messrs Weber and McClelland is evident in the Global Entrepreneurship Monitor (GEM) a report published in late 2002 by London Business School. This reckons that nearly 18 per cent of India's workforce is engaged in some form of entrepreneurial activity as compared to 2 per cent in Japan and 10.2 per cent in the US (the global average is 7 per cent). Only Thailand ranks higher. Such entrepreneurial activity is most evident in new industries. Infosys was promoted by N.R. Narayana Murthy (he would have been a priest by Weber's calculations) and five others; Dr. Reddy's laboratories and Apollo Hospitals were both promoted by professionals (doctors, actually); and one of India's largest mobile telephony companies was founded by Sunil Mittal, who started off with a bicycle spare parts business in Ludhiana. Better still, armed with defection capital, a growing number of executives are opting for the risky life of an entrepreneur over their 'safe jobs'. Low achievement motivation, indeed.

The retarding economic factors for entrepreneurship growth are inadequate infrastructural facilities, short-age of capital and technical know-how, transport and communication facilities, absence of cheaper and regular supply of power and raw materials. These constraints are exiting more in rural areas. The environmental factors discouraging entrepreneurship are unstable state governments, lack of security, absence of ideal market conditions and business and corruption in administration.

**Box 2**
**SMALL SCALE UNIT**

By taking charge of my future,
I join hands with India's prosperity.
By starting a small scale unit,
I inspire more people to be entrepreneurs.
By beginning a new venture,
I give jobs to my fellow citizens.
By starting my own little industry,
I improve the business of my suppliers.
By improve the business of my suppliers.
By adding to my local economy,
I add to the wealth of the nation.
By being a partner in India's progress,

## Entrepreneurship Stimulants

A variety of social, economic, political and cultural factors are stimulating entrepreneurial activity and thus generating more robust economic development. These stimulants are as follows:

(1) An increasing focus on capital formation. A availability of capital is a stimulant to an entrepreneur to start a new firm and/or give birth to a new idea.

(2) The ability to transform scientific and technical developments through new institutional development through is a second stimulant.

(3) A third stimulant is the supportive government programmes.

(4) A availability of required training and inputs in the fourth stimulant.

(5) A collaborative relationship between business and research and their direct attempts to transfer technology to the market place may provide stimulus to a number of entrepreneurs who seek the opportunity to commercialised their ideas.

(6) Finally, an endeavour to create an environment conducive to innovation will provide a much-needed stimulant to entrepreneurial activities.

## INTEGRATED RURAL DEVELOPMENT PROGRAMME

Poverty eradication has been one of the major objective of planned development. The strategy and policy of direct attack on poverty by way of target approach for rural poor came into being in the Fourth Five year plan. With the main objective of improving the asset base of the poor and to involve the poor in the production/income generation processes of the economy. Integrated Rural Development Programme (IRDP) was initiated. IRDP was taken up initially in 2300 blocks and has been extended to all the blocks of the country since 2nd October, 1980.

### Programme Implementation

IRDP aims at providing income generating assets and self-employment opportunities for the rural poor. Assistance under IRDP is given to a target group of rural poor belonging to families Below Poverty Line (BPL), in the form of subsidy by the Government and term credit by financial institutions.

### Criteria for Allocation of Funds to the States

Allocation of funds to states is being made by the central government in proportion to the poverty levels in each state on the basis of official estimates of the Planning Commission. These official estimates of poverty are arrived at by the Planning Commission based on the National Sample Survey Organisation. Consumer Expenditure Surveys conducted every five years.

Devolution of funds to districts is based on a formula evolved by the respective state governments. Further devolution to the blocks is done by the governing body of the DRDA based on the criteria approved by it.

### Target Group

The target group consists of families of small and marginal farmers, agricultural labourers and rural artisans etc. Whose per capita monthly expenditure does not exceed the poverty line (ranging been Rs. 216.65 and Rs. 327.48 for different States/UTs) as estimated by the Planning Commission. Currently, the Below Poverty Line census is being carried out in all the states and the revised poverty line will be used to categorise BPL families. Within the target group, special safeguards have been provided by reservation of

- 50% benefits for SCs/STs;
- 40% for women and;
- 3% for physically handicapped persons;
- Priority is also to be given to women headed households, assignees of surplus land, freed bonded labourers and acceptors of small family norm. However, this should not in any way adversely affect the safeguards provided for SCs/STs, women and physically handicapped persons;

- The flow of financial assistance (subsidy + credit) to the categories described above should be commensurate with the percentage of the physical coverage.

## Pattern of Subsidy

Pattern of subsidy is:

- 25% for small farmers;
- $33\frac{1}{3}$% for marginal farmers, agricultural labourers, and rural artisans; and
- 50% for SCs/STs beneficiaries and physically handicapped persons.

The ceiling on subsidy in respect of individuals is:

- Rs. 4,000 in normal areas;
- Rs. 5,000 in DPAP/DDP areas;
- Rs. 6,000 in SC/ST families and physically handicapped persons;
- Rs. 7,500 or 50% of the project cost, whichever is less for unemployed educated youth; and
- For activities involving at least 5 persons, the ceiling has been fixed at Rs. 1.25 lakhs or 50% of the project cost, whichever is less.

## Implementing Agency

District Rural Development Agency/Zilla Parishad is the implementing agency for this programme. The Government Body at the district level provides guidance and directions to DRDAs. It includes local MPs, MLAs, and Chairman of Zilla Parishad, Heads of District Development Departments and representative of SCs/STs, women and NGOs. At the grassroots level, the programme is carried out by Block Development Officer, and the other block staff with the help of the village level functionaries.

## Funding Pattern and Release of Funds

IRDP is financed on a 50:50 cost-sharing by the Centre as well as by the states. The funds are released differently to the DRDAs.

## BPL Census and Selection of Beneficiaries

In order to target assistance to poor families, a BPL census is conducted at the beginning of each plan period by the states, at the behest of Ministry of Rural Areas and Employment. The Gram Sabha is involved in the identification and selection of beneficiaries under IRDP from the initial stage itself. After the survey census is completed, the same is verified in the Gram Sabha and once it is approved, such a list is drawn up. The same is sent to the Panchayat samitis/ blocks and DRDAs for record.

*Fig. 1. An IRDP beneficiary with his cow*

## Identification Thrust Areas and Selection of Projects for Beneficiaries

The project profiles to be taken up for beneficiaries, take into account the beneficiary's needs and includes and the local resource endowment. The investment target for the year, the choice of the BPL family for the activity, forward and backward linkages and infrastructural support, etc, are also taken into account while making a project profile. The activities can be taken up in primary sectors, secondary sectors and tertiary sectors.

**Box 3**

**BENEFITS OF IMPROVED TECHNOLOGY IN THE SMALL-SCALE INDUSTRIAL SECTOR**

Small-scale industries provide almost 40 per cent of india's manufacturing sector output and 35 per cent of total exports. These account for 95 per cent of all industrial units in the country, employ nearly 20 million people, and produce a wide range of some 7,500 goods. The sector is also one of the largest polluters and one that is difficult to monitor. One of the major reasons for the poor environmental and energy use performance of the sector is the continuing use of outdated technological options.

The foundry sector is one of the largest energy-intensive small-scale sectors in India. In recent times the foundry industry has been facing intense market competition and environmental pressures. TERI, with support from the Swiss Agency for Development and Cooperation (SDC), has demonstrated the energy-efficient, divided-blast cupola (DBC) and pollution control system for small-scale foundry units. The techno- logy helped reduce the energy consumption in melting by about 35 per cent and led to improvements in the quality of finished products. The pollution control system helped bring down the particulate and sulphur dioxide emissions of cupola stack gases to below the more stringent emission norm (150 mg/Nm$^3$ for suspended particulate matter and 300 mg/Nm$^3$ for sulphur dioxide) specified by the Central Pollution Control Board.

Encouraged by the success of the technology demonstration, many more foundry units have shown interest and are replicating the technology.

## Credit Target

At the beginning of the year target for credit for RDI at the all-India level as well as the state level are fixed. This is done in consultation with the RBI, NABARD and the participating banks. Credit should normally flow in the ratio 2:1 to subsidy. However, the effort is to see that credit-subsidy ratio exceed 2:1. The ceiling limit for collateral free loans is Rs. 50,000.

## Acquisition of Assets and Cash Disbursement Scheme

The assets procured should be of standard quality at economic prices and to the satisfaction of the beneficiary.

Beneficiaries under IRDP are generally given assets and not the cash. However, sometimes the quality or the price is not to the satisfaction of beneficiaries for the purchase of quality assets and to minimize the leakage in its disbursement if the assistance is given to the beneficiary in cash. Experience has shown that reliance can be placed on the good sense of the beneficiaries in purchasing of assets subject to some safeguards. Disbursement of money in cash to a beneficiary improves his/her bargaining power and has the added advantage of reducing delays and other malpracticed precedent in disbursement in kind. Hence, with effect from the year 1991-92 it was decided to permit disbursement of assistance in cash under the Cash Disbursement Scheme with a view to giving greater choice to beneficiaries in purchasing assets. Initially it was implemented in 50% of the blocks. With effect from the year 1996-97, it is extended to all the blocks of the country.

*Fig. 2. Power Tiller provided to a group under IRDP*

## Release of Subsidy (Back-end Subsidy)

Earlier, simultaneously with the disbursement of loan by the bank, the subsidy amount was debited from the DRDA account and credited to the account of the beneficiaries. Thus is effect, the beneficiary was burdened only with the bank credit portion. This adjustment of subsidy at the beginning itself was termed as front-end subsidy. It was, however found that the beneficiaries were repaying the loan immediately, thereby availing of amount of the subsidy. This in effect meant misuse of subsidy. To make beneficiary utilise the loan for sustainable income generation, the system of front-end subsidy was stopped. The subsidy would be adjusted only in the last few instalments. At the some time a lock-in period for subsidy has also been stipulated and the subsidy would be adjusted only in the last few instalments and it will not be allowed in the event of the repayment made before the stipulated lock-in period. The loan document would be taken by the bank for the full project cost and it would be inter-alia stipulated that in case of misutilisation of the loan, the entire amount of subsidy would be forfeited. Such forfeited amount of subsidy will be available to the bank for adjustment against the borrower's dues.

## Why Credit Plan

A new project of Family Credit Plan (FCP) has been launched in the year 1994-95. It is in operation in 316 selected districts. Under this scheme, more than a single member of the family can be given assistance, subject to the normal subsidy limits for the family. The banks mobilize higher credit for families selected under this scheme. The current levels of investment under FCP have crossed Rs. 26,110 at the all-India level.

*Fig. 3. A beneficiary of IRDP, operating a machine*

## Monitoring and Supervision

IRDP is being monitored from the central level down to grassroots level. At the state level, a State Level Coordination Committee (SLCC) monitors and reviews the implementation of the scheme and lays down policy guidelines. A High Level Coordination Committee on credit support to IRDP also functions at the central level to monitor and review all aspects relating to credit linkage for IRDP. The progress under IRDP is being monitored on a monthly, quarterly, half-yearly and annual basis through reports and returns submitted by DRDAs/States. The shortfall, if any, in the performance under IRDP has been brought from time to the notice of all concerned states/UTs for corrective measures. Over and above, the implementation of the Programme is monitored through the annual Project Directors' Workshop and periodic meetings with the State secretaries. At the Block/DRDA level monitoring is done through field visits and physical verification of assets for which an inspection schedule for the district and block functionaries has been laid down.

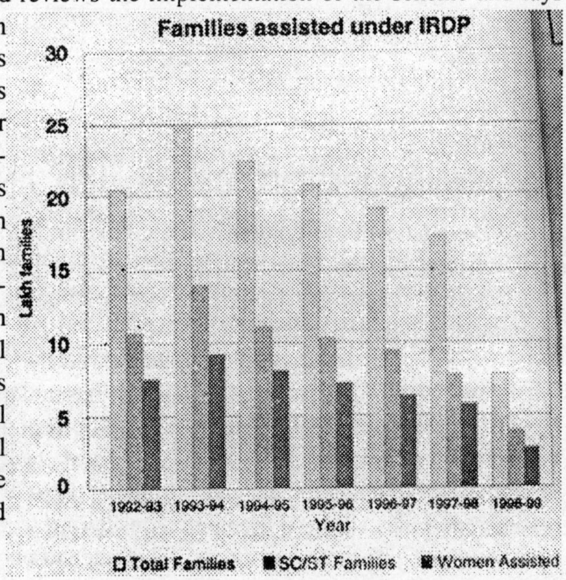

## Risk Fund for Consumption Credit

To meet the small consumption needs of weaker sections of society, a scheme of Risk Fund for Consumption Credit has been in operation as a no-plan scheme since 1977-98. The scheme is intended to enable commercial banks, cooperative banks and regional rural banks to provide consumption loans, not exceeding Rs. 1,000 per borrower to weaker sections of society.

## Insurance Cover for Various Assets

Insurance cover is available for livestock assets given under the programme. The General Insurance Corporation provides this cover on certain terms and conditions.

## Review of Progress (1992-97)

During the Eighth Five Year Plan, more than 108 lakh families have been assisted. There has been a shift of emphasis from mere coverage of families to qualitative aspects of the programme through enhancement of the average level of per family investment. Credit targets have been fixed from 1995-96 onwards. As a result of these interventions, the average level of investment per family which was Rs. 7,889 at the beginning of the Eighth Plan period rose to more than Rs. 14,950 during 1996-97 and further increased to Rs. 17,771 during the current year.

**Table 1**
**PERFORMANCE DURING THE EIGHTH AND NINTH PLAN**

| *Year* | *No. of Families Assisted (No.in lakhs)* | *Subsidy Disbursed (Rs. in crores)* | *Credit Mobilisation (Rs. in crores)* | *Total investment (Credit+Subsidy)* | *Subsidy Credit ratio* | *Per family investment (Rs.)* |
|---|---|---|---|---|---|---|
| **PERFORMANCE DURING THE EIGHTH FIVE YEAR PLAN** | | | | | | |
| 1992-93 | 20.69 | 579.68 | 1036.80 | 1616.48 | 1:1.79 | 7889 |
| 1993-94 | 25.39 | 800.82 | 1408.44 | 2209.26 | 1:1.76 | 8746 |
| 1994-95 | 22.15 | 818.30 | 1450.58 | 2268.88 | 1:1.77 | 10313 |
| 1995-96 | 20.89 | 870.20 | 1701.33 | 2571.53 | 1:1.96 | 12310 |
| 1996-97 | 19.24 | 905.94 | 1969.16 | 2874.10 | 1:2,17 | 14943 |
| **PERFORMANCE DURING THE NINTH FIVE YEAR PLAN** | | | | | | |
| 1997-98* | 17.07 | 863.11 | 1996.64 | 2859.75 | 1:2.31 | 16753 |
| 1998-99** | 7.82 | 407.98 | 980.72 | 1389.69 | 1:2.40 | 17771 |

* Provisional
** Up to Nov. '98

# DEVELOPMENT OF WOMEN AND CHILDREN IN RURAL AREAS

Development of Women And Children In Rural Areas (DWCRA) was launched as a sub-scheme of IRDP during the year 1982-83 in 50 districts. It subsequently expanded to cover all the districts in the country by 1994-95. The flow of benefits to poor women, in spite of reservation, under various poverty alleviation programmes viz. IRDP and TRYSEM were found to be not making much impact. Therefore, in order to overcome this situation and to involve the rural women more intensely in economic activities and matters that concern the rural community. One of the initiatives taken by this Ministry was the introduction of an exclusive programme for women viz. Development of Women and Children in Rural Areas. Since economic empowerment involves provision of additional channels of funds in the form of working capital and crèdit, training, employment, management skill etc. DWCRA with exclusive focus on economic empowerment of women provides all these inputs by considering women as critical to development. This intervention aims at not only raising the incomes of rural women of poor households, but also enabling organized participation of groups of women provides all these inputs by considering women as critical to development. This intervention aims at not only raising the incomes of rural women of poor households, but also enabling organized participation of groups of women in the programmes of credit, skill training and infrastructure support for self employment. Who cannot take up economic activities individually or on their own. DWCRA was introduced for ensuring that the benefits of IRDP programme reach women directly. The programme seeks to improve the access of rural women to health, education, safe drinking water, sanitation, nutrition etc., thereby bringing about an enhancement in the quality of the general well-being of women and children.

## Strategy

The basic unit under DWCRA is a group of 10-15 poor women who have come together to help each other in order to use their collective strength to break social bonds that have denied them income generating and self-fulfilling opportunities. The group size may be smaller in difficult terrain and far-flung areas. One woman amongst the members functions as the group organizer who helps in the choice of activity, procurement of raw material, marketing of products. Before undertaking the activities women are made aware of the objectives and benefits of group information under the scheme; undertaking their potential and recognizing their strength. At the operational level inputs/coaching for such an exercise by the group is given by Gram Sevika for a period of two years, who not only creates a group but also nurtures the group and orients them in availing of benefits of various other programmes/schemes.

*Fig. 4. Cane and Bamboo products units under DWCRA in Mathura village of South Andaman*

## Implementing Agency and Staffing Pattern

DWCRA is being implemented by the District Rural Development Agencies. To facilitate the implementation of scheme, one post of Assistant Project Officer (Woman) has been sanctioned to be part of the DRDA team. One additional post of Gram Sevika has also been sanctioned at the block level to look after the activities of the groups. This is addition to the two Gram Sevika in the normal block pattern.

The Assistant Project Officer (APO), the additional Gram Sevika along with two Gram Sevikas and Mukhya Sevika already available with CD Block form a team to help in the implementation of DWCRA. They conduct preliminary surveys of the area, and establish contacts with the rural women, identifying their constraints and needs. The team is responsible for monitoring and follow up. The APO is to help in establishing contacts with different agencies, in mobilisation of resources and training facilities, also to look after the day to day administration of the scheme within the DRDA. Implementation of DWCRA is the overall responsibility of the entire DRDA team headed by the Project Officer or Project Director.

*Fig. 5.*

## Community Based Convergent Services

The Community Based Convergent Services (CBCS), as a component of DWCRA was started in 1991 in a few districts of the country as a pilot programme. The objective was to create greater awareness among the village communities to enable them to demand social services provided by the state in a better manner and also share responsibilities in the management and implementation of these services, thus, leading to sustainable development. Traditional methods like visuals, role play, folk art, puppetry, dance and drama etc, are some of the means employed for sensitizing the community to the basic needs. The programme seeks to strengthen existing organisation of rural poor women, encourage the level of social and economic status of women. The programmes of ICDS, Rajiv Gandhi National Drinking Water Mission, National Literacy Mission are some of the programmes which are sought to be converged at the grassroots level. 298 districts Community Based Convergent Services (CBCS) with cent per cent Central assistance at Rs. 5.00 lakhs per district.

*Fig. 6. DWCRA groups engaged in income generating activities*

## Child Care Activities

Child Care Activities (CCA) has been incorporated in DWCRA programme during 1995-96 with the following objectives:

- To provide creche services for children of working DWCRA women.
- Setting up of literacy centres of DWCRA women with specific emphasis on girl child dropouts and illiterate members of the DWCRA groups.
- Filling up critical gaps in the areas of immunization, nutrition etc. for the children of DWCRA members with special focus and emphasis on the girl child to reduce gender disparities in the infant girl child care.
- To provide some relief to the physically handicapped children of DWCRA members. To provide immediate relief and pay for legal assistance in case of redressal of physical abuse of the girl child.

Children below 6 years are the target group under Child Care Activities. Each DRDA is to receive Rs. 1.50 lakhs (Rs. 1.00 lakh as Central Share and Rs. 50.000 as State Share) for Child Care Activities.

## Funding Pattern

Each DWCRA group gets Rs. 25,000 as Revolving Fund to meet capital expenditure requirement of economic activities. Expenditure on revolving fund was being shared equally by the Central Government, State Government and UNICEF till 1994-95. UNICEF assistance was not available from 1.1.96. The revolving fund has been increased from Rs. 15,000 to Rs. 25,000 from 1995-96. Presently, the expenditure for revolving fund is being shared by the centre and state on 50:50 basis.

## Marketing of Products

Since the focal point of the scheme is income generating activities for women, it is necessary that their activities must be economically viable. Marketing of products of the women's group is, therefore, very important. The interest of women in the programme can be sustained only when a proper market outlet is available for their products. Some State Government like Haryana, Andhra Pradesh have issued orders declaring the DWCRA groups as approved sources for the supply of bulk articles required by the Government Departments. The Gram Stree Melas organised by CAPART are also used as outlets for the sale of DWCRA products. Setting up of supportive institutions for marketing like District Supply and Marketing Societies (DSMS) are being encouraged by the states. These district level agencies must be multi-faceted and also support non-credit inputs like purchase of raw materials and sale of goods where sectoral linkages cannot be established. Recently, efforts are also on at state level to create market for the products manufactured under DWCRA/Integrated Rural Development Programme. The state of Kerala and Orissa have created state level organisations like KERAMS and ORAMS. The State of Andhra Pradesh is encouraging organisation and melas. A DWCRA mela was organised, with the state government support at Hyderabad which has reported very good response. The State of Haryana encourages DWCRA groups for supply of nutrition providers for ICDS programme. The momentum has to be sustained if the money invested through DWCRA groups has to receive significant returns. A wide range of DWCRA products need improvement in designing and packaging. Such improvements need to be carried out by involving professional bodies. The supply of raw material and its quality, quality control of finished products is an area of concern.

## Coverage

Initially no specific coverage of vulnerable groups such as SC/STs was fixed. However, during the year 1997-98, it has been made compulsory that 50% of the groups have to be women belonging to SC/ST. Priority has to be given to physically handicapped persons and also girls and women rehabilitated from prostitution. The coverage achieved during each plan period is shown in Table 2:

**Table 2**

| *Plan* | *Target No. of Groups* | *No. of Groups formed* | *No. of Women benefitted* |
|---|---|---|---|
| Sixth Plan | 6,035 | 3,308 | 52,170 |
| Seventh Plan | 35,000 | 28,031 | 4,69,707 |
| Annual Plan 1990-91 | 7,500 | 7,139 | 1,09,557 |
| Annual Plan 1991-92 | 7,500 | 9,378 | 2,08,012 |
| Eighth Plan | 91,900 | 1,41,514 | 22,68,327 |
| Ninth Plan | 91,850 | 56,093 | 6,95,803 |

**PHYSICAL AND FINANCIAL ACHIEVEMENT UNDER DSCRA SINCE INCEPTION** *(Rs. in lakhs)*

| *Plan* | *Target (No. of Groups)* | *Achievement (No. of Groups)* | *Women Benefitted* | *Central Assistance Released* |
|---|---|---|---|---|
| Sixth Plan | 6036 | 3308 | 52170 | 298.53 |
| Seventh Plan 1985-86 | 5000 | 6008 | 101056 | 630.70 |
| 1986-87 | 7500 | 5545 | 96132 | 786.33 |
| 1987-88 | 7500 | 5968 | 98636 | 738.21 |
| 1988-89 | 7500 | 5551 | 90294 | 901.00 |
| 1989-90 | ** | ** | ** | ** |
| Total | 35000 | 28031 | 469707 | 3663.53 |
| Annual Plan 1991-91 | 7500 | 7139 | 109557 | 898.00 |
| Annual Plan 1991-92 | 7500 | 9378 | 208012 | 962.72 |

| | | | | |
|---|---|---|---|---|
| Eighth Plan | | | | |
| 1992-93 | 7500 | 9029 | 128744 | 1548.17 |
| 1993-94 | 11000 | 15483 | 268525 | 2365.00 |
| 1994-95 | 13400 | 37964 | 592026 | 3100.00 |
| 1995-96 | 30000 | 37576 | 697088 | 6365.00 |
| 1996-97 | 30000 | 41462 | 581944 | 5696.00 |
| Total | 91900 | 141514 | 2268327 | 19074.17 |
| Ninth Plan | | | | |
| 1997-98 | 30000 | 36436 | 460409 | 4145.43 |
| 1998-99 | 61850 (*) | 19657 (*) | 235394 (*) | 8354.68 |
| Total | 91850 | 56093 | 695803 | 8354.68 |
| G. Total | 239785 | 245463 | 3803576 | 33251.632 |

(*) – Position as on 21.1.99.

## TRAINING OF RURAL YOUTH FOR SELF-EMPLOYMENT

Started as a centrally sponsored scheme on 15th August, 1979. Training of Rural Youth for Self-Employment (TRYSEM) aims at providing basic technical and entrepreneurial skills to the rural youth from families below the poverty line to enable them to take up self-employment in the board fields of agriculture and allied sectors, industries, services and business activities. This objective was subsequently enlarged in the year 1983 to include taking up of wage employment also to the trained youth. TRYSEM plays an important role in facilitating diversification of activities taken up under IRDP. Diversification away from the primary sector to secondary and tertiary sectors requires acquisition or upgradation of skills relevant to industries and business enterprises. TRYSEM seeks to impart new skills, and upgrade existing skills of beneficiaries who are by and large attuned only to stagnant levels of agricultural or artisan skills.

### Salient Features

The rural youth in the age group of 18-35 years from families below poverty line are enlisted for training under the scheme. The minimum age for providing training under TRYSEM is relaxed to 16 years for inmates of orphanages in rural areas. The upper age limit of 35 years is relaxed to 45 years in case of widows, freed bonded labourers, freed convicts, persons displaced due to large development projects and cured leprosy patients. There is no age limit for rural artisans. A minimum of 50% of selected youths should belong to the scheduled caste and scheduled tribe communities, 40% should be women and 3% of the trainees should be physically handicapped persons.

The duration of training courses is normally six months. However, the State Level Co-ordination Committee (SLCC) can change the duration and prescribe duration for new trades. There are no educational qualifications prescribed for selection of trainees.

The TRYSEM trainees are paid a stipend varying from Rs. 200 to Rs. 500 per month during the training. To enable the participants to take up employment there is a provision of Rs. 800 as an allowance for purchase of toolkits by the trainees.

### Pattern of Assistance

*(a) Recurring Expenses:* The share of the Centre and States is on 50:50 basis. In case of UTs the funding is 100% by the Centre. The assistance is released to the DRDAs in two instalments.

*(b) Non-Recurring Expenses for TRYSEM Training Infrastructure:* The assistance to the State Governments on 50:50 basis and the central share is limited to Rs. 20 lakhs per exclusive TRYSEM Training Centre (ETTC) or 50% of the total cost of the centre whichever is less. The funds are released directly to the state governments.

## Performance During the Eighth Five Year Plan

During the Eighth Plan period (1992-93 to 1996-97) total releases by the Centre and State Governments were Rs. 353.94 crores out of which Rs. 365.80 crores have been utilised which is 103.35%. During the same period against the target of 16.12 lakhs rural youth, 15.17 lakhs youth have been trained which is 94.10%. Details are given below:

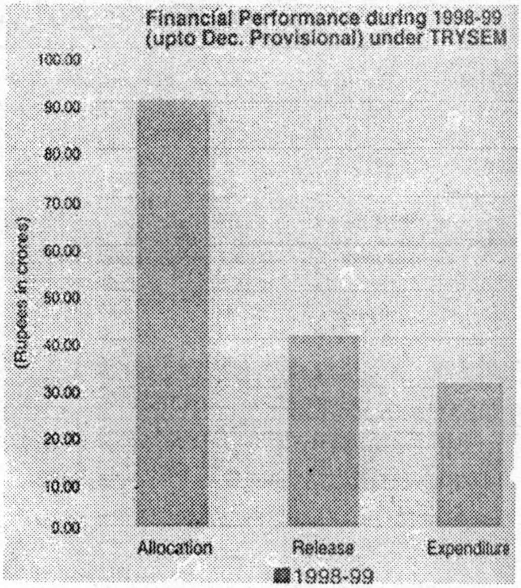


**Table 3**

*[Rs. in crores] (No. in lakhs)*

| *Year* | *Allocation* | *Release* | *Expenditure* | *Target* | *No. of youths trained* |
|---|---|---|---|---|---|
| 1992-93 | 39.87 | 47.04 | 47.50 | 3.00 | 2.76 |
| 1993-94 | 111.24 | 89.45 | 55.02 | 3.50 | 3.04 |
| 1994-95 | 89.16 | 74.03 | 68.46 | 3.18 | 2.82 |
| 1995-96 | 90.25 | 73.31 | 94.55 | 3.54 | 2.91 |
| 1996-97 | 90.25 | 70.11 | 100.27 | 2.90 | 3.64 |
| Total | 420.77 | 353.94 | 365.80 | 16.12 | 15.17 |
| **PERFORMANCE DURING NINTH FIVE YEAR PLAN** | | | | | |
| 1997-98 | 90.00 | 68.08 | 80.74 | 3.04 | 2.51 |
| 1998-99* | 89.76 | 40.61 | 30.86 | 2.92 | 0.66 |

Up to November 1998.

**Table 4**

**PHYSICAL PERFORMANCE UNDER TRYSEM**
**(Number of Trained Youth Employed)**

| *Year* | *No. of youth to be trained* | *No.of youth trained* | *Self employed* | *Wage employed* | *Total* |
|---|---|---|---|---|---|
| 1992-93 | 300000 | 275993 | 99334 | 42058 | 141392 |
| 1993-94 | 350000 | 303821 | 107919 | 43004 | 150923 |
| 1994-95 | 318436 | 281874 | 86466 | 44965 | 131431 |
| 1995-96 | 353980 | 291450 | 92665 | 48450 | 141115 |
| 1996-97 | 290079 | 364377 | 130812 | 51725 | 182537 |
| 1997-98 | 304129 | 251387 | 73358 | 39384 | 112742 |
| 1998-99 | 292485 | 66016 | 12988 | 11175 | 31535 |

**NUMBER OF SC/ST AND WOMEN AMONG TRAINED YOUTH**

| Period | SC/ST | Women |
|---|---|---|
| 1992-93 | 116464 | 134929 |
| 1993-94 | 145298 | 153981 |
| 1994-95 | 126978 | 137822 |
| 1995-96 | 133930 | 124462 |
| 1996-97 | 173502 | 195522 |
| 1997-98 | 118379 | 132841 |
| 1998-99 | 40073 | 46390 |

* Up to November, '98.

*Computer Training imparted under TRYSEM – Rajbagh,*

**Table 5**

**DEPARTMENT OF RURAL DEVELOPMENT APPROVED OUTLAYS IN RESPECT OF PLAN**

*(Rs. in crores)*

| Name of the Schemes | Approval outlays | | |
|---|---|---|---|
| | 1997-1998 | 1998-99 | 1999-2000 |
| Rural Water Supply Programme | 1302.00 | 1627.00 | 1800.00 |
| Rural Sanitation | 100.00 | 100.00 | 110.00 |
| Strengthening of State Training Centre | 3.25 | 3.25 | 3.25 |
| Assistance to CAPART | 12.00 | 12.00 | 13.00 |
| Org. of Training Courses Seminars | 0.50 | 0.50 | 1.25 |
| Strengthening of Ext. Training Centre | 3.00 | 3.00 | 3.00 |
| Assistance to Assignees of Selling Surplus Land | 0.01 | 0.01 | 0.00 |
| Grants-in-aid to Institute for Agrarian Studies | 0.68 | 0.68 | 0.00 |
| Computerisation of Land Records | 20.00 | 30.00 | 33.00 |
| Strengthening of Revenue Machinery & Updating of L.R. | 18.80 | 8.00 | 10.00 |
| Committee on Land Reforms | 0.01 | 0.01 | 0.00 |
| Communication Cell | 4.00 | 4.00 | 10.00 |
| Promotion of Voluntary Schemes | 10.00 | 20.00 | 26.00 |
| Organisation of Beneficiaries | 3.50 | 3.50 | 4.00 |
| Panchayat Development and Training | 3.00 | 3.00 | 3.00 |
| Roads in Special Problem Areas | 2.00 | 1.50 | 0.50 |
| NSAP | 700.00 | 700.00 | 725.00 |
| Agricultural Marketing | 7.25 | 7.25 | 0.00 |
| Monitoring Mechanism | 0.00 | 0.50 | 2.00 |
| Total | 2195.00 | 2530.00 | 2750.00 |

**Table 6**
**FINANCIAL SUPPORT UNDER TRYSEM**

*(Rs. in lakhs)*

| *Period* | *Recurring Expenses* | *Infrastructure* |
|---|---|---|
| 1992-93 | 4703.96 | 600.00 |
| 1993-94 | 8944.67 | 795.55 |
| 1994-95 | 7403.25 | 899.42 |
| 1995-96 | 7331.26 | 2591.68 |
| 1996-97 | 7071.25 | 1628.78 |
| 1997-98 | 6807.55 | 893.01 |
| 1998-99 | 4061.34 | 893.01 |

* Up to December, 98

## Steps for Strengthening the Scheme of TRYSEM

1. The stipend rates, honorarium and other allowances etc. under the TRYSEM recurring expenses have been enhanced appreciably from 1st June 1994 with a view to make the training more effective and meaningful.
2. States and Union Territories have been asked to set up a sub-committee under SLCC exclusively for TRYSEM. A district level committee exclusively for TRYSEM already exists.
3. The State/Union Territories have been advised to explore the possibilities of setting up of production groups from amongst TRYSEM production groups from amongst TRYSEM trainees for undertaking the ancillary activities like manufacture and assembly of modern items of production.

*Fig. 7. Mat Weaving training under TRYSEM: Lakkireddipalle, A.P.*

4. A scheme regarding setting up of Exclusive TRYSEM Training Centres in each block, where no organised training facility exists, to strengthen training infrastructure under TRYSEM for imparting training to the rural youth in different traditional trades has been introduced.

## Linkage with IRDP

The linkage forged between TRYSEM and IRDP has so far been weak. The fourth round of IRDP concurrent evaluation revealed that only 3.88% of IRDP beneficiaries received training under TRYSEM. The findings of the 'Quick Evaluation of TRYSEM' (June-August 1993) also indicate that of the total number of beneficiaries who got training under TRYSEM, roughly 53.57% trained youth did not apply for assistance under IRDP and of the remaining youth only about 50% were given assistance under IRDP. To ensure proper linkage of TYRSEM with IRDP it has been made incumbent on the DRDAs, the block authorities and the training institutions to complete all the required formalities for sanction of IRDP loans to TRYSEM trainees. During the training period itself, the loan application forms will be sent to the banks so that the bankers in turn can interact with the trainees. This will significantly reduce the chances of such sponsored applications being rejected later and generate interest in the trainee to take up self-employment.

## SUPPLY OF IMPROVED TOOLKITS TO RURAL ARTISANS

The scheme was launched as a sub-scheme of IRDP in July, 1992, with the objective to enabling the rural artisans Below Poverty Line to enhance the quality of their products, increase their production and income and ensure a better quality of life with the use of migration to urban areas.

### Salient Features

Artisans from a variety of crafts, except weaving, tailoring, needle-workers and beedi-workers are to be supplied with suitable improved hand tools or a set of tools. The average cost of a toolkit is Rs. 2,000 and in case of power driven tools the average cost is Rs. 4,500. 90% of the cost of the toolkit is a subsidy from the Government of India and 10% is to be contributed by the beneficiary and there is no State share. The unit cost is to be fixed by the District Rural Development Agency (DRDA) concerned. DRDA is the implementing agency.

Prototypes of improved tools in pottery, carpentry, blacksmith, leather work, woodcraft, metal craft and lacquerware have been developed by the National Small Industries Corporation, Regional Design and Technical Development centres under Development Commissioner (Handicrafts) and similar other organisations. The State Government have been authorized to choose methods/tools, which suit the needs of their artisans.

### Target Group

There is 50% reservation for SC and ST communities. Wherever SC/ST persons are not available, the DRDA governing body can decide to allocate the percentage meant for SC/ST to other categories of artisans. There is no provision of reservation for women and physically handicapped persons. However, if eligible, preference will be given to such person over other person.

### Performance During Eighth Five Year Plan

During the Eighth Five Year Plan (1992-93 to 1996-97) a sum of Rs. 149.07 crores was released out of which Rs. 120.08 crores has been utilised which works out to be 80.55%. Against the target of covering 8.32 lakh beneficiaries, 6.52 lakh beneficiaries have been covered which works out to be 78.36%. Details are given in Table 7:

**Table 7** *(Rs. in crores) (No. in lakhs)*

| *Year* | *Allocation* | *Release* | *Expenditure* | *Target* | *No. of toolkits distributed* |
|---|---|---|---|---|---|
| 1992-93 | 16.85 | 16.85 | 13.86 | 0.98 | 0.83 |
| 1993-94 | 23.22 | 23.22 | 18.60 | 1.29 | 1.09 |
| 1994-95 | 29.00 | 29.00 | 22.91 | 1.61 | 1.25 |
| 1995-96 | 40.00 | 40.00 | 28.69 | 2.22 | 1.54 |
| 1996-97 | 40.00 | 40.00 | 36.02 | 2.22 | 1.81 |
| Total | **149.47** | **149.07** | **120.08** | **8.32** | **6.52** |
| **Ninth Plan** | | | | | |
| 1997-98 | 35.00 | 30.82 | 34.37 | 1.94 | 1.62 |
| | 59.00 | 26.87 | [illegible] | 3.27 | 1.32 |

Up to November, '98

## Areas Identified for Further Improvement

Based on the feedback gathered and with a view to further improving the implementation of the scheme and its efficacy, the following areas would receive attention in the Ninth Plan:

- The source of supply of toolkits would be wholly guided by the quality and cost parameters, the reputation and expertise of manufacturers, timely delivery and pre-delivery extension and post-delivery service facilities offered and suitability of the toolkits to the need of specific artisan groups.
- White it may be true that a majority of the rural artisans would be illiterate and therefore, cannot have access to documented literature, the need for such literature with plenty of graphics and illustrations cannot be discounted altogether. Efforts should therefore be made to prepare such literature and supply a copy to the artisans covered.
- Marketing linkages need to be established for more effective use of improved toolkits so that higher productivity and enhanced production can be absorbed leading to higher earnings for artisans. state government have been advised to make institutional arrangements for establishing such linkages.
- The State Government have been requested to interact with the Department of Science and Technology, NSIC and IITs for the development of appropriate technology and designs for improved toolkits for various artisan groups.
- The Scheme would henceforth place due emphasis on the choice of the artisans. The designing and manufacture of tools should at least emerge from a wider level of consultations with groups of artisans. The process of consultation should be continued even after the supply of tools have been effected to find out whether these have fulfilled the objectives of the scheme and the needs of the artisans.
- There are pockets of rural technology, which have survived the onslaught of modern technological innovations by virtue of the sturdiness; and locale specific utility. These need to be identified and replicated elsewhere.
- The scheme's objective also needs to include upgradation of skills through technological innovations resulting in additional income generation. The scheme would aim at capturing markets beyond the nearest rural areas wherever feasible.
- Research and Development must be given due emphasis. States have been advised to take the initiative in developing toolkits at least in the case of one artisan trade to start with. Similar initiatives will have to be taken by the Small Industries Services Institutes.
- State Government have been advised to sponsor evaluation of the scheme though institutions having an expertise in the field, experience of extension work and involvement in the field of technological and marketing promotion.
- For dissemination of technology. States have been advised to organise exhibitions in several locations on important occasions.

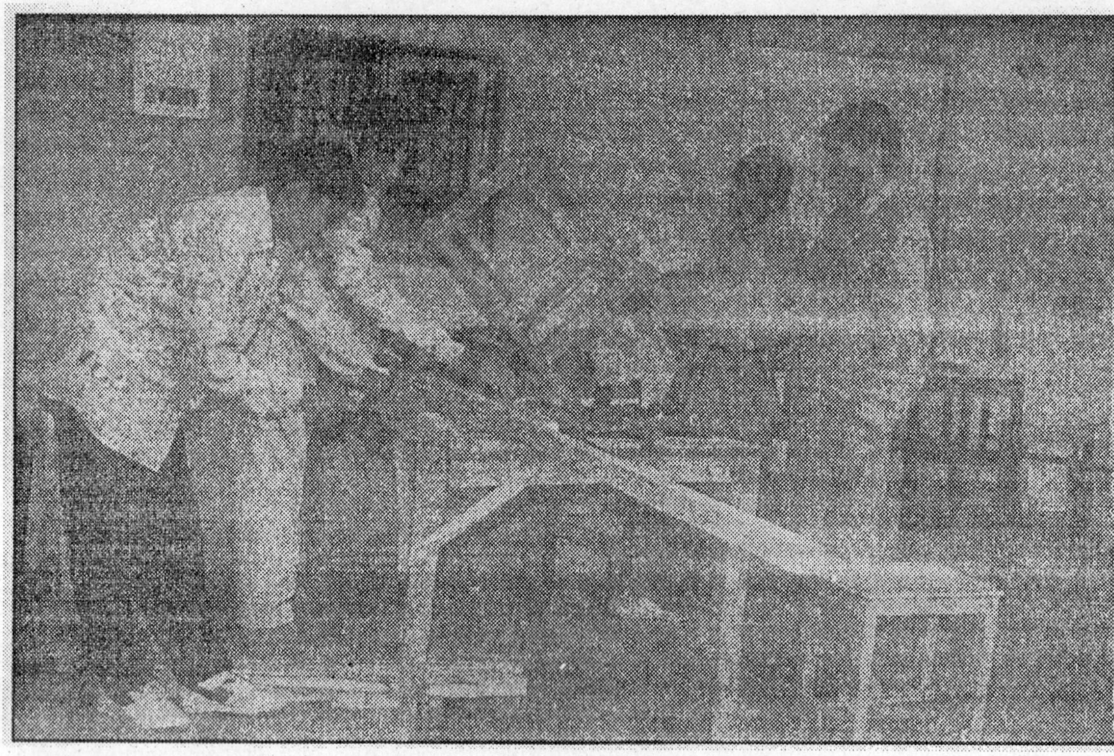

*Fig. 8. Deft hands at work: Improved toolkits to rural artisans*

## GANGA KALYAN YOJANA

Ganga Kalyan Yojana (GKY) was launched as a sub-scheme of Integrated Rural Development Programme (IRDP) during 1996-97 with effect from 1.2.1997 and is being continued as an independent scheme with effect from 1.4.1997.

### Objective

The objective of the scheme is to provide irrigation through exploitation of groundwater (borewells and tubewells) to individuals and groups of beneficiaries of small and marginal farmers belonging to the below poverty line.

### Programme Strategy

The individual/groups are assisted through subsidy by Government and term credit by financial institutions including SC/ST/BC Finance and Development Corporation.

### Target Group

The beneficiaries under the scheme are small and marginal farmers living below the poverty line. Other than those who have already been assisted under any minor irrigation programme of State or Central Government.

### Safeguards for SCs and STs

At least 50% of the funds have been earmarked for SCs and STs.

## Funding Pattern

The funding pattern is 80:20 *i.e.* 80% by Central Government and 20% by the State Government.

## Allocation of Funds to the States

The funds are allocated to the States according to the criteria fixed for IRDP allocation. The States are required to make district wise allocation taking into consideration the potential for exploitation of ground-water resources, economic viability of exploiting such potential and other relevant considerations.

## Subsidy

75% subsidy is allowed for SCs/STs and physically disabled groups and 50% for others. The monetary ceiling of subsidy per group (5 to 15 members) is Rs. 40,000 and for individual beneficiaries the subsidy is Rs. 5,000 per acre of land under the scheme subject to a ceiling of Rs. 12,500 per beneficiary. 5% of the project cost per annum is permissible as additional subsidy for SC/ST/physically disabled groups as part of operation and maintenance cost for 3 years. For other groups and individual schemes, no subsidy on operation and maintenance is admissible.

## Implementing Agency

The scheme is being implemented by the DRDAs/Zilla Parishads.

# SWARNJAYANTI GRAM SWAROZGAR YOJANA (SGSY)

The Swarnjayanti Gram Swarozgar Yojana (SGSY) has been launched with effect from 1.4.1999 as a new Self-employment Programme. With the coming into effect of the SGSY, the earlier programmes of Integrated Rural Development Programme (IRDP), Training of Rural Youth for Self-Employment (TRY-SEM), Development of Women and Children in Rural Areas (DWCRA), Supply of Toolkits in Rural Areas (SITRA), the Ganga Kalyan Yojana (GKY) as well as the Million Wells Scheme (MWS) are no longer in operation.

**Box 4**

- Swarnjayanti Gram Swarojgar Yojana (SGSY) – a holistic programme for promoting self employment of rural poor.
- Covers all aspects of self employment of rural poor-organisation of rural poor into Self Help Groups (SHGs), capacity building of the Group through financial assistance, training, selection of key activities, infrastructure build up, technology and marketing support.
- Swaranjayanti Gram Swarojgar Yojana (SGSY) – a holistic programme for promoting self employment of rural poor.
- Self Help Groups (SHGs) to be a national movement – 11.47 lakh Self Help Groups already formed.
- Involvement of NGOs/CBOs/Animators for social mobilisation, training and capacity building of Self Help Groups.
- 15% of the central allocation earmarked for sanction of projects for development of infrastructure and activity cluster.

## Objective

The objective of the SGSY is to bring the assisted poor families (Swarozgaris) above the poverty line by providing them income-generating assets through a mix of bank credit and governmental subsidy. The programme aims at establishing a large number of micro enterprises in rural areas based on the ability of the poor and potential of each area.

## Salient Features

The salient features of the Swarnjayanti Gram Swarozgar Yojana (SGSY) are given below:

- The Swarnjayanti Gram Swarozgar Yojana aims at establishing a large number of micro-enterprises in the rural areas, building upon the potential of the rural poor.
- The SGSY emphasises on the cluster approach for establishing the micro-enterprises. For this, 4-5 Key Activities have to be identified in each block. The major share of the SGSY assistance has to be in activity clusters. The SGSY adopts a project approach for each key activity. Project Reports are to be prepared in respect of each of the identified Key Activities. The banks and other financial institutions have to be closely associated and involved in preparing these Project Reports, so as to avoid delays in sanctioning of loans and to ensure adequacy of financing.
- The existing infrastructure for the cluster of activities should be reviewed and gaps identified. Critical gaps in investments have to be made up under the SGSY, subject to a ceiling of 20% (25% in the case of North Eastern States) of the total allocation made under the SGSY for each District. This amount is maintained by the DRDAs as 'SGSY – Infrastructure Fund'.
- In the planning of the Key Activities, care has to be taken to ensure that the maximum numbers of Panchayats are covered without jeopardising the quality of the Programme.
- The assisted families may be individuals or groups (Self-Help Groups). The SGSY, however, favours the group approach.
- The Gram Sabha authenticates the list of Below the Poverty Line families identified in the BPL Census. Identification of individual families suitable for each Key Activity is to be made through a participatory process.
- The group approach involves organisation of the poor into Self-Help Groups (SHGs) and their capacity building. Efforts have to be made to involve women members in each SHG. Besides, exclusive women groups are also to be formed. At the level of the block, at least half of the groups should be exclusively women groups. Group activities are given preference and progressively, majority of the funding should be for Self-Help Groups.
- The SGSY is a credit-cum-subsidy programme. However, credit is the critical component of the SGSY, subsidy being a minor and enabling element. Accordingly, the SGSY envisages greater involvement of the banks. They are to be involved closely in the planning and preparation of Project Reports, identification of activity clusters, infrastructure planning as well as capacity building and choice of activity of the SHGs, selection of individual Swarozgaris, pre-credit activities and post-credit monitoring including loan recovery.
- The SGSY seeks to promote multiple credit rather than a one-time credit 'injection'. The credit requirements of the Swarozgaris need to be carefully assessed; the Swarozgaris are allowed and, in fact, encouraged to increase credit intake, over the years.
- The SGSY seeks to lay emphasis on skill development through well-designed training courses. Those, who have been sanctioned loans, are to be assessed and given necessary training. The design, duration of training and the training curriculum is tailored to meet the needs of the identified Key Activities. DRDAs are allowed to set apart up to 10% of the SGSY allocation on training. This may be maintained as 'SGSY – Training Fund'.

- The SGSY attempts to ensure upgradation of technology in the identified activity clusters. The technology intervention seek to add value to the local resources including processing of the locally available material from natural and other resources for local and non-local market.
- The SGSY provides for promotion of marketing of the goods produced by the SGSY Swarozgaris, which involves provision of market intelligence, development of markets and constancy services, as well as institutional arrangements for marketing of the goods including exports.
- The SGSY is implemented by the DRDAs through the Panchayat Samitis. The process of planning, implementation and monitoring integrate the Banks and other financial institutions, the Panchayati Raj Institutions (PRIs), Non-Government Organisations (NGOs), as well as Technical Institutions in the District.
- 15% of the funds under the SGSY are set apart at the national level to try new initiatives for self-employment of the rural poor through "Special Projects", in conjunction with other Departments or Semi-Government/International Organisations, which includes initiatives to be taken in individual districts or across the districts.

## Strategy

The SGSY is different from earlier programmes, in terms of the strategy envisaged for its implementation, and has been conceived as a holistic programme of self-employment covering all aspects of self-employment, *viz.*, organisation of the rural poor in to self-help groups and their capacity building, training, planning of activity clusters, infrastructure build-up and technology and marketing support.

## Activity Clusters — Planning and Selection

There are two key aspects of the SGSY, namely, Activity Clusters and the Group Approach. Each block has to concentrate on 4-5 key activities based on local resources, occupational skills of the people and availability of markets so that the Swarozgaris can draw sustainable incomes from their investments. Selection of these activities has to be done with the approval of the Panchayat Samitis at the block level and District Rural Development Agency/Zilla Parishad at the district level. These key activities should preferably be taken up in clusters so that the backward and forward linkages can be effectively established.

The SGSY also focuses on organisation of the poor at grassroots level through a process of social mobilisation for poverty eradication. Social mobilisation enables the poor to build their own organisations Self-Help Groups (SHGs) in which, they participate fully and directly and take decisions on all issues that will help them in enhancing their income to come above the poverty line. A SHG may consist of 10-20 persons belonging to families below the Poverty Line and a person should not be a member of more than one group. In the case of minor irrigation schemes and in the case of disabled persons, this number may be a minimum of five (5).

*Fig. 9. Saras fair at Dilli Haat-Promoting marketing of products of rural artisans*

## Project Approach

The SGSY adopts a Project approach for each Key Activity. Project Reports are to be prepared in respect of each identified Key Activity. The Banks and other financial institutions have to be closely associated and involved in preparing these Project Reports, so as to avoid delay in sanctioning of loans and to ensure adequacy of financing. Project report should include all aspects like level of investment required at Swarozgaris level, economies of group lending, return from the activity, repayment schedule, technical input required by Swarozaris, training requirement and mode of training, credit, infrastructure and marketing requirement and identification of resources to develop them, net accruable income from activity.

## Target Group

Below the Poverty Line families in rural areas constitute the target group of the SGSY. Within the target group, special safeguards have been provided to vulnerable sections, by way of reserving 50% benefits for SCs/STs, 40% for women and 3% for disabled persons.

**SUCCESS STORY**

**Dry Flowers Blossom Their Lives : Dindigul (Tamil Nadu)**

45 women from BPL families organised themselves into 3 Self-Help Groups (SHGs) namely; Annai Indira Women Self-Help Group, Vilpatti Annai Teresa Women SHG, Attuvampatty and Johnsi Rani Women Self-Help Group, Vilpatti, in the Dindigul district of Tamilnadu. The members of the groups were trained to take up thrift and credit activities. The members were trained in leadership, group process, accounting and financial management through training and capacity building input by an NGO engaged as facilitator under the SGSY. The M.G. Art Gallery Kodai Kanal came forward to give training to the groups in "Dry Flower" arrangements an innovative and new activity in the area. Each group was sanctioned Rs. 2.25 lakhs under the SGSY. In November, 2000 as a cluster approach three SHGs under one roof have started this economic activity. These three SHGs have formed a federation and named their federation as "Biriza". The monthly sales within six months of commencement of the activity was Rs. 70,000/- which fetches the members an average net income per month of Rs. 1,500/-. This helped them to increase their average family income from the earlier level of Rs. 7,000/- to Rs. 18,000/- per annum. Before taking up this activity, the members of the SHGs were agricultural labourers and doing hard work in the fields. From the first month itself, the family income of the SHGs have gone up. Every week, each member gets about Rs. 600/-. Thus, it not only helped the members to improve their economic status and standard of living but gave a big boost to their self confidence towards achieving self-reliance. These SHG members are also actively participating in social work. They have fought against illicit arrack and male chauvinism. Liberty, equality and fraternity are their guiding force. Sizeable amount to the extent of about Rs. 11.00 lakhs has been raised by the community as the community funds, matched by the contribution from the NGO which would be very useful in institution building and sustaining the activities in the area.

**Financial Assistance**

Assistance under the SGSY to individual Swarozgaris or Self Help Groups, is given in the form of subsidy by the Government and credit by the Banks. Subsidy under the SGSY to individuals is uniform at 30% of the Project Cost subject to a maximum of Rs. 7,500. In respect of SCs/STs, the subsidy is 50% of the Project Cost, subject to a maximum of Rs. 10,000. For groups of Swarozgaris, the subsidy is 50% of the cost of the Scheme, subject to a ceiling of Rs. 1.25 lakh. There is no monetary limit on subsidy for Irrigation Projects; subsidy is back ended.

## Funding Pattern

The Swarnjayanti Gram Swarozgar Yojana (SGSY) is financed on 75:25 cost sharing basis between the Centre and the States.

## Performance of scheme since inception (up to December, 2007)

| | | | |
|---|---|---|---|
| (i) | No. of SHGs formed | : | 27,41,081 |
| (ii) | No. of Swarozgaris assisted | : | Total : 93,32,572 |
| | (a) SHGs Swarojgaris | : | 58,12,645 |
| | (b) Individual Swarojgaris | | 35,19,927 |
| (iii) | Subsidy disbursed | : | Rs. 6,612.02 crores |
| (iv) | Credit disbursed | : | 13,538 crores |
| (v) | Per Capital Investment (Av./Per year) | : | Rs. 21,832/- |

## Problems with Banks

- The major complaints of the swarozgaris were non co-operation from the banks, delay in bank procedures and delay in disbursement of loans.
- 52% of the swarozgaris reported that the loan amount was provided in a single dose.
- Delay in sanctioning of loans, non-co-operation of the banks, lack of proper guidance have been creating problems in the smooth development of group activities.
- Credit portion of the Revolving Fund was found to have been postponed in certain cases.
- Lack of co-ordination between banks and block officials was also noted.
- No effective follow up was being made after sanctioning loans to the Swarozgaris.

## Training, Skill Development, Product Design and Product Development

SGSY is a process-oriented scheme which involves organization of rural poor into Self Help Groups (SHGs), their training and capacity building to enable them to evolve into a self managed organization. Here the role of facilitators/Self Help Promoting Institutions (SHPIs), field level functionaries of banks and development functionaries is critical in successful implementation of the scheme. It is beyond doubt that wherever functionaries have been trained in the concept of functioning of SHGs, group dynamics, guidelines of the scheme, marketing and entrepreneurship development etc., the quality of groups as well as overall implementation of the programme has been qualitatively better. It has also been observed that large number of development functionaries do not have access to well organized training programmes. Keeping this in view, the Ministry has earmarked a separate budget in the current financial year for organizing training programmes for Training of Trainers (TOTs), Facilitators/SHPIs, Bank Officials and Development functionaries at various levels.

The SGSY seeks to lay emphasis on skill development through well-designed training courses. Those, who have been sanctioned loans, are to be assessed and given necessary training. The design, duration of training and the training curriculum is tailored to meet the needs of the identified Key Activities. The DRDAs will be entitled to meet the expenses, incurred by the training institutions for both Basic Orientation and Skill Development Training from out of the SGSY funds. However, the total expenditure on Basic Orientation and Skill Development Training will not exceed Rs.5,000/- per trainee. Duration of Skill Development will be decided by the State Government depending upon the activities and skill level of Swarozgaris.

- Though 20 States have identified State Level agencies for training purposes, yet only 12 were able to organise State Level Training Programmes.
- Only 10 States took steps for ensuring exclusive mechanisms for providing product design and product development.
- 66.50% individual beneficiaries had not undergone any kind of skill development.
- 53.36% of the sample group swarozgaris did not undergo training for skill development.
- The products produced by the Swarozgaris were found to be of inferior quality due to non-adequate training and skill development facilities.

## Social Upliftment

- 67.44% of the total sample beneficiaries were women and 46.79% were from SC & ST category and physically challenged constituted 2.45%.
- 60% of the total swarozgaris were found to be illiterate and 50.92% were agrarian.
- 93.37% of sample beneficiaries participated in group decision-making process.

## Infrastructure Development

The SGSY provides for review of existing infrastructure for the cluster of activities and identification of gaps. Critical gaps in investments have to be met from the funds available under the SGSY programme infrastructure, subject to a ceiling of 20% (25% in the case of North Eastern States) of the annual allocation made under the scheme for each District.

## Marketing and Technology Support

The SGSY attempts to ensure upgradation of technology in the identified key activity. The technology intervention seeks to add value to the local resources, including processing of the locally available material from natural and other resources for local and non-local market.

The SGSY provides for promotion of marketing of the goods produced by the Swarozgaris, by organizing exhibitions/melas at District/State/National/International levels for exhibition and sale of goods produced by the Swarozgaris, provision of market intelligence, development of markets and consultancy services, as well as institutional arrangements for marketing of the goods including exports. DRDAs could spend up to Rs. 5.00 lakh per annum for management of professional input related to identification of viable activities, preparation of projects for product and design development, value addition, packaging etc.

## Assets under SGSY

- Most of the assets (45.52%) created under the SGSY were livestock assets.

## Implementing Agencies

The SGSY is being implemented by the District Rural Development Agencies (DRDAs), with the active involvement of Panchayati Raj Institutions (PRIs), the Banks, the Line Departments and Non-Government Organisations (NGOs).

## Monitoring

A comprehensive system of monitoring has been adopted under the SGSY. The programme is monitored from the central level down to the grass-roots level. At the central level, the Central Level Co-ordination Committee (CLCC) monitors and reviews the implementation of the programme and lays down Policy Guidelines for all aspects related to credit linkages for the SGSY. The Performance Review Committee of the Department of Rural Development also reviews the implementation of the SGSY. At the State level, a State Level Co-ordination Committee (SLCC) monitors the programme. In addition, the progress under the SGSY is monitored periodically through Reports and Returns submitted by DRDAs/States. Detailed monitoring formats for reporting progress of the programme have been circulated to all the DRDAs. Implementation of the programme is monitored and reviewed through the Project Directors' Workshops and periodic meetings with the State Secretaries. At the Block/DRDA level, monitoring is done through field visits and physical verification of assets. Efforts are underway to bring all the DRDAs of the country within online networks for smooth flow of information from the Districts to the Centre and the States/UTs.

## Innovative Micro-spinning Project under SGSY

The Ministry of Rural Development has sanctioned an innovative Micro-Spinning Project under SGSY to the Anna University, Chennai with total project cost of Rs. 59.50 lakh. The technology for the project has been developed by Vortex Engineering Pvt. Ltd. The technology developed is able to bring the spinning process to such a small level that women can do it in their houses. The conventional spinning mills are very expensive (Rs. 50 to 100 crore) and large in its scale because the processes preparatory to spinning are very complex. This can be greatly simplified if pressing of cotton into bales and its transportation to distant places is avoided. Micro-spinning takes advantage of this idea to provide a low-cost economic method of spinning on a small scale. This is suitable specially for handloom sector and can provide the variety of types of yarn needed.

The technology developed by Vortex pertains to the stages preparatory to spinning (pre-spinning). This can be coupled with a conventional spinning frame to produce yarn economically at a scale that is 1/100th of the prevailing scale. The technology integrates the operation of seed-removal (Ginning) with *in-situ* handling of fibres to produce slivers. The slivers so produced on a small scale can then be converted into yarn at the same venue. These projects are suitable to be implemented near to the places of cotton cultivation.

## Innovative Employment Generation through Farm Mechanisation and Farmers' Service Centres in Assam

Agriculture is the backbone of Assam's economy and a large number of people depend on it. If the productivity of land and labour can be increased by providing technological, managerial and other inputs then it has ripple effect in the area and creates employment opportunities. Two special project namely 'Special Project for Establishment of Farmer Service Centre at Block Level in all districts of Assam' with project cost of Rs. 8.16 crore were sanctioned by the Ministry and have been completed.

Recurrent floods leave a very small flood free season for cultivation in the State and this time has to be utilized in the best possible way. The introduction of power tillers/tractors through formation of Self Help Groups was found to be the answer which has increased the production levels to a significant level along with other benefits like attracting younger generation to modern agricultural practices, multiple cropping, increase in income, confidence in people etc. The increasing production lead to increasing demand of various inputs (such as fertilizers, seeds, insecticides, different farm implements etc.) and services such as tractors, supply of spare parts, maintenance etc. The concept of Farmers' Service Centre in each block to be managed and run by Self-Help Groups was introduced with a view to provide farm inputs and services at single place. This has resulted in substantial improvement in farm practices and production in the area along with employment generation.

## Handloom Sector Interventions Under SGSY

The Textile Industry encompasses the organized mill sector, the organized decentralized sector consisting of handlooms, khadi and powerlooms. The handloom sector at present accounts for 18.75% of the total cloth production in the country. The major contribution of Handloom sector is in terms of providing employment to 24 lakh persons and stands next to agriculture. 60% of those employed in the sector are women, 12% SC and 20% ST. There are 38.91 lakh handlooms in India. The total share in textile exports is 10%. The labour intensive character of the sector, decentralized nature and optimum utilization of scarce capital resources gives it a unique position in Indian economy and hence, eligible for assistance under SGSY.

The Ministry of Rural Development has sanctioned 16 Special Projects (3 in Andhra Pradesh, 3 in Punjab, 2 in Assam and 1 each in Gujarat, Jharkhand, J & K, Madhya Pradesh, Tamil Nadu, Manipur, Nagaland and Tripura) under SGSY for this sector with total investment of Rs. 11,211.80 lakhs. The State-wise projects sanctioned in the sector are :

Andhra Pradesh: (1) 'Action Plan to Create Technologically Qualified Global Workers' which is being implemented in Rangareddy, Medak, Nalgonda and Warangal Districts of AP; (2) Special Project for Income Generation of SHGs through Imparting Skills in Textile Processing and Garment Manufacturing, Visakhapatanam and (3) Special Project for Income Generation through Fashion Designing and Garment Manufacturing by Women SHGs, East Godavari'.

Punjab: (1) 'Special Project for Setting Up of Handlooms in Bhatinda, Punjab' with a total cost of Rs. 797.5 lakhs (2) 'Special Project for Insfrastructure Development for Carpet Weaving, Amritsar, Punjab' with a total cost of Rs. 529.00 lakhs and (3) 'Special Project for Infrastructure Development for Setting up of Handlooms in Firozpur District in Punjab' with a total cost of Rs. 755.30 lakhs.

Gujarat: 'Design Intervention for Skill Upgradation and Product Diversification in Handicraft and Handloom Clusters in Gujarat' with a total project cost of Rs. 540.00 lakhs. The project is being implemented by GRIMCO.

Jharkhand: 'Special Project for Blacksmithy and Handloom Weaving' Was sanctioned for the Deoghar DRDA with a total cost of Rs. 600.00 lakhs during 2001-02.

J&K: 'Special Project for Blacksmithy and Handloom Weaving' was sanctioned during 2003-04 with a total cost of Rs. 278.75 lakhs.

Madhya Pradesh: 'Development of Carpet Craft in Sidhi District' was sanctioned during 2001-02 with a total cost of Rs. 242.74 lakhs.

Tamil Nadu: 'Special Project for Economic Upliftment of Weavers in 13 Districts of Tamil Nadu' with a total cost of Rs. 1,447.92 lakhs was sanctioned during 2003-04.

## RURAL EMPLOYMENT GENERATION PROGRAMME (REGP)

**(Gramdyog Rojgar Yojana)**

### Introduction

The KVIC launched the Rural Employment Generation Programme (REGP) on 01 April 1995.

### Main Objectives

The main objectives of REGP are as under:

- To generate employment in rural areas.
- To develop entreprenurial skills and aptitude among rural unemployed youth.
- To achieve the goal of rural industrialization.
- To facilitate participation of banks in the village industries sector so as to ensure higher credit flow to these industries.

### Silent Features of REGP

- The programme is applicable to all village industry projects set up in rural areas.
- The eligible beneficiaries under the programme are (i) individuals (rural artisans/entrepreneurs), (ii) institutions, co-operative societies, trusts & Self Help Groups (SHGs) for projects costing upto Rs. 25 lakh.
- Partnership firms private/public limited companies, joint ventures, joint borrowers, co-obligators of HUF are not eligible.
- The permissible margin money assistance is as detailed in the Table below:

**Table 8**

**MARGIN MONEY ASSISTANCE UNDER REGP**

| *S. No.* | *Category of beneficiary* | *Project cost* | *Margin money assistance* |
|---|---|---|---|
| 1. | General | Up to Rs. 10 lakh | 25 per cent of project cost |
| | | Above Rs. 10 lakh and up to Rs. 25 lakh | Rs. 2.5 lakh plus 10 per cent of balance project cost |

| 2. | SC/ST/OBC/Women/PH/ Ex-servicemen/ NE Region/Hill areas | Up to Rs. 10 lakh | 30 per cent of project cost |
|---|---|---|---|
| | | Above Rs. 10 lakh and up to Rs. 25 lakh | Rs. 3 lakh plus 10 per cent of balance project cost. |

*Note:* SC/ST-Scheduled Caste/Scheduled Tribe; PH-Physically Handicapped: NE-North Eastern

- The borrower is required to invest his own contribution of 10 per cent of the project cost. In case of SC/ST and borrowers from other weaker sections, the beneficiary's contribution is 5 per cent of the project cost.
- Banks will sanction loan of 90 per cent of the project cost in the case of general category borrowers and 95 per cent of the project cost to the weaker section beneficiaries/institutions. After the sanction of the credit facility by the Bank branch, eligible amount of margin money will be kept in term deposit of two years in the account of the borrower at the leading bank branch, which will be credited to the borrower's loan account after a period of two years from the date of first disbursement of loan.

## Definition of "Rural Area" and "Village Industries"

The term 'rural area' as per amended KVIC Act, 1956 has been defined as under:

"**Rural Area** means the area comprised in any village, and includes the area comprised in any town, the population of which does not exceed twenty thousand or such other figure as the Central Government may specify from time to time."

Similarly, the term 'Village industries' has been redefined in amended KVIC Act, 1956 as 'any industry located in a rural area which produces any goods or renders any service with or without the use of power and in which the fixed capital investment per head of artisan or worker does not exceed Rs. one lakh (Rs. one lakh and fifty thousand in case of village industry located in a hilly area) or such other sum as may, by notification in the *Official Gazette*, be specified from time to time by the Central Government.'

All activities which do not appear in the negative list circulated by KVIC are eligible for financing under the scheme.

All activities which do not appear in the negative list circulated by KVIC are eligible for financing under the scheme.

## Implementation

KVIC is implementing REGP through:

- All public Sector Banks
- All Regional Rural Banks
- Co-operative Banks approved by State/U.T Governments, KVIBs, Private Commercial Banks approved by the State KVIBs; and
- Other Financing Institutions of State & Central Government as approved by KVIC.

## Sponsorship

Sponsoring of Project by any agency is not mandatory. However, KVIC's State/Regional Offices and State KVI Boards/District Industries Centre (DIC) may sponsor the project, if approached.

## Entrepreneurship Development Programme (EDP)

Once the project is sanctioned by the financing branch of the Bank, before releasing the second installment of loan, beneficiary is to be imparted a 3-day EDP training arranged by the State/Regional Director.

## Status and Progress of REGP

Since the commencement of REGP, 2,36,355 projects have been financed and 33.74 lakh job opportunities have been created up to 31.03.2006. Keeping in view REGP's potential, the Government revised the target of creating 20 lakh additional jobs to 25 lakh additional jobs during the 10th Plan.

During 2005-06, against the target of generating 5.50 lakh additional job opportunities under REGP, 5.68 lakh job opportunities have been generated, thus recording a 7.16 per cent growth in employment generation as compared to that during 2004-05 (5.31 lakh against the target of generating 5.25 lakh job opportunities). The target for 2006-07 is to generate 5.90 lakh additional employment opportunities.

During 2006-07 (up to December 2006), 10,747 projects have already been set up, generating 2.36 lakh additional employment opportunities as against the target of creation of 5.90 lakh job opportunities. A large number of projects are at 'sanction' stage and it is expected that the target set under the programme would be achieved going by the trends of 2005-06 as well as the results of assessment made by KVIC of the progress.

The details of achievement during the 10th Plan are as under:

| *Year* | *Target for employment generation (lakh opportunities)* | *Employment generated during year (lakh opportunities)* | *Number of projects set up* | *Margin money released (Rs. crore)* |
|---|---|---|---|---|
| 2002-03 | 4.00 | 3.61 | 21024 | 193.72 |
| 2003-04 | 5.00 | 4.71 | 24747 | 268.75 |
| 2004-05 | 5.25 | 5.31 | 23453 | 292.40 |
| 2005-06 | 5.50 | 5.68 | 26650 | 320.96 |
| 2006-07* | 5.90 | 2.36 | 10747 | 240.43 |

*up to 31 Dec., 2006

## Category-Wise Distribution of Projects among Beneficiaries

Of 2,36,355 units that have been set up since the inception of REGP and upto 31.03.2006, approximately 7.71 per cent of the projects have benefited persons from the Scheduled Castes, 5.45 per cent from Scheduled Tribes and 13.75 per cent from OBCs, while 15.87 per cent have helped women entrepreneurs secure gainful employment. Following is the share of distribution of the projects sanctioned in 2006-07, upto December 2006:

| *Sr. No.* | *Category* | *No. of Projects* | *Percentage* |
|---|---|---|---|
| 1. | Scheduled Castes | 824 | 7.67 |
| 2. | Scheduled Tribes | 1,403 | 13.05 |
| 3. | OBC | 2,953 | 27.48 |
| 4. | Minority Community | 1083 | 10.07 |
| 5. | Ex-Servicemen/physically handicapped | 78 | 0.72 |
| 6. | General | 4,406 | 40.99 |
| | **Total** | **10,747** | |
| | Women | 2794 | 25.99 |

## Backward and Forward Linkages

The KVIC provided financial assistance to its State Offices as well as the State Khadi and Village Industries Boards for establishing backward and forward linkages of the entrepreneurs/institutions under REGP. These linkages include EDP Trainings, exhibitions of products manufactured by REGP entrepreneurs, district/state level workshops and awareness camps, identification of success stories and their dissemination, etc. An amount of Rs. 629.34 lakh have been released towards backward-forward linkages which was utilised towards organising workshops, 141 awareness camps and 30 exhibitions. 6,009 persons have undergone EDP training during 2006-07 (up to December 2006).

## Other Initiatives

For better implementation of the REGP, the KVIC has taken the following initiatives:

(i) Decentralisation of the implementation of the scheme by releasing margin money through State Offices and State KVI Boards;

(ii) Financing of units based on coir as raw material;

(iii) Financing of auto-rikshaws in Andaman and Nicobar Islands, house boat, shikara and tourist boat in Jammu and Kashmir under rural transport, keeping in view the special requirement of the UT/State:

(iv) For providing information/guidance to the new entrepreneurs, REGP 'help counters' were opened in all the field offices of the KVIC and the State KVI Boards;

(v) 10 per cent of the total budget under REGP allocated exclusively for the States of North Eastern Region;

(vi) 40 per cent of the total target has been identified for the Agro & Food Based Industries in each State/Division/UT;

(vii) 30 per cent of the total target as been fixed for allocation to women entrepreneurs;

(viii) Self-Help Groups (SHGs) also to be provided assistance under REGP Scheme;

(ix) State Level Task Force Committees constituted for better monitoring and implementation of REGP;

(x) Rural Industries Consultancy Service Cells (RICS) opened in 49 places for guiding and preparing projects for first generation entrepreneurs;

(xi) 178 Training Centres identified for providing EDP training to REGP employment throughout the country;

(xii) For placing margin money in advance with nodal branches of banks at state level, 214 nodal branches of public sector banks identified by state/divisional offices and 132 nodal branches of public sector banks identified by State/KVI Boards in the country;

(xiii) Funds provided to State/Divisional Offices for conducting awareness camps, workshops, and exhibitions, etc., as support services under backward-forward linkages. 50 per cent of the same allocated to State/UT KVI Boards;

(xiv) 25 per cent of the stalls in each exhibition of REGP to be allotted for disadvantaged section beneficiaries including women beneficiaries;

(xv) To mitigate the problems of the rural entrepreneurs, who are otherwise required to furnish collateral security for projects under REGP, coverage under Credit Guarantee Trust Fund for Small Industries (CGTSI) provided;

(xvi) An MoU has been signed between KVIC and Army Wives Welfare Association (AWWA) in June 2006 for extending REGP to the war widows, ex-servicemen, etc., in the AWWA fold and to encourage convergence of marketing activities of AWWA and KVIC through their respective outlets;

(xvii) Another MoU has been signed between KVIC and Nehru Yuvak Kendra Sangthan (NYKS) in July 2006 which carries out self-development programme for Rural Youth through clubs to conduct awareness camps and entrepreneurs' workshops for REGP amongst the Rural Youth with focus on SC/ST/minority and women beneficiaries;

(xviii) An MoU has also been signed by KVIC with Department of Women and Child Development, Ministry of HRD, New Delhi for convergence in the area of credit linkages, marketing tie-up, etc., through SHGs for bettering the cause of SHGs and rural employment.

### Quality is the Main Attraction

| | | |
|---|---|---|
| Name & Address of Entrepreneur | : | Shri Gurupada Roy, Itabhata, Shiwalik Park, Silchar (Assam). |
| Name of the Activity | : | : |
| Project Cost | : | Rs. 7,37,000/- |
| Commencement of Production | : | 2001-02 |
| Annual Turn Over | : | Rs. 9,54,700/- |
| Employment Generated | : | 7 persons |
| Monthly Income | : | Rs. 8,000/- |

Shri Gurupada Roy is a young undergraduate from a family with business background. His family business was trading in groceries. He tried to get Govt. job but was unsuccessful. He got inspiration from his family members and started thinking in terms of self employment. Since his family grocery shop along-with other items, used to deal with spices, which is considered to be quite remunerative, he developed an interest to take up work dealing with spices.

The common raw materials like Haldi, Chili, Dhania are locally grown and consumption is very high. From DICC he came to know about REGP of KVIC and he approached Indian Overseas Bank to get the finance. He purchased required machinery and procured attractive printed packing pouches of different capacities. At present one expert operator and 2 semi skilled workers are working with him. He ensures procurement of quality raw material by himself as also quality product with due hygiene arranged in attractive packing. He conducted displays of his products at various popular places. His efforts and aggressive zeal have started paying him dividends. He got Agmark for his products.

The entrepreneur wishes to become one of the leading spice suppliers in future. The speed at which the unit and the product is gaining market is such that it would certainly carry a good socio economic impact in the vicinity and contribute to the image of the KVIC.

### No Looking Back

| | | |
|---|---|---|
| Name & Address of Entrepreneur | : | Shri Zatwana Chawnpuri Veng, Thiak Village |
| Name of the Activity | : | Tyre Retreading Unit |
| Project Cost | : | Rs. 5,56,000/- |
| Commencement of Production | : | 1999-2000 |
| Annual Turn Over | : | Rs.7,60,000/- |
| Employment Generated | : | 7 persons |
| Monthly Income | : | Rs. 15,000/- |

Shri Zatwana Chawnpuri, belonged to Veng village and came to Aizawl city in search of job for better living. His younger brother established Tyre Retreading Unit and he started helping him. Slowly he learnt the work sufficient enough to manage the industry independently and opened a new unit at 75 km. away from Aizawl with one show room in a rented shop.

He approached Mizoram Rural Bank for assistance under REGP of KVIC and after getting the loan, he purchased all new machinery. Now he takes up retreading work of all types of vehicles. His two sons are working with him and 7 others are also employed in the working of the unit.

Although he is not educated, he has no problem in the management of his industry. His unit is flourishing well. He constructed residential building also lately.

## Prime Minister's Rozgar Yojana (PMRY)

The Prime Minister's Rozgar Yojana (PMRY), a credit linked subsidy scheme to provide financial assistance to less educated and poor unemployed youth in the country was launched on 02 Oct.,1993.

Since 1994-95, PMRY is being implemented in both urban and rural areas.

An educated (up to viii standard) unemployed person living in any part of the country is eligible under the scheme.

The unemployed youth is trained in his selected project. State/UT Governments provide infrastructure support to the entrepreneurs on priority basis. In addition, general tax concessions/incentives may also be provided to the beneficiaries.

District Industries Centre (DIC) is the implementing agency. The field agencies in consultation with the banks of the respective areas, are responsible for formulation of self-employment plans, their implementation and monitoring under the overall guidance of the district PMRY committee.

During the Tenth plan (2002-2007) out of the 23,35,012 applications received, 14,21,932 were given assistance and Rs. 7,442 crore was disbursed to 11,92,531 entrepreneurs providing employment to 14,91,847 people.

The Central Government assists the entrepreneurs through capital subsidy and provides funds to states for entrepreneurial development.

Evaluation studies have shown that the employment generation was around 1.95 per functioning unit. 39.1 per cent of beneficiaries are from rural areas. Assets have been created in 89.7 per cent of the cases where loans were disbursed. About 36.4 per cent of the beneficiaries were repaying the loan instalment on time the average amount of loan disbursed was Rs. 64,000 per unit.

PMRY has been successful in motivating people in rural areas towards self-employment and entrepreneurial activities.

*Fig. 10. Shoe unit setup with financial assistance under PMRY scheme at Dholpur after receiving training under the scheme.*

## ELIGIBILITY NORMS UNDER THE PMRY SCHEME

### Age :

- 18 to 35 years for all educated unemployment in the country except for North Eastern States, Uttaranchal, Himachal Pradesh and Jammu & Kashmir.
- 18 to 40 years for all educated unemployed in North Eastern States, Himachal Pradesh, Uttaranchal and J & K.
- 18 to 45 years for Scheduled Caste/Scheduled Tribes, Ex-servicemen, Physically Handicapped and woman.

**Educational Qualification:** VII standard passed. Preference will be given to those trained in any trade in Government recoginsed/approved institutions for at least six months.

**Family Income:** The income of the beneficiary and the spouse along with the income of the parents of the beneficiary should not exceed Rs. 40,000 per annum.

**Residency:** Beneficiary should be a permanent resident of the area for at least 3 years (relaxed for married men in Meghalaya and for married women in rest of the country). For married men in Meghalaya and for married women in rest of the country, the residency criteria applies to the spouse or in-laws.

**Creditworthiness:** The beneficiary should not be a defaulter to any Nationalised Bank/Financial Institution/Co-operative Bank. Further, a person already assisted under other subsidy linked Government schemes would not be eligible under the Scheme.

**Reservation:** Preference should be given to the weaker sections including women. The Scheme envisages 22.5 per cent reservation for SC/STs and 27 per cent for other Backward Classes (OBCs). In case SC/ST/OBC candidates are not available, State/Union Territories (UT) Government will be competent to consider other categories of candidates under PMRY.

## FINANCIAL TERMS UNDER PMRY

### Project Cost:

- Rs. 1.00 lakh for business sector
- Rs. 2.00 lakh for other activities.
- Loan to be of a composite nature.
- If two or more eligible persons join together in a partnership, projects costing up to Rs. 10.00 lakh can be covered. However, assistance shall be limited to individual admissibility.
- Self Help Groups (SHG) can be considered for assistance under the scheme.

### Subsidy & Margin Money:

Subsidy is provided @ 15 per cent of the project cost subject to a ceiling of Rs. 7,500 per beneficiary. In the North Eastern states is Rs. 15,000 per beneficiary.

## Scheme of Fund for Regeneration of Traditional Industries (SFURTI)

In pursuance of the National Common Minimum Programme (NCMP), a scheme titled the SFURTI has been notified in October 2005 for Regeneration of Traditional industries and development of 100 clusters (25 Khadi, 50 village industries and 25 coir industry) over a period of five years.

The main objective of SFURTI is to establish a regenerated, holistic sustainable and replicable model of integrated cluster-based development of traditional industries. This will primarily mean:

(i) more competitive traditional industries with more market-driven, productive, profitable and sustained employment for the participents;

(ii) strengthen local socio-economic governance system of the industry clusters, with the active participation by the local stakeholders that can help them to continue and undertake development initiative by themselves; and

(iii) building up innovative and traditional skills, improved technologies, advanced processes, market intelligence and new models of public-private partnerships, so as to gradually replicate similar models of cluster-based regenerated traditional industries.

KVIC and Coir Board are the Nodal Agencies for disbursing of funds to the identified Implementing Agencies.

Until December 2007, 124 clusters (34 khadi, 64 village industries and 26 coir) have been approved by the scheme Steering Committee for development.

SFURTI Plans to take up the following support measures:

- Replacement of charkhas and looms in khadi sector.
- Setting up of Common Facility Centres (CFCs).
- Development of new products, new designs for various khadi and village industry (VI) products, new/improved packaging, etc.
- Market promotion activities.
- Capacity building activities, such as exposure visits to other clusters and institutions, need-based training, support for establishment of cluster level networks (industry associations) and other need based support.
- Other activities identified by the implementing Agency (IA) as may be necessary for the development of the cluster.

SUFRTI is the first organised systematic attempt at introducing cluster-based development approach in rural and traditional sectors. Almost all the clusters are in a take of stage in 2007-08. The scheme will go a long way in increasing employment opportunities in rural areas.

❑ ❑ ❑

*"Drought Prone areas are characterized by large human and cattle populations which are continuously putting heavy pressure on the already degraded natural resources for food, fodder and fuel. The major problems are continuous depletion of vegetative cover, increase in soil erosion and fall in ground water levels due to continuous exploitation without any effort to recharge the underground aquifers."*

# Chapter 13

# SPECIAL AREA DEVELOPMENT PROGRAMMES

## Introduction

Drought and desert have always been features of life in some pockets of India. Uncertainty regarding the availability of water makes many susceptible to drought and desertification. In this chapter, Special Areas Development Programmes of the government are discussed.

## What is Drought?

Drought is a normal, recurrent feature of climate. It occurs almost everywhere, although its features vary from region to region. Defining drought is therefore difficult; it depends on differences in regions, needs, and disciplinary perspectives. Based on the many definitions that have appeared in literature, for example, we might define drought in Libya as occurring when annual rainfall is less than 180 mm, but in Bali, drought might be considered to occur after a period of only six days without rains! In the most general sense, drought originates from deficiency of precipitation over an extended period of time, resulting in a water shortage for some activity, group or environmental sector. Whatever the definition, it is clear that drought cannot be viewed solely as a physical phenomenon.

## Drought Management

Drought can cause great damage in terms of human suffering, economic loss, and environmental impact. Drought can affect every region of the country and every sector of the economy. The total economic impact on agriculture, energy, transportation and recreation/tourism associated with any drought could be billions of dollars. The nature of drought, and response to it, is aptly summarized in the legislative record of the National Drought Policy.

In many respects, drought presents one of the most challenging dilemmas for policy makers, managers and citizens. It can be both pervasive and covert, moving slowly yet steadily into an entire region. This "creeping phenomenon" also differs from other natural hazards, such as tornadoes or flash floods, in that it lacks any precise or universally accepted definition, seldom results in structural damage, and can linger for lengthy periods of time in affected areas. The result is that, compared to other disasters, drought often receives minimal attention in advance or uncoordinated, delayed responses. drought, like other types of disasters, tends to prompt a crisis management, rather than risk management approach.

Planning for drought to mitigate its effects allows decision-makers to take actions that reduce the most damage at the least cost. States, tribes, farmers, ranchers, municipal water suppliers, and water users should develop a contingency plan that includes short and long-term mitigation actions.

## DROUGHT PRONE AREAS PROGRAMME

Drought Prone Areas Programme (DPAP) is one of the area development programmes launched by the Government in 1973-74 to tackle the special problems faced by those fragile areas which are constantly affected by severe drought conditions. These areas are characterized by large human and cattle populations which are continuously putting heavy pressure on the already fragile natural resource base for food, fodder and fuel. This continuous biotic pressure is leading to fast and continuous depletion of vegetative cover, less and less rainfall, increasing soil erosion and fast receding ground water levels due to continuous exploitation without any effort to recharge the under ground acquifers.

Though the programme created some positive impact in terms of creating durable public assets in the programme areas, the overall impact of the programme in effectively containing the adverse effects of drought was found to be not very encouraging. In addition, many of the programme States had also been demanding inclusion of additional areas under the programme. Keeping this in view a High Level Technical Committee under the Chairmanship of Prof. C.H. Hanumantha Rao, Ex-Member, Planning Commission critically reviewed the contents, methodology and implementation processes of all area development programmes and suggested suitable measures for improvement.

Based on the recommendations of the Hanumantha Rao Committee, comprehensive Guidelines for Watershed Development commonly applicable to the DPAP, DDP, IWDP, EAS (50% allocation in DPAP and DDP areas) were issued in October, 1994 which came into effect from 1995-96.

### Objectives

The basic objective of the programme is to minimise the adverse effects of drought on production of crops and livestock and productivity of land, water and human resources ultimately leading to the drought proofing of the affected areas. The programme also aims to promote overall economic development and improving the socio-economic conditions of the resource poor and disadvantaged sections inhabiting the programme areas, through creation, widening and equitable distribution of resource base and increased employment opportunities. The objectives of the programme are being addressed in general by taking up development works through watershed approach for land development, water resource development and afforestation/pasture development.

### Strategy

The common Guidelines for Watershed Development provide for a uniform strategy in the implementation of all area development programmes *viz.* DPAP, DDP, IWDP and EAS. The main features of this strategy are:

- Area development programmes to be implemented exclusively on watershed basis.

- Programme activities to the confined to the identified watershed of about 500 hectares and are to be executed on a project basis spanning over a period of four years.
- Watershed project to cover a village, as far as possible.
- Elaborate institutional mechanisms at various levels clearly defined for effective participation of the local people and the Panchayati Raj institutions in all stages of project management.
- DRDA/ZP to be the nodal Government agency at the district level to act as a facilitator and provider of finances and technical assistance to the people's organizations executing the watershed projects.
- Voluntary agencies to be given effective role in the implementation of the programme particularly in motivating people, community organisation and training.

## Coverage

At present DPAP is in operation in 961 blocks of 180 districts in 16 States. The corresponding physical area for treatment under the programme works out to approximately 7.45 lakh square kilometers. The States where DPAP is under implementation along with number of districts and blocks may be seen in the Table 1.

**Table 1**

| *Sl. No* | *States* | *No of Districts* | *No of Blocks* | *Area in Sq kms.* |
|---|---|---|---|---|
| 1. | Andhra Pradesh | 11 | 94 | 99,218 |
| 2. | Bihar | 6 | 30 | 9,533 |
| 3. | Chhattisgarh | 8 | 29 | 21,801 |
| 4. | Gujarat | 14 | 67 | 43,938 |
| 5. | H.P. | 3 | 10 | 3,319 |
| 6. | J & K | 2 | 22 | 14,705 |
| 7. | Jharkhand | 15 | 100 | 34,843 |
| 8. | Karnataka | 15 | 81 | 84,332 |
| 9. | M.P. | 24 | 105 | 89,101 |
| 10. | Maharashtra | 25 | 149 | 1,94,473 |
| 11. | Orissa | 8 | 47 | 26,178 |
| 12. | Rajasthan | 11 | 32 | 31,969 |
| 13. | Tamil Nadu | 17 | 80 | 29,416 |
| 14. | Uttar Pradesh | 15 | 60 | 35,698 |
| 15. | Uttarakhand | 7 | 30 | 15,796 |
| 16. | West Bengal | 4 | 36 | 11,594 |
| | **Total** | **185** | **972** | **7,45,914** |

*Fig. 1. Dryland Cultivation: Tank (Rajasthan)*

## Funding Pattern

The programme allocation is shared on 50:50 basis between the Centre and the State Governments. The cost norms adopted under DPAP for various ecosystems depending on the severity of the problem are as below:

**Table 2**

| S. No. | Ecosystem Type | Per Ha. Cost Average (Rs.) | Watershed Project Cost (Rs. in lakhs) |
|---|---|---|---|
| 1. | Semi-Arid Region | 4,000 | 20.00 |
| 2. | Dry Sub-Humid Region | 3,000 | 15.00 |
| 3. | Dry Sub-Humid (Hill) Region | 4,000 | 20.00 |

Under DPAP, a total of 10,020 watershed projects covering an area of 41.68 lakh hectares at a total cost of Rs. 1666 crores were under implementation on end March, 2001.

## Rainwater Harvesting

An old technology is gaining popularity in a new way. Rainwater harvesting is enjoying a renaissance of sorts but it traces its history to biblical times. Extensive rainwater harvesting apparatus existed 4000 years ago in the Negev Desert. In ancient Rome, residences were built with individual cisterns and paved courtyards to capture rainwater to augment water from the city's aqueducts. And as recently as early in this century, rainwater was the primary water source on many ranches, with stone and steel cisterns still standing today on homesteads upon which wells were long ago drilled.

Rainwater offers advantages in water quality for both irrigation and domestic use. Rainwater is naturally soft (unlike well water), contains almost no dissolved minerals or salts, is free of chemical treatment, and is a relatively reliable source of water for households. Rainwater collected and used on site can supplement or replace other source of household water.

One of the beauties of rainwater harvesting systems is their flexibility. A system can be as simple as a whiskey barrel placed under a rain gutter downspout for watering a garden or a complex as an engineered, multi-tank, pumped and pressurized construction to supply residential and irrigation needs.

Although configurations vary with each installation, most systems include five basic components:

(1) A catchment area, which could be the roof of a house or an open-sided barn sheltering cisterns;

(2) Gutters and downspouts to channel water from the catchment to storage;

(3) Cisterns and storage tanks;

(4) A conveyance system, either gravity-fed or pumped;

(5) Water treatment.

Cost of a rainwater harvesting system is comparable to that of a drilled well and pump. The primary expense is the storage tank. Operating costs can be less than those of a well, since rainwater eliminates the need for water softening treatments.

## Water Efficiency Measures

Efficient use of water, through behavioural, operational, or equipment changes, and practiced broadly in farm and rangeland, municipalities, and rural areas can help mitigate the effects of drought. Water efficiency measures by sector are presented below. These measures will be most effective in mitigating drought impact if implemented in advance of a drought on a long-term basis. This list of measures is not meant to bee comprehensive.

## Water Efficiency Measures for Agricultural Districts

- Provide adequate water measurement and accounting
- Adopt water-pricing structure that encourages efficiency
- Provide information and education services for water users
- Designate a water efficiency coordinator
- Encourage on-farm management measures such as :
  - — ditch lining
  - — development of water reuse systems
  - — installation of surge valves and gate pipes
  - — sprinkler systems
  - — field leveling
  - — soil treatments
- Incentives for on-farm water efficiency measures include in-kind services, educational programmes, demonstration projects, and financial incentives, including tax incentives, low-interest loans, equipment purchase subsidies, and water discounts or rebates

# DESERT DEVELOPMENT PROGRAMME (DDP)

The Desert Development Programme launched in 1977-78 aim at checking the further desertification of the desert areas and raising the productivity of the local resources to achieve higher income and employment levels for the local inhabitants. The programme covers hot arid desert areas of Ladakh, Jammu and Kashmir and Himachal Pradesh. The programme will continue to be implemented both in the hot and cold arid zones of the country during the Sixth Plan. The emphasis will be on arresting desertification through activities which restore the ecological balance, stabilise sand dunes, and facilitate soil and water conservation. The plantation of shelter belts, the adoption of water harvesting techniques and the development of pastures to sustain the livestock economy will be vigorously pursued. The exploitation of the natural resources of these areas will be closely linked to the replenishment of these resources. It has been proposed to encourage innovative use of land for fodder crops, pastures and fuel and fodder plantations. This diversification is expected to improve the economy of the desert areas in keeping with their ecological requirements. In the cold arid zones of Ladakh and Sikkim irrigated agriculture and improved animal husbandry practices would be among the activities to be encouraged.

## Objectives

The programme has been conceived as a long term measure for restoration of ecological balance by conserving, developing and harnessing land, water, livestock and human resources. It seeks to promote the economic development of the village community and improve the economic conditions of the resource poor and disadvantaged sections of society in the rural areas. The major objectives of the programme are as under:

- To mitigate the adverse effects of desertification and adverse climatic conditions on crops, human and livestock population, combating desertification.
- To restore ecological balance by harnessing, conserving and developing natural resources *i.e.* land, water, vegetative cover and raising land productivity.
- To implement developmental works through the watershed approach, for land development, water resources development and afforestation/pasture development.

## The Strategy

The strategy of the programme is to arrest desertification and the following activities are taken up under the programme:

(*a*) afforestation (with special emphasis on shelter belt plantation), grassland development and sand dune stabilisation;

(*b*) ground water development and utilisation;

(*c*) construction of water harvesting structures;

(*d*) rural electrification for energising tube-wells and pumpsets;

(*e*) development of agriculture, animal husbandry, dairy, horticulture and sericulture suited to the agro-climatic conditions of the area.

*Fig. 2. Check-dam to prevent soil erosion*

At present, 232 blocks in 40 districts of 7 states are covered under the programme. The States where DDP is under implementation along with the number of blocks and area are indicated in the table below:

**Table 3**

| *Sl. No.* | *State* | *Number of districts* | *Number of Blocks* | *Area in sq. kms.* |
|---|---|---|---|---|
| 1. | Andhra Pradesh | 1 | 16 | 19136 |
| 2. | Gujarat | 6 | 52 | 55424 |
| 3. | Haryana | 7 | 45 | 20542 |
| 4. | Himachal Pradesh | 2 | 3 | 35107 |
| 5. | Jammu & Kashmir | 2 | 12 | 96701 |

| | | | | |
|---|---|---|---|---|
| 6. | Karnataka | 6 | 22 | 32295 |
| 7. | Rajasthan | 16 | 85 | 198744 |
| | Total | 40 | 235 | 457949 |

As at end March, 2008, 15,746 Watershed Development Projects and special projects covering an area of 78.73 lakh hectares at a cost of Rs. 2,060.17 crores were under implementation in different states.

## Administration

The programme has been administered by the state governments through the DPAP/SFDA (now District Rural Development Agencies, DRDA) agencies. The outlay envisaged under the programme is at the rate of Rs. 15 lakhs per block subject to a minimum of Rs. 25 lakhs per district, The allocation is shared equally between the centre and the state governments. 100 per cent of the cost of the scheme was borne by the central government prior to 1979-80 when the funding pattern was changed to matching grant basis. Central assistance was provided at the rate of Rs. 7.50 lakhs per block with an equal contribution from the concerned state government.

## RURAL ROADS

Rural roads form the crux of infrastructure. It is one of the core of rural development. Rural roads provide connectivity with urban areas and opens up multiple opportunities to the rural people, it brings in change and socio-economic development.

*Fig. 3. Combination of community development interventions, ecological restoration, and support to livestock and livelihoods*

The Government of India has identified 'rural roads' as one of the six components of 'Bharat Nirman', with a goal to provide connectivity to all habitations with a population of 1000 persons and above (500 persons and above 250 in the case of hilly or tribal areas) with an all-weather road by 2009. A total of 66,802 habitations was proposed to be covered under Bharat Nirman. This would involve construction of 1,46,185 kms. of rural roads. In addition to new connectivity, the programme envisages upgradation of 1,94,130 kms (of which 60% length is to be funded by the Central Government and the remaining 40% length is to be covered under 'renewal' by the States as part of maintenance) of existing rural roads. At present, out of the 8,48,894 rural habitations, 3,29,898 (38.8%) rural habitats are unconnected.

## Pradhan Mantri Gram Sadak Yojana

Pradhan Mantri Gram Sadak Yojana (PMGSY) was launched on 25th December 2000. It is a fully funded scheme to provide good all-weather roads in rural areas of the country. The programme envisaged connecting all villages with a population of 200 persons and above.

Under the programme, upto November, 2007, 44,290 road works measuring 14,046 km have been completed incurring Rs. 26,277.80 crore.

PMGSY is a 100% centrally sponsored scheme to provide connectivity to the eligible habitations.

However, the projects are executed by the state government agencies SRRDA (State Rural Roads Development Agency), Programme implementation units at district level. National Rural Roads Development Agency (NRRDA) has been set up on 14-01-2002 to provide technical support to the programme.

❑ ❑ ❑

*"Housing is a basic need which is critical for determining the quality of human life. A roof over the head endows a shelterless person, with an essential asset and improves his physical and mental well-being. Hence, fulfilling the need for rural housing and tacking rural housing shortage is an important task to be undertaken as part of the poverty alleviation efforts of the government."*

# Chapter 14

# RURAL HOUSING PROGRAMMES

## Introduction

Housing is one of the basic requirements for human survival. For a normal citizen, owning a house provides significant economic security and dignity in society. For a shelterless person, possession of a house brings about a profound social change in his existence, endowing him with an identity, thus integrating him with his immediate social milieu.

There is a clear correlation between the poverty and the housing condition. The poor person either does not have a house or lives in an unserviceable kutcha house.

Housing is one of the most serious challenges facing India's socio-political economy today. While food security has been largely achieved and clothing today is not a serious problem for the poor, shelter remains beyond the reach of millions in India even after 50 years of the country's independence. This is a matter not merely of deep concern but also a matter that requires immediate attention and urgent action. For a normal citizen, owning a house provides significant economic security and status in society. For shelterless persons, a house brings about a profound social change in their existence, endowing them with an identity, thus integrating them with their immediate social milieu.

## Housing Shortage

According to the 1991 Census, the rural housing shortage was 13.72 million consisting of 3.41 million households without houses and 10.31 million living in unserviceable kutcha houses. It has also been estimated that another 10.75 million houses would be needed to cover the population growth during 1991-2002 at the rate of an annual growth of 0.89 million houselessness. Thus, a total of 24.47 million houses need to be constructed or upgraded to achieve the target of providing shelter to all in the rural areas by 2002 A.D. of the above 24.47 million houses. 5.7 million houses have been added by various agencies until 31.3.1997. It is anticipated that around 6.17 million houses will be added by different agencies by 2002. Thus the housing shortage to be tackled is 12.60 million houses, of which 10.31 million houses need upgradation and 2.29 million new houses wilt need to be constructed.

The Central Government announced in 1998, the National Housing and Habitat Policy which aims at providing 'Housing for All', with an emphasis on extending benefits to the poor and the deprived. Government is committed to the goal of ending all shelterlessness by the end of the Ninth Plan period and conversion of all unserviceable kutcha houses to pucca/semi pucca by the end of the Tenth Plan Period. For achieving these objectives, a comprehensive Action Plan for Rural Housing has gone onstream.

The Action Plan for Rural Housing consists of the following elements:

- Provision for upgradation of unserviceable kutcha houses in Indira Awaas Yojana (IAY) in addition to new construction.
- Pradhan Mantri Gramodaya Yojana: Gramin Awaas.
- Credit-cum-Subsidy Scheme for Rural Housing.
- Innovative Stream for Rural Housing & Habitat Development.
- Rural Building Centres.
- Samagra Awaas Yojana.
- Enhancement in equity contribution by Ministry of Rural Development to HUDCO.
- National Mission for Rural Housing & Habitat.

## INDIRA AWAAS YOJANA

The Government of India is implementing Indira Awaas Yojana (IAY) since the year 1985-86 with the objective of providing dwelling units free of cost of the members of Scheduled Castes, Scheduled Tribes and freed bonded labourers living below the poverty line in rural areas. From the year 1993–94, its scope has been extended to cover non-scheduled castes and scheduled tribes rural poor subject to the condition that the benefits of the scheme have also been extended to families of servicemen of the armed and paramilitary forces killed in action, 3% of the houses are reserved for the below poverty line disabled persons living in rural areas.

IAY operates as a 100% subsidised centrally sponsored programme with the resources being shared on 75:25 basis between Centre and the States, Funds under the scheme allocated to the States/UTs are further distributed to the districts in proportion to the SC/ ST population in the district.

*Fig. 1. A View of the Houses constructed under IAY*

The allotment of house under the scheme is done in the name of the female member of the beneficiary household. Alternatively, it can be allotted in the name of both the husband and wife. The beneficiaries are to be involved from the very beginning in construction work and have to make their own arrangements for construction to suit their requirements. As far as possible houses are built in clusters so as to facilitate provision of common facilities. The permissible construction assistance per house Rs. 25,000 in plain areas and Rs. 27,500 in hilly or difficult areas.

District Rural Development Agencies/Zilla Parishads on the basis of allocations made and targets fixed shall decide the number of houses to be constructed Panchayat wise under IAY during a particular financial year. The same is intimated to the Gram Panchayat. Thereafter, the Gram Sabha selects the beneficiaries from the list of eligible households according to IAY guidelines are as per priorities fixed, restricting this number to the target allotted. No approval of the Panchayat Samiti is required. The Panchayat Samiti is however, sent a list of selected beneficiaries for their information.

*Fig. 2.*

The nutritional status of women and children in rural areas is a matter of concern. Most of the rural women and children belonging to families below poverty line and found to be suffering from various ailments related to malnutrition. It is, therefore necessary to focus attention on the need for improvement in nutritional status of our rural population by encouraging the cultivation of fruits and vegetables which can be grown easily in the backyard of rural houses. Accordingly instructions have been issued to implementing agencies for popularising the production of fruits and vegetable at household level particularly in houses constructed under IAY.

The IAY is implemented through District Rural Development Agencies specially set up in each district of the country for the implementation of Rural Development Programmes or through Zilla Parishads. At the field level the block machinery is entrusted with the responsibility for implementing the programme. At the village level the Gram Sabha is responsible for selection of beneficiaries.

Fuel efficient chullahs have been developed and are being manufactured at several places. The Department of Non–Conventional Energy Sources is encouraging installation of such chullahs. It is ensured that every house constructed under the Yojana is provided with the fuel efficient chullah.

Construction of sanitary latrines forms an integral part of IAY house. It has, however, been observed that in a large number of cases either the sanitary latrines in these houses are not constructed or if they are constructed, these are not put to proper use which is mainly due to the old habits of the people.

*Fig. 3. Houses free of cost to the poor under IAY*

While fixinḡ technical specification, efforts are to be made to utilise to that maximum extent, local material and low cost technology developed by various institutions. Technology using bricks, cement and steel on large scale is not be encouraged. As far as possible, cement is substituted by lime and lime surkhi manufactured locally. Due to increase in price of bricks, it is considered desirable to substitute burnt bricks with sun dried bricks of earth–soil-cement. Bricks manufactured by the beneficiaries themselves instead of its purchase may also be undertaken for reduction of cost and better wages employment.

## Programme Performance

The IAY has proved to be a popular programme and targets have exceeded in almost every year since its inception. A total of around 171,69,130 houses have been constructed from 1985-86 till February 12, 2008, with an expenditure of Rs. 34,435.39 crore under the scheme.

Besides, the Ministry of Rural Areas and Employment in Coordination with Nirmithi National Institute of Habitat Management, Thiruvananthapuram organised a Study Tour to Kerala State Nirmithi Kendra (KES-NIK) from 7th – 9th October,1998 in order to sensitise the State Secretaries of Housing, Heads of Housing Departments etc. about alternative cost, effective environment-friendly technologies, materials and designs.

**Table 1**

**Physical and Financial Achievements under Indira Awaas Yojana since inception upto 12-02-2008**

| *Year* | *Expenditure (Rs. In Crores)* | *Number of houses built* |
|---|---|---|
| 1985-86 | 57.93 | 51,252 |
| 1986-87 | 149.18 | 1,60,197 |
| 1987-88 | 235.37 | 1,69,302 |
| 1988-89 | 149.65 | 1,39,192 |
| 1989-90 | 188.50 | 1,86,023 |
| 1990-91 | 213.07 | 1,81,800 |
| 1991-92 | 263.01 | 2,07,299 |
| 1992-93 | 238.81 | 1,92,585 |
| 1993-94 | 481.00 | 3,72,535 |
| 1994-95 | 500.38 | 3,90,482 |
| 1995-96 | 1,166.36 | 8,63,889 |
| 1996-97 | 1,385.92 | 8,06,290 |
| 1997-98 | 1,591.48 | 7,70,936 |
| 1998-99 | 1,803.88 | 8,35,770 |
| 1999-2000 | 1,907.63 | 9,25,679 |
| 2000-2001 | 2,185.80 | 11,70,926 |
| 2001-2002 | 2,149.55 | 11,71,081 |
| 2002-2003 | 2794.96 | 15,48,641 |
| 2003-2004 | 2580.09 | 13,61,230 |
| 2004-2005 | 3262.09 | 15,21,305 |
| 2005-2006 | 3654.09 | 15,51,923 |
| 2006-2007 | 4253.42 | 14,98,367 |
| 2007-2008 | 3223.15 | 10,92,426 |
| **Total** | **34,435.39** | **1,71,69,130** |

| | | |
|---|---:|---:|
| Seventh Plan | 780.63 | 70,05,966 |
| Annual Plans | 476.08 | 3,89,099 |
| Eighth Plan | 3772.51 | 26,25,781 |
| Ninth Plan | 9638.36 | 48,74,392 |
| Tenth Plan | 16,544.66 | 74,81,466 |
| Eleventh Plan one year | 3223.15 | 10,92,426 |

## New Initiatives

Government has recognised shelter as a basic human requirement which needs to be met on a priority basis. It has announced a National Housing and Habitat Policy which aims at providing 'Housing for All' and to facilitate construction of 13 lakhs additional housing units in rural areas annually with an emphasis on extending benefits to the poor and the deprived. An Action Plan for Rural Housing has accordingly been prepared. The Action Plan comprising of a series of recommendations for policy, institutional and schematic interventions has attempted to address the various issues related to rural housing in a holistic fashion and yet emerge with workable and practical interventions. Among the highlights of the Action Plan for the construction of 13 lakh additional houses in rural areas are:

## Conversion of Unserviceable Kutcha Houses into Semi-pucca/Pucca Houses

There are 103.1 lakh unserviceable kutcha houses requiring upgradation in the rural areas. It is therefore, proposed to convert unserviceable kutcha houses to semi–pucca/pucca houses under this scheme with an assistance of Rs. 10,000, per unit utilising the 20% of available funds for IAY. Conversion will necessarily include a provision of sanitary latrine and smokeless chullah.

## Credit-cum-Subsidy Component of IAY

There are a large number of households in the rural areas who have not been covered under IAY, since they do not fall within the Below Poverty Line category. They also do not have high repayment capacity to take benefit of loan based programmes as offered by housing finance institutions. The needs of this large majority located just above the poverty line can be met through a sub–scheme of IAY, which is part credit and part subsidy based. The Finance Minister in his Budget Speech had also announced the credit-cum-subsidy based sub-scheme would be an important step in the direction of redefining the role of government from that of a 'provider' to a 'facilitator' as envisaged in the new National Housing and Habitat Policy, 1998. It is, therefore, proposed to initiate a credit-cum-subsidy component of IAY, which will be targeted to the group just above the poverty line having income limit of Rs. 32,000 annually. It is proposed that the upper ceiling limit of assistance will be restricted to assistance limit under Indira Awaas Yojana (presently Rs.20,000 for plan areas and Rs.22,000 for hilly/difficult areas). The subsidy will be restricted to a maximum of 50% of IAY assistance limit.

## Innovative Stream for Rural Housing and Habitat Development

Presently under IAY, it is left to the beneficiary to select building/housing design technology and materials. In fact houses being built under IAY suffer from inadequacies such as the use of expensive materials, technology and design, lack of thermal comfort and the inability to withstand natural calamities. An important and collinear area of concern which needs to be tackled along with housing is the deteriorating habitat and non-availability of quality infrastructure support services. In view of this, an Innovative Stream for Rural Housing and Habitat Development is proposed to be initiated.

Under this scheme it is proposed to provide financial assistance for efforts initiated on a project basis by organisations such as HUDCO/Building Material Technology Promotion Council (BMTPC) Central Building Research Institute (CBRI)/NGOs etc.

## Institutional Mechanisms for Improved Shelter Delivery

At present there are virtually no institutional structures available in the country to support rural housing initiatives, whether we consider housing finance or the areas of housing construction technology, designs or habitat. A series of initiatives are therefore being proposed to address these glaring inadequacies.

## Setting up of Rural Building Centres

The primary objectives of setting up of a building centre are:

*(i)* Technology transfer and information dissemination

*(ii)* Skill upgradation through training and

*(iii)* Production of cost effective and environment friendly material components.

In other words, a building centre will be involved in transfer of technology from 'lab to land', production of cost effective building materials for sale and providing training to carpenters, masons, etc.

The Rural Building Centre Programme is proposed to be implemented through one or more agencies contributing to the rural housing/rural development programmes such as HUDCO, BMTPC or well known state organisations involved in setting up of such centres. These rural building centres are intended to be located within the close reach of rural populations. It is proposed to provide one time grant for setting up of a building centre at the State of Rs. 5 lakhs.

*Fig. 4. Promotion of cost effective and environment friendly materials through Rural Building Centres*

## National Mission for Rural Housing

The National Housing and Habitat Policy, 1998 states: "At present the rural housing and to a large extent informal housing do not benefit from the outcome of research and development. Efforts will be made to disseminate information about new technologies and provide training to construction workers in the use of new technologies. In this regard a mission approach may be adopted." Adoption of a 'mission' approach will significantly alter the rural housing scenario, by enabling the induction of science and technology inputs on a continuous basis into the sector and providing convergence to technology, habitat and energy related issues. Moreover, this will sought to be achieved within a specified timeframe and through community intermediation. It is, therefore proposed to set up a National Mission for Rural Housing.

Construction design, materials and technologies are culturally rooted and region specific, these need to be documented/located with reference to past practice and accumulated knowledge systems and thereafter disseminated through a people centered, region specific information, education and communication strategy. Hence housing and habitat related problems would be dealt with through the co-ordinated effort of various agencies and local communities, within specified time frames and low cost, replicable solutions evolved. A threefold strategy of strengthening of supply lines for technologies, materials, awareness creation among the rural populace and improvement in skills of rural sector professionals will be its centerpiece. This will enable qualitative improvement in both quality of construction techniques, habitats and in maintenance practices.

## Setting up of Rural Housing and Habitat Development Corporation

Presently the outreach of housing finance institutions in the rural areas is negligible. There is virtually no institutional finance going in for the creation of infrastructure support services in the rural areas. For instance, the definition adopted by the National Housing Bank for rural areas, enables it to extend loaning under the Golden Jubilee Rural Housing Finance Scheme to residents of townships having population up to 50,000. It would be pertinent to mention that about 83% urban local bodies fall in this category. To facilitate and co-ordinate the rural housing programme, through a multipronged approach of evolving strategies for extending the outreach of housing finance in the rural areas, sourcing of capital from both internal and external sources and the development of a menu approach for housing and habitat development, it is proposed to set up a Rural Housing and Habitat Development Corporation under the administrative control of the Ministry of Rural Areas and Employment. The setting up of a separate Rural Housing and Habitat Development Corporation dedicated to the cause of enabling the creation of quality and cost effective rural human settlements will go a long way in achieving the set goals of 'Housing for All'.

## Impact of IAY

Providing houses to the poorest has a positive impact on people's physical and mental health. It also has a bearing on children's education, sanitation and on better standard of living. Since, the construction of an IAY house is the sole responsibility of the beneficiary, it has raised the participation of people in the programme.

## Success Stories in Rural Housing & Habitat Development

Shri Bhagyamma w/o Late Chikkaraju of Alkere village in Mandya Taluk is from BPL family. She is wage labourer and a widow who belongs to Scheduled Caste having two female school going children, one is in the 7th and the second one is in the 5th standard. She is the only wage earner in the family. Before she was staying in a thatched hut. Grama Sabha decided her name for house grant under the Indira Awaas Yojana (IAY) and to construct house herself without involving contractor. She came forward and constructed house to her own satisfaction along with smokeless chulha and sanitary latrine as per guidelines. Now she feels much better having her own pucca house to live.

## Provision of Urban Amenities in Rural Areas

The Scheme of Provision of Urban amenities in Rural Areas (PURA) was announced by the Hon'ble Prime Minister in his speech on 15 August 2003 based on the concept promoted by the Hon'ble President of India to bridge the rural-urban divide and achieve a balanced socio-economic development.

The scheme aims to meet the gaps in physical and social infrastructure in the identified rural clusters consisting of 10-15 villages around towns with population of one lakh or less to further their growth potential.. The identified areas of intervention and support are:

- Road, transportation and power connectivity
- Electronic connectivity in the form of reliable telecom, internet and IT services
- Knowledge connectivity in the form of good educational and training institutions
- Market connectivity that would enable farmers to get the best price for their produce
- Provision of drinking water supply and up-gradation of existing health facilities.

These facilities are expected to be created by the implementing Agencies by converging resources of the on-going Central and State Government programmes. If there is any gap which cannot be funded under any scheme or the available funds under the existing schemes are insufficient for the purpose, such gaps will be funded through PURA. The PURA builds on the existing schemes while providing funds for critical gaps.

Ministry of Rural Development in consultation with Planning Commission decided to launch a pilot phase for implementation of PURA in seven States selecting one cluster of 10-15 villages in each State. The seven clusters selected for the pilot phase are Rayadurg (district Annanthpur in the State of Andhra Pradesh), Gohpur (district Sonitpur in the State of Assam), Motipur (district Muzzafarpur in the State of Bihar), Basmath (district Hingoli in the State of Maharashtra), Kujunga (district Jagatsinghpur in the State of Orissa), Shahpur (district Bhilwara in the State of Rajasthan) and Bharthana (district Etawah in the State of Uttar Pradesh).

A Steering Committee on PURA under the chairmanship of Secretary (RD) has been constituted to examine, sanction and monitor the implementation of the project under PURA. The Committee in its meeting held on 11th January 2005 decided that each cluster under PURA scheme would be financed to the tune of Rs. 4-5 crores over the period of three years. Based on the decision of the Steering Committee, funds are released to the States. The budget provision has been Rs. 10 crore per year in 2004-05, 2005-06 and 2006-07. So far, Rs. 20.50 crores have been released to the States against which an expenditure of Rs. 20.27 crores as on 31.12.07 has been reported.

At present, based on the experience of pilot phase, the Scheme is being restructured for implementation of a full fledged Scheme. A note on restructured PURA Scheme prepared by this ministry was considered by Committee of Secretaries (COS) in its meeting on 19th September 2006. COS recommended implementation of PURA as a regular scheme during the 11th Five Year Plan, covering all the districts in rural areas.

❑ ❑ ❑

*"The Directive principles of state policy in the constitution (Article 41) of India directs the state to provide public assistance to its citizens in case of unemployment, old age, sickness and disablement within the limit of its economic capacity and development."*

Chapter 15

# NATIONAL SOCIAL ASSISTANCE PROGRAMME

## Introduction

The National Social Assistance Programme (NSAP) which came into effect from 15th August 1995 represents a significant step towards the fulfilment of the Directive Principles in Article 41 and 42 of the Constitution. It introduces a national policy for social assistance benefit to poor households in the case of old age, death of primary bread-winner and maternity. The programme has three components, namely:

(1) National Old Age Pension Scheme (NOAPS)

(2) National Family Benefit Scheme (NFBS)

(3) National Maternity Benefit Scheme (NMBS)

These schemes were modified in 1998 based on the feedback received from the state governments. The salient features of these schemes in their present modified form are given below:

## NATIONAL OLD AGE PENSION SCHEME

Under this scheme, central assistance is available as per the following criteria:

- Age of the applicant (male or female) is 65 years or more.
- The applicant is a destitute in the sense of having little or no regular means of subsistence from his/her own sources of income or through financial support from family members or other sources.
- The amount of old age pension is Rs. 75 per month for the purpose of claiming central assistance.

## NATIONAL FAMILY BENEFIT SCHEME

Central assistance is available under this scheme for a lump sum family benefit for households below the poverty line on the death of the primary bread winner in the bereaved family subject to the following conditions:

- The 'primary bread winner' is the member of the household, male or female whose earnings contribute substantially to the total household income.
- The death of such a primary bread winner occurs while he or she is more than 18 years of age and less than 65 years of age.
- The bereaved household qualifies as one below the poverty line according to the criteria prescribed by the Government of India.
- The amount of benefit available is Rs. 10,000 in the case of death of the primary bread winner irrespective of the cause of death — natural or accidental.
- The family benefit is paid to such surviving member of the household of deceased who after local enquiry, is determined to be the head of the household.

## NATIONAL MATERNITY BENEFIT SCHEME

Under this scheme, maternity benefit is provided as a lump sum cash assistance to women of households below the poverty line, subject to the following conditions:

- The maternity benefit is restricted to pregnant women for up to the first two live births provided they are of 19 years of age and above.
- The beneficiary belongs to a household below the poverty line as per criteria prescribed by the Government of India.
- The amount of the benefit is Rs. 500.
- While the benefit should be disbursed 8-12 weeks prior to delivery, in case of delay the benefit may be disbursed even after the child is born.

Under the modified guidelines the state government would be free to adopt any mode of disbursement of benefits, namely, cash, money order, bank account of beneficiaries in the post office saving bank/commercial bank. The benefit under NOAPS could be disbursed in not more than two instalments in a year. In case of cash disbursement, the payment shall be made in public meetings preferably of Gram Sabha in villages and in neighbourhood/mohalla committee meetings in towns.

*Fig. 1. Helping the old and the destitute under NOAPS*

### Objectives of the Programme

The NSAP is a 100% centrally sponsored programme. The NSAP aims at ensuring minimum national standards in providing social assistance benefits to poor households. These are in addition to the benefits that the states are currently providing or might provide in future. The intention in providing 100 per cent central assistance is to ensure that social protection to the beneficiaries everywhere in the country is uniformly available without interruption. Accordingly, it should be ensured that central assistance does not displace states' own expenditure in this respect and States/UTs may expand their own coverage of social assistance independently wherever they wish to do so.

The NSAP provides opportunities for linking social assistance packages to schemes for poverty alleviation and provision of basic needs. Specifically, old age pension can be linked to medical care and other benefits for the old and the poor. Integrated Rural Development Programme/Nehru Rozgar Yojana assistance may be provided in addition to the family benefit for the families of poor households who suffer the loss of the bread winner. Maternity assistance can be linked to maternal and child care.

## Implementation of the Programme

The NSAP is implemented in the States/UTs though Panchayats and municipalities. The panchayats and municipalities are encouraged to involve voluntary agencies to the extent possible in taking the benefits to the poor households for whom they are intended. The States/UTs have already taken various steps to appropriately implement the programme.

The Gram Panchayats/Municipalities are expected to play an active role in the identification of beneficiaries under the three NSAP Schemes. The State Government may thus, communicate the targets for NOAPS, NFBS and NMBS to the Panchayats/Municipalities so that the identification of beneficiaries can suitably be made by the Gram Panchayats/Neighbourhood/Mohalla Committees in line with these targets. Further, Central Assistance under NOAPS, NFBS and NMBS may also be preferably disbursed in public meetings, such as Gram Sabha meetings in the rural areas and Neighbourhood/Mohalla Committee meetings in urban areas. The Panchayats/Municipalities are responsible for disseminating information about NSAP and the procedures for obtaining benefits under it. In this task, they may encourage the involvement and cooperation of voluntary organisations also.

**Table 1**

**THE SCHEME WISE DISBURSEMENT OF SOCIAL ASSISTANCE TILL DECEMBER 2000**

| *Scheme* | *Budgetary Allocation (Rs. Crores)* | *Beneficiaries (in Lakh)* | *Assistance Released Rs. Crores* |
|---|---|---|---|
| NOAPS | 447 | 55.45 | 347.62 |
| NFBS | 193 | 1.00 | 142.86 |
| NMBS | 73 | 6.46 | 55.80 |
| Total | 713 | 62.91 | 546.28 |

❑ ❑ ❑

*"The key to Swaraj is not with the cities but with the villages. When I succeed in ridding the villages of their poverty, I have won Swaraj for you and for the whole of India."* — *Mahatma Gandhi*

Chapter 16

# RURAL WATER SUPPLY PROGRAMME

## Introduction

In terms of human needs, water availability is highly variable across Indian states. Water is a basic need. The availability of decent water supply and sanitation system goes a long way to improving the quality of life for rural people.

## States' Responsibility

Provision of safe drinking water in the rural areas is the responsibility of the States. Funds are being provided for provision of the facility in the state budgets right from the First Five Year Plan period. The Accelerated Rural Water Supply Programme (ARWSP) was introduced in 1972-73 by the Government of India (GOI), to assist the States and Union Territories to accelerate the pace of coverage of drinking water supply. To ensure maximum inflow of scientific and technical input into the rural water supply sector to improve the performance, cost effectiveness of the on-going programmes and ensure adequate supply of safe drinking water, the entire programme was given a mission approach. The Technology Mission on drinking water and related water management was launched in 1986. It was also called the National Drinking Water Mission (NDWM) and was one of the five societal missions launched by the Government of India. The NDWM was renamed Rajiv Gandhi National Drinking Water Mission (RGNDWM) in 1991.

It was realised that the objective of supplying safe water would not be achieved unless the sanitary aspects of water and the issue of sanitation are addressed together. The Centrally Sponsored Rural Sanitation Programme (CRSP) was launched in 1986 with the overall objective of improving the quality of life of the rural people.

It is envisaged that the two programmes, the ARWSP and the CRSP, implemented simultaneously would help break the vicious circle of disease, morbidity and poor health, resulting from water borne diseases and insanitary conditions.

## ACCELERATED RURAL WATER SUPPLY PROGRAMME

The Accelerated Rural Water Supply Programme (ARWSP) aims at providing safe and adequate drinking water facilities to the rural population by supplementing the efforts made by the State Governments/UTs under the State Sector Minimum Needs Programme (MNP). Keeping in view the different kinds of problems arising while providing potable water in the rural areas, 56 mini-missions (pilot projects) were identified covering all States/UTs. These pilot projects helped to evolve models that are replicable and can be incorporated in the on-going programmes.

### Objectives

The prime objectives of the ARWSP are:

*(a)* to ensure coverage of all rural habitations especially to reach the unreached with access to safe drinking water.

*(b)* to ensure sustainability of the system and sources; and

*(c)* to tackle the problem of water quality in affected habitations and to preserve quality of water by institutionalising water quality monitoring and surveillance through a Catchment Area Approach.

### Norms

The provision of drinking water facilities in the problem villages is based on the following norms:

- 40 litres of safe drinking water per capita per day (lpcd) for human beings.
- 30 lpcd additionally for cattle in the Desert Development Programme (DDP) areas.
- One hand pump or stand post for every 250 persons.
- The water source should exit within the habitation or within a distance of 1.6 km, in the plains and within 100 metres elevation difference in the hills.
- Drinking water is defined as safe if it is free from bacteria contamination, chemical contamination *viz.*, fluoride, iron, arsenic, nitrate, brackishness is excess or beyond permissible limits.

### Priorities

Viewing the objective of providing safe drinking water facility in all the villages, there is need for a certain order of priority which is as follows:

- To cover the "Not Covered" (NC) habitations.
- To fully cover the "Partially Covered" (PC) habitations getting less than 10 lpcd.
- To cover all habitations having water quality problems.
- To supply water to all habitations with per capita supply of less than 40 lpcd at the rate of 40 lpcd.
- To provide water supply facilities for the scheduled castes (SC), scheduled tribes (ST) and the landless agricultural labourers.
- To provide safe drinking water in every rural primary school.

  Once the task of providing every village with at least one source of safe drinking water is completed, the enhancement and expansion process may be initiated to provide adequate drinking water. The above mentioned norms can then be liberalised so as to now cover:

- Villages that do not have an assured source of safe drinking water within a distance of 0.5 km. (as against 1.6 km)
- To enhance the per capita rate of supply (as against the 40 lpcd rate)
- Adopting the above norms would mean providing once source for every 150 persons (as agains one source for every 250 persons).

*Fig. 1.*

## ARWSP Allocation Criteria

The allocations are subject to matching provision by States under their MNP. The criteria for allocation of funds is as given below:

**Table 1**

| *Component* | *ARWSP funds* | *Purpose* | *Funding pattern* |
|---|---|---|---|
| ARWSP (Natural Calamity) | 5% | For restoration of water supply suffered on account of any kind of natural calamity | 100% GoI funding |
| ARWSP (DDP Areas) | 5% | For drinking water supply in DDP blocks/areas | 100% GoI funding |

| ARWSP (Support activities/programme) | 2% | For various support activities relating to rural, water supply viz. MIS, IEC, HRD water quality monitoring & surveillance, etc. | 100% GoI funding |
|---|---|---|---|
| Sub-Mission on Water Quality | Up to 20% | For addressing quality problems in the affected habitations | 75:25 GoI and State |
| ARWSP (Normal) | Rest of the funds | -up to 5% of total funds for sustainability, -up to 15% for operation & maintenance, and remaining amount for coverage | 50:50 GoI and State |

| *Weightage for* | *Percentage* |
|---|---|
| Rural Population | 40 |
| States under DDP, DPAP, HADP & special category hill States in terms of rural areas | 35 |
| Not Covered/Partially Covered village (at 2:1 ratio) | 15 |
| Quality affected village (40:40:15:5)* | 15 |
| **Total** | **100** |

| *Weightage for* | *Percentage* |
|---|---|
| Proportionate rural population in DDP blocks | 40 |
| NC/PC habitations (at 2:1 ratio) | 35 |
| Quality affected habitations | 25 |

The States/UTs have to earmark 25% as minimum outlay for SC and 10% as minimum outlay for STs, for taking up water supply schemes exclusively for them. The ARWSP guidelines state that at the time of scheme formulation, the coverage of SC/ST should be given first preference so as to ensure equal access to water supply facilities.

*Fig. 2. Community participation for safe and adequate drinking water*

# PHYSICAL AND FINANCIAL PROGRESS

## Physical Progress

- More than 3.50 million handpumps installed.
- Over 1 lakh piped water supply schemes installed.
- Coverage of habitations:

As per information received from the States/UTs till November, 2000, the status of coverage of rural habitations is as under:

**Table 2**

| *Type of coverage* | *Number of habitations* | *Percentage of total habitations covered* |
|---|---|---|
| Total | 1,422,664 | |
| Fully Covered (FC) | 1,203,323 | 84.58 |
| Partially Covered (PC) | 1,95,426 | 13.74 |
| Not Covered (NC) | 23,915 | 1.68 |

*(Number of habitations)*

| *Year* | *Target* | *Achievement* |
|---|---|---|
| 2002-03 | 63,869 | 39,250 |
| 2003-04 | 1,11,051 | 39,736 |
| 2004-05 | 74;868 | 69,639 |
| 2005-06 | 56,270 | 97,215 |
| 2006-07 | 73,120 | 1,07,350 |
| **Total** | **3,79,178** | **3,53,190** |

## Financial Progress

Government has invested more than about Rs.30,000 crores for the programme since its inception. Details regarding the investment made in the sector during the Ninth Plan are as under:

**Table 3**

*(Rs. in crore)*

| *Year MNP* | *Release* | *ARWSP Expenditure* |
|---|---|---|
| 1997-98 | 1,299.91 | 1,676.44 |
| 1998-99 | 1,610.64 | 1,896.35 |
| 99-2000 | 1,717.91 | 2,456.16 |
| 2000-2001 | 1,326.19 | 988.23* |
| Total | 5,954.65 | 7,013.74 |

* provisional

*(Amount Rs. in crore)*

| *Year* | *ARWSP* | | *State share* | |
|---|---|---|---|---|
| | *Allocation* | *Release* | *Provision* | *Expenditure* |
| 2002-2003 | 2,100.70 | 2,100.70 | 2,698.46 | 2,395.65 |
| 2003-2004 | 2,565.01 | 2,564.90 | 2,821.52 | 2,488.06 |
| 2004-2005 | 2,900.00 | 2,930.79 | 3,380.19 | 2,971.52 |
| 2005-2006 | 4,060.00 | 4,098.03 | 3,931.05 | 3,165.26 |
| 2006-2007 | 4,560.00 | 4,560.00 | 5,150.46 | 4,192.23 |
| **Total 10th Plan** | **16,195.01** | **16,254.43** | **17,981.68** | **15,212.72** |

## Policy Initiative

The Ministry has revamped the Rural Water Supply Programme which, with a view aims to usher in reforms by institutionalising community participation in the rural water supply sector with a view to gradually replace the government oriented, centralised, supply-driven and non-people participating Rural Water Supply Programme by a people oriented, decentralised, demand-driven and community-based Rural Water Supply Programme. 20% of the annual ARWSP outlay would be given to those State Governments who undertake community-based Rural Water Supply Programmes by adopting the demand-driven approach based on empowerment of villagers to ensure their full participation in the project, through a decision-making role in the choice of key design and management arrangements, and part of capital cost and 100% O&M cost to be borne by the users.

The reforms, are, at this stage being implemented through specific projects in 58 pilot districts identified by the State Governments. These projects are mainly IEC-based and would commence with start-up activities and a heavy component of awareness and HRD campaigns.

The IEC campaigns would be aimed at educating the rural people about the need for them to actively participate in the programme, various technologies available, its capital cost, operation and maintenance costs, etc., of each of the possible technology options and the benefits of the people planning, funding, implementing, owning, operating, maintaining and replacing the water supply schemes of their choice. The HRD campaigns would be aimed at giving the rural population the requisite training to carry out the responsibilities indicated above. The physical work under the project would commence only subsequently on the basis of the awareness and demand generated by the campaigns in the first stage. Even though, the requirement of funds is likely to be slightly higher, it is expected that it would be a one-time investment as by the time the project is completed the beneficiaries would be sufficiently equipped to operate and manage their rural water supply schemes and to plan, fund and implement the replacement schemes after the expiry of the life of the existing schemes.

Project in respect of fifty seven districts identified by the State Governments for implementing the sector reform projects on a pilot basis, have already been sanctioned for implementation.

## Involvement of Women

Since women are the principal beneficiaries of this programme, it is of crucial importance that women are involved at all the stages of Rural Water Supply Schemes, particularly while making decisions on the location of the standpost/spot sources in the villages/habitations. Information about sources of water should be obtained from women by the surveyors of the Schemes. They should also be involved in the following manner:

(*a*) At least 30% of handpump mistries under NHRD, TRYSEM and other training schemes, should be women of the local areas/habitations as they can take better care of the operation and maintenance of the handpump schemes than others.

(*b*) There should be women caretakers for handpumps in the habitations.

(*c*) Certificate about satisfactory completion of the Schemes may be obtained from women groups in the habitations.

(*d*) Prominent women from the habitation should be represented on the Village Level Water Monitoring Committees.

Experience has shown that where women are involved in such consultation and in the maintenance of the spot sources, the performance of the water-supply system has been effective.

## HUMAN RESOURCE DEVELOPMENT

Sustainable management of rural water supply and sanitation needs not only the engineering systems but also community participation and empowerment, together with adequately trained professional and sensitised planners, administrators and decision makers. To build up a human resource base of appropriately trained personnel to serve the needs of the rural water supply and sanitation sector, the National Human Resource Development Programme (NHRDP) was launched in 1994. The major objectives of the NHRDP are *(a)* to train at least one beneficiary, especially women, at the grassroots level in each village of the country, *(b)* improve the productivity of sector professionals through specialised courses and *(c)* to introduce rural orientation in technical education sector coupled with publication of manuals on rural water supply and rural sanitation.

The implementation of the NHRDP involves:

- Creating a resource pool of trainers for training grassroot level trainees in the villages through the Indian Training Network (ITN).
- Establishing Human Resource Development (HRD) cells in all the states to undertake HRD activities in the states, based on trainer assessment.
- Networking with NGOs, Technical Teacher Training Institute, community polytechnics, training institutes/ organisations etc.
- Conducting specialised courses and experience sharing workshops for sector professionals, in India and abroad.
- Evolving courses, for introduction at diploma and degree levels, to introduce rural orientation and appropriate technologies and practices.

HRD Cells are functioning in 24 States. Up to November, 2000, 28 crores had been released to the states, for HRD activities.

Four workshops have been held so far for operationalising grass-root level training programmes. Four multimedia packages, focusing on four focal themes given below, have been prepared by the Technical Teachers' Training Institute for conducting Grassroots Level Training Programmes.

- Operation and Maintenance (O&M) of handpumps.
- Construction of sanitary toilets and other rural sanitation facilities.
- Motivation for community support mobilisation.
- Health education and hygiene promotion.

Under the programme for development of capability of in-house training instructors, the course on Ground Water Development which was being conducted in United Kingdom through the Overseas Development Agency (ODA) assistance has now been fully transferred to the Gujarat Jal Sewa Training Institute, Ahmedabad, one of the seven key institutions selected under the ITN.

## Conclusion

In order to achieve the objective of sustainable human development at the village level, rural water supply Programme is brought under the Prime Minister's Gramodaya Yojana (PMGY) Programme.

The PMGY-Rural Drinking Water Programme is to be implemented in accordance with the guidelines issued by the Government of India. Under this Scheme, minimum 25% of the total allocation for the component is to be utilised by the respective States/UTs on projects/schemes for water conservation, water harvesting, water recharge and sustainability of the drinking water sources in respect of DDP/DPAP areas, over exploited dark/grey blocks and other water stress/drought affected areas and the balance 75% of the allocation can be used for tackling water quality and coverage of Not Covered (NC) and Partially Covered (PC) habitations.

The hope for the future lies in doing for water productivity what the green revolution did for crop productivity. This "blue revolution", as it has been termed by various scientists and water planners, would dramatically improve the efficiency of fresh water use. Adopting socially inclusive policies to spread the benefits of water resource development to the poor and others, benefits society as a whole by improving living conditions, health, social stability, and opportunities for productive employment.

❑ ❑ ❑

*"Rural Sanitation improves the health and quality of life of rural people and provide privacy and dignity to women. Total sanitation is key to rural development."*

# Chapter 17

# RURAL SANITATION

## Introduction

Rural Sanitation is a state subject. The efforts of the states are supplemented by the central government. The centrally sponsored Central Rural Sanitation Programme (CRSP) was launched in the year 1986 with the objective of improving the quality of life of the rural people and to provide privacy and dignity to the women. The concept of sanitation including safe disposal of solid and liquid waste including human excreta, personal, domestic and environmental hygiene. The central funds allocated under the CRSP/TSC supplement the state sources made available under the State sector MNP.

## Objectives

- Accelerate coverage of rural population, specially among households below poverty line (BPL), with sanitation facilities, complementing the effort in Rural Water Supply.
- Generate felt need through awareness creation and health education involving Voluntary Organisations (VO) and Panchayati Raj Institutions (PRIs).
- Eradicate manual scavenging by converting all existing dry latrines into low cost sanitary latrines.
- Encourage cost effective and appropriate technologies to support other objectives.
- The Total Sanitation Campaign (TSC) launched in 1999 focuses on awareness generation to create demand for sanitation facilities.

The main objective of the TSC are:

(i) Bring about an improvement in the general quality of life in rural areas.

(ii) Accelerate sanitation coverage.

(iii) Generate demand through wareness and health education.

(iv) Cover all schools and anganwadis in rural areas with sanitation facilities and promote hygiene behaviour among students and teachers.

(v) Encourage cost effective and appropriate technology development and application.

(vi) Endeavour to reduce water and sanitation related diseases.

*Fig. 1. Towards setting up of sanitary marts.*

## Programme Components

- Construction of individual sanitary latrines for households below poverty line with subsidy (80%) where demand exists.
- Encourage other households to buy facilities through markets, including sanitary marts.
- Assist in setting up of sanitary marts.
- Launch intensive awareness campaigns in selected areas.
- Establish sanitary complexes exclusively for women.
- Encourage locally suitable and acceptable models of latrines.
- Promote total sanitation of village through construction of drains, soakage pits for liquid and solid waste disposal.

## Brief details of each Component

### Construction of Individual Household Latrines

Construction of individual household latrines by persons below poverty line may be supported in cluster of 20 or more in a village.

The unit cost of construction should be limited to Rs 2,500 of which 80% could be paid as subsidy to the selected beneficiaries below the poverty line. In case the unit cost exceeds Rs. 2500 the additional cost should be borne by the beneficiaries or specific approval of the Government of India may be obtained before execution. Out of the total annual funds a minimum 20% should be earmarked for paying subsidy to the individual households from SCs and STs below the poverty line where the percentage of SC/ST population to the total population below poverty line is less than 20%. Where the SC/ST population below poverty line is more than 20% of the total population below poverty line earmarking should be enhanced at least to match the percentage of SC/ST population. The proportion of rural families with access to toilets has gone upto 49 percent in 2007.

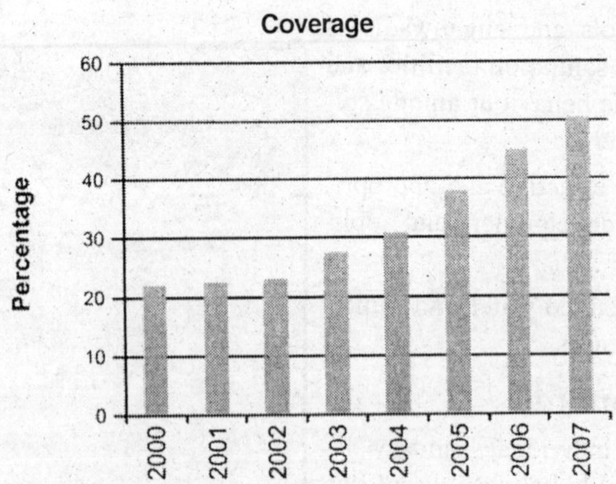


*The proportion of rural families with access to toilets has been increasing*

## Technological Options

The Mission has already circulated the report of the Expert Committee, which has recommended a vast range of (27 Nos.) Technical Options with cost estimates, keeping in view the concept of vertical upgradation, varying soil and hydrogeological conditions and acceptability and affordability of the beneficiaries.

In order to explore for additional models and to supplement the information provided in the report of the National Expert Committee on Technological Options for the implementation of the rural sanitation programme in the country, a committee has been constituted under the Chairmanship of the Mission Director. The committee will suggest additional models/technologies to supplement the information provided in the Handbook on Technological Options with special emphasis to waterlogged/rocky areas and the islands.

## Village Sanitation Complexes for Women

Though public latrines have not proved to be very successful in past, in view of the difficulties experienced by rural women in some areas, where individual household latrines are not feasible, village sanitary complexes exclusively for women could be attempted on a pilot basis. Up to 10% of the annual funds can be utilised to provide public latrines in selected villages during the plan period, where the panchayats/charitable trust/NGO offer to construct and maintain village complexes exclusively for the use of women.

*Fig. 2. Rural Sanitary Mart*

## Rural Sanitary Marts

United Nations International Children's Fund (UNICEF) have successfully demonstrated the validity of the concept of sanitary marts by implementing the scheme through voluntary organisations in Uttar Pradesh and the Ramkrishna Mission in Midnapur district, West Bengal. Rural Sanitary Marts (RSMs) are outlets dealing with materials required for construction of latrines and other sanitary facilities. Besides, it also keeps the designs of various low-cost sanitary facilities showing estimated costs and the list of trained masons. Rural Sanitary Marts also serve as service centres. UNICEF provides assistance of Rs 50,000 for each mart with turnover of Rs 2 lakhs per annum. Managerial subsidy is provided up to Rs 18,000 per annum for a period of two years One time assistance up to Rs 12,000 is provided for publicity etc.

Where UNICEF assistance is not available for setting up RSMs, the State Governments/UT Administrations can set up Rural Sanitary Marts with assistance from the Central Government through reputed Voluntary Organisations/Panchayati Raj Institutions in difficult areas where proper marketing facilities for sanitary components do not exit. Such voluntary organisations should be carefully selected, based on the assessment of their ability to carry out the task.

## Total Sanitation of Village

Other sanitation facilities such as drains, soakpits, solid and liquid waste disposals etc. should be taken up as far as possible under Jawahar Rozgar Yojana or any other programme for civic amenities in the Panchayat. Where this is not feasible due to other priorities and non–availability of adequate financial resources, the facilities can be taken up under CRSP/TSC.

## Campaign for Creation of Felt Need

While government machinery for publicity may be useful to some extent, a well orchestrated programme of publicity, health, education and creation of required facilities only can make any change in the attitude of the people. Support of the reputed local voluntary organisations, autonomous institutions, social, political and religious organisations who carry conviction with the people can be enlisted in creating the felt need. These organisations should be selected for their reputation for good and adequate infrastructure already available with them.

## Model Village

Assistance is also given to states to develop model villages under the programme. A model village is covered with facilities like sanitary latrines, garbage pits, soakage pits, drains, paved lanes, sanitary latrines in village institutions (school, health centre, panchayat ghar, aanganwadi), smokeless chullahs, clean tanks, ponds and surroundings, sanitary wells and safe drinking water sources (handpumps, stand posts) with platforms for bathing and washing and drains.

So far, the States of Andhra Pradesh, Bihar, Assam, Karnataka, Kerala, Tamil Nadu, Madhya Pradesh, Maharashtra, Orissa, Rajasthan and Uttar Pradesh have taken up the model village scheme.

## Extent of Subsidy

The extent of subsidy from Central/State Governments and contribution from persons below poverty line/panchayat for various components of the Programme are as follows:

| *Components* | *Subsidy* | | *Contribution by User/panchayat* |
|---|---|---|---|
| | *Centre* | *State* | |
| Construction of sanitary latrines and conversion of dry latrines for individual households below poverty line | As per the | Table – 2 under | TSC |
| School sanitation | 60% | 30% | 10% |
| Village complex for women | 40% | 40% | 20% |
| Total sanitation package for villages | 50% | 40% | 10% |
| Awareness campaigns, health education, demand creation etc. | Up to 15% of annual allocation | | Nil |
| Administrative cost | Up to 5% of annual allocation | | Nil |
| RSM/PC | Up to 5% of annual allocation | | Nil |

## Physical Progress:

As on December, 2007, 578 projects in the country are under implementation. The main physical components sanctioned in the 578 projects to be achieved over a period of 4-5 years are as follows:

i) Construction of 569.53 lakh individual household latrines for BPL families

ii) Construction of 614.97 lakh individual household latrines for APL families

iii) 11.21 lakh toilet units for schools

iv) 4.11 lakh toilets for Balwadis/Anganwadis

v) 27,661 community sanitary complexes

vi) 4,248 Rural Sanitary Marts/Production Centers.

About 223.31 lakh household toilets for BPL and 163.67 lakh for APL have been constructed with support from the TSC. Besides, 4.92 lakh school toilets, 1.55 lakh anganwadi toilets, 11,922 community complexes and 7,531 production centers/rural sanitary marts (RSMs) have been set up.

| *Financial Year* | *IHHL BPL* | *IHHL APL* | *Total IHHL* | *School Toilets* | *Sanitary Complex* | *Balwadi Toilets* |
|---|---|---|---|---|---|---|
| 2001-2002 | 638660 | 0 | 638660 | 10210 | 512 | 674 |
| 2002-2003 | 662130 | 0 | 662130 | 11197 | 428 | 979 |
| 2003-2004 | 5577528 | 620350 | 6197878 | 66230 | 1580 | 9589 |
| 2004-2005 | 2737178 | 1716690 | 4453868 | 55236 | 1623 | 10631 |
| 2005-2006 | 4161145 | 5650437 | 9811582 | 88109 | 2880 | 36074 |
| 2006-2007 | 4800192 | 5093124 | 9893316 | 131952 | 3018 | 53179 |
| 2007-2008* | 3750474 | 3285878 | 7036352 | 128757 | 1881 | 44481 |
| Total | 22327307 | 16366479 | 38693786 | 491691 | 11922 | 156607 |
| (As on 31.12.2007) | | | | | | |

For sanitary marts, the assistance will be limited to as interest free loan as revolving fund of Rs 50,000 per mart for the purpose, which would be repayable at the end of three years. Adequate funds for this purpose can be provided from the funds released to the States/UTs depending upon the actual need.

## NANDIGRAM II BLOCK ACHIEVES FULL SANITATION COVERAGE

The year 2002 witnessed historical achievement in the Rural Sanitation Sector when Nandigram II block of East Medinipur district of West Bengal achieved full sanitation coverage. All the rural households (18,003) have got sanitation facilities and open defeaction has been stopped in all 7 Gram Panchayats in the block. The success in Nandigram II has been due to sincere involvement of Rama Krishna Mission Lok Siksha Parishad and its cluster NGOs, active PRI system in the Medinipur district and support by district administration as well UNICEF. The success of Nandigram II has motivated many blocks in West Bengal and other parts of the country to attain full sanitation coverage. A multi-disciplinary Review Mission consisting of representatives from Government of India, leading NGOs and UN agencies visited the Nandigram II to assess the extent of success and its impact.

## CRSP/TSC Allocation Criteria

Funds available under the Annual Plan are allocated to the States/UTs in accordance with the following:

- 50% weightage given to incidence of poverty in the State/UT.
- 40% weightage given to rural population.

- 10% weightage given to recognised hill states and hilly areas on the basis of their population.

## New Initiatives

The Programme has been radically changed with effect from Ist April, 1999. The restructured CRSP moves away from the principle of statewise allocation primarily based on poverty criteria to a "demand-driven" approach in a phased manner with a view to widen the coverage of rural population by the end of the 9th Plan period. The revised criteria are as under:

- 50% allocation for Total Sanitation Campaigns (TSCs) in select district during the first year.
- Balance 50% for the existing but modified "allocation- based" programme.
- Progressively phasing out the "allocation based" programme.

In India, sanitation coverage in rural areas is only 20%, as a result a large number of people practice open defecation. This is the root cause for various water-borne diseases and incidence of diarrheal cases. In addition to the health hazard, lack of sanitation facilities causes a great inconvenience to the people particularly women in the rural areas.

## Conclusion

Rural sanitation is one of the key components of rural development, it strives to improve the health of rural people. The Central Rural Sanitation Programme (CRSP) provides for construction of sanitary latrines for rural households. This essential step towards clean living also ensures privacy to women. Separate bathing and washing places are also provided for women. Up to 10% of the annual funds can be utilised to provide public latrines in selected villages during the plan period, where the panchayats/charitable trusts/non-governmental organisations offer to construct and maintain village complexes exclusively for use by women.

The Total Sanitation Campaign (TSC) focuses on awareness generation to create demand for sanitation facilities. Financial support is given for construction of individual household toilets by the below poverty line (BPL), school toilets for all governments schools in the rural areas with emphasis on separate toilets for girls in all co-educational schools, toilets for Anganwadi and Balwadi centres, Community Sanitary Complexes for women in villages where land availability with individuals is a problem and people are ready to own, operate and maintain such complexes. In addition to meet the demand generated for sanitation facilities alternative delivery mechanism in the form of Production Centres and Rural Sanitary Marts are being set up. It is being implemented in 185 districts of the country.

❑ ❑ ❑

# ANNEXURE

## Alternative Service Delivery Arrangements

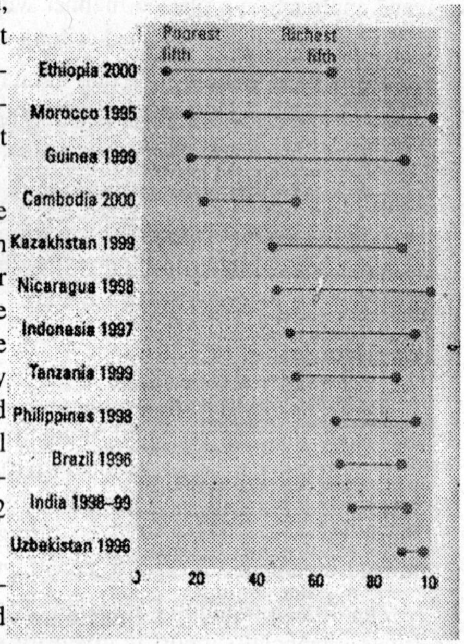


Ensuring access to basic services such as health, education, water, energy, and sanitation is a public responsibility today, but it has not always been. Nor do governments discharge this responsibility solely through central-government provision. Throughout history and around the world, societies have tried different arrangements—with mixed results.

- Some governments contract services out to the private sector, to non-governmental organisations (NGOs), even to other public agencies. In the aftermath of a civil war Cambodia introduced two forms of contracting for the delivery of primary health care ("contracting out" whole services and "contracting in" some services). Randomly assigning the arrangements across 12 districts (to avoid systematic bias), it found that health indicators, as well as use by the poor, increased most in the districts contracting out. Whether this can be scaled up beyond 12 districts in Cambodia is worth exploring.
- Governments also sell concessions to the private sector—in water, transport, electricity—with some very good and some very bad results. Privatising water in Cartagena, Colombia, improved serivces and access for the poor. A similar sale in Tucuman, Argentina, led to riots in the streets and a reversal of the concession. Overall, though, privatizing water in Argentina, by expanding access of poor communities to clean water and sewage treatment, appears to have had a favorable effect on health. One study estimates that it prevented about 375 deaths of young children a year.
- Some societies transfer responsibility (for financing, provision, and regulation) to lower tiers of government. Again, the record has varied—with potentially weaker capacity and greater political patronage at the local level and the reduced scope for redistribution sometimes outweighing the benefits from greater local participation. Local government delivery of infrastructure in South Africa improved service provision in a short time. But decentralising social assistance in Romania weakened the ability and incentives of local councils to deliver cash transfers to the poor. The program is now being recentralised.
- Responsibility is sometimes transferred to communities—to or the clients themselves. El Salvador's Community-Managed Schools Program (Educo) gives parents' associations the right to hire and fire teachers. That, plus the monthly visits to the schools by the parents' associations, has reduced teacher—and student—absenteeism, improving student performance.
- Still other programs transfer resources and responsibility to the household. Mexico's Education, Health, and Nutrition Program (Progresa) gives cash to families if their children are enrolled in school and they regularly visit a clinic. Numerous evaluations of the program shows consistently that it increased school enrolment (eight percentage points for girls and five for boys at the secondary level) and improved children's health (illness among young children fell 20 per cent).

With all these innovations, of course, comes the challenge of understanding what works—where, how, and why—so that, with enough resources, successful results can be replicated on a broad scale.

## SECTION FOUR

# APPROACH TO RURAL DEVELOPMENT

A dynamic approach or the new look is needed for alleviation of poverty, elimination of inequality and tackling the problem of unemployment and under-employment in rural sector. There should be strong stress on rural development in the formulation of plans for economic advancement. Development and anti-poverty programmes must go hand-in-hand. Local resources and skills must invariably be kept in view for economically viable household units. The household unit should be a multi-input multi-output firm for generating adequate results *viz.*, and *(i)* production at least cost so as to make it competitive, and *(ii)* generation of adequate surplus for the purpose of investment. Programmes so far have failed to achieve these twin objectives.

Rural Development is a complex phenomenon covering a wide spectrum of activities meant to ameliorate the condition of people, especially the poor people, living in rural areas. The development aspects of the rural people can broadly be stratified in five groups:

*(i)* HEALTH, hygiene, family welfare and the like covering an individual from cradle to grave;

*(ii)* AGRICULTURE, land soil, water management, transportation, storage, processing, marketing of foodgrains along with allied agricultural activities like animal husbandry, fishing, etc., which form the main source of livelihood of majority of rural population and accelerate the process of sustainable development.

*(iii)* INDUSTRIES, cottage, small scale and medium scale which forms occupation of the artisans and population other than in the agriculture sector;

*(iv)* INFRASTRUCTURE, buildings, roads, engineering and technological tasks in other sectors such as energy;

*(v)* EDUCATION, primary, secondary, non-formal, adult and other learning activities catering all the age groups of population.

But top priority in any scheme of rural development be acceded to alleviation of poverty, increased opportunity for gainful employment and elimination of inequality.

There is need for widening and sharpening the focus of several existing programmes. Supply of assets followed by credit-cum-input supply system should aim at the small and marginal farmers. As far as agricultural labourers are concerned, they should be ensured full time employment through rural industrialisation and higher level of economic activities in the agricultural and allied agricultural sectors like agricultural product-processing and agro-based industries.

The strategy for agricultural development, mostly under rainfed conditions, hinges on a comprehensive and integrated package which includes measures to improve the moisture content in the soil and reduce soil erosion, as well as measures for the adoption of cropping and improved management practices (such as appropriate time of sowing, weeding, protective irrigation etc.) Small and marginal farmers are given a subsidy for the purchase of inputs and agricultural implements. Agro-service centres provide mechanised farming services on hire and help in timely preparation of lands to increase productivity significantly. In order to ensure an adequate flow of credit to small and marginal farmers, their co-operative societies have been revitalised through various credit support measures such as the provision of risk fund contribution loans for share capital contribution, managerial subsidy and the like. Besides, such farmers are educated in the adoption of established dry farming practices. Towards the end, a comprehensive crop demonstration programme was organised on the fields of small and marginal farmers. Subsidy up to 50 per cent of input/costs was given and the extension apparatus — for example credit and marketing structure — was geared to assist farmers.

The development of irrigation was oriented towards the overall needs of the area and not towards conferring economic benefits on a few beneficiaries. For instance, in the digging of wells and construction of tanks, bunds, etc., small farmers received special attention. Assured supply of water for agriculture was a limiting factor in these areas. The cultivation of high duty crops was, therefore, gradually reduced and green fodder and perennial legumes were developed to stimulate diary development in the nearby towns and metropolis. Time constraint in developing an advanced weather forecast system and evolving suitable dryland cropping practices call for the development of cattle, sheep and poultry breeding, which can well thrive in adverse weather conditions with relatively much lower investment. The production of animal feed and fodder was stepped up in irrigated and dry areas by re-seeding with high-yielding and perennial species of grasses, legumes and similar crops under management practices.

For agricultural labourers and other rural poor, who have no assured source of income, various options are open. Some of these are poultry, piggery, sericulture, fisheries, lacworks, village crafts and marketing of milk, mutton, wool etc. The various programmes may be interlinked. For instance, community irrigation works and pastures may be developed exclusively for the benefit of agricultural labourers. Co-operative societies may be organised for them to enable them to undertake the execution of works, etc., and participate in other productive occupations.

Various operational and action-oriented research studies have been sponsored under the programme to test-check the strategy of development and the adequacy of the existing organisation, credit structure, etc., to meet and implement the plan postulates. The setting-up of the Agency to advise, execute, monitor, evaluate and modify the programme augurs well for the realisation of the objectives of growth with equity.

A reconsideration of the cropping pattern in areas where the monsoon is most unpredictable has become possible following the preparation of the latest objective map of Maharashtra on the monsoon and the cropping pattern, which specified the monsoon dates as most likely in different regions of the state and the likely deviations in precipitations along with their ancillary determinant factors. This map throws a new light on many aspects—like sowing dates. Crop periods and cropping patterns. A seeds supply organisation for expeditious supply in the event of the loss of the first sown seed due to a dry spell, will have, however, to be built up.

Some of the important approaches of the programme are:

*(i)* Development and management of water resources;

*(ii)* Soil and moisture conservation measures;

*(iii)* Afforestation, with special emphasis on social and farm forestry;

*(iv)* Development of pasture lands and range management in conjunction with the developmen^ of sheep husbandry;

*(v)* Livestock development and dairy development;

*(vi)* Restructuring of the cropping pattern and changes in agronomic practices; and

*(vii)* Development of subsidiary occupation.

The long term strategy should take into account the overall growth of rural economy. It needs a strong political will to reverse a large segment of urban biased policies. The long-term strategy should concentrate on one child family formal education, strengthening of rural infrastructure, providing motivations improving the process of democratisation at the grassroot level, strengthening the co-operatives, the schools and creating wider markets for the processed goods, raw materials, etc. The panchayat, the school, the bank and the co-operative society act as a corner stone of accelerated growth of rural economy.

These centres so as to ensure a ready market for rural products. The programmes aimed at employment generation in rural areas should aim at regular employment of at least 300 days per worker in a year in order to ensure a minimum standard of living to them. Thus, well conceived and objectively structured economic programmes are necessary for speedier rural development and eradication of poverty. There is a need to improve the effectiveness of the programmes so as to ensure that the benefits flow to those for whom they are intended.

Rural development administration should be streamlined and be made more effective for encouraging local initiative and participation. It must be free from bureaucratic tutelage and must promote the independent functioning of the elected Panchayat leaders.

# Chapter 18

# AGRICULTURE AND RURAL DEVELOPMENT

## Introduction

Agriculture occupies a key position in the Indian economy and more particularly in accelerating the process of rural development. Its role stimulating rural development is unique. It contributes to overall economic growth through supplies of food for sustenance, raw materials for industries, and export, earning valuable foreign exchange. it is a source of livelihood for a majority of the rural population and provides a large market for non-agricultural goods and services.

Agriculture and rural development are interwoven. Rapid development in agriculture and allied activities will improve the quality of life of the rural people. A close integration between agriculture and industry holds better prospects for rural development and advancement of forces of production for skill formation and positive attitudes to development. This may also accentuate rural inequalities. But this increased inequality within rural areas may be preferable to the state of rural under-development obtaining under conditions of industrial development confined to metropolitan centres whose only link with the rural economy is by way of receiving raw materials and other marketed surplus from there and selling consumer non-agricultural goods, including edible oil and kerosene, but contributing little by way of providing employment and reducing poverty.

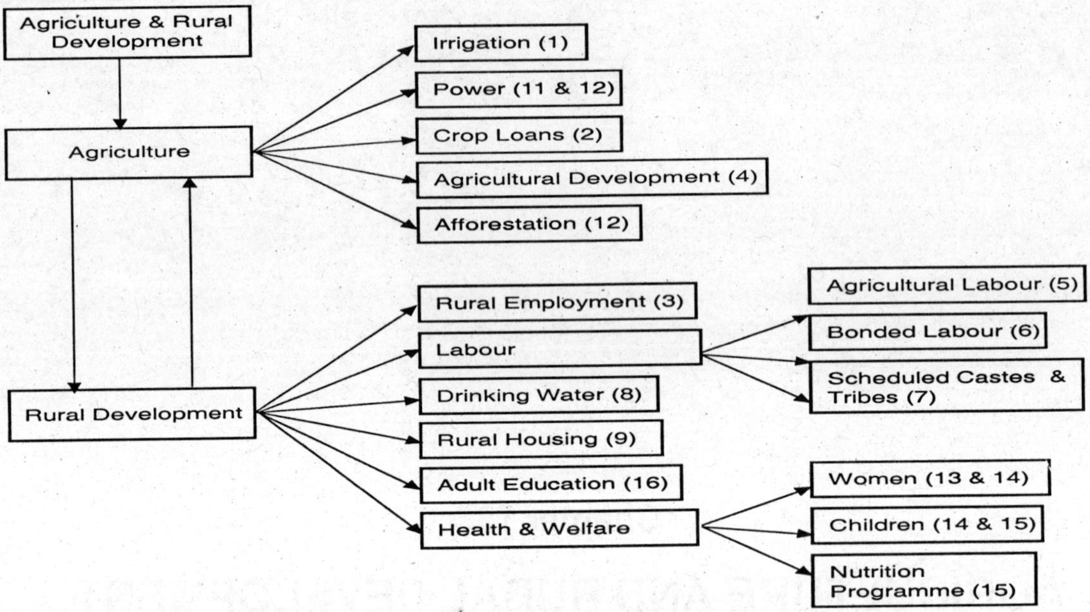


*Fig. 1. Components of Agriculture and Rural Development*

## Dependence on Industry

In the fifties and early sixties, industrial development depended on import substitution. It is quite likely that the slackening of industrial growth rate since mid-1960 may be due to the demand constraint. The factors leading to demand restrictions in the capital goods industry are different from those in the consumer goods industries. The latter are influenced by the performance of the agricultural sector.

The agriculture sector influences the industrial sector on the supply side through the availability of the raw materials required for industries. The agro-based industry covers an important segment of the industrial sector. In the early 1950, the agro-based industry had a weight of about 60 per cent in the total industrial output. This has now declined to 33 per cent.

The Leontief Input-Output Technique is suitable for ascertaining the inter-relationship between different industries and sectors. Based on this technique, the latest CSO input-output table for the Indian economy shows the dependence of different industries on other sectors. On the basis of these data the direct requirements have been estimated from other sectors of the economy for every Rs. one million output of individual group of industries.

For the manufacturing sector as a whole, factor inputs account for 36.4 per cent of the ex-factory value of output, the remaining 63.6 per cent being accounted by the non-factor inputs. Of the non-factor inputs, comprising commodity and service inputs, the former accounts for 73.3 per cent and the latter 22.7 per cent. Agricultural commodities account for 36.8 per cent of all commodity inputs directly required by the manufacturing sector. It also supplies 24.8 per cent of the non-sector inputs used by the manufacturing sector. Agriculture and allied activities will accelerate the process of rural development in India.

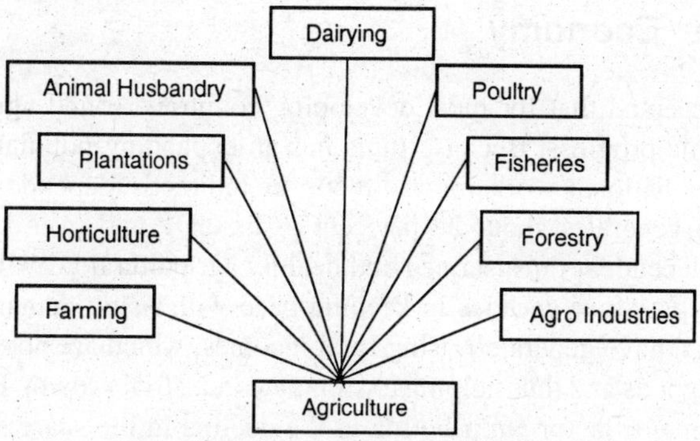


*Fig. 2. Elements of Agricultural Sector*

Agriculture and allied sectors have a great potential of creating employment opportunities to absorb the rising rural labour force. The greater generation of employment in the agricultural sector is linked with the growth of agriculture, which is caused by both an increase in productivity and an increase in employment. Additional income in rural areas will thus be generated for rural development and go a long way in improving the standard of living of the rural people—poor and rich alike. Above all, agriculture is a way of life, unique and irreplaceable in human values.

Sugar, food, tobacco products, cotton textiles, jute textiles, wood and wood products, etc., depend heavily on the agricultural sector for raw materials. For instance, cotton textiles require two-thirds of its commodity inputs, from the agricultural sector; again, for every Rs. one million output of the cotton textile industry, the direct requirements from the agricultural sector exceed Rs. 3,38,000. The sugar industry requires 92 per cent of its commodity input from the agricultural sector. Out of every Rs. one million output of the sugar industry, the direct requirements from the agricultural sector are Rs. 6,07,000. The food (excluding sugar) industry purchase 78 per cent of its commodity inputs from the agricultural sector. For every Rs. one million output of this industry, the requirement from the agricultural sector is Rs.5,75,000. Another important influence of agriculture on industry is via the demand route. The rural consumption of consumer goods like clothing, sugar, footwear, edible oils, etc., is nearly 2.5 times that of urban consumption. It is quite likely that fluctuations in agricultural output may, with some time-lag, have a considerable impact on the demand for industrial consumer goods.

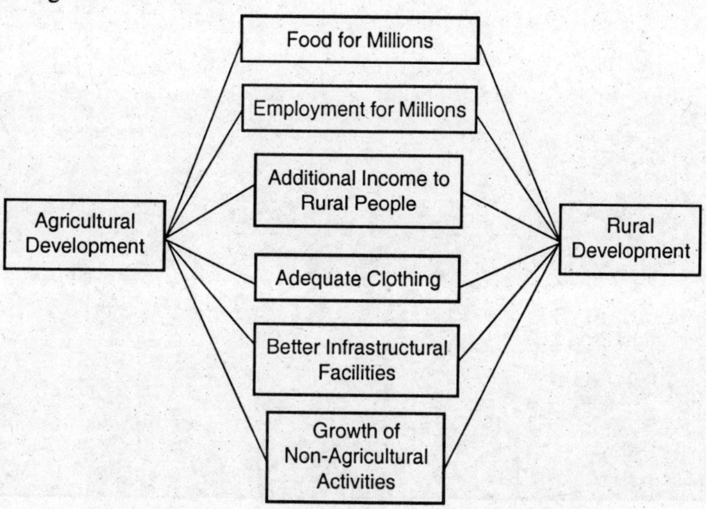


*Fig. 3. Links between Agriculture and Rural Development*

## Agriculture in the Economy

It is now widely accepted that for most developing countries, sound agricultural development is essential to overall economic progress. Because India has an expanding population of 1001 million to feed, has over two-thirds of its national work force directly or indirectly dependent on agriculture and has an agricultural sector which generates about 28 per cent of its GDP and over 15 per cent of its exports, its economy is particularly dependent on sustained and healthy agricultural growth. The agricultural sector has been successful over the past four decades in keeping pace with rising demand for food. Sectoral growth and product diversification have generated rising rural incomes, which are now having an important impact on demand for consumer goods and thus helping to stimulate industrial growth. Furthermore, increased yields per hectare have been a major factor contributing to the decline in the share of the rural population living in poverty.

Increased foodgrains production through the uptake of Green Revolution technology has been the cornerstone of India's agricultural success. Effective development programmes for milk, oilseeds, poultry, fish and horticultural development have followed. Demand for all these commodities will continue to rise in response to further population growth and rising incomes. A slowing in the demand for foodgrains for human consumption will be offset by increased allocations to livestock feed. Foodgrains production rose from 51 million tons in 1950-51 to a record 191 million tons in 1994-95 and stands at 196 million tons for 1997-98 but India's Ninth Five-Year Plan estimates that 230 million tons will be needed by 2002. Rising consumer prosperity and the search by farmers for higher incomes will simultaneously drive crop diversifica- tion. Export opportunities for agricultural products are also expected to continue to grow, provided India can meet the stability, quality and presentation standards demanded by foreign trade and consumers and maintain its comparative advantage as a relatively low cost producer. At the same time there is an urgent need for more effective sectoral development programmes to improve food security and nutritional adequacy among the poor; an estimated 20 per cent of the population, including a disproportionate share of preschool children, remain malnourished. The Green Revolution had generally by-passed vast rained tracts, especially arid zones, hill and mountain ecosystems and coastal regions, thus, exacerbating agro-eco-regional and social disparities.

*Fig. 4. Agriculture in the Economy.*

## Agriculture and GDP Growth

With an increase in agricultural production both foodgrains and non-foodgrains (mainly industrial raw materials), the marketable surplus of food crops and the supply of industrial raw materials increase. This, in turn, generates an additional volume of trade, transport, banking and other activities. Thus, the agricultural output directly influences not only the growth of the industrial sector but also that of other sectors.

The total influence, direct and indirect, of the agricultural sector on economic growth has been estimated by using the relevant data pertaining to the period from 1970 to 1984. In the first stage, the net influence of agriculture on industrial growth was determined by assuming that industrial output in any year depends on:

*(i)* Agricultural production with a time lag of six months; and

*(ii)* Gross domestic product originating in all other sectors of the economy, excepting agriculture and industry.

Logarithmatic relationship among the variables have been used for this purpose. The 'fit' was very good, the square of the co-efficient of multiple determination being as high as 0.9895. The elasticity co-efficient are of the proper sign with low standard errors.

The elasticity co-efficient indicate that:

*(i)* For every 10 per cent increase in agricultural production, industrial output increases by 2.37 per cent; and

*(ii)* A 10 per cent increase in the output of other sectors gives rise to a 7.39 per cent increase in the industrial production.

In the next stage, agricultural influence on the output of trade, transport, banking, business service, etc. (hereafter referred to as the T sector) has been ascertained by fitting the logarithmatic curve on the assumption that the 'T' sector's output depends on agricultural and industrial output. In this case also, the square of the co-efficient of multiple determination is very high (0.9924). The elasticity co-efficient are of the proper sign with low standard errors.

The co-efficients indicate that:

*(i)* A 10 per cent increase in agricultural output raises the T sector's output directly by 2.10 per cent; and

*(ii)* A 10 per cent increase in industrial output directly pulls up the T sector's output by 9.87 per cent. Since agriculture influences industrial growth, its indirect influence on the T sector's output is to raise by 2.34 per cent for every increase of 10 per cent of its own output.

In the final stage, it has been assumed that the GDP growth directly depends on the growth of agricultural and industrial production and on the T sector's output. The logarithmatic functions fitted to the relevant data give a very high co-efficient multiple determination (the square of the co-efficient being 0.9995). The elasticity co-efficient are of the proper sign with low standard errors. These indicate that:

*(i)* Every 10 per cent increase in agricultural output raises the gross domestic product by 3.33 per cent directly;

*(ii)* A 10 per cent rise in industrial output directly raises the GDP output by 0.64 per cent; and

*(iii)* A 10 per cent increase in T sector's output directly helps in pushing up the GDP by 4.94 per cent.

Since the growth of industrial and T sector's output depends on agriculture, and since the GDP growth rate depends on the last two sectors as well, agriculture is also indirectly responsible for GDP growth.

For every 10 per cent increase in agricultural output, the rate of increase in GDP is as follows:

| | |
|---|---|
| *Direct* | 3.33 per cent |
| *Indirect* | |
| Via industrial sector only | 1.15 per cent |
| Via industrial sector as well as T sector | 0.15 per cent |
| Via T sector only | 1.04 per cent |
| Total *indirect* | 2.34 per cent |
| Total *direct and indirect* | 5.67 per cent |

## Some Policies for Agricultural Development

Agricultural development is necessary for the rapid economic growth of our country. It contributes the largest share of the national income. Over the years, there has been a reduction in agriculture's share in national output. This was expected; but what is amazing is the fact that the rate of change has been rather slow.

Agriculture is a major source of livelihood in India. The latest population census shows that more than three-fourths of our people live in villages and that 87.4 per cent of them are directly dependent on agricultural for their livelihood. Most of the remaining rural people are indirectly dependent on agriculture. The occupational structure in our country has shown a lack of flexibility—the larger proportion of the increasing labour force as been absorbed in agriculture. This is mainly due to the absence of alternative employment opportunities. The increasing labour force in agriculture only adds to the already low productivity and disguised unemployment. Unless proper steps are taken to raise the level of productivity in time and create alternative employment opportunities, the economic situation will not change very materially.

In the post-Green Revolution period, there has been improvement in the productivity of various groups of crops, specially in the second half of the period. However, barring wheat, potato, dry chillies, tobacco and rice, the productivity growth is negligible—less than 2 per cent per annum. In spite of an appreciable growth in productivity, the yield rate of wheat and rice, the two most important crops in our country, has not been very satisfactory in comparison with international standards. As shown in terms of yields, India stands fifth among the major wheat producing countries in the world—its average yield of 1,714 kgs per hectare is 14.8 per cent less than the corresponding world average, and about two-thirds of the average yield of China, which occupies the first position. In the case of paddy, India's average yield is only 1,938 kgs per hectare, which is 31.3 per cent less than the world average and only one-third of the yield rate of Egypt, which occupies the first position.

The rate and pattern of industrialisation did not produce any significant structural transformation; nor did it bring about a large-scale transfer of population from rural to urban areas. As a result, rural economy is required to support a vast and growing population. The agricultural sector in turn will be required to shoulder a greater responsibility in providing food and nutrients to both rural and urban population, industrial raw materials, employment opportunities and foreign exchange earnings.

A lack of growth in the agricultural sector overheads in the form of irrigation facilities, roads, transport, electrification, markets. will add to the process of growth of the economy through backward and forward linkages, and generate substantial employment. Agricultural development will also lead to more non-agricultural activities like education, training, research and extension, and the provision of supplies and services, etc.

## Price Policy

A higher growth in agriculture stimulates the economic growth of our country. Faster agricultural growth requires higher growth in agricultural productivity. If productivity in agriculture increases, agricultural incomes and incentives will grow at the same time, and agricultural prices will decline. However, there is a fundamental difference between measures such as price controls, taxes and subsides, etc., which artificially lower the prices of food and other agricultural products, and measures which stimulate investments in farms, effect technological advances and promote rural infrastructural development (such as roads, electricity, water etc). These, too, lower prices by reducing the real cost of production.

A price policy is very important in the context of agricultural development. The policy of the Government of India, in this regard, seems to be to keep the prices of food and other agricultural commodities at relatively lower levels. This is evident from the fact that the terms of trade index in favour of the non-agricultural sector increased from 100 in 1970-71 to 132.5 in 1988-89.

The comparative price parity index between the output price of agricultural commodities and the cost of material inputs (that is, the ratio of the output price index to the index of the cost of material inputs) declined from 100 in 1970-71 to 96.5 in 1988-89. However, if the government did not give high subsidies for fertilisers and supply electricity and seeds at subsidised rates, the parity index would have declined further.

The terms of trade policy against agricultural is probably based on the following assumptions:

*(i)* The chief beneficiaries of higher price would be the large-sized farmers;

*(ii)* High food and other agricultural related prices, such as clothing (essential commodities), would most adversely effect the low income consumers.

In contrast to this policy, the price policies followed by industrial countries have been distorted in favour of the farmers, creating problems of over production of agricultural commodities. The European Economic Community pays its farmers the current world market prices to grow each lb of sugar. With such rewards, European farmers increased output from 10.8 million to 13.8 million tonnes from 1977, when the EEC began to export more sugar than it imported. In United States, sugar farmers are getting 17.75 cents a lb or about 4 1/2 times the world price. As a result, American sugar imports have fallen from 6 million tonnes a year a decade ago to less than 3 million tonnes now.

According to one study, greater productivity of crops per hectare of land in industrial countries than in developing countries has occurred mainly in the last 50 years when a differential price policy has been pursued. In 1934-38, grain yields were on an average 1.15 tonnes per hectare in industrial countries as against 1.14 tonnes in developing countries. By the end of the 1970s, grain yields in industrial countries were more than double the yields in developing countries—3.0 tonnes per hectare against 1.4 tonnes per hectare.

These differences cannot be ascribed to price policies only. However, it is likely that in industrial countries, more favourable farm prices and more rapid growth of farm yields reflect efforts to support farm income.

## Productivity

Production in irrigated areas is much higher than in un irrigated areas. But only 18 per cent of all agricultural holdings in the country are wholly irrigated, 24 per cent partly irrigated and the balance of 58 per cent unirrigated. Unless relatively less capital intensive methods are evolved to irrigate land, production cannot be raised through multiple cropping as well as through increased productivity with the help of fertilisers.

Fertiliser consumption per unit of gross cropped area varies widely from one state to another and from one district to another in the same state. Fertiliser consumption per unit of gross cropped area in Punjab was

158.5 kgs in the year ending June 1988, whoreson Assam, it was only 4.6 kgs. The all India average was 49.7 kgs per hectare.

Irrigation facilities can be increased in the areas which entirely depend on the monsoon by trapping the monsoon water into ponds and tanks. This is very important because a considerable part of rain water during the monsoon goes back to the sea, creating floods in a number of areas. With the trapping of water in ponds and tanks, multiple cropping can be used in the dry season.

India is fortunate to have a clear sky for more than 6 months in most of the areas which receive abundant sun. This solar energy should be utilised effectively to operate irrigation pumps.

The production of oilseeds fluctuates widely from year to year due to weather conditions, since only 8 to 10 per cent of the total area under oilseeds is irrigated. Moreover a substantial part of the rain-fed area under oilseeds consists of marginal land. The plant population is mostly sub-optimal due to use of poor quality seeds and wide spacing. The combination of weeds, pets, etc., causes a great deal of loss both during the early stage of plant growth and at crop maturity. Lack of rain at a critical stage before maturity also causes significant losses in yields, particularly in the yield of groundnut. Poor post-harvest technology, including deficiency in marketing support and storage and processing arrangements, has had an adverse effect on returns to growers.

With a view to raising production, the production strategy for important oilseeds like groundnut and rape seeds and mustard should involve the launching of an integrated oilseeds yield maximization programme with emphasis on:

*(i)* Production and distribution of improved seeds;

*(ii)* Popularising application of fertilisers, specially phosphatic fertilisers, to groundnut and soyabean crops;

*(iii)* Adoption of adequate and timely plant protection measures on yearly basis;

*(iv)* Inclusion of oilseeds crop in irrigated crop rotation;

*(v)* Expansion of area under non-traditional crops like soyabean and sunflower; and

*(vi)* Demonstration of improved practices.

The Planning Commission has recently divided the country into 15 agro-climatic zones on the basis of soil type, climate and water resources available in the various parts. To select the states/districts and the crops which should initially receive maximum thrust within each zone, such features as soil type, major constraints on higher production, historical data on the achievements of agricultural sector, existing level of irrigation along with assured increase by 1989-90, technological package available and the coverage under existing thrust programmes such as National Wasteland Development Programme (NWDP), Special Rice Production Programme (SRPP), National Oilseeds Development Programme (NODP), etc., were taken into consideration.

On the basis of the above features, a total of 169 districts in 14 states were tentatively identified as having immediately releasible potential for higher foodgrains production. Among these districts, 108 were selected for rice, 68 for wheat, 27 for maize, 28 for gram and 20 for arhar. Production credit planning will, hopefully, become more systematic and scientific when these programmes become operational.

## Alternative Uses of Agricultural Commodities

In order to minimise yearly fluctuations in the output and prices of agricultural commodities, it is necessary to carry out extensive research to find alternative industrial uses of these commodities. For example, from potato, sugarcane, tapioca, etc., alcohol can be produced; and if sufficient demand for industrial alcohol can be generated, then, the fluctuations in such commodities can be reduced. Brazil is producing ethanol from sugarcane and using it as fuel for automobiles in place of petrol. In California, substantial investment have been made to use ethanol for automobiles. India has taken steps to increase its automobile production within a few years. If we produce ethanol from sugarcane, potato, etc., and use it as a fuel for automobiles it will lessen the pressure on petrol. It is necessary to establish research organisations in various parts of the country to carry out research on alternative uses of agricultural commodities.

## Agricultural Growth as a Development Strategy

Of late, economists are convinced that a more appropriate development strategy will be one that gives primary emphasis to agricultural growth: Agricultural growth in itself only serves as an intermediate objective. The mechanism of agricultural growth and the generation of intersectoral linkages with the rest of the economy represent the key to rapid broad based, and self-sustaining economic development. It is demonstrated that the agricultural demand-led strategy "generates the same rate of industrialisation as does export-led growth but leads to a higher rate of labour absorption, a better distribution of income, better balance-of-payments result, less poverty, and a higher rate of growth of per capita gross national product than export-led growth." The leads to greater increase in the real incomes of rural households, which account for a very high proportion of the poverty population. More importantly, the substantial increase in the rate of return on agricultural investment raises the level of rural incomes that raises the rural savings. The strategy properly implemented will accelerate the process of rural development.

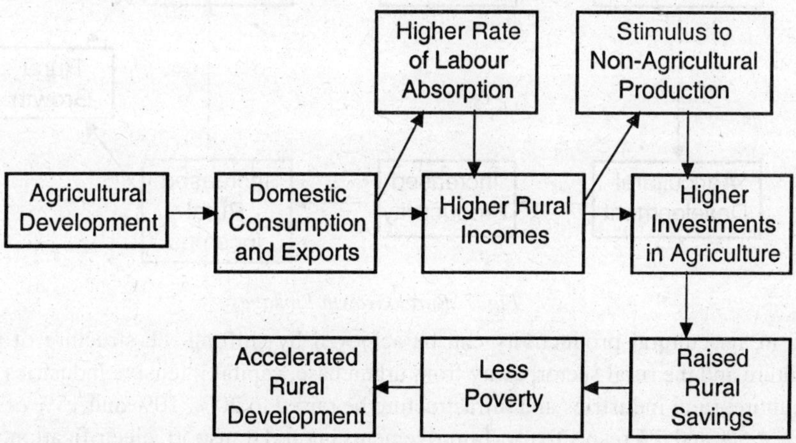


*Fig. 5. Agricultural Demand-led Strategy*

The development of rural infrastructure goes a long way in achieving rapid productivity growth in agriculture. The development and maintenance of rural infrastructure requires huge capital investment. Additionally, the stimulus to non-agricultural production induced by increased rural incomes, due to rising agricultural prices and productivity. This form of rural growth linkages is at the heart of an agriculture based development strategy.

The effectiveness of an agriculture-based development strategy depends crucially on the expansion of the real income of rural household from agri- cultural growth. It underlines that prod- uctivity in agri culture is expected to increase substantially, to give the farmers a significant marketable surplus and the agricultural produces get a reasonably higher price, both to cover cost of production at the same time give a reasonable return. Increased rural incomes will generate an increased demand for agricultural inputs and, more importantly, for food and labour intensive industrial goods and services that are consumed by rural people. It will set in motion a sequence of employment and income multiplier effect on the rural economies

*Fig. 6.*

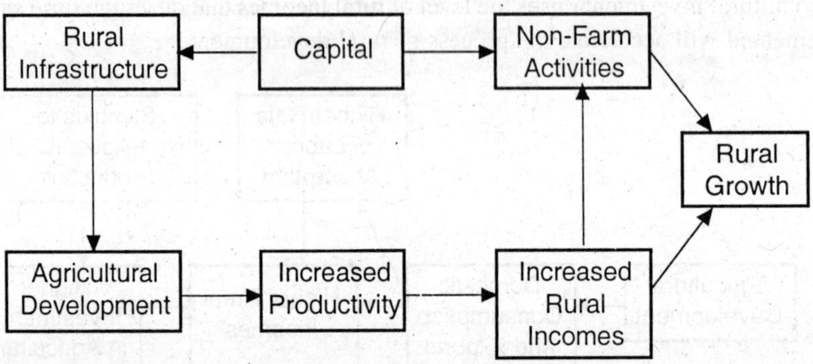


*Fig. 7. Rural Growth Linkages*

Increase in agricultural productivity can be achieved by shifting the structure of public investment toward agriculture and the rural sector, away from urban base, capital intensive industries. To start with, the share of agriculture, rural industries and infrastructure be raised to 20%, 10% and 15% of public investment as against 10%, 1.5% and 5% respectively. Improvements in rural transport, electrification, agricultural credit and irrigation will increase the agricultural supply response to price incentives. The entire gamut of agriculture growth needs to be strengthened by enforcing effective linkages with the rest of the economy. Agriculture or rural sector is part of the whole economic system. What is more, production technologies should be conducive to local conditions and more particularly suited to small producers in regionally dispersed areas. The need of the hour is labour intensive technologies.

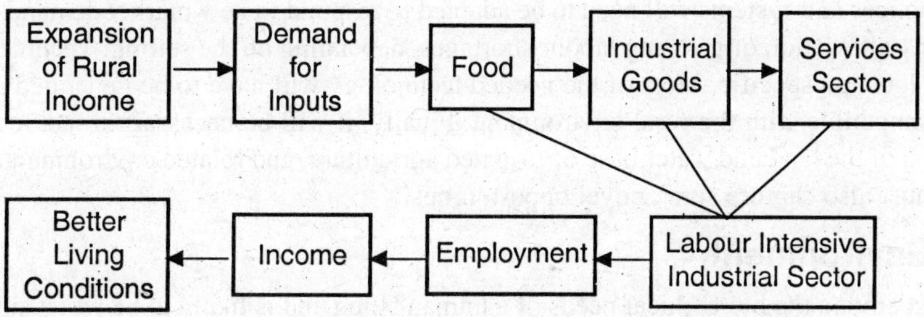


*Fig. 8. Multiplier Effects on the Rural Economies*

The magnitude of rural growth linkages is also determined by the labour intensity in agricultural and non-agricultural sectors. Increase in employment in rural areas, raises their real wages, the purchasing power of rural people. The multiplier effect will reduce rural poverty.

To achieve a broad based, self-sustaining growth process in rural areas it is required to promote rural industries that have been neglected or discriminated. If need be protection and other incentives may also be provided. These considerations point to the desirability of mobilizing resources like infrastructure, electricity, biomass energy, technology, labour training, and credit and substantial participation by the rural wage earners. Indeed, as one observer has noted, the agricultural based development strategy "lends itself well to decentralized, democratic process, decentralized in decision making geographically and individually to a myriad of small rural entrepreneurs and small farmers." Thus, agricultural and non-agricultural growth in the rural sector increases rural employment, rural income, purchasing power, saving capacity and improves their standard of living. In the initial stage greater government support is necessary to set in motion a sequence of employment and income multiplier effect on rural economies. The agricultural development strategy should not only be for growth programmes but also for employment, anti-poverty and income redistribution programme.

## Emerging Needs, Opportunities and Constraints

Given its range of agro-ecological setting and producers, Indian agriculture is faced with a great diversity of needs, opportunities and prospects. Most importantly growth needs to be more rapid, more widely distributed and better targeted in order to reduce the absolute number of people living in poverty and to reduce regional imbalances. In responding to these challenges, more efficient and sustainable use will have to be made of increasingly scarce land, water and germplasm resources. The well-endowed irrigated areas which account for 37 per cent of the country's cultivated land currently contribute about 55 per cent of agricultural production; it is projected that a significant part of the further required increases in production will still have to come from these areas. However, of late, deceleration in production and of factor productivity growth in some of the major irrigated production systems, such as the rice-wheat system, have been recorded. Those areas in which yields from Green Revolution technology are already high will have to raise total factor productivity and break through the present yield ceilings, which for the major food grains are often below those of East Asia. Rained agriculture, which covers 63 per cent of the total cultivated land, accounts for only 45 per cent of agricultural production; in these less favourable areas, yields are not only low but also highly unstable and technology transfer gaps are much wider as compared to those in irrigated zones. Areas where productivity lags (particularly the rainfed rice areas of eastern Indian) will have to be brought closer to their existing productive potential. All areas where rainfed farming is dominant—whether in the central plains, hill, semi-arid or coastal lands—will have to contribute more to poverty alleviation, augment food security by producing marketable surpluses more reliably.

Production practices and systems will need to be adapted to respond to new market demands and export opportunities, poverty alleviation or growing labour shortages, depending on the setting. Technical solutions will be increasingly location specific. Most of the needed technology will have to be generated and adapted locally to make it compatible with the rural environment. Finally, it will be necessary to address to natural resource conservation of the land and water base of irrigated agriculture, and related environmental concerns. Indian agriculture must also capture some novel opportunities.

## Climate and Environment

Food is the first among the hierarchical needs of a human being and is likely to be worst sufferer under conditions of global warning and sea level rise. Therefore, bridging the available yield gap using clean technologies is the need of the hour.

Population is still growing and per capita land and water resources are shrinking, this will be a disaster. Therefore, it is urgent that we strengthen our agricultural production systems under conditions of uncertain weather patterns. Fortunately, weather forecasting techniques are improving. Given the prediction of a normal southwest monsoon this year, we should launch immediately a "bridging the yield gap movement" using clean technologies associated with conservation farming and green agriculture. The idea of the movement is to bridge the prevailing gap between potential and actual yields.

## Bridging the Yield Gap

Over sixty per cent of our cultivated area is still rain fed. The yield gap analysis for rain fed crops in India undertaken by the International Crop Research Institute for the Semi Arid Tropics (ICRISAT) led consortium has indicated that the productivity of many crops such as kharif sorghum and pearl millet can be increased many times from their current levels of productivity. The same is true for the productivity of legumes and oilseeds. Supplemental irrigation using harvested rain water would further increase these yields. Our committed goal should be to increase average productivity of selected crops in rain fed areas by at least 50% by 2010. This can be accomplished through the following steps:

- Achieve convergence and synergy among various ongoing programmes by creating clear command chain.
- Adopt a holistic "Seed to Consumer" chain strategy.
- Establish participatory action research-cum-demonstration trials.
- Ensure availability of quality inputs in a timely manner.
- Assess and improve soil health.
- Identify high yielding cultivators preferred by the farmers in target districts.
- Establish village seed and food banks in each target district by providing financial, technical and institutional support including policy support.
- Establish Agri-clinics and Agri-business centres to provide equipment relevant to the production and post harvest phases of crop cultivation.
- Ensure procurement by providing an attractive procurement price based on national and global markets.

## An Important Development Tool

On the one hand, transgenic technology may hold the greatest potential to increase food (production, reduce the use of harmful chemical, pesticides, and provide nutritional foods.

Ultimately, biotechnology is more than just a new and useful agricultural tool. It could also be a hugely important instrument of economic development in many poorer regions of the globe. By making agriculture more productive, labour and resources could be freed for use in other areas of economic growth in nations where farming currently occupies 70 or 80 per cent of the population. This, in turn, would be an important step in the journey toward genuine food security. The choice is clear. Innovators must proceed with due caution and transform the Indian agriculture.

## ISSUES

Agriculture desperately needs spread of irrigation, rise in productivity and hybrid grains and high technology such as combined harvesters and other equipment to move into high gear.

But, India's bane has been its landholdings — among the smallest in the world. There are some 100 million fragmented landholdings and an average Indian farmer holds about 2-3 acres of land, which makes the use of technology difficult. Then, there are an estimated 40-50 million landless labourers, who often work on large farms and whose presence and low costs mean that the need for high technology is rarely felt. Figures available for a decade ago show over 71 million marginal holdings, over 21 million small holdings, 14 million semi-medium holdings, 7 million medium, and just 1.4 million large holdings.

*Fig. 9. A foodgrain vendor: no worry this year*

"A way out could be to form farm co-operatives, where ownership stays with the farmers but adjoining land is combined to allow high technology," says Ranade, pointing out that co-operation has worked well in the milk sector and the aim should be to replicate the model for agriculture.

The Central government is also exploring ways and means of promoting investments. Recently it has undertaken an ambitious Rs.25,000 crore project which will plough more funds for improving productivity in the sector. A part of the Food Security Mission, this project proposes to give a matching grant to states making additional allocations in agriculture. Around 16 states have already inked agreements with the Central government. Some other states are also doing their mite in contributing to this productivity drive.

The Punjab government for instance has decided to impose a 1 per cent fee on purchase of food grains to revive the 150-year-old canal system of the state. The state also plans to utilise other resources to ensure sufficient water availability.

## Eliminating the Middleman

The private sector has made a beginning with various corporate giants entering the retail space seeking to deal with farmers directly. The farm to fork chain is complicated with a number of middlemen who are crucial to the marketing of agricultural produce. One way of keeping costs down and increasing the margin for farmers is to eliminate the middlemen, something the large retailers have begun to try. Yet, such steps are in their infancy and years away from complete realisation.

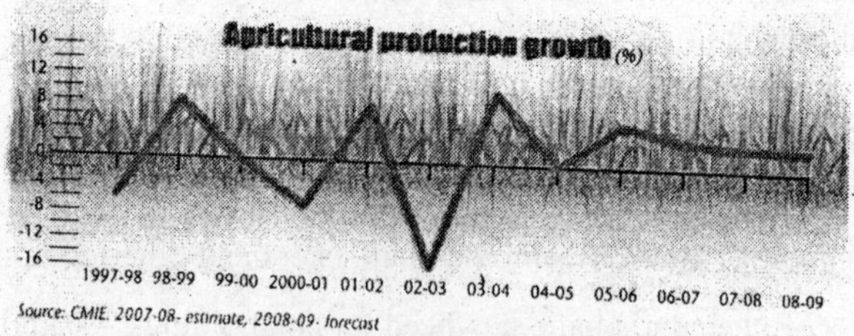

Source: CMIE. 2007-08- estimate, 2008-09- forecast

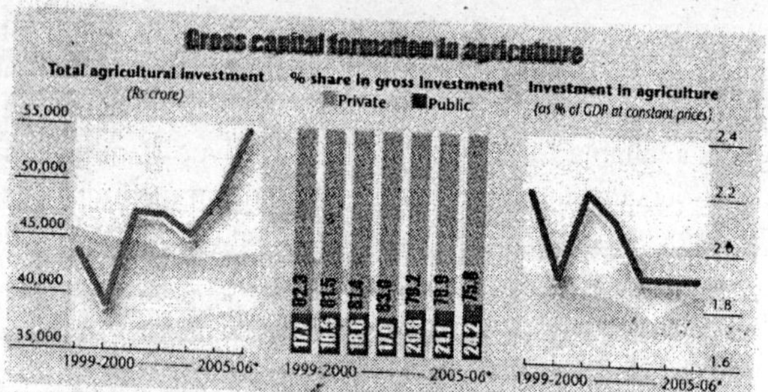

*Quick estimates. Source: CSO

A combination of wastage, poor management and high profits makes for the high margins. Companies can try and ensure better logistics and storage to cut the wastage. Farmers and corporates will need to join hands, perhaps in the form of getting farmers to form co-operatives and sell the produce directly to the corporations, given the restrictions in buying farmland. In the meantime, the government, in a show of populism, makes various announcements that only compound the problems in the end. It needs to be remembered that, while agriculture contributes about 18 per cent to the GDP, around some 60 per cent of the population lives in villages. A way has to be found to give them employment in the service sector in the rural areas and to provide employment by agro-based industries and cold storages to preserve perishable items like fruits and vegetables.

## Conclusions

INDIAN agriculture has witnessed significant transformation over the past few decades. The changes range from new entrants into the sector to new and improved technologies to farming becoming more mechanised, to weather, soil and environmental changes, to new markets and demand, and most importantly to agriculture evolving from just a way of life to a full-fledged business — agribusiness. These changes have unfortunately not been accompanied by changes on the institutional and policy front. Even in instances where amendments have been introduced on the policy front they have not necessarily been accompanied by changes on the organisational and institutional fronts. This disconnect has limited the growth potential of this vital sector.

The need to develop a long-term strategy that would reduce the vulnerability of the farming community and accelerate agricultural growth is thus imperative. What are required are institutional reforms and technological are technological breakthroughs, which trigger agricultural transformation. It is here that the central and state governments play a key role through national and state research systems as the future and success of the agricultural sector in India depends on how the Centre and states function with respect to each other and how they facilitate the sector across the country.

Fluctuations in the growth rate of national income are a regular phenomenon in the Indian economy. Since agriculture contributes the largest share of national income, violent fluctuations in agricultural production bring about significant variations in the level of national income. It has already been pointed out that a 10 per cent increase in agricultural production raises, directly and indirectly, the national output by 5.7 per cent.

The rapid economic growth of the country requires faster agricultural development. This is necessary not only to raise output but also employment, increase foreign exchange earnings, etc. The latest census shows that 7 out of every 8 persons in rural areas directly depend on agriculture for their livelihood. A majority of the other rural people, too, are indirectly dependent on agriculture.

The occupational structure of the country has not undergone any significant change. A larger portion of the increasing labour force has been absorbed in agriculture. This is mainly due to the absence of alternative employment opportunities. The agricultural sector, therefore, has to shoulder a great responsibility in providing employment. It will also have to supply food and nutrients to both rural and urban populations, raw materials to industry and foreign exchange earnings for the whole economy. A lack of growth in the agricultural sector and therefore a lack of increase in the purchasing power of the vast agricultural population can be serious bottlenecks to the growth of the gross domestic product.

A higher growth in agriculture stimulates the economic growth of the country. Faster agricultural growth requires higher growth in agricultural productivity. If the relative productivity of agriculture vis-a-vis other sectors increases, agricultural income and incentives will grow at the same time when agricultural prices fall.

The government should follow a price policy which will give incentives to agriculturists to produce more and also attract investment to the agricultural sector so that new technologies may be developed and adopted. Irrigation facilities should be increased in the areas which depend entirely on the monsoon.

The panchayati raj institutions also need to be re-integrated fully into the agricultural system for sustainable and equitable growth. The hitherto problem of non-involvement of farmers in the planning process will be addressed by involving the panchayati system in the process of agriculture planning by introducing the three-tier system. This again would require certain institutional and policy reforms along with facilitating mechanisms that would ensure a smooth participative system.

All of the above would require focused and strategically designed institutional reforms that would facilitate the movement towards a robust agricultural sector jointly driven by the public and private sector. An in-depth analysis of the situation, and the required institutional and legal structure reforms that emerge therefrom, could also involve a review of the redundant aspects in the constitutional framework to enable some of the changes. The need of the hour is an in-depth analysis and review of the current system, identification of the problem areas and the subsequent formulation of institutional and policy reforms that would ensure an efficient governance mechanism to facilitate the new/reformed system — a system that allows for a smooth functioning of the Centre, states and private sector players in a combined effort to boost Indian agriculture.

A well developed food value chain is essential for the development and success of the Indian agribusiness sector. This, however, requires the identification and implementation of appropriate projects and interventions. Lack of agri infrastructural facilities can severely affect, and in fact nullify, the gains in value and efficiency in the agricultural sector. These bottlenecks need to be dealt with and removed in a focused manner. This can be done by facilitating and extending Public Private Partnership (PPP) principles from the infrastructure sector to the agribusiness sector.

# Annexure - I

## NATIONAL AGRICULTURE POLICY

The first ever National Agriculture Policy was announced on 28th July, 2000. The formulation of Agriculture Policy had been under consideration of the Government for the last few years as a comprehensive National Agriculture Policy was absolutely essential to build on the inherent strength of the agriculture and allied sectors to address the constraints and to make optimal use of resources and opportunities emerging as a result of advancement in science and technology and emerging of a new economic regime.

The National Agriculture Policy seeks to actualise vast untapped growth potential of Indian agriculture, strengthen rural infrastructure to support faster agricultural development, promote value addition, accelerate the growth of agro business create employment in rural areas, secure a fair standard of living for the farmers and agricultural workers and their families, discourage migration to urban areas and face the challenges arising out of economic liberalization and globalization over the next two decades, it aims to attain:

- A growth rate in excess of 4 per cent per annum in the agriculture sector;
- Growth that is based on efficient use of resources and conserves our soil, water and bio-diversity;
- Growth with equity, *i.e.* growth which is widespread across regions and farmers;
- Growth that is demand driven and caters to domestic markets and maximises benefits from exports of agricultural products in the face of the challenges arising from economic liberalisation and globalisation;
- Growth that is sustainable technologically, environmentally and economically.

A nine pronged strategy has been devised to meet the challenges of enhancing production and strengthening rural economies while taking care to promote technically sound, economically viable, environmentally non-degrading and socially acceptable use of country's natural resources—land and water in particular.

The unutilised wastelands will be put to use for agriculture and afforestation besides reclamation of degraded lands. Integrated and holistic development of rainfed areas, conjunctive use of surface and ground water, on farm water management, sensitization of farming community with environmental concerns will be given priority. Survey and evaluation of genetic resources and safe conservation of both indigenous and exogenously introduced genetic variability in crop productivity and utility needs particular attention. The use of bio-technologies will be promoted for evolving plants which consume less water, are drought resistant, pest resistant, contain more nutrition, give higher yields and are environmentally safe. Conservation of bio-resources through their ex situ preservation in gene banks, as also in-situ conservation in their natural habitats through bio-diversity parks, etc, will receive a high priority to present their extinction.

A regionally differentiated strategy for development of crops horticulture, floriculture, roots and tubers, plantation crops, aromatic and medicinal plants, bee keeping and sericulture shall be adopted. Live-stock breeding, dairying, poultry, agriculture shall be promoted through generation and dissemination of appropriate technologies. Research and extension linkages will be broad based and strengthened to improve effective use of new technologies. Adequate and timely supply of quality inputs such as seed, fertilisers, plant protection chemicals, bio-pesticides, agriculture machinery and credit at reasonable rates to farmers will be the endeavour of the Government.

Agriculture in India has suffered for want of infrastructural facilities. The National Agriculture Policy gives emphasis on stepping up public investment for narrowing regional imbalances, accelerating development of supportive infrastructure for agriculture and rural development particularly rural connectivity. A conducive climate will be created through a favourable price and trade regime to promote farmers' own investments as also investments by industries producing inputs for agriculture and agro based industries. High priority is also given to rural electrification, development of market infrastructure and setting up of agro processing units to reduce wastage, particularly, of horticulture produce, and to enhance value addition with the objective to create off-farm employment in rural areas. To safeguard the interest of farmers, National Agriculture Insurance scheme covering all farmers and all crops throughout the country with built in provisions for insulating farmers from financial distress caused by natural disasters and making agriculture financially viable will be made more farmer specific and effective. Endeavour will be made to provide a package insurance policy for the farmers, right from sowing of the crops to post-harvest operations, including market fluctuations in the prices of agricultural produce.

Indian agriculture is characterised by pre-dominance of small and marginal farmers. Institutional reforms will be so pursued as to channelize their energies for achieving greater productivity and production. The approach to rural development and land reforms will focus on the following areas:

- Consolidation of holdings all over the country on the pattern of north western States;
- Redistribution of ceiling surplus lands and waste lands among the landless farmers, unemployed youth with initial start up capital;
- Tenancy reforms to recognize the rights of the tenants and share croppers;
- Development of lease markets for increasing the size of the holdings by making legal provisions for giving private lands on lease for cultivation and agri business;
- Updating and improvement of land records, computerization and issue of land pass-books to the farmers; and
- Recognition of women's rights on land.

People's participation through Panchayati Raj Institutions, voluntary groups, social activists and community leaders shall be adequately encouraged for implementation of programmes. Progressive institutionalisation of rural and farm credit for providing timely and adequate credit to farmers will be continued. Cooperative sector shall be strengthened by:

- Structural reforms for promoting greater efficiency and viability by freeing them from excessive bureaucratic control and political interference;
- Creation of infrastructure and human resource development;
- Improvement in financial viability and organisational sustainability of cooperatives;
- Democratisation of management and increased professionalism in their operation; and
- Creating a viable inter-face with other grassroot organisation

Sophisticated techniques including latest information technology, remote sensing technology, etc. will be used for compilation and dissemination of information in the process of planning and policy making.

❑ ❑ ❑

# Chapter 19

# IMPERATIVES FOR WISE WATER MANAGEMENT

## Introduction

Water is a prime natural resources, a basic human need and a precious national asset. It is needed in all aspects of life and health, for producing food, industrial activities, energy generation and maintenance of environment for sustenance of life and development.

The total water resources of the country are approximately four percent of the world's fresh resources, whereas the country's population is slightly more than 16 per cent of the global population. As per estimate of National Commissioner for Integrated Water Resources development total annual water resources of the country is 1953 $km^3$. However, the utilisable quantities of water drawable from the annual resources are only 1086 $km^3$ which is the sum of 690 $km^3$ drawable from surface water resources and 396 $km^3$ drawable from groundwater sources. Thus water availability is adequate to meet the requirement at the national scale.

The seventies have witnessed the emergence of a major policy focus in development planning. For the first time, development avenues for the rural poor were explored and given due importance. Primarily, the rapid development of agriculture and allied activities goes a long way in developing rural areas, for, a strong agriculture base is an essential requirement of rural development. The accelerated development of agriculture and allied activities is based on the extension of irrigation, effective water management and effective use of modern science and technology. This apart, the rural sector has to harness forestry and cottage industries for their benefit. Briefly, development avenues for the rural poor can be opened up in the field of agriculture and allied activities, cottage industries, and forestry.

## IMPORTANCE OF WATER

Water is a basic component. The vital importance of water must be recognised—equitable provision of water for human needs, protection of water quality, and conservation of a natural environment are development prerequisites of the highest priority.

Although the poor are disadvantaged in terms of access to the benefits of improved water supply and sanitation, providing water supply and sanitation is pivotal to improving both the social and economic status of rural poor. Hence, water is one of the basic component in reducing poverty in rural areas.

The most important factors for improvement in agricultural yields are the availability of adequate and timely water supply and the adoption of modern agricultural technology. In the present section has been assessed the role of irrigation and modern technology in improving agricultural production in India.

**Box 1**
**Manila Case Study**
**WATER AND POVERTY**

Winnie lives in Block A of the Kabusig, Floodway Cainta metro Manila. She is 34 and earns $ 162 per month as a domestic helper. Her husband a messenger, earns $ 138 per month. They support a family of seven, which includes Winnie's mother-in-law and four children. They rent a 20 square metre room and share a kitchen and toilet with another family. With monthly expenses of $ 125 for food, $ 50 for transport, and $ 38 for rent, there is little left to cover costs of power, water, gas, medicines and schooling.

Water costs Winnie $20 per month, or seven percent of their household income. She used to pay $ 12.50 per month for a metered piped supply from a deep tubewell operated by a private contractor. However, the supply was only for one hour twice a day. She paid another $ 7.50 per month for drinking water purchased by the container from another contractor. The source was purported to be from the concessionaire's piped supply.

Recently, there was trouble with both sources of water at the same time. The deep tubewell closed down due to pump problems. Diarrhoea and typhoid broke out in the neighbourhood. One of Winnie's boys had to be hospitalised.

Now Winnie has a connection to a more distant deep tubewell and is selling water (not fit for drinking) by the container to five of her neighbours who do not save water. At $ 1.25 for the first 10 cubic metre ($m^3$) and $0.40 per $m^3$ thereafter, she fears she may not have collected enough to pay the excess charges at the end of the month as well as the instalments on the $50 connection fee.

*The message brought home by Winnie's case study is that the poor can and do pay for water. Local governments should ensure that piped water supplies reach the poorest areas, and that the poor are assisted to make use of such supplies.*

Ironically, there are some mainstream economists and policymakers who argue that the monsoon's impact on the economy has actually reduced over the past decade. The strength of this point of view derives largely from the fact that the share of agriculture and allied activities in the country's overall GDP has steadily declined over the years. Agriculture used to contribute over 40 per cent of the GDP in the 1970s, and just over 22 per cent at the start of the present decade. Currently, the sector's contribution to the overall GDP stands at 17.5 per cent. Moreover, the monsoon's detractors point out that India's recent growth has been fed largely by exports of manufactured goods and services, as well as a marked increase of domestic urban markets that are also large consumers of the same category of goods and services.

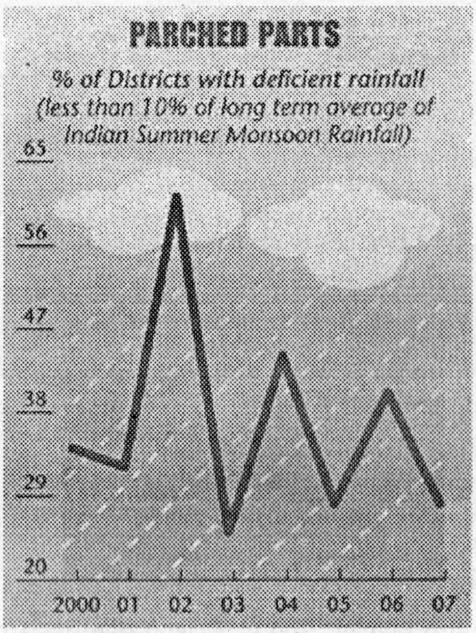


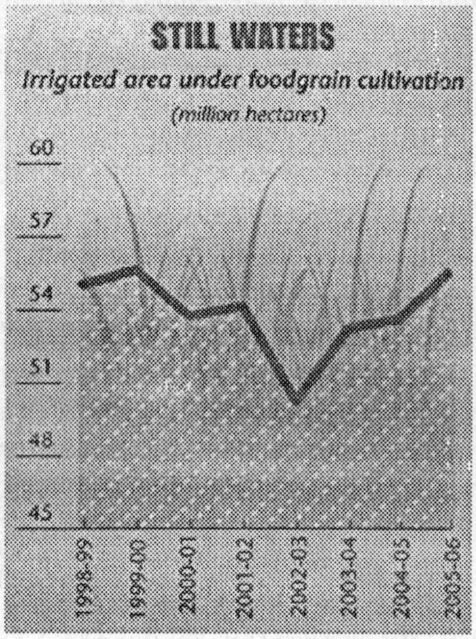


*Source: Economic Survey 2007, Government of India*

However, there is also the fact of life that offers strong discomfiture to those who argue for the reducing economic impact of the ISMR. Even though the share of agriculture in overall GDP has declined drastically, this hardly changes any reality of existence for 60 per cent of the Indian population whose lives and earnings are still tied to agriculture and allied activities. The mónsoons are a godly phenomenon for these 600 million odd Indians because Indian agriculture continues to be critically dependent on rains.

## Irrigation Limits

The limits of irrigation fed agriculture are an overt aspect of this harsh reality. Only 40 per cent of the net cultivated area in India, amounting to a total of 142 million hectares, is fed by irrigation systems. Of course, this produces most of the farm output, including 56 per cent of foodgrains' production. The rest of the cultivated area, amounting to 60 per cent of the total, is entirely rain fed in its output. This basic data also points to the relative poverty of the un-irrigated areas that gets accentuated with any adverse variation of the annual rains. Over the decades, the government — at the Centre as well as in the states has found it dauntingly difficult to expend the country's irrigated agricultural zones.

## Need for Irrigation

The importance of irrigation to the predominantly agricultural economy of the country needs no emphasis. Irrigation is a key input for increasing agricultural production. Rural India depends heavily on agriculture as a means of livelihood. First, agriculture in India suffers from the vagaries of a notoriously capricious rainfall. Droughts alternating with floods in a one part of the country or another are a common feature, resulting in famine conditions, sometimes over very extended areas. Irrigation, therefore, is necessary in one form or the other in all parts of the country, where the mean annual rainfall is less than 75 cms. It is indispensable for the economical use of land. Second, with irrigation, both land and labour can be put to profitable use throughout the year. Third, crop yields can almost be doubled and money return increased by growing commercial crops with a high export potential. Fourth, irrigation contributes substantially to agricultural price stability by removing, to a large extent, the element of uncertainty in agricultural production.

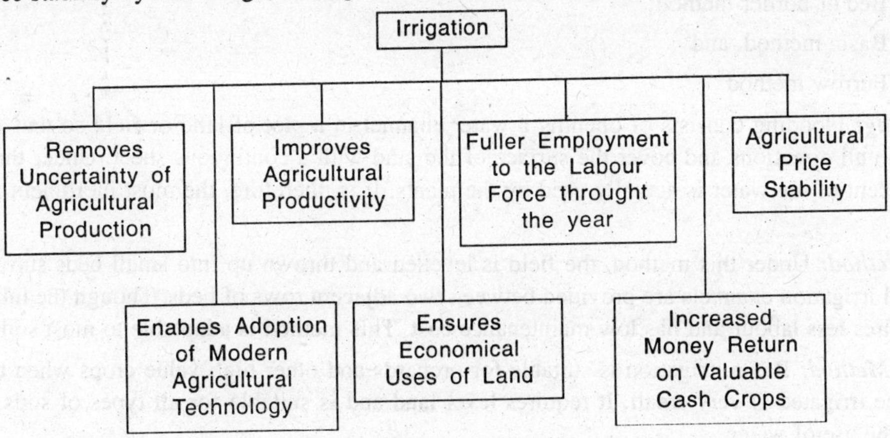


*Fig. 1. Importance of Irrigation*

## Historical Perspective

Irrigation has been practiced in India since times immemorial. The diversion of floods through inundation canals, lift irrigation, storage of rain water in tanks and reservoirs and numerous other water conservation systems were introduced in different parts of the country. The Grand Anicut across the river Cauvery was built in the second century. From times immemorial, tanks were invested with religious significance. Every village had a temple and a tank. Besides, surface wells and ponds provided water for drinking purpose as well as for irrigation from very ancient times. At the beginning of the 19th century, irrigation works included numerous wells all over the country. Between 1836 and 1866, Upper Ganga Canal, the Upper Bari Doab Canal and the Krishna and Godavari delta system were constructed.

## Evolution of Government Policy

The attention of the government was drawn to the need for irrigation works by the various famines that ravaged the country in the 19th century. The first Famine Commission of 1880 emphasized the need for direct state initiative in the development of irrigation, particularly in drought-prone areas. The famines of 1897-98 and 1899-1900 led to the setting up of the first Irrigation Commission in 1901 to ascertain the utility of irrigation as a means of protection against famine, the extent of irrigation development and the scope for future irrigation works. The gross area irrigated by public works in British India was about 7.5 million hectares, of which 3 million hectares were irrigated by minor works—by tanks, inundation canals, etc. An additional 5.7 million hectares were irrigated privately, of which 70 per cent were by wells. There was a spurt in protective irrigation works in the first two decades of the present century. The overall irrigation outlay doubled from Rs. 40 crores in 1901 to Rs. 79 crores in 1920-21. The Bengal famine of 1943 underlined the urgency of increasing agricultural production to meet the needs of the growing population. The Grow More Food (GMF) Campaign, launched in 1942, relied mainly on the development of minor irrigation works for speedy results. The construction of tubewells in the Indo-Gangetic Valley and in Gujarat, taken up in the thirties, received a fillip in the early fifties. The advent of independence provided the necessary impetus for the evolution of a national policy on irrigation.

## Methods of Applying Irrigation Water

There are three principal methods of irrigation, *viz.,* surface, subsurface and aerial.

***Surface Irrigation:*** There are four variations under this method;

*(a)* Flooding;

*(b)* Bed or border method;

*(c)* Basin method; and

*(d)* Furrow method.

***Flooding:*** Flooding consists of opening a water channel in a plot of land or field so that water may flow freely in all directions and cover the surface of the land with a continuous sheet. Under this method, only 20 per cent of the water is actually used by the plants. It is, therefore, the most inefficient method of irrigation.

***Bed Method:*** Under this method, the field is levelled and thrown up into small beds surrounded by bunds. Small irrigation channels are provided between two adjacent rows of beds. Though the initial cost is high, it requires less labour and has low maintenance cost. This method is adaptable to most soil textures.

***Basin Method:*** Basin irrigation is suitable for orchards and other high value crops when the size of the plot to be irrigated is very small. It requires level land and is suitable for all types of soils. It is also efficient in the use of water.

***Furrow Method:*** In furrow irrigation, water is led through the furrow opened between crop rows. There is great economy in the use of water which is a great consideration in lift irrigation.

## Sub-surface Irrigation

Sub-surface irrigation may be natural or artificial. Natural sub-surface irrigation is possible where an impervious layer exists below the root zone. Water is led into a series of ditches dug up to impervious layers, which then moves laterally and wets the root zone. It artificial sub-surface irrigation, perforated or porous pipes are laid underground below the root zone and water is led into the pipes by suitable means. It is very efficient in the use of water, for evaporation is completely eliminated. It involves a high initial cost but its maintenance is very cheap. As it requires special soil conditions for successful operation, its use is very limited.

## Aerial, Overhead or Sprinkler Irrigation

It ensures a uniform distribution of water, adaptable to most kind of soils and offers no hindrance to the use of farm implements. In sprinkler irrigation, water is conveyed under pressure through pipes to the area to be irrigated, where it is passed out through sprinklers. The system comprises of four parts;

*(i)* Power generator;

*(ii)* Pump;

*(iii)* Pipe line; and

*(iv)* Sprinkler.

The original cost is very high. So is the cost of operation and maintenance.

## Major and Medium Irrigation Schemes

The important schemes initiated during the first two plan periods and the Bhakra-Nangal, the Rajasthan Canal, the Gandhisagar Dam and the Gandak, Kosi, Nagarjunasagar, Hirakud, Tungabhadra, Malaprabha and Ghataprabha projects. Later, the multipurpose Beas Project, Ramganga Dam and canals, Tehri, Sri Ramsagar, Jayakwadi, Ukai, Kadana, Sardar Sarovar, Tawa, Teesta, etc., were taken up for a proper utilisation of the monsoon waters. With the strengthening of survey and investigation organisations in the states, more projects are expected to be formulated during the Eighth Plan period to harness the monsoon waters.

**Box 2**

Reservoirs created by dams are essential for supplying water for human needs. They conserve water that would otherwise flow out of the river basin, and thereby enable release of water when river flows are insufficient. They enable the development of towns, industries, and irrigation with all of their economic and social benefits. They also provide hydroelectric power, flood mitigation, and recreational facilities. Water can be released to maintain environmental flows, dilute pollutants, and flush sediments out of the lower river reaches, thereby promoting healthier instream conditions and improving navigation.

Until the early 1980s, systematic evaluation of their environmental and social impacts was not mandatory. Such impacts are frequently serious but difficult to predict and quantify. The displacement of people to make way for the construction of dams and their reservoirs can cause great suffering and social dislocation. The negative ecological impacts can extend upstream into the reservoir and downstream to the sea.

There is now growing opposition in most countries to new large dams, and several projects have recently been canceled due to public opposition. There is also a stricter regulatory framework for such projects. International non-government organisations have played a role in fostering independent scrutiny of large dam projects, and they have emboldened the affected communities to seek a greater role in decisions that impact directly on their lives.

The good dam sites (and many not so good sites) have already been used, and strict environmental and social conditions are now imposed.

Some of the major deficiencies in the major and medium schemes were:

*(a)* Need for modernisation of the preplan and early plan systems to provide water at the outlet delivery points to farmers at the right time and in the right quantity;

*(b)* Lack of adequate drainage, resulting in waterlogging conditions due to excess water used in irrigating crops as well as due to soil factors;

*(c)* The absence of a distribution system within the outlet and the non-introduction of rotational distribution of water to the farmers;

*(d)* Inadequate attention to land consolidation, levelling and all other aspects which promote a better on-farm management of water;

*(e)* Lack of anticipatory research in optimum water use, particularly in black soils with considerable moisture retention capacity;

*(f)* Lack of suitable infrastructure and extension services;

*(g)* Poor co-ordination between the concerned government organisation in the command areas.

## Modernisation

Irrigation projects, sanctioned for execution up to 1965, were designed to meet the pattern of irrigation of traditional crops. With the introduction of high yielding varieties of seeds since 1965, several earlier projects have proved inadequate to meet the rather exacting demands for water following the use of high yielding varieties of seeds. Work on the modernisation of irrigation system will be taken up actively in each state during the Sixth Plan.

## Minor Irrigation Programme

Minor irrigation includes all ground water development and surface water development by means of irrigation projects having CCA up to 2,000 hectares. There have been two significant developments in the field of irrigation. The first relates of the recognition of the facts that irrigation is not merely one of the inputs but a pre-requisite infrastructure on the basis of which the use of other inputs and better cultivation methods can be effectively planned. The second relates to the explosive expansion in the development of ground water through dug wells, shallow tubewells and pumpsets. This provided the farmer instant and controlled irrigation most suited to the growth of new high yielding varieties.

Minor irrigation programmes suffered a setback on account of the shortage of EC grade aluminum. In fact, the shortage affected the electrification programme, which was most vital for ground water development and surface lift irrigation schemes.

## Irrigation and New Farm Technology

With the expansion of irrigation facilities, there is scope for enlarged adoption of the new farm technology in terms of application of HYV seed, chemical fertiliser, pesticides, etc. As discussed earlier in such states where there are relatively better irrigation facilities, we notice relatively more area under the HYV programme, higher doses of fertiliser application and better yields.

## Water Resources Management

Water resources management implies the efficient management of available water resources so as to ensure optimum utilisation. It aims at harnessing the water resources for irrigation for stepping up of farm production. Water resources management has different aspects like water management in flood prone areas, surface water management and ground water management.

## Water Management in Flood-prone Areas

The task of water management in flood-prone areas needs investigation with a view to arriving at some optimal solution to the problems of diversion and storage. This is necessary to even out the flow and also to conserve our precious water resources for use in water scarcity regions, particularly during the dry seasons. The National Commission on Flood (1980) suggested that, measures, primarily for conservation (like small, medium and large reservoirs, natural detention basins, ground water storage, etc.) which help in moderating run-offs depending on their capacity, should be the first task for flood management in any basin. Reservoirs costing heavily are not usually planned for flood control only. It forms only a part of multi-purpose projects.

*Construction of Checkdam at Kattumalai Channel After Work (District: Dindigul, Tamil Nadu)*

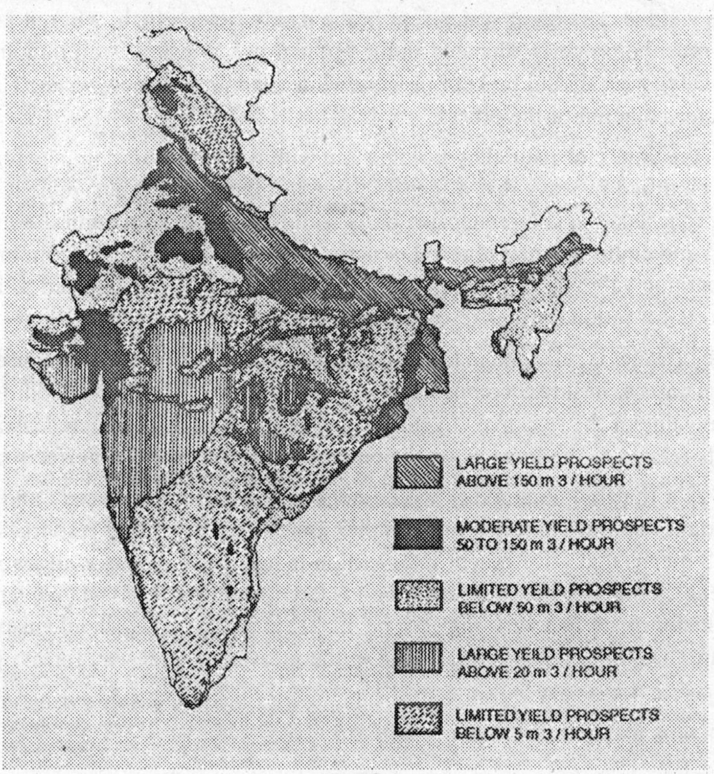


*Fig. 2.*

## Surface Water Management

The surface water is released from the reservoirs and dams through a network of main canal, distributaries and minors and water courses. Proper water management in this case requires certain steps:

(1) The losses due to seepage and percolation in the canals should be minimised;

(2) The irrigated area should have suitable crop planning to achieve maximum production;

(3) The number of waterings and the water depth in field should be optimal so as to avoid wastage in deep percolation below the root zone;

(4) The drainage of irrigated areas should be properly planned so that there is no danger of water-logging or soil salinity;

(5) There should be efficient system of measuring and controlling of water outlet;

(6) To ensure even supply of water to the entire area, it is of utmost importance that land shaping is properly done, fields are levelled and water courses and field channels are constructed; and

(7) For equitable distribution of water from the headworks up to the tail-end of the canal, warabandi system should be adopted so that the minimum waterings are provided to the tail-end farmers also to get the optimum crop yield from the entire command area.

## Ground Water Management

Ground water being a major source of irrigation in dry areas, its management assumes crucial importance. In pumping out water and in taking it to the field, care should be taken to avoid wastages. The water-lifting equipment must be appropriate and it must be in good condition. The water channel from the well to the field must be properly maintained. The illiterate farmers sometimes may be under the wrong impression that more yield is possible if water dept in the paddy field is high, without knowing its adverse effects. The farmers must be properly educated in the optimal use of water. A minimum space required in between wells of all categories should be kept in view while planning for new wells. This avoids one well drawing away the water potential of the other.

The river basin constitutes the natural hydrologic unit within which users compete for the same resource and water quality is modified in ways that affect its value to other users. Management of water resources must therefore be approached on a comprehensive basis within this hydrologic unit. Beyond the basic needs for human well being and environmental renewal, scarcity of water is largely an economic issue. This idea, that water has an economic value in all its competing uses and should be recognized as an economic good, must underlie all efforts for rational water resource management.

Part of the value of water is reflected in the costs of extraction and delivery to the users. As a minimum, users should pay these costs to ensure accountability and financial sustainability. In addition, the opportunity cost, representing the value of the resources to some other user, must be considered. And finally, there are also the external costs related to the impacts on the environment and the health effects of polluted water.

Treating water as a tradable commodity would help ensure greater efficiency and productivity in its use. However, important cultural concerns and complex issues exit regarding resources sustainability and natural habitat, which means that government intervention is needed in resource allocation and investment decisions. Government should also provide financing for large water projects—dams, large scale irrigation, flood control—for which private financing may not be readily available. They should also intervene, directly or indirectly, to ensure that water resources are used in the most beneficial way for the greater society.

The development of freshwater resources for human uses has compromised natural ecosystems that depend on these resources for their continued integrity.

**WATER STRESS**

Water stress for a river basin is defined in degree of annual water use (that is, water withdrawn from a surface or groundwater source for human purposes) as a percentage of the total water resources available in that basin. Water stress for a country is the summation of water stress for all its river basins. Water stress begins when withdrawals of freshwater rise above 10 per cent of renewable resources. Medium to high stress translates as water use that exceeds 20 per cent. Countries experience high water stress when the ratio of water use to supply exceeds 40 per cent. At such levels, their patterns of use may not be sustainable and water-scarcity is likely to become the limiting factor to economic growth.

Freshwater ecosystems, comprising lakes, rivers and wetlands, have already lost a greater proportion of species and habitant than land or ocean ecosystems. Unrestricted development of surface water and groundwater has altered the hydrologic cycle and threatens the natural functions of deltas and wetlands. Wetlands have been converted to croplands, and rivers that channelled water to estuaries and deltas, have dried up.

## Wise Water Management

The past century has seen enormous changes in the way society conducts the business of economic development, food production, and trade. Concurrently, and especially in the latter part of the century, there has been an explosion in the construction of large projects for water storage, flood control, irrigation and hydro power. These were conceived and realized in an atmosphere of challenge: how to tame nature to serve the needs of humanity. The limits to the scale of the projects were set by the ingenuity of engineering solutions. The driving forces were population growth, food security, and industrial development.

Most large-sale projects have been financed by governments, and governments have naturally assumed responsibility for their management. The absence of private investors reflects not only the scale of the investments required, but also the fact that for some of these projects there were political objectives: for example, to encourage development in remote areas or to distribute development funds among regions. In many cases, it was assumed that users would repay the investment costs through water and other charges. This did not always happen. The repayment obligations have been eased and the cost of providing the services has frequently become institutionalised as a direct subsidy.

Water planners and developers have always worked from projections based on population growth, industrial and agricultural production, and level of economic and social development to determine demand, and hence to formulate engineering solutions to provide the appropriate freshwater supply. However, because of natural resource constraints and the accumulating adverse environmental impact of past projects, changes are beginning to be made in the way planners approach the problems of water supply. This is evident as a discernible shift from water resources development towards supply and demand management. The tightening fiscal environment, recent financial crisis, and reduction in the potential for developing additional surface water and groundwater supplies have added impetus to this shift in the last decades. In addition, people the world over now place a higher value on maintaining the ecological action of freshwater ecosystems. There is also growing public pressure for the costs and benefits of water development projects to be shared more equitably and prudently and for investment to be directed towards satisfying basic human needs rather than benefiting elite groups at a high cost to the community at large.

The agriculture sector is, therefore coming under increasing pressure to release water to meet other, more productive needs. for producing high value crops in water-scarce areas, new irrigation techniques have been shown to be highly efficient and cost-effective. Even simple improvements in surface canal systems, which are used almost exclusively in developing countries, can lead to impressive gains in efficiency. Efforts to increase efficiency in water use could, however, have serious impacts on poor farmers, who may not be able to finance technological improvements. Hence, special assistance may be required to help poor farmers move up the technological ladder. Potentially greater saving can be achieved in delivering water, and the incentives for such improvements should be structured in such a way that the major beneficiaries (those who will avail of the "saved" water) contribute their share of the costs.

## Swajaldhara

The Government of India has been emphasizing the need for taking up community based rural water supply programmes, and now has decided to open up the reform initiatives in the rural drinking water supply sector through out the country. This programme is called **Swajaldhara**. The key elements are *(i)* demand driven and community participation approach; *(ii)* panchayats/communities to plan, implement, operate, maintain and manage all drinking water schemes; *(iii)* partial capital cost sharing by the communities upfront in cash; *(iv)* full ownership of drinking water assets with Gram Panchayats; and *(v)* full operation and maintenance by the users/panchayats.

Beneficiary groups, Gram Panchayats and blocks adopting the reforms principles will be eligible for Swajaldhara Projects. 10% community contribution of the estimated capital cost of the schemes upfront (5% in case of predominantly SC/ST habitations as per 2001 census) will be integral part of the project. The cost of the project excluding community contribution will be fully met by Government of India. The important features of this scheme is that the rural people should feel as the owner of the Scheme. Moreover, people and their Gram Panchayat must shoulder fully the operation and maintainance responsibility of the Schemes.

The community contribution must come only from the users. The Panchayats and State Governments should not provide any government fund as substitute for community contribution, as this will not confirm to the principles of the Swajaldhara. The users will implement the scheme and undertake its O&M, only when they contribute towards the project cost. Therefore, people's contribution is a non-negotiable ingredient of Swajaldhara.

## Looking Ahead: Working for a Blue Revolution

The hope for the future lies in doing for water productivity what the green revolution did for crop productivity. This "blue revolution," as it has been termed by various scientists and water planners, would dramatically improve the efficiency of freshwater use, particularly in agriculture. The revolution will begin with greater public awareness of the potential dangers of a business as usual approach: help create policies, strategies, and incentives needed to establish integrated water resource management on a global basis; and culminate in the allocation of resources to effect the social, institutional, and technological changes necessary for efficient water allocations and use.

In rural India, consultations resolved that:

- Sustainability of water resources, institutions, and financing is critical to poverty reduction;
- National water policies need to adopt cross-sectoral approaches and be practical and implementable;
- Water institutions need to be reformed to deal with cross-sectoral dimensions through approaches that involve stakeholders at all levels; and
- Participatory planning and management need to focus on people's needs, equity, gender and accountability.

The following policy elements are at the core of water policy.

- Promote effective national water policies and action programmes;
- Apply principles of socially inclusive development to improve the equitability of water service delivery; support adoption of appropriate pricing policies to promote greater efficiency; and encourage decentralisation and autonomy to foster increased private sector participation and to improve service accountability;
- Foster integrated approach to management of water resources;
- Foster the efficient and sustainable use and conservation of water;
- Promote cooperation for beneficial use of shared resources within and between countries;
- Facilitate stakeholder consultation and participation at all levels; and
- Improve governance through capacity building, monitoring, and evaluation.

Despite the difficult choices that must be made worldwide to ensure sustainable water use and management, there is some cause for optimism. Commitment to stricter environmental controls and their enforcement does help to maintain healthier ecological condition and can restore the severely degraded environment. The efficiency of water use can be improved without sacrificing quality of life and such improvements can alleviate if not completely avoid the looming water crises. Adopting socially inclusive policies to spread the benefits of water resources development to the poor and other traditionally disadvantaged members of the community benefits society as a whole by improving living conditions, health, social stability, and opportunities for productive employment.

## Conclusion

The Union ministry of water resources reports that there are nearly 395 incomplete irrigation projects in the country. Forty of these are still in the construction stage despite dating back to the early 1970s (and even earlier). Another 300 were launched prior to 1992. Last year, the office of the Comptroller and Auditor General said Rs. 78,450 crore had been spent on these irrigation projects, with a further Rs. 89,873 crore required for completion. All these projects put together are envisaged to bring in a further 20 million hectares under irrigation. That is a huge amount land, but a much bigger chunk of cultivated land will continue to depend on the rains. Moreover, even irrigation projects depend on the Indian Summer Monsoon Rainfall (ISMR) to fill up water reservoirs, tributaries and provide snow in the Himalayas.

For all these reasons, key economic institutions and research agencies factor in the role of the ISMR in the country's economic prospects explicitly. The level of water in designate reservoirs is used as a vital input by the Reserve Banks periodic reviews of the economy, Further, experts such as Sulochana Gadgil and Siddhartha Gadgil from the Indian Institute of Science have also carried out rigorous econometic analysis that points to the strong and abiding impact of the monsoons on foodgrains output and overall GDP. A significant finding of their research is a marked asymmetry of the Indian economy's response to annual variation in the ISMR. According to their research, and which has been corroborated by other eminent economic institutions, a deficiency in the ISMR has very strong negative impacts on the GDP and agricultural output – often showing up in economic data for the following year. In contrast, a surplus rainfall has a relatively smaller positive impact.

Again, there are less complex indicators of the overall economic impact of the rains. A normal rainfall enables large sections of the agriculture-based population to find incomes to consume new goods and services. This year, manufacturers of fertilisers, tractors, FMCGS and other consumer durables are looking to the play of the ISMR.

❑ ❑ ❑

# Chapter 20
# ENERGY MANAGEMENT

## Introduction

Growth of India's agricultural sector is essential pre-requisite for wider national development and for poverty alleviation. Energy has increasingly given agriculture a boost. Energy has also given humanity power over environment. As for agriculture, energy plays a unique role in irrigation, storage etc. Socially, it provides a phenomenal push to modernisation. Energy and rural development are interwoven. Hence, a prudent management of energy is a must in the present context.

## Rural Electrification

Rural electrification, coupled with the assured supply of power, is the backbone of the minor irrigation programme, particularly that of ground water development, because it promotes the most economical and efficient means of lifting water. Diesel pumping and the use of animal-operated water lifting appliances are the alternatives; but they are comparatively more expensive in operation. Short supplies and price hikes in the cost of imported diesel have become constraints on the minor irrigation programmes in recent years. The situation makes it imperative that the rural electrification programme be given an added momentum. The Seventh Plan has accorded the highest priority to the energy sector.

The Rural Electrification Corporation Limited set up by the Government of India in July 1969 in pursuance of the recommendations of the All-India Rural Credit Review Committee, has played a significant role in accelerating the rural electrification programme and putting it on a sound technical footing.

Over the years, the REC has evolved a number of loan categories, with varied terms and conditions suited to the socio-economic and geographical diversity of the country, and in accordance with the government directives. The states have been classified into above average (AA), average (A) and below average (BA) categories. The average in this case is been classified into ordinary advanced (OA), ordinary backward

(OB) and specially underdeveloped categories. The terms and conditions of loans for backward and specially underdeveloped areas are much softer than those for advanced areas.

Rural Electrification Schemes are formulated and implemented by the States and Union Territories and are financed both from the state resources and loans from the Rural Electrification Corporation.

Special attention is being paid to increase household connections in electrified villages to extended the benefit of electricity to the rural community.

**Table 1**

**ELECTRIFICATION OF VILLAGES: 1947-1994-95**

| *At the end of* | *Villages Electrified* | |
|---|---|---|
| | *Number* | *As % of total no. of villages* |
| 1947 | 1,500 | 0.3 |
| 1950-51 | 3,061 | 0.5 |
| 1955-56 | 7,294 | 1.3 |
| 1960-61 | 21,750 | 3.8 |
| 1965-66 | 45,144 | 8.0 |
| 1970-71 | 1,06,774 | 18.5 |
| 1975-76 | 1,85,806 | 32.3 |
| 1976-77 | 2,02,843 | 35.2 |
| 1977-78 | 2,16,863 | 37.7 |
| 1978-79 | 2,32,770 | 40.4 |
| 1979-80 | 2,49,799 | 43.4 |
| 1980-81 | 2,72,625 | 47.3 |
| 1981-82 | 2,94,900 | 51.2 |
| 1982-83 | 3,20,083 | 55.6 |
| 1984-85 } Promoted by Ministry of Energy | 3,50,000 | 60.8 |
| 1994-95 } | 5,76,126 | 100.0 |

In a Conference of the Chief Ministers, held in March, 2002, it was resolved that village electrification may be completed by 2007 and full coverage of all households be completed by 2012. To achieve these objectives, village electrification is now treated as a Basic Minimum Services under the Pradhan Mantri Gramodaya Yojana (PMGY) from the year 2001-02. For the year 2001-02, an allocation of Rs. 421 crore was made and Rs. 412 crore were released to the States. During 2002-03, a sum of Rs. 360 crore has been allocated for rural electrification. Besides availability of funds for village electrification under PMGY, Central Plan Assistance is also available to the States for village electrification under Minimum Needs Programme (MNP). During 2002-03, an allocation of Rs. 600 crore was made under MNP and the same was released to the states in two equal installments.

## Highlights

- With all the flaws noted below, the progress in respect of rural electrification should be regarded as a major achievement of post-independence India. A good part of the credit for this should go the Rural Electrification Corporation established by the central government in July 1969.

- When is a village regarded electrified? Officially it is defined thus: Even if a single connection is supplied to a village, it is considered as having been electrified. But even for this, the capital expenditure can be pretty heavy. For giving even a single connection in a village, it is necessary to set up one 11/22 KV line, one transformer.
- At the end of March 1988, 4.26 lakh villages were electrified, *i.e.* 74% of the total number of 5.76 lakh villages in the country. The population coverage of these villages is, however, substantially higher than 76% The perspective plan of the states provides for electrification of all the villages by 1994-95.
- The Working Group on Energy (Chairman: Mr. N.B. Prasad) has observed: "Inspite of electrifying all towns and about 44 percent of villages, the percentage of households electrified remains at about 14 percent only. Even with the acceleration in the pace of electrification in the seventies, the number of new electricity connections to houses has increased at the rate of about one million households a year, while the number of new households has been increasing at the rate of about 2.2 million per year. In other words, the number of non-electrified houses is steadily increasing inspite of the accelerated rural electrification programmes."
- This basically reflects the poverty of rural and urban India.
- The most scandalous aspect of rural electrification, however, is the intolerably frequent breakdown of power supply. So much so that many a farmer who can afford it installs a diesel engine (as a stand-by) along with an electrically-run pump to draw water from his well. A major drive to improve the transmission and distribution network of State Electricity Boards (hardware as well as personnel) is urgently required.

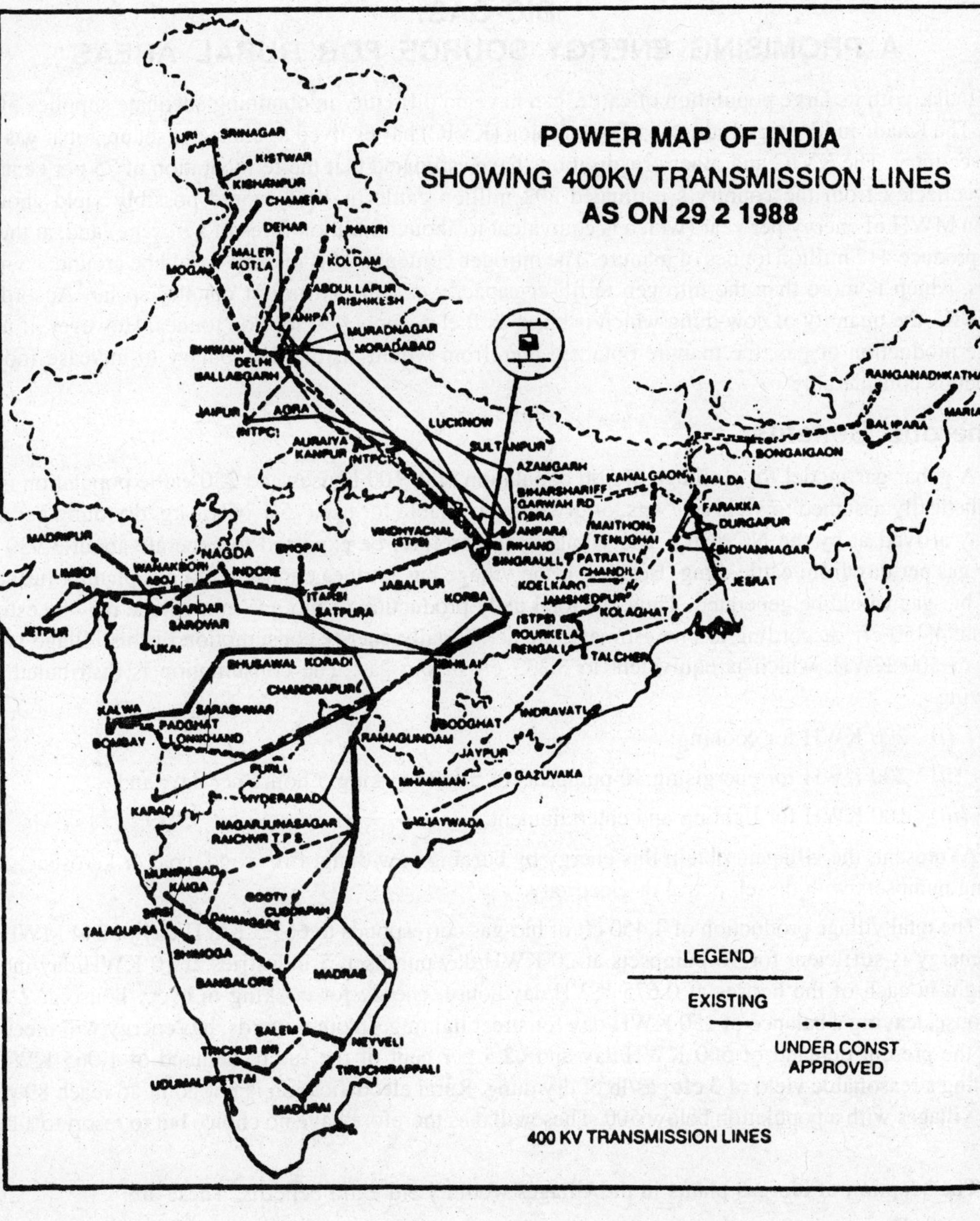


*Note:* The locations/sites of the power stations and sub-stations shown in this are approximate.

The administrative head quarters of chandigarh, haryana and punjab are at chandigarh based upon survey of india map with the permission of the surveyor general of india. The territorial waters of india extend into the sea to a distance of twelve nautical miles measured from the appropriate base line.

The boundary of meghalaya shown on this map is as interpreted from the north eastern areas (reorganisation) act 1971. But has yet to be verified.

# BIO-GAS: A PROMISING ENERGY SOURCE FOR RURAL AREAS

India, with its large population of cattle, can have no difficulty in obtaining adequate supplies of cattle dung. The Khadi and Village Industries Commission (KVIC) has evolved a scheme to set up gobar gas plants in the country. The KVIC and other organisations have estimated that the fermentation of 75 per cent of the dung collected from the country's estimated 392 million cattle in 1983 would possibly yield about 337 million MWH of energy per year (which is equivalent to about 42 billion litres of kerosene) and, at the same time, produce 412 million tonnes of manure. The nitrogen content of this manure would be around 3.5 million tonnes, which is more than the nitrogen fertiliser capacity established in our country so far. According to the KVIC, the quantity of cow dung which is burnt as fuel is about 400 million tonnes. However, if utilised for the production of gas, the manure obtained therefrom would enable the country to increase foodgrain production considerably.

## Numerous Benefits

A gobar gas model for a village of 500 population with 100 houses and 250 cattle population may be hypothetically assumed to yield 597 kgs. of dry dung available for use (75% of 3.2 kg. dry dung per animal per day arrived at by the NCAER). The village can therefore, be expected to generate about 3,950 cft of gobar gas per day from cattle dung. Besides, if the village has latrines connected to gas plant, a further 500 cft of bio-gas would be generated. Thus, the total daily production of bio-gas in a village may be estimated at about 4,450 cft. According to one estimate, the actual daily energy consumption of this village is of the order of 500 KWH, which is equivalent to 3,333 cft of bio-gas. The consumption is distributed in the following

*(i)* 200 KWH for cooking;

*(ii)* 200 KWH for energising 10 pumpsets of 5 HP working 5 hours per day; and

*(iii)* 100 KWH for lighting and entertainment.

At present, the villagers obtain this energy by burning cow dung, fire wood, coal or kerosene, and by running pumpsets with diesel, petrol or electricity.

The total village production of 4,450 cft of bio-gas corresponds to 667.5 KWH/day or 244 MWH/year. This energy is sufficient for 10 pumpsets at 20 KWH/day/pumpset, 5 industries at 10 KWH/day/industry, one light in each of the houses at 0.675 KWH/day/house, energy for cooking in every house at 2 KWH/day/house, leaving a balance of 150 KWH/day for street lighting. In other words, bio-energy will meet 1,335 times the present demand of 500 KWH/day and 62.5 per cent of the future demand of 1,065 KWH/day, assuming a reasonable yield of 3 cft gas/lb of dry dung. Rural electrification is not going to reach 89 percent of the villages with a population below 500. These villages therefore have no choice but to resort to a bio-gas plant.

The adoption of bio-gas plants in the villages would yield extra benefits. These are:

*(i)* Dispersal of production units to the villages;

*(ii)* Saving in capital and foreign exchange;

*(iii)* Generation of more employment for less skilled workers;

*(iv)* Production for fertiliser at the source where it is consumed, thus relieving the burden on the transport system.

Based on this study by Prof. A.K.N. Reddy at the Institute of Science, Bangalore, the United Nations Environmental Programme (UNEP) points out that 26,150 bio-gas plants will produce as much fertiliser as a single $ 140 million coal-based plant. But the bio-gas plant will require an investment of $ 14 million and will generate 130 times as much employment, What is more, the added prosperity will be diffused over 26,000 villages instead of being concentrated in a single township; and since the fertiliser will be consumed where it is produced, it will eliminate the need for packaging, transport and storage.

## Community Gobar Gas Plant

A community gobar gas plant project has been set up at village Dhaneev in Thane district near Mumbai under the auspices of the KVIC. The first of its kind in the country, the project aims at supplying gobar-gas/bio-gas for cooking and, if possible, for lighting to about 40 hamlets of the village. The villagers owning about 100 cattle would supply cow dung every day as feedstock for the plant. The project has now commenced producing gas. What remains to be done is to give connections to the residents. It is a chain of three gas plants which produces gas from cow dung, night soil and agricultural waste respectively. Each of these plants is capable of producing about 1,500 cubic feet of gas per day.

The first gas plant will be fed with cow dung. After taking about 70 to 80 per cent of the gas, the slurry in the digester will be transferred to another tank, which will produce gas from night soil. For this purpose, about 8 latrines have been constructed and are directly connected to the digester of the new plant. This has to be done because night soil does not ferment properly without the addition of cow dung to the slurry, although it gives the maximum amount of gas. The slurry from this plant is then transferred to the third plant which produces bio-gas from agricultural waste and some plants, like the hyacinth. Each of these link plants produces 1,500 cubic feet of gas or a total of about 4,500 cubic feet of gas per day. The project has to far cost Rs two lakhs and about Rs 40,000 is required for giving connections to every house in the village. The KVIC plans to make use of surplus gas for running a water pump at the village well. Water drawn from the well will be stored in an overhead tank and supplied to the villagers through a pipeline.

**Table 2**

**LARGE-SCALE COAL-BASED VS. BIO-GAS FERTILIZER PLANTS**

| | | *Coal-Based* | *Bio-Gas Based* |
|---|---|---|---|
| *(i)* | Annual production/unit | 5,00,000 tonnes urea | 590 tonnes compost |
| *(ii)* | Annual nitrogen production | 2,30,000 tonnes | 8.8 tonnes |
| *(iii)* | Capital cost/unit | Rs. 120 crores | Rs. 41,000 |
| *(iv)* | Foreign exchange component | Rs 50 crores | Nil |
| *(v)* | Employment/unit | 1,000 | 5 |
| *(vi)* | Sale @ Rs.4,350/tonnes N | Rs. 100 crores | Rs 38,280 |
| *(vii)* | Capital turnover ratio | 1.20 | 1.07 |
| *(viii)* | To produce 2,30,000 tonnes N | | |
| | *(a)* Number of units | 1 | 26,150 |
| | *(b)* Capital cost | Rs.120 crores | Rs 107 crores |
| | *(c)* Foreign exchange | Rs.50 crores | Nil |
| | *(d)* Employment | 1,000 | 1,30,750 |
| | *(e)* Energy | Consumption | Generation |

The most urgent need of the time is to provide low-cost fuel to farmers to run their engine pumpsets because of the exorbitant increase in the price of petrol, diesel, crude and kerosene oil. The only way out is to instal biogas engine pumpsets. On an average, about 15 cubic feet of gas is required per horse power per hour to run an engine. In other words, a 5 HP engine would require 300 cubic feet of gobar gas plant to run for four hours every day. Basically, gobar gas dual fuel engine requires 15 per cent diesel and the balance of the energy can be obtained from gobar gas. The normal specific fuel consumption of a 5 HP engine running for four hours every day for 25 days at 183 gms/bph/hr would be $\frac{183 \quad 5 \quad 4 \quad 25}{1000 \quad 0.83}$ = 110.24 litres of diesel. For running the 5 HP engine on gobar gas, only 16.53 litres of diesel oil would be required as against 110.24 litres. Thus, 93.71 litres of diesel per month would be saved which would amount to over Rs.181 per month.

The National Project on Bio-gas Development with a target of 400,000 bio-gas plants for the Sixth Plan period was sanctioned only in November, 1981. The state-wise targets which were provisionally drawn at the stage were subsequently firmed up on yearly basis.

## New and Renewable Sources of Energy

The broad objectives of the development of new and renewable sources of energy in the Sixth Plan are:

*(a)* To implement on a large scale programmes, such as those of energy forestry and bio-gas, where technology development has already reached a stage which permits field application;

*(b)* To carry field testing and demonstration on a country-wide basis of technologies which have the potential to become commercially viable in the next five to seven years; and

*(c)* To intensify research in, and development of, other technologies where the potential is likely to be available over a longer time horizon.

The programme covers all the important new and renewable sources of energy, such as solar, wind biomass, chemical and geothermal energy and their application to agriculture, transportation and other sectors. In order to give an impetus to the development of renewable sources of energy, an Alternative Engeries Commission has been set up.

## Energy Forestry

In the emerging energy situation, the role of non-commercial fuels acquires a new significance. Rather than proceed on the assumption that the substitution of non-commercial by commercial fuels is inescapable, a systematic effort has now to be made to sustain the supplies of such fuels and to improve the efficiency with which they are utilised. Firewood, it is well know, is the most important among the traditional fuels, accounting for almost two-thirds of the total energy contribution from non-commercial sources. It is becoming increasingly scarce; and in many parts of the country, it has already ceased to be non-commercial in the strict sense. The ecological damage caused by extensive denudation of forests for fuel and other requirements is too well know to need any elaboration here. There is, no doubt, the problem of pressure on land and the competition for land use for agriculture, industrial and housing activity. Recent experience, however, shows that even in the thickly populated areas of the country, sufficient land is available along roads, railway lines and canals and in the degraded forests and community lands for developing wood lots to provide fuel to the local communities. Energy forestry would have be regarded as an important component of our energy strategy, because rural communities will continue to depend heavily on firewood for several decades to come. A large programme of fuel and farm forestry has therefore been taken up in the Sixth Plan, the target being 13 lakh hectares of plantation.

## Bio-gas

The technology for the conversion of animal wastes into bio-gas is well-established and a fairly large number of bio-gas plants are already in operation. While the pioneering work in this field has already been carried out by the Khadi and Village Industries Commission, a number of agencies are currently involved in a nationally co-ordinated programme; and the research effort aims at raising the efficiency of gas generation and bringing down the capital cost of the bio-gas units. Some new designs have already become available; for instance, 'Janata' bio-gas plants, which are built of bricks, have become very popular in Uttar Pradesh. Ferro-concrete is another material which holds out possibilities of displacing steel and reducing the cost of the construction of bio-gas plants. Some innovative solutions to the problem of poor gas generation under conditions of low ambient temperature also appear to be in sight. Further research efforts will be directed at cost reduction brought about by improvements in the design and use of materials, as also by the use of crop residues and water hyacinth in bio–gas production. Problems relating to the use of bio-gas for motive power and the generation of electricity will also be taken up.

The bio-gas programme, as is well-known, not only provides the much needed energy to rural families and reduce the pressure on firewood supplies, but yields valuable organic manure, improves environmental health in rural areas and reduces the drudgery of women. Having regard to the large potential of local sources of energy supply, an ambitious programme for the installation of bio-gas plants has been launched. About one million family size plants and 100 community plants are to be set up during the Sixth Plan. While financial provision has been made in the Plan for the payment of appropriate subsidies to those who install bio-gas units, institutional funds will have to be harnessed for the prospective owners to meet the initial capital cost. It will also be necessary to strengthen the machinery for providing technical guidance, assistance in installation and post-commissioning services in rural areas and to initiate a programme for the dissemination of information relating to bio-gas and its applications.

## Integrated Rural Energy Systems

The possibility of decentralised energy production and distribution deserves serious consideration, particularly for meeting the energy needs of the dispersed rural population. Such energy systems would have to be based on a systems approach, which takes into account all the available energy resources in a given location, with particular emphasis on new and renewable energy technologies. The optimal mix of energy supply technologies for each location would have to be individually evaluated.

## Conclusion

The rural electrification and energisation of pumpsets have played a very important role in improving the agricultural production. It has helped in exploitation of underground water resources in many parts of the country which improved crop intensity considerably. Commercial banks have been playing a major role in rural electrification through direct and indirect lendings. Commercial banks provide term loans for tube wells and energisation of pumpsets. Banks also provide finance to REC and State Electricity Boards through purchase of bonds issued by them.

All along, rural areas should also harness alternative sources of energy to enrich their lives as well as improve the rural environment. This will lead to conservation of natural resources like forests, improves water shed and foster rural arts and crafts. Above all, it also provides a big relief to rural women to channelise their energies more productively and creatively.

❑ ❑ ❑

*"TECHNOLOGICAL SUPPORT FOR RURAL development requires first, technology backup to a process of widespread agricultural growth, organisation of delivery system for different inputs along modern lines and efficient procurement and processing of agricultural sector in rural areas. This will have to be organised in the context of spreading agricultural and rural growth and employment in the diverse conditions of the different agroclimatic regions of India and for supporting the small peasant and producer base of the agrarian economy."*

# Chapter 21

# MODERN AGRICULTURAL TECHNOLOGY

## Introduction

Indian agriculture has made significant strides in the past 50 years, demonstrating unique resilience in becoming a significant contributor to the Indian economy. It has also thrown enormous challenges before the scientists, planners and policy makers in view of its diversity, while at the same time it has absorbed improved technologies in order to ward off the challenge to food scarcity that loomed large around the sixties. It has also demonstrated the huge potential for employment generation, reducing rural poverty, generating exports and above all meeting the challenges, towards household food security despite the rise in population and exploitation of our natural resources. It is these challenges, growing in their dimensions day by day, that have prompted the Ministry of Agriculture to assess the strengths and weaknesses of our Research and Development system and evolve a holistic strategy to strengthen our interface for generation and dissemination of new technologies, especially by taking advantage of the rich experiences so gained.

Production practices and systems will need to be adapted to respond to new market demands and export opportunities, poverty alleviation or growing labour shortages, depending on the setting. Technical solutions will be increasingly location-specific, matched to the huge diversity of India's 20 agri-ecological regions, 60 sub-regions and 120 agro-climatic zones.

The term modern agricultural technology refers to the use of fertiliser, and better high yielding seeds, and the application of agricultural engineering. Agricultural engineering is defined as the application of the knowledge, techniques and disciplines of various fields of engineering to the solutions of problems arising in the field of agriculture and rural living, with the object of reducing labour, improving productivity per worker, raising the standard of living of the farmers and increasing the overall earnings of the individual worker.

## Fertiliser Consumption

Fertilisers and pesticides occupy the second rank in importance in their contribution to agricultural production. Chemical fertilisers yield the optimum results when used with irrigation facilities. The importance given to manures and fertilisers has been clearly brought out by the Famine Enquiry Commission:

"Next to the provision of an assured supply of water, the use of manure offers the most important single means of increasing the yield of crops. Experience has shown that the plant food, abstracted by the low yielding varieties of crops, is replaced through the operation of the natural recuperative powers of the soil, assisted by the small quantity of manure occasionally applied, and that the fertility of the soils in India has thus become stabilised at a low level. If, therefore, the yield of crops is to be increased; in particular, if the full benefit is to be derived from improved varieties, plant food must be added to the soil in very considerable quantities." The problem of the low fertility of Indian soils was recognised by the planners in the very beginning; and they have accorded prime importance to fertilisers in successive Plans. The importance of fertilisers was further enhanced with the adoption of the Intensive Agricultural District Programme (IADP) in 1960, and the high-yielding varieties programme (HYVP) in 1966.

During 2001-02 the per hectare consumption of fertilisers in India has been 90.12 kgs as compared to 1,285 kgs in New Zealand, 743 kgs in the Netherlands, 530 kgs in Belgium and 450 kgs in Japan. The consumption of fertilizers in India has been increasing from 66,000 tonnes in 1951-52 to 174 lakh tonnes in 2001-02. As a result, the per hectare consumption increased from 0.5 kg to 90 kg.

The following measures have been taken to promote their use:

**Table 1**

**PER HECTARE CONSUMPTION OF FERTILIZERS FOR CROPPED AREA DURING 2001-02**

| *S. No.* | *State / U.T.* | *2001-02* |
|---|---|---|
| 1. | Andhra Pradesh | 143.46 |
| 2. | Karnataka | 101.48 |
| 3. | Kerala | 60.72 |
| 4. | Tamil Nadu | 141.55 |
| 5. | Gujarat | 85.52 |
| 6. | Madhya Pradesh + | 39.96 |
| 7. | Maharashtra | 78.24 |
| 8. | Rajasthan | 38.88 |
| 9. | Haryana | 155.69 |
| 10. | Himachal Pradesh | 41.40 |
| 11. | Jammu & Kashmir | 64.55 |
| 12. | Punjab | 173.38 |
| 13. | Uttar Pradesh ++ | 130.44 |
| 14. | Bihar | 87.39 |
| 15. | Orissa | 40.91 |
| 16. | West Bengal | 126.82 |
| 17. | Arunachal Pradesh | 2.88 |
| 18. | Assam | 38.81 |
| 19. | Tripura | 30.45 |
| 20. | Manipur | 104.94 |
| 21. | Meghalaya | 17.16 |
| 22. | Nagaland | 2.13 |
| 23. | Mizoram | 13.72 |
| 24. | Sikkim | 9.72 |
| | All India | 90.12 |

\+ Includes Chhatisgarh

++ Includes Uttaranchal

*Source:* Ministry of Chemicals & Fertilizer.

Fertilisers are being made available at subsidised rates. The quantum of subsidy on fertilisers has increased from Rs 24 crores in 1977-78 to Rs. 7,004 crores in 2002-03.

Short terms loans are also made available at concessional rates of interest for purchase and distribution of fertilisers, seeds and pesticides.

In 2002-03 fertilizer production (N&P) is expected to rise to 15.23 million tonnes (10.83 million tonnes of nitrogen and 4.40 mt of phosphate) as compared to 1.06 million tonnes in 1970-71.

Soil testing facilities have been intensified in 60 selected rainfed districts in 16 states.

Fertilisers are made available in small packs of 25 kgs.

The system of lead fertiliser supplies introduced in 1986-87 is being continued. The lead suppliers nominated prepare detailed action plans and chalk out strategy for increased fertiliser consumption for their district for the next five years.

An assured supply of water is a prime condition for an intensive application of fertilizers. The absence of this condition over large parts of the country is one of the important factors which hamper a more rapid increase of fertilizer consumption in India. This apart the steep increase in fertilizer prices during recent years has adversely affected its use. It is now conceded, at least in principle, that organic manures should receive greater attention in coming years.

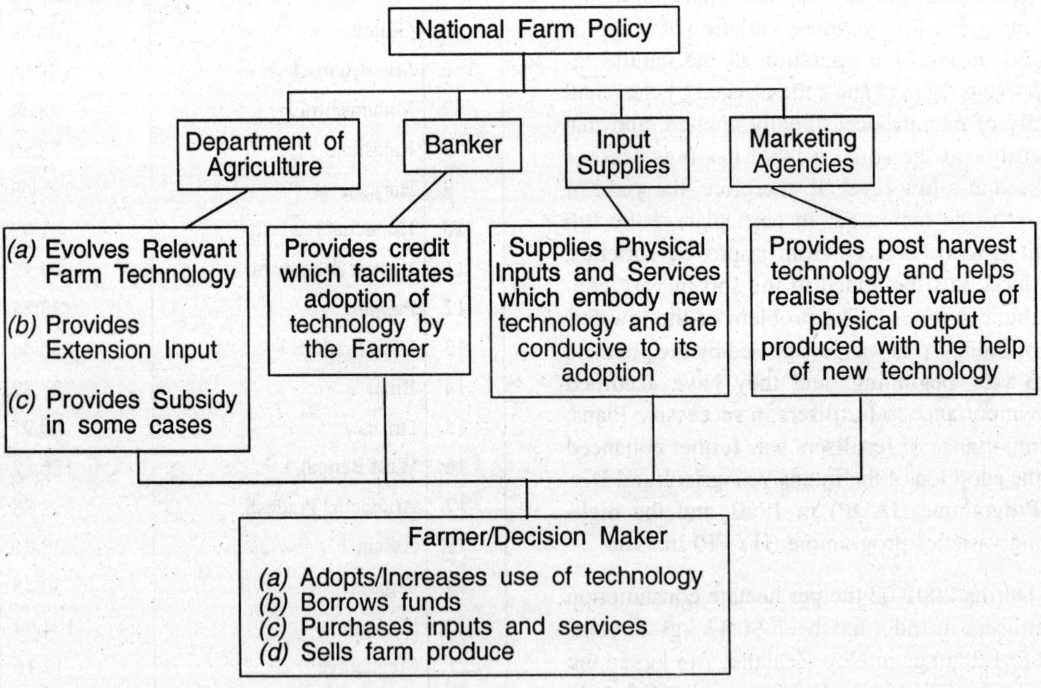


*Fig. 1. National Farm Policy*

*Source:* Banker and the Farm Development System

The objectives of the Ninth Plan are:

(*a*) To have an equitable and efficient fertilizer distribution system in the country, together with a proper infrastructural and organisation support;

(*b*) To reduce regional disparities in fertilizer consumption;

(*c*) To ensure that the benefits of fertilizer use are received by all the sectors of the farming community, especially by small and marginal farmers; and

(*d*) To promote an integrated nutrient supply system by a better and increased mobilisation of organic and bio-fertilizer resources in order to supplement and optimise the use of chemical fertilizers, as also to maximise the efficiency of fertilizer use.

## Improved Seeds

The National Seeds Policy 2001 provides the framework for growth of the Seed Sector. It seeks to provide the farmers with a wide range of superior quality seed varieties and planting materials. The production/distribution of certified/quality seeds since 1997-98 is given in Table 2.

**Table 2**

**PRODUCTION AND DISTRIBUTION OF QUALITY SEEDS**

| *Type* | *Unit* | *1997-98* | *1998-99* | *1999-2000* | *2000-01* | *2001-02** | *2002-03*** |
|---|---|---|---|---|---|---|---|
| Breeder Seed | Qtls | 46,134 | 38,994 | 51,131 | 42,690 | 47,021 | 49,000 |
| Foundation Seed | '000 Qtls | 684 | 675 | 466 | 591 | 550 | 600 |
| Certified Quality Seed Distribution | '000 Qtls | 7,879 | 8,497 | 8,798 | 8,627 | 9,100 | 9,300 |

* Expected

** Target

*Source :* Ministry of Agriculture.

The Seed Bank Scheme introduced in 1999-2000 with the basic objective of making available seeds for meeting any contingent requirement is currently implemented through the National Seeds Corporation, State Farms Corporation of India and 12 State Seeds Corporations. During 2002-03, the Seed Bank had a physical target of maintaining over 1,33,200 quintals of Certified Seeds and 9,000 quintals of Foundation Seeds of various major crop varieties, besides 11,000 quintals of Certified Seeds for the North Eastern States.

The augmentation of such infrastructural facilities as the setting up of processing plants, seed certification agencies and seed testing laboratories is a part of some of the important programmes. The creation of Seed Technology Units in 12 agricultural universities and a few ICAR institutions for breeder and foundation seeds is also a part of this programme. The projects, in brief, aim at placing the seed industry on a scientific footing by reorganising the functions of various institutions in a systematic manner.

It has been felt that it would be very difficult to produce large quantities of breeder seeds if only 3 stages of multiplication up to the stage of certified seeds are adhered to, as has been the practice so far. Hence, only two stages of foundation seeds—Stage I and Stage II—have been introduced. Taking into account the requirements of reserve stocks of seeds for foundation and certified seeds, the total requirements in the terminal year of the Seventh Plan would be about 60 lakh quintals of certified seeds, 5.0 lakh quintals of foundation seeds, and 20,000 quintals of breeder seeds. These figures include a massive increase in the production of seeds of pulses and oilseeds, keeping in view the national priority for increasing the production of these crops and the vital role that quality seeds play in promoting good plant population and performance.

It has been observed in the past that the production of certified seeds has been limited because of the non-availability of an adequate quantity of breeder and foundation seeds. Plan provisions have been made to strengthen the National Seeds Corporation with a view to enabling it to assume direct responsibility for the production of breeder and foundation seeds so that the shortage exhibited at the national level in the past may be eliminated. The National Seeds Corporation is expected to be strengthened for the production of vegetable seeds.

The State Farms Corporation of India, too, will play a bigger role in the production of certified seeds of imported cereals and other crops, especially oilseeds, vegetables, etc. on its large and scientifically managed farms.

The National Seed Project aims at assisting farmers by ensuring timely availability of quality seeds of suitable varieties at economical prices, through the expansion and modernisation of the seed industry.

In order to improve agricultural productivity, a New Policy on Seed Development has been formulated which is effective from 1st October, 1988. The new policy has been evolved with special emphasis on *(a)* the import of high quality seeds of oilseeds, coarse grains, vegetables and seeds/planting materials of flowers and fruits, *(b)* a time bound programme to strengthen/modernise plant quarantine facilities and *(c)* encouraging the domestic seed industry to make the country self-reliant in the seed sector. The new policy while providing access to the best planting material to the Indian farmer should go a long way in stepping up productivity and providing enhanced income to the farmers.

The National Seeds Projects Phase III was approved by the World Bank on 25.8.88. The total outlay for the project is Rs. 239 crore. The World Bank will provide US $ 150 million. The main objectives of these project is to ensure timely and adequate availability of quality seeds of suitable varieties at economical prices.

A buffer stock scheme has been in operation since 1978 for meeting unforseen contingency arising out of natural calamities like drought, floods, disease, etc. From 1987-88, the scheme has been modified as a Centrally Sponsored Scheme to include participation of the state governments. Under the revised scheme, NSC will be the implementing agency in respect of the north-eastern region. The State Seeds Corporation will maintain buffer stock for their states at 50:50 cost sharing basis. The buffer stock of foundation and certified seeds of pulses, oilseeds and coarse grains, namely, bajra, jowar and maize will be maintained for the states other than north-eastern states. For the north-eastern region, in addition to pulses and oilseeds, the seeds of paddy and maize are also being maintained. Under the SFPP, a buffer stocking scheme for seeds of identified varieties has also been sanctioned. To review the status and strategy of seed production and distribution, an Expert Group on Seeds has been constituted.

## Plant Protection

Recurrent attacks of pests and diseases have been causing considerable damage to crops. Unless these pests and diseases are kept under check, efforts to boost agricultural production will not succeed. Recent studies have revealed that, in 1986-87, about 20.8 per cent of the cropped area suffered from the depredations of pests and diseases but the area treated with pesticides was only 7.2 percent of the affected area. The crops that suffered most were groundnut (47 per cent) and cotton (28 per cent). Even a conservative estimate of the loss of 10 per cent to 15 per cent in the total agricultural output should amount to thousands of crores of rupees in a single year.

The major emphasis in respect of plant protection continued to be on Integrated Pest Management. To ensure that the chemicals used had the requisite degree of efficacy, quality control of pesticide was accorded the highest priority. In addition, action was initiated to evolve a package of measures to make Plant Quarantine procedures more effective and to expedite quarantine clearance.

The Finance Minister, while presenting the 1988-89 Budget, announced reduction of import duty on 15 pesticides from 105 per cent to 70 per cent, reduction in import duty on raw material used in the production of some technical grade pesticides from 147 per cent to 60 per cent, and full exemption of excise duty on 23 indigenously produced intermediates used for the manufacture of pesticides.

The demand for pesticides (technical grade material) has been estimated at 84,675 tonnes for 1988-89. The availability of pesticides, their raw materials and solvents were kept under constant review, and remedial action taken wherever the possibilities of any shortage were apprehended. Heliothis and whitefly in cotton in Guntur and Prakasam District of Andhra Pradesh were found to have developed resistance to existing pesticides and, therefore, the Government of India, as a special case, permitted the immediate import of four new pesticides, namely, Methomyl, Triazophos, Fluvalinate and Fenpropathrin for controlling these pests in Andhra Pradesh.

In view of the serious locust situation in African countries and anticipating the possible threat of a locust invasion, extensive and intensive field surveys were conducted by the 34 locust outposts in the scheduled desert areas of Rajasthan, Gujarat and Haryana where the locust is an endemic pest. The Field Research Unit at Bikaner continued the studies on various aspects of locust biology and ecology in the field for improving the control techniques.

In order to popularise and propagate the Integrated Pest Management approach among the farmers, field demonstrations at 32 locations in farmers' field were organised by the field units of Central Directorate of Plant Quarantine. To minimise the dependence on the use of chemical methods of plant protection, increased emphasis has been laid on the use of biological means for effective management of crop pests/weeds.

The consumption of pesticides in the country was negligible in the early fifties. Starting from a low figure of 100 tonnes of pesticides consumed in the agricultural sector at the beginning of the First Five-Year Plan, the country is now consuming 84,675 tonnes of technical grade pesticides. However, the consumption varies considerably from state to state. Whereas Tamil Nadu consumes more than 1.8 kgs of formulated pesticides on each hectare of cropped area, Madhya Pradesh hardly consumes 1/10 of a kg of formulated pesticides in an equal area. The high rainfall areas in the eastern part of the country, which are more prone to the attacks of weeds, pests and diseases, do not consume any sizable proportion of pesticides.

The objectives during the Tenth Plan period are:

*(a)* To minimise the losses arising out of pests and diseases;

*(b)* To expand the area under plant protection from 80 million hectares to 100 million hectares;

*(c)* To increase the consumption of pesticides from 60,000 tonnes to 80,000 tonnes of technical grade material;

*(d)* To strengthen surveillance against pests and diseases and determine economic thresholds with a view to making a more efficient use of pesticides. Surveillance in the tribal areas will be given special attention;

*(e)* To strengthen quality control arrangement and set up a Central Insecticides Laboratory and Regional Laboratories;

*(f)* To expand the work on "integrated pests control" and intensify the control of pests by biological means; and

*(g)* To continue the scheme of "Control and Eradication of Pests and Diseases of Agricultural Importance, including Weed Control in Endemic Areas."

The Protection of Plant Varieties & Farmers' Rights Legislation has been passed by the Parliament and Gazette notification has been issued. The objective of this legislation is to provide an effective system for the protection of plant varieties and farmers' rights which will also stimulate investment for research and development both in public and private sector for development of new plant varieties by ensuring appropriate returns on such investment.

## Implements and Machinery

Technology changes in general and mechanisation in particular have been taking place in India, mainly on the large farms in the high income and high growth pockets. Agricultural implements and machineries play a crucial role in increasing agricultural productivity. The main incentives for the adoption of innovations have been high yield, high profit and low cost. On the average, the cost of mechanisation was lower than the cost of biological sources of energy (e.g., human and bullock labour). Further, mechanisation, i.e, tractorisation, energisation, etc., has been associated with an increase in output and employment. Improved technology has resulted in an increase in output profit and growth.

The declining share in the use of animal power from 45.30 percent in 1971-72 to about 9.50 percent now signals the increasing role of machine power in substituting drought animals. Tractors and power tillers have become the main source of motive power for tillage, threshing and transport, contributing about 44 percent of the total farm power requirement compared to that 7.75 percent in 1971-72.

There has been a steady progress in the use of improved implements and machinery in Indian agriculture. Between 1951 and 2002, the number of tractors has increased from 9,000 to 22.5 lakhs; oil engines, from 82,000 to 82 lakhs; and electric pump sets, from 26,000 to 112 lakhs. The Prasad Committee has projected a further increase in farm mechanisation in the eighties. Farm mechanisation, though impressive, is largely confined to rich farmers.

The programmes of research and development taken up by the agricultural universities have enabled them to identify the implements which are suitable for use in different areas. But what is lacking is a programme of demonstration to motivate the farmers in the use of improved implements and infrastructure at the state level with a view to co-ordinating the demand with production, quality control, distribution and supporting services related to the farmers' education, credit, repair and maintenance facilities. Agro-industries corporations have been set up in different states to strengthen these activities. Another programme is for the establishment of agro-service centres to be handled by self-employed engineers. This was taken up to achieve the objectives of employment generation and provision of supplies and services to farmers. Under this programme, about 3,160 centres were set up. The State Agro-Industries Corporation have taken up a wide range of activities which have a bearing on the production of inputs for agriculture and for use in the processing of agricultural products. The funds available for them have, however, been utilised for activities which are connected with the supply of inputs and services. On the financial side, their performance has not been very satisfactory.

In the central sector, attention has been given to the training of personnel in the operation, maintenance and management of agricultural machinery and in the testing of different types of machinery for their functional performance and durability at the two central institutions at Budni and Hissar. These institutions are to be strengthened so as to meet the regional needs for training and testing. The development of hill areas under a programme of training in the selection and use of the tools and equipment appropriate for these areas will also receive high priority.

Keeping in view the constraints and requirements of the programme of agricultural machinery, the strategy for the Tenth Plan aims at:

*(i)* The introduction and popularisation of selected implements, particularly those which benefit small and marginal farmers, with emphasis on the requirements of ecologically handicapped areas and areas where a higher potential for improvement of agricultural production exists;

*(ii)* Strengthening the supporting services and infrastructure for demonstration and popularisation;

*(iii)* Testing and quality control;

*(iv)* Training; and

*(v)* The promotion of agro-industries and agro-services.

Farmers' Agro Service Centres will be set up for the training of, and assistance to, entrepreneurs, groups of farmers, the personnel of co-operatives etc., with the help of the multi-agency approach. It is proposed to set up 500 such centres in different parts of the country during the Sixth Plan period. Their main objective will be to organise supplies and services for the benefit of small and marginal farmers. This programme will be supported by national and regional centres for technology transfer.

## Agricultural Extension and Training

It is a well known fact that there is a wide gap between the production potential and the actual field harvests of most agricultural crops. Adequate technology is available for transfer from research laboratories and experimental stations to farmers' field and homes. Besides, agricultural technology is developing very rapidly. In order to keep pace with it and to improve the economy of the farmers, the machinery involved in the transfer process should be strengthened and attuned to meet the growing and changing needs. In the past the agricultural administration had not received adequate attention in most states, with the result that policy goals were not often supported by an implemention machinery. Recently experiments in the reorganisation and strengthening of the agricultural extension service under the "training and visit" (T and V) system in Rajasthan and Madhya Pradesh have yielded very encouraging results. This T and V system is already working satisfactorily in 17 states. During the Seventh Plan period, it will be introduced on a nation-wide basis with a view to improving the education and technical competence of the extension functionaries and bringing about better linkage between agricultural universities and extension wings of the state governments and farming communities.

The need for the training of women in agriculture cannot be overemphasised because more than fifty percent of the agricultural operations are carried out by them. In order to improve their technical competence and economic conditions, more intensive training programmes for women in agriculture will have to be organised. There are four categories of labour involvement by women. These are:

*(i)* Field labour—sowing, transplanting, harvesting, threshing;

*(ii)* Skilled operations—plant protection, plant propagation, hybridisations, as in cotton;

*(iii)* Post-harvest operations, such as cotton grading, processing and vending of various agricultural commodities; and

*(iv)* Farm management and supervision of farm operations.

In all these areas, farm women should be given training to improve their efficiency.

The labour force in many areas belong to the lowest strata of society. Almost all the scheduled castes and tribes depend on their meagre earnings from farmlands particularly horticultural crops; so do the tribals. Their skills in agriculture are mostly inherited. There is ample scope for the improvement of these skills under specially organised training programmes to suit their background and culture with a view to reducing their drudgery in agricultural operations and improving their economic status. Some sectors of society, such as ex-service personnel who enter agriculture, need special attention in our training programmes. They have to be given tailor made courses to meet their requirements. Likewise, progressive farmers and farm youths should be trained to take to new crops under export promotion, multiple and mixed cropping, etc.

In some respects, the agricultural sector can provide opportunities for the gainful employment of the physically handicapped. This is so because of the variety of operations involved in agriculture and post-harvest processing. Such employment, however, would call for specialised training for handicapped persons, taking into consideration the needs of the situation.

**Chart : 1**

**FARM TECHNOLOGY SOME CHARACTERISTICS**

| *Category of Technology* | *Major Components* | *Main Function* | *Economic impact on the Farm* | *Duration of Life and Coverage* | *Cost and Other Implications* | *Main decision Maker* | *Other Participating Agencies* |
|---|---|---|---|---|---|---|---|
| *(i)* Pre-production Stage | Land and soil improvement measures, irrigation development, farm mechanisation, improved breeds of farm animals, etc. | Facilitating adoption of production stage technology and hence indirectly improving farm productivity. | Laying the foundation of increased physical yield of the farm. | Life covers more than one production period and technology encompasses the farm partly or wholly. | Huge cost and investment finance and hence farm loans. | Govt and/or farmer individually or in group. | Govt., banker, other input suppliers. |
| *(ii)* Production Stage Proper | New crops and improved crop varieties, chemical fertilizers, plant protection measures, improved breeding, feeding and management practices for farm animals, improved cultural practices for crops. | Directly improves the productivity of the basic resources of the farm, *i.e.*, land and livestock. | Increases the physical yield of the farm. | Life synchronizes with one production period and hence the technology has to be adopted afresh every time the production is planned. The technology is crop or animal specific. | Most of the elements need working capital or short-term finance. Some of them need only change in the method of working, and may or may not require additional working finance. | Farmer himself. | Banker, other input suppliers and Govt. |
| *(iii)* Post Harvest Technology | Processing preservation and marketing arrangement. | Adds to the form, time and space utility of farm produce. | Increase money value of farm produce. | Longer life and encompasses more than one production unit/farm. | Huge cost, investment finance and long-term credit needs. | Govt. public corporations, private companies. | Former/Group of Farmers, banker, input suppliers and marketing agencies. |

## Dry Farming Technology

*Fig. 2.*

Given the limited scope for expansion of irrigation in drought-prone areas attention has to be focused on other possible ways of reducing the effects of drought. One of the methods could be to improve the productivity of rainfed areas in these districts. The Indian Council of Agricultural Research (ICAR) and International Crop Research Institute for Semi-Arid Tropics (ICRISAT) have developed technologies for red and black soils for rainfed farming, which cover *(a)* soil and water management, *(b)* use of high yielding and short maturity crop varieties, *(c)* optimum plant population and *(d)* crop management involving operations like sowing, pre-and post-sowing tillage, fertiliser use and pest and weed control. The technologies also incorporate contingency crop plans for taking care of the aberrations in rainfall. The National Bank has held detailed discussions with ICAR and ICRISAT scientists on the technology package developed by them with a view to identifying areas where the National Bank can promote pilot rainfed areas farming projects for transfer of dry farming technology with the necessary institutional credit support. After taking up the matter with the state governments in order to ensure their active involvement, the Bank has now initiated rainfed farming projects on pilot basis in three identified watersheds with a rainfall range of 750 mm to 1,250 mm, one each in Andhra Pradesh, Tamil Nadu and Karnataka. These projects have been formulated in consultation with the concerned state governments. Additionally, the National Bank has adopted a policy measure by which short-term credit will be provided to the beneficiaries in these water sheds on a cyclical basis to facilitate technology adoption. The beneficiaries will be assured of production credit for every season over the entire weather cycle and the recoveries of the entire crop loan dues will be made over the cycle. GOI has also formulated a dryland farming project called National Watershed Development Programme for Rainfed Agriculture, which is being implemented in 99 districts covering 16 states. The National Bank will collaborate with the GOI for extending credit support in these pilot rainfed farming project watersheds. In these watersheds the GOI and the state governments will implement the community items of work of soil and moisture conservation from budgetary resources and credit will be extended by the banks to farmers for adopting technology package.

*Fig. 3 Dry Farming Technology*

"Choupal", International Business Division's novel web-based initiative will connect Indian farmers with world markets. Farmers can access latest local and global information on the weather, scientific farming practices as well as market prices at the village itself on a computer screen all in the local language. Choupal will also facilitate supply of high quality farm inputs and purchase of farm produce at the farmer's doorstep.

## Contribution of Technology Generation, Assessment, Refinement and Transfer to Sectoral Growth

If it is to respond successfully to these challenges, agriculture will have to become more knowledge-intensive. Investments in research will be needed to generate the new knowledge. Greater attention will have to be paid to information-based technologies. Strengthened means of dissemination will be needed to transmit this information to farmers. Both technology generation and transfer will have to focus more strongly than before on the themes of optimisation in the management by producers of their available resources, sustainability, coping with diversity by adapting technology more specifically to agro-ecological or social circumstances and raising the economic efficiency of agricultural. To make information transfer more cost effective, greater use will need to be made of modern information technology in communication between researches, extensionists and their farmer clients. The techniques of frontier sciences for instance biotechnology will have to be further developed nationally, where necessary supplemented by imports, and increasingly applied. Because the new knowledge will be generally focused on management of resources and systems, disadvantaged and risk prone areas, and because the majority of users of this knowledge will be small-scale, poor or women farmers, India will have no choice but to continue to rely largely on government funding to generate the quintessential public goods. While there is greater scope to draw other actors—the corporate sector, NGOs or associations of technology users themselves—into implementing government-funded programmes, the public sector research and technology transfer system itself must nevertheless remain strong and responsive to meet these national priorities.

The rationale for establishment of ATIC are:

*(i)* to provide diagnostic services for soil and water testing, plant and live stock health, *(ii)* to supply research products such as seeds and other planting materials, poultry strains, livestock breeds, fish seed,

processed products, etc. emerging from the institution for testing and adaptation by various clientele; *(iii)* providing information through published literature and communication materials as well as audio-visual aids; and *(iv)* providing an opportunity to the institutes/SAUs to generate some resources through the sale of their technologies. The project will also be supporting the district level project on innovation in technology dissemination through Agricultural Technology Management Agency (ATMA) in 24 pilot districts.

The important criteria of Agricultural Technology Information are *(i)* availability (or accessibility) of new technologies, *(ii)* relevance of new technologies, *(iii)* responsiveness of new technologies to the needs of different categories of farmers, *(iv)* varied requirements for different categories of farmers and *(v)* sustainability of such a unit within the overall institutional system. The management as well as the functioning structure of ATIC have been indicated in Annexures 3-6 and 3-7.

The Agricultural Technology Information Centre (ATIC) is a "single window" support system linking the various units of a research institution with intermediary users and users (farmers) in decision making and problem solving exercise.

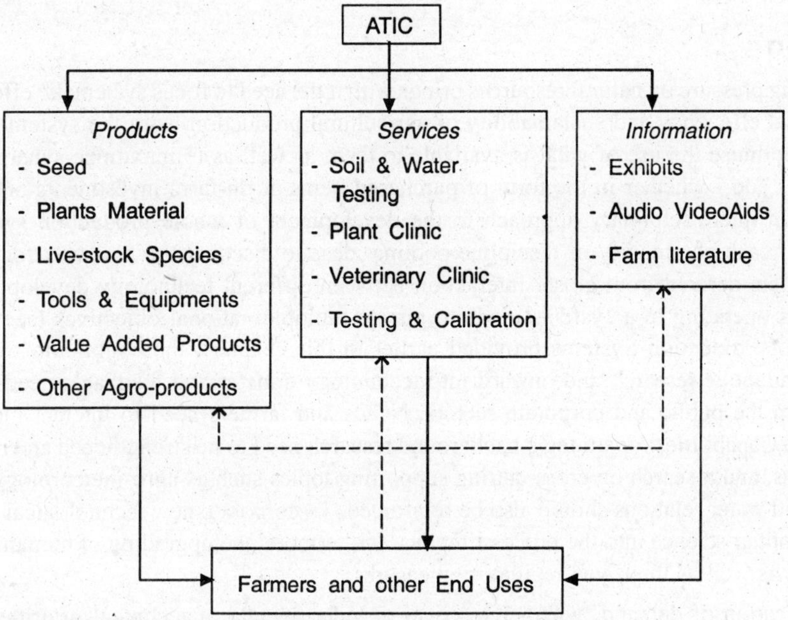


*Fig. 4. Farmers and Other End Users*

*N.B.:* The products and services to be provided by ATIC will depend on the areas of technology development involved by the Institute

The objectives for establishment of ATIC centres as a single window systems are as follows:

*(i)* to provide a 'single window' delivery system for the products and species available from an institution to the farmers and other interested groups as a process of innovativeness in technology dissemination at the institute level;

*(ii)* to facilitate and direct the farmers' access to the institutional resources available in terms of technology, advice, technology products, etc., for reducing technology dissemination losses, and

*(iii)* to provide mechanism for feedback from the users to the institute.

There was consensus among villagers regarding the overwhelming impact of technology on the village life resulting in changes in the standards of rural life and agricultural productions. However, the detailed analysis of the perceived impact of technology in various areas at individual, village, and societal levels revealed that the economic prosperity and life comforts were accompanied by social, political, religious and cultural problems. In addition, the impact of technology was neither uniform across various areas nor consistent across different levels. The analysis of specific consequences indicated that technology had changed significantly the style of the use of human energy. The pattern of investment of human effort and labour is being remodelled in the light of advancing technologies innovations. In contrast technology is also viewed as a source of certain problems including threat to life and environmental pollution.

It was evident that the farmers from the developed villages who were more achievement-oriented than villages, their counterparts of undeveloped villages, had a more positive image of technology. They had greater experience of the uses of technology in different areas. As a result they were also more sure about the potential uses and consequences of technology. In contrast, the villagers from undeveloped areas, who were deprived of socio-economic benefits and lacked the necessary infrastructure at the level of village, displayed certain degree of ambivalence towards technology. Also, they had limited experience of technology and constraints in their thoughts because of lack of requisite personal as well as environmental resources at the village level.

## Conclusion

Increasing pressure on natural resources brings with it the need to focus systematic efforts more strongly on the technical efficiency and sustainability of agricultural production, with the system geared to helping producers to optimise the use of what is available to them as well as to maximize synergy with what they can themselves add—whether in the form of purchased items or on-farm investments or their own labour. This implies an interdisciplinary approach to the development of whole production systems, with those responsible for each commodity or discipline pooling ideas to discover the best way forward. Along with greater synergism derived from closer interaction between different technology development programmes and disciplines operating in a systems mode to pursue multiple national objectives (see Box on National Prioritisation of Production Systems provided earlier in this chapter), the continuum from basic through strategic into adaptive research and onward into technology transfer and feedback, needs to be improved. Stakeholders in the public and corporate sectors, NGOs and farmers need to interact more closely in the whole process. Capabilities for strategic background research need to be strengthened and re-oriented to feed into the process, and research on cross-cutting supporting topics such as agro-meteorology, maintenance of soil fertility and water relations should also be reinforced. To corporate new technological opportunities and advances in frontier science into the process implies, furthermore, the upgrading of human skills and institutional support, as well as improved regulatory measures.

Diversification of demand, whether to cover a wider agenda of technical priorities or client types, implies greater location specificity. To tailor technologies to local needs requires that those working within the system obtain a better understanding of the circumstances of different categories of technology users—their resource availabilities, survival strategies, attitudes to risk and cultural preferences. Interactive, participatory approaches, new skills in social and economic assessment and often a change of mindset by the responsible scientists are pre-requisites for success.

Coping at the same time with scarcity of public funding calls for greater operational efficiency within the public funding calls for greater operational efficiency within the public part of the system for technology generation, assessment and transfer. This implies not only the easing of generic constraints which bind the public services in India, such as poor information access and sharing, bureaucratic procedures, excessive centralisation and poor staff incentives. It also implies the existence of priority setting and resources allocation mechanisms which can respond appropriately to evolving national policies and needs: these mechanisms need to focus the use of public resources on the provision of the new public goods which are required when dealing with topics such as sustainability of production systems. New mechanisms of funding should be exploited where possible and where the benefits of new technology can be privately appropriated, R&D responsibilities should be transferred to the private sector or to the users themselves.

## ANNEXURE-I

## STAGES IN THE EVOLUTION OF FARM DEVELOPMENT AND THEIR CHARACTERISTICS

| | *Characteristics* | *Single Enterprise subsistence* | *Diversified* | *Specialised* |
|---|---|---|---|---|
| 1. | Pattern of Enterprise | One/few crops or one dominant / activity—rearing of livestock—Non descript breeds. | Crop + Animal Husbandry | One dominant enterprise *i.e.*, cash crops or highly specialised animal breeds |
| 2. | Principal Purchase of Production | Domestic Consumption (No gap between produced/consumed form of consumption, sometimes inverse relation with price.) | Domestic Consumption and market; sheep husbandry is highly market oriented. The nature of product / product mix and the type of market differs from the highly specialised one. | Serving the market: form of product and type of market is quite different from earlier stages. |
| 3. | Employment Pattern | Seasonal-precarious<br>*(i)* during off season no gainful employment and lack of food<br>*(ii)* family labour getting part employment in a year<br>*(iii)* most of the labour is supplied by the family<br>*(iv)* specialised and yet unskilled less efficient labour/workforce. Specialised for the enterprise not specialised for activity. One labourer does all type of jobs. | Balanced/Established<br>Family labour getting stable employment. | Somewhat seasonal: but high level of employment. Per unit of land/other production unit employment higher. Changes in the roles and proportion of family and hired labour in total employment in the farm. Fall in the marginal significance of the family labour as a source of income. |
| 4. | Income Levels | Low | Medium | High |
| 5. | Stability of income flows | Low because of natural forces leading to starvation-precarious position of the family. | High | Low (because of market forces) but no starvation. Farm business income has no direct impact on the standard of life of the farmer. |
| 6. | Internal Saving | Low/nil/negative | Low | High |
| 7. | Percentage share of family incomes in the value of total output | High | in between | Low |
| 8. | Risk-bearing capacity | Negative | Fairly good | High |

| | | | | |
|---|---|---|---|---|
| 9. | Level and pattern of Capital Investment Absolute and relative | Low/absolute as well as per unit of labour, therefore more labour per unit of land and also per unit of capital (Land value is low and animals are cheaper). | Medium | High/absolute as well as per unit of labour: therefore more capital per unit of land and per unit of labour. |
| 10. | Productivity per unit of land/labour | Low | Medium | High |
| 11. | Farmer's knowledge regarding agriculture | Low and specialised (New opening restricted). Sources of knowledge is father and family. | Medium and Diversified | High and specialised: Sources of knowledge are insitutionalised (Radio, news medium, TV, formal education). |
| 12. | Need and nature of dependence on supporting system | None (either because support is not available or there is nothing to make use for). | Partial | Full. The role involvement of the supporting system in the farm business is very essential. The farmer is able to easily indicate the need for such support. |

*Source :* This table is adopted on the basis of the Table quoted by Roanum Weitz, in his book. *From Peasant to Farmer* p. 20 published by Columbia University Press, 1971.

1. At the single enterprise subsidence level, the family labour gets an exclusively large share in total employment. The labour is specialised so far as enterprise is concerned. As regards activity, the same labour does all types of jobs from preparing the field to harvesting and threshing. There is some division between male, female and child labour. The nature of work schedule also is such where a single labour unit can take up one operation (land-tilling threshing, etc.) after another because there is only one type of crop or crops of similar agronomic characteristics.

❑ ❑ ❑

*Forestry represents the second-largest land use in India after agriculture, but contributes merely 1% of GDP. This points to the dormant potential to this sector. China's experience also shows what can be unleashed by developing a competitive wood-based industry. According to a Study by the Center for International Forestry Research (CIFOR) and others. Chinese exports of Forest Products, in a span of just 8 years preceding 2005, rose from US $ 3.6 billion to US $ 17.2 billion, and in specific products like plywood, the increase was as much as ten-fold, making China one of the world's largest exporters. The United States and European Union were the main buyers with imports increasing 700 to 900%.*

***A concerted export to promote wood plantations in degraded wastelands in India could potentially change the fortunes of small and marginal farmers and consequently the opportunities in Rural India.*** *Degraded wastelands in the country are estimated at 60 million hectares by the Planning Commission, out of which 33 million hectares constitute degraded forest lands. By converting these wastelands into productive and renewable agro-forestry resources, strong economic multipliers can be unleashed to significantly mitigate the challenges of livelihood, energy and environmental security. Let me briefly outline some of these multiple possibilities.*

# Chapter 22

# SOCIAL FORESTRY

## Introduction

Rich productive forestry, along with productive agriculture development, will solve the problem of population pressure. The experience of developed districts in India clearly shows that when there is productive economic activity, the ensuing prosperity results in the withdrawal of women and children from the work force (a shift to lighter home duties and to schools) leading to a reduction in the demand for employment. The rapid development of secondary and tertiary sectors also flows from this prosperity, causing a decline in the number of people available and willing to work in the arduous and monotonous business of agriculture. The shift to better jobs in local industries and trade can only happen after there in increased purchasing power through better income. Improving the quality of work will prove more important for development than increasing the number of low grade jobs. Massive efforts for forest development with parallel agricultural development of these areas will redress the balance of development and ensure that the benefits of development are more equitably spread to both the richer and the poorer areas on an economically viable basis.

## Social Forestry

The concept of social forestry was introduced by the National Commission on Agriculture in 1976; but although it is quite recent, it was in vogue in a different form and with a different content for a long time. In the past, farm forestry was adopted as means of creating raw wood resources and replacing wood harvests on farm lands, community lands, etc. Farm forestry is defined as the "practice of forestry in all its aspects on farms or village lands generally integrated with other farm operations." In other words, when forestry has linkages with farm operation, it is known as farm forestry. In actual practice, however it would be better to refer to it as extension forestry, with farm forestry as its integral part. The afforestation of farm lands refers to extension forestry linked with farm operations; and extension forestry includes the activities of raising trees on farm lands, village waste lands and community forestry areas and on lands along the sides of roads, canal banks and railway lines. But development has not been uniform in all the states. Even where it was, the practice did not stem entirely from the concept of producing from forest or tree lands a flow of physical benefits and social values.

- As a source of renewable and carbon-neutral biomass energy, agro-forestry can generate 1000 MW of power from plantation of half a million hectares. This has the potential to substantially reduce the dependence on carbon generating fossil-fuel based energy. Specially suited for distributed energy systems in rural India, power generated from biomass can either meet the needs of smaller rural communities or be fed into the grid. **Renewable plantations in 10 million hectares can produce as much as 20,000 MW of power, almost one-fourth of the total capacity addition proposed in the 11th Five Year Plan from conventional sources.**
- **Given the major environmental advantage of wood as a carbon sink, greater usage of wood in housing is a better alternative** than the use of cement and steel which have much large ecological footprints. By 2010-12, more than 500 million sq.ft. of space in expected to be built in India, mostly in urban areas. Even a limited use of wood for door and window frames, flooring, wooden cabinets etc. would mean a demand for wood products valued at US $ 3 billion. **With greater usage of wood as a predominant material for housing, in rural and urban areas, this potential can increase exponentially.**
- **The wood-based industry is growing rapidly with increasing demand for furniture, housing construction material, packaging, agricultural implements, sports goods, plywood, veneer, matches,** and so on. The Indian furniture market is estimated at US $ 8 billion, and today employs around 3,00,000 people. Wooden home furniture is the largest segment. Imports of furniture are growing at a fast clip with a rate as high at 60%. Total wood-based import for various uses today is already over US $ 1 billion. Depending on the regeneration of wood and the changing demand profile, India is likely to face a wood deficit of 20 to 70 million cubic metres by 2020. Certainly, the case for agro-forestry is obvious.
- **Trees are also a valuable source of bio-chemicals.** The cellulose part of the structure, used primarily for pulp and paper, represents only 20 to 30% of the total, and the balance can be a valuable resource for extraction of bio-chemicals with wide applications from food to medicine. **Non-Timber Forest Produce, also lends itself to medicinal and herbal applications,** and is a very important source of sustenance of forest dependent population. It is estimated that over 75% of forest export revenue comes from these sources.
- The societal benefits of agro-forestry outweigh that of many other sectors. **One of the most important is in its role as an instrument of climate change mitigation.** Potentially, the greening

even 10 million hectares of degraded forest lands, nearly 500 million MT of carbon dioxide can be sequestered. This implies a compensatory sequestration for as much as 500 million MWh of electricity generated from fossil-fuels. Plantations also contribute to other ecological benefits in terms of arresting top soil erosion, and enabling greater ground water recharge.

- **In addition, the livelihood creation potential of agro-forestry makes it an extremely important investment option for the country.** For example, in wood pulp based plantations, every hectare of plantation creates approximately 450 person days of employment. Extrapolating this to cover the degraded forest lands estimated at 33 million hectares implies a potential of nearly 15,000 million mandays of employment. **Taken together, the wood-based value chain, including plantations, has the potential to create sustainable livelihoods for nearly 100 million people.**
- In addition, creation of forests and natural parks has been known to boost eco-tourism and innovative initiatives here could also make it a source of sustainable livelihoods. Agro-forestry also supports a number of handicrafts, including wooden jewellery and gift items, potentially another revenue stream in appropriate areas.

The Prime Minister's Council on Climate Change recently unveiled its National Action Plan. As part of the 8 Millions announced, the National Mission for a Green India envisages the afforestation of 6 million hectares to enhance forest and tree cover to 33%. The Mission will be taken up on degraded forest lands with an initial corpus of Rs. 6000 crores. This is indeed a very welcome initiative. I understand that the Ministry of Environment and Forests had earlier estimated that nearly Rs. 70,000 crores would be necessary to enhance the tree cover to targeted dimensions. **Given the massive investment requirements, larger corporate participation in renewable agro-forestry cannot only multiply the initiative launched by the Prime Minister significantly, but with the right policy support, create tremendous value across the entire spectrum of the wood-based value chains.**

## National Commission on Agriculture

In the context of the slow and uneven growth of forestry in India, the National Commission on Agriculture (1976) stressed the need for social forestry as a means of developing the economy. It focused attention on the socio-economic importance of social forestry as a means of developing the economy. It focused attention on the socio-economic importance of social forestry in the rural community and the management of forest resources. It had realised that, by taking up the programme of raising of trees, grasses and fodder on the farmer's own land, village commons, waste lands and degraded forests close to habitations, it would be possible to meet the requirements of fuel wood, fodder and small timber for rural housing and agricultural implements, thorns for fencing etc.

## Definition

Social forestry covers farm forestry, extension forestry, reforestation of degraded forests and recreation forestry. It also covers waste lands, panchayat lands, village commons and lands on the sides of roads, canal banks and railway lines, which may be brought under forest plantations, shelter belts and mixed forestry, and lands on which grass and leaf fodder may be raised and on which fruit trees and fuel wood trees may be grown.

Social forests also include "minor forests" as well as such lands as are dedicated to recreation forestry.

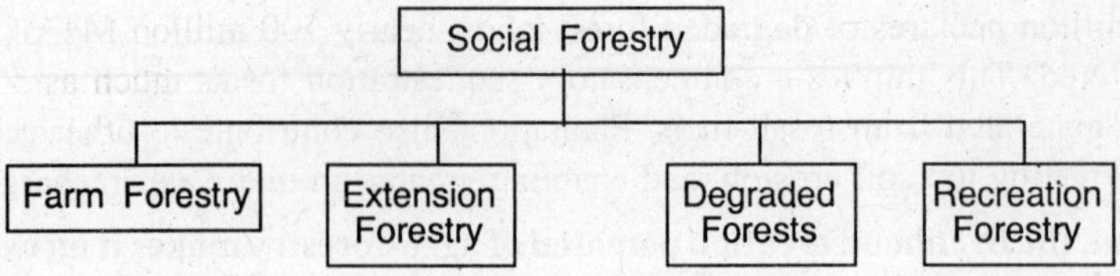


*Fig. 1. Forms of Social Forestry*

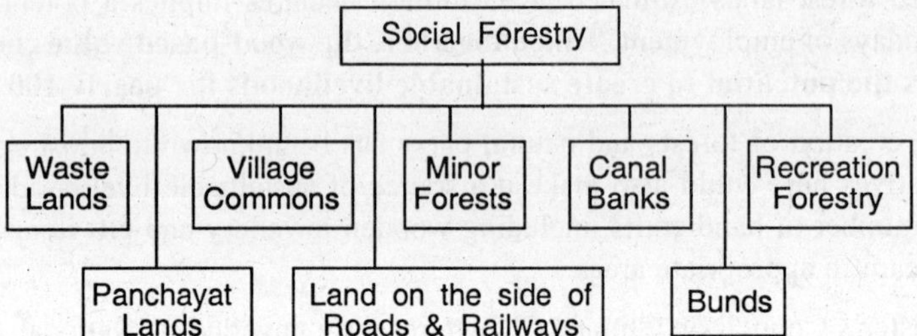


*Fig. 2. Coverage of Social Forestry*

*Social forestry—A Group Panchayat Project in DRDA, Silvassa, Dadra and Nagar Haveli*

## Objectives

The social functions of forests is to provide basic infrastructure to the rural community, such as;

(*a*) Agriculture timber and fuel wood;

(*b*) Grazing lands and grasses; and

(*c*) Recreation

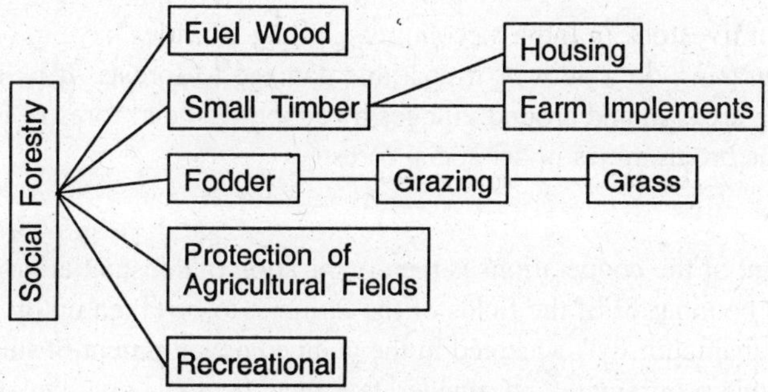


*Fig. 3. Objectives of Social Forestry*

The Commission (NCA) has adopted the following objectives of social forestry, which are the basic and economic needs of the community and which aim at bettering the conditions of the rural people:

*(i)* Fuel wood supply to rural areas and replacement of cow dung, which may be better used as manure;

*(ii)* Small timber supply for rural housing and agricultural implements;

*(iii)* Fodder supply;

*(iv)* Protection of agricultural fields against wind and wild animals; and

*(v)* Meeting the recreational needs of the rural population.

## Socio-economic Benefits

Agricultural small timber and fuel wood should be made available to the rural population at a reasonable price, considering that the viability of the rural economy is greatly dependent upon the ready supply of the timber required for agricultural implements, housing and other miscellaneous uses and of fuel wood as a source of domestic energy. In this way, rural people will save a considerable amount of cow dung for purposes of manure. Moreover, by using leaves and grass, they can produce additional compost manure to supplement their manure requirements. Research has shown that this manure has more nutritional value than other kinds of manures. For a considerable time, rural people have met their needs from products in the forests and, in doing so, have reduced them to minor forests. They have over-exploited forest resources for sundry purposes and in an ad hoc manner, without contributing to their maintenance or regeneration. One of the principal objectives of social forestry is to make it possible for the government to meet in full these needs of the village folks, and so lighten the burden on production forestry.

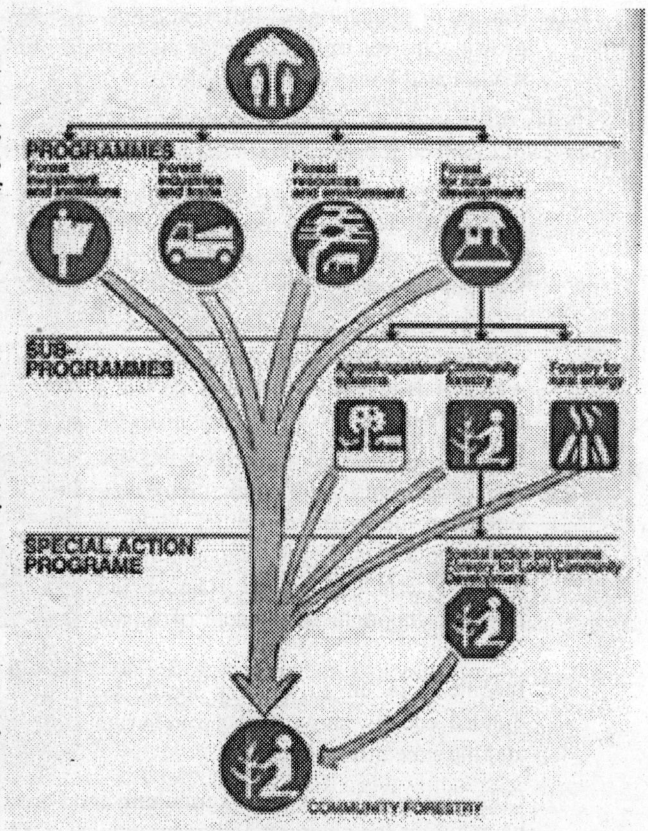


*Fig. 4. FAO and Community Forestry.*

In view of the role of livestock in India's economy, grazing facilities have to be provided in an around forests. Goat and sheep grazing do a allot or irreparable damage to forests. It is, therefore, imperative to provide additional grazing areas in and around villages by adopting social forestry in an extensive way. Let us now discuss the various programmes under social forestry.

## Farm Forestry

This basic component of the cooperations is the organisation of substantial programme of the planting of trees on the bunds and boundaries of the fields of the farmers, to be taken up by the farmers themselves. The basic objective of "vanamahotsav", accepted in the planned development of forestry, was to encourage farmers to participate in this programme and regenerate forests for their own benefit. The government has exempted the value of trees standing on agricultural land from wealth tax. Even in advanced countries like the UK and the USA, special incentives are given to farmers in the form of exemption of wood lands from estate duty, wealth tax, etc., to encourage them to take to tree planting.

## Extension Forestry

Extension forestry programmes cover:

*(i)* Mixed forestry on waste lands, panchayat lands, village commons;

*(ii)* Raising of shelter belts in arid regions; and

*(iii)* Raising of plantations of different quick-growing species on lands on the sides of roads, canal banks and railway lines.

The NCA has suggested the following important steps in regard to mixed forestry and shelter belts:

*(i)* Any programme of mixed forestry in village waste lands and panchayat lands should be such as is acceptable to the village population;

*(ii)* The programme should be undertaken only in those areas where the incidence of waste lands in sufficiently high, so that a part of them can always be kept apart for the satisfaction of the rights of villagers;

*(iii)* The programme should take into consideration the need for a quick yield of such products as are the villagers, immediate concern. Fodder and grass should form an important component of mixed forestry;

*(iv)* Income from mixed forestry should be divided equally between the panchayats and the state government;

*(v)* Co-ordinated efforts by the Agriculture and Forest Department of the State Government should be made for the planning and creation at shelter belts;

*(vi)* Research should be carried out on a priority basis by the concerned institutions to determine the regions where shelter belts should be planted, their effect on hydrology and crop yield, and their composition and management; and

*(vii)* There should be an element of subsidy, to be shared between the central and state governments, that has to be built into programmes during the first round of 15 to 20 years.

Mixed forestry and shelter belts programmes should be implemented by villagers under the supervision of village panchayats and in close cooperation with the state government's forest departments. The effects of mixed forestry on the lives of the rural community are far-reaching, and it is in their own interest that work on this programme should be implemented in stages.

In the prevailing conditions of increasing demand for forest produce and shrinking forest areas, the strips of land on the sides of roads, canal distributories and railway tracks assume a very great importance and should be planted with trees. The planting of such trees as the neem and other oilseed trees would increase revenue. This programme should be treated as a commercial investment to be met by the railway and public works and irrigation department in close collaboration with the forest authorities.

## Reforestation in Degraded Forests

Agri-silviculture is an adopted forest plantation technique. The adoption of this practice in a reforestation programme will provide employment to many a landless labourer, and increase forest production.

## Recreation Forestry

Recreation forestry contributes to social development and education in environmental matters. Better landscape effects are achieved by easing out the edges of copses and adding a few ornamental species in a more frequented or frequently viewed site. With the planting of such trees as the pipal and semuel, the landscape brightens up. These trees are not only ornamental but attract birds and add colour and life to the environment. In urban areas, parks and gardens are a city's lungs; they lend colour and life, and bring recreation to urban people. Since the maintenance of parks and gardens is expensive, larger areas may be planted with suitable trees and shrubs to provide a forest atmosphere. Such forest parks are very popular and contribute to the general uplift of the health of the urban population. The development of wild life should be as much for recreational forestry as for its scientific importance.

## Organisation

The development of social forestry depends on organisational capabilities, initiative, innovation and imagination. The implementation of social programmes demands tact, resourcefulness, preserverance, a sympathetic attitude, and above all, lot of tolerance. The Royal Commission on Agriculture (RCA) 1928, had suggested an organisational pattern. In each Province (State), it said, the Forest Department should be constituted along the following lines.

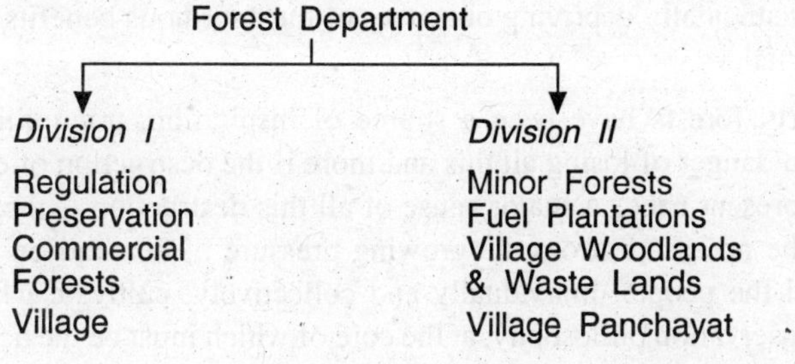


*Fig. 5.*

The NCA has suggested the involvement of three basic village institutions, namely, local panchayats, and co-operatives and village school staff in demonstrations. The extension organisation would work closely with agricultural departments and village panchayats in the implementation of mixed forestry programme.

## Forest Preservation

The importance of forests in soil conservation and in modifying the hydrology of watersheds has been well recognised. The term conservation refers to the management of the biosphere, the eco-system and the species for human use, so that these may yield the greatest benefit to the present generation, while maintaining their potential to meet the needs and aspirations of future generations. For this purpose, it is essential that we protect our forest and preserve the eco-system, for these constitute the most effective means of conserving and ensuring the long-term productivity of the soil and water resources. Many people do not appreciate the extraordinarily effective role that virgin forests play, and believe that similar benefits can be achieved from man-made forests. It takes little observation to appreciate the remarkably efficient manner in which nature has clothed and protected the areas covered by these forests, and the way in which it has provided for the existence of a great diversity of vegetation of tall trees which form the top canopy of the jungle, the smaller trees which form the middle hampers, still smaller trees and shrubs which form the lower hampers, and finally the enormous variety of low-growing vegetation — bushes, ferns, grasses, mosses and the like—which form the ground cover.

All of these together, with their intricate network of widespread and deep-root systems, contribute to the formation of the vital top soil, and provide protection against the erosion of such soil from wind and the rapid run-off of rain water. They also ensure that these areas hold moisture for gradual release during the dry months through springs and streams. A failure to realise this, and a wanton and shortsighted felling of trees in the catchment areas, have resulted in the loss of valuable soil, and silt has set in progressively.

But these are only some of the many benefits that virgin forests offer. The natural eco-systems which they support provide genetic pools of irreplaceable botanical and zoological species which may one day prove to be our saviours against existing and hitherto unknown diseases. We are fortunate that, up to the present, nature's munificence has been so great that we have not yet been forced to exploit the vast majority of these species, many of which can offer untold scientific and economic benefits to our country and to the world. They constitute a storehouse of enormous wealth and capital that, left to nature's own dynamics rather than human contriving, may grow at a rate far greater than would be possible in any commercial or financial institution of human design.

In emphasizing the importance of conserving and enlarging our forests, therefore, it is necessary to emphasis the importance of our wild life—which includes animals, birds, reptiles, insects, marine life, and not by any means the least, our plant life — in all its wide and wondrous diversity. It hardly needs stressing that these represent our greatest and most valuable heritage in the present generation. This invaluable legacy is, however, one that most of us take for granted. As responsible citizens, it is our bounded duty to see to it that all these various species are protected from the consequences of improvident use and destruction. In our ignorance, we are almost suicidally depriving ourselves of the enormous benefits these confer on us—economic, aesthetic and spiritual.

To the human spirit, forests have been a source of inspiration, tranquillity and solace from times immemorial. We stand in danger of losing all this and more if the destruction of our forests, both virgin and others, continues at the present pace. A major cause of all this destruction is the pressure of population. In the long run, there can be no escape from the growing pressure of demand on our forests and all natural living resources until all the people, individually and collectively, cultivate what may be described as a conservation ethics, a conservation philosophy, at the core of which must be the acceptance of a value system based upon the satisfaction of only our minimal material needs.

## Less Consumption for Greater Happiness

The complete protection of our virgin forests and a total moratorium for a given period on any exploitation of them is the single most effective way of protecting our wild life and ourselves. But to implement this effectively, a solution to a human problem of great complexity and magnitude must first be found. Consistent with sound production forestry; it is necessary to ensure that forest produce is made available in sufficient quantities to meet the essential needs of the people.

The fuel and fodder requirements of the majority of the people come from wild uncultivated trees and plants which supply their basic and essential needs. This may compel us to apply our talents in a sustained manner to the problem of utilising solar energy.

Many industries today depend on forests for their sources of raw materials. These requirements, too, must be met. The only solution lies in a system of agro-forestry based on intensive cultivation and cropping on a multi-purpose basis on specially demarcated areas outside our virgin forests. This would include industrial and social forestry, as the terms are now understood, by both of which a rapidly increasing proportion of the country's requirement of fuel, fodder and industrial raw materials must be met.

Forests, however, must be husbanded and protected so as to secure and stabilize the soil and water regimen of this country, and sustain the agricultural productivity of our major tracts by preventing rapid surface run-off and consequent erosion. Billions of tons of the country's most fertile top soil and organic nutrients are lost each year, and we cannot afford this luxury much longer.

According to authoritative information, satellite imagery pictures have discerned a massive island which is coming up south of the Sunderbans, variously estimated in extent at between 25,000 and 50,000 sq kms, from silt discharged into the sea by the Ganga and the Brahmaputra river systems. The loss we have sustained in this matter is phenomenal, and our soils are today greatly the poorer.

Many of our so-called forests have long since disappeared, and many of the areas recorded as forests are, in fact, barren tracts no longer capable of carrying strands of perennial vegetation without a major investment of resources.

It is often authoritatively stated that India has nearly 75 million hectares of forests, constituting approximately 23 per cent of its total geographical area. Both these figures are extremely misleading without numerous qualifications. The nominal or national area under forests includes the perpetually snow-bound alpine areas, deserts, extensive marshy areas, extremely degraded rocky areas bereft of any vegetation, and large stretches of scrub land. If due allowance is made for all these factors, it would be evident that no more than half of this area can properly be classified as forest area capable of performing its protective and productive functions. The rest is only semi-productive or unproductive degraded land, which is more a potential danger to the maintenance of the ecological balance of the environment than an agency of conservation. This is reflected in the fact that only 66 per cent of the so-called forests are taken cognisance of by the Forest Department, and are covered by regular working plans and working schemes; and that a large part of this two-thirds is merely fit for classification as suitable for protection, and for which hardly any scientific management practices are laid down.

Another disturbing feature is the legal status of the forests in the country. Barely half of 75 million hectares are Reserved Forests, to which a reasonable degree of protection can be extended. Nearly one-third are Protected Forests, in which the degree of control varies from almost nil to just acceptable, depending on their composition, density but, above all, their nearness to human habitations. The nearer they are to inhabited areas, the more vulnerable and degraded they become. The status of the so-called unclassed forests, which account for 17 per cent of the total area, is so poor that it is a travesty of fact to call them forests at all, unless they happen to be so located as to be unapproachable by reason of physical remoteness and lack of any means of communication worth the name.

Happily, the view is now gaining support that an investment of the country's resources in protecting existing forests and in reforestation should be given far higher priority than it has hitherto received, and that the direct and short-term economic and social pay offs would amply justify this investment.

Of late, the forests in the Himalayan region and the wild life they contain have come in for some harsh treatment. The Himalayas, stretching nearly 2,700 kms, have from times immemorial, held an indescribable charm and spiritual significance for the millions in the Indian sub-continent. It is only in modern times that man has begun to look at the abode of the gods for the exploitation of its material resources. This is due to the increasing need of the local communities for fuel wood and grazing lands, and for construction purposes. These demands underscore the need for sound forestry practices so that sustained yields may be realised without impairing the ecology of the areas.

Forests and forestry have a special place in the lives of the people in the Himalayan region. Forests serve a host of needs not only of the local communities, but of people far beyond. Besides their commercial value, the Himalayan forests have an important ecological role in controlling soil erosion and consequent silting of the rivers, streams and irrigation canals in the plains.

The natural resources of the Himalayan region are very vast indeed. The great rivers which spring from the snowy expanse hold an immense potential for a multiplicity of uses, of which power generation, irrigation and navigation are the three most important. An integrated plan for the management of these water resources to benefit not only the northern states but the entire country is overdue.

The role and importance of forests in the general economic development of the country in terms of protection of the eco-system and supply of various forest products has now been better appreciated. The task of bringing one-third of the geographical area of the country under tree-cover has become a vital need and all possible efforts have to be made to achieve the target by the turn of the century. The objective of the conservation, protection and development of forests in proposed to be achieved through the strategy and approach which inter alia include *(i)* conservation of ecologically fragile ecosystem and preservation of biological diversity in terms of fauna and flora, *(ii)* increasing substantially the vegetative cover by massive afforestation—through social and farm forestry and other plantation programmes, *(iii)* meeting the basic needs of the people in respect of fuel wood, fodder, minor farm produce and small timber, *(iv)* ensuring close linkages between forest programmes and welfare of the tribal and other communities traditionally dependent upon forests, *(v)* special emphasis on forestry research, education, training and extension, *(vi)* creating a massive people's movement for achieving the objectives.

The National Commission on Agriculture has estimated that 40 million hectares will have to be brought under wood production for various purposes including fuel, and 10 million hectares each for production of crops and fodder. To this, we have to add the additional area which may have to be diverted for non-agricultural uses, particularly for urbanisation, by 2000 AD.

This future scenario, therefore, calls for effective steps towards social forestry so that loss of soil due to water and erosion is halted for protecting land. We need to achieve maximization of the bio-mass on the limited land resource so as to be shared by all concerned in the rural community. The present efforts in this direction are just not adequate to meet the actual requirements in times to come. The per capita availability of the forest area in the country is only 671 square metres as per the estimates of the National Remote Sensing Agency as against the requirement of 1605 sq. metres. The availability of forest which is only 41.8 per cent of the needs must increase by at least 2.39 times.

## Conclusion

In India, land is limited. With steady increase of population, the pressure on land is more than double. This calls for better management of land, water and the eco-system. With modernisation and proper management of land and water, it is possible to raise productivity as well as improve the living standards of rural people. There is thus a need for a long term policy to develop rural areas, keeping in mind the process of growth and its impact or rural environment and social fabric. Here an emphasis should be laid on harnessing the human resources, which is abundant in rural areas, for the growth of the economy in coming years.

Rural development cannot be planned and achieved in isolation. For the overall development of India, both rural development and urban development become necessary. The development of these two sectors is interlinked. We cannot conceive of rural development without the urban development. They are interdependent, one supporting the other and in the process both are being benefited. Rural development is a comprehensive programme of activities which include agricultural growth, development of village industries, development of housing for the poor, planning for public health, education, provision of adult education, including functional literacy, development of rural transport and communication, family planning care for livestock, etc. In each one of these different aspects of rural development, urban support in terms of goods and services is required. Modern agricultural inputs like chemical fertilisers, pesticides, pump-sets, tractors etc., required for agricultural development have to be supplied by the urban sector. Again, urban people have to supply different types of improved tools and implements for the development of rural industries, rural transport and communication. Many urban-based goods and services are required for rural house construction and rural electrification. Education, health and medical and other professional services needed for rural development are to be provided by the urban-based people. Certain food items are processed and supplied by urban people to the rural consumers also the demand for different rural products is generated by urban consumers, part from providing marketing services. There is a greater need to establish proper linkages between various sectors as well as rural and urban spheres. If need be to reverse a few policy measures and implement harsh measures—in the interest of rural poor.

## Planet Earth

There's so much pollution in the air now that if it weren't for our lungs there'd be no place to put it all. *– Robert Orben*

Nature provides a free lunch, but only if we control our appetites. *– William Ruckelshaus*

We never know the worth of water till the well is dry *– Thomas Fuller*

The earth will continue to regenerate its life sources only as long as we and all the people of the world do our part to conserve its natural resources. It is a responsibility which every human being shares. *– Gerald Ford*

We must not be forced to explore the universe in search of a new home because we have made the Earth inhospitable even uninhabitable. For if we do not solve the environmental and related social problems that beset us on Earth-pollution, toxic contamination, resource depletion, prejudice, poverty, hunger—those problems surely accompany us to other worlds. *– Donald G. Kaufman and Cecilia M. Franz*

It isn't pollution that's harming the environment. It's the impurities in our air and water that are doing it. *– Dan Qualye*

The environment is man's first right. Without a safe environment, man cannot exist to claim other rights, be they political, social, or economic. *– Dean Rusk*

The reason lightening doesn't strike twice in the same place is that the same place isn't there the second time *– Willie Tyler*

The sun, the moon and the stars would have disappeared long ago... had they happened to be within the reach of predatory human hands. *– Havelock Ellis*

Modern technology owes ecology an apology. *– Alan M. Eddison*

I think the environment should be put in the category of our national security. Defense of our resources is just as important as defense abroad. Otherwise what is there to defend? *– Robert Redford*

Let us.. permit nature to take her own way; she better understands her own affairs than we. *– Montaigne*

Your grandchildren will likely find it incredible – or even sinful – that you burned up a gallon of gasoline to fetch a pack of cigarettes! *– Dr. Paul MacCready, Jr.*

I have no doubt that we will be successful in harnessing the sun's energy... if sunbeams were weapons of war, we should have had solar energy centuries ago. *– Sir George Porter*

The use of solar energy has not been opened up because the oil industry does not own the sun. *– Ralph Nader*

We abuse land because we regard it as a commodity belonging to us. When we see land as a community to which we belong, we may begin to use it with love and respect. *– Aldo Leopold*

❑ ❑ ❑

*"There are 100 ways in which to stay alive and stay alive well, and the rural industry has an important role to play in this.... Agro and rural industries are the backbone of Indian economy and it is the priority of the government to strive for their continuous progress.... In accordance with this, we need to create such employment opportunities that meet the needs of today, go hand with the new technology."*

*Extracts of speech by Prime Minister at National convention on Rural Industrialisation.*

# Chapter 23

# RURAL INDUSTRIALISATION

## Introduction

In recent economic literature and economic thinking, industrialisation has been considered as a key to rapid economic development. It offers prospects of a growing availability of manufactured goods, increased employment opportunities, improved balance of payments position, and greater efficiency and modernisation throughout the economy. Industrialisation is characterised by technological innovation, the development of managerial and entrepreneurial talent, and improvements in technical skills, which lead to higher productivity. "India lives in its villages." More than 76 percent of the population live in rural India. Even by 2000 AD, over 70 per cent of the expected population will continue to live in 3.75 lakh villages. In absolute numbers, there is likely to be more pressure on land. As at present over fifty per cent of the people in rural areas live below the poverty line drawn in 1978-79. If upward adjustment is made in view of the rising trend in the cost of living. more than 60 per cent of rural people continue to live below the poverty line. Whereas, the father of our nation, Mahatma Gandhi cherished that. "the quality of life in the villages should be the same, if not better than that of urban habitations... the village people should not only be self-sufficient and self-reliant but also participate in matters of their own development."

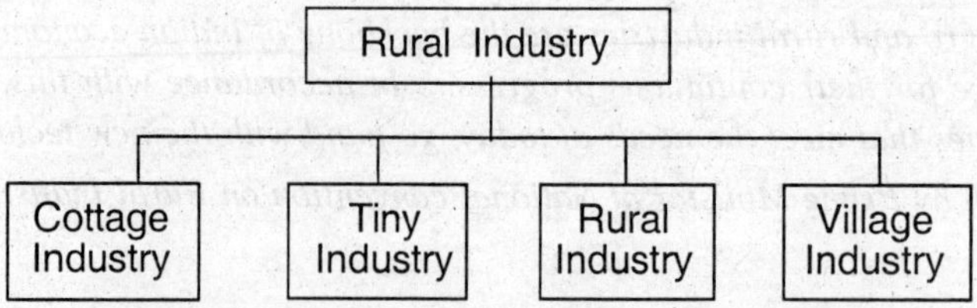


*Fig. 1. Main Components of Rural Industry in India*

## WHAT IS A RURAL INDUSTRY?

A rural industry could be defined as one which is located in a large village/cluster of villages with a population of 10,000 to 50,000. In order short and long term lending policies of the financial institutions is streamlined, the rural industries investment limits of minimum-maximum amounts on plant and machinery and working capital may be fixed at: *(i)* Rs. 10,000-15,000 for machinery and as much for working capital for small artisan type of units, (also called tiny sector sometimes) and *(ii)* Rs. 50,000 to 1,00,000 for machinery and as much for working capital for other rural artisan industries.

- *"Rural Area"* means the area comprised in any village, and includes the area comprised in any town, the population of which does not exceed twenty thousand or such other figure as the Central Government may specify from time to time.
- The term *"Village Industries"* has been redefinded in the amended KVIC Act, as "any industry located in a rural area which produces any good or renders any service with or without the use of power and in which the fixed capital investment per head of artisan or worker does not exceed Rs. one lakh (Rs. one lakh and fifty thousand in case of village industry located in a hilly area) or such other sum as may, by notification in the *Official Gazette*, be specified from time to time, by the Central Government".

### Benefits of Rural Industrialisation

(1) Rural industries provide, additional employment opportunities, raise production and improve economic conditions in rural areas.

(2) Rural industries are labour intensive. They provide additional employment to men and women. Ensures decentralisation of economic power and elimination of monopolistic exploitation.

(3) Decentralised production through a network of well-knit rural industries obviates the necessity of complicated managerial and competitive marketing techniques, thus reducing the costs on account of overheads.

(4) Rural industrialisation leads to the development of rural areas thereby lessening the disproportionate growth in large cities, reducing the growth of slums, social tensions, exploitation and atmospheric pollution.

(5) Rural industries will strive to build up village republics and human resources development.

(6) Rural industrialisation provides ample scope for the promotion of artistic achievement and creativity that has been suppressed in rural areas..

Although, agriculture is the mainstay of the rural economy, rural industry in a complementary industry. The pressure of population on land is already high and increasing. In the process, it has resulted in a large surplus of labour, both educated as well as uneducated in rural areas. Agriculture alone cannot absorb the entire surplus force and hence the need for rural industries. If we consider rural industry as a main stay, agriculture is an important part of this process. Rural industrialisation aims at the maximum productive employment of local resources, revival and development of traditional industries and skills, establishment of new units and integration of agricultural and industrial development in rural areas, so as to provide increasing employment to local people, add to local prosperity, progressively narrow down the disparities between urban and rural incomes, prevent migration of rural population. More so, rural industrialisation has been assigned a crucial role in the development of industrially backward areas in rural India.

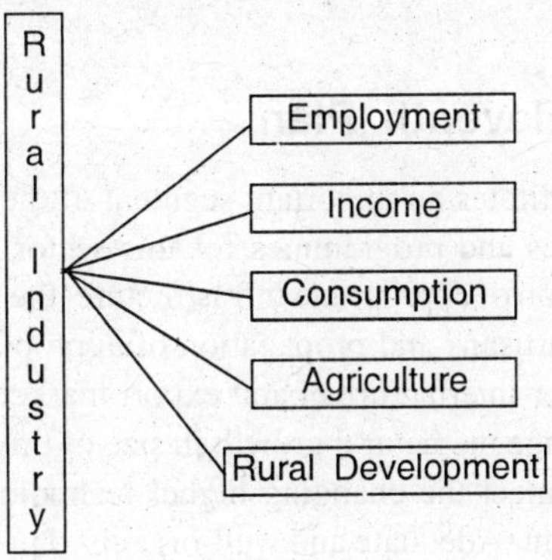


*Fig. 2. Importance of Rural Industry*

## Gandhian Viewpoint

From the Gandhian viewpoint, "Rural Industrialisation" should not merely amount to industrialisation of rural India. It should in fact lead to 'ruralisation' of Indian industries wherein production apparatus and technology suitable to Indian ethos and culture and rural needs and aspirations would play a decisive role in generating and sustaining real happiness while ensuring harmony with Nature. The following basic inferences are derived from the Gandhian economic approach to rural industrialisation:

- In Gandhian perspective, rural industrialisation is welcome as it promotes decentralization of industry and it is not city based.
- Gandhiji was not against mechanised industries—big or small provided they subserve the overall interests of the rural people.
- Priorities of production have to be planned and implemented to suit the real needs of the masses.
- Industries should be labour-intensive, generating more employment.
- The village and cottage industries should be encouraged side-by-side.
- Industries should be labour-intensive, generating ecology of the region but should promote the quality and well-being of the rural masses.
- Application of new technologies should be appropriate to the regional needs, making use of indigenous resources. Efforts should be made to reduce the disparities in income, with a guarantee of reasonable minimum 'living income'.

Since Independence it has been one of the basic objectives of planning to revive and rejuvenate village and cottage industries through various measures. The revival of such industries was aimed at providing alternative sources of employment to the rural people whose only source of livelihood has become agriculture. The increasing pressure on land made the opening of several avenues of employment an urgent necessity. Rural industrialisation is commonly understood as meaning merely rejuvenation and development of traditional and village industries. To some, it seems merely the introduction of small units of large scale mechanised industries in rural areas. In fact, rural industrialisation signifies much more than these. It means the integration of industry in the life of the people in the rural areas. In this sense it would mean not only the introduction of new technology in the villages but also the optimum utilisation of local raw materials and manpower. If industry is to be integrated into the life of the people in rural areas the type of industry that can be run profitably will vary from area to area. It should be on the availability, among other things, of the raw materials, power and technically trained personnel and the possibility of their introduction into the area from outside without generating further imbalances in the already aggravated rural economy. Rural industrialisation has to contend with all these difficulties if it has to become really an effective programme to ameliorate rural poverty.

## Rural Industries in the Eleventh Plan

The rural industries sector constitutes an important segment of the rural economy in terms of employment-output and exports. The policies and programmes for this sector should emphasise rationalisation of the fiscal and taxation regime, provision of appropriate infrastructure, the introduction of modern management techniques, upgradation of skills of artisans and propagation of appropriate technology and the adoption of a coherent marketing strategy both for internal urban and export marketing. The policies should not, on the other hand, be such as would discourage the natural growth in size of tiny rural industries. The organisational set up will have to be revamped to meet the changing higher technological needs in terms of a well-programmed human resource development. Adequate and well-organised programmes of extension, training and entrepreneurial motivation will have to be undertaken. Research and Development efforts will have to be stepped up and commercial production and distribution of improved tools and equipment undertaken. The financing of dispersed sector will have to be modified in relation to the economic status of the beneficiaries. New initiatives are required for increased production of ancillaries, as adjuncts to parent plants both in the private and the public sector. Effective implementation of all programmes will also require strengthening of the data base and monitoring arrangements.

Industrial development strategy has to be based on adequate infrastructural development, incorporating the growth centre concept and nucleus plant approach together with initiatives for increased ancillarisation. The policy framework must also disperse industry away from urban concentrations. In the north-eastern region, particularly, industrial growth will have to be promoted keeping in view the totality of facilities and incentives and infrastructure that is made available, and not merely in terms of financial concessions like investment and transport subsidies.

Processing facilities for upgrading the quality of khadi and a marketing strategy for diversification of its use will be pursued and organic linkages established between KVIC and the state-level Khadi & Village Industries Boards. Commercial borrowings, where necessary, assisted by differential interest rates subsidised by KVIC financing. Village industries and handicrafts development will be pursued, through appropriate policies. To ensure faster growth of rural industries and handicrafts, the need for establishment of separate commissions will be examined.

The coir industry should direct research and development efforts towards diversification into new products and uses, and the Coir Board will have to be revamped for rapid development of the coir industry.

An expanding role is envisaged for the handloom sector including the production of the entire requirement of Janata cloth. However, the handloom sector continues to retreat before the growth of the powerloom sector. The position of the powerloom sector needs to be clearly defined is satisfying the textile demand and given its rapid (and unlicensed) proliferation, it will have to be assigned some specific role co-extensive with the handloom sector, so that both can develop optimally.

Sericulture has been experiencing a slow rate of growth primarily on account of the non-availability of basic seed and insufficient attention to genetic upgradation. Considerable attention should be focused on basic research, propagation of multivoltine hybrids, seed preparation and maintenance. The emphasis on rural industrialisation will continue with better planning, closer monitoring and tighter organisation for effective implementation. Backward and forward linkages will be fully provided so that beneficiaries are able to make full use of the assistance.

The strategy of the Eleventh Plan will be that the programme and policies have to be oriented to the objective of providing productive employment to everyone seeking it and, in every sector, priority has to be given to activities which contribute most effectively to this purpose. The implications of such restructuring of growth for employment and income generation for the poor need to be worked out.

## Importance of Rural Industrialisation

Rural industrialisation is important not only as a means of creating employment for the labour force and raising the real income of the nation, but because it contributes to the development of agriculture and urban industries. Without rural industrialisation, it would be considerably more difficult to solve the problem of agricultural unemployment and widespread under-employment. Rural industrialisation promotes agricultural development and agricultural development promotes rural industry. The development of rural industries increases the level of income in rural areas, and tends to breakdown the old self-sufficiency of the family and to lessen its cohesiveness, creating opportunities for youth, women and the able bodied as well as changing the pattern of leisure and work. Rural industrialisation should be looked upon not merely as a way of containing the rural workers and stopping them from migrating to urban areas by providing them some kind of remunerative employment in the villages, but as a dynamic element in the process of raising the productivity and income levels of the workers in rural areas.

Rural industrialisation has taken roots in the rural economy in India. This is so because simple forms of manufacture typical of consumer goods industries and varied service industries, are everywhere developed before the more complex process involved in the production of capital goods, and because the size of the home market at the time of industrialisation prohibits the establishment of optimum-sized plants in the production of certain capital goods.

## Towards Rural Development

Rural development involves a strategy to improve the economic and social life of rural people with particular emphasis on the rural poor. The government envisaged to reduce the level of the poverty of the population to 10 per cent by the end of the Eighth Plan in 1994-95. Rural industrialisation can serve as an effective means of reducing the imbalance between agriculture and modern industry and accelerating the process of rural development. This could be achieved in two ways. Firstly, by developing agriculture and allied activities. However, there are a number of limitations in this regard and whatever the positive gains achieved in the post-independence period have invariably gone to the rich people. All along, rural population continues to grow at an alarming rate and a large segment is pushed below the poverty line. To meet this peculiar situation, the other alternative open is the expansion of rural industries based on indigenous technical know-how and labour-intensive techniques. What is actually needed is a broad-based economic policy in which traditional village (rural) cottage industries get a prominent place in the rural economy. Over the period, development of rural industries has come to be regarded as an integral part of rural development, and to the extent it included the small-scale industries, also an element in the overall programme of industrialisation.

In fact, rural areas, to some extent, possess the requisite infrastructural facilities for the promotion of some key industries which can play a catalytic role in developing rural industries. They occupy an important place in the framework of socio-economic development of rural areas. The development of village industries help in the emergence of efficient, decentralised sectors of the economy. They create more avenues of employment and contribute to the process of self-sustaining economy. What is more, the growth of rural industries in rural environment reduces the pressure on land and in particular on agriculture. Rapid growth of village industries in rural areas help in the economic amelioration of the rural people, by imparting a new look at their occupational structure.

Rural industrialisation is a key to rural development and rural prosperity. It constitutes a significant link in the process of socio-economic transformation of rural areas. Primarily, it provides additional opportunities of employment, income, better standard of living and thereby enriches the cultural heritage of the varied social structures in rural areas. Rural industries programme should not be drawn in isolation. It should be drawn up keeping in mind the long-term industrial development plan under a broad framework for developing not only manufacturing industries but also industry related activities to generate income and employment in the country, particularly for the vulnerable section of the society in backward regions. The development of rural industries should also take into account of enriching the environment, particularly the eco-system in the rural hinterland. Yet another policy measure adopted and implemented shall be to use products manufactured by rural industries in preference to imported goods, particularly in urban market segment. This will open up a vast market both in urban as well as rural areas for the goods manufactured by rural industries and pave the way for its rapid growth in the coming years.

The programme for rapid growth of rural industries should be launched like a mass movement, with the emphasis on rural brand. Efforts should be made to carry the message of rural development to the rural people. This apart, a sure market is created for the rural consumer goods. And, the urban and international markets are developed for artistic works. The rural industrialisation is an integral part of the overall rural economy and it will hasten the integrated rural development.

## Strategy of Rural Industrialisation

The framework of a strategy of rural industrialisation should consist of attempts towards rejuvenation of traditional village industries by bringing improvement in their technology, dispersal of modern manufacturing activity in the countryside with or without a linkage to the existing village industries as also production of any type of commodities that would cater to the needs of the country's population and that may or may not be based on the local resources. The rural industries would continue to be supplementary source of income as well part/full time employment activity for the rural artisans, landless labourers, women, and educated unemployed. Progressive expansion and modernisation of rural industry could be best brought out by the establishment of small industrial units along with the necessary services in large villages and small towns located all over the country.

The non-traditional industries also seem to be capable of breaking the caste-industry nexus and reducing the rigidities of social stratification in rural areas. Their entrepreneurs come from a wider cross-section of rural society, while the caste-industry identification has been more or less complete in the traditional occupations, may well accentuate the social distance among the caste groups, despite the betterment they may bring about in the economic conditions of artisans and craftsmen. No doubt, even non-traditional activities exhibit concentration by social groups, though to a smaller extent than the traditional industries; but such concentration is primarily based on class distinction in terms of ownership of resources, rather than on the traditional caste-occupation association.

Most rural industries, however, have a limited capacity for generating even a subsistence income for those engaged in them and have not shown a very encouraging record of growth in the recent past. Only blacksmithy, carpentry and handloom have shown a good promise in so far as the value added per worker is high enough to provide a subsistence income for the workers and their dependents. The new industries—wiremeshing, lamp shade and hub-brush manufacturing—meet the criterion easily; and food and oil products, the two old industries but run on modern lines and on a larger scale, have brought prosperity and effluence to their entrepreneurs.

The basic reason for their low income-generating capacity lies in their tiny size in terms of their physical volume of output. Most units are run on a household basis, and do provided full employment to all the household workers. Low level of productivity, prevalence of traditional technology, lack of knowledge of the new innovations and development in the field of production, inadequate infrastructure, inadequate finance, absence of marketing skills, lethargy, inefficiency, non-availability of skills and entrepreneurial ability, administrative snags have been enumerated as the constraints in the task.

The supply of raw materials, which mostly are a free gift of nature, has already started posing a problem, and is likely to taper off with the passage of time. It is, therefore essential to concentrate on the development of such traditional rural industries as have a positive income elasticity of demand for their products, and are not faced with the danger of inevitable extinction; such as have the potential for the technological flexibility which is necessary before they are able to cope with the changes in the demand pattern. Blacksmithy, carpentry, handloom and leather products fit quite well in this category. In order, however, that rural industrialisation becomes an effective tool for the development of rural areas as well as for the better integration of the rural and urban sectors, equal emphasis should be laid on the development of non-traditional industries in these areas. Many of them may not be linked with rural areas in terms either of use of local materials or of having a local market, but would be effective in providing productive employment to rural labour.

Rural industrialisation should be looked upon as a dynamic process in raising the productivity and income levels of people in rural areas. It should also be looked upon as a means of rural development. The first issue relates to the treatment of rural industrialisation, as an aspect of industrial location or as a programme primarily for the development of rural areas. The long term strategy of rural industrialisation would require not merely the development of traditional rural industries, but also a programme of infusing increasingly a larger component of modern consumer and other industries in rural areas. The promotion and development of "dynamic" rural industries, not doubt, needs emphasis, but in the interest of long term growth on a sustained basis, rural industrialisation should be looked upon as an integral part of the programme of rural development. It means effective linkages with the medium and large industries in urban areas.

Further, it is important not only to accelerate development of rural areas, but also to reduce the economic and technological gap between rural and urban areas, and seek to achieve a greater degree of integration between the two. The development of low technology and low productivity industries located in rural areas should generate not only linkages, to the extent possible, in the villages, but become a link in rural-urban integration. Besides reducing the income gap between the two sectors,it is also desirable that rural industries use technologies which are in line with the technological pattern of the emerging industrial structure in the country as a whole. The upgradation of the technologies of "dynamic" rural industries and the introduction of relatively modern-technology industries in rural areas alone are likely to make rural industries an integral part of the industrialisation process in the country. The technology used in rural industries varies in terms of machinery, equipment, non-human energy, and therefore, of capital intensity but, by and large, the activities in which mechanical devices and capital equipment are used yield a reasonable income only to those who are engaged in them. At the same time the use of such devices and equipment does not turn these industries "capital intensive" nor does it reduce the employment potential. It only makes employment more effective in terms of income generation.

One of the reasons which accounts for the fact that the productivity an income aspects of rural industries have received less attention than employment creation lies in the assumption that these industries are subsidiary activities on the part of the households, for which agriculture or some other activities is their main occupation, and that, therefore, they only reduce under-employment and supplement their income from their major activity. In fact, however, this assumption is not valid. For the households and workers engaged in rural industries, their occupation in them is their sole or at least the main source of income. Most of them do not even have another activity as a subsidiary occupation. These industries will, therefore, have to be seen as the effective means of providing full employment and as the only source of income for those engaged in them. The need for industrial employment on a full-time basis is likely to increase, for the development of agriculture, even if rapid, will absorb only a part of the increasing rural labour force.

It is necessary to spell out the concept of rural industrialisation. It begins with the assessment of resources, human and material, locally available in a selected area. Assessment is also made of the pattern of demand. Present and future and an area-wise production plan is formulated for ensuring minimum needs of the people by using local resources, skills and appropriate technology.

As rural industries play an important role in the national economy, particularly in rural economy, modernisation and improvement of efficiency of these industries has assumed greater importance. A main element in the success of the modernisation programme is to train and bring awareness about the new technology to the people who will implement it. As rural industries increase in progress, in number and diversity, and as their share of industrial production begins to grow, it becomes even more important that they improve efficiency in their operations. Five main elements in the success of these programmes are: the orientation of the rural entrepreneurs and rural artisans to a more forward-looking approach and flexibility of loan basis to meet the cost of modernisation and the role of appropriate technology and marketing in modernisation and improvement efficiency of rural industries. The basic objective of the programme is to set the rural industries—traditional and non-traditional—on a path of growth so that they are able to compete, on more equal terms, with the urban industries.

## Promotional Measures

For a massive rural industrialisation, the following measures may have to be taken in coming years.

Firstly, the scope of promotional measures undertaken for the development of rural industries would have to be extended to all the industries located in rural areas, and not limited merely to the specified village industries and crafts. Secondly, the measures emphasising mainly the creation of a protected market should be at least equally matched by efforts to raise productivity, even if it implies technological changes and increase in the capital intensity of these industries. Thirdly, the need for strengthening the productive potential of existing units should be given precedence over the efforts to multiply the number of units in order to ensure that rural industrialisation does not result in the creation of a larger amount of spurious employment without subsistence income for workers. Finally, it must be noted that the protective and promotional measures should aim at increasing the growth potential rather than mere survival of rural industrial units. An approach mainly relying on subsidy and assistance on individual basis may help them to survive; but it will not enable them to grow. It is necessary, therefore that emphasis should be laid on "planning" for the development of industries in rural areas and that the exclusive reliance, so far placed on the "assistance" approach is given up. Fourthly, a co-ordinated approach be adopted by the multi-agencies operated in the province of rural industrialisation. DRDA, FSS, RRB, KVIC, DIC, NABARD, SSIC, commercial and co-operative banks, IDBI are the prominent ones. For a planned development at a district level, DRDA should be authorised to co-ordinate the activities as well as monitor and evaluate the programmes relating to rural industrialisation. At the apex level, the programme should be overseen by the Ministry of Industry. Fifthly, a large number of consumer industries be located in the vicinity of rural areas. An effective linkage of large and small units through a system of job work and sub-contracting be established. This system has to be encouraged deliberately for making the small units, village industries viable and stronger. Sixthly, cater to the basic needs of the rural people by expanding and exploring potential rural markets. Finally, entrepreneurial development in rural areas would be ensured by encouraging the urban based entrepreneurs to come back to the rural areas. It would be feasible as they have the rural background, requisite experience of industrial activity, awareness of new technology, trade links, savings, etc. Group entrepreneurship of such persons can also be encouraged.

The programme of rural industrialisation has endeavoured to take industrial and manufacturing activity to the rural areas through a process of dispersal as also developing on sound footing the existing traditional units thereby creating an industrial climate in the country side. For effecting this, creation of growth centres and provision of infrastructural facilities in the rural areas should be planned carefully. Setting up of nucleus plants in districts or at potential block level will promote as many ancillaries, small and cottage units as possible. The interlinkages will strive for integrated industrial development in rural areas. Development of focal points in specific regions by providing different kinds of complementary facilities on the lines of Punjab is considered worth emulating. This will facilitate better planning, greater optimal use of resources, better control and higher productivity and profitability. And, setting up of agro-industrial service complexes and non-traditional industries in planned manner will lead to gradual urbanisation of the rural areas. This will in turn stop migration from the villages and may enable return flow to rural areas. Rural industrialisation is, therefore, integral part of rural development. A 'cluster of villages' approach would also be beneficial if adopted sagaciously and without undue interference of exogenous elements. Thus, rural industrialisation provides the necessary impetus to rapid rural development.

Rural industrialisation is an important plank of rural development. The process involves enlarging employment avenues, offering higher income and better standard of living to the people living in rural areas. The basic need of the hour is to make rural industrialisation as an effective instrument of rural development. Towards this end, the programme has to be interlinked harmoniously with the rural activities, with particular stress on agriculture and forestry.

## ASSESSING TECHNOLOGY INFRASTRUCTURE

The strength of the technology infrastructure can be assessed by considering three aspects.

First, the technology and technological capability levels of individual element of the technology infrastructure need to be assessed.

Secondly, the level of interaction among the elements, as measured by the flow of resources (sharing of technology components, technological capability and financial resources), need to be analyzed. Active interaction among the elements helps in complementing and supplementing their technology and technological capability. For successful innovation there should be a minimum critical mass of resources available.

Thirdly, one needs to assess the continuity of the technology development chain. There should not be any missing link in the creation-application spectrum consisting of product development, process development and market development. A possible methodology to assess the strength of technological infrastructure is presented in Figure 3. The five steps in this procedure are elaborated below.

**ASSESSMENT OF THE TECHNOLOGY INFRASTRUCTURE IN AN INDUSTRY SECTOR**

| | |
|---|---|
| Step – 1 | Identification of the major value addition activities in the sector and the possible areas of innovation |
| Step – 2 | Identification of available unit technologies and technological capability needs of the manufacturing enterprise, and existing linkages among the technology infrastructure elements |
| Step – 3 | Development of a set-of-indicators for assessing the technology and technological capability of technology infrastructure elements and the level of interaction among them |
| Step – 4 | Benchmarking |
| Step – 5 | Identification of areas of weakness |

### Multi-Pronged Action

The existing programmes for rural industrialisation are mainly based on the 'industry' approach which have, no doubt in many cases led to increase in production and employment but have not helped in raising to an appreciable extent the level of income of the artisan. The rural artisans are scattered and they find it difficult to obtain credit and raw materials, the size of the market is small and even at places where there are clusters of artisans engaged in specific industries, their operations are not viable. A strategy based on industry-cum-area development approach leading to vertical and horizontal integration of the programmes is the appropriate approach to sustain industries in the rural areas. This calls for an integration of beneficiary oriented schemes with the overall 'area' development plans to be drawn up after taking the resource endowments into account. All types of industries cannot be developed everywhere. There are certain areas where the clusters of artisans already exit; there may be certain areas which have the potential for development of specific industries. For such a group of artisans and crafts men, the approach should be to provide a package of assistance including setting up of functional industrial estates so that the clusters could turn into growth centres. In fact, the emphasis should be on selected industries with maximum potential rather than spreading the efforts thinly in propagating all types of industries in the same area.

More effective measures including incentives and assured supply of raw materials and power would also have to be provided to induce entrepreneurs to occupy sheds in already built industrial estates in the rural and backward areas. It would also be necessary to provide common service facilities, technical guidance, etc. so that the entrepreneurs in these areas are not in a disadvantaged position vis-a-vis those in urban industrial estates.

## Innovation Process

Innovation processes fail to take off because of the inadequate strength of linkages among the various institutional actors and the sub-critical mass of resources allocated to them. I today's era of globalisation and liberalisation, with increased competition, industries cannot afford to continue to use obsolete technology. Indeed, they need to be able to use technology as a competitive weapon. In this context, R & D orgainsations and educational institutions, for their very survival, cannot remain insulated and aloof from industry. Gone too are the days of grants and subsidies. R & D orgainsations have to earn their expenses and working with industry is perhaps a pragmatic approach to generate revenue while simultaneously establishing credibility.

It is common knowledge that establishing strong linkages with R & D institutes is an effective way to complement and supplement the technological capabilities of a firm. Most firms recognise the importance of linkages and explicitly incorporate their establishment in their corporate objectives. However, due to the lack of practical and realistic interventions, the establishment and utilization of such linkages tend to be very weak. One of the key problems that leads to the withering away of the linkage establishment objectives appears to be the lack of a methodology to asses the potential of the actors within a national technology infrastructure and the strengths of their linkages with a firm. Unfortunately, the literature on management of technology has not paid adequate attention to the assessment of a national technology infrastructure.

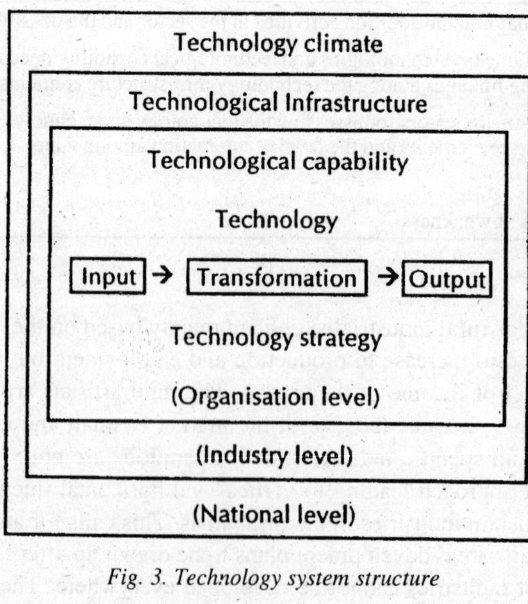


*Fig. 3. Technology system structure*

**Table 1**

| | **Technology Assessment Criteria** |
|---|---|
| *Criteria* | *Evaluation attribute* |
| Technoware level | Material, labour and energy, productivity, quality of output, pollution characteristics scale of operation, proximity to the state of the art. |
| Humanware level | Operation and maintenance skill level. |
| Inforware level | Level of operation and maintenance documentation, proximity to the state of the art. |
| Orgaware level | Level of relevant organisational system, proximity to the state of the art. |
| Cost | Unit cost of technoware and humanware |
| Interaction | The type of interaction the technology has with other technologies. currently being used by the organisation. |

**Table 2**

| | **Indicators of the Assessment of the Strength of Linkage** |
|---|---|
| *Types of Linkage* | *Possible Indicators* |
| Technical linkage | Equipment-hours shared and the total cost of sharing as a per cent of total cost of innovation, Person-hours shares, number of interactions made and the total cost of sharing as per cent of total cost of innovation, Documents developed jointly. |
| Financial linkages | Ratio of outside sponsorship to in-house project development. |
| Market linkage | Extent of involvement of marketing personnel in idea generation, preliminary assessment, concept development, product development, testing, trial launching and final launching. |
| Organisational linkage | Mobilising support for a shared goal. Number of outside members (from other organisations of technical infrastructure) in the management and other committees, percentages of outside members in various committees. |
| Generating commitment through superordinate goal | Availability of charismatic product champion, Cohesive strength of design team. |

## Necessary Corrective Action

Rural industrialisation constitutes the key link in the process of socio-economic transformation of under-developed rural areas as well as social structures. In view of its importance and problems, it is necessary to take some corrective actions to rejuvenate rural industries and rural artisans to play a pivotal role in the development process.

Some of the necessary ingredients of successful rural industrialisation may be briefly stated as follows: *(i)* the industry should be based on locally available resources, *(ii)* there should be rural-urban, local-national and wherever possible, even foreign trade, linkages. The concept of 'village republics' is no longer valid, *(iii)* there should be comprehensive planning, especially with regard to the availability of ready markets, *(iv)* there should be a nationwide organisation, with separate sections for each product or group of products which are produced in the rural industrial sector. The existing organisations like the Khadi and Village Industries Board, Handlooms Board and Handicrafts Board can be utilised for the products which they are already handling, *(v)* up-to-date technology should be used so that the industrial units can be competitive; obsolete technologies should not be adopted in the name of 'appropriate technology' etc., and (vi) while the government may provide necessary benefits, the units should be set up on a co-operative basis or through individual enterprise and not by government departments.

**Table 3**

| *States* | Details of Rural Industries Programme | |
|---|---|---|
| | *Districts* | *Agency* |
| Madhya Pradesh | Betul & Dhar | Centre for Entrepreneurship Development, Madhya Pradesh (CEDMAP), Bhopal |
| Chhattisgarh | Raipur | Centre for Entrepreneurship Development, Madhya Pradesh (CEDMAP), Bhopal |
| Jharkhand | Hazaribagh & Koderma | Nav Bharat Jagriti Kendra (NBJK), Hazaribagh |
| | Palamu | ACIL Navsarjan Rural Development Foundation (ANARDE Foundation), Mumbai |
| | Ranchi | Society for Human Ability and Right Endeavour (SHARE), Ranchi |
| Bihar | Bhagalpur | Science & Technology Entrepreneurship Development Project (STEDP), Bhagalpur |
| | Buxar | Asian Society for Entrepreneurship Education & Development (ASEED), New Delhi. |
| | Vaishali & Muzaffarpur | EDA Rural Systems, Gurgaon |
| Orissa | Mayurbhanj, Balasore, Bhadrak & Jaipur | Organisation for Social Change and Rural Development (OSCARD), Bhubaneswar |
| | Nayagarh & Keonjhar | Centre for Development Research & Training (CENDRET), Bhubaneswar |
| Uttar Pradesh | Mirzapur | Asian Society for Entrepreneurship Education & Development (ASEED), New Delhi |
| | Pratapgarh | Society for Entrepreneurship, Environment & Human Resource Development (SEEHURD), New Delhi |
| | Etah | Integrated Management Group (IMG), Lucknow |
| | Ghazipur | Purvanchal Grameen kalyan Sansthan (PGKS), Ghazipur |
| | Varansi (Rural) Jaunpur | IEDUP, Lucknow |
| Tamil Nadu | Salem & Namakkal | Industrial and Technical Consultancy Organisation of Tamil Nadu Ltd. (ITCOT), Chennai |
| Rajasthan | Alwar | Matashree Gomati Devi Jan Seva Nidhi, Fort Road, Rajgarh, Alwar |
| | Bharatpur | Lupin Human Welfare Research Foundation (LHWRF), Bharatpur |
| | Jaipur, Ajmer & Dausa | EDA Rural Systems, Gurgaon |
| | Jhalawar | Shri Pramod Paliwal, Indian Institute for Rural Development (IIRD), Jaipur |
| Karnataka | Bijapur & Shimoga | Association of Women Entrepreneurs of Karnataka (AWAKE), Bangalore |
| | Dharwad & Hassan | Centre for Entrepreneurship Development of Karnataka (CEDOK), Dharwad |
| | Udupi | Rural Development and Self Employment Training Institute (RUDSETI), Ujire, Karnataka |
| Assam | Barpeta | Indian Institute of Entrepreneurship (IIE), Guwahati, Assam |
| Himachal Pradesh | Kangra & Kulla | Himachal Consultancy Organisation Ltd. (HIMCON), Shimla |
| Andhra Pradesh | Anantapur, Warangal, Chittoor, Karimnagar, Vizianagaram & East Godavari | Andhra Pradesh Industrial Technical Consultancy Organisation Ltd. (APITCO), Hyderabad |
| | Nellore | Shri M.V. Ramanan, Principal Director, Andhra Pradesh Productivity Council Hyderabad |

| | | |
|---|---|---|
| West Bengal | Malda & Murshidabad | Shri Sanjay Sinha, Director, EDA Rural Systems, Gurgaon |
| | Howrah | West Bengal Consultancy Ltd. (WEBCON), Kolkata |
| | Midnapore | Midnapore Planning & Development Society (MPDS), Midnapore |
| Sikkim | East & South District | Sikkim Consultancy Centre (SICON) |
| Gujarat | Bhachau region of Kutch District | Shri Pramod Paliwal, Indian Institute for Rural Development (IIRD), Jaipur |
| Tripura | West Tripura District | Tripura Industrial Development Corporation (TIDC) |

*Source:* SIDBI.

## Toward Rural Prosperity

Rural industrialisation is a key to rural development and rural prosperity. It constitutes a significant link in the process of socio-economic transformation of rural areas. Primarily, it provides additional opportunities of employment, income, better standard of living and thereby enriches the cultural heritage of the various social structures in rural areas. Rural Industries Programme should not be drawn in isolation. It should be drawn up keeping in mind the long-term industrial development plan under a broad framework for developing not only manufacturing industries but also industry-related activities to generate income and employment in the country, particularly targetted towards vulnerable sections of the society in backward regions. The development of rural industries should also take into account enriching of the environment, particularly the ecosystem in the rural hinterland. Yet another policy measure adopted and implemented shall be to use products manufactured by rural industries in preference to imported goods, particularly in the urban market segment. This will open up a vast market both in urban as well as rural areas for the goods manufactured by rural industries and have the way for its rapid growth in the coming years.

## A Mass Movement

The programme for rapid growth of rural industries should be launched like a mass movement, with emphasis on the rural brand. Efforts should be made to carry the message of rural development to the rural people. This apart, a sure market is created for the rural consumer goods, and the urban and international markets are developed for artistic works. Rural industrialisation is an integral part of the overall rural economy and it will hasten the integrated rural development.

The traditional village industries and crafts continue to play a pivotal role in providing new markets, particularly in case of handicrafts, handlooms and other varied crafts. However, till today, the rural potential has not been effectively utilised. Besides, a number of industrial activities have begun to play a significant role in employment generation and income in rural areas. Most of these activities have been economically more rewarding than the traditional ones, and have been providing remunerative employment and shown relatively better growth potential. The emerging pattern of rural industries and their relative performance, therefore indicate that rural industrialisation is an effective means for the generation of growth and employment in rural areas by utilising the potential of new industries and of the existing traditional ones.

## Conclusion

The rural industries and handicrafts have to grow, change and enhance their productivity as part of the integrated growth process of the rural economy. It is abundantly clear that the policy of rural industrialisation needs a fresh look along with all its assumptions. All this requires a greater consciousness of the issues and problems involved before making policy pronouncements or even financial provisions under the plan. Since the problem involved has large implications for national development generally, but more particularly for rural development.

The programme of rural industrialisation has endeavoured to take industrial and manufacturing activity to the rural areas through a process of dispersal as also developing on sound footing the existing traditional units thereby creating an industrial climate in the country side. For effecting this, creation of growth centres and provision of infrastructural facilities in the rural area should be planned carefully. Setting up of nucleus plants in districts or at potential block level will promote as many ancillaries, small and cottage units as possible. The interlinkages will strive for integrated industrial development in rural areas. Development of focal points in specific regions by providing different kinds of complementary facilities on the lines of Punjab is considered worth emulating. This will facilitate better planning, greater optimal use of resources, better control and higher productivity and profitability. And setting up of agro-industrial service complexes and non-traditional industries in planned manner will lead to gradual urbanisation of the rural areas. This will in turn stop migration from the villages and may enable return flow to rural areas. Rural industrialisation is therefore, an integral part of rural development. A 'cluster of villages' approach would also be beneficial, if adopted sagaciously and without undue interference of exogenous factors. Dr. Duraid Yawer has aptly said that, "the emphasis of rural industrialisation should be placed on the people themselves, their aspirations and motives and their capacity for utilising the available resources." Rural industrialisation is, therefore, a fore-runner to rural development. It is complementary to agriculture. Rural industrialisation, implemented in an integrated manner will generate vast employment opportunities, raise income and contribute to rapid economic growth.

**Annexure 1**

# IDEAL FOR RURAL INDUSTRIALISATION

Mrs. Vandana Agrawal right from her childhood was having urge either to join in Government sector or to start own business. But as she was from middle class society, after graduation, she got married to a C.A. After a few years of her marriage when she became little free from her responsibilities, she expressed her wish to start some work. Her husband supported her idea and as he was a C.A. he was aware of the Rural Employment Generation Programme of KVIC and suggested her to start Steel Furniture manufacturing unit. She got the loan within a short time.

She started manufacturing work but for marketing she had to compete with Delhi products. As she was local, she was able to develop confidence among the people and the quality of her products was good. This has benefited her a lot and she could overcome the marketing problem. As business started expanding her husband and elder son also started helping her.

| | | |
|---|---|---|
| Name & Address of Entrepreneur | : | Smt. Vandana<br>W/o. Shri Vinit Agrawal,<br>M/s. Vandana Ent. VPO<br>Amleshwar, Dist. Durg,<br>Chhattisgarh |
| Name of the Activity | : | Mfg. of Steel Furniture |
| Project Cost | : | 9.98 lakhs |
| Commencement of Production | : | 2000-01 |
| Annual Turn Over | : | Rs. 33,00,000/- |
| Employment Generated | : | 30 persons |
| Monthly Income | : | Rs. 11,000/- |

This enterprise has improved her socio-economic status. At present 30 employees are working with her. She became free of her all worries. According to her, Rural Employment Generation Programme of KVIC is a very good means for rural industrialzation.

She desires that all the ladies of Chhattisgarh area should come out of all traditions and should become self-sufficient.

**Annexure 2**

# WHERE THERE IS A WILL, THERE IS A WAY

Being driven in by monetary considerations, the Yadav couple decided to start something of their own. Husband Rambachan used to work in a Namkeen preparation factory, whereas Neelam had every idea about how to prepare Farsan of various types. They have decided to start their own unit in Farsan/Namkeen making.

With the financial assistance of Dena Bank, Gomati Nagar to the tune of Rs. 9.00 lakhs, the unit R.B.N. Food products started in the year 1999.

Within four years, the business grew rapidly and every shop in Eastern Uttar Pradesh have the Farsan of R.B.N. Brand. It is the will power of the couple along with the financial assistance under REGP that leads their way to success.

| | | |
|---|---|---|
| Name & Address of Entrepreneur | : | Smt. Neelam Yadav<br>Gram-Anowra<br>Po-Chinahat,<br>Lucknow, U.P. |
| Name of the Activity | : | Mfg. of Farsan/Namkeen |
| Project Cost | : | Rs. 10,00,000/- |
| Commencement of Production | : | 1999-2000 |
| Annual Turn Over | : | Rs. 40,00,000/- |
| Employment Generated | : | 20 persons |
| Monthly Income | : | Rs. 15,000/- |

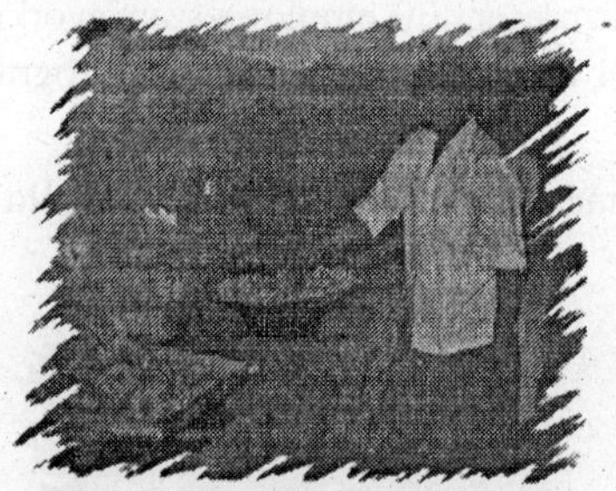

**Annexure 3**

# MAJOR CRAFTS PRACTISED IN DIFFERENT STATES

| *States* | *Major Crafts* |
|---|---|
| Andhra Pradesh | Carpets, ikat, himroo, lace, kalamkari, banjara embroidery, brassware, bidri, silver filigree, wood work, nirmal work, jewellery, etc. |
| Assam | Cane and bamboo, brass and bell metal, ivory, pottery, solapith, fibre (kuhila), jewellery, mirijimask. |
| Bihar | Folk painting (madhubani), sikki, lacquerware, aplique, wood work, papier machie, brass and bell metal, carpet and durries. |
| Gujarat | Embroidery, applique, bead work, handprinting, bandhani, durries, namdahs, shawls, wood carving, lacquer, marquetry, patara, silver smithy and agate. |
| Haryana | Durries, carpets, druggest, embroidery, brassware, moorah, jewellery, pottery, toys and dolls. |
| Himachal Pradesh | Shawls, rugs, namdahs, chamba rumals, costumes, metal crafts, jewellery, woodcraft and paintings. |
| Jammu & Kashmir | Shawls, embroidery, namdahs, chain stitched rugs, carpets, wood carving, papier machie, metal ware, widkerwork, turquoiseware, jewellery. |
| Karnataka | Wood carving, wood inlay, lacquerware, bidriware, stone carving, embroidery, durries, matweaving, jewellery, pottery, painting, ivory. |
| Kerala | Wood carving, ivory, horn carving, bell metal, koftgiri, lace, mat weaving, fibre crafts, cane and bamboo, lapidiary, coconut stem and shell articles. |
| Madhya Pradesh | Handprinted textiles, woodcraft, dhokra, papier machie, lacquerware, jewellery, rag dolls, terracotta. |
| Maharashtra & Goa | Copperware, silver jewellery, bidriware, leather craft, agate, sisal work, folk painting (worli), paithani. |
| Manipur | Cane and bamboo, embroidery, bell metal, artistic weaving. |
| Meghalaya | Cane and bamboo, carpets, musical instruments, jewellery, fibre crafts, textiles. |
| Nagaland | Textiles, cane and bamboo, wood work, pottery, jewellery. |
| Orissa | Ikat, applique, stone carving, folk painting (pattachitra), silver filigree, dhokra, horn carving, grass and solapith crafts. |
| Punjab & Chandigarh | Embroidery (phulkari), carpets, durries, jewellery, ivory inlay, leather jooties, wood turning and lacquerware. |
| Rajasthan | Handprinted textiles, bandhani, carpets, art metalware, wood carving, ivory, folk painting, embroidery (textiles and leather), jewellery, stone carving, pottery, etc. |
| Sikkim | Carpets, lepcha weaving, cane and bamboo, wood carving and folk painting. |
| Tamil Nadu | Bronze casting and wood carving, grass and fibre articles, cane articles, pottery and clay crafts, embroidery and shell crafts. |
| Tripura | Cane and bamboo, wood craft, textiles crafts, sitalpati, bell metal, jewellery. |

| | |
|---|---|
| Uttar Pradesh | Carpets, art metalware, handprinted textiles, embroidery, wood carving, stone inlay, zardozi, jewellery, pottery. |
| West Bengal | Cane and bamboo, sitalpati, embroidery (kantha), artistic weaving (jamdani), solapith, shell products, horn crafts, clay craft, papier machie, pattachitra, jewellery, ivory, bell metal. |
| Andaman Nicobar, | Cane and bamboo, shell crafts, coconut shell crafts, mat making. |
| Arunachal Pradesh | Textiles crafts, carpets, cane and bamboo, wood carving painting. |
| Delhi | Lace, embroidery, zari, hand printing, jewellery, woodware, ceramics and pottery, stoneware, metalware etc. |
| Mizoram | Artistic textiles, woodware, cane and bamboo, stoneware, etc. |
| Pondicherry | Cane, bamboo and straw, art textiles, carpet, etc. |

*Source:* Press Information Bureau, Government of India (press release dated December 14, 2000).

❑ ❑ ❑

# KHADI AND VILLAGE INDUSTRIES

## Introduction

Most people living in the rural areas of the country draw their livelihood from agriculture and allied sectors. Accordingly, the strategy of the Government has been to improve the economic and social conditions of the underprivileged sections of the rural population with emphasis on agricultural production and also the non-farm sector to promote productive employment opportunities, by integrating traditional production infrastructure, skills and locally available raw material.

The rural non-farm sector in India has been growing in aggregate size and increasingly contributing to rural income generation. The growing pace of international trade and globalisation presents both opportunities and challenges for the Indian economy, including the small enterprises sector, which consists of small scale, agro & rural industries and service/business entities.

Recognising that long-term development of Indian economy depends critically on the effective exploitation of the productive potential of the rural non-farm sector and development of village industries.

The development of village and khadi industries provide opportunities for work, albeit part time work, in certain cases, and thereby helps to mitigate the severity of rural unemployment and under-employment. With this end of view, the Khadi and Village Industries Commission (KVIC) was established in April 1957, under the Khadi and Village Industries Commission Act, 1956.

Under the guidance of Mahatma Gandhi, provisional activities of Khadi were started in 1922, when they were symbolic of the 'fight for freedom'. The Khadi Programme was thus closely linked with the struggle for freedom. The All-India Congress Committee, then known as the All-India Spinners' Association (AISA), was established in 1925 to organise hand-spinning and hand-weaving. This was followed by the establishment of another organisation in 1935, called the All-India Village Industries Association (AIVA), to monitor and look after other village industries such as hand-pounding of paddy, ghana oil, palm gur, bee-keeping, hand-made paper etc. The establishment of the Khadi Commission was the culmination of the efforts to organise cottage/village industries during the freedom movement. In 1951, the Sarva Sangh took over the work of AISA and AIVA, as a part of an integrated plan for rural industrialisation.

The Government of India evolved a general policy framework for the development of these industries. In the First Plan, these industries were treated as an integral part of agriculture; and emphasis was on local consumption. In the Second Plan, on the advice of the Village and Small-Scale Industries Committee (Karve), 1955, and in consonance with the Industrial Policy Resolution of 1956, Khadi and Village Industries programmes were made an integral part of the whole plan for the country's industrialisation.

The Third Plan retained the emphasis on these programmes while highlighting the need for an integrated approach. In the successive plans, emphasis and policy shifted from one of protection of such industries to positive forms of assistance - such as improving skills, supplying technical guidance, better equipment and adequate credit with a view to increasing productivity and reducing cost.

The Government is committed to the encouragement of the production of textile and textile products in the Khadi sector. Considering its large employment potential, it would be the endeavour of the Government to make the products of this sector more competitive and of better quality.

The infrastructure for the distribution of controlled cloth, particularly in rural areas, will be strengthened and streamlined. State Governments will be encouraged to open more rural outlets and exercise stricter control over distribution.

## Functions of KVIC

The functions of KVIC also comprise building up a reserve of raw materials and implements for supply to producers, creation of common service facilities for processing, marketing and training.

To promote the sale and marketing of Khadi products of village industries or handicraft, the KVIC may forge lines with established marketing agencies wherever necessary and feasible.

The KVIC is also charged with the responsibility of encouraging and promoting research in the production techniques employed in the khadi and village industries sector and providing facilities for the study of the problems relating to it, including the use of non-conventional energy and electric power with a view to increasing productivity, eliminating drudgery and otherwise enhancing their competitive capacity and to arrange for the dissemination of salient results obtained from such research.

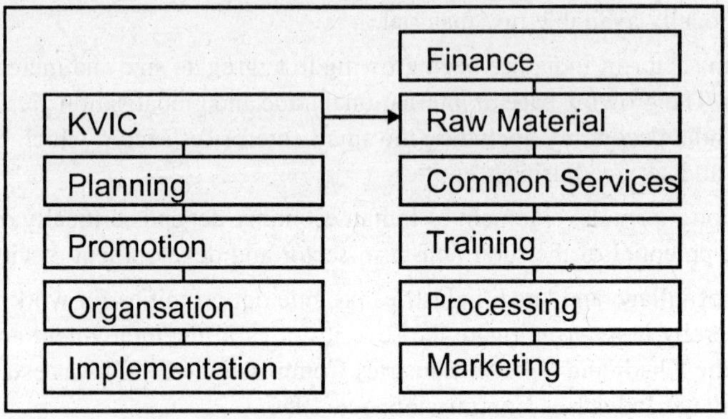


Further, the KVIC is entrusted with the task of providing financial assistance to institutions or persons engaged in the development and operation of Khadi and Village industries and guiding them through supply of design, prototypes and other technical information.

In implementing KVI activities, the KVIC plans to initiate steps to ensure genuineness of the products and to set up standards of quality and ensure that the products of these industries do conform to the standards including issue of certificates or letter's of recognition to the concerned.

The KVIC may also undertake directly or through other agencies studies concerning the problems of Khadi or Village Industries besides experiments or pilot projects for the development of these industries and Rural Artisans and Rural Industries.

The KVIC is authorised to establish and maintain separate organisations for the purpose of carrying out any or all of the above matters, besides carrying out any other matters incidental to its activities.

## Organisational Set Up

KVIC is functioning under the administrative control of the Ministry of Micro, Small and Medium Enterprises, Government of India. The Commission functions with its Head Office at Mumbai and six Zonal Offices, located at Delhi, Bhopal, Bangalore, Kolkata, Mumbai, Guwahati and 29 state offices to facilitate speedy implementation of KVI programmes. At the Central Office level, different directorates have been constituted in order to co-ordinate the functions like Training, Marketing, Funding, Economic Research and Rural Employment Generation Programmes etc. The Commission also undertakes training activities through its 38 departmental and non-departmental training centres. Similarly, in case of marketing, Market Promotion programmes have been taken up through 12 departmentally run Khadi Gramodyog Bhawans/Vastragars and 7050 sales outlets located in different parts of the country. As an endeavour to provide quality raw materials to Khadi institutions, six Central Sliver Plants (CSP) have also been set up.

## Implementing Agencies

KVI programmes are implemented through 5,549 Registered Institutions, 30,000 Co-operative Societies, 33 State/UT KVI Boards and 27 Public Sector Banks, RRBs and few selected Co-operative Banks. Khadi programmes are implemented only though Registered Institutions, for which they are to be registered either with KVIC or KVIBs. The village industries programmes, apart from directly registered institutions/Co-operative Societies, are also implemented through individual entrepreneurs by availing credit from banking sector.

## Group of Industries

While the Khadi programmes comprise of hand spun and hand woven cotton, woollen, muslin and silk varieties, the Village Industries programmes have been classified into seven broad groups. They are :

(i) Mineral Based Industry;

(ii) Forest Based Industry;

(iii) Agro Based and Food Processing Industry;

(iv) Polymer and Chemical Based Industry;

(v) Rural Engineering and Bio-technology;

(vi) Hand Made Paper & Fibre Industry; and

(vii) Service Industry.

*Fig.*

## Box 1
## INDUSTRIES UNDER THE PURVIEW OF THE KVIC I KHADI (COTTON, SILK AND WOOLLEN) II VILLAGE INDUSTRIES

Following Village Industries/Schemes under the purview of KVIC are grouped in seven major groups as under :

**Group-I: Mineral Based Industry:** (1) Cottage pottery industry; (2) Limestone, lime shell and other lime products industry; (3) Stone cutting, crushing, carving and engraving for temples and buildings; (4) Utility articles made out of stone; (5) Slate and slate pencil making; (6) Manufacture of plaster of paris; (7) Utensil washing powder; (8) Fuel briquetting; (9) Jewellery out of gold, silver, stone, shell and synthetic materials; (10) Manufacture of gums and resins; (11) Manufacture of bangles; (12) Manufacture of paints, pigments, varnishes and distemper.

**Group-II: Forest Based Industry:** (13) Hand made paper; (14) Manufacture of katha; (15) Manufacture of gums and resins; (16) Manufacture of shellae; (17) Cottage match industry, manufacture of fireworks and agarbatties; (18) Bamboo and cane work: (19) Manufacture of paper cups, plates, bags and other paper containers; (20) Manufacture of exercise book, binding, envelope making, register making including all other stationery items made out of paper; (21) Khus tattis and broom making; (22) Collection, processing and packing of forest products; (23) Photo framing; (24) Manufacture of jute products (under fibre Industry).

**Group-III: Agro-Based and Food Industry:** (25) Processing, packing and marketing of cereals, pulses, spices, condiments, masala etc., (26) Palm gur making and other palm products industry; (27) Manufacture of cane gur & khandsari; (28) Bee-keeping; (29) Fruits and vegetable processing preservation and canning including pickles; (30) Ghana oil industry; (31) Fibre other than coir; (32) Collection of forest plants and fruits for medicinal purposes; (33) Processing of maize and ragi; (34) Pithwork-manufacture of pith mats and garland, etc; (35) Cashew processing (36) Leaf cup making.

**Group-IV: Polymer and Chemical Based-industry:** (37) Flaying, curing and tanning of hides and skins and ancillary industries connected with the same and cottage leather industries; (38) Cottage soap industries; (39) Manufacture of rubber goods (diped latex products); (40) Products out of rexins, PVC etc; (41) Horn and bone including ivory product; (42) Candle, camphor and sealing wax making; (43) Manufacturing of essential oils, (44) Manufacture of bidi; (45) Manufacture of mehendi; (46) Manufacture of sandal oils; (47) Manufacture of shampoo; (48) Manufacture of hair oils; (49) Detergents and washing powder making (non-toxic).

**Group-V: Engineering and Non-conventional Energy:** (50) Carpentry; (51) Blacksmithy; (52) Manufacture of household aluminium utensils; (53) Manufacture and use of manure and menthane (gobar) gas from cow-dung and other waste products (such as flesh of dead animals, night soils etc.); (54) Manufacture of paper pins, clips, safety pins, stove pins etc.; (55) Manufacture of decorative bulbs, bottles, glass etc. (56) Umbrella assembling; (57) Solar and wind energy implements; (58) Manufacture of handmade utensils out of brass; (59) Manufacture of handmade utensils out of copper; (60) Manufacture of handmade utensils out of bell metal: (61) Other articles made out of brass, copper and bell metal; (62) Production of radios; (63) Production of cassette olayer whether or not fitted with radio; (64) Production of cassettes recorder whether or not fitted with radio; (65) Production of voltage stabilizer; (66) Manufacture of electronic clocks and alarm time pieces; (67) Carved wood and artistic furniture making; (68) Iron grills making; (69) Motor winding; (70) Wire net making; (71) Iron grills making; (72) Manufacture of rural transport vehicles such as; hand carts, bullock carts, small boats, assembly of bicycles, cycle rikshaw, motorised carts etc., and (73) Manufacture of musical instruments.

**Group-VI: Textile Industry (Excluding Khadi):** (74) 'Poly Vastra' which means any cloth woven on handloom in India from yarn handspun in India from a mixture of man-made fibre with either cotton, silk or wool or with any two or all of them or from a mixture of man-made fibre yarn handspun in India or with any two or all of such yarn; (75) Manufacture of Lok Vastra cloth; (76) Hosiery; (77) Tailoring and preparation of Readymade Garment; (78) Fishing nets out of Nylon/Cotton by hand; (79) Batic Work; (80) Toys and Doll Making; (81) Thread Balls and Woollen Balling, Lacchi Making; (82) Embroidery; (83) Manufacture of surgical bandages; (84) Stove Wicks.

**Group-VII: Service Industry:** (85) Laundry; (86) Barber; (87) Plumbing; (88) Servicing of electrical wiring and electronics-domestic appliances and equipment; (89) Repairs of diesel engines, pumps etc. (90) Tyre vulcanising unit; (91) Agriculture servicing for sprayers, insecticides, pump-sets etc.; (92) Hiring of sound systems like loud speaker, amplifier, mike etc.; (93) Battery charging; (94) Art board painting; (95) Cycle repair shops; and (96) masonry.

The KVI sector makes significant contribution to the Indian economy.

**KVIC Performance**

*(Value - Rs. crore)*
*(Employment - lakh persons)*

| Year | Production | | | Employment | | |
|---|---|---|---|---|---|---|
| | Khadi | VI | Total | Khadi | VI | Total |
| | Value Rs. | Value Rs. | Value Rs. | | | |
| 2002-03 | 443.07 | 8,126.30 | 8,569.37 | 8.58 | 57.87 | 66.45 |
| 2003-04 | 451.93 | 9,228.27 | 9,680.20 | 8.61 | 62.57 | 71.18 |
| 2004-05 | 461.54 | 10,458.89 | 10,920.43 | 8.64 | 68.14 | 76.78 |
| 2005-06 | 468.30 | 11,915.54 | 12,383.84 | 8.68 | 74.09 | 82.77 |
| 2006-07* | 491.52 | 12,383.19 | 14,018.71 | 8.84 | 80.08 | 88.92 |

## NEW INITIATIVES IN KVI SECTOR

### (a) Quality Control in Khadi

In order to increase the appeal of Khadi while maintaining its handcrafted quality, KVIC forged tie-up arrangements with the National Institute of Design (NID), Ahmedabad; Dastakar, Andhra Pradesh, IIT Delhi and Textiles Committee, Mumbai. The IIT, Delhi developed stiff and soft processing techniques as distinct characters of khadi. The process was implemented as a project at Kshetriya Shree Gandhi Ashram, Barabanki in U.P. Building on the success of the project, replication of such facilities as common facility centers in other parts of the country are also being done.

A Memorandum of Understanding (MoU) was signed with the Textile Committee, a statutory body under Ministry of Textiles, which has extended facilities of their 16 laboratories in the country for testing of Khadi at concessional rates. Under the arrangement, the quality of Khadi would receiver a fillip, thus further increasing its marketability.

### (b) Product Development Design Intervention and Packaging (PRODIP) Scheme

The Product Development, Design Intervention and Packaging (PRODIP) scheme was launched in November 2002 with a view to improving the quality of khadi products and also to diversify into new products. The scheme envisages improvement in product quality, introducing new designs and better packaging of products.

The scheme has gained acceptance as would be evident from the progress achieved so far. During 2003-04 to 2007-08 there were 592 projects.

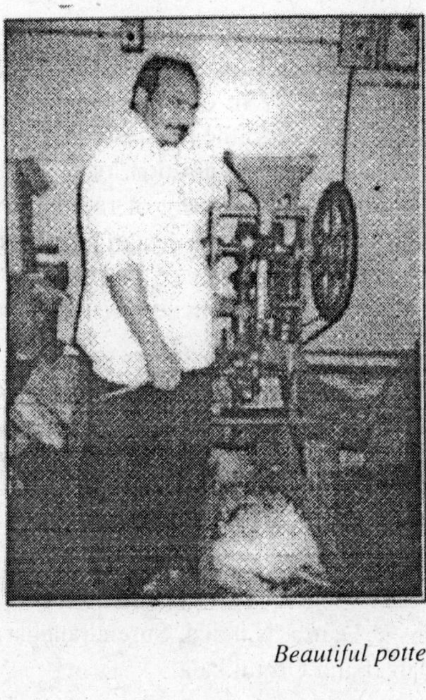

*Beautiful pottery item manufactured under KVI sector.*

With a view to improve the quality of Khadi products and also to diversify into new products, capacity building programmes were organized under PRODIP scheme such as:

- Training for production of knitwear organized at Khadi Gramodyog Vidyalaya, Tamil Nadu and Sarvodaya Sangh, Tirupur.
- Training for Readymade Garment manufacturing at NID, Ahmedabad premises.
- Training for Readymade Garments manufacturing, conducted at Multi Disciplinary Centre, Patna, a departmental unit of the Commission.
- Training for manufacturing of Readymade Garments which included design development, pattern making, stitching etc., were organized at Kshetriya Shri Gandhi Ashram, Varanasi and Meerut and Khadi Gramodyog Vidyalaya, Tirupur.

## (c) Rural Industries Service Centers (RISC)

The KVIC is implementing the Rural Industries Service Centers (RISC) Scheme from 2004-05 onwards to provide infrastructural support and services to units to upgrade their production capacity, skill upgradation and market promotion. RISC inter alia provides for:

- testing facilities by establishing laboratory to ensure quality of the products.
- improved machinery/equipment to be utilised as common utility facilities by the nearby units/artisans to enhance production capacity or value addition of the product.
- attractive and appropriate packaging facilities and machineries to the local units/artisans for better marketing of their products.
- training facilities to upgrade artisans' skills in order to increase their earnings.
- new design or new products, diversified product in consultation with experts/agencies for a value addition of rural manufacturing units.

This scheme is implemented through KVIC/KVIBs, National level/State level Khadi and VI Federations, Khadi and VI Institutions affiliated to KVIC and KVIBs and NGOs who have already worked in the implementation of programmes relating to rural industries.

## (d) Rural Industries Consultancy Service (RICS)

The KVIC launched a Rural Industries Consultancy Service (RICS) in order to help the potential entrepreneurs for providing guidance for technical and managerial support to the prospective entrepreneurs which includes preparation of projects, liaison with banks/other agencies/organisation/local authorities in respect of the project, assistance and support to implement the project, procurement of raw materials, machinery, installation, quality control for acceptability and reliability, packaging and design for better marketing, marketing support for sustainability of the unit, etc.

## (e) Central Sliver Plants (CSPs)

As a step towards improving the quality of raw material and in order to enable the khadi institution to access these sources of quality raw material, KVIC continued to operate its 6 CPs at Kuttur, Chitradurga, Sehore, Raibareilly, Etah and Hajipur. During the year 2006-07, the khadi institutions purchased slivers/rovings from these plants to the extent of 25.94 lakh kgs valued at Rs. 2,236.00 crore.

## (f) Raw Material Godowns

In order to facilitate continuous use of slivers/rovings by Khadi institutions faced with resource crunch, the KVIC continued operation of 9 local raw material godowns at Dausa, Nanded, Surendranagar, Bijnour, Wavilala, Metapalli, Karimnagar, Sangaraligapuram, Murshidabad and Orutukkala.

With a view to making the khadi industry more competitive with more market-driven, profitable, production, capacity building sustained employment at increased level of wages to khadi artisans by replacement of obsolete and old machinery and equipment and repairs to/renovation of existing/operational machinery and equipment, increase value to the existing khadi production by converting from fabric to readymade garments; and to provide appropriate incentives to shift from the existing rebate framework to market driven approach.

## Conclusion

Khadi and village industries has been playing a catalystic role in rural industrialisation and more importantly in generating rural employment and accelerated development of rural areas.

❑ ❑ ❑

*Agrarian reforms have been a core issue for rural reconstruction as a means of ensuring social justice to actual tillers and the landless rural poor, thereby creating a sustainable base for the overall growth of the industrial and tertiary sectors of our economy. Generating greater access of landless rural poor to land is considered an important component of the effort aimed at poverty alleviation.*

# Chapter 24

# LAND REFORMS AND RURAL DEVELOPMENT

## Introduction

The term land in the economic sense connotes the total natural and cultural environment within which production takes place. It encompasses the flora and fauna, and the factors governing the productivity of land. Land is the basic input of development. In India, of the total geographical area of 328.8 million hectares, 142.9 (43.5 per cent) million hectare are under cultivation, and 67.4 million hectares (22.1 percent) are under forests. Land resources are, therefore, limited. The net sown area is likely to increase marginally by 7.1 million hectares to 150 million hectares by 2000 AD, on an average, by 0.3 per cent per annum. The limitations are many.

Land plays an important role in agricultural and rural development. The defective agrarian structure is one of the causes of the low productivity of agriculture in India. Dr. R.K. Mukerjee aptly observes; "The standard of living of the Indian peasants cannot rise until a change in land system supplies the essential economic basis of more efficient farming. Neither scientific agriculture nor co-operation can make much headway unless we reform the land system." (Dr. R.K. Mukerjee, *Land Problems of India*).

The National Planning Committee, too, spoke in the same vein. "Ownership of all forms of natural wealth must belong to, and vest absolutely in, the people of India collectively... No intermediary parasite—zamindars, talukdars, malguzars, etc.—should be recognised... All rights belonging to these classes should be bought out, and steps should be taken to consolidate all holdings into standard units, and minimise the human effort involved. No sub-division of agricultural land by any incidence of inheritance, mortgaging, or alienation should be permitted." *(N.C.P. Report on Land Policy and Agriculture, pp. 48-49).*

## Agrarian System

According to a UNO Report, the present agrarian system is a powerful obstacle to economic development in three ways. First, the tenant has little incentive to increase his output, for a large share accrues to the landowner who incurs no cost. Second, a very small margin is left with the actual cultivator, and this amount is quite insufficient to provide for capital investment in the land. Third, wealth is held in the form of land, and the tenants secure no benefit of working with better equipment or with better seeds. In other words, under the present agrarian system, the landlords grew richer, the intermediaries continued to flourish, the state was deprived of its share of legitimate increase in revenue and the cultivator-tenants lived on a hand-to-mouth existence.

When India became independent, it was faced with the problem of an antiquated system of land ownership which it had inherited from the past. Many of these systems were unjust and oppressive, demanding high rents from farmers and destroying the incentive to improve farms and farm method. Besides, there were gross inequalities in land ownership. Insecure tenures not only perpetuated social and economic injustice, but turned out to be formidable stumbling blocks in the path of the modernisation of Indian agriculture.

# LAND REFORMS AND POVERTY REDUCTION

India embarked on a programme of land reforms soon after Independence. The first stage of land reforms abolition of landed intermediaries achieved limited and variable success. The consolidation of land holdings also conceived as a component of the land reforms programme but without any explicit redistributive content, met with considerable success in many states. Moderate land reforms, as in Kerala, West Bengal and Karnataka, have helped to diffuse economic and political concentration and provided a more adequate basis for promoting participation, improving the prospects for labour and accelerating poverty reduction. But ambitious programmes of tenancy reform and implementation of land ceilings have been largely unsuccessful in most states. On the other hand, large regions in many of the states which have a poor record in human development and poverty reduction (Bihar, Uttar Pradesh, Madhya Pradesh, Rajasthan) are characterised by unequal ownership of land, absentee land ownership and insecure tenancies. In these states, legalising tenancies (as advocated in the Ninth Plan Approach Paper) or facilitating the entry of the rural poor into the rural land market will improve agricultural growth and reduce poverty (Shankar, forthcoming). One study (Bandopadhyay, 1986) shows that an important factor affecting labour market participation in recent decades has been the broadening of access to land. In the 1970s, according to the NSS 37th Round, there was a 30 percent increase in landowning families compared to a 26 percent increase in the number not owning any land. Nearly one-fifth of the new holdings were acquired through modest land reforms. While many of the new holdings were small, they nevertheless enabled the poor to achieve a modicum of security (in the form of a marketable asset and some certainty in income flows) and social status. Even a small hutment lot with space for a garden can make a qualitative difference in a household's livelihood strategy. A study by ICRISAT found that increased access to land played a large role in the real income gains of the poor in the semi-arid zone in the 1970s and the early 1980s (World Bank 1990). More recent evaluations carried out by the National Academy of Administration have confirmed the importance of even modest land reforms in the livelihood strategies of the poor.

Agrarian reforms have also been a core issue of the National Agenda for Rural Reconstruction as a means of ensuring social justice to actual tillers and the landless rural poor, thereby creating a sustainable base for the overall growth of the industrial and tertiary sectors of our economy. Generating greater access of landless rural poor to land is considered an important component of the effort aimed at poverty alleviation.

## Agrarian Reform

A high-powered committee, with Shri Jawaharlal Nehru as chairman, reported in 1948: "All intermediaries between the tiller and the state should be eliminated, and all middlemen should be replaced by non-project taking agencies... Land should be held for use as a source or employment... In the case of minors and the physically handicapped persons, a share of the produce of the land should be given to them... The maximum size of holdings should be fixed and the surplus land over such a maximum should be acquired and placed at the disposal of the village co-operatives. Small holdings should be consolidated and steps should be taken to prevent further fragmentation."

The Agrarian Reforms Committee, with Shri J.C. Kumarappa as chairman, laid down the guidelines for the formulations of land reform policies in Independent India. It recommended:

*(i)* All intermediary interests should be abolished and the land should belong to the tiller.

*(ii)* Leasing of land should be prohibited except in the case of widows, minors and other disabled persons.

*(iii)* All tenants, who had been cultivating land continuously for a period of 6 years, should be granted occupancy rights.

*(iv)* The tenants should have the right to purchase the holdings at reasonable prices to be determined by a land tribunal.

*(v)* The agrarian economy should provide an opportunity for the development of the farmers' personality.

The Committee further emphasised that:

*(i)* There should be no scope for exploitation of one class by another;

*(ii)* There should be maximum efficiency of production; and

*(iii)* The scheme of reform should be within the realm of practicability.

The most radical view on the agrarian question is perhaps reflected in the recommendations of the Committee on the Size of Holdings (of the Land Reform Panel of the Planning Commission), which declared: "Among all resources, the supply of land is the most limited and the claimants for its possession are numerous. It is, therefore, obviously wrong to allow the exploitation of any large surface of land by a single individual or a state unless other overwhelming reasons make this highly desirable. Further, in the light of the available supplies of land, labour and capital, it would be undesirable to encourage the capital intensive method of production. Moreover, whatever the economies of large-scale management, they should, in the congested state of our countryside, accrue to collective or co-operative bodies of cultivators rather than to an individual family. Lastly, in the context of the current socio-political climate, redistribution of land would appear to be imperative..."

*Agricultural reform is a core issue of rural reconstructions*

"A successful agrarian reform, which strengthens the economic position of the rural population, undoubtedly helps to develop the qualities of intellect, commonsense, morale, energy, resourcefulness and prudence, which are necessary to economic progress. For necessary spirit and drive can come only when the entire agricultural population is involved in the process of change and development. The people must be convinced, not only that general progress is possible, but that it is actually under way."

In the rural economy, "the agriculturist is the lynch-pin of the whole social chariot," and in order to revitalise the rural economy, it is he who should be given a sense of participation. Mr. Chester Bowles, emphasizing this factor writes: "Without awakening the enthusiasm and co-operation of the masses, often buried under centuries of hopeless repression, development is impossible. This underscores the need for a reasonable, equitable and speedy distribution of tangible benefits and the cultivation of a widespread sense of personal participation."

The World Bank Paper on Land Reform makes a distinction between land reform on one hand and agrarian reform and rural development on the other.

"In the main, land reform is seen as a means of bringing about structural changes in the agricultural sector, thereby altering the size distribution of holding or the distribution of income... Agrarian reform may or may not include land reform, since it involves a modification of a wide range of conditions that affect the agricultural sector. Broader still is the concept of rural development, since it embraces all the dimensions of the rural sector, agricultural and non-agricultural, and is more concerned with the welfare of the rural people than with agricultural output or productivity as an end itself." Warriner defines land reform as "redistribution of property or rights in land for the benefit of small farmers and agricultural labourers." Byres rejects the narrow definition used by Warriner for the benefit of small farmers or agricultural labourers as excessively restrictive. He includes in land reform programmes of the removal of land from large feudal landowners vesting it in rich peasants. Raj Krishna classifies land reform measures as:

*(i)* Liberative;

*(ii)* Distributive;

*(iii)* Organizational; and

*(iv)* Developmental.

He, moreover, categorises the first three under land reform. The abolition of intermediaries is placed under liberative; the distribution of ownership and consolidation and tenancy reform under distributive; and the choice of form of organisation as co-operative, collective, etc., under organisational.

Land Reform is now taken to mean by most writers as:

*(a)* Redistribution of property in favour of landless or small cultivators with or without co-operativisation or collectivisation; and

*(b)* Tenancy reform;

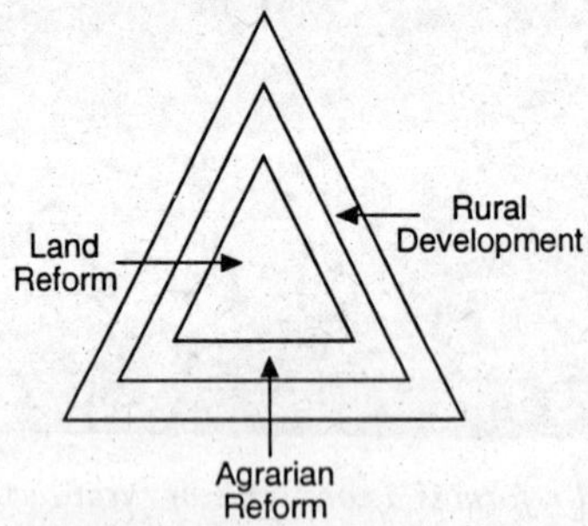


*Fig. 1 Varying Definitions of Land Reforms*

A recent study of land reforms by a political scientist defines them as public programmes that seek to restructure equitably and rationally defective land tenure system by compulsory, drastic and rapid means. The objective is the attainment of just relationships among the agricultural population, and improvements in the utilisation of land. The emphasis is well placed on redistribution as the essence of land reform. Land reform should then serve the ends of equity as well as productivity.

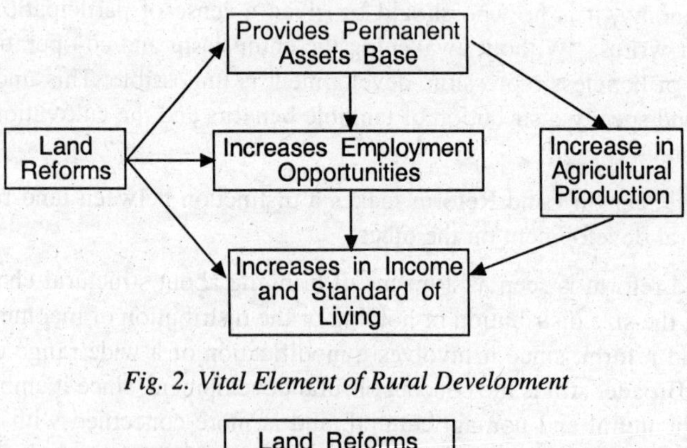


*Fig. 2. Vital Element of Rural Development*

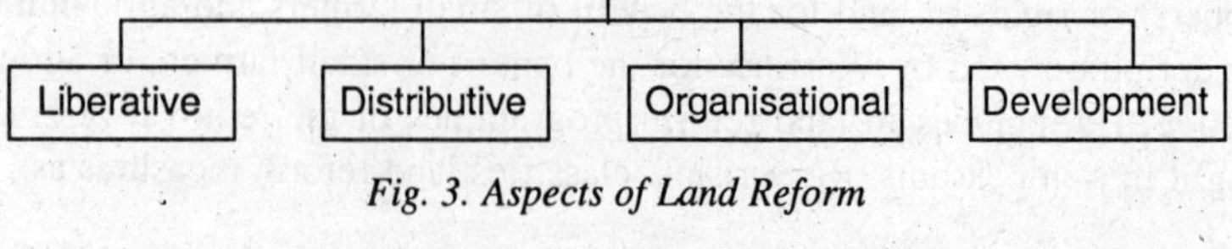


*Fig. 3. Aspects of Land Reform*

## Objectives of Land Reforms

Agrarian reforms have been a core issue for Rural Reconstruction as a means of ensuring social justice to actual tillers and the landless rural poor, thereby creating a sustainable base for the overall growth of the industrial and tertiary sectors of our economy. Generating greater access of landless rural poor to land is considered an important component of poverty alleviation.

The major objectives of Land Reforms have been the re-ordering of agrarian relations in order to achieve an egalitarian social structure, elimination of exploitation in land relations, realising the age old goal of land to the tiller, enlarging the land base of the rural poor, increasing agricultural productivity and infusing an element of equality in local institutions. The following main items of land reforms have been implemented in fulfilment of this objective:

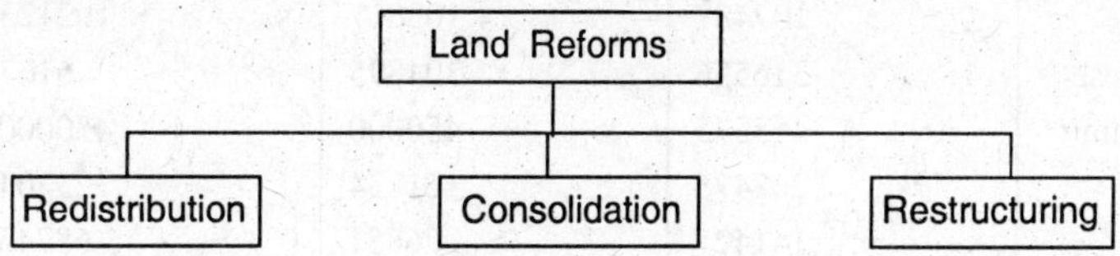


*Fig. 4. Phases of Land Reforms*

(*a*) Abolition of intermediary tenures;

(*b*) Provision of security to tenants with the ultimate objective of conferring ownership rights on them;

(*c*) Imposition of land ceiling on agricultural holdings and distribution of surplus land to landless agricultural workers as well as small landholders;

(*d*) Preparation and maintenance of land records; and

(*e*) Consolidation of agricultural land holdings.

In a broad sense, the term land reform refers to improvements in the institutions of land tenure of the agricultural organisation, including not only in the redistribution of property rights in land but such measures as would effect improvements in the conditions of tenancy, the viability of farm holdings, agricultural credit, co-operative organisation, marketing, advisory and demonstrative services. Prof. Gunnar Myrdal refers to the crucial role in development of agrarian reform of one sort or another, adjusted to the conditions and opportunities in the several underdeveloped countries, but aimed at creating such a relationship between man and land that the tiller has opportunities, and feels incentives, to exert himself; the need for such a redirection of all other institutional reforms—providing and subsidizing agricultural extension, market outlets, and availability of fertilizers, water, seeds, machinery and other agricultural implements—so that they may serve the masses and not, as now, cause a widening of the gap between the rich and the poor; and the importance of agrarian reform for making that redirection of other reforms effective. All these reforms in the interest of greater equality are required to spread technological advances and raise labour utilisation and yields. This also creates a situation where the labour force has the opportunities, and feels the incentives, to exert itself to the utmost. In its broadest context, land reform is a social change, affecting the lives of farm people in rural areas. It aims at creating a new social order in rural India, with a rational distribution of agricultural income and the growth of higher agricultural productivity. In particular, it lays emphasis on rapid rural development.

## DISTRIBUTION OF CEILING SURPLUS LAND

Since inception of the ceiling laws on agricultural holdings, according to reports received up to the end of March, 2000, the total quantum of land declared surplus in the entire country is 73.73 lakh acres, out of which about 65.01 lakh acres have been taken possession of and a total area of 53.93 lakh acres have been distributed to 56.47 lakh beneficiaries, of whom around 36% (20.30 lakh) belong to the Schedule Castes and around 15% (8.30 lakh) belong to the Scheduled Tribes.

Table 1

**THE DISTRIBUTION OF CEILING SURPLUS LAND AS ON 31ST, MARCH 2000**

| S. No. | States/UTs | Area Declared Surplus | Area taken possession of benefit | Area Distributed to indv. | Total No. of Benefit |
|---|---|---|---|---|---|
| 1 | 2 | 3 | 4 | 5 | 6, |
| 1 | Andhra Pradesh | 799663 | 641655 | 582319 | 540344 |
| 2 | Assam | 613400 | 575377 | 545870 | 445848 |
| 3 | Bihar | 415447 | 390752 | 306964 | 379528 |
| 4 | Gujarat | 227404 | 160801 | 139853 | 32308 |
| 5 | Haryana | 107487 | 103017 | 102123 | 29228 |
| 6 | Himachal Pradesh | 316556 | 304895 | 6167 | 6259 |
| 7 | Jammu & Kashmir | 455575 | 450000 | 450000 | 450000 |
| 8 | Karnataka | 268478 | 161834 | 123204 | 33610 |
| 9 | Kerala | 141427 | 96851 | 68745 | 166814 |
| 10 | Madhya Pradesh | 298763 | 260323 | 186942 | 74705 |
| 11 | Maharashtra | 740002 | 670449 | 642835 | 140850 |
| 12 | Manipur | 1830 | 1685 | 1682 | 1258 |
| 13 | Orissa | 179176 | 167253 | 156948 | 139595 |
| 14 | Punjab | 223115 | 105834 | 104232 | 28574 |
| 15 | Rajasthan | 611096 | 569211 | 461847 | 81808 |
| 16 | Tamil Nadu | 200920 | 191628 | 181295 | 143683 |
| 17 | Tripura | 1995 | 1994 | 1598 | 1424 |
| 18 | Uttar Pradesh | 374125 | 341464 | 258698 | 294062 |
| 19 | West Bengal | 1383852 | 1294739 | 1064044 | 2651619 |
| 20 | D&N Haveli | 9406 | 9305 | 6851 | 3353 |
| 21 | Delhi | 1132 | 394 | 394 | 654 |
| 22 | Pondicherry | 2326 | 1209 | 1070 | 1464 |
|  | Total | 7373175 | 6500620 | 5393681 | 5646988 |

## Distribution of Government Wasteland and Bhoodan Land

In addition to the distribution of 53.93 lakh acres of ceiling surplus land to 56.47 lakh beneficiaries, distribution of government wasteland has been one of the key strategies of land reforms in the country. Till end March, 2006 an area of 153.22 lakh acres of government wastelands has been distributed amongst landless rural poor.

Table 2

**DISTRIBUTION OF GOVERNMENT WASTELANDS AS ON MARCH, 2006**

| S.No. | Name of State/UT | Area Distributed in Lakh Acres |
|---|---|---|
| 1. | Andhra Pradesh | 43.93 |
| 2. | Assam | 5.89 |
| 3. | Bihar | 13.21 |
| 4. | Chhatisgarh | 2.10 |
| 5. | Gujarat | 13.21 |
| 6. | Haryana | 0.00 |

| | | |
|---|---|---|
| 7. | Jharkhand | 0.65 |
| 8. | Himachal Pradesh | 0.17 |
| 9. | Karnataka | 13.72 |
| 10. | Kerala | 4.57 |
| 11. | Madhya Pradesh | 0.79 |
| 12. | Maharashtra | 10.23 |
| 13. | Manipur | 0.32 |
| 14. | Punjab | 1.10 |
| 15. | Orissa | 7.34 |
| 16. | Tamil Nadu | 2.89 |
| 17. | Tripura | 1.32 |
| 18. | Uttar Pradesh | 24.89 |
| 19. | West Bengal | 4.32 |
| 20. | Goa | 0.05 |
| 21. | Mizoram | 0.74 |
| 22. | Rajasthan | 1.12 |
| 23. | Delhi | 0.06 |
| | Total | 153.22 |

In addition 16.66 lakh acres of land under the Bhoodan Movement was distributed among the landless rural poor. Comparatively, the movement has been more successful in Bihar, Orissa, Uttar Pradesh, Andhra Pradesh and M.P.

**Table 3**

**DISTRIBUTION OF BHOODAN LAND (UP TO MARCH, 2000)** *(Area in lakh acres)*

| *S.No.* | *States* | *Area* | | |
|---|---|---|---|---|
| | | *Donated* | *Distributed* | *Balance* |
| 1. | Andhra Pradesh | 2.52 | 1.10 | 1.42 |
| 2. | Assam | 0.01 | 0.01 | Nil |
| 3. | Bihar | 3.57 | 2.01 | 1.56 |
| 4. | Gujarat | 0.34 | 0.27 | 0.07 |
| 5. | Haryana | 0.02 | 0.02 | Nil |
| 6. | Himachal Pr. | Neg. | Neg. | Neg. |
| 7. | J & K | Neg. | Neg. | Neg. |
| 8. | Karnataka | 0.11 | 0.05 | 0.06 |
| 9. | Kerala | 0.01 | 0.01 | Nil |
| 10. | Madhya Pr. | 1.72 | 1.41 | 0.31 |
| 11. | Maharashtra | 1.04 | 0.27 | 0.77 |
| 12. | Orissa | 6.39 | 5.80 | 0.59 |
| 13. | Punjab | 0.05 | 0.01 | 0.04@ |
| 14. | Rajasthan | 1.15 | 1.14 | 0.01 |
| 15. | Tamil Nadu | 0.24 | 0.21 | 0.03 |
| 16. | Uttar Pr. | 4.37 | 4.21 | 0.16 |
| 17. | West Bengal | Neg. | Neg. | Neg |
| | Total | 21.70 | 16.66 | 5.04 |

Area not taken possession

## Conferment of Ownership Rights to the Tenants

Legislative provision have been made in extensive areas of the country providing for conferment of ownership rights on tenants or allowing cultivating tenants of acquire ownership rights on payment of a reasonable commendation to the landlords. Some of the states have acquitted ownership of land from the landowners and have transferred it to the tenants who have to pay a certain amount of premium to the state. Sub-tenancies are generally prohibited except in certain cases *viz.* widows, member of armed forces, minors, unmarried women, persons suffering from disabilities etc.

## Consolidation of Land Holding Programme

Consolidation of fragmented agricultural holdings form an integral part of land reforms policy. Successive Five Year Plans have accordingly been laying stress on the importance of its implementation for planned development of villages and increased agricultural output. This operation is considered necessary for planned development of villages and achieving efficiency and economy in agriculture. In pursuance of this strategy, a number of states have enacted legislation for carrying out consolidation of holdings. However, it appears that the programme of consolidation of agricultural land holdings has virtually stopped all over the country except in the state of Uttar Pradesh, where annually about 9,000 to 10,000 villages are being covered under the programme. So far an area of 1739.01 lakh acres have been consolidated in the country.

**Table 4**

**CONSOLIDATION OF LAND HOLDINGS – STATEWIDE INFORMATION AS ON MARCH, 2006**

*(Area in lakh acres)*

| S.No. | States/UTs | Area Consolidated |
|---|---|---|
| 1. | Andhra Pradesh | 8.18* |
| 2. | Bihar | 96.05* |
| 3. | Gujarat | 65.28 |
| 4. | Haryana | 104.38 |
| 5. | Himachal Pradesh | 29.91 |
| 6. | Jammu Kashmir | 1.37* |
| 7. | Karnataka | 26.76# |
| 8. | Madhya Pradesh | 95.53 |
| 9. | Maharashtra | 526.50$ |
| 10. | Orissa | 29.74 |
| 11. | Punjab | 121.81 |
| 12. | Rajasthan | 43.51@ |
| 13. | Uttar Pradesh | 587.66 |
| 14. | Delhi | 2.33 |
| | Total | 1,739.01 |

*Notes:*

* Scheme has been discontinued (w.e.f. July 92 in Bihar) and re-started from 15-03-2004.

\# Consolidation of Holding Act, 1996 has been repealed in '91.

@ Scheme discontinued from 1965.

$ Implementation of the scheme stopped w.e.f.1.4.93.

## Implementation

It is widely recognised that implementation of land reforms has not been satisfactory. Lack of clear direction from the State Governments has been one of the factors responsible for this situation. Rural society in India is a highly unequal society and characterised by the skewed nature of land and asset owning patterns.

This fact is compounded by inter-twinning of castes and classes. A small group of land owners exercises social and political power, totally disproportionate to their number. When faced with progressive land reform laws, these rural rich maintain their position through use of muscle power and manipulation of administrative and judicial processes. It is lack of determination to act against this class which has stood in the way of effective land reforms. The ambivalence at the political level has its effect on administrative style in the bureaucracy. A good officer is one who avoids conflict and can settle things tactfully and amicably. Such a style of functioning accomplishes "token" implementation but is appreciated by vested interests. On the other hand the rural poor are unorganised and are unable to exert requisite pressure. The need of the hour is that necessary change should be brought about in the judicial and revenue processes so that cases are settled speedily at the village level and substantive justice is available to the rural poor in a simple manner.

It is recognised that significant success in implementation of land reforms can be achieved with the active help and co-operation from revenue officers, police, organisation of rural poor voluntary agencies and other related representative bodies.

## Formulation of the National Land Records Modernization Programme (NLRMP)

It has been proposed to merge the two Centrally-sponsored schemes, namely, Computerisation of Land Records (CLR) and Strengthening of Revenue Administration and Updating of Land Records (SRA & ULR) in the shape of the National Land Records Modernization Programme (NLRMP). The NLRMP has been conceptualized as a major systems reforms initiative that is concerned not namely with computerization, updating and maintenance of land records and validation of titles, but also as a program that will add value and provide a comprehensive tool for development planning wherever location specific information is required. Three layers of data: (a) spatial data from satellite imagery/aerial photography, (b) topographic maps and other data from the Survey of India and Forest Survey of India, and (c) land records data – both records of rights (RoRs) and maps will be integrated and harmonized on a geographic information system (GIS) platform. The primary focus of the programme will be on (i) providing citizen services, such as providing records of rights (RoRs) with maps to scale; other land-based certificates such as caste certificates, income certificates (particularly in rural areas), domicile certificates; information for eligibility for development programmes; land passbooks, etc., and (ii) developing a comprehensive tool for supporting and planning developmental, regulatory, and disaster management activities, wherever land-based information is required.

## Conclusion

To sum up, land reform has been recognised as an important instrument of economic and social change. In the pre-independence period, the agrarian structure was characterized by wide-ranging inequalities, high degree of concentration of land ownership and exploitation of the rentier class. It was in this backdrop, that land reforms were adopted to achieve the twin objectives of increasing agricultural production and social justice. Land reforms policy during the post-Independence period has undergone a radical change and has acquired a new content and direction. The policy recommendations made by successive five-year plans, as also by various governmental commissions and committees discussed above, reflect a totally new outlook on agrarian relations. In a sense, they are indicative of the aspirations of the Indian people, after independence, for basic institutional and structural changes. It is now generally recognised that without restructuring rural society and transforming agrarian economic relations in such a manner as would unleash and develop the production capacity and initiative of the vast mass of cultivators, who are actual tillers of the soil, no far-reaching and permanent advance in the agricultural sector would be registered. The question is not merely that of meting out social justice to the rural poor. Land reform is a state subject and its implementation rests with state governments. Legislative measures enacted and adopted in this regard, therefore, vary from one state to another to suit local conditions. The main elements of the land reform policy have been five-fold *viz.*, abolition of intermediary tenures, tenancy reforms comprising regulations of rent, security of tenure and conferment of ownership rights on tenants, ceiling on agricultural holdings, consolidation of holdings, and compilation and updating of land records.

The question is essentially an economic one having a bearing on our national life as a whole. Unless the agrarian society is regenerated and converted into a dynamic and rapidly growing system, both the base and superstructure of the national economy will remain weak and unstable. The concept of economic holding was spelled out by the Hyderabad Agrarian Reforms Committee (1949). An economic holding may be construed as "one which in a normal year and with the present methods of cultivation, allows a cultivator a chance of producing a surplus, after meeting all necessary and incidental expenses sufficient to provide him a fair standard of living and allows him to keep himself and his family in a reasonable minimum of comfort according to Indian standards and without obliging him to incur debts."

On this presumption, about 6 wet acres, about 25 good dairy acres and about 75 poor dry acres constitutes a family economic holding. As against this, up to September 1998 nearly 55.37 lakh landless persons had been allotted 63.05 lakh hectares of ceiling surplus land or on an average 1.08 hectares. This means that more and more uneconomic holdings have been created. It is observed that productivity per acre (both in physical and value terms) decreases with increasing size of holding in practically all the regions. The explanation put forth is that smaller holding in practically all the regions. The explanation put forth is that smaller holdings have more intensity of input than large holding; high fertility is built up on smaller holdings due to maximum application for available human labour. Provided the allottee is in the know-how of agriculture and possess necessary skills.

However, a few field studies indicate that there has not been any noticeable change in the pattern and level of production between the two time periods. It is argued that tenancy reform so far has been a failure and unless the reform goes to the root of the agrarian structure, chances are very meager that supply of adequate technical know-how, credit and other facilities would make any strong impact on the level of agricultural production. The critics express the view that two years or five years (as covered by most studies) are too short a period to expect a tenancy legislation to provide any observable increase in agricultural yields.

About 8.43 lakh hectares of land declared surplus remains to be taken possession of and distributed as at end September 1998. In view of the above analysis, this land be put to better economic use, provided it is cultivated on large scale rather than showing small mercies without having any impact on the agricultural economy. Alternatively, the surplus land may be handed over to village panchayats for cultivation, social forestry and other allied activities and thereby augment resources for development.

The quality of land records leaves much to be desired. In several areas the last survey and settlement operations were conducted so long ago that the records have lost all connection with existing realities of ownership and possession. Even where the record of rights were prepared fairly recently, lapses in continuous updating have led to its obsolescence. For quite sometime record maintenance work by revenue functionaries has not been supervised and the records, prepared with considerable effort and at great cost, have become prematurely out of date. A proper land revenue and land records system is crucial to agricultural development programmes.

Co-operative effort in rural life is as old as the village community. For mutual advantage and benefit, the villagers come together on many occasions and carry out their operations such as ploughing, sowing, harvesting, etc., together. Co-operative thinking has been formalized by way of co-operatives such as co-operative farming societies, co-operative credit societies and co-operative marketing societies.

A co-operative farming society is one where each cultivator would retain his rights in his own land, but cultivation operations would be carried out jointly. The need for co-operative farming has been well recognised long back. Mahatma Gandhi wrote, "I firmly believe that we shall not derive the full benefits of agriculture until we take to co-operative farming." The Congress Agrarian Reforms Committee under the chairmanship of J.C. Kumarappa stated: "Without various co-operative moulds, co-operative better farming for family farms and co-operative farming for holding below basic—the efficiency of agriculture cannot be substantially increased."

Land reforms are interlinked with rural development. It should become the nucleus around which other rural development programmes can be developed. The land belongs to the people. And, everyone has a share in its productivity, profit. Land reform should aim at equitable distribution of income generated by the land. The measures to be taken in its totality of rural development and not in its literal meaning. It is the most crucial test which our political system has to pass to survive.

## Annexure 1

# STATE-WISE LEGISLATION ON ABOLITION OF INTERMEDIARIES

(1) The Uttar Pradesh Zamindari Abolition and Land Reforms Act, 1950.

(2) The Bihar Land Reforms Act, 1950.

(3) The West Bengal Estates Acquisition Act, 1953.

(4) The Orissa Estate Abolition Act, 1951.

(5) *(i)* The Hyderabad Abolition of Cash Grants Acts, 1952.

*(ii)* The Andhra Pradesh (Telangana Area) Abolition of Inams Act, 1954.

*(iii)* The Andhra Pradesh Absorbed Enclaves Act, 1955.

*(iv)* The Andhra Pradesh Jagir Regulation Act 25 of 1948.

*(v)* The Andhra Pradesh Estates Act, 1948.

(6) The Rajasthan Land Reform and Resumption of Jagir Act, 1952.

(7) The Tamil Nadu Estates Abolition Act, 1948. (12 different Acts were passed to abolish all types of intermediaries).

(8) 17 Land tenure abolition laws have been enacted in Maharashtra since 1949 to do away with all inams, jagirs and other special tenures.

(9) The Madhya Pradesh Abolition of Proprietary Rights Act, 1950.

(10) The Intermediaries like Watandars, Inamdars, Jagirdars were abolished by passing 10 Acts, since 1950.

(11) Two Acts were passed in Assam to abolish all intermediary rights.

(12) The Kerala Agrarian Relations Act, 1960.

(13) The Gujarat State has enacted thirty laws to abolish all grades of intermediary tenures.

(14) Four Acts were passed in Punjab to extinguish the rights of the intermediaries and superior interests.

(15) All the laws which were in force in the composite state of Punjab (including Haryana) continued to be in force in Haryana.

## Annexure 2

# STATE-WISE LEGISLATION IN TENANCY REFORMS

(1) The Andhra Pradesh (Telangana Area) Tenancy Act, 1950.

(2) The Andhra Pradesh Tenancy Act, 1956.

(3) Assam Tenancy Act, 1971.

(4) Bihar Land Reforms Act, 1961.

(5) The Bombay Tenancy Act and Agricultural Lands Act, 1948, as amended from time to time up to 1981, is applicable to the State of Gujarat.

(6) Tenancies in Haryana are regulated by the Pepsu Tenancy and Agricultural Land Act, 1955.

(7) The Himachal Pradesh Tenancy and Land Reforms Act, 1972.

(8) Jammu and Kashmir Agrarian Reforms Act, 1972.

(9) The Karnataka Land Reforms Act, 1961.

(10) The Kerala Land Reforms Act, 1963

(11) The Madhya Pradesh Land Revenue Code Act, 1959.

(12) The Bombay Tenancy and Agricultural Land Act, 1948.

(13) The Orissa Land Reforms Act, 1960.

(14) The Punjab Security of Land Tenures Act, 1953.

(15) The Rajasthan Tenancy Act, 1955.

(16) The Madras Cultivating Tenants Protection Act, 1955.

(17) The Uttar Pradesh Zamindari Abolition and Land Reforms Act, 1950.

(18) *(i)* The West Bengal Estates Acquisition Act, 1953.

*(ii)* The West Bengal Restoration of Alienated Land Act, 1973.

## Annexure 3

### STATE-WISE REGULATION OF LAND REFORMS

| *Sr. No.* | *States* | *Regulation of Rent* | *Security of Tenure* |
|---|---|---|---|
| 1. | Andhra Pradesh | Andhra area: 1/2 of gross produce, 28-1/3% of produce on land by bailing; Hyderabad area; lesser of 1/5 produce or 3 to 5 assessment; 1/4 irrigated land. | Andhra area: Ejection of tenants prohibited; Hyderabad: tenants in possession 6 years protected from eviction; landlord resumption limited to 3 family holdings. |
| 2. | Assam | 1/4 of produce if landlord supplies bullocks; 1/5 of produce if tenant supplies bullocks. | Right of resumption expired in 1963. Occupancy riot has permanent transferrable interest. Non-occupancy riots and under riots no security. |
| 3. | Bihar | 1/4 of gross produce. | Tenant obtains occupancy right after 12 years of possession; under riots have little security. |
| 4. | Gujarat | Lesser of 1/6 of gross produce or 2 to 5 assessment. | Tillers deemed to be owners. Resumption for personal cultivation by landlord restricted to 1/2 the holding, except for surrounded land. |
| 5. | Kerala | Paddy land 1/8 to 1/4 produce; garden 1/10 to 1/3; of normal gross produce for dry land 1/8 for cultivated. | Tenure for all tenants permanently fixed. Talent purchase ownership for 16 times fair rent. |
| 6. | Madhya Pradesh | 2 to 4 assessment. | All tenants were occupancy tenants. |
| 7. | Tamil Nadu | 40% of normal gross produce for wet land; 33⅓% of normal gross produce for dry land. | Tenants have rights to be restored if evicted up to 6-2/3 acres of wet land. |
| 8. | Maharashtra | Lesser of 1/6 of produce or 2 to 5 assessment. | Compulsory transfer. |
| 9. | Karnataka | 1/5 to 1/4 of produce depending on land class. | Tenure is fixed subject to landlord resumption up to 1/2 the leased area. |
| 10. | Orissa | 1/4 of produce. | Tenure is fixed. |
| 11. | Punjab and Haryana | 1/3 gross produce | Tenure is fixed. Tenants have purchase option. |
| 12. | Rajasthan | 1/6 of gross produce | Khatedari tenants have fixity of tenure. |
| 13. | Uttar Pradesh | 1/2 the gross produce | Fixity of tenure (permanent and heritable rights). |
| 14. | West Bengal | 1/4 the gross produce. | If the area is less than 7-1/2, landowner is permitted to resume the entire area. Share croppers do not have tenancy status. |
| 15. | Jammu and Kashmir | 1/4 of the wet land, 1/3 of dry land, 1/2 the produce from wet or dry land if landlord holds less than 12-1/2 acres. | Tenants in possession have right of purchase but a limit has been placed on the extent of land which a landowner may resume. |
| 16. | Himachal Pradesh | 1/5 of the gross produce. | Landowners are permitted to retain a limited area for personal cultivation. |

**Annexure 4**

# STATE-WISE LEGISLATION ON CEILING ON HOLDINGS

(1) The Andhra Pradesh Land Reforms (Ceiling on Agricultural Holdings) Act, 1973.

(2) The Assam Fixation of Ceiling of Land Holding Act, 1956.

(3) The Bihar Land Reforms (Fixation of Ceiling Area of Acquisition of Surplus Land) Act, 1961.

(4) Gujarat Agriculture Lands Ceiling Act, 1960.

(5) The Haryana Ceiling on Land Holding Act, 1972.

(6) The Himachal Pradesh Ceiling on Land Holding Act, 1972.

(7) The Jammu and Kashmir Agrarian Reforms Act, 1972.

(8) The Karnataka Land Reforms Act, 1961.

(9) The Kerala Land Reforms Act, 1963.

(10) The Madhya Pradesh Ceiling on Agriculture Holding Act, 1960.

(11) The Maharashtra Agricultural Lands (Ceiling on Holdings) Act, 1961.

(12) The Orissa Land Reforms Act, 1960.

(13) The Punjab Land Reforms Act, 1972.

(14) The Rajasthan Imposition of Ceiling on Holding Act, 1973.

(15) The Tamil Nadu Land Reforms (Fixation of Ceiling on Land) Act, 1961.

(16) The Uttar Pradesh Imposition of Ceiling of Land Holding Act, 1960.

(17) The West Bengal Estate Acquisition Act, 1953 and the West Bengal Land Reforms Act, 1955.

## Annexure 5

# FIFTY-FIVE LAND LAWS TO BE INCLUDED IN THE NINTH SCHEDULE. CONSTITUTION (SIXTY-SIXTH) AMENDMENT BILL INTRODUCED IN PARLIAMENT ON 19.04.1990.

The Constitution (Sixty-sixth) Amendment Bill has been introduced in the Lok Sabha on April 19,1990 to include 55 land reforms laws in the Ninth Schedule of the Constitution so that these are not challenged in courts.

The fifty-five land laws largely cover legal provision relating to protection of tribal land against alienation, ceiling on agricultural holdings, tenancy reform measures, etc. The Bill seeks to ensure that implementation of these laws in not adversely affected by litigation.

Of the 55 laws, (5 each in Andhra Pradesh and Bihar) 10 in West Bengal, 7 in Gujarat, 6 in Madhya Pradesh, 4 each in Orissa and Tamil Nadu, 3 each in Maharashtra and Rajasthan, 2 each in Himachal Pradesh, Kerala and Pondicherry and 1 each in Karnataka and Uttar Pradesh.

## Why Protection of the Ninth Schedule

National Land Reforms policy consists of among others the following redistribution measures:

*(a)* abolition of intermediary tenures;

*(b)* provision of security to tenants with ultimate object of conferring ownership rights on them;

*(c)* imposition of land ceilings on agricultural holdings and distribution of surplus land to landless agricultural workers as well as small landholders.

All these measures extinguish or curtail the existing rights of holders of land and their power in society, they usually halt/stall this process of redistribution by challenging the validity of the law itself in higher courts. The challenge is made most effective by establishing that fundamental rights guaranteed by the Constitution have been violated by the laws enacted by the State. Since a fundamental right guaranteed by the Constitution cannot ordinarily be taken away by any statute, such a challenge on constitutional grounds in the higher courts provides an instant remedy for invoking judicial intervention.

Article 31-A of the Constitution protects agrarian reform laws against being declared void on the ground that they take away or abridge fundamental rights conferred by Articles 14 and 19 of the Constitution. Article 31-C protects a law giving effect to the policy of the State towards securing the directive principles laid down in Part IV of the Constitution from any challenge on the ground that it takes away or abridges any of the rights conferred by Article 14 or 19. The protections are further reinforced by Article 31-B which provides a complete umbrella of protection against the entire Part III of the Constitution of the Acts and Regulations specified in the Ninth Schedule. This protection is available to such laws with retrospective effect.

Thirteen land reform laws were included in the Ninth Schedule by the first Constitutional Amendment Act. the Ninth Schedule has been amended more than once subsequently and more land reforms laws have been included. It will also be seen that amending land reforms legislation have been included in the Schedule because the courts have taken the view that while legislatures are competent to amend the scheduled Acts, the amendments do not automatically enjoy the protection of the Ninth Schedule. The last such amendment was carried out in 1984. Since then additional proposals have been received from state governments for inclusion of their laws in the Ninth Schedule. The Constitution (sixty-sixth) Amendment Bill covers all these proposals.

## Restructuring of Land Reforms

Land reforms policy pursued since independence has the objectives of breaking feudal socio-economic structure of land ownership, eliminating exploitation in agrarian relations and establish a more egalitarian society. Redistributive measures have also been considered vital for increased productivity in agriculture and also for alleviation of poverty. Among the measures pursued in this connection are abolition of intermediary tenures, regulation of rent and provision of security of tenure to tenants and share croppers with the ultimate objective of conferring ownership rights on them;

imposition of ceiling on agricultural land holdings and distribution of surplus land to landless agricultural workers and small holders; consolidation of land holdings and updating and maintenance of land records.

In pursuance of these objectives legislative measures have been enacted almost all over the country since early 50s. Great deal of progress has also been registered in achievement of these objectives.

## Abolition of Intermediary Tenures

As a result of abolition of intermediary tenures more than 20 million tenants have been brought in direct contact with the State. A large portion of estimated 6 million hectares of waste, fallow and other classes of land vesting in the state has been distributed to landless and marginal farmers. In the field of tenancy reforms legislative provisions have been made in extensive areas of the country providing for conferment of ownership rights on payment of a reasonable compensation to the landlord. Some states have acquired ownership rights of land from landlords and have transferred it to the tenants who have to pay certain amount of premium to the state. As a result of these measures an estimated 7.72 million tenants have acquired ownership of about 13.84 million acres of land. Besides, provisions for security of tenure have been made in the law of most of the states which do not provide for conferment of ownership rights on tenants, sub-tenants and share-croppers. Legislative provisions have also been made in most states. Fixing rents payable by the tenant to the land-owner and prohibiting eviction except on specified grounds. But there are still some areas of tenancy reforms which need urgent attention such as recording of informal/concealed tenants and share-croppers, elimination of absentee landlordism by withdrawal of exemptions, providing assistance to tenants to acquire ownership rights where they have been unable to mobilise necessary purchase price, etc.

## Land Ceilings

As a result of implementation of ceiling laws around 73 lakh acres of land has been acquired of which 48 lakh acres have been distributed but the total amount of land that could be acquired is short of expectations. This is on account of various loopholes in the provisions of laws and unsatisfactory implementation in many places. Among the problems which require attention for more effective implementation of ceiling laws are review of the definition of family unit, withdrawal of exemptions, application of appropriate ceiling to irrigated lands, reconsideration of ceiling limits, ensuring possession over the allotted land and provision of financial assistance to allottees for making their lands more productive. Where land acquired under Bhoodan has still remained undistributed review of existing legal provisions and administrative structures also require attention.

While in the field of consolidation of land holdings which is being implemented on a voluntary basis in most states the problems which need attention are priority to be given to areas falling within the command of irrigation projects and ensuring that small farmers do not get a raw deal in this programme. Protection of tenants and share-croppers should also be a pre-requisite before taking up consolidation programme.

## Land Records

Land records are in a pretty bad shape all over the country. They have suffered neglect over the years. The revenue machinery which look after their maintenance and updating is inadequate and is serviced by very poor infra structure. Preparation, maintenance and updating of land records require considerable resources, trained manpower, induction of high technology on an urgent basis. It is, therefore necessary to ensure that requisite resources are ploughed into this work both by the state government and the central government. The entire structure of revenue administration and land records, management also needs to be looked into in considerable depth so that system changes more appropriate to the work could be introduced.

## Structural Impediments

Implementation of land reforms has also suffered on account of structural factors such as pressure of influential land-owners, lack of organisation among the beneficiary groups, excessive litigation, lack of proper orientation in the bureaucracy, and dilutory judicial system etc. These areas also require urgent intervention.

## The Government's Commitment

The Government has made a commitment to revise the existing agrarian laws to bring about more equitable distribution of land and to make the tiller of the land its owner. With a view to achieve this objective it is therefore proposed to have a discussion with the State Governments in the Inter-State Council covering the whole ambit of land reforms policy. It may be relevant to mention that such a comprehensive review of land reforms policy has not been undertaken for a long time. The last such review was undertaken on the programme of ceiling on agricultural holdings in 1972 in which the chief ministers participated. The proposed discussion with chief ministers on the wide range of agrarian reform measures is, therefore, a major step forward to implement the commitment of the Government.

❑ ❑ ❑

## SECTION FIVE

# FINANCING RURAL DEVELOPMENT

The policy towards financing rural development has seen a sea change and has also undergone a rapid structural transformation over the last four decades. The scale and scope of its activities has scaled new high keeping in view of the rapid changes in the social, economical, political and cultural environment in the country. The financial system is diversifying itself to cater to the growing needs of the rural sector and have been experimenting with innovative schemes dovetailed to meet the needs of the rural sector. This recognition has led to the development of the concept of planning at the grass-root village level and adoption of a service area approach strategy. Thus rural lending would be more purposive based and at the same time accelerate the process of village development. The paramount need is to ensure higher productivity of institutional credit and better recycling of funds. There is also a growing need for encouraging non-agricultural activities in the rural sector. The All-India Debt and Investment Surveys (AIDIS) have brought out the crucial role played by institutional agencies in the extension of the credit delivery system in the rural sector.

The total credit flow to agriculture and allied sector during the Ninth Plan (1997-02) is expected to have reached Rs. 2,33,700 crore as against the projection of Rs. 2,29,000 crore. For the Tenth Plan Period (2002-07) the credit flow into agriculture and allied activities from all banking agencies is projected at Rs. 7,36,570 crore, which is more than three times the credit flow during the Ninth Plan. The target for credit flow for the agriculture and allied sector for the year 2002-03 is Rs 82,073 crore.

The thrust of rural credit policy has been on the provision of timely and adequate flow of credit, especially to meet the requirements of small and marginal farmers and the weaker sections. The flow of institutional changes in agricultural technology, although there are areas where credit deepening as well as widening is needed.

The main objectives of the institutional credit policy are:

*(i)* To secure an increase in the total volume of institutional credit for agriculture and rural development;

*(ii)* To direct a larger share of the credit to the weaker sections;

*(iii)* To reduce the regional imbalances in the availability of credit;

*(iv)* To bring about greater co-ordination between different credit institutions under the multi-agency systems; and

*(v)* To improve the recovery of institutional loans to ensure continuous re-cycling of credit.

The entire problem of rural credit should be viewed in the light of providing an integrated rural credit service, *i.e.* provision of credit along with facilities for its conversion into the inputs and services required by farmers to use the credit effectively. This service should be made available to small and marginal farmers and agricultural labourers who want to upgrade their technology and productivity. The service must cover not only a complete range of farm produce up to the marketing stage but ancillary form of occupations, such as those of rural artisans and craftsmen, who provide services to industries producing the farm products to meet the consumption needs of the farmers. It should also look after the requirements of credit, inputs and other services required by animal husbandry (including poultry farming, piggery, sheep rearing, etc), dairying, fisheries, horticulture, floriculture, farm forestry and other enterprises allied to agriculture and rural development. Financing rural development strives for timely credit to all rural activities which are related to development and growth.

### THE FIVE PRINCIPLES OF DEVELOPMENT THROUGH CREDIT

(1) Credit must be used in accordance with the most suitable methods of science and technology.

(2) The terms and conditions of the credit (or techno-economic parameters) must be fully respected.

(3) Work must be done with skill so as to increase productivity and income.

(4) A part of the additional income created by credit must be saved.

(5) Loan instalments must be repaid in time and regularly so as to recycle credit.

**FLOW OF INSTITUTIONAL CREDIT TO AGRICULTURE** *(Rs. crore)*

| *Institutions* | *1997-98* | *1998-99* | *1999-00* | *2000-01$* | *2001-02@* | *2002-03 Target* |
|---|---|---|---|---|---|---|
| Co-operative Banks | 14,085 | 15,957 | 18,363 | 20,784 | 27,080 | 35,111 |
| Percent share | 44 | 43 | 40 | 39 | 42 | 43 |
| Short-term | 10,895 | 12,571 | 14,845 | 16,564 | 21,542 | 24,711 |
| Medium/Long-term | 3,190 | 3,386 | 3,518 | 4,220 | 5,538 | 10,400 |
| Regional Rural Banks | 2,040 | 2,460 | 3,172 | 4,219 | 4,956 | 5,745 |
| Percent share | 6 | 7 | 7 | 8 | 8 | 7 |
| Short-term | 1,396 | 1,710 | 2,423 | 3,239 | 3,415 | 3,145 |
| Medium/Long-term | 644 | 750 | 749 | 980 | 1,541 | 2,600 |
| Commercial Banks | 15,831 | 18,443 | 24,733 | 27,711 | 31,964 | 41,217 |
| Percent share | 50 | 50 | 53 | 53 | 50 | 50 |
| Short-term | 8,349 | 9,622 | 11,697 | 13,480 | 16,004 | 17,073 |
| Medium/Long-term | 7,482 | 8,821 | 13,036 | 14,231 | 15,960 | 24,144 |
| Total | 31,956 | 36,860 | 46,268 | 52,714 | 64,000 | 82,073 |
| Percent increase | 21 | 15 | 26 | 14 | 21 | 28 |

$ Provisional

@ Estimated

*Source :* NABARD

Institutional credit to agriculture stood at Rs. 1,37,759.56 crore (Rs. 33,070.17 crore co-operatives, Rs.35,924.56 crore RRBs & Rs.88,764.83 crore (CBs) as on 30-11-2007.

**NUMBER OF KISAN CREDIT CARDS AND AMOUNT SANCTIONED**

| *Agency* | *1999-2000* | | *2000-2001* | | *2001-2002* | | *As on March 31, 2007* | |
|---|---|---|---|---|---|---|---|---|
| | *No. of cards issues (lakh no.)* | *Amt. sanc. (Rs.cr)* | *No. of cards issued (lakh no.)* | *Amt. sanc. (Rs.cr)* | *No. of cards issued (lakh no.)* | *Amt.sanc. (Rs.cr)* | *No. of cards issued (lakh no.)* | *Amt.sanc. (Rs.cr)* |
| Co-op Banks | 35.95 | 3606 | 56.14 | 9412 | 54.36 | 15,952 | 22.98 | 13,141 |
| RRBs | 1.73 | 405 | 6.48 | 1400 | 8.33 | 2382 | 14.06 | 7,373 |
| Comm. Banks | 13.66 | 3537 | 23.90 | 5615 | 30.71 | 7524 | 37.67 | 19,786 |
| Total | 51.34 | 7548 | 86.52 | 16427 | 93.40 | 25858 | 74.21 | 40,300 |

*Source :* NABARD

**GROSS CAPITAL FORMATION IN AGRICULTURE AT 1993-94 PRICES** *(Rs.crore)*

| *Year* | *Total* | *Public* | *Private* | *Percentage of Share Public* | *Private* | *Investment in agriculture as per cent of GDP* |
|---|---|---|---|---|---|---|
| 1993-94 | 13523 | 4467 | 9056 | 33.0 | 67.0 | 1.6 |
| 1994-95 | 14969 | 4947 | 10022 | 33.0 | 67.0 | 1.6 |
| 1995-96 | 15690 | 4849 | 10841 | 30.9 | 69.1 | 1.6 |
| 1996-97 | 16176 | 4668 | 11508 | 28.9 | 71.1 | 1.5 |
| 1997-98 | 15942 | 3979 | 11963 | 25.0 | 75.0 | 1.4 |
| 1998-99 | 14895 | 3870 | 11025 | 26.0 | 74.0 | 1.3 |
| 1999-00 | 17304 | 4222 | 13082 | 24.4 | 75.6 | 1.4 |
| 2000-01 | 16687 | 3919 | 12768 | 23.5 | 76.5 | 1.3 |
| 2001-02* | 18057 | 4794 | 13263 | 26.5 | 13.5 | 1.3 |

* Quick estimates

*Source :* Central Statistical Organisation

*"The formal Rural Financial System (RFS) in India comprises National Bank for Agriculture and Rural Development (NABARD), Small Industries Development Bank of India (SIDBI), Commercial Banks (CBs), Regional Rural Banks (RRBs) and the Co-operative Banks (COBs). In the recent past, private non-banking finance companies are also found to be active in the rural areas albeit in a small measure. The co-operative banks include the short-term (ST) co-operative credit structure and the long-term (LT) co-operative credit structure.*

*The ST co-operative credit structure has three tiers, i.e., State Co-operative Banks (SCBs) at the state level, District Central Co-operative Banks (DCCBs) at the district level and the Primary Agricultural Credit Societies (PACS) at the village level. The ST co-operative credit structure provides mainly loans for crop production, marketing of crops, purchase and distribution of inputs, etc. the currency of these loans is one year.*

*The LT co-operative credit structure is federal in 12 states and unitary in eight states and the loans are provided for investment purposes with a loan maturity varying from 3 to 15 years. The co-operative credit structure functions on democratic principles.*

# Chapter 25

# CREDIT NEEDS OF THE RURAL POOR

## Introduction

The promotion of agriculture and other allied economic activities through credit intervention for ensuring integrated rural development and securing the prosperity of the rural areas is a central objective of India's development planning. In pursuance of this, formal credit institutions have been guided by the principle of growth with equity and a large share of the credit disbursed for various activities was channelised towards the weaker sections of the society. With the aid of the several poverty alleviation programmes, the number of people below the poverty line has increased from 272.7 million in 1984-85 to 370.20 million in 2000-03, which still constitutes over 37 per cent of the population. The number of operational holdings is expected to have crossed the 100 million mark with more than 80 per cent being small and marginal holdings.

By the turn of the century, the number of cultivator households and other rural households will have steadily grown. The institutional credit system will need to meet the challenge of delivering credit to an ever increasing number of rural people who will need greater access to formal credit. It may have to reinforce its own structure at the grass-roots. It may also have to devise new ways of reaching out to the rural poor.

## EVOLUTION OF THE RURAL CREDIT SYSTEM IN INDIA

Rural financial market development is a complex process. The creation of the formal credit structure for financing agriculture and other rural activities commenced in India in the early part of this century with the introduction of co-operatives. It received a big push during the plan era. The All India Rural Credit Survey Committee (AIRCS) 1954, forms the edifice for the policy towards the development of the institutional credit structure. The committee highlighted the awful inadequacy in the supply of institutional credit to the rural sector and proposed an integrated scheme of re-organisation many more committees and recommendations. Priority sector lending, lead bank scheme, services area approach, setting up of NABARD, are some of the outcomes of the repeated scrutiny of the system.

Coming to the recent committees, the Agriculture Credit Review Committee (ACRC) 1989, examined the existing rural credit system in detail. It highlighted the yawning gap between income generated and costs incurred by rural credit institutions, necessitating external assistance. The committee recommended greater autonomy for commercial banks; the weakness of RRBs were seen as endemic to the system with non-viability built into them. Co-operatives were sought to be strengthened through thrust on deposit mobilisation and reduction of political interference. The Narsimham Committee on Financial Sector Reforms 1991, among other things, recommended a redefinition of priority sector, gradual phasing out of directed credit programmes to 10% of aggregate bank credit and deregulation of interest rates.

Looking at the situation today, the exercises seem to have resulted in a scenario where "an imposing superstructure of credit institutions has been built which one Committee after another has kept reshuffling or adding to." (Dandekar, 1993). Commenting broadly on the exercise in developing countries (to which the Indian experience seems to be no exception), Braveman & Guasch, 1986, see most of the changes in institutional design as largely superficial, window dressing type rather than substantial. "The institutions have been perceived more like a welfare agency than a commercial undertaking. There seems to be little effort to integrate deposit taking activities or to generate saving mobilisation—a vital activity for the long run success of a credit institution. No provisions were made to deal with non-compliance, or to implement a reasonable system of incentives to both lenders and borrowers to induce the desired objectives."

The major problems of the rural credit system thus evolved are as follows:

(1) It has not produced desired results in terms of the direction, quantum, and quality of the flow of credit.

(2) It is afflicted by alarmingly high overdues, bad debts, loan defaults, unviability, low profitability, overburdening of staff, declining control and deteriorating customer services. It is estimated that the overdues of credit institutions have increased from Rs 2,818 crores to Rs 9,661 crores during 1983-93.

(3) The complex tiering of funds through RBI-NABARD-Commercial banks-State Co-operative Banks (SCBs)-District Co-operative Banks (DCBs)-Primary Agricultural Credit Societies (PACS), has tended to unduly increase the cost of banking.

(4) Features of rural credit markets in developing countries may be understood as responses to the problems of adverse selection, moral hazard, and enforcement (Karla Hoff & J.E. Stiglitz, 1990). Imperfect information in this sense creates problems from the perspective of constrained Pareto efficiency. In the Indian case too, information imperfections have contributed to inefficiencies like high transaction costs and low recycling of credit.

(5) From the institutional perspective, role of an appropriate institution as an enforcer and transmitter of incentives and motivator and inducer of saving is essential for development. The institutional design should serve to promote and facilitate functioning at the levels of both the lenders and the borrowers. This factor seems to have been largely overlooked in the Indian case. Motivating to perform has not been given due importance.

(6) Directed credit programmes and subsidized lending have badly affected viable functioning of credit disbursing units. The entire exercise has largely comë to be characterized by tiering of funds from above to borrowers who often tale as a gift that need not be returned.

## NATIONALISATION OF BANKS

A major objective of the nationalisation of commercial banks (CBs) in 1969 was to improve the access of the rural households, particularly the rural poor, to institutional credit and to reduce their dependence on informal sources of credit. To ensure that the relatively weaker sections have access to credit, the Reserve Bank of India (RBI) stipulated that at least 40 per cent of the advances of the CBs should be earmarked for the priority sectors as defined by it (18 per cent as "direct" loans for agriculture and 10 per cent as advances to weaker sections). A multi-agency approach for rural credit delivery was also adopted involving CBs co-operative banks and regional rural banks (RRBs). The RRBs were, by deliberate policy, to confine their lending to the target groups of weaker sections. A vigorous rural branch expansion programme was also launched to increase the rural credit delivery outlets for facilitating easy access to credit.

A number of special programmes aimed at meeting the credit needs of the small and marginal farmers and agricultural labourers were launched and implemented through agencies, such as Small Farmers Development Agency (SFDA) and Marginal Farmers and Agricultural Labourers (MFAL). The experience of the implementation of these programmes led to the introduction of the Integrated Rural (IRDP) with the specific objective of raising the poor rural families above the poverty line, Credit support from banks was considered as an important input in taking up economic and gainful activities by such families.

Notwithstanding these impressive achievements in the expansion of the credit delivery system and the special programmes, nearly half the indebted rural households are still outside the ambit of the institutional credit system. They approach the moneylenders for meeting their consumption and production needs in the absence of institutional support. Some of the poor who have not been reached, even by the vast network of the institutional credit delivery system have, however, organised themselves into self help groups (SHGs) and many such groups have come into existence either spontaneously or with the active involvement of the Voluntary Agencies (VAs) which motivated the rural poor to pool their meagre financial resources for meeting their small and frequent consumption and production credit needs. The role which VAs can play in poverty alleviation was recognised by the Planning Commission which highlighted in the Seventh Plan document the need for associating the VAs in such programmes.

This chapter reviews some of the experiences of the past two decades and discusses the need to bring about the linkages between the formal credit structure and SHGs to the mutual advantage of both, Such linkages can improve the access of the poor to formal credit and can also provide an effective instrument of credit delivery to be used by the formal credit agencies. The Chapter also delineates the steps to be taken for overcoming the inherent limitations of the formal credit structure in servicing a large number of very small borrowers and examines the constraints in adopting an innovative approach with respect to SHGs, the likely pitfalls on the way and suggests solutions and precautionary measures.

### Rural Poverty and Credit in Perspective

The extent of poverty generally depends upon the extent of ownership of productive assets and the access to gainful employment opportunities. It is well established that due to the lack of such productive assets and regular employment, the burden of unemployment/underemployment and poverty falls mainly on the rural poor. There is a clear inverse relationship between the assets held by the households and the incidence of poverty and the consequent need to incur debt for meeting household expenditure. (All India Debt and Investment Survey, 1981-82.) The question that arises is how do the poor who, by definition, lack adequate purchasing power, make both ends meet and survive? Generally, the gap between current income as consumption is usually bridged through occasional hand loans from relatives and friends. In some cases, the rural poor are even compelled to borrow on extremely exploitative terms making them bonded labourers to the creditors.

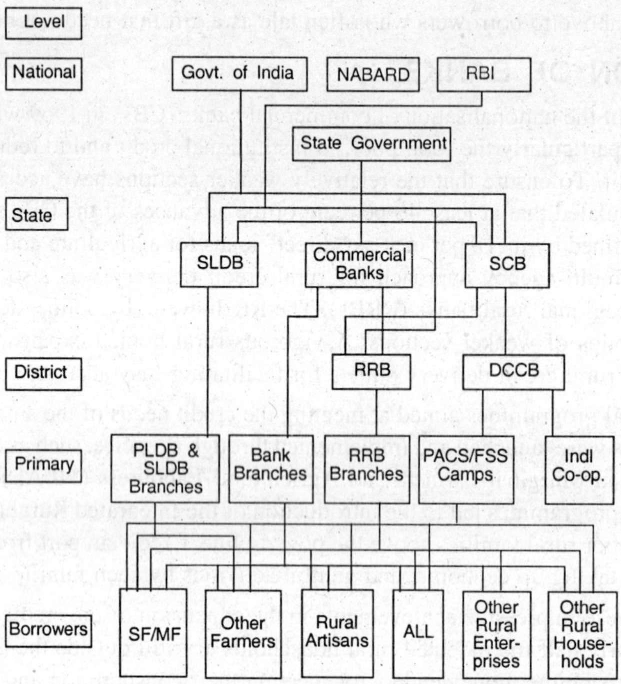


*Fig. 1. Multi Agency approach for Rural Finance*

The dependence of the rural poor on the informal sources of credit for meeting their production/ consumption needs on exploitative terms is one of the cause that perpetuates poverty. Such dependence restricts their power to generate surplus from their small economic enterprises as also their potential to participate effectively in the production process. The links that the poor establish with the suppliers of credit are often used to siphon off the meagre surplus generated by the poor (see Box 1). Where the poor are concerned, credit has been an important element in linking the factor and commodity markets, especially in the rural areas.

## Credit Institutions and the Rural Poor

The rural credit structure in India has completed 95 years and is unparalleled in the world. It serves around 120 million rural households in about seven lakh villages through its 92,000 primary agricultural credit societies, 11,426 branches of short-term cooperatives, 2,213 branches of commercial banks and 11,426 branches of regional rural banks. After Independence, the rural credit system has disbursed credit for farm development.

The massive branch expansion of banks coupled with policy initiatives taken by the government to provide to the rural poor easy access to institutional credit had brought about perceptible improvements. However, the dependence of the cultivator-borrowers on informal sources of credit for household expenditure between 1971 and 1981 fell more sharply than of the non-cultivator borrowers who largely constituted the rural poor. The poor household need to contract debt for household expenditure stands in sharp contrasts with the cultivator households. Further, 63 per cent of the non-cultivator borrowers continued to depend on informal sources of credit in 1981.

**Box 1**

**BANKER FILLING THE ROLE OF MONEYLENDER**

In most of the tribal areas borrowing for consumption purpose against the pledge of standing crops is a common practice. Such borrowing is particularly heavy when it is undertaken for celebrating festivals or discharging religious responsibilities after the death of a family member. The trader-money lender who advances the loan usually charges very high interest rates, sometimes even beyond 100 per cent on an annualised basis. Usually, the interest charged is not explicit but is implicitly contained in the difference between the market price of the produce and the sale price to the trader-moneylender. This system, called by various names, such as, "palemode" in the tribal parts of Thane district is one of the mechanisms by which the surplus generating capacity of the poor tribals gets eroded. A reduction in poverty among tribals will be achieved even if such usurious activities are eliminated.

The Gram-Vikas Development Society (GDS) operating an the Kalahandi district of Orissa has attempted an intervention in precisely such a situation. The GDS finance villages committees to step into the shoes of the moneylender-trader. The village committees and the GDS together finance the consumption needs of the farmers against the pledge of the farmers' produce and also undertake trading of the produce after harvesting. The interest rates charged by the banks. The GDS makes a profit in the trading activity by selling produce in the competitive market. The profit made is distributed back to the village committee and the members. Since the trade is handled by the Village Committees and the GDS, the full recovery of the previous consumption loans is ensured. Interestingly, the GDS generates part of the finance for this activity by drawing trade credit at commercial interest rates from the banks operating in that area.

As observed earlier, a number of programmes aiming at poverty alleviation were introduced culminating in the launching of the credit linked IRDP from 2nd October 1980. Inspite of the massive financial assistance of credit and subsidy provided under this programme, the achievements in the form of households crossing the poverty line income level have not met the expectations. According to the Concurrent Evaluation Study Report of the Government of India (GOI) 1990, for the survey period January 1989 to December 1989, about 67 per cent of the families assisted had crossed the earlier poverty line income level of Rs 3,500 and only 16 per cent of the families had crossed the poverty line income level of Rs 6,400.

## Rural Banking Set-up

The spectrum of rural financial institutions broadly consists of commercial banks, RRBs and co-operative societies. The commercial banks and RRBs are playing a catalytic role in rural India through their 32,856-branch network and numerically 93,314 primary agricultural credit societies continued to occupy a predominant position in the co-operative credit structure, Out of the total number of societies, 89,727 were active covering 6,10,088 villages and serving 94 million members.

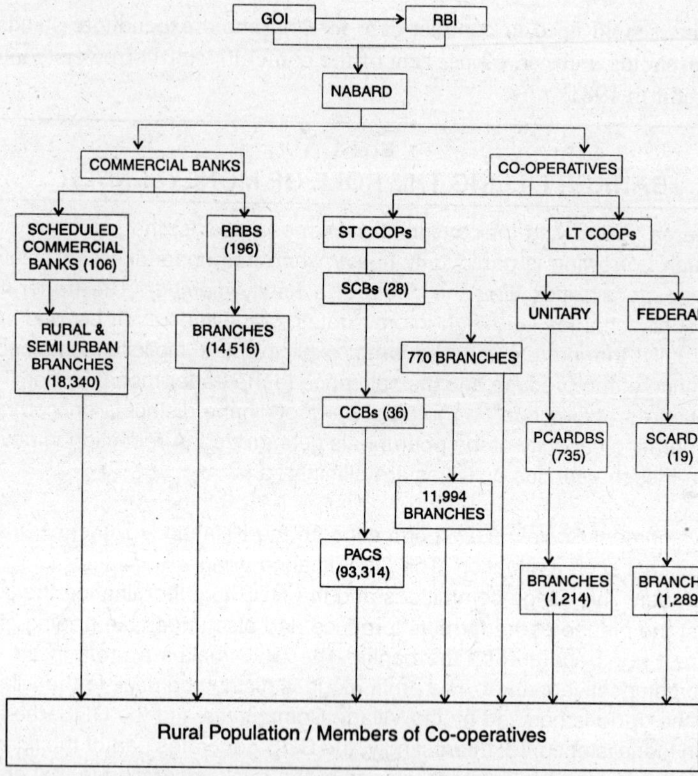


*Fig. 2. Rural Financial Institutions in Operation*

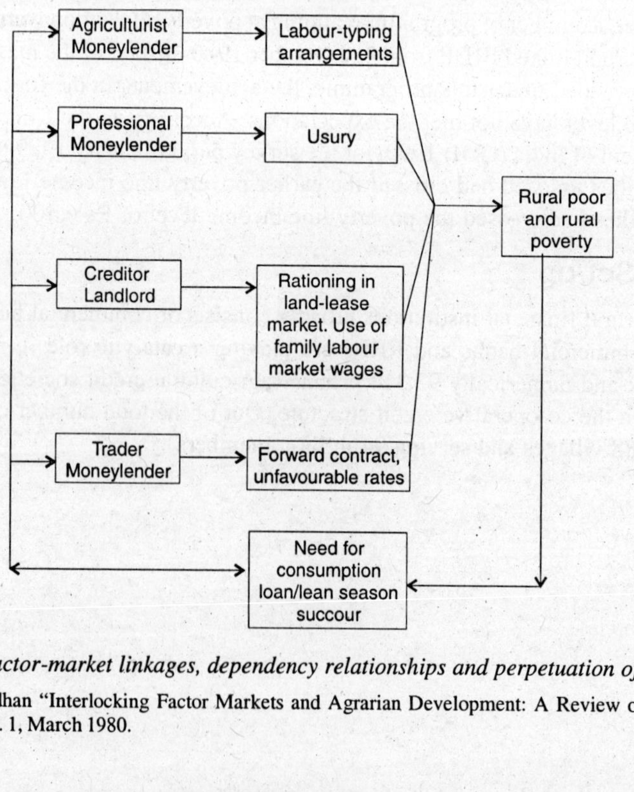


*Fig. 3. Factor-market linkages, dependency relationships and perpetuation of poverty*

*Source:* Adapted from Bardhan "Interlocking Factor Markets and Agrarian Development: A Review of Issues," Oxford Economic Papers, Vol. 32, No. 1, March 1980.

In the multi-agency system, while in theory the three sets of institutions are expected to supplement the efforts of one another, in actual practice, is inevitable.

When there is a level playing field in the matter of interest rate policy, cross-subsidisation and depoliticisation, the competitive strength of each of the institutions would depend upon their ability to raise resources at reasonable volumes of business, and to attract farmers with high-value business proposals.

The experience so far indicates that commercial banks with their 'one window' approach ability to attract deposits, and to cross-subsidise weaker section loans, availability of expertise etc., have been in a comparatively better position to meet the rural credit needs. This is not to say that they experience no problems, their Achilles' heel being their staff attitudes.

One reason which contributed to this result was the manner in which the beneficiaries were identified. The IRDP was on out-growth of the experiences under the SFDA/MFAL Schemes which were launched with the idea of identifying the problems of "potentially viable" small and marginal farmers, helping them to undertake appropriate productive activities and supporting them with the needed inputs, service and credit. It was envisaged that assistance would be provided to each of the identified families for package of activities so as to enable each family to cross the poverty line once and for all. While such quantum jumps over the poverty line would be possible in the case of "potentially viable poor families a large number of poor families may not be prepared by way of skills, attitudes and enterprise to manage activities currently undertaken by them. Considerably more effort than ascertaining the income levels is therefore, involved in identifying the beneficiaries."

**Box 2**

**DAPS AND MOU**

**DAPs aim to sensitise the co-operative banks for providing commercial orientation to their business planning, to the concepts of:**

Cost effectiveness,
Recycling of funds,
Professionalisation,
Accountability and
Viability

The institution specific DAPs which are based on SWOT analysis cover financial aspects as also organisational and HRD aspects, systems and procedures etc., having a bearing on their viability.

MoU which are intended to facilitate effective implementation of DAPs spell out the performance obligations under various financial parameters and package of measures to be taken by the banks and the concerned state governments. These measures include:

Democratization and functional autonomy through amendment/adoption of state legislation on the lines of model act as recommended by Chaudhary Brahm Perkash Committee;

Professionalisation in management, particularly at the top executive level;

Human resource management and development;

Minimising state control and interference particularly in lending and recovery; and

Revamping the system of audit to ensure timely and qualitative audit by professionally qualified persons.

To supplement the efforts of the co-operative banks in implementation of their DAPs, the National Bank provides assistance out of its Co-operative Development Fund (CDF) for various purpose such as infrastructure development for deposit mobilisation and recovery efforts, studies in important areas like HRD and MIS, appointment of financial analysts, etc. and renders professional advice for improving their recovery performance, operations and profitability.

The National Bank Study of 1985 observed that the banks found it difficult to associate their staff in the identification of the beneficiaries because of the acute shortage of field staff in all the rural branches. The study recommended that the role of the banks needed to be improved upon with due emphasis on their close involvement in the process of identification, follow-up and supervision of the end-use of credit. The augmentation of the field staff of the rural branches of banks was considered to be one the solutions to ensure proper planning and implementation. While this seems to be a desirable course to follow, the banks have not shown much enthusiasm to pursue it, largely because of the significantly higher costs involved. In the long run, it may be worth their while to meet such additional costs in the interest of fostering a better system of delivering credit to the poor. Even now wherever it is feasible, the banks should be encouraged to augment the staff.

However, in a large segment of the banking sector, insufficient manpower will continue to inhibit a larger role for the banks in meeting the credit needs of the rural poor. The Agricultural Credit Review Committee (ACRS), 1989, appointed by the RBI noted, "the bulk of the lending, much more than the stipulated norm of 40 per cent of the total lending in the rural branches of the CBs is to priority sector and consists of a large number of small advances. the borrowers of these branches are located in far-flung areas and commuting facilities for reaching such borrowers are very often non-existent. Obviously, the sanctioning and monitoring of advances to clients of this nature is time-consuming and requires disproportinately more manpower than what is necessary in urban centres, a single officer can supervise at the most up to 750 accounts. Even this norm is on the high side, if the borrowers are scattered over a wider area. Many of the rural branches were inadequately staffed. As many as 1,700 accounts had to be managed by a single field officer in many branches. In view of the large number of accounts to be covered by field officers, supervisory work in many branches came to be neglected. The staff gave priority to the routine housekeeping work including the submission of returns. Due to their reduced profitability, the controlling offices tried to economise the costs in the rural branches in several ways and cutting down on the staff strength was frequently resorted to." The phenomenon of handling a large number of small accounts gives rise to high transaction costs in dispensing credit. This, obviously, puts considerable pressure on the small margins available to the banks and tend to make such financing unviable.

When a large number of small accounts are to be handled by the limited field staff, the quality of lending and supervision of credit are generally the first casualty. This handicaps the banker in faithfully following the credit cycle starting with the assessment of needs, appraisal, disbursement and monitoring including ensuring the end-use of credit and recovery.

**Box 3**

**RESTRUCTURING OF REGIONAL RURAL BANKS**

RRBs were established as a new set of state sponsored, rural-oriented region based low cost banks having the ethos of co-operative and business acumen of commercial banks for providing credit in the rural areas, particularly to the relatively weaker section of the society. Though the RRBs succeeded in spreading banking services to far-flung rural areas, mobilizing rural saving, opening up more avenues for rural poor through institutional credit and generating employment opportunities, the mandate of financing only the target group borrowers coupled with administered interest rate structure, poor recovery performance, increasing establishment costs, low level of operational efficiency, etc., resulted in RRBs incurring losses right from their inception.

With a view to enabling the RRBs to achieve current and sustainable viability, several policy measures were initiated including revamping or RRBs by infusion of capital. The concept of DAPs was initiated by the National Bank and the RRBs and sponsor banks signed the MoU for ensuring performance obligations/ commitments.

The experience of other developing countries underscores one other important fact of financing the rural poor in India. The report of the study of "Linking Self-Help Groups and Banks in Developing Countries" commissioned by the Asian and Pacific Regional Agricultural Credit Association (APRACA) and Gesellschaftfur Technische Zusammenarbeit (GTZ), West Germany, 1989 pointed out that low interest rates set below the market rates and the cost of funds inhibited the banks from covering a large number of the poor and that the lending portfolio remained limited as local resources were not mobilised and the programme depended mainly on outside funds. It also highlighted the fact that the credit programmes with international debt, shortage of internal resources and growing dissatisfaction with state-nurtured and seemingly not so effective credit-linked programmes have led to a rethinking on development policies, both at the international and national levels, centering on such concepts as self-reliance, self-sufficiency and self-help.

## Agriculture Insurance Corporation

Budget 2002-03 proposed setting up of a separate Corporation for Agriculture Insurance to be promoted by the existing public sector general insurance companies. A Task Force was constituted to oversee the setting up of the Agriculture Insurance Corporation. It was decided by the Task Force that the new company will be named as "Agriculture Insurance Company of India Ltd" and will be registered under the Companies Act, 1956 with the capital participation from General Insurance Corporation of India (GIC), four public sector general insurance companies *viz. (i)* National Insurance Co. Ltd., *(ii)* New India Assurance Co. Ltd., *(iii)* Oriental Insurance Co. Ltd. and *(iv)* United India Insurance Co. Ltd. and NABARD. The promoters' subscription to the paid-up capital will be: 35 per cent by GIC, 30 per cent by NABARD and 8.75 per cent each by the four public sector general insurance companies. The authorised capital of the new organisation will be Rs. 1500 crore, while the initial paid-up capital will be Rs. 200 crore. NAIS shall be transferred to the new organisation and shall form the core of business to begin with. Transition to actuarial regime will be made over a period of time. The new organisation will, in due course, cover other allied rural/agricultural risks in addition to crop insurance.

The Registrar of Companies (Delhi & Haryana) has approved the name of the new company as "Agriculture Insurance Company of India Ltd." The new company has since been incorporated under the Companies Act. 1956 on 20.12.2002. It has yet to obtain registration from Insurance Regulatory and Development Authority under Insurance Act, 1938.

## The Prospect

Despite the implementation of target-oriented programmes like the IRDP and the opening of a large number of retail credit outlets, a substantial number of the rural poor do not have access to assistance from the formal credit institutions. This arises because of the risks and credit worthiness of the borrowers as perceived by the banks, limitations imposed by the legal framework on their operations and above all, in their inability to deal efficiently and economically with a large number of small borrowers. By the turn of the century the problems of numbers will surely overwhelm the banks and alternative solutions will have to be found. The self-help groups will be a good alternative to explore and support.

In the new liberalised policy with phasing out of concessionality of interest rates, the co-operative sector's viability would significantly improve, When viability improves and deposits with PACS get the insurance cover from the DICGC, they will be able to attract more deposits. With larger local resources at their command PACS, dependence on loan resources from the NABARD would go down and their operations can significantly expand. Improved viability and capacity to pay for better qualified staff, would improve the quality of lending.

Competition from commercial banks would tend to put pressures on the cooperative societies to improve their functioning. Side by side with liberalisation, therefore, Khusro Committee's recommendations on training and manpower planning in the co-operative credit sector would need to be implemented, so that the competitive position of the co-operatives would improve and in the process, the entire rural credit structure will get toned up.

A thorny problem of rural credit in India is one of financing small and marginal farmers. So far, mandatory provision ensured credit supply to them. The Narasimham Committee, no doubt, would like the mandatory provisions to be in place so far as credit needs of weaker sections are concerned, covering entirely the small and marginal farmers. But if the mandatory stipulations are lifted, with their credit needs be looked after by banks considering their poor viability and the high risks? Banks will tend to finance the sounder and more viable proposals from amongst those emanating from this sector, but what about the rest?

The crux of the matter is to improve the viability of these production units, say, by securing for them inputs, marketing and processing facilities, extension services etc. They should be encouraged to move into more remunerative occupations from cultivation, (or in addition to it) such as horticulture, dairying, poultry, sericulture etc. If there is organisational support to provide backward and forward linkages for these activities, their viability would be improved, banks would find it easier to finance these tiny business, as their risks would be reduced. Credit is necessary for viable business but experience of the banks in recent years shows that credit cannot make non-viable business units viable. Organisational support, which can improve backward and forward linkages of such small businesses can improve their viability and credit worthiness. Proposal of the Government of India to promote "small farmers' agri-business consortium" would go a long way to improve the viability of small business. Rather than compelling banks to grant loans to weaker sections, Government. should strengthen the economic strength of the weaker sections. Once these become viable, they will automatically become credit-worthy.

**Box 4**

**SMALL LOANS BIG IMPACT**

***More than 40,000 women in Nepal have found that small loans can build businesses — and elevate their status within their families***

Seven years ago, 42-year-old Junumaya Gautam was down and out. Her husband had died; she had three small children—and no income. That same year, a landslide had swept away her hillside house in Kavre District, Nepal. With nothing left in Kavre, Ms. Gautam moved to Kathmandu to work as a housemaid. Her sister introduced her to a non-government organisation (NGO), Creative Women Development Association, that helped her get a small loan from the Microcredit Project for Women, supported by ADB.
She has not looked back since.

With the $60 loan she received from the project, Ms. Gautam bought vegetables from wholesalers on the outskirts of Kathmandu to sell in the city. She made a small profit and used this to pay off the loan. She then borrowed $260, and later $450 from the project to run two businesses. In the mornings, Ms. Gautam sold vegetables; in the afternoons, she sold peanuts at bus stops. She not only paid off her loans on time, but also managed to send her children to school, buy a small piece of land, and build a modest house in Kathmandu. She is currently renovating her house and replacing the temporary roof with a concrete casting.

**Expanding Business**

In addition to her two businesses, Ms. Gautam now owns a tea stall, which is managed by a business partner. She also lent some money to her partner so she could also start a business. "The Project helped me when I was poor," she says. "Now that I can afford it, I want to help other poor and needy people like me."

The project, completed in 2002, has benefited thousands of women. Santa Kumari Gurung, of Chitwan, is another example. Her unemployed husband used to while away his time drinking alcohol and playing cards. They had no property and no source of income. She borrowed money from the project through the Pragati Women's Savings and Credit Cooperatives to buy livestock and rent land for vegetable farming. Now both husband and wife work on the farm and make a good income. Ms. Gurung is happy that the project provided the money to start her business, and provide employment for her husband. "I am very grateful to the project for giving me the loan," she says. "I am happy that my husband is working now and not wasting his time."

Though the individual loans may seem small, they have had a big impact on the lives of the poor who would otherwise have no access to capital.

By increasing women's access to funds, the project has also helped enhance the role of women within the family. Women have used loans to open shops and provide work for their otherwise unemployed relatives. Some women have even bought rickshaws for their husbands.

*Source:* ADB Review May-June 2003

## Community Development Society (CDS) Alappuzha, Kerala — A Micro Credit Breakthrough

Poor women in Alappuzha and Malappuram districts of Kerala have demonstrated that by pooling together their resources they can prove to be better credit managers, if proper environment is created by the supporting system including the Government.

Two programmes know as the 'Urban Basic Services for the Poor' (UBSP) and 'Community Based Nutrition Program' (CBNP) were launched by the State and Central Governments with UNICEF assistance. The programmes aimed at providing basic food and hygienic needs of the poor with focus on women and children. The poor women were identified by the community through a survey using an independent set of indicators on poverty. One women each from every family so identified become a member of Neighbourhood Group (NHG) of 15-30 members. Each NHG had a five-member committee. The NGHs were federated into ward level Area Development Societies (ADS) and further into Panchayat or town level Community Development Societies (CDS). The entire CDS structure comprised only poor women. Over 1,60,000 poor women are today the members of the NHGs in Alappuzha and Malappuram districts.

The National Bank developed a simple effective accounting system and facilitated training programmes to train women volunteers in 'group management'. The Bank also provided through banking system appropriate financial support to take up a wide range of income generating activities. The repayments from the members to NHGs are 100 per cent.

### Box 5
### CREDIT FLOW TO AGRICULTURE

Agriculture credit, by promoting agricultural and related business, plays an important role in poverty alleviation and creation of employment. Keeping this in view, the Tenth Five Year Plan envisaged a substantial increase in credit flow to agriculture to Rs. 7,36,570 crore as compared with that of Rs.2,29,956 crore achieved during the Ninth Plan period. On June 18, 2004, the Government announced a comprehensive policy envisaging the doubling of credit to agriculture in the next three years through commercial banks, co-operative banks and RRBs. During 2004-05, with an aggregate disbursement of Rs.1,15,243 crore, the targetted credit was exceeded by 10 per cent (Table). Continuing on the same path, the Union Budget 2005-06 proposed to increase the flow of credit by another 30 per cent by commercial banks, RRBs and co-operative banks. Further, the public sector banks were advised to increase the number of borrowers by another 50 lakhs.

Major developments relating to agricultural credit in the recent years included, *inter alia*, (a) periodic review and enhancement of credit delivery to agriculture; (b) exclusive focus on the development of rural infrastructure in view of its implications for long-term sustainable agricultural growth; and (c) innovative ways of providing access to institutional finance to the rural poor by promoting micro-finance and other initiatives.

The Reserve Bank has advised public sector banks to prepare Special Agricultural Credit Plans (SACPs) on an annual basis. For the financial year 2004-05, disbursements to agriculture under the plan aggregated Rs.65,218 crore as against the projection of Rs.55,616 crore. As recommended by the Advisory Committee on Flow of Credit to Agriculture and Related Activities from the Banking System (Chairman: Prof. V.S. Vyas) and announced in the Mid-Term Review of Annual Policy Statement for 2004-05, the SACP mechanism has been made applicable to private sector banks from 2005-06. Banks were advised to fix the SACP target for 2005-06 indicating a growth rate of 30 per cent over disbursements during 2004-05. Public sector banks were also advised to make efforts to increase their disbursements to small and marginal farmers to 40 per cent of their direct advances under SACP by March 2007. Banks were allowed to waive margin/security requirements for agricultural loans up to Rs.50,000 and in the case of agri-business and agri-clinics for loans up to Rs.5 lakh. Interest rates on the Rural Infrastructure Development Fund (RIDF) were revised downwards in alignment with the softening of the interest rate structure over the years. It was decided to continue with the National Agricultural Insurance Scheme (NAIS), introduced in *rabi* season 1999-2000, in its present form for *kharif* and *rabi* seasons 2005-06.

Two innovations, *viz*., Micro-finance and the *Kisan* Credit Card (KCC) Scheme have emerged as the major policy tools in addressing the problems associated with the distributional aspects of rural credit in recent years. The growing popularity of the KCC scheme reflects its effectiveness in ensuring the timeliness, hassle-free operations as also availability of credit with minimum transaction cost and documentation. During 2004-05, public sector banks issued 43,95,564 KCCs. Cumulatively, the number of KCCs issued by public sector banks increased to 1,83,55,173 till June 2005.

With a view to further increasing the flow of credit to agriculture, several measures were announced by the Reserve Bank in its Annual Policy Statement for 2005-06. These include: (i) setting up of an Expert Group (Chairman: Shri Y.S.P. Thorat) to formulate strategy for increasing investment in agriculture (see Book II.1); (ii) conducting a survey with the help of an outside agency to make an assessment of customer satisfaction on credit delivery in rural areas by banks; and (iii) to increase the limit on loans to farmers through the produce marketing scheme from Rs.5 lakh to Rs.10 lakh under priority sector lending.

Rural credit has emerged as an important growth opportunity. Several new areas such as agri-clinics, contract farming and rural housing are fast becoming viable revenue propositions for banks. Although rural credit witnessed higher growth during the year, there is still need to further enhance credit to the new emerging areas of economic activity in rural areas. In order to enhance the flow of credit to these emerging areas, the Reserve Bank has been undertaking measures to remove the impediments on timely availability of credit through various means. First, the coverage of rural credit has been extended to include facilities such as storage as well as credit through NBFCs. Second, procedural and transactional bottlenecks are sought to be removed by reducing margins, redefining overdues to coincide with crop-cycles, new debt restructuring policies, one-time settlement and relief measures for farmers indebted to non-institutional lenders. Third, public and private sector banks are being encouraged to enhance credit-delivery in rural areas. Finally, banks are urged to price the credit to farmers based on actual assessment of individual risk rather than on a flat rate, depending on the category of borrower or end-use while ensuring that interest rates charged are justifiable as well as reasonable. As productivity and incomes increase in rural areas, banks will need to serve the credit needs of the full supply chain activities as they emerge, along with those of other service and manufacturing activities. Banks will also need to devise appropriate risk assessment and management strategies and develop technical capabilities to serve the emerging needs.

Micro-finance institutions (MFIs) now provide several non-credit services such as capacity building, training, marketing of the products of the SHGs and micro insurance. The focus of discussion is expanding beyong the narrow domain of micro-credit to encompass micro-finance. This underscores the need for a clearer policy framework to cover the non-credit financial services by MFIs as well as the need to evolve a differentiated legal framework as per the organisational form. Micro-finance process would also need to iron out several operational issues as well as putting in place co-ordinating mechanisms amongst the various regulatory agencies. The policy environment has been fine-turned such that the micro credit extended by banks is presently reckoned as part of their priority sector lending. Banks have been provided the freedom to devise appropriate loan and savings products in this regard. Use of intermediaries or franchise agents could emerge as a mechanism to reduce transaction costs. The thrust is on enhancing credit delivery within the existing legal and institutional framework.

**Table 1**

**FLOW OF INSTITUTIONAL CREDIT TO AGRICULTURE** *(Rs. crore)*

| *Agency/Years (Estimated)* | *1997-98* | *1999-2000* | *2002-03* | *2003-04* | *2004-05* |
|---|---|---|---|---|---|
| Co-operative Banks | 14,085 | 18,363 | 24,296 | 26,959 | 30,638 |
| RRBs | 2,040 | 3,172 | 5,467 | 7,581 | 11,718 |
| Commercial Banks | 15,831 | 24,733 | 41,047 | 52,441 | 72,886 |
| **Total** | **31,956** | **46,268** | **70,810** | **86,981** | **1,15,243** |

*Source:* NABARD.

## Conclusion

Liberalisation will improve the business environment of rural credit institutions but each of the institutions will have to tone up its organisation set-up and operational efficiency, to take the fullest advantage of the new policy environment. In the case of public sector banks, initiatives may have to come from government, though one sees no reason why individual, public sector banks cannot be given the freedom to decide the course of action, within certain parameters. For private banks and co-operatives, however, initiative for reform will have to come from within the institutions themselves. Liberalisation will lead to organisation strengthening, if there is a genuine effort on the part of the institutions themselves, to tone up their own functioning. Regulatory bodies should facilitate and directly encourage such internal efforts in the public sector and co-operative organisations, so that these can reap the full benefits of the atmosphere of liberalisation and improve their contribution to the rural economy.

❑ ❑ ❑

Chapter 26

# THE NATIONAL BANK FOR AGRICULTURE AND RURAL DEVELOPMENT

## Introduction

The National Bank for Agriculture and Rural Development (NABARD), is an apex development bank for promotion and development of agriculture, small scale industries, cottage and village industries, handicrafts and agricultural credit/other allied activities in rural areas.

As an apex level development financial institution committed to rural prosperity, NABARD has been a key player in the country's rural economy. It provides refinance to banks and loans to the State Governments, takes development and promotional initiatives to improve the impact of credit on rural development and attempts to bring about equity and justice in such development. It also supervises the operations of rural financial institutions like co-operative banks and the regional rural banks.

In the field of agricultural credit, the emphasis has been to ensure an adequate flow of credit to the weaker sections of the community. Special assistance has been provided to co-operatively backward states in order to reduce regional imbalances. Following the enactment of debt relief legislation in the states, the co-operative credit institutions have been reorganised and strengthened to bridge the credit gap by providing consumption credit to the weaker sections of the community. A recent review by the Department of Co-operative Development shows that considerable progress has been made by co-operative credit institutions in the matter of the reorganisation of primary agricultural credit societies and of Farmers' Service Societies and large sized multi-purpose societies, the appointment of full-time paid secretaries, deposit mobilisation and universalisation of membership.

Special emphasis continues to be laid on institutional credit for the weaker sections. The loaning procedure and policies of credit institutions have been under continual review during the last few years in order to make agricultural credit production-oriented rather than security-oriented and also to assist the weaker sections of the farming community to obtain credit with greater facility. The liberalisation of share capital requirements, loans without insistence on mortgage security, lower margin and a longer repayment schedule which were introduced in the Fourth Plan period – these are some of the facilities which have been continued during the Sixth Plan.

A significant experiment was launched during the Fifth Plan by organising Farmers' Service Societies in pursuance of the recommendations of the National Commission on Agriculture. The societies provide integrated credit, supplies and services. While the membership of the society is open to all the cultivators within its jurisdiction, the control over the management is vested in the weaker sections, who have two-thirds of the seats on the board of management.

Institutional credit for the secondary and tertiary sectors had assumed great importance since the IRD programme covers these sectors too, and the KVIC implements several schemes in this field. While one of the reason for the inadequate flow of credit to these sectors was the lack of availability of refinance from ARDC, the situation has changed with the setting up of the National Bank for Agriculture and Rural Development (NABARD).

## THE NATIONAL BANK FOR AGRICULTURE AND RURAL DEVELOPMENT (NABARD)

The establishment of the National Bank for Agriculture and Rural Development (NABARD) on 12 July 1982 is a milestone in the history of banking in India, for it has accelerated the process of development of agriculture, rural industries and allied activities and, more particularly rural development. Inaugurating the Bank, the Prime Minister declared: "It would be a dynamic service institution for rural development and the people should regard it as a friend and a guide." The NABARD aroused a new awakening and doubts among those who are interested in rural development.

### Historical Perspective

The evolution of rural development and institutional support indicates that the constitution of NABARD as an apex body was first visualised by the National Commission on Agriculture in 1976. Various earlier committees had rejected the idea of a separate national apex bank for agriculture. It may be recalled that the proposal to give off agricultural credit from the RBI and create a National Level Agricultural Bank was rejected by the All India Rural Credit Review Committee (1969) in the following words:

"On all relevant considerations, such as those associated with the refinancing functions of the Reserve Bank, its role as a financier and adviser to the state government on matters of co-operative credit, the statutory responsibility of the central bank of the country for ensuring the safety of the depositors' interests and regulating the credit operations in the economy and the experience and expertise which the bank has built up over the years, we are convinced that the Reserve Bank should continue to discharge the functions which it undertakes at present in the field of agricultural credit. A new institution in this context at the all-India level will only add to the cost of credit and the red-tape associated with its procedures without adding to the resources or the efficiency of the system or the service to the cultivator. It is, therefore, our considered view that there is no justification for having any national level institution for agricultural credit outside the Reserve Bank."

### Functions

In view of these varied aspects, the Report of the Committee to Review Arrangements for Institutional Credit for Agriculture and Rural Development (CRAFICARD) recommended the setting up of a new national level bank known as the National Bank for Agriculture and Rural Development (NABARD), which is a logical step in the organisational evolution of the RBI.

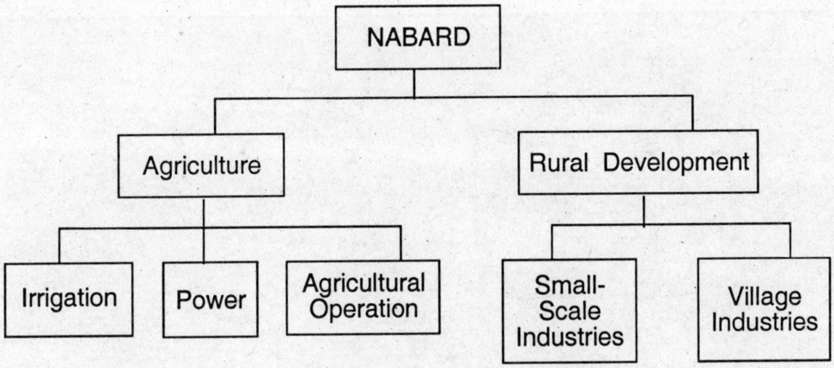


*Fig. 1. Operation of NABARD*

The functions of NABARD are:

*(i)* Developmental policy, planning and operational matters relating to credit for agriculture, allied activities, rural artisans and industries and other rural development;

*(ii)* Training, research and consultancy relating to credit for agriculture and development;

*(iii)* Refinance (short-term, medium-term, long-term) to the co-operatives and RRBs including co-operative marketing and distribution;

*(iv)* Refinance to commercial banks against term lending (medium-term and long-term) short-term accommodation for special purposes;

*(v)* Direct lending, singly or through consortium arrangements in special cases;

*(vi)* Co-ordination and monitoring of all agricultural and rural lending activities with a view to typing them up with extension and planned development activities in the rural sector;

*(vii)* Inspection of co-operative banks and RRBs; and

*(viii)* Advice and guidance to state governments, Federations of Co-operatives, the NCDC, etc., on the co-operative movement inclose collaboration with the RBI and the central government.

The NABARD has close links with the RBI (CRAFICARD) has spelt out the more important of these. It said:

*Financing of SHGs — SBOP, Sidhari and Chinmaya Tapovan Trust, District — Kangra, Himachal Pradesh*

**Table 1**

**THE REFINANCE FACILITIES PROVIDED BY NABARD TO ELIGIBLE INSTITUTIONS CAN BE SUMMED UP AS FOLLOWS:**

| | *Type of refinance accommodation* | *Purposes for which sanctioned* | *Eligible institutions* |
|---|---|---|---|
| 1. | Short-term (ST) (up to 18 months) | *(i)* Crop Loans<br>*(ii)* Marketing of crops<br>*(iii)* Inputs distribution<br>*(iv)* Working capital to co-operative sugar factories<br>*(v)* Procurement of raw materials<br>*(vi)* Production and marketing activities of weavers' and other industrial societies.<br>*(viii)* Production and marketing activities of rural artisan | SCBs on behalf of CCBs in the states with three-tier co-operative credit structure where such structure does not exit, limits are sanctioned to SCBs. |

| | | | |
|---|---|---|---|
| 2. | Medium-term (MT) (18 months to 7 years) | *(i)* Approved agricultural purpose | SCBs and RRBs |
| | | *(ii)* Purchase of shares of processing societies | SCBs |
| | | *(iii)* Conversion of ST crop loans into MT loans due to natural calamities and enemy action | SCBs and RRBs |
| 3. | Medium and Long-term (Not exceeding 25 years) | Fixed investment in agriculture and non-farm rural activities under schematic lending | SCBs<br>LDBs<br>RRBs<br>CBs |
| 4. | Loans to state governments (Not exceeding 20 years) | For contribution to share capital of co-operative credit institutions | State governments |
| 5. | Composite credit limit | All purposes mentioned against 1 and 2 above except 1 *(iv)* and 2 *(ii)* | |

*(i)* Unlike in the case of the IDBI, the RBI must own 50 per cent of the share capital of NABARD. The balance of 50 per cent will be held by the central government.

*(ii)* It would be necessarily advantageous to have some common members on the boards of the RBI and NABARD. The Board of NABARD may be a nominated board, consisting of experts in the related fields. Considering the fact that agriculture and rural development are state subjects, some state government officers may be appointed on the board with a view to bringing knowledge of different areas to it. The strength of the board may not exceed 15, and not less than 3 directors, excluding the Chairman, may be from among the Directors of the central Board of the RBI.

*(iii)* A Deputy Governor of the Reserve Bank of India should be appointed as the Chairman of the Board (as is presently the case with the ARDC). This will also help maintain a proper perspective in NABARD on credit and monetary policies and training.

*(iv)* The Managing Director should be appointed by the Board after consultation with the RBI.

## Microfinance Innovations

The SHG Bank Linkage Programme being propagated by NABARD for providing access to micro finance services to the rural poor attained new heights. The programme envisages organising rural poor, especially women, into small informal affinity groups called Self Help Groups (SHGs), training the group members to learn the art of thrift and credit management, facilitating door-step saving facilities to the members, meeting emergent and small credit needs and then providing access to larger resources in the from of bank loans. Besides providing an enabling environment to the poor for a meaningful participation in economic activities, the programme, which is already a mass movement in several states, has succeeded in socio-economic empowerment of large number of poor women.

## Opening of New Lines of Credit

With a view to augmenting credit flow for handicrafts and other rural crafts which have large export potential, a new line of credit has been opened for financing State Handicrafts Development Corporations through the Scheduled Commercial Banks and State Co-operative Banks.

To improve availability of credit to cultivators against pledge of their agricultural produce, particularly in the context of surplus production of certain crops in various states and non-availability of adequate storage capacity, the existing scheme for financing marketing of crops was reviewed and suitably modified, to make it more user-friendly. Rate of interest reduced from 10% to 8.5% on refinance, extension of coverage of non-borrowing members/non-members of PACs, direct loans to farmers, increase in ceiling to Rs. 1 lakh per borrower, etc.

## Rural Entrepreneurship Development Programme (REDP)

As a part of capacity building of the rural unemployed, NABARD had been supporting conduct of Rural Entrepreneurship Development Programmes (REDP), all over the country. During the year 1017 REDPs were supported, enabling training of 25,425 rural youth. Of these, NABARD has supported more than 5000 REDPs since the inception of the programme in early nineties. Through these programmes, about 1.50 lakh rural youth have been trained which has generated about 2 lakh additional employment. Of these, about 1 lakh persons were trained over last 5 years.

## NABARD and Rural Development

As a development bank for the rural sector, NABARD will have special responsibility to ensure that the training facilities for the bank staff engaged in rural lending are adequate. To the extent that the training schemes are sponsored and financed by the ARDC, these will automatically stand transferred to NABARD. This is a field in which the RBI should continue to take active interest and take the necessary measures to strengthen the efforts of NABARD at improving and expanding the training facilities for project and programme lending.

The National Bank, through its operations and policy initiatives endeavoured to foster development of the agricultural and other rural sectors of the economy. While the Bank's refinance operations both in the short-term and the long term structures scaled new heights, its developmental initiatives and efforts at improving the health of rural credit institutions received added impetus during the year.

Sustainability is at the core of NABARD's Mission of Rural Development. NABARD itself has been formed to promote sustainable and equitable agriculture and rural prosperity through effective credit support, related services, institutional development and other innovative initiatives. Our efforts and functions are directed towards achieving this mission. Some ideas on sustainability and the initiatives being taken by NABARD to achieve sustainable rural development are: NABARD believes that both farm and the non-farm activities have to be simultaneously encouraged if overall development of the rural sector is to be achieved. Credit as a policy instrument is crucial in channelising the direction of private sector investments in consonance with the national objectives and priorities. NABARD, as an apex institution vested with the responsibility of assisting in securing rural prosperity, has played a definitive role in ushering in sustainable programmes of rural development through aligning its refinance and development policies in line with such requirements.

The major initiatives of NABARD in attaining the objective of sustainable rural development are as follows:

(1) Credit planning at the block and district level.

(2) Harnessing water resources and its judicious management.

(3) Understanding the needs of the people and enlisting their co-operation and participation in rural development programmes.

(4) Ensuring Self Help Group-NABARD linkages

(5) Water shed development programme

(6) Rural infrastructure development

(7) Wadi development programme

(8) Animal husbandry activities

(9) Fisheries
(10) Post Harvest Management
(11) Agro/Food Processing
(12) Transfer of Technology
(13) Promoting rural non-farm sector for generating sizeable income and employment in rural areas
(14) Micro-financing
(15) Empowering women; and
(16) Institutional development

Some of the other noteworthy initiatives of NABARD are:

*(i)* Promotion of Kisan Credit Cards and its effective use.

*(ii)* Capacity building of bankers NGOs, SHGs VVVs and other grassroot level organisations for banking with the poor.

*(iii)* Infrastructure development support, computerisation and other efficiency improvement measures for co-operative credit institutions.

*(iv)* Helping RRBs and co-operatives in the preparation of their development action plans for long term viability, entering into Memoranda of Understanding, monitoring and supporting achievements of these institutions.

*(v)* Capacity building of NGOs, watershed management committees and other village level organisations in execution of watershed development projects.

*(vi)* Support to research and development projects, studies, seminars, conferences etc, on matters relating to agriculture and rural development.

*(vii)* Assisting non-farm development activities through entrepreneurship development assistance and assistance for formulation of viable projects through bank finance.

*(viii)* Formulation of potential linked credit plans of every district of the country, background papers for district credit plans and monitoring of achievements of banks under annual action plans.

*(ix)* Preparation of model schemes/projects suited to specific areas for new activities.

*(x)* NABARD provides consultancy services to various client institutions and individual investors in the area of appraisal of multi-disciplinary agro-based projects, micro-finance, institutional development, infrastructure, training, working capital assessment, marketing, product and development, innovative working practices, research and value addition.

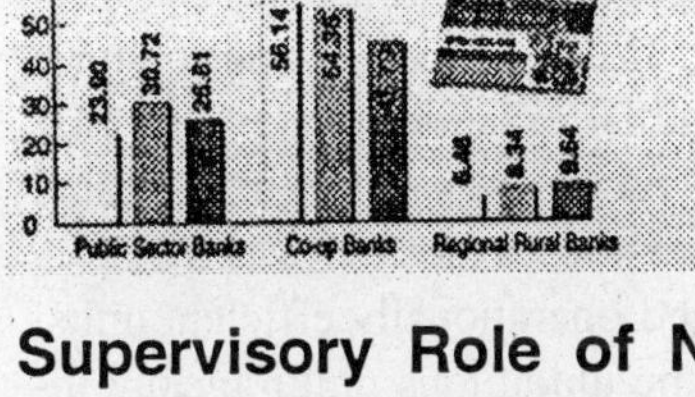


**Box 1**

**Farmers get on the credit card bandwagon**

The Kisan Credit Card scheme, launched by NABARD in 1998-99 to cover short-term and medium-term farm credit needs, has shown an appreciable growth in penetration in the rural areas. In 2002-03, public sector banks issued 26.81 lakh KCCs, while co-operative banks issued 45.79 lakh cards and rural banks gave away 9.64 lakhs of them.

## Supervisory Role of NABARD

Over 600 rural financial institutions fall within the supervisory purview of NABARD. During the year off-site surveillance and supplementary appraisals were introduced to improve the effectiveness of biannual inspection of these institutions. In consultation with Reserve Bank of India, a Board of Supervision has also been set up to help NABARD effectively perform its supervisory functions. The knowledge and skills of supervisory personnel together with technological support to them was given added importance. The Y2K compliance of the rural finance institutions was closely monitored and ensured that these institutions met the needed standards of compliance well before the targeted date.

**Box 1**

**CREDIT ASSESSMENT – THE ASSEFA WAY. DO BANKERS EMPLOY SUCH METHOD?**

The Association of Sarva Seva Farms (ASSEFA) was set up as an agency to provide guidance and assistance to allottees of land under the Bhoodan Movement for raising agricultural production on the newly allotted lands. Over the years, the character of ASSEFA has changed and they have expanded their work to cover farmers other than Bhoodan allottees. Though ASSEFA's primary work is in the area of development, they have been running some very interesting credit related activities as part of the development work in the Vidharba region of Maharashtra as well as in Dindigul – Madurai districts of Tamil Nadu.

When the ASSEFA undertakes developmental work in any village, the first step is to organise the Gram Sabha where all adult members are eligible to participate. In the Gram Sabha the villagers discuss their developmental problems and try to seek solutions. As one of the possible solutions, the members are encouraged to start a small savings fund called the Gram Kosh. This is built up from small contributions of the order of Re. 1 to Rs. 5. The Gram Kosh is utilised to assist members for emergent needs such as medical or educational expenses as well as for production loans.

ASSEFA volunteers observe the practice of self-management of the Gram Sabha and the Gram Kosh for a period of six months to one year. To ensure that the work of the Gram Sabha is truly participatory, no elected leader is encouraged in the initial years and the monthly Gram Sabha meetings are chaired by different members.

Over a period of 6 months to a year when the self-management capacity of the members becomes evident and the members themselves start dealing with the constraints on mutual help through small savings, they approach the ASSEFA for assistance in taking up bigger investments for development. The ASSEFA contributes from its own resources to the Gram Kosh. The Gram Sabha is advised to utilise the greater portion of funds at its disposal for assisting its members in the manner and for the purpose they choose. Obviously, the recovery of the funds from the members is the responsibility of the Gram Sabha. The usual experience of ASSEFA has been that once responsible self-management has set in, recoveries are almost cent percent. In rare cases where recoveries are not forthcoming from a substantial number of persons, the ASSEFA has withheld further help to the Gram Sabha and advised them that the Gram Kosh money belongs to the ASSEFA has withheld furhter help to the Gram Sabha and advised them that the Gram Kosh money belong to the Gram Sabha and further developmental work may be undertaken by the Gram Sabha from the limited funds available with them. After such experience, even recalcitrant members have behaved more responsibily and the fruitful association of the Gram Sabha and ASSEFA continues.

## LOOKING AHEAD

An effective rural credit delivery system is a sine qua non for smooth flow of credit for agricultural and rural development. The process of institutionalisation of rural credit had two distinct phases, the first was expansion of the network of branches in order to improve the access of the rural population to institutional credit and other banking facilities even in the remotest parts of the country, while the second was transformation of these institutions into organisationally strong, financially viable and operationally efficient units. Institutionalisation of rural credit has been achieved to a large extent with the ubiquitous multi-agency institutional arrangements for provision of credit for agriculture and rural development. The second phase of institutional development witnessed several initiatives taken by RBI and National Bank for rehabilitation of weak units in the co-operative sector. These included 12-point programme for rehabilitation of weak DCCBs,

15-point programme for rehabilitation of ground level co-operative institutions, 10-point programme for rehabilitation of weak PLDBs and lastly the institutional strengthening programme covering 'non-solvent' and 'near-non-solvent' banks. While the first three programmes were not able to make any serious impact on the working of the weak units mainly because of lack of adequate resources support, and low recoveries, the fourth programme *viz.*, institutional strengthening programme was a non-starter as it did not find favour with the State Governments mainly due to their inability to found their share as envisaged under the programme. However, the latest initiative taken by National Bank for revamping both the co-operatives and RRBs, through DAPs and MoU, has received a much greater impetus with the reforms initiated in the financial sector by the Government.

The current initiative for strengthening the RRBs through restructuring and infusion of capital to cleanse their balance sheets, hinges primarily on the earnestness with which the State Governments, the sponsor banks and RRBs themselves implement the key action points incorporated in the MoU. During the restructuring process of RRBs, several issues particularly relating to staff matters, return on SLR and non-SLR funds, interest rates and margins, branch licensing policy, expansion of business avenues and multiplicity of agencies exercising control over the working of RRBs, have come to fore. It is hoped that the expert group recently appointed by RBI to look into all such problems, on an on-going basis, will help in resolving these issues with positive approach and active support of all the concerned agencies.

The success of the current initiatives for strengthening the co-operatives through DAPs/SAPs will largely depend on the seriousness with which certain vital issues affecting their working are addressed to. They relate to recovery, resource mobilisation, operational efficiency, productivity improvement and cost effectiveness which would determine the viability of their operations. Business diversification, broadening and deepening of credit along with the quality of service offered to farmers are equally important in the changing economic environments. Human resource development and systems improvements also deserve focused attention. The problem of carry over of accumulated losses and loss assets has also to be tackled through evolving a suitable mechanism for mobilisation of resources required to cleanse their balance sheets.

The co-operatives, as they are conceived, have to be run by democratic managements so that they can truly function as peoples' institutions and meet the aspirations of the people for whom they are established. The Model Co-operative Societies Act, proposed by the Committee under the Chairmanship of Choudhary Brahm Perkash seeks to achieve this objective. With a view to facilitating the democratisation process it would be necessary to enact legislations on the lines of the model act, albeit, with relevant modifications to suit local conditions. The recent initiative taken by the Government of Andhra Pradesh for introducing the bill for enactment of the "Andhra Pradesh Mutually Aided Co-operative Societies Act, 1995" is a welcome attempt to provide for the voluntary formation of co-operative societies as accountable, competitive and self-reliant business enterprises, based on thrift, self-help and mutual aid and owned, managed and controlled by members for their economic and social betterment.

The importance of a dynamic and highly motivated leadership in the development of co-operative can hardly be overemphasised. The 'peer influence' has, indeed, been the desideratum in motivating the members to involve themselves in the development of their co-operatives. The pre-eminent position of many of the co-operatives, especially in the states of Gujarat and Maharashtra could be attributed largely to the good and strong leadership provided by the non-official co-operatives have caused greater damage to the concept of co-operation by stultifying leadership, generating member apathy and curbing local initiatives at the grass root level. Steady depoliticisation, combined with the renewed capacity of non-official elected leadership to rise above political persuasions, is imperative to motivate the members to take pride in the success of their co-operative institutions. To recapture the spirit of co-operation, a climate conducive to democratic governance and development of strong co-operative leadership needs to be achieved. While adoption of the Model Co-operative Societies Act, would bring about greater democratisation and minimise interference in the functioning of the co-operatives, a suitable strategy for transforming the co-operative leadership into a real 'peer' through suitable training programmes, publication of pamphlets/books in local language etc., for the benefit of non-official office bearers of co-operatives needs to be evolved.

In a long-term perspective, though the commercial banks are expected to meet their share of growing demand for rural credit, the co-operatives and RRBs which enjoy a pivotal position with a good network of branches in rural areas will have to shoulder a major responsibility in supply of rural credit. And, therefore, these institutions need to be adequately strengthened, to enable them to play an effective and meaningful role in meeting fully the credit demand of the rural sector.

The task of sustainable rural development is an enormous one. An important requirement in the agriculture sector is to give greater emphasis on increasing productivity and profitability through conserving natural resources. Therefore, the role of universities in research and development and later that of extension services for dissemination of the findings and right application of technology and information becomes crucial. This requirement of focused research and its linkage with extension education has been rightly recognised in the National Agricultural Policy. Unified strategies including watershed management, promotion of technologies like integrated plant nutrient management, integrated pest management, etc., could result in judicious use of vital resources like soil, water etc., ultimately leading to the conservation of natural resources. Simultaneously, thrust is also required to prepare strategies which would generate income potential through other non-farm activities by building the entrepreneurial capacity of the villagers and providing them with ideas, resources to set up their own micro-enterprises. Knowledge on availability of market for the products, which is the most crucial for micro-enterprises in case of non-farm sector, needs to be tapped for them to become sustainable.

## Conclusion

NABARD is a unique development finance institution committed to rural development. It provides refinance to banks and the State Governments, takes development and promotional initiatives to improve the impact of credit on development and attempts to bring about equity and justice in such development. It also supervises the operations of rural financial institutions like Cooperative Banks and the RRBs. NABARD has been making progressively much greater efforts towards improving the access of the rural poor to formal banking services through the self help groups and other macro finance initiatives. The financial assistance from banks through over 7 lakh SHGs is estimated to have benefitted 1.12 crore very poor families as on 31st March 2003.

NABARD, through the focus on a thrust of areas, is pursuing policies, initiating promotional programmes, developing innovative credit products and extending refinance support with an objective of securing prosperity in rural areas. To meet this end, NABARD is examining the scope for re-engineering the organisation in the light of ongoing change in the rural financial sector.

## NABARD – Highlights of Achievements during 2003-04

Refinance for Production Credit limits aggregating Rs.9864.48 crore were sanctioned to Cooperatives and RRBs during 2003-04 as against Rs.8752.93 crore sanctioned during 2002-03 registering a growth of 11%.

Refinance for investment credit: Disbursed Rs.7605.29 crore. Growth rate over previous year's achievement (Rs.7418.77 crore) is 2.5%.

The ninth tranche of RIDF: Against an allocation of Rs. 5,500 crore, loans amounting to Rs. 5,437.51 crore, loans amounting to Rs. 5,437.51 crore were sanctioned. An additional Rs. 176.20 crore was sanctioned under AICF taking the total sanctions to Rs. 5613.71.

To give a greater boost to exports of agri produce refinance of Rs. 160 crore as against that of Rs. 45 crore in the previous year for activities in 48 notified AEZs spread over 193 districts of 19 states.

Watershed development projects covering 3 lakh hectares of land under Indo German Watershed Development Programme and Watershed Development Fund.

Provided refinance of Rs. 2050 crore for lending for Rural Non Farm Sector activities. Of this, Rs.930 crore was for supporting housing.

230 cold storage units with a capacity of 8.20 lakh MT were sanctioned, against the target of 7.2 lakh MT allocated to NABARD by GOI taking the cumulative achievement to 734 units with a capacity of 31.63 lakh MT since commencement of the scheme in April 1999.

1774 units with a capacity of 23.57 lakh MT were sanctioned during the year under Investment Subsidy Scheme for construction/renovation/expansion of rural godowns taking the cumulative sanctions to 2769 units with a capacity of 82.86 lakh MT since commencement of the scheme in April 2001.

2.25 lakh new SHGs provided with bank loan (up to 15 March 2004); (cumulative 9.42 lakh). Rs. 1191.71 crore loans disbursed by banks to SHGs (up to 15 March 2004); (cumulative Rs. 3,240.38 crore). NABARD refinance is Rs. 706 crore; (cumulative Rs. 2125 crore). Bank loan has reached more than 14 million poor families. Over 90% SHGs were exclusively of women.

Cooperative Banks, RRBs and Commercial Banks (up to 31 January 2004) have together issued 3.85 crore Kisan Credit Cards. It is expected that by the end of March 2004, over 4 crore farmers would have been brought under the ambit of the KCC Scheme.

To facilitate easy access to credit artisans and self employed persons in the country, a new credit card called Swarozgar Credit Card (SCC) was introduced during the year. Launched formally in September 2003 and during the last 6 months, a total of about 16500 cards were issued making available credit to the tune of Rs. 36 crore.

During the year 1017 REDPs were supported for training of 25,425 rural youth. The self employment units are expected to provide employment opportunity to about 30,000 persons in the rural areas.

Under District Rural Industrialisation Programme, 16 additional districts were covered during the year, taking the total number of the districts covered since 1993-94 to 80.

Under Cluster Development Programme, taken up as a part of National Programme for Rural Industrialisation, initiated by Government of India, 65 clusters have been identified and 55 have been launched, so far.

100 Women Development Cells have been supported between 1995 to 2003. During the year, 9 such cells were supported.

An amount of Rs. 7834.15 crore was mobilised by NABARD through instruments such as Capital Gains bonds, Tax-free bonds, Priority sector and non-priority sector bonds etc.

8 new District Development Managers' (DDM) Offices in five States were opened taking the total number of DDM Offices to 338 as on 31st March 2004. Further, 102 district were tagged with the neighbouring DDM Offices.

945 VVV Clubs have been formed taking the total clubs formed so far to 9417.

The PLPs prepared by the Bank have projected a credit potential of Rs. 72015 crore for Production Credit, Rs. 28357 crore for Investment Credit for agriculture and allied activities and Rs. 69564 crore for rural non farm sector and other priority sector advances for the year 2004-05.

**Annexure**

# TYPE OF CREDIT FACILITIES WHICH CAN BE PROVIDED BY THE NATIONAL BANK UNDER THE NABARD ACT, 1981

| | *Purpose with relevant section of the NABARD Act* | *1981* | *Eligible institution* |
|---|---|---|---|
| I. | **Short term credit (Section 21(1))** (*i*) Agriculture Operation or marketing of crops | (*a*) State Co-operative Banks, (*b*) Regional Rural Banks, (*c*) Any other financial institutions as may be approved by RBI | Repayable on demand or on the expiry of fixed periods not exceeding 18 months. |
| | (*ii*) Marketing and distribution of inputs necessary for agriculture for rural development | | |
| | (*iii*) Any other activity for the promotion of or in the field of agriculture or rural development. | | |
| | (*iv*) Bonafide commercial or trade transactions | | |
| | (*v*) Production or marketing activities of industries in the tiny and decentralised sector, rural artisans, small scale industries, village and cottage industries, those engaged in the field of handicrafts and other rural crafts. | | |
| II. | **Medium-term Credit** | | |
| (a) | **Conversion loan for Production Credit (Section 22)** | | |
| | Conversion of short-term loans into medium term loans under circumstances owing to drought, famine or other natural calamities, military operations or enemy action. | (*a*) State Co-operative Banks, (*b*) Regional Rural Banks, (*c*) Any other financial institutions as may be approved by RBI | Not exceeding 7 years. |
| | Financial assistance for enabling the borrowing bank or institution to: financial institution as may be approved by RBI | | |
| | (*i*) Pay any dues to the National Bank for credit extended for financing agricultural operations or marketing of crops: or | | |
| | (*ii*) make loans and advances to central co-operative banks or primary rural credit societies by way of reimbursement of loans and advances made by such co-operative banks or societies for agricultural operations or for reimbursement of such loans or advances which have been converted into medium-term loans or advances | | Not less than 18 months and not exceeding 7 years. |
| (b) | **Rescheduling facilities to artisans, small-scale industries etc. (Section 23)** | | |
| | Where owing to unforeseen circumstances, rescheduling of loans and advances made to artisans, small-scale industries, industries in the tiny and decentralised sector, village and cottage industries and those engaged in the field of handicrafts and other rural crafts is considered necessary by the NABARD | (*a*) State Co-operative Banks, (*b*) Regional Rural Banks, (*c*) Any other financial institution as may be approved by RBI | Not less than 18 months and not exceeding 7 years. |

| | | | |
|---|---|---|---|
| (c) | **Medium-term investment credit (Section 24)** | | |
| | Investment credit connected with agriculture, rural development or such other purposes as the National Bank may; from time to time determine. | *(a)* State Co-operative Banks, *(b)* Regional Rural Banks | Not less than 18 months and not more than 7 years. |
| III. | **Long Term Credit** | | |
| (a) | **Other Investment Credit (Section 25)** | | |
| | *(i)* Refinance for promoting agriculture and rural development and allied activities such as minor irrigation, land development, soil conservation, dairy, poultry, piggery, sheep rearing, farm mechanisation, plantation/horticulture, forestry, fishery, storage and market yards, agricultural aviation, bio-gas and other alternative sources of energy, sericulture, pisciculture, animals and animal driven carts, agro-service centres, compost plants, modern abattoir, pumpsets, energisation etc. | *(a)* State Land Development Banks, *(b)* State co-operative Banks, *(c)* Scheduled commercial banks including the RRBs, *(d)* Any other Financial Institution as may be approved by RBI. | Whether originally or by rescheduling the payment thereof, the period should not exceed 25 years. |
| | *(ii)* Purchasing or selling or subscribing to the bonds or debentures issued by any bank or approved institution as specified in Col.2 | | Not exceeding 25 years |
| | *(iii)* Refinance for artisans, small scale industries, industries in the tiny and decentralised sector, village and cottage industries and those engaged in the field of handicrafts and other rural crafts and also rescheduling the payment of such loans and advances. | State Co-operative Banks or Scheduled Commercial Banks including RRBs | Not exceeding 25 years whether originally or by rescheduling the payment thereof. |
| | *(iv)* Short-term credit in connection with any financial assistance under clauses *(a)* or *(b)* or *(c)* referred to above including rescheduling of the same into long-term loans. | *(a)* State Land Development Banks, *(b)* State Co-operative Banks, *(c)* Scheduled Commercial Banks including the RRBs. | Not exceeding 18 months by way of refinance as also rescheduling the payment of such loans and advances for such period as is deemed fit by the National Bank. |
| (b) | **Loans to State Govts. for share capital contribution (Section 27)** | | |
| | For making loans and advanced to state governments out of National Rural Credit (Long-term Operations) Fund for enabling them to subscribe directly or indirectly to the share capital of a co-operative credit society. | Any co-operative credit institution through the State Government. | Not exceeding 20 years. |

❑ ❑ ❑

## Chapter 27

# TECHNIQUES OF LENDING TO AGRICULTURE

### Introduction

Agricultural projects focusing on production are a key to reducing poverty. Agricultural investments tend to create more jobs than equivalent investment in other sectors and can directly target pockets of poverty. In fact, microfinance strategy enhance farm incomes through improved productivity, diversification into high value crops, and improved input and market linkages.

Credit is a crucial input for increasing agricultural production and productivity. A multiagency network consisting of Commercial Banks (CBs), Regional Rural Banks (RRBs) and to the farming community has been set up. In terms of network, coverage and outreach, the co-operatives account for 46 per cent share in rural credit flow for agriculture, 31 per cent in rural deposits and the small farmers constitute 42 per cent of their total membership. However, the percentage share of production credit of the total institutional credit disbursed through the network is at present estimated to be around 60 per cent. The coverage of village in the country by PACs/PCARDBs is about 99 per cent with a membership of over 11.00 crore.

There has been a major change in the banks' lending patterns and policies to agriculture in the post-nationalisation period for the purpose of raising the productivity of the rural poor and productivity in agriculture.

## AGRICULTURAL ADVANCES

Agricultural advances are broadly classified into direct and indirect.

The direct advances are those granted directly to agriculture. They are further classified into short, medium and long-term advances, depending on their repayments period.

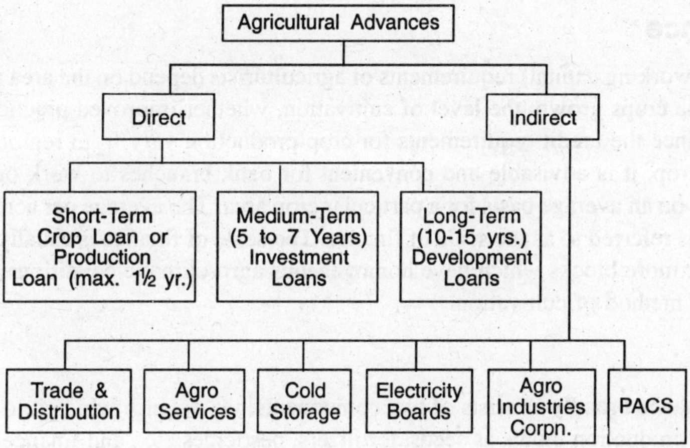


*Fig. 1. Types of Agricultural Advances*

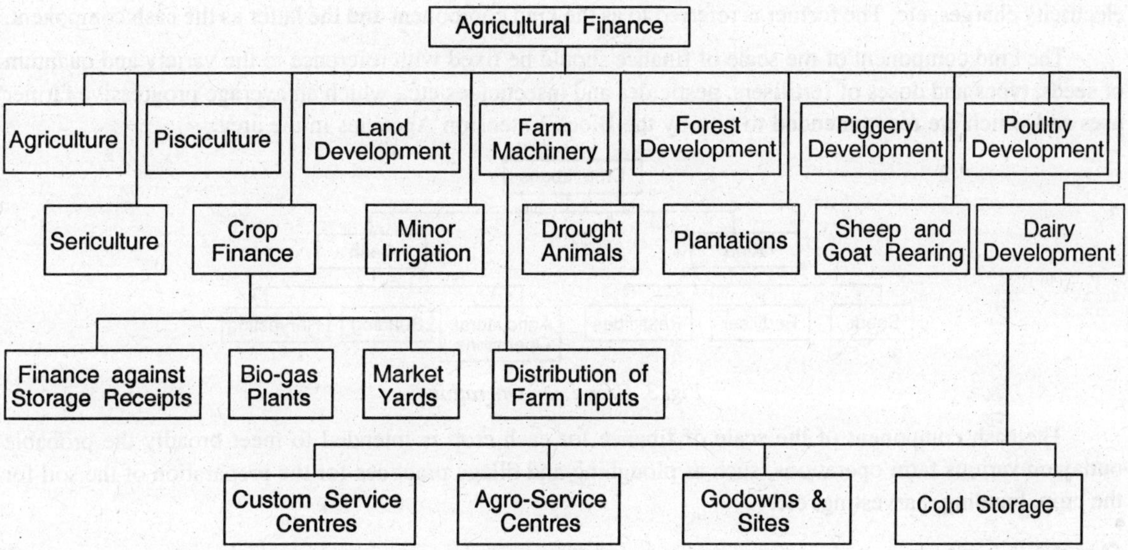


*Fig. 2. Schemes of Agricultural Finance*

## Short-term

Short-term advances are for a maximum period of 18 months and are given to farmers for the purchase of production inputs (seeds, fertilisers, pesticides) and to enable them to meet the cost of cultivation, including labour charges for agricultural operations, irrigation and power charges. These advances are popularly know as crop loans or production loans.

The objectives of the scheme is to meet the genuine credit needs of farmers and enable them to move to a higher technological plane of production activity with a view to improving the productivity of their farms, maximising farm income and raising the level of their living conditions. Crop loans are repayable when the crops are harvested and marketed.

Banks considered these loans as demand loans. To large farmers having a multiple cropping programme, a cash credit facility is given with a suitable schedule of disbursement and repayment, which is worked out on the basis of the cropping pattern followed in different crop seasons in the year.

## Scale of Finance

The crop loan (working capital) requirements of agriculturists depend on the area and type of cultivated land, the nature of the crops grown, the level of cultivation, whether improved practice of cultivation have been adopted, etc. Since the credit requirements for crop production vary from region to region, farmer to farmer and crop to crop, it is advisable and convenient for bank branches to work out crop-wise per acre finance requirements on an average basis for a particular crop area. The average per acre finance requirement for a particular crop is referred to as the scale of finance. The scale of finance is usually related to a compact area, covering one or more blocks which have homogeneous agro-climatic conditions, and follow the same cropping pattern and method of cultivation.

## Components

The scale of finance broadly consists of two components, *viz.* finance which it to disbursed in kind for the purchase of such production inputs as seeds, fertilizers, pesticides etc., and finance that is required to be disbursed in cash to enable the farmer to meet cultivation expenses such as the payment for hired labour wages, payment for carrying out tillage practice, hire charges for tractor and other agricultural machinery, electricity charges, etc. The former is referred to as the kind component and the latter as the cash component.

The kind component of the scale of finance should be fixed with reference to the variety and quantum of seeds, types and doses of fertilisers, pesticides and insecticides etc., which an average progressive farmer uses and which are recommended to him by the Block Extension Agencies in the area.

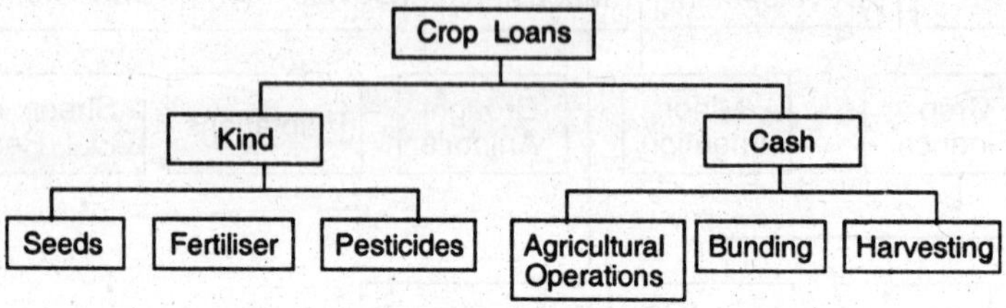


*Fig. 3. Crop Loan Operation*

The cash component of the scale of finance for each crop is intended to meet broadly the probable outlay on various farm operations, such as ploughing and tillage practices for the preparation of the soil for the crop, bunding, harvesting, etc.

## Credit Limit

Normally, the quantum of loan is 75 per cent of the scale of finance. Wherever a mortgage is obtained as security, the loan amount is considered as under:

| *Sanctioned Limit* | *% of Scale of Finance* |
|---|---|
| Up to Rs.1,000/- | 100 |
| Rs.1,000/- to Rs. 10,000/- | 90 |
| Rs.10,000/- and above | 80 |

The agricultural borrowers' capacity to repay the loan is affected by unrealistic repayment schedules and heavy consumption expenses. More over, other problems are likely to arise because of the following reasons:

*(i)* Natural calamities like floods, droughts, pest attacks, etc affecting the whole area and setting at naught the efforts of the farmers.

(ii) Death or physical incapacity of the borrower or any unusual circumstances beyond his control, consequent upon which there is a setback in his farming activities.

When such calamities occur, special measures are necessary to ensure that there is no permanent cessation of farming activities, for farmers do not have the requisite strength to bear the losses. To meet these contingencies, there is a built-in provision in the scheme of agricultural credit. The banks offer two types of facilities in the event of such calamities:

(i) Conversion of a crop loan into a term loan for seasonal agricultural operations: and

(ii) Rescheduling of the repayment programme for term loans sanctioned for investment purposes.

Let us consider the details of these two facilities.

## CONVERSION OF A CROP LOAN INTO A TERM LOAN

When a crop loan is sanctioned to a farmer to enable him to carry on his seasonal agricultural operations, it is made repayable out of the sale proceeds of the harvested produce. If, however, the crops raised with bank finance are affected by natural calamities, or if the borrowers faces some unforeseen contingencies resulting in considerable damage to the crop, he suffers a heavy loss. His capacity to repay the crop loan is therefore eroded. At this stage, not only will he require a postponement of the crop loan repayment, but he will need additional support from the bank so that he may resume cultivation activities during the next season. To meet such a requirement, the scheme provide for the transfer of the balances in the short term loan account, which is usually in the form of a cash credit facility, to a medium-term loan account, with a repayment schedule generally extending over a period of three years, depending upon the repaying capacity of the farmer. A fresh crop loan is sanctioned for the farmer to enable him to carry on his cultivation activities in the next agricultural season.

The farmer requires time to repay the current loan and financial support to take up the cultivation of the next crop. Once this facility is provided, he will be capable of generating in the ensuing years enough income not only to repay the current crop loan but the instalments of the converted crop loan as well. This means that the facility cannot be extended in all cases whenever there is a crop failure. It is not an act of sympathy alone on the part of the banker. It is sympathy combined with the judgement of the field staff about the borrower's capacity to recoup the losses in the future.

The Deposit Insurance and Credit Guarantee Corporation extends its guarantee support for conversion facilities, covering the dues in respect of even three agricultural seasons. The bankers, however, seem to be very reluctant to extend these facilities even to those who genuinely need them. The reluctance for the extension of these facilities on the part of the field staff may arise out of the following apprehensions:

(i) If the facility is extended in a few deserving cases, they amy be confronted with a spate of requests from a large number of farmers, in which case it will be difficult to distinguish genuine cases from those which are not genuine.

(ii) In the case of conversion, the loan burden of the farmer for the future years is increased. Why take the risk of financing a farmer again, when he is not clear the present loan? In the co-operative sector, we have the spectacle of a series of crop loan converted into term loan which are not repaid. Why invite such a risk?

(iii) The desk work and procedural requirements in extending the facility are time-consuming.

In agricultural finance, it is needless to reiterate the need for the close contacts which the field staff are expected to maintain with the farmers. When there are such contacts, and when proper information about the operations of the borrowers is available, the field staff is aware of the progress and problems of the farmer-borrowers in the area. In such a situation, they have a difficulty in weeding out the spurious cases clamouring for this facility. On the other hand, the facility extended to deserving farmers helps in establishing the image of the bank in the community as an institution which has not only replaced the moneylender, but is one which cares for the people.

For small/marginal farmers. the imputed value of family labour and farmyard manures, which they put into farm operations, may be considered as margin money contribution. Accordingly, a 100 per cent of the scale of finance is considered for advance facility.

## Medium-term

The medium-term advances, which are for a period up to 5 years and, in the case of small farmers, 7 years, are granted for development purposes and are, therefore, often know as investment loans. The loans for the following purposes may be classified as medium-term loans, provided of course, that their term does not exceed 5-7 years:

(a) Minor irrigation development through dugwells/borewells/tubewells, revitalisation of existing wells; lift irrigation schemes installation of pumpsets;

(b) Purchase of draught animals like bullocks,

(c) Construction of farm houses, such as cattlesheds, implement shed;

(d) Farm mechanisation with the purchase of tractors and accessories, power tillers, sprayers, threshers and other agricultural machinery/equipment;

(e) Land improvement schemes, such as land reclamation, levelling bunding, terracing, etc;

(f) Construction of godowns/silos;

(g) Setting up of dairy, poultry, fishery, apiculture, sericulture and other allied activitities.

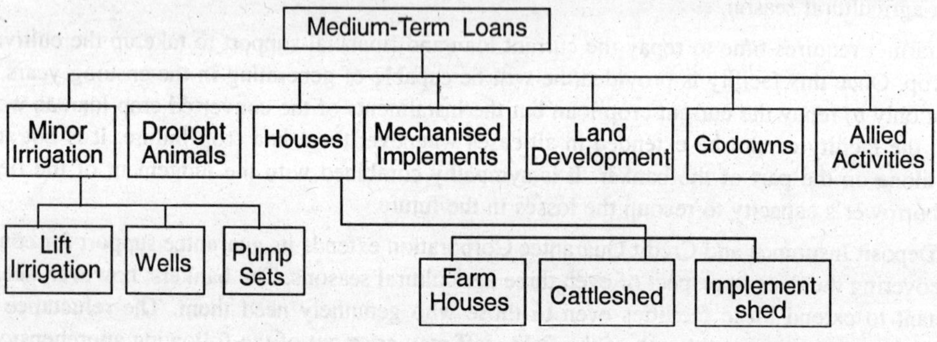


*Fig. 4. Coverage under Medium-term Loans*

## Long-term

Where a scheme has a long gestation period, and as a result, repayment is spread over a period of 10 to 15 years (with requisite moratorium), the advances for it are classified as long-term loans. Long term advances are granted for the following purposes:

(a) Development of plantation crops, such as coffee, cardamom, tea and rubber;

(b) Development of horticulture crops, such as coconut, cardamom, tea and rubber;

(c) Integrated schemes for the development of dairy, poultry, fishery;

(d) Development of farm forestry.

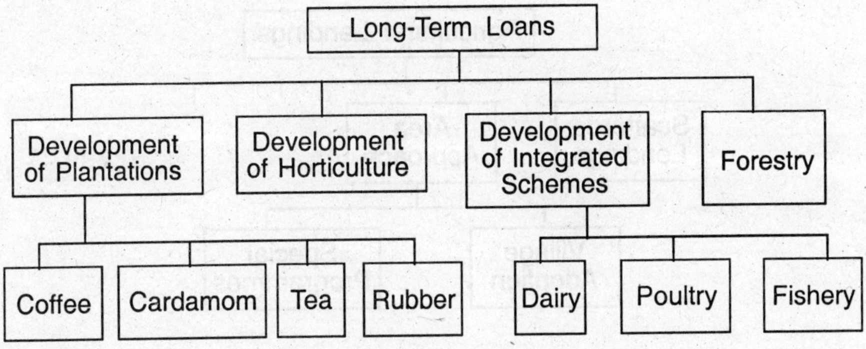


*Fig. 5. Coverage under Long-term Loans*

## Indirect Advances

Banks also finance such agricultural service activities as marketing agro-service units, etc. The following are the sources of indirect advances:

- *(a)* Loans for the working capital requirements of wholesale/retail traders/distributors/co-operative marketing societies for the procurement/distribution of agricultural inputs, such as fertilisers, pesticides, seeds;
- *(b)* Loan for setting up a custom service unit/agro-service centre to provide the services of agricultural machinery to agriculturists on a contract/hire basis;
- *(c)* Loans for setting up cold storage plants for the storage of potatoes, fish;
- *(d)* Loan to electricity boards for their well-energisation programmes;
- *(e)* Loan to Primary Agricultural Credit Societies which will then be granted to agriculturists;
- *(f)* Loans to Agro-Industries Corporations and other public sector bodies for their agricultural development activities. Depending on the period for which they are required, these indirect advances are again classified as short-term, advances. Loan repayable in 5-7 years are medium-term loans and those for a longer period are long-term loans.

## Area Approach

By and large, co-operative and commercial banks have distributed loans to agricultural in a free manner in order that they may show a better quantitative performance. This posed many a problem relating to service and recovery. It was realised that scattered lendings were not convenient, for they entailed a number of operational difficulties, particularly those of supervision, follow-up and recovery. Restricting the area of operation then become a need, and the area approach become an alternative to scattered lendings. The approach basically involved the identification of compact and contiguous area, comprising a cluster of villages for the purpose of agricultural advances. However, the approach was meant to be broadbased. It was thought that, by adopting the area approach, it would be possible to effect an intensive coverage of all viable and potentially viable farmers in a given area. It was also felt that it would be possible for a bank to provide complementary services such as arrangements for timely and adequate supply of inputs, technological guidance, marketing, etc and that this would go a long way in improving the economy of the area. Besides, it was presumed that, by following the area approach it would be easier to co-ordinate with other agencies and that, operationally, it would be more convenient to supervise, follow-up and recover advances. The approach therefore aimed at intensive coverage, effective co-ordination and operational convenience at the micro level. Village adoption came later s a further refinement of the area approach, in which the focus was narrowed down to the village.

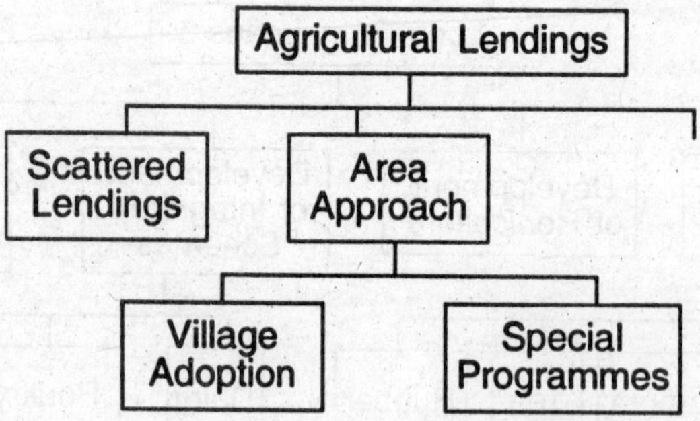


*Fig. 6. Lending Patterns in Agriculture*

From the operation angle, the area approach has several merits which scattered lendings do not have. The most important among them are:

*(i)* Coverage of a large number of farmers by a small number of field staff and field visits;

*(ii)* Curtailed requirements of transport; and

*(iii)* Easier and less expensive supervision, follow up and recovery.

From the broader and more important point of view of modernising and developing agriculture as an industry, however, many other opportunities are offered by the area approach. These opportunities are:

*(i)* Modern methods of cultivation call for a number of inputs, such as fertilisers, improved varieties as seeds, insecticides, etc., and also certain infrastructural facilities, such as storage, marketing and transport. To provide these inputs and infrastructural facilities, it is necessary to build a dependable system in an organised manner. For any viable system, however, there has to be a scope of its optimum utilisation. For example, if marketing arrangement is a system for serving a specific area, its is necessary to have an optimum level of utilisation of this system by the farmers in that area, so that it may function as a viable unit. The optimum demand for the utilisation of any system can be built up only when a sufficient number of farmers, requiring the facilities offered by the system, are available in a compact area. Only the area approach of lending can create such a situation.

*(ii)* Second, the adoption of modern methods of cultivation can be achieved by intensive extension work. Even today, a large number of farmers are hesitant to give up their traditional methods. They have to be educated and convinced that modern technology and scientific methods of farming can turn agriculture from a way of life into a commercial proposition. This type of education and necessary motivation can be possible and effective only when a sizable number of borrowers are located in one place. The area approach strategy offers such an opportunity. Another method for effectively rendering extension service is demonstration. By and large, farmers believe more readily what they see, than what they hear. Banks can afford to spend some money on demonstrations provided that a large number of borrowers benefit from these efforts.

*(iii)* The success of the extension service depends largely upon the confidence and trust which the target group places in the extension workers. These are built up only when extension workers repeatedly and frequently visit farmers and help solve their problems. This can be achieved only when attention is focused on a limited area for an intensive coverage.

(iv) When a large number of farmers are involved within a compact area, other agencies working towards the betterment of agriculture can be meaningfully associated, and concerted effort can be made for an all-round improvement.

(v) There are certain activities which can be successfully taken up only with group participation because individual investments, either due to lack of facilities or because of heavy outlays, are not feasible. Minor irrigation for small farmers and non-land based activities, either allied to agriculture or cottage and rural industries, have a special significance in this regard. By following the area approach strategy, it would be possible to motivate a group of potential borrowers to collaborate in joint efforts for their own economic betterment.

(vi) In the area approach strategy, a specific area, instead of an individual farmer, is viewed as a unit, suitable location specific projects can be planned, taking into account the resources available in that area and the scope for the maximum exploitation of these resources. Such projects benefit the entire community and have a wholesome effect on the rural economy.

(vii) Lastly, scattered lendings over a vast area do not create any impact of bank credit on agricultural development. The impact becomes pronounced and observable only when credit is intensively given in a compact area. This can then be assessed and evaluated. Without proper evaluation, effective improvement in lending schemes, as also in the style of lending, cannot be implemented.

It is obvious from these fact that the area approach strategy for agricultural lendings not only serves the interest of banks, but is the only systematic method of achieving the goal of development in the field of agriculture in consonance with the national policy.

## Problems

The increasing expectations from the banking system during the Sixth Plan indicate that there will be a four-fold increase in short-term loans. Accordingly, the task assigned to the banks to deploy funds for agriculture aggregating Rs 51,460 crores will pose several problems, and calls for a better co-ordination of credit policies.

***(a) Number of Accounts:*** The main problem would be to cope with a large number of small accounts, particularly because another parameter of progress enjoined on the banks is that the share of small and marginal farmers in the total direct farm credit will have to be 50 per cent. Lending involves decision making, it starts right from identifying borrowers to disbursement of loan. Due to various concessions and facilities available for agricultural credit, there are chances that groups of wrong elements will put pressure for availing the loan facility. The availability of subsidy is another reason for attraction of bad elements for credit who also put pressure on field functionaries to sanction and disburse loan. Due to increase of loan accounts and work pressure field attention and inquiries about the borrowers are not getting due importance. Further the involvement of different agencies in selection of beneficiary; providing subsidy etc., also influences the banker to entertain the proposal relying on the information given application form.

The disbursement of credit of such magnitude will involve a tremendous extension effort, particularly among the small and marginal farmers, where the average amount per account is very small. Further a mere disbursal of credit would not be enough. Its end-use will also have to be very closely supervised in order to ensure that the credit disbursed leads to the desired development, which would make the recovery of loans possible.

***(b) Recoveries:*** The problems of the recovery of agricultural advances will also become increasingly difficult. As it is, agriculture is subject to the vagaries of nature; large areas in the country are periodically affected by recurrent floods or drought. The problem is further complicated by certain unhealthy trends which are developing in rural areas, where defaulters tend to be shielded by the political elite. So far as the weaker sections are concerned, their projects are often of marginal viability, so that even a small rise in the sustenance needs of their families or in the production costs is enough to upset their repayment capacity.

As the banks increase the coverage of small and marginal farmers, the problem of recovery would become more difficult. It is essential, therefore, that state governments should support the efforts to recover the dues. In many states, legislative measures have been passed to enable designated revenue officials to assist commercial banks in recovering their dues. There are, however, practical difficulties in the implementation of the scheme. In some states, the number of recovery officers appointed for the purpose is small; and in addition, they are burdened with other work. Besides, there are some loopholes which enables the defaulters to escape. The effective assistance in the recovery of overdues available to commercial banks is not always satisfactory and adequate. There is, therefore, a need for passing such legislation in all the states, and improving the efficiency of the administrative machinery set up for the purpose in those states where legislation has already been passed.

***(c) Cost:*** As a result of the appointment of a large complement of technical staff and field staff, the administrative cost of handling a large number of small agricultural loans spread over a number of villages is mounting. As it is, the wage structure in commercial banks is more costly than in other financial institutions operating in rural areas, and the necessity of appointing specialised staff for handling the work has further enhanced the cost of credit. Studies by the State Bank of India have indicated that agricultural loaning is making a negative contribution to the bank's profitability.

Further, the variable costs of agricultural loaning, which increase in direct proportion to the volume of advances, are considerably high. Consequently, agricultural financing is becoming an increasingly costly proposition for commercial banks. With the increase in the volume of agricultural credit envisaged in the Sixth Plan, the profitability of banks is likely to be under great strain.

***(d) Lack of Trained Staff:*** In order to cope with such a large volume of agricultural credit, it would be necessary for banks to appoint a large number of technical and non-technical personnel and to train them for the purpose. In the backward states, where technical persons are in short supply, the staff will have to be taken on deputation from the state governments. In very backward areas, such as the tribal areas of the north-eastern region, Orissa, Madhya Pradesh, or Bihar, communication with the local tribal population presents many problems. In these areas, it may be necessary to take village level workers on deputation. But before the new staff becomes operationally effective, it would be necessary to give them intensive training in the banks' accounting procedures and practices.

Some banks have recently created a new cadre of rural development officers from amongst their technical staff. But the need for creating adequate training facilities for the increasing number of rural development officers is so pressing that they have, in fact, to think in terms of setting up a separate training institute to meet their specialised training needs. Other commercial banks are experiencing similar difficulties.

***(e) Supporting Package of Services:*** What the agriculturist needs is not merely credit, but also a package of services. This is particularly relevant in the case of small and marginal farmers. Since the size of their marketable surplus is small, and since it is sold in small lots, small farmers do not get remunerative prices; and the viability of their production operations, already tenuous, suffers. It is, therefore, necessary to develop the supporting services to meet the needs of small farmers for the supply of inputs, the marketing of produce, the supply of energy, machinery and equipment, for storage and warehousing facilities, etc., through appropriate institutional machinery. Unless institutional support for improving the viability of small and marginal farmers is strengthened, the efforts of commercial banks to improve their lot will be infructuous; and the weaker sections will be saddled with loans which they cannot repay.

## Strategy to Meet the Challenges

It is evident that credit absorption in agriculture sector depends on various other factors apart from policies and systems of the credit institutions. Basically capital (credit) is one ingredient of factors of production although most influencing but its intake naturally depends if production is assured to the desired level. Thus proper strategy to improve and strengthen the associated factors requires to be planned out. Associated factors like marketing, weather risk and uncertainties, storage facilities, insurance, weather forecast and pricing of agriculture produce etc., also need due attention of policy makers and others concerned. Thus agricultural lending is affected by different direct and indirect factors resulting in poor credit intake. The following strategies may be helpful in enhancing agriculture lending but coordinated effort will yield encouraging result.

Credit Planning.

Awareness building.

Availability of infrastructural Inputs.

Meeting risk of uncertainties.

Simplification of Procedures.

Encouraging Self Help Groups.

Training and skill building.

Innovating agricultural activities.

Thus challenges before agricultural lending can be faced by removing the barriers coming in the way through strategic planning and by providing awareness on various issues directly and indirectly influencing the factors of production. The various departments/agencies involved in improving agricultural output should develop better co-ordination among themselves with the object to making agriculture more profitable venture which will not only increase income and standard of living but also restrict rural migration.

## Conclusion

In the post-independence period, more particularly since the nationalisation of 14 major banks in 1969, the infrastructure for resource mobilisation and channelising productive credit in rural areas has been strengthened. There is a strong demand for agricultural credit in India. It must be stressed, though that credit, while often necessary, is only one instrument for promoting agricultural development. In most advanced states, where agriculture is commercialised, credit is needed to sustain technological changes. However, the rich farmers benefitted by these programmes. Banks or co-operative societies should revamp their schemes to help the poor. The financial institutions have abundant resources. The need of the hour is the will to accelerate the process of rural development from village to village. There is no dearth of resources, both financial and human. Both are to be put to maximum use. The bank, co-operative society, the school and the village panchayat co-ordinate development activities, plan for development, raise resources, implement the schemes, monitor the schemes and bring the fruits of development to all the people in the villages.

**AGRICULTURE CREDIT—CREDIT FLOW-GROWTH RATE AND AGENCY-WISE SHARE**

*(Rs. in crore)*

| Year | Production (ST) Credit | | | Investment (MT/IT) | | | Total | | |
|---|---|---|---|---|---|---|---|---|---|
| | Co-ops' Share % | RRBs' Share % | CBs' Share % | Co-ops' Share % | RRBs' Share % | CBs' Share % | Co-ops' Share % | RRBs' Share % | CBs' Share % |
| 1995-96 | 8331 (57) | 849 (6) | 5345 (37) | 2148 (29) | 532 (7) | 4827 (64) | 10479 (48) | 1381 (6) | 10172 (46) |
| 1996-97 | 9328 (55) | 1121 (7) | 6549 (38) | 2616 (28) | 563 (6) | 6234 (66) | 11944 (45) | 1684 (6) | 12783 (49) |
| 1997-98 | 10895 (53) | 1396 (7) | 8349 (40) | 3190 (28) | 644 (6) | 7482 (66) | 14085 (44) | 2040 (6) | 15831 (50) |
| 1998-99 | 12320 (52) | 1691 (7) | 9622 (40) | 3596 (27) | 847 (6) | 8821 (67) | 15916 (43) | 2538 (7) | 18443 (50) |
| 1999-00 | 15619 (57) | 2025 (8) | 9566 (35) | 5046 (29) | 1418 (8) | 11001 (63) | 20665 (46) | 3443 (8) | 20567 (46) |

*Source:* Rural Credit of NABARD

❑ ❑ ❑

# Chapter 28

# AREA AND PROJECT APPROACH TO BANK LENDING

## Introduction

The credit needs of the Indian rural economy are met by both the organised and unorganised credit agencies. The organised sector consists of the Reserve Bank of India, National Bank for Agriculture and Rural Development, commercial banks, regional rural banks and co-operative banks and specialised financial institutions. The unorganised sector is largely made up of indigenous bankers and money lenders.

The commercial banking system consists of state sector comprising of 28 banks with a market share of 85 per cent, regional rural banks sponsored jointly by the government and commercial banks, Indian banks in the private sector, incorporated outside India and non-scheduled commercial banks. The co-operative credit structure for short and medium-term credit is a three-tier system, with a state co-operative bank at the apex level in each state, the central co-operative bank at the district level and the primary credit societies at the base—agricultural credit societies in village and urban banks as other non-agricultural credit societies mainly in towns and cities. For long term credit, there is a central development bank in each state operating through branches in some states or through primary land development bank at taluka or district level. There are in addition a few industrial co-operative banks at the state or district level.

## PLANNING

Planning is the codification and quantification of strategy, research and development of specific project—*e.g.*, strategic acquisitions. It is a continuous movement towards desired goals. The precise formulation of plan objectives adopted in the successive five-year plans has varied. The essential goals of Indian planning have been growth, removal of poverty and achievement of self-reliance.

The planning process has been accepted as a sure tool of rapid development, and has been in operation in various fields of economic activity. Banks, in particular, resorted to credit planning as a means of allocating their loanable funds to various sectors.

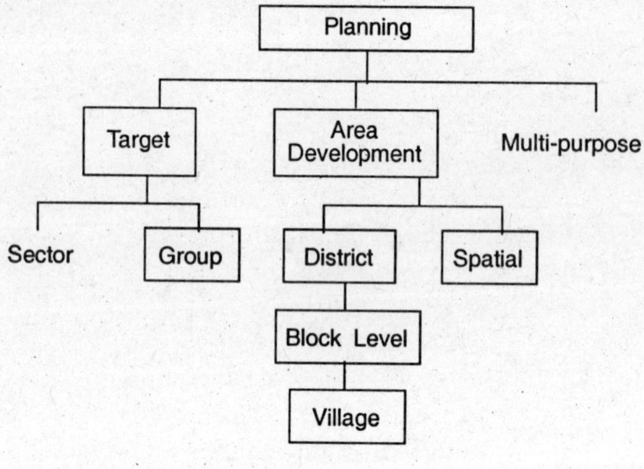


*Fig. 1. Planning Approach*

Under the lead bank scheme, banks have adopted district credit and block level planning as a means of integrated rural development. Meaningful solutions of the problems of poverty, under-employment and unemployment can only be found within the framework of a rapidly expanding economy.

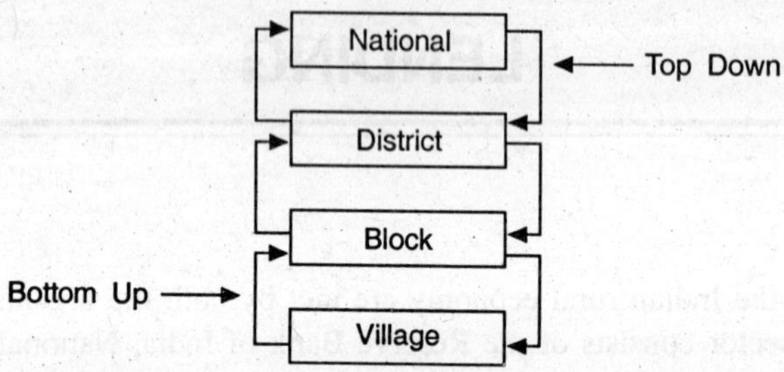


*Fig. 2. True Planning*

## Credit Planning

Credit planning was introduced in the wake of bank nationalisation to redirect the flow of bank credit into the priority sectors in accordance with the overall national policies. It is a conscious effort on the part of banks to allocate their loanable funds to various sectors. Till recently, the Reserve Bank had guided banks in credit planning at the micro level. It had already set up a credit planning cell on an annual basis, But the credit planning attempted so far had been on an annual basis, covering the traditional slack and busy seasons. Credit budgets were discussed in detail by the RBI with the top management of individual banks.

Credit discipline is a significant aspect of credit planning. the concept of production-oriented credit assumes that, for every manufacturing activity there is a minimum credit need which must be satisfied, and that every increase in production is expected to lead to a corresponding increase in the need for credit. Since bank credit forms a fraction of aggregate credit (the average level of the ratio of bank credit to the total liabilities of industries was 17.7 per cent — varying from 0.2 per cent for the match industry to was 34.7 per cent of jute textiles, and the average level of the ratio of bank credit to current assets was 32.7 per cent — varying in magnitude from 0.3 per cent 52.2 per cent), credit planning by banks alone will not bring about credit discipline. At the macro level, total credit created from various sources in the economy — and not the increase in bank credit alone — will have to be matched with the increase in production at the micro level; and the total availability of funds to a unit will have to be kept under observation to ensure an alignment with production trends. Only then will credit planning succeed effectively as an instrument of monetary policy. For this purpose, the role non-institutional agencies in the financial market has to be reduced. Credit planning, credit discipline and credit management are three important tolls of future lending operations.

## DISTRICT UNION OF FARMERS' SERVICES SOCIETIES

The National Commission on Agriculture has recommended that there should be a Union of Farmers' Services Societies at the district level for consultation and for a co-ordination of policies in the district. Various types of facilities, especially the facilities for storage, purchasing, processing and marketing required by the member, are best organised at the district level. Where such services can be organised on a viable basis, and the Farmers' Services Societies consider that they must directly be involved in organising these services, the district union can take over this function on behalf of the Farmers' Services Societies. Where the purchase, marketing and processing of any agricultural produce assume large proportions — particularly of such commodities as milk, cotton, oilseeds, etc. — it may be desirable to establish a separate functional district union. Such functional district organisation for particular commodities may formed separately at the district level.

The working funds for the union's commercial activities will be drawn from the lead bank. Depending upon the area and its needs, each union's activity may grow along different lines. Where separate functional unions do not exit, they may start with one or two specialised activities of marketing and processing, and gradually cover the other needs.

### Area Approach

The Study Group, set up October 1968 under the chairmanship of the late Dr. D.R. Gadgil with the approval of the National Credit Council, recommended that an area approach should be adopted by commercial banks to identify and study local problems and evolve an integrated credit plan for the area. The Group was of the view that the lowest unit under the area approach should necessarily be identified with the district, which is the main administrative unit of the country. On the lines of this recommendation, the Reserve Bank of India accepted the principle of the Lead Bank Scheme. Accordingly, 406 district have been allotted to lead banks.

In this connection, it may be pointed out that a lead bank is responsible for surveying the resources potential to facilitate the expansion of branches and diversification of credit facilities in the district allotted to it. While other banks are not precluded from opening branches, the lead bank is expected to act as the consortium leader and enlist their co-operation in the mobilisation of deposits, and the location of actual and potential credit needs. In allotting districts to lead banks, the Reserve Bank has kept in view the factors of continuity in order to ensure the viability of operation, provision of control points for development work and branch expansion, and a broad correspondence between the responsibilities allocated in terms of the number of districts and the resources base of each bank:

**Box 1**
**IFAD ASSISTED MAHARASHTRA RURAL CREDIT PROJECT (MRCP)**

The IFAD assisted Maharashtra Rural Credit Project (MRCP), approved for implementation in four districts of Maharashtra has been launched with the overall objective of making a large number of poor as bankable clients either directly or through villages based intermediaries. The specific objectives of the project are:

- to upgrade the capacity of rural branches of commercial banks to lend efficiently to the small target group borrowers
- to demonstrate the impact of improved procedures, practices and staff performance on bank's profitability; and
- to develop the capacity of Self Help Groups (SHGs) to improve credit reception and to act as financial intermediaries to banks and borrowers.

The unique feature of the project is that it is being implemented jointly by the National Bank and Government of Maharashtra with active participation of other field level functionaries such as banks, National Institute of Bank Management (NIBM), Mahila Arthik Vikas Mahamandal (MAVIM), Maharashtra Industrial and Technical Consultancy Organisation (MITCOM), Maharashtra Centre for Entrepreneurship Development (MCED) and Non Government Organisations (NGOs) which will promote and support Self Help Groups to provide training and technical expertise in the project areas. All these agencies work together for creating awareness among the beneficiaries about the various economic activities such as sericulture, backyard poultry, basket making, food processing, agro-forestry, etc., which have markets in and around the village, systematising off-farm skill training and developing the local youth to work as agricultural extension workers, health workers, Self Help Group animators, etc. Intensification of on-site monitoring of the project implementation, stimulation of savings habit, creation of awareness on village resources management and preparation and use of appropriate audio-visual material to facilitate quick replication of the project objectives in new districts are some other yardsticks which distinguish MRCP from other projects of poverty alleviation in the country. The project is closely monitored by a high powered Project Steering Committee under the chairmanship of the National Bank Chairman.

The project with a total outlay of US $ 48.3 million was launched in 1994 and has made rapid strides in its implementation. The innovativeness of the project and the extent of success achieved give enough encouragement for its replication in a few other states of the country.

## Spatial Planning

In working out the spatial plan, the economists divide the aggregate economy into regions which are homogeneous in characteristics—natural, physical, sociological, economic, etc. Thus river valley areas, or urban rural areas under the influence of a city centre or a tribal area are examples of the earmarking of special areas from the point of view of spatial planning. The working of Tennesse Valley Authority under David Lilienthal has provided a pioneering example of spatial planning. In India also, in the Fifth Five Year Plan, 55 areas under the major irrigation projects have been selected for command area development. The major irrigation projects in this country created substantial irrigation potential but its utilisation was somewhat tardy in the absence of integrated irrigation development plan. The concept is therefore now accepted that an integrated area development plan must be prepared for the command area. Such integrated command area irrigation development plans will include a series of inter-connected items like the construction of canals, distributors, water courses and field channels and drops, levelling and reshaping of land, drainage facilities, agriculture extension, training of farmers in irrigation development, prescription of an appropriate cropping pattern, supply of agricultural inputs, rural communication, marketing, storage, processing and town and country planning in the developing area. The irrigation development plan has necessarily to be evolved with the co-operative and conjoint efforts of the various departments like PWD, agriculture, co-operation, revenue, development, etc.

The concept of spatial planning is also linked with another approach evolved by the demographers, *viz.*, that of identification of growth centres. The basic idea behind this is that development does not take place without some pattern and the pattern is that of a series of linked centres of growth, each growth centre providing a stimulus to the surrounding areas. An approach to planning which does not take into account the growth centres is bound to lose sight of the dynamics of economic development. The concept of growth centre has received a great deal of attention from the regional scientists and considerable literature has grown. An attempt has also been made to apply these concepts of regional and district planning also to evolve concrete plans which make these growth centres the nodal points in the framework of planning. This approach envisages a planning hierarchy of growth centres. Four hierarchies of centres have been distinguished:

*(i)* Central villages providing minimum facilities to a cluster of villages like primary school or a health dispensary, etc.

*(ii)* A service centre providing all basic facilities like a market centre.

*(iii)* A growth point providing market-cum-service centre to 5-10 service centres of category (II). Such a growth point can provide scope for industrial growth.

*(iv)* A growth centre serving 5-10 growth points with a number of secondary and tertiary activities and specialised facilities. These growth centres provide consumer products both finished and semi-finished of the lower hierarchy. They have a large number of processing activities. Planning for such growth centres would ensure best use of investment in a region since—

  *(a)* if concentrates resources in growth centres in such a manner as to have the maximum spread effect, and

  *(b)* they take into account linkages between the growth centres.

## District Planning

The concept of block as the unit of planning and development was also related to the structure of the panchayat samiti at the block level. It is true that the block was chosen as a unit of planning and development, the idea was that of the three-tier local self-government institutions or panchayat raj institutions, at the district, block and village levels. Out of these, panchayat samiti at the block level should be the most crucial agency for local planning. However, later on when in the states of Maharashtra and Gujarat, district was chosen as a more viable unit for planning and development agency. The development plans at the district level were, therefore, attempted in all those states where zilla parishad was the most effective unit. Zilla parishad had more resources, more competent technical staff and therefore had greater strength to attempt planning for development. However, the nature of planning attempted by the panchayat samitis remain at the block level. It is true that the local sector at the zilla parishad level attempted to cover a much larger spectrum of schemes within the budget of the zilla parishad and the allocation of the state government at the district level could not be considered to be an adequate arrangement of horizontal planning at the district level.

## Integrated District Plans

The district plans will have to integrate all these different approaches and components within an overall framework. The following components will, therefore, have to find a place in an integrated district plan:

*(i)* Identification and full utilisation of natural resources,

*(ii)* Full utilisation of the manpower resources,

*(iii)* Building institutions and organisations and using them for maximum productive effort,

*(iv)* Mobilisation of efforts of financial institutions of for mopping up savings and their productive investment,

*(v)* Building up of infrastructure facilities,

*(vi)* Identification and development of growth centres,

*(vii)* Provision of minimum needs of social consumption, and

*(viii)* Plan for technological development in rural areas.

Each of these elements would have to be incorporated in the area or horizontal development planning for a district.

The entire development process may be looked upon as the end product of the effort of individuals and institutions. A network of institutions is need to initiate support for the development process. In the process of local planning, the institutions which are to play a prominent role are the following:

*(a)* At the village level, the village panchayat, primary co-operative society or the newly set up farmers' service society and auxiliary institutions like the youth and women's clubs, etc.

*(b)* At the tehsil/block level, the tehsil/block development board, land development bank, branches of commercial banks, taluka agricultural produce marketing society, the Agricultural Produce Marketing Society (AMPS), etc.

*(c)* At the district level, the zilla parishad, or district development council, district central co-operative bank commercial banks, etc.

Each of these institutions has a definite role to play and each must prepare a development plan for its own area of activity. Thus, the village panchayat, the tehsil development board and the zilla parishad or the district development council have to produce general development plan while the co-operative and the commercial banks have to prepare credit plans. The marketing society and the agricultural produce marketing societies have to produce marketing plans. Finally, youth and women's institutions and similar other institutions may prepare their plans limited to their purpose.

*(i)* It will designate the bank branch (either its own or that of another bank) with which each society will have banking transactions, and will lend for development purpose.

*(ii)* It will initiate and assist in the functioning of the Farmers' Services Societies;

*(iii)* It will formulate guidelines for

- *(a)* The grant of loans to members by each society;
- *(b)* Giving finance to the society by each branch, both for loans to members and the society's commercial transactions; and
- (c) Giving finance to viable units for the supply of inputs and services;

*(iv)* It will ensure that bank finance is available for the suppliers of inputs and services organised on commercial lines;

*(v)* It will contribute to the share capital and a part of the pay bill for the extension staff of each society. It will advice each society on the selection of managerial and extension staff and participate in the deliberations of the Board of Directors.

**CHART NO. 1**

**MACRO LEVEL**

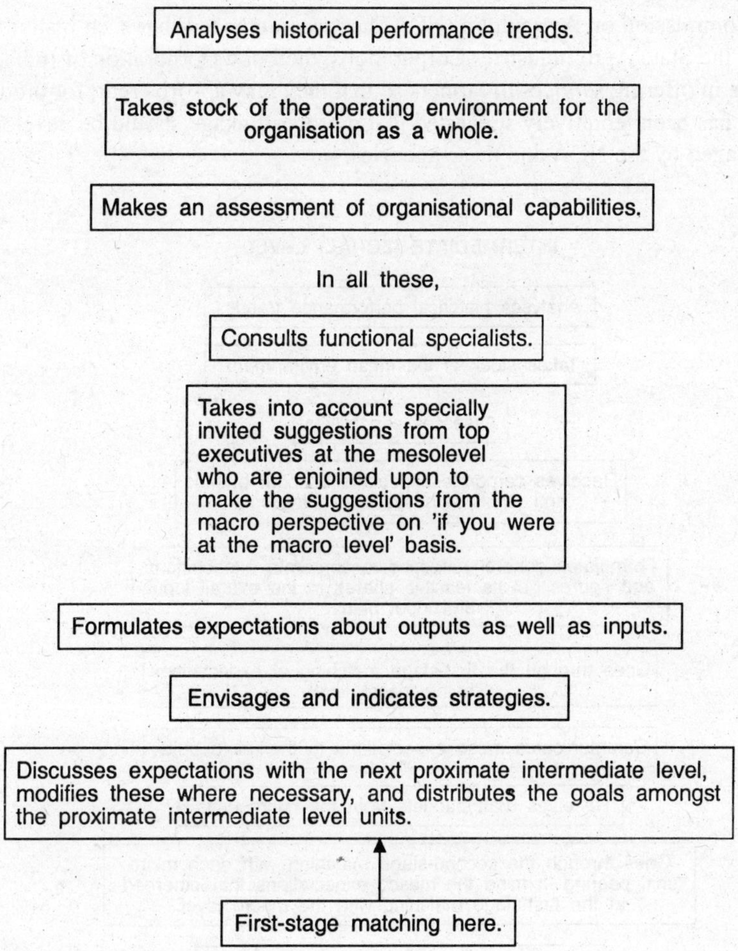


## Linkage with other Agencies

An integrated agricultural credit system, based on the concept of credit service, economic viability and the development of borrowers into a self sufficiency of working funds, would invigorate the process of capital formation in the rural economy. It would facilitate resources mobilisation and investment. The primary aim of the integrated credit system is to provide to the farmer one contact point where he may obtain his credit and input requirements. Besides co-operative, there are certain other agencies which tender credit assistance to small and marginal farmers. The Land Development Bank, for instance, acts as a service agency for handling land development and works connected with the prevention of soil erosion, drainage digging of wells, etc., for the member of each Farmer's Service Society. In this way, it assists in the conversion of medium/long-terms loans granted by banks into productive assets.

Agro-industries corporations have been set up in several states with the objects of providing the means for agricultural operations and for undertaking the distribution of agricultural machinery. These corporations should act as promoters and initiators of processing industries, and keep in close touch with each service society and the district union. The Food Corporation of India and other commodity corporations may also render assistance and use the District Union of the Farmers' Services Societies as their agency for the procurement, storage and despatch of their purchase.

The National Commission on Agriculture (NCA) has recommended that such institutions as the Land Development Banks, the State Agro industries Corporations, the Food Corporation of India, etc should play a vital supporting role in offering services to farmers so that they may absorb credit for productive purposes. In this connection, it has been tentatively suggested that a proper linkage should be developed between the credit structure envisaged by the NCA and these agencies.

**CHART NO. 2**

**INTERMEDIATE (ZONAL) LEVEL**

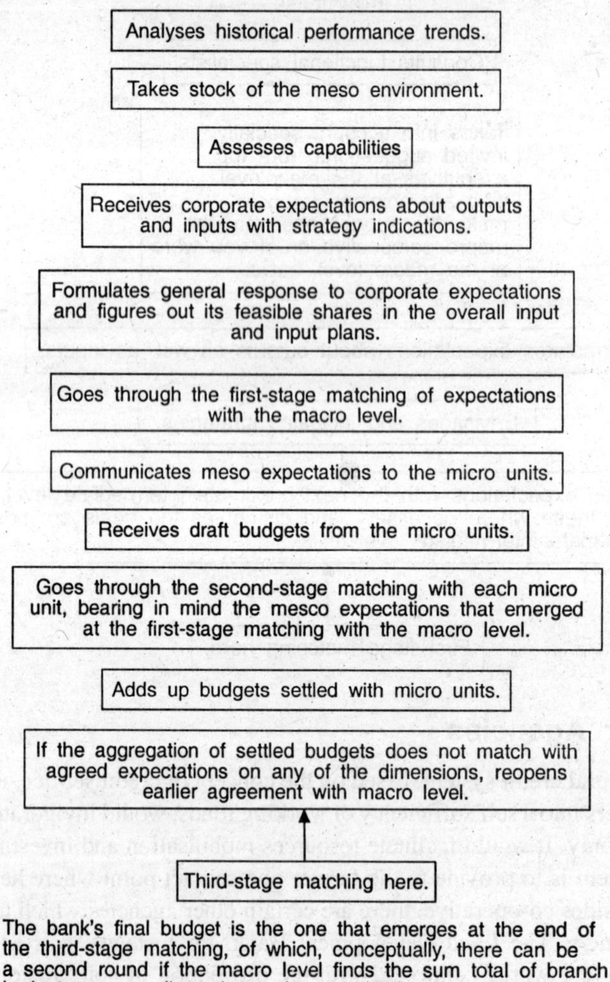


The bank's final budget is the one that emerges at the end of the third-stage matching, of which, conceptually, there can be a second round if the macro level finds the sum total of branch budgets on any dimension to be completely off the mark.

Commercial bank, too, should have access to refinance by the Agricultural Refinance Corporation and Life Insurance Corporation for long term loans to the Farmers' Services Societies (for their own operations as well as their members) and the Union. When the object of finance qualifies a co-operative credit organisation for the allotment of funds at concessional rates of interest from Reserve Bank of India's allocation for agricultural credit, commercial banks must have access lo these funds for their short and medium-term lending to the Farmer's Service Societies. What is relevant is the end object of the loan and not the channel through which it is distributed. The fact that a commercial bank comes in the chain of operations instead of a co-operative bank should not deprive the loanee, and particularly the small and the marginal farmer and the agricultural labourer, of the special benefits of the concessional credit given by the Reserve Bank of India.

As already stated, the small and marginal farmers own 19 per cent of the cultivated area. Assuming that the per acre credit needs of the small and marginal farmers are twice as large as those of others, and taking note of the fact that the requirement of agricultural labourers, too, have to be met, it is but appropriate that at least 40 per cent of the total agricultural credit should go to small and marginal farmers and agricultural labourers. In this context, it may even by necessary to lay down a broad guideline at the national level that at least 40 per cent of the funds allocated for agricultural credit by the Reserve Bank of India and of commercial bank loan to agriculture should go to small and marginal farmers and agricultural labourers, together with facilities which would enable them to use these funds productively. Based on the experience gained in the implementation of this programme, the reservation limit of finance for these categories of rural population may be raised further in subsequent years. The Farmers' Service Societies at the tehsil/block level should be able to get all the facilities available under the different schemes for the benefit of small farmers, marginal farmers and agricultural labourers and for the special programmes for animal husbandry, village artisans, etc. In any case, it is necessary that the funds required by the tehsil/block Farmers' Service Societies should be made available by the banking system and that they should not be subjected to any restrictions on the availability of credit because of a credit squeeze or other contingencies.

With the changing socio-economic environment in the rural areas, the task of integrated rural development and rural lending should be assigned to bank branches. Here in, the villages will be allotted to each branch of the commercial bank. The branch/bank will conduct village economic surveys, prepare village plans, mobilise resources and provide a package of assistance including finance. This integrated credit management will accelerate the process of rural development.

## Project Approach to Bank Lending

The objective of lending is to assure that loans are used for the most productive purposes. These different sorts of undertaking are, for the purposes of banking lending, considered to be projects.

The term "project" is interpreted as comprising a homogeneous investment or a series of related or similar investments in a particular sector or in different sectors. Some 'Projects' only provide technical assistance for the preparation of specific investment, or for more general investigation or studies. A project can also consist of a loan to a financial intermediary to finance its activities generally, or specific development programme in a particular sector.

The former is typically the case in loans to development finance institutions which relend to sub-borrowers in the industrial sector. Illustrations of the latter are loans to agricultural finance institutions to finance specific programmes, such as dairy, pasture, piggery, fishery, irrigation and farm distribution system, or the introduction of mechanical equipment, fertilizer, pesticides and seeds. Project consists of the construction of civil works or the provision of equipment and institutional improvements, policy changes and training of management and staff.

**CHART NO. 3**

**MICRO LEVEL**

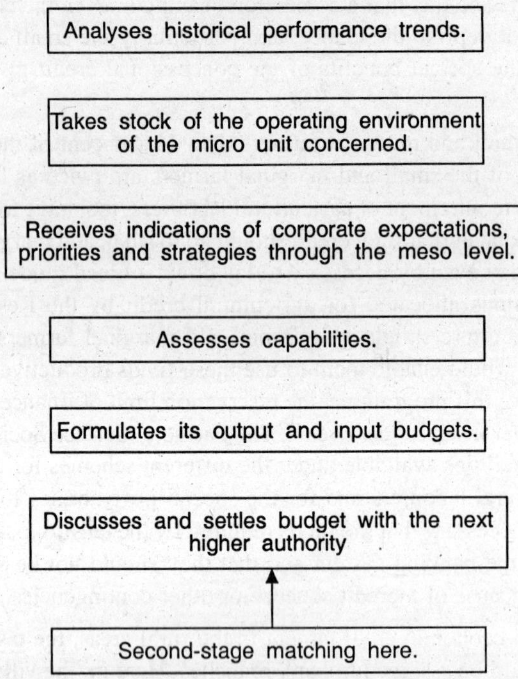


In regard to the development of agriculture and rural development, banks have to formulate and finance both tangible and intangible projects. The project finance is within the area approach system of lending in rural areas.

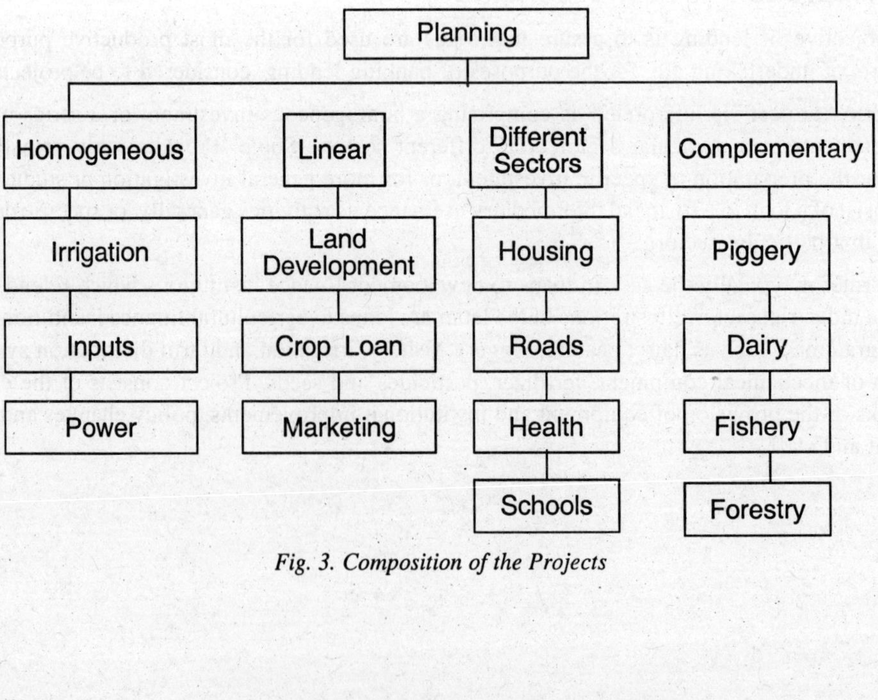


*Fig. 3. Composition of the Projects*

Thus, the more comprehensive view of the development process by the World Bank has led to an increasingly integrated approach to lending by incorporating into projects a variety of activities which embraces many sub-sectors and often cut across sectoral lines. In the final analysis, development can have no meaning unless it brings a better, fuller and more productive life to the mass of the underprivileged in rural areas. The concept of project lending aims at achieving this goal of integrated development of rural areas.

## Conclusion

The commercial banking system has become a vital tool in the functioning of the economy as well as conducive to accelerated economic development, with their experience and the just need of the rural economy and the economic compulsions the banks have adopted innovative schemes of lending. Among new innovations, area approach and project lending stand out as outstanding programmes meeting with the demands of the rural economy.

Banks are catalystic agents of economic growth. Besides providing a wide variety of financial and non-financial services to individuals and group of individuals, corporate bodies or governments. Through their penetration in the hitherto neglected areas in rural India, they have been inculcating banking habit, thrift, by their social lendings they have not only broad based the employment horizon but also increased the standard of living of the poor people. By their education and housing policies, they are serving the rural community in a big way.

❑ ❑ ❑

## Chapter 29

# DECENTRALISED CREDIT PLANNING

### Introduction

Credit in an important input for the development process. Its impact being pervasive on various sectors of the economy, the mobilisation or resources by the financial system and their allocation to sectors and projects in conformity with priorities underlying the development plans have become integral parts of the overall planning process. Planned allocation of the scarce credit resources among different sectors of economy in accordance with priorities implicit in the development plans has come to be accepted as a strategic instrument in planning. Given the natural tendency for credit to gravitate towards sectors and activities capable of yielding high rewards irrespective of their contribution to the overall balanced economic development. It a developing economy, rural markets are generally characterized by large imperfections, and as such, the free market forces are unlikely to provide the right incentive or the required momentum for optimum utilisation of scare capital resources. In contrast, the planned system could ensure better allocation of the available limited resources among various competing demands. Credit planning assumes greater importance especially in the context of substantial reliance on fixed capital formation from the private sector for promoting agriculture and rural development. A substantial proportion of gross fixed capital formation in agriculture, ranging between 60 and 70 per cent, takes place in the private sector. Though the growth in gross fixed capital formation (in real terms) in agriculture (private and public) has just been around 3 per cent (compound) between 1970-71 and 1984-85, the gross fixed capital formation in agriculture in the private sector, in absolute terms, had increased, in current prices, from Rs. 919 crores to Rs. 4,320 crores during this period. This increase has been possible because of large expansion in institutional credit, which as a proportion of private sector gross fixed capital formation increased from 25 per cent in 1970-71 to 54 per cent in 1984-85. Further, in a situation where the flow of credit has been found to be rather uneven as between various sectors of the economy and between different regions in the country, credit planning, especially when it is decentralised, assumes considerable importance. While the need for decentralised credit planning may be readily accepted, it has, however, to be recognised that no meaningful progress can be made in this direction unless the process of development planning is also suitably decentralised.

## Development Planning

The process of planning for economic development of the country was developed initially as a centralised approach, perhaps, for the reason that the process involved a high degree of technical expertise and skills and that the major emphasis was to develop the public sector as an engine of growth. In this task, the major concern of the central planning agency, *viz.*, the Planning Commission, was to take the national economy on the long term growth path through consistent and optimal allocation of scarce investible resources between the different sectors of the economy keeping in view the long term perspective. The initial thrust of planning was on building up a strong industrial base and strengthening the infrastructure for which a centralised system of planning was well suited. However, the experience of implementation of successive five year plans has demonstrated the weakness of a centralised planning approach particularly in respect to its linkages with realities at the grass-root levels. Thus, the planners have recognised the need for decentralised planning which seeks to link organically the various unit plans so as to present an integrated plan for a given region. The disillusionment with the results of centralised planning and implementation of development activities undertaken during the fifties and sixties, awareness in the seventies of the need to ensure equity alongside growth, and the realisation among the planners that it was difficult to plan and administer effectively from the centre as societies become more complex and government activities expanded led to the efforts towards decentralisation.

The idea of decentralised planning was given shape in the Third Plan which outlined detailed methodology for the preparation of rural development plans at the district and block levels. Despite the recognition that better planning at the grass-root level is likely to contribute to substantial improvement in the quality of national planning, decentralisation of the planning process was rather slow because of the non-availability of adequate machinery and expertise at the state level to undertake decentralised planning. The Planning Commission, therefore, launched a scheme in 1972 for strengthening the planning machinery at the state level which led to setting up of state Planning Boards/State Planning Commissions.

## Rationale of Decentralised Planning

The relevance of decentralised planing is, however, greater for the agriculture and rural development sector, than for other sectors of the economy. The advantage of decentralised planning is derived from its ability to discover dormant resources and skills and its endeavour to activise them. The structural, institutional and organisational constraints to overall growth rate said to be better identified when planning is done in close proximity to the area and the people. Decentralised planning has the advantage of realistic appreciation of local needs and participation of people in planning which factors are crucial to the success of the planning effort.

While the merits of decentralised planning are appreciated, it is necessary to recognise that in certain areas it may not be adequate to fulfil the tasks. Local resources may be better utilised under a decentralised planning system but there are several areas where centralised planning system initiative will be indispensable. The development of backward regions may call for transfer of more resources which can be achieved only through a centralised planning system. Similarly, multi-purpose river valley projects involving inter-regional co-ordination call for more centralised effort, whereas minor irrigation projects based largely on institutional credit support should appropriately be accompanied by more decentralised efforts. This underlines the need for adoption of a judicious mix of both centralised and decentralised planning approaches so as to ensure the accelerated development of the economy.

An agricultural development plan, though a country wide plan in terms of coverage, has to be location-specific in its details. The highly localised aspects of agricultural development planning arises from various reasons. Firstly, there is a high degree of variability in climate, soil, water resources, drainage, etc., in different regions from village-to-village and even from field to field. The above conditions determine, to a large extent, the type of agricultural production and technology, which can be effectively taken into account only under decentralised micro level planning. Secondly, the conservation and development of natural resources like soil, water and vegetation is extremely important for agriculture. If the nature of the problem as well as the great variations in the characteristics of resources from area to area are to be taken into consideration in planning for development, the programmes would need to be planned at micro-level, preferably, on the basis of a watershed which may encompass a geographical area cutting across administrative boundaries. Thirdly, the family farms, which are the basic units of production in agriculture, are small and scattered. Planning for agriculture necessarily means influencing and motivating these units to take to improved technology, use of yield-increasing inputs and switching over to imported crop patterns leading to more optimal use of resources. Thus, the basic problem of agricultural planning tantamounts to directing numerous and scattered individual cultivators to act in the desired manner which is possible only under a micro-level planning system.

## The Unit of Planning

Decentralised planning would mean planning at different levels *viz.* , state, district, block and village. What is the ideal level at which decentralised planning is to be undertaken? The idea of planning from below stretched to its logical end would suggest the village which is the lowest administrative unit. However, the various experts who have examined the issue in depth feel that village is too small to be seriously considered as a planning unit. Many of the problems of villages stem from sources outside it and for which solutions are to be found outside. Below the state level, whether the district or block is more suitable for planning need not be viewed with rigidity. The general agreement on this issue appears to be that planning unit should be small enough for people to participate effectively and large enough to ensure efficiency and economy. The consensus of opinion appears to favour the district as the appropriate unit because of various advantages like administrative convenience, availability of better technical expertise and better data base for planning.

## Attempts at Decentralisation

Planning in India has generally been identified as planning at the national level, although there have been attempts to initiate planning at lower levels of state, district and even below. Following the report of the Balwant Rai Mehta Study Team, the Third Plan advocated the people's participation in local level planning under the framework of democratic decentralisation called Panchayati Raj. The Third Plan also provided a methodology for preparing state plans for rural development on the basis of district and block plans. Under the Fourth Plan, an attempt was made to give a more concrete shape to district planning by issuing guidelines for its formulation. However, the progress achieved in decentralizing the planning process at the district level was constrained by various factors. Firstly, the shift of the traditional revenue administration to development administration took place only with regard to implementation of policies and not their planning. Secondly, overriding consideration following the food crisis and the introduction of programmes like Integrated Area Development Programme (IADP) and High Yielding Variety Programme (HYVP) aiming at quick results and involving high technical expertise, perhaps, contributed to the centralisation of efforts.

Notwithstanding the limited success achieved in introducing planning at the district level, the demand for the adoption of decentralised planning has steadily grown, probably, in the context of development programmes meant for weaker sections, meeting the ecological needs for various regions and ensuring the efficient implementation of development projects.

❑ ❑ ❑

# Chapter 30

# DISTRICT CREDIT PLANS

## Introduction

Planning for credit had not received much attention in development planning for the agricultural sector prior to the nationalisation of commercial banks. The scheme of social control over banks was initiated by the Government of India (GOI) in December 1976 to bring about wider diffusion of banking facilities and changes in the pattern of lending. The system of credit planning which has become an integral part of credit policy and the Lead Bank Scheme (LBS) which seeks to make the banking system function as an instrument of development are the outcome of social control. The adoption of the area approach for the development of credit and banking in the country on the basis of local conditions was first recommended in October 1969 by the Study Group of the National Credit Council on "Organisational Framework for Implementation of Social Objectives." The group suggested earmarking the district to commercial banks (Lead Bank of the district) so that they could act as pace setters in these districts in providing integrated banking facilities. The Reserve Bank of India (RBI) accepted the recommendation and the LBS was formulated towards the end of 1969. The Lead Bank was to act as a consortium leader for co-ordinating the efforts of all credit institutions in the district for branch expansion and meeting the credit needs. The first set of DCPs was prepared and launched in 1978. These plans, however, reflected significant differences among themselves in regard to approach, methodology, quality, etc. Though considerable efforts were put in by Lead Banks in their preparation, the DCPs could not fully serve the purpose. As commented by Committee to Review the Arrangements for Institutional Credit for Agriculture and Rural Development (CRAFICARD) in their report, the plans were not aligned with development schemes of the district and even the emphasis on agriculture and allied activities which constitute the mainstay of the rural economy was not adequate. Besides, these plans did not adequately take into account the role of the co-operatives which were an important source of credit. The major gain in this exercise, however, was the awareness of the problems of credit planning that it created amongst all concerned.

## Objectives

The DCPs will have the same objectives as those of the National Plan. It is therefore, important to emphasise the principal objectives of the National Plan, namely:

*(i)* Removal of unemployment an under-employment;

*(ii)* Appreciable rise in the standard of living of the poorest sections of the population; and

*(iii)* Provision of some of the basic needs of the people belonging to the poorer sections.

From these objectives, the main objectives for bank loans follow. These are:

*(i)* Loans for labour-intensive schemes which generate employment;

*(ii)* Loans to increase the productivity of land and other allied sectors to reduce under-employment and increase income levels;

*(iii)* Loans to the weaker sections of the population (marginal and small farmers, agriculture labourers, rural artisans, and scheduled castes and scheduled tribes) for productive purposes to the maximum extent possible; and

*(iv)* Provision for some consumption component to the low income groups as a part of loans for production and investment purposes.

All District Development Plans are expected to take care of these three basic objectives, and clearly indicate where the banks can step in and meet the demand for loans for bankable schemes. Considered this way, the DCP is only an amplification of certain programmes included in the overall District Development Plan. Care, however, has to be taken to ensure that the credit plan for the district is formulated in line with the development strategy worked out for the district.

In this connection, it may be pointed out that banks have to ensure that:

*(a)* The share of small and marginal farmers in the total direct credit to agriculture would reach 50 per cent by the end of plan period, i.e. by 1984-85;

*(b)* The banking sector's lendings to the priority sector should reach a level of not less than one-third of outstanding credit; and

*(c)* The credit-deposit ratio for rural and semi-urban branches should reach at least 60 per cent within a stipulated period of time.

Budgeting in stages has certain advantages. First, it is less complicated to solve budget problems in a number of successive steps than to approach them within an integrated system of data. Second, budgeting in stages makes it easy for one to determine at what points in the process policy decisions relating to a long-term plan or budget are requited. Third, since the planning authority functions in stages, budgeting in stages offers effective co-ordination between planning and the operating departments.

The following order of operational procedures in the preparation of the budget would seem to be the most logical:

*(i)* The determination of the level of government expenditure for the next budget period;

*(ii)* The setting of general priorities among and within the various sectors or main fields of government activity by the planning authority;

*(iii)* The formulation of proposed projects by the operating departments;

*(iv)* A review of the selection of projects by the planning authority;

*(v)* The submission of financial estimates of the projects to the budget office for review and inclusion in the budget;

*(vi)* The establishment of the final form in which the budget estimates will be presented to the legislature;

*(vii)* The discussion and authorisation of the budget by the legislature.

## NEW DEVELOPMENTS

The Planning Commission has now placed special emphasis on block level planning. According to available information, out of 5,011 blocks in the country, a programme of integrated rural development (IRDP) combining the special programmes, is to be undertaken in all the blocks in 1983-84. Moreover, it has been proposed that 300 blocks should be taken up each year for intensive block level planning and development for a period of 5 years, starting from 1978-79. An amount of Rs. 2 lakhs per block has been earmarked for block level planning. The main objectives of the IRDP in selected blocks is to provide full employment and a better standard of living by implementing productive programmes within a definite time frame for the identified target groups consisting of small and marginal farmers, sharecroppers, agricultural labourers, rural artisans and persons belonging to scheduled castes and scheduled tribes. The emphasis now is on the block for the purpose of planning, and hence the DCP work has to be taken up on a block basis.

The Government of India has approved 395 District Industrial Centres (DICs) covering 403 districts out of a total of 406 districts, to promote rural industries and to maximise the employment potential. The main thrust of this programme is on the development of such industrial units in the rural areas and small towns of the country as would create wider employment opportunities in these areas.

Following the Ashok Mehta Committee Report on Panchayti Raj, there has been an increasing emphasis on the decentralisation of decision making and development planning. In the states where Panchayat Raj institutions are already working, functional co-ordination and alignment of lending programmes under the DCP with the activities of the Panchayati Raj institutions are essential. The Antyodaya Scheme, too, has to be taken into account.

The Government of India has decided to set up industrial promotional agencies (IPA) at the district level to play a catalytic role in generating opportunities for self-employment in close co-operation with the District Manpower Planning and Employment Generation Council.

### Methodology for the Next District Credit Plan

The DCP has to be based on:

*(a)* The existing pattern of economic activities and the potential for development;

*(b)* The Sixth Five-Year Plan (1980-85) targets and annual budgetary provisions;

*(c)* The performance of financing agencies under the previous DCP and their potential capacity in respect of the availability of funds as well as man power; and

*(d)* Likely demand for credit in respect of specific projects, different sectors and different blocks in the district.

The period of the next DCP should synchronises with the period of the Sixth Plan, subject to minor adjustments.

In the preparation of the District Credit Plan, one has to be as realistic and precise as possible. The lead banks have already brought out two previous documents, namely, the district survey report and the first DCP report, which provide the necessary background. The new plan did not therefore take the from of a district survey report containing avoidable description material, but was a credit plan framework giving need-based estimates of credit requirements block-wise, scheme-wise and bank-wise, with full explanatory details for important and specified items.

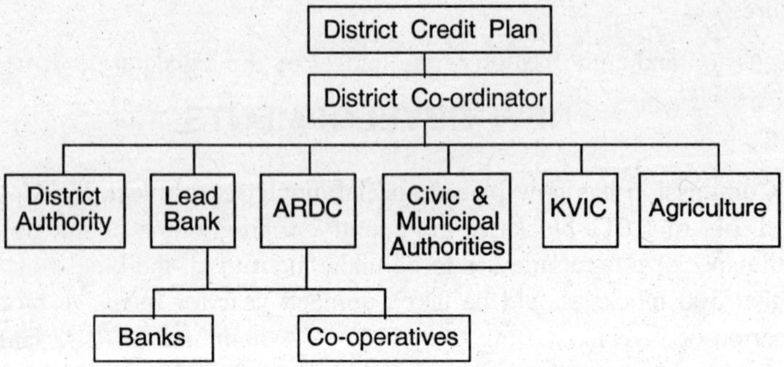


*Fig. 1. District Credit Plan*

The starting point for the formulation on the DCP is the assessment of the capacity and role of each of the commercial banks, co-operatives and RRBs (if there is any) in the district, and arriving at a consensus about the specific nature and magnitude of the lending programme each can undertake.

To arrive at such consensus and to fix the responsibility of each credit agency, the time-table given below has been suggested.

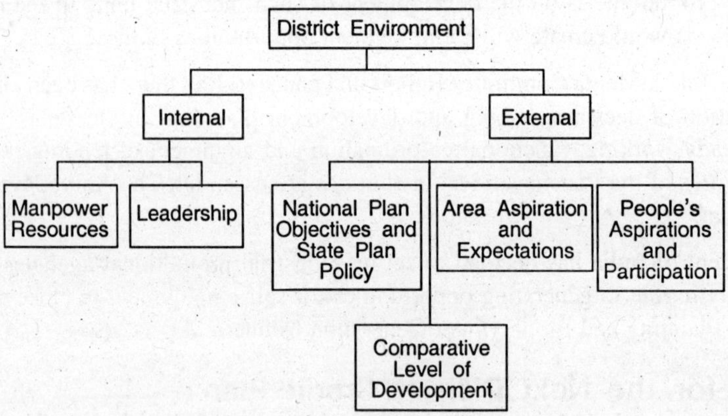


*Fig. 2. District Environment*

## Plan to Work

Taking into account the past experience and the present requirements, the preparation of the district credit plan for 1980 was taken up in nine consecutive stages. These were:

| | *Stage* | *When to be taken up* |
|---|---|---|
| 1. | Updating of block data | |
| 2. | Marshalling together Sixth Plan data for the district | April |

| | | |
|---|---|---|
| 3. | Review of implementation of previous district credit plan and ascertaining the capability and role of commercial banks, central co-operative banks and RRBs (if there are any) in the district. | May |
| 4. | New District Credit Plan formulation. | June-July |
| 5. | Circulation of the Draft Credit Plan to all the financial institutions and concerned development department in the district for their comments. | August |
| 6. | Revision of the District Credit Plan in the light of comments received. | September-October |
| 7. | Meeting of the District Consultative Committee to finalise the District Credit Plan and allocation under it. | November |
| 8. | Finalisation and issue of the District Credit Plan to all the concerned financial institutions and district development departments. | |
| 9. | Allocation of shares by each of the financial institutions to its individual branches. | December |

## Uniformity in Approach

There is a need for a minimum uniformity of approach in presenting, in the DCPs, the estimates of credit outlay, *i.e.* the estimated credit demand under the various bankable schemes to be implemented during the plan period. The DCP involves three estimational exercises *viz.*, outlay on crop loans, outlay on working capital finance. Crop loans are allowed for relatively short periods, *viz.*, for the agricultural seasons and there is a periodical recycling of funds. The total disbursal by way of crop loans in the terminal year of the plan period is therefore considered as the credit outlay on crop loans. As against this, the outlay on term loans represents the cumulative disbursements to be made during each of the years of the entire plan period. As regards working capital finance, *i.e.*, cash credit/overdrafts (including export credit), the total limits in force at the end of the plan period should be taken to indicate the total amount of finance made available under this head. This indicates the additional limits that may be sanctioned during the plan period.

For crop loans, the DCP Convertor/Task Force has to examine carefully the farm extension programme in the district, the preparedness of farmers to use modern inputs after taking loans, the past experience of fertilizers, etc., and arrive at the likely need-based demand for credit, and how much of this may be met by credit agencies. The crop loan estimate thus arrived at has to be allocated among banks. The aggregate of the committed crop loans figure is relevant for the DCP.

## Estimation of Crop Loan Requirements

As regards the estimational exercise regarding the crop loan requirements, the estimate has to be arrived at on the basis of the gross cropped area under different crops in the district after taking note of the break-up into irrigated and unirrigated areas. The possible increase in the cultivable area and the likely changes in the cropping pattern in the district as result of *(a)* The increase in irrigation facilities, *(b)* The rise in the acreage under hybrid, high yielding varieties, *(c)* The introduction of new crops and *(d)* Pursuant to the setting-up of processing units for agricultural produce such as sugar factories, spinning mills are taken note of. On the basis of the estimated gross cropped area under different crops and the realistic crop wise scales of finance for irrigated and unirrigated areas, for high-yielding varieties and normal, as recommended by the Agricultural Department, the total cultivation requirements of the district are computed.

Since a portion of the outlay on cultivation is met by the farmers, particularly the bigger farmers, from their own resources, and since not all the cultivators go in for the recommended doses of fertilizers and pesticides, the short-term credit requirements for agricultural production to be met by institutional agencies may be taken at around 50 per cent of the total costs of cultivation in the district.

To cross check the estimate of credit requirement thus arrived at, it is worthwhile to work out that estimate by another method. The total estimate of the cost of cultivation thus arrived at may be divided further into that for the land cultivated by:

*(i)* Small farmers (bottom one-third of the farmers according to the frequency distribution of operational holdings in the district available from district-level authorities);

*(ii)* Middle farmers (middle one-third); and

*(iii)* Large farmers (top one-third).

The crop loan needs to each of these groups may be taken as under:

*(i)* Small farmers: 100% of their requirements

*(ii)* Middle Farmers: 50% of their requirements

*(iii)* Large Farmers: 25% of their requirements

The above approach to a crop loan estimate is based on the need for ensuring that the credit needs of small and marginal farmers are given due weighage. As the National Commission on Agricultural (NCA) has stated:

"Credit cannot, however, be distributed over the different socio-economic classes in the rural economy on a pro rata basis according to land."

The aggregate credit estimate thus arrived at may be compared with the aggregate credit estimated at 50 per cent of the total cost of cultivation in the district. An average of the two estimates may be considered as the need based crop loan requirement of the district.

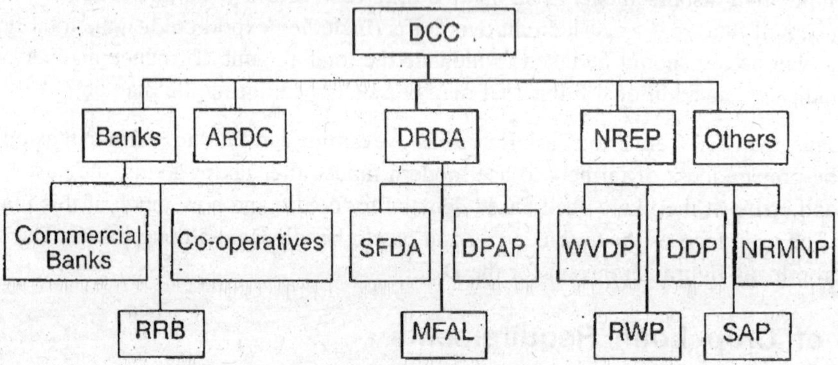


*Fig. 3.*

The difference between the estimated credit requirement thus arrived at and the total of the allocations accepted by the different lending institutions in the district indicates the gap in the crop loan availability from institutional sources. Banks have to take steps to strengthen their organisational set-up for this purpose.

## Organisational Set-up at the District Level

Though non-lead banks had been advised to designated district co-ordinators for each district, the progress in the matter was tardy; even where district co-ordinators had been designated, they were not able to play an effective role because of inadequate staff support, their pre-occupation with day-to-day duties at the branch, and certain administrative bottlenecks. In the circumstances, non-lead banks, particularly those having a large number of branches *i.e.*, say, five or more branches, were advised to create a Lead Bank Cell under the charge of the district co-ordinator and attend to all matters arising out of the Lead Bank Scheme. Further, adequate staff, including technical staff, and other facilities for an individual branch or on a pool basis, depending upon the circumstances, should be provided to the cell to enable it to function effectively.

## District Level Planning

The strength of the Indian economy and the stability of our social and political system will increasingly depend on effective performance in a large number of programmes aimed at meeting basic needs, providing employment on a decentralised basis, improving land and water management and enhancing the productivity of resource use in small enterprises. These programmes, unlike investments in energy, transportation, communication and large industries, cannot be formulated or implemented in a centralised fashion. Hence, the shift in the core areas of concern for planning has to be matched by more effective district planning which can provided greater flexibility and efficiency in the use of scarce resources and wider opportunities for articulating aspirations. District planning will also help to secure better integration of employment generation and anti-poverty programmes with local needs, resources and development potential.

Fig. 4. Shows the district level economic development in Karnataka and its relation with district credit plans. What is true of this state is true for other states.

With the extension of the IRDP to all the blocks in the country from October 1980, the Government of India decided to merge the existing SFDA and DPAP agencies, and reconstitute them into the District Rural Development Agency (DRDA). A new DRDA would be set up where SFDA and DPAP do not exist. This agency has been entrusted with the responsibility of monitoring the formulation and implementation of IRD Programmes in the district. The lead banks were asked to take the initiative in the preparation of banking plans, in line with the guidelines provided by the ARDC, for the implementation of the IRD Programmes. They were drawn up to cover all the activities to be undertaken under the IRD Programme during the calendar years 1981 and 1982. The various schemes covered in such plans were included in the AAPs for the respective years, with the outlay earmarked for each programme shown separately. These banking plans were finalised by the Standing Committee of the DCC and approved by the later.

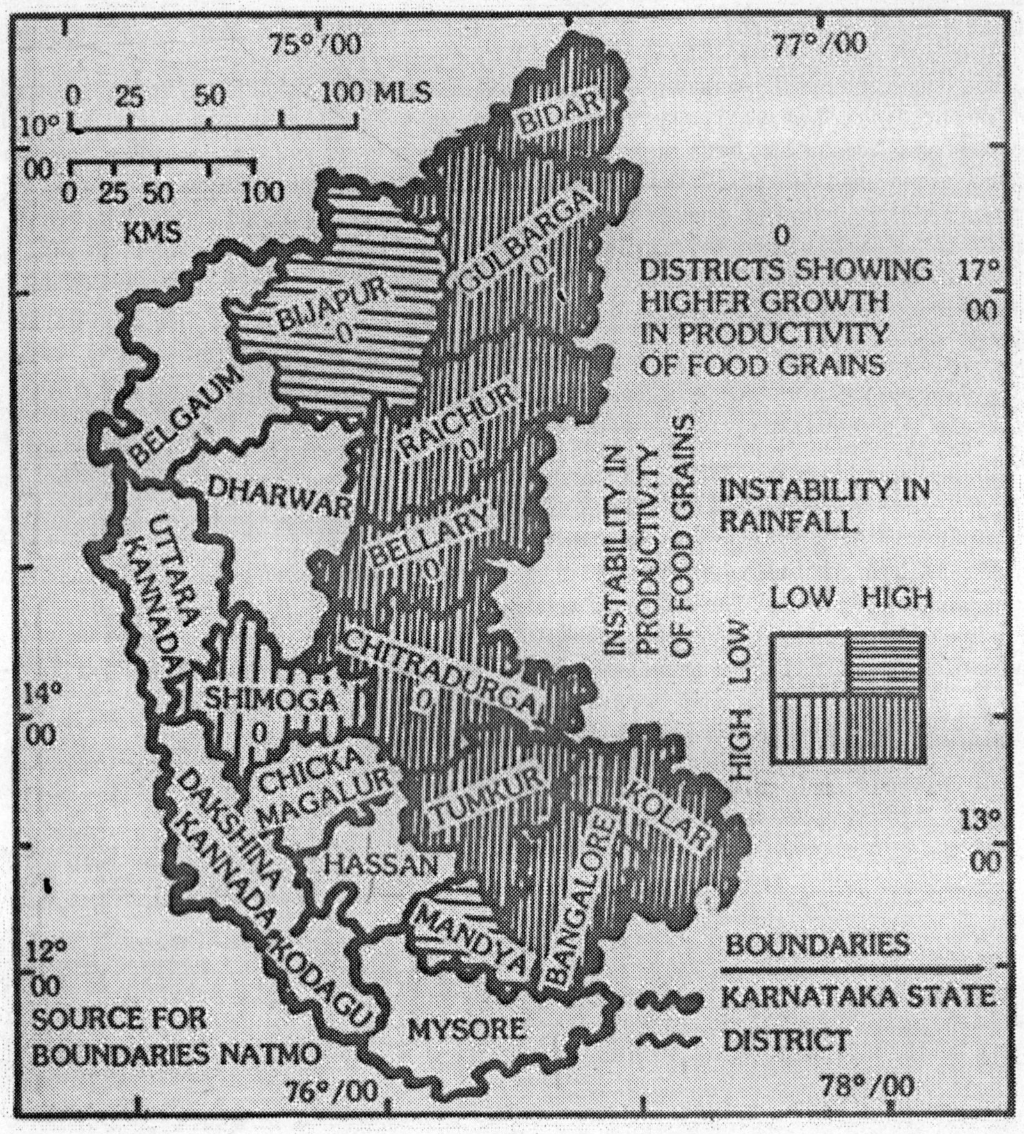


*Map*

The banking plan of each block should clearly specify the scheme under each sector so that the purposes eligible for refinance may be straightaway taken by the NABARD for sanction. The NABARD treats the banking plan itself as a scheme and sanctions refinance for the participating banks for loans given for agriculture and allied activities. The regional office of the NABARD is invited to attend the meetings of both the Standing Committee and the DCC, at which the banking plan for the IRD Programme is considered.

❑ ❑ ❑

**Table 1**
**MAJOR SECTORS IN DIFFERENT PROGRAMMES**

| Sl. No. | Major Sector | Drought prone area Programme | Hill area Development Programme | Tribal area Development Programme | Command area Development Programme | Small and Marginal Farmers Development Programme | Revised minimum Needs Programme | Normal state Government Programme |
|---|---|---|---|---|---|---|---|---|
| 1. | Agriculture | 0 | 0 | 0 | 0 | 0 | – | 0 |
| 2. | Minor irrigation | 0 | 0 | 0 | 0 | 0 | – | 0 |
| 3. | Soil and water conservation | 0 | 0 | 0 | 0 | 0 | – | 0 |
| 4. | Land Development | – | 0 | 0 | 0 | 0 | – | 0 |
| 5. | Animal Husbandry | 0 | 0 | 0 | 0 | 0 | – | 0 |
| 6. | Horticulute | – | – | 0 | – | 0 | – | 0 |
| 7. | Forestry | 0 | 0 | 0 | 0 | 0 | – | 0 |
| 8. | Village industries | 0 | 0 | 0 | 0 | 0 | – | 0 |
| 9. | Co-operation | 0 | 0 | 0 | 0 | 0 | – | 0 |
| 10. | General education | – | – | – | – | – | 0 | 0 |
| 11. | Technical education/training | 0 | – | 0 | – | 0 | – | 0 |
| 12. | Health and sanitation | – | – | – | – | – | 0 | |
| 13. | Sewerage and water supply | 0 | – | – | – | – | 0 | 0 |
| 14. | Housing | – | 0 | – | – | – | 0 | 0 |
| 15. | Urban Development | – | – | – | – | – | 0 | 0 |
| 16. | Roads | 0 | 0 | 0 | 0 | 0 | 0 | 0 |
| 17. | Power | 0 | – | – | – | – | 0 | 0 |

0 Sectors included — Sectors not included.

*Source* : Compiled.

**STATEMENT 1:**
**COMPOSITION OF DISTRICT LEVEL PLANNING BODY IN THE STATES**

| *State* | *Name of the Planning Body* | *Chairman/Vice-Chairman* | *Member* |
|---|---|---|---|
| Andhra Pradesh | Not known | Not known | Not known |
| Assam | District Development Committee | Deputy Commissioner | District Heads of all Development Committees. |
| Bihar | Not known | Not known | Not known |
| Gujarat | District Planning Board | A minister from the district, District Collector (VC) president District Panchayat (Co-VC) | All MLAs, mayor of Municipal Council, president one of Municipal Panchayat and most of the Head Development Departments, Representatives of Lead Bank and Cooperative Bank. An expert from Research Institution. District Planning officer Member-Secretary. |
| Himachal Pradesh | District Planning Committee | Not known | Not known |
| Jammu & Kashmir | District Development Board | Not known | State Cabinet Members |
| Karnataka | District Development Council | Deputy Commissioner | MLAs, MPs, Presidents of Taluk Boards. Heads of all Development Departments, District Planning Officer, and Member-secretary. |
| Kerala | Not known | Not known | Not known |
| Madhya Pradesh | District Planning Board | District Collector (Secretary), District Planning Officer Deputy Secretary | MLAs, MPs, three prominent social workers, President of District Panchayat, Urban local body, District co-op. Bank, District Mortgage Bank, Manager of lead Bank. |
| Maharashtra | District Planning and Development Council | Designated Ministers of the District. Other Ministers and Divisional commissioner (VSs) | MLAs, MPs, MLCs, President of zilla parishads, Mayor of Municipal Corporation, one President each from 'A' class, 'B' class and 'C' class Municipal Council in the district, chairman of district Central Cooperation, Regional Manager of lead Bank, Chairman of Maharashtra village and Khadi Industries. |

## Statement 1 (Contd.)

| *State* | *Name of the Planning Body* | *Chairman/Vice-Chairman* | *Member* |
|---|---|---|---|
| | | | Board, Superintendent of Post Offices, Chief Executive Officer of Zilla Parishad and 13 non-official members nominated by state government. Deputy Commissioner is Member-Secretary. |
| Meghalaya | District Board | Non-official Chairman and Deputy Chairman either from MLAs, MPs for prominent citizens | MLAs, MPs and other prominent citizens and Deputy Commissioner. District Planning Officer is the Member-secretary. |
| Nagaland | District Planning Board | Deputy Commissioner | District Head of all Development Committees prominent personalities in the district. District planning officer is Member-secretary. |
| Orissa | District Development Board | District Collector | Head of all Developments and MLAs, and MPs, District Planning Officer is Member-secretary. |
| Punjab | District Planning Committee | Deputy Commissioner | MLAs, Chairman Zilla Parishad and Block Samitics in the district, representative from Lead Bank, Heads of all Development Departments, One Development minded non-official of the district. Planning Officer is Member-secretary. |
| Rajasthan | District level Planning Committee | District Collector | MLAs, MPs of the district. Heads of all Development Departments of the district, Circle Superintendents of post office. |
| Uttar Pradesh | District Plan Advisory Committee (there is also Divisional Level Committee) | A Minister from the Division (group of districts) | Not known |
| West Bengal | District Co-ordination Committee | District Magistrate | Heads of all Development Departments in the district. |

**STATEMENT 2:**
**COMPOSITION OF DISTRICT PLANNING ORGANISATION IN THE STATES**

| *State* | *Name of the District Planning Organisation* | *Heads of the Organisation* | *Other Officers* |
|---|---|---|---|
| Andhra Pradesh | District Planning (Work) | Assistant Director of Statistics | One Senior investigator and Project Officers of SFDA, DPAP and ITDA. |
| Bihar | District Planning Unit District Executive Planning Committee | District Planning Officer District Collector | Necessary supporting staff. |
| Gujarat | District Executive Planning Committee | District Collector | There MLAs by rotation, President of District Panchayat, District Development Officer, Project officer of Tribal Area Sub-Plan. District Planning Officer is Member-Secretary, District Statistical Officer is Addl. Member-Secretary assisted by Research Officer and Research Assistant, Statistical Assistant and other service staff. |
| Jammu & Kashmir | District Development Commission | Not known | Not known |
| Karnataka | District Planing Committee | Deputy Commissioner | Project Director District Development Society, General Manager of District Industry Centre, District Development Asst. District Statistical Officer and District Publicity Officer and District Planning Officers is Member-Secretary. |
| Kerala | District Planning Unit | District Planning Officer | Research Officers and Research Assistants |
| Madhya Pradesh | District Planning Committee | District Director | Heads of all Development Department. |
| Maharashtra | District Planning Unit | District Planning Officer | Two Research Assistants and One Planning Assistant. |
| Manipur | District Planning Unit | District Planning Unit | One Research Assistant |
| Orissa | District Planning Unit | District Planning Officer | Not known |
| Rajasthan | District Planning Unit | District Planning Officer | Not known |
| Tripura | District Planning Unit | District Planning Officer | One Economist, One Cartographer, One industry Officer, one Co-op. Officer, One Agronomist, Five Research Investigators. |
| Uttar Pradesh | District Plan Co-ordination and Implementation Committee | Economic Officer, District Statistical Officer Regional Deputy Director of Economics and Statistics. | |

**STATEMENT 3:**
**SECTORS IDENTIFIED FOR DISTRICT PLAN**

| | *Karnataka* | *Maharashtra* | *Uttar Pradesh* | |
|---|---|---|---|---|
| 1. | Agriculture Production | Agricultural Production | Agriculture | (21) |
| 2. | Soil conservation | Medium & Minor Irrigation | Horticulture | (15) |
| 3. | Forest | Soil Conservation | NREP, | |
| 4. | Fisheries | Ayacut development | Agricultural Marketing | (3) |
| 5. | Animal Husbandry | Forest | Land & Water Conservation | (7) |
| 6. | Minor irrigation | Marketing & Warehousing | Area Development | (2) |
| 7. | Ayacut development under Minor irrigation | Co-operation | | |
| 8. | Primary & Secondary | Community development | Animal Husbandry | (44) |
| 9. | Education | Small Scale Industries | Dairy Development | (4) |
| 10. | District & village Roads | Primary and Secondary Education | Fisheries | (8) |
| 11. | Health | Social Welfare | Community development | (5) |
| 12. | Water Supply & Sanitation | Backward classes | Rural electrification | , |
| 13. | Urban Development | Rural Housing | Small and Village Industries | (3) |
| 14. | Welfare and Backward classes | Community Listening Facilities | Village roads | |
| 15. | Social Welfare | Tahsil Information Centre | Tourism, | |
| 16. | Housing | Youth Hostels | Primary, Secondary & Adult Education | |
| 17. | Cooperation | Promotion of scientific storage of food-grains, sugar Cane development (2) Labour Welfare of SC/ST social Welfare | Adult Education Ayurvedic Hospitals & Dispensaries Rural development | |

*Note :* The figures in brackets indicate number of schemes under each sector included in district plan.

**STATEMENT 4:**
**ALLOCATION FORMULA FOR DISTRIBUTING DISTRICT SECTOR OUTLAY AMONG DISTRICTS**

*Gujarat*

| | Criterion | % |
|---|---|---|
| 1. | Population (excluding towns having population of 50,000 and above) | 40 |
| 2. | Population of SC & ST, Small & Marginal, farmers, population of agricultural labourers other than SC/ST | 15 |
| 3. | Agricultural backwardness | 10 |
| 4. | Irrigation backwardness | 10 |
| 5. | Industrial backwardness | 10 |
| 6. | Backwardness in spheres of road and drinking water | 5 |
| 7. | Backwardness in respect of | 10 |
| | the targets of other selected | 5 |
| | Incentive provision | 5 |
| | Total | 100 |

*Karnataka*

| | Criterion | % |
|---|---|---|
| 1. | Population | 50 |
| 2. | Agri. production as measured by value of agricultural output | 5 |
| 3. | Backwardness in Irrigation as measured by area irrigated to net area sown | |
| | Industrial backwardness as measured | 2.5 |
| 4. | by the value of industrial output | |
| | Backwardness in communication as | |
| 5. | measured by road and railway length in kms per 100 sq. kms. area and per lakh population | |
| | Backwardness in financial | 5 |
| 6. | infrastructure as measured by size of population served by each coml. & co-op. Bank | |
| 7. | Backward in medical and health facilities as measured by the number of | 2.5 |
| 8. | hospitals per 1000 population/bed population ratio. | 2.5 |
| 9. | Backwardness in power supply | 2.5 |
| | *(a)* As measured by the proportion of | |
| 10. | villages electrified | 2.5 |
| 11. | *(b)* Per Capita power consumption | 5 |
| | Problems of weaker sections | |
| 12. | *(a)* As measured by the proportion of SCs/STs population | 2.5 |
| | *(b)* As measured by the proportion of landless agri. labourers | |
| | Local tax effort | 5 |
| | Special problems of Maland areas and drought prone areas | |
| | *(a)* As measured by the area under forests | |
| | (b) As measured by the rural population of drought prone area | |
| | Incidence of unemployment measured by the proportion of registrants at the employment exchange. | |

*Maharashtra*

| | Criterion | % |
|---|---|---|
| 1 | Population | 60 |
| (i) | Urban population | 5 |
| (ii) | SC/ST population | 5 |
| 2. | Backwardness in | |
| (i) | Agriculture | 5 |
| (ii) | Irrigation | 5 |
| (iii) | Communication | 5 |
| (iv) | Industries | |
| 3. | Special Problems | 3 |
| (i) | Drought-prone area | 15 |
| (ii) | Coastal district | 1.5 |
| (iii) | Forest areas | 5 |
| 4. | Unallocated amount for meeting special problems | 10 |
| | Total | 100 |

*Uttar Pradesh*

| | | |
|---|---|---|
| 1. | Population | 50 |
| 2. | Population of SC/STs | |
| | No. of small farmers | 5 |
| 3. | Backwardness in agriculture | 10 |
| 4. | Backwardness in industry | 5 |
| | Backwardness in roads | 5 |
| 5. | Backwardness in | |
| 6. | electrification of villages | 5 |
| | Backwardness in hospital | |
| 7. | beds | 5 |
| | No. of scarcity problem | |
| 8. | villages (Drinking water Facility) | 5 |
| | | 5 |
| 9. | | 5 |
| | Special problems | |
| 10. | | |
| | Total | 100 |

# Chapter 31

# BLOCK LEVEL PLANNING

## Introduction

A micro-level plan has the advantage of not only reflecting local needs and requirements in a better way but also of explicitly taking cognisance of the types of structural relations obtaining in small rural societies and developing credit based development interventions consistent with local ethos and institutions. For instance, for the development of a tribal area, the basis of investment could be the resources of the entire village and not of individual households. Some observers are of the view that the structure of financial institutions ought to be different for meeting the needs of tribals for the following reasons. The local economies are only partly monetized; apart from communal system of access to resources, there is much community activity for the maintenance of infrastructure; there are culturally determined moral norms guiding the circulation of surplus.

## BLOCK LEVEL PLANNING

With a view to achieving full employment the Planning Commission appointed a Working Group under the chairmanship of Prof. M. L. Dantwala to prepare guidelines for block level planning in the country. The Working Group drew up detailed guidelines for block level planning. The terms of reference of the group were:

*(i)* Definition of the exact sphere of block level planning and the way in which it should be co-ordinated;

*(ii)* The method of selecting a block;

*(iii)* The essential pre-requisites of block level planning;

*(iv)* The agency for preparing and implementing block level plans, and where and how voluntary agencies should be associated with block level planning and/or implementation;

*(v)* The question of how to integrate, particularly where there are more than one implementing agencies;

*(vi)* The cost involved in preparing a block plan;

*(vii)* The relationship between the agency preparing the plan and the agency implementing it.

The Working Group appointed five sub-groups to consider various aspects, such as organisation and planning machinery, institutional support to block level planning, the problems of institutional credit for area development, resources inventory and other information to be collected for preparing block level plans and for considering the various aspects of training in relation to block level planning.

## Objectives of Block Level Planning

*(i)* Optimum utilisation of the area leading to an increase in income and employment;

*(ii)* Ensuring that the gains of development accrue to the weaker sections of the population, small and marginal farmers, sharecroppers, agricultural labourers, and rural artisans;

*(iii)* Fulfilment of the minimum needs programme—health and medical facilities, drinking water, housing, education and supply of essential commodities through the public distribution system;

*(iv)* Build-up of social and economic infrastructure to achieve the above objectives;

*(v)* Reorientation of the existing institution/organisation, in order to protect the interests of the poor;

*(vi)* Building up of appropriate organisations of the poor to protect them from exploitation;

*(vii)* Augmentation of the duration and productivity of employment to the poor and the under-employed in their existing occupation, inter alia by upgrading technology, imparting skills and setting up non-exploitative institutions with credit, marketing and extension services; and

*(viii)* Alleviating chronic unemployment by employment in public works.

## Flexibility Needed

In taking a block as a unit of planning, the group has clarified that no rigidity should be employed in the choice. Different programmes and schemes will need coverage appropriate to their operational requirements. In any case, keeping in view the imperative of vertical and horizontal linkages, the group has recommended the placement of a planning team at district headquarters to ensure the integration of the block plan with district plan.

While taking note of the proposal of the Government of India to introduce block level planning in 35,000 blocks in the next five years, the group has suggested the policy of "hastening slowly" in the initiation of this proposal. It feels that the planning machinery in several states, particularly at the district level, is very weak, if not non-existent, and that a hasty adoption of the proposal may prove self-defeating. The group has noted that, in 2,945 block out of 5,000 one or more of the special programmes (SFDA, DPAP and CAD) are already operating. Keeping these facts in view, it has recommended that, beginning with 100 block level planning each year may be progressively increased to 500 (additional) in the terminal year of the Sixth Plan. It has endorsed the criteria indicated by the Government of India for the selection of additional blocks for intensive development.

Since the major objective of block level planning is the elimination of poverty and unemployment, top priority will have to be given to those districts/blocks in which the intensity of unemployed is very acute. The group has suggested that the exercise, undertaken by the Planning Commission, by which "group of regions" have been ranked in terms of the intensity of backwardness, should be carried further, and a priority list of districts may be prepared. It feels that the responsibility for the selection of block from priority districts should be that of the state government. It recommends that, at least one block should be taken up for intensive development in every district in the country. The group considers it essential that the components of all the special programmes operating in the selected blocks should be merged in the block level plans, and funds allocated to these programmes should be placed at the disposal of the block level planning authority.

## Core Group

The Working Group has stressed the need for strengthening planning capabilities at the district level. It has recommended that the planning team at the district level should consist of a core group, with a chief planner, economist/statistician, cartographer, agronomist, engineer, industry officer, and a credit planning officer. In addition to the above core staff, specialists may be engaged according to the needs of the area or the programme.

According to the report, another highly debatable issue pertains to the authority which the Panchayti Raj institutions (Zilla Parishad, for example) the Group fully endorses the philosophy of decentralisation in decision making, it points out that two problems should first be sorted out. First, in a large number of states, Panchayati Raj institutions are either non-existent, or are in a moribund state. The reality has to be reckoned with in making any recommendation which is meant for immediate implementation. Second there is a widespread feeling that, by and large, Panchayati Raj unsteadiness do not reflect the interests and needs of the weaker section of the community. Given the structure of ownership of land and other assets in rural and urban areas, a powerful ideological commitment would be required for implementing a plan deliberately biased in favour of the poor. Keeping these facts in view, the group suggests that the decision in this regard should be taken after an appropriate appraisal of the full-fledged representative character of Panchayati Raj institutions.

The Working Group is of the opinion that the country's social and economic problems are so vast that the government's administrative machinery alone cannot tackle them. Keeping in view the significance of the technical component in planning and the fact that very few voluntary agencies have the requisite competence for it, the group feels that the responsibility for preparing an integrated area plan must be shouldered by the government. The planning team at the district level should consult and actively seek the assistance of the voluntary agencies in their area while preparing the plan, and selectively entrust to them the implementation of some sectoral plans in which they may have the requisite expertise and experience. It can be a joint venture; but the ultimate responsibility should be that of the planning team. The group feels that the state governments, if they so wish many entrust the task of preparing a certain number of block plans to voluntary agencies. In the same manner, professional institutes may be actively associated with the planning exercise, though the total responsibility for the preparation of the plan remains with the government.

## Public Participation

The group has emphasised the necessity and importance of public participation at the different stages of planning. At the same time, it has drawn attention to the limits to such participation. Since the rural community is not homogeneous, it would be necessary to make a special endeavour to ensure the participation of the weaker sections in the planning process. Also, the public will have to be familiarised with the problem of the financial and technical constraints of planning, so that it may recognise the need for exercising restraint in presenting the planner with a catalogue of demands, and get used to the inevitability of mutual adjustment.

To integrate the block and district plans into the overall state plan, the state planning team will have to give to the block level team a broad indication of the entire state plan and its priorities, the financial parameters within which to plan, and the continuing schemes to which a part of the plan expenditure is committed. The group has suggested that the compilation of a resource inventory may be deferred till the planning teams know exactly what they want for the purpose of inventory and why. It has emphasised the fact that the resource inventory should be more in the nature of a series of "Status Papers" containing an analysis of performance, identification of constraints and developmental potential. Of particular importance would be the "Status Paper on the weaker sections, their needs and their disabilities."

The group has attached great importance to the reform of the agrarian structure and institutional set-up so that they may effectively serve the needs of the rural poor and protect their interest. It is convinced that in the absence of adequate structural and institutional support, the proposed step up in the allocation of financial resources for the elimination of destitution and augmentation of employment opportunities will not achieve the desired objectives. The absence of basic records of rights in land in many districts has proved a major obstacle in the implementation of land reforms extension of irrigation facilities, supply of inputs and deployment of credit. If such reforms do not exit or are in arrears, their preparation should receive high priority in the block level plan.

The group recommends a two-pronged strategy for employment generation. Since under-employment constitutes a large component of the total "unemployed mandays." it has been suggested that the development projects and planned investment should be directed towards in their existing occupations. The measures suggested for this purpose are intensification and diversification of agriculture and rehabilitation of rural industries. Second, there is a hard core of wholly unemployed persons who possess neither assets nor skills to get assimilated in the mainstream of economic activities. For them, a massive programme of public works would be an appropriate strategy of employment planning.

The Working Group has argued that institutional credit should be tapped to augment the scope and coverage of the development programme. A major obstacle in this is lack of proper liaison between development agencies and the institutional credit system. The group has suggested that a credit planning officer should be included in the planning team to cover this lacuna. It says that, during the last decade, there has been a marked expansion and diversification in, and innovative approaches to, the provision of credit to rural areas; but a feeling still persists that credit institutions are hesitant and conservation in providing the necessary credit to the rural economy. In this connection, the group has taken note of the Committee Working Groups recently appointed by the Reserve Bank of India and has expressed the hope that their recommendations would help to remove many of the deficiencies in the flow of credit to rural borrowers.

## PLANNING PROCESSES AND DECENTRALISATION

The block as a unit of planning has been accepted by the government. It is sufficiently small in terms of area and population to promote intimate contact and understanding between the planners, those responsible for the implementation of the plan, and the people. Block level planning has to be viewed, not as an isolated exercise, but as a link at all levels—from a cluster of villages below the block level to the project, district and state level.

In the preparation of a block plan, planners should first:

*(i)* Ascertain specifically the physical and human resources potential;

*(ii)* Identify the constraints inhibiting socio-economic and technological growth;

*(iii)* Understand the felt needs of the people and the factors inhibiting the uplift of the block, and, in particular, the weaker section;

*(iv)* Expand the area of people's participation in the formulation and implementation of plans;

*(v)* Formulate production programmes suited to the capacity and needs of the areas in the light of their resource potential;

*(vi)* Undertake an exercise in manpower planning and skill development in relation to the production programmes; and

*(vii)* Formulate programmes for institutional support.

Block level planning call for co-ordination at the district level so that a proper programme may be worked out and the best deployment of resources particularly for such schemes and programmes as cut across the boundaries of more than one block, maybe secured. Efforts should be made to ensure that the block plan does not become a lone and truncated exercise, and must be closely co-ordinated with planning at the district and states levels. This would be all the more important in respect of such items as expansion of infrastructure, provision of essential inputs, administrative interaction and adaptation. In order to facilitate such interaction and integration, a sort of perspective and indicative plan should be prepared for all the backward areas, covering more than one block within the district, and constituting a project or project comprising two to three blocks with similar problems. Planning and co-ordination would also be necessary to eliminate contradictions, inconsistencies, discrepancies and overlaps among the schemes worked out by the different departments, and to render the block level schemes mutually compatible and supportive in order to increase their overall development impact. While preparing district plans, it should be ensured that district level elected representatives are fully associated with finalising the programmes and their implementation. So, too, the elected representatives of the poor and disadvantaged people in the district. The methodology for associating the elected representatives of the poor and disadvantaged and other concerned non-governmental and local governmental bodies in the district has been discussed in detail in a separate section.

The district plans, prepared for all the districts where backward areas lie, should then be forwarded to the state government, which would co-ordinate them and give them the shape of a "Sub Plan" for the development of backward areas.

In order to ensure that the necessary direction and guidance on major policy issues connected with the development of backward areas, particularly in block level planning and implementation, are available, there should be a high-powered Steering Committee at the state level under the chairmanship of the Chief Minister and consisting of the minister for the key sectors in rural development, such as agriculture, industry, health, education, irrigation, etc. as members. A senior officer of the rank of Commissioner may be Secretary of this Steering Committee. The state level department responsible for the planning and development of backward areas should be responsible for the following functions:

- *(a)* Issue of guidelines;
- *(b)* Allocation of material and financial resources;
- *(c)* Provision for the monitoring of performance and benefits;
- *(d)* Corrective reorientation; and
- *(e)* Training.

## Methodology of Central and State Plan Allocations

In the case of the State Plan, it has been recommended that each ministry should work out a list of schemes which, it considers, can be classified as divisible. Once this exercise has been carried out, the total outlay available for these divisible schemes should be apportioned between the backward and non-backward areas of the country on the basis of a weightage of 50 per cent for population and 50 per cent for the backward areas of the country. Ideally, of course, the backward area formula is to work out allocations for the backward areas on the basis of 50 per cent population, 30 per cent for area and 20 per cent for the income generated in the backward areas. Unfortunately, the amount of the income generated in these areas is not yet available. Till such time, however as reliable indices are available, the rough and ready formula is to give a weightage of 50 per cent for population and 50 per cent for area, as pointed out earlier.

Once this exercise has been carried out, the central ministries may undertake specific schemes in accordance with their existing guidelines. For the central schemes for which sharing is on the basis of a 50 per cent grant from the central government, it should be ensured that matching grants are always available from the central ministries when the governments have made a provision for these schemes for the backward areas. The intention here is that if adequate funds are not available with the central ministries to meet the entire 50 per cent matching grant, priority should be given to schemes for backward areas.

## Identification of Beneficiaries

It is necessary to be clear about who are the least advantaged in backward areas for the purpose of designing policies and programmes for them, or who are the people who should be regarded as the "target group" to be accorded the first priority in planning and implementing comprehensive area development strategies. Certain exercises would appear to be essential. If resources are unlimited, there would be taken up for simultaneous development, priority being accorded to the poorest. But this is not so. One has to accept this hard reality that resources—physical, financial and personnel—are limited. Development strategies and plans have, therefore, to be formulated by keeping in view the available and foreseeable resources within a time frame, and give priority to the poorest among the poor in the backward areas. It is therefore essential to define who should be the "beneficiaries".

# ORGANISATIONAL SET-UP FOR PLANNING AND IMPLEMENTATION

The concept of planning for development and its execution as a time bound programme requires as well-considered counterpart administrative input. Unity of command is often considered an essential element of any administrative system. But unified command requires a capability on the part of the command to deal with all the details in all the hierarchies of the administration, institutions and local bodies. A good and efficient administrative system is *inter alia*, expected to play the role of an innovator and pacesetter for socio-economic changes in rural areas, with the effective participation of the people. Programmes which are likely to be undertaken should be varied enough to require an adequate and a high level of inputs, both technical and non-technical. A strong multi-disciplinary leadership at the field level will have to conceived. Whatever organisation is entrusted with the task of developing the rural areas will have to constantly address itself to the need for achieving efficiency.

The strategy of development in backward areas should maximise productivity in the crop production sector. Because of the fundamental backwardness of these areas, the inherent potential for agricultural growth and the application of the latest technology which increases productivity have not yet been realised. The initial thrust will, therefore, have to be on substantial increases in agricultural productivity by suitable land use, multiple cropping practices and larger applications of inputs. This will necessitate the marshalling of input supplies, particularly fertilizers, pesticides, power, irrigation, equipment, credit, etc. As a result of these, productivity increases, greater and wider employment opportunities will be generated and a greater consumption demand will develop for consumer goods which, in turn, will give a boost to animal husbandry, pisciculture, agriculture, horticulture and village and small industries producing good and services for local consumption. The strategy will be to suitably phase this secondary development in a suitable time frame and adjust to available demand. A parallel effect of the development of consumer industries will be to raise a demand for such services as transport and marketing, which will generate further employment in the tertiary sector. Suitable skills will have to be developed to enable the agricultural labourers to avail themselves of the new labour opportunities that will arise in the secondary and tertiary sectors of growth. The whole process of adjusting the new economy to the rural environment will require the active participation and co-operation of the rural population, particularly of the rural poor. It is, therefore essential that, from the very commencement of the programme itself, the people whose lot is intended to be improved, are enabled to play an effective role in the planning and implementation process. There will thus have to be a multi-pronged attempt to tackle the problem of backward area development.

Till recently, the major thrust towards the development of the rural areas has been for the development of agriculture. Agriculture is, by and large, a private enterprise, involving millions of farmers—large, medium, small and marginal. Dry-farming technology, intensive horticulture, farm forestry and inland and brackish water fisheries are recent additions to the available technologies for maximising returns on land according to the environment. The future of rural development and the abolition of poverty will depend very largely on an intensive and widespread dissemination of these technologies in the field.

Rural development may be achieved only when the various production opportunities are brought to the doors of the rural household. Each of the sectors, comprising agriculture, rural industry, tertiary sector opportunities and labour opportunities, is comprehensive and multi-disciplinary. Each calls for the integration and co-ordination of the efforts of scientists and technologists, extension workers and institutions, and for services, marketing facilities and training of all those participating in the vast complicated structure. First, there has to be co-ordination in the chain of technology transfer from the laboratory to the field. Second, there has to be co-ordination between the technical programme and the other requirements. Third, and the most important of all, there has to be overall integration of, and coordination between, the several sectors in order to make a comprehensive package of services for the households according to their capacities to absorb them.

Co-ordination is management problem. The essential needs of co-ordination are:

*(i)* The co-ordinator must have a bird's eye view of the whole complex, and broadly understand the interplay of the several parts in the functioning of the system;

*(ii)* When systems are large, each function should be given full freedom to work and authority should be decentralized so that the head of each function may perform effectively;

*(iii)* The co-ordinator should not treat himself as an expert in any of the functions and overrule the head in charge of the function, but uncover the problem in the co-ordination level for a consensus.

*(iv)* The co-ordinator does not impose decisions but arrives at an acceptable consensus in which he will take a guiding role on the basis of his understanding of the interplay of the functions in the system.

Considering the experience of the various models attempted so far for specific programmes, and the fact that the new strategy envisages a comprehensive development approach, what has to be aimed at is not the creation of a new organisation, but a suitable restructuring and remoulding of the existing set-up. The administrative set-up for integrated rural development should be area-based, with built-in multi-purpose characteristics for a well-defined area. The set-up should cover all the rural development activities, which should function in a co-ordinated way. In order words, the set-up would largely be an entity comprising the existing administrative units in the given area, with such innovation and modifications as are necessary to achieve the ends in view.

A question at this stage may arise: Will such an approach have any special characteristics which will distinguish it from the traditional administrative structure? If, under the new dispensation, the proposed organisation is a conglomeration of the existing units, it may, in reality, be merely a new name for the old system. If the present system has not delivered the goods, how can it be expected that a mere renaming and certain modifications would give it the necessary drive and dynamism? Past experience has shown that a new body/organisation, set up with the best of intentions, loses, with the passage of time, its initial drive and becomes dysfunctional. Whatever may be the rationale for the creation of a totally new organisation, it only adds to the mess. It would be best, therefore, to introduce such innovations as are necessary to fit in with the total development approach and the full involvement of the people. Such innovations would succeed only if they area introduced within the existing structure by changing, re-moulding and fusing them together, without addition to the mess, but strengthening them, where necessary.

## Proposed Set-up

As discussed earlier, a comprehensive development project should be implemented on the basis of "project approach" on the pattern of the Integrated Tribal Development Project for the total development of the project area. This project should cover the entire non-regulatory administrative apparatus in the project area. An important question has to be settled as to the role Panchayati Raj in the structure. At the block level, the Panchayat Samiti is an elected body with certain powers of policy formulation. The actual field picture of the powers and authority of the Panchayat Samiti varies very substantially from state to state. The only fixed authority at this level is the Block Development Officer; and there is an agreement for co-ordination of the other hierarchies at that point for certain accepted policies. The project approach, dealing with more than one backward block, has the capacity to coordinate satisfactorily the work of the Panchayat Samiti in the field and the work of the other departments and institutions within the project area. There is no conflict between Panchayat Raj and the project authority at this level. The chairman of the Panchayati Samiti should be included as a member on the Board of Management at the project level to bring about the necessary co-ordination.

## DISTRIBUTION OF FUNCTION AT VARIOUS LEVELS

### Block Level

(1) Education up to higher secondary level, where possible;

(2) Elementary health services;

(3) Agricultural extension;

(4) Supply of agricultural inputs;

(5) Elementary veterinary services;

(6) Multi-purpose co-operative societies providing the integrated services of credit marketing, supply of inputs, smaller godowns in market centres;

(7) Organisation of local panchayats;

(8) Household industries; and

(9) Village approach roads.

### Local Planning

Block level planning will have to be given full support in order to ensure that development of agriculture and rural activities receives the necessary fillip. Further, for conservation and optimum utilisation of moisture and water resources, civil engineering projects will have to be formulated on the basis of watersheds, village-wise or depending on the size of watersheds, clusters of villages or for block. Once water availability for crops in ensured, suitable steps for identifying the best crops and ensuring availability of water for such crops will have to be taken up, by preparing various projects for water-economizing irrigation-development. Development of irrigation, horticulture and agriculture will need to be supported with credit facilities and from this angle, the banks' credit programmes will have to closely follow the programmes to development based on the local development and planning effort. Thus, development of economic activities at the grassroots levels will have to be carefully planned, through preparation of various projects—some supported out of the carefully planned, through preparation of various projects—some supported out of the revenues of the state government or local bodies and others out of private savings and loans from banks and other financial institutions. Local planning effort will have to be carefully fostered through formulation of inter-related projects at the grassroot levels.

Under the Service Area Approach, the planning exercise will be expected to start at the grassroots level. Each branch manager will have to draw up the credit plan for his service area, which will also form the basis for the performance budget of the branch and he would be accountable for the implementation of the plan.

Even if the planning is to commence from the branch level, the district level would be relevant for provision of infrastructure and linkages on which credit extension would still depend. Lead bank officers have over the years acquired skills in credit planning and preparation of bankable schemes relevant to the district. Under the new approach, the lead bank officer will prepare bankable schemes for reasonably large areas such as blocks, will hold seminars of branch managers block-wise to explain the details of the schemes and the factors which should be taken into account for determining the number of feasible units in different areas. The Branch Manager will study the village data and in consultation with village/block level staff, decide schemes and viable number of units thereunder, which he will be able to finance in a given time-frame. The annual lending programme drawn up by each branch can be aggregated into annual credit plan for the block. Thus, the branchwise programmes will be aggregated into block-wise credit plans and further into annual credit plan for the district. Under the new system of credit planning, the annual action plan will improve in its contents, as it would become a consolidation of realistic plans drawn up by implementing branches. Branch Managers' commitments to fulfilling the targets will also improve and the targets themselves would have real meaning.

The initial exercise of allocation of villages as service area among the rural and semi-urban branches of commercial banks including the RRBs has been more or less completed. The bank branches have also been conducting surveys of the villages included in their services area and under the guidance of the Lead Bank Officers, they would soon start preparing their annual lending programmes, covering both farm and non-farm sector activities, for the service areas. The lending programmes would reflect on the one hand the credit needs of the villages, carefully assessed by the branch managers in the framework of viable schemes and existing market potential and availability of infrastructure and other linkage-support and organisational capabilities of the branch to handle rural lending, on the other.

❑ ❑ ❑

## Chapter 32

# 20-POINT PROGRAMME AND RURAL DEVELOPMENT

## Introduction

The government has played a major role in the development process to promote the interest of the poor, reduce disparities in income and wealth, curb regional inequalities in the level of development, protect the environment, strengthen the scientific-technological base for long-term growth and safeguard the interests of future generations. These are matters which cannot be left to the free play of market forces. Purposive government intervention in these crucial areas is central to India's rural growth strategy.

During the last one decade (1975-1986) three sets of 20-point programmes were launched. Though, these points started as stray thoughts, they received the sanction of the government and turned out to be a programme. Although the 20-points conflict with other programmes in operation then, these were of significance as a plan of action.

There are three sets of 20-points which have by and large aimed at eradication of poverty, development of agriculture along with other social measures. In this chapter, we discuss the role of the 20-point programme in relation to rural development. In short, 20-point programme is a multi-pronged attack on poverty. It consists of economic programmes as well as ameliorative measures conducive for growth.

## THE GENESIS

The 20-point programme, firstly initiated by the Prime Minister on July 1,1975 as a step to ushering a new era for the poor and the downtrodden was refurbished on January 14, 1982. The announcement of the new 20-point programme was, however, a logical extension of the 20-point programme announced in 1975. In the words of the Prime Minister, "This agenda for the nation has been development. It pinpoints the areas of special thrust which will show immediate tangible results for various segments." The 20-point economic programme is a multipronged attack on poverty. Some of the points are ameliorative in nature and some others aim at breaking stagnation for generating growth and welfare in rural areas. Growth is possible through strengthening of infrastructure, mobilising and utilising resources and increasing productivity through various strategies, including investment in human capital and through agricultural and industrial development. Further, in formulating the 1983-84 annual plan, the government's primary concern had been to provide maximum support to those projects and programmes which are of immediate benefit to the economy and especially to the weaker sections to the society. The outlays for the new 20-point programme have been enhanced to Rs 10,000 crores and special thrust is being given to the programmes that benefit the poor directly. The revised 20-point programme has acquired a national status and all the states have agreed to implement them without reservation. Addressing a conference of Chief Ministers convened to review the progress of the revised 20-point programme on April 4, 1983, the Prime Minister stated that "this (revised 20-point) programme should not be treated as her programme. It is a national programme. It is designed for the entire nation to participate in its implementation. Its only politics is the good of the people." The Chief Ministers agreed to implement the revised 20-point Economic Programme with greater co-operation of the people and voluntary agencies. Although the progress of the revised 20-point economic programme had been encouraging, there is a need to dovetial the programme into a general plan so that it would serve as a dynamic instrument of production as well as the welfare of the people. Consistent with the social objectives placed before the banking system, the aspects of the 20-point programme listed above have a special relevance to it. The banking system has to play an important role in assisting the fulfilment of the aims and objectives of programme by so orienting its credit policy as to provide one of the essential input necessary, namely, credit, for the successful implementation of the various programmes. The concept of priority sector lending has been evolved to ensure that assistance from the banking system flows in an increasing measure to certain vital sectors for the economy and according to national planning priorities. This concept has been reviewed from time to time with a view to ensuring that necessary changes are brought about by banks in their credit deployment policy.

The advances to the weaker sections as identified should reach a level of 25 per cent of priority sector advances or 10 per cent of total bank credit by the end of March 1985.

Sustained efforts are called for on the part of the banking system to achieve the estimated increase in the level of outstanding credit to weaker sections.

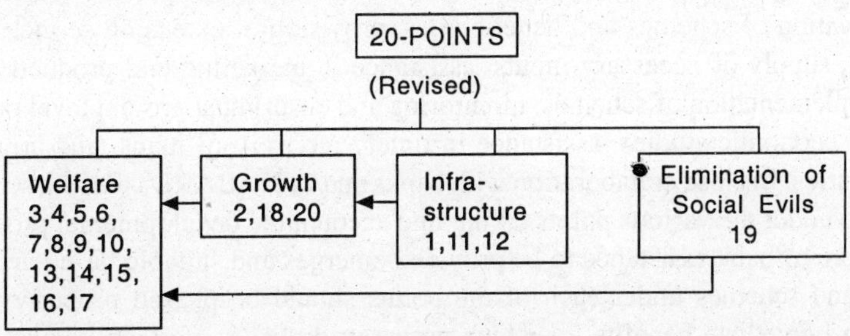


*Fig. 1. Classification of the Revised 20-Point Economic Programme According to Broad Goals*

The field level machinery has to be geared up to achieve this task. The systems and procedure have to be suitably simplified keeping in view the type of beneficiaries to be financed and the same should be implemented effectively at the field level. The state government and their agencies have a variety or responsibilities like systematic identification of schemes and beneficiaries, provision of extension services, linkages and infrastructural facilities, provision of necessary inputs and assistance in marketing end products, technical support in preparation and implementation of schemes, monitoring and ensuring at ground level proper implementation of schemes, conducting techno-economic studies, assisting the timely recovery of loan arrangements for imparting training to beneficiaries. The achievement of the targets for assisting the weaker sections depended critically upon the co-ordinated and effective performance of their respective roles by banks as well as government agencies.

There is no scope for raising the targets of one per cent prescribed for DRI advances. There is, however need for more precise means of identifying the beneficiaries under the DRI Scheme. The government and Reserve Bank may consider this on the basis of the finding of the study carried out by NIBM. It is not considered necessary to make any change in the existing target for credit-deposit ratio of rural and semi-urban branches. The credit deposit ratio on an area-wise basis is not a perfect guide to measure the performance of banks. It may not be feasible to achieve the target of 40 per cent set for priority sector advances uniformly in all states. It will not also be practicable to fix different targets on a state-wise basis.

## Role of Co-operative and Regional Rural Banks

The co-operatives and RRBs have an important role to play in the implementation of the new 20-point programme. In this context, there is a need for effective co-ordination between commercial banks, RRBs, and co-operatives in implementing DCPs. For ensuring effective participation of the co-operatives, it is necessary to take certain steps such as *(i)* implementing a time-bound programme for re-organisation and revitalization of weak co-operative banks, primary agricultural societies and industrial societies, *(ii)* provision of adequate trained personnel, *(iii)* setting up of separate monitoring cells in the co-operative department and District Co-operative Banks to review the performance of co-operatives in the matter of implementation of the 20-Point Programme etc. Weakening of financial institutions particularly co-operatives, as a result of accumulation of overdue and consequent non-recycling of funds should be considered as a matter of concern not only to the financial institutions but also to state government and developmental agencies concerned. Concerted efforts should therefore be made all around to promote a healthy recovery atmosphere and ethics.

Co-operative banks may ensure that the share of the weaker sections is not less than half of the total credit advanced by co-operatives during a year. RRBs should draw up plans to ensure sizeable participation by them in financing the 20-Point Programme.

## Role of State Governments

For ensuring smooth flow of financial assistance from banks to the 20-Point Programme beneficiaries, supportive action on the part of state government and their agencies is essential. Their responsibilities include systematic identification of schemes and beneficiaries, provision of extension services, linkages and infrastructural facilities, supply of necessary inputs, assistance in marketing end-products, technical support in preparation and implementation of schemes, monitoring and ensuring at ground level proper implementation of schemes techno-economic studies, assistance in timely recovery of loans, and arrangements for giving training to beneficiaries. In close collaboration with banks and/or NABARD, specific schemes/plans of action should be drawn up under the various points taking into account the developmental programmes in the states so that a clear picture of bank assistance to be provided emerges and suitable tie-up arrangements are made. The programmes and schemes under each of the points should be phased properly with priorities fixed. Schemes providing immediate benefits for which necessary linkages are readily available can be taken up initially.

State governments may actively consider the question of setting up suitable intermediary organisation with appropriate back-up facilities at field level for disbursing credit to weaker sections in rural and semi-urban areas. Apart from organising state corporations and agencies, the weaker section beneficiaries may be organised into homogeneous functional groups for ensuring more meaningful extension of institutional credit, required support from development agencies in matters like technical advice input-supply and marketing, better supervision and improvement in the economic life of target groups. The block level functionaries should encourage formation of such groups wherever possible and render active assistance to them. Concerted efforts should be made to promote a healthy atmosphere and ethics for recovery of overdue. Field level staff of state governments should be apprised of their role in the various areas indicated above, in order that efficient co-ordination between banks and state government staff at field level in ensured. Necessary steps should be taken to make to state level plans and to discuss the various developmental programmes contemplated in the state with district-wise allocations, so that the institutional financing arrangements are properly integrated with them.

There has to be a proper phasing of the programmes and schemes under each of the point and fixation of priorities by the stage governments. Schemes which will provide immediate benefits and for which necessary linkages and readily available resources may be taken up initially. Banks should integrate assistance to 20-point beneficiaries under DCPs/AAPs by including all viable/bankable schemes drawn up under the programme.

The guidelines issued by RBI for making the DCC an effective instrument of co-ordination need to be implemented by banks and state governments. Similarly the SLCC should also be made an effective instrument of co-ordination at the state level. The question of setting up suitable intermediary organisation, with appropriate back-up facilities, may be considered by state governments to facilitate credit flows in an organised manner to the weaker sections as well as assistance regarding input supply and marketing.

The successful implementation of the new 20-point programme also needs that a more serious attempt is made to weed out corruption from the administration. And this again can only succeed if the ruling party is able to project a clean image. People will draw their own conclusions from the fact that while the new 20-point programme refers to action against smugglers, hoarders, tax evaders, black-marketeers it says nothing about ending corruption in the administration.

## THE NEW 20-POINT PROGRAMME

(1) Increase irrigation potential, develop and disseminate technologies and inputs for dryland agriculture.

(2) Make special efforts to increase production of pulses and vegetable oil seeds.

(3) Strengthen and expand coverage of Integrated Rural Development and National Rural Employment Programmes.

(4) Implement agricultural land ceilings, distribute surplus land and complete compilation of land records by removing all administrative and legal obstacles.

(5) Review and effectively enforce minimum wages for agricultural labour.

(6) Rehabilitate bonded labour.

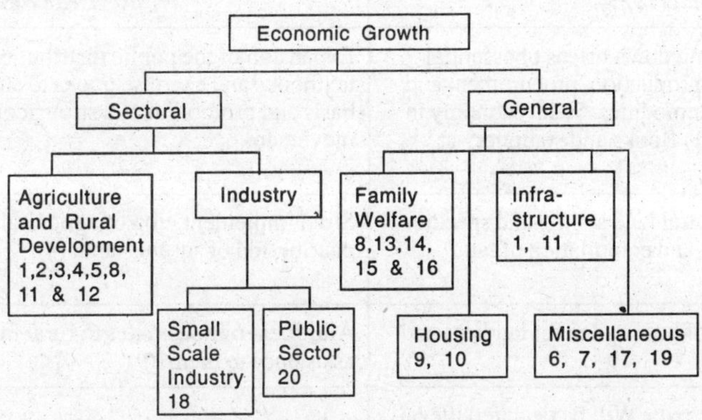


*Fig. 2. A Broad Sectoral Classification of the Revised 20-Point Economic Programme Pertaining to Growth and Development are grouped*

(7) Accelerate programmes for the development of Scheduled Castes and Tribes.

(8) Supply drinking water to all problem villages.

(9) Allot house sites to rural families who are without them and expand programmes for construction assistance to them.

(10) Improve the environment of slums, who are without them and house building for economically weaker sections, and take measures to arrest unwarranted increase in land prices.

(11) Maximise power generation, improve the functioning of electricity authorities and electrify all villages.

(12) Pursue vigorously programmes of afforestation, social and farm forestry and the development of bio-gas and other alternative energy sources.

(13) Promote family planning on voluntary basis as a people's movement.

(14) Substantially augment universal primary health care facilities, and control of leprosy, TB and blindness.

(15) Accelerate programme of welfare for women and children and nutrition programmes for pregnant women, nursing mothers and children, specially in tribal, hill and backward areas.

(16) Spread universal elementary education for the age-group 6-14 with special emphasis on girls, and simultaneously involve students and voluntary agencies in programmes for the removal of adult illiteracy.

(17) Expand the public distribution system through more fair price shops, including mobile shops in far-flung areas and shops to cater to industrial workers, students' hostels and make available to students textbooks and exercise books on a priority basis and to promote a strong consumer protection movement.

(18) Liberalise investment procedures and streamline industrial policies to ensure timely completion of projects. Give handicrafts, handlooms, small and village industries all facilities to grow and to update their technology.

(19) Continue strict action against smugglers, hoarders and tax evaders and check black money.

(20) Improve the working of the public enterprise by increasing efficiency, capacity utilisation and the generation of internal resources.

**COMPARATIVE STUDY OF 20-POINT ECONOMIC PROGRAMME COMMON POINTS**

| *Original (1975)* | *Revised (1982)* |
|---|---|
| Continuance of steps to bring down prices of essential commodities. Streamlined production, procurement and distribution of essential commodities. Strict economy in government expenditure. (1) Books and stationery at controlled prices (19) | Expansion of the public distributing system, supply of textbooks and exercise books to students on a priority basis and promotion of a strong consumer protection movement. |
| Implementation of agricultural land selling and speedier distribution of surplus land and compilation of land records. (2) | Strict implementation of agricultural land ceiling and distribution of surplus land. (4) |
| Stepping up of provisions of house sites for landless and weaker sections. (3) | Allotment of house sites to rural families and construction assistance to them. (9) |
| Bonded labour wherever it exits. Will be declared illegal. (4) | |

| *Original (1975)* | *Revised (1982)* |
|---|---|
| Review of laws on minimum agricultural wages. (6) | Review and effective enforcement of minimum wage for agricultural labour. (5) |
| Five million more hectares to be brought under irrigation. National programme for use of ground water. (7) | Increase the irrigation potential, develop and disseminate technologies and inputs for dryland agriculture. (1) |
| An acceleration in power programme. Super thermal stations under Central control (8) | Maximisation of power generation, electrification of all villages. (11) |
| Socialisation of urban and urbanisable land. Ceiling on ownership and possession of vacant land on plinth area of new dwelling units. (11) | Improving the environment of slums and house-building schemes for economically weaker sections. |
| Special squads for valuation of conspicuous construction and prevention of tax evasion. Summary trials and deterrent punishment of economic offenders. (12) | Continued strict action against smugglers. |
| Special legislation of confiscation of smugglers'/offenders' assets. (12), | |
| Liberalisation of investment procedures. Action against misuse of import licences. (14) | Liberalisation of investment procedure and streamlinning of industrial policies to ensure timely completion of projects, all facilities to handicrafts, handlooms, small and village industries to update technology. (18) |

| *Point Omitted* | *Action Taken* |
|---|---|
| Plan for liquidation of rural indebtedness. Legislation for moratorium on recovery of debt from landless labourers, small farmers and artisans. (5) | The central government suggested to the state governments that all non-financial debts of cultivators holding land up to 2.5 acres of unirrigated land should be totally liquidated and those of cultivators holding between 2.5 acres and 5 acres of land should be scaled. |
| New development plan for development of handloom sector. (9) | Adequate steps have been taken to rehabilitate handloom industry and to improve the lot of the weavers. The National Handloom Development Corporation has put at reasonable prices throughout the year. |
| Improvement in quality and supply of people's cloth. (10) | With the increase in production of textile cloth, necessary improvement in quality and supply of people's cloth has been ensured. Under the Sixth Plan, production of cotton cloth has to go up from 7,540 million metres to 9,250 million metres by 1984-85. |
| New schemes for workers association in industry. (15) | The government has extended the scheme of workers' participation in industry to commercial and service organisation. |
| National permit scheme for road transport (16) | Under the National Permit Holders' Act, national road permits for haulage of long distance interstate goods traffic by road area issued and liberal finance is being made available for acquisition of vehicles and working capital. |

| *Original (1975)* | *Revised (1982)* |
|---|---|
| Income-tax relief to middle class. Exemption limit place at Rs 8,000/- (17) | During the last five years, the Income-tax exemption limit for individual assesses has been raised in three stages from Rs.8,000/- to Rs. 15,000/- by the government in order to ensure that persons whose incomes are just enough to make a living are not called upon to pay income-tax. The amount of the tax exemption limit was raised from Rs 8,000/- in 1976-77 income year to Rs 10,000/- in 1977-78, Rs 12,000/- in 1980-81 and further to Rs. 15,000/- in 1981-82. |
| Essential commodities at controlled prices to students in hostels. (18) | Efforts are made to supply essential commodities to student community through the Book and Stationery Stores run by schools and colleges. |
| New apprenticeship scheme to enlarge employment and training, especially of weaker section. (20) | Under the Apprenticeship Act of 1961, the central government, in consultation with the Apprenticeship Council, has specified the industries and designated the trades to be covered. The number of specified industries rose from 53 in 1962 to 216 in May 1976 and the number of designated trades from 14 to 103. |

| *In Perspective* | *New Points* |
|---|---|
| A new point introduced with a view to augment production of pulses and vegetable oil-seeds and bring down prices to an optimum level. | Special efforts to increase production pulses and vegetable oilseeds. (2) |
| Alleviation of rural poverty is the prime objective of the Sixth Plan. The IRD Programme aims at strengthening the socio-economic infrastructure of development in rural areas, alleviating rural poverty and reducing regional disparities. Under NREP Programme, development project and target group oriented employment generation projects will be closely interwined. | Strengthening and expanding coverage of integrated rural development and national rural employment programme. (3) |
| This point was one of the point of the five-points social programme. It has been conceded that the scheduled castes and tribes had been submerged far too long and needed special concession. | Accelerated programmes for the development of the scheduled castes and tribes. (7). |
| This point aims at supplying of drinking water to all problem villages. This is in furtherance of the Drought Prone Area Programme | Supply of drinking water to all problem villages. (8) |
| This point was one of the point of the five-point social programme. Forests are a renewable asset. They can be perpetuated through a judicious and discriminating use, and they can be pressed into service to produce a wide range of goods and services which are so essential for the socio-economic well-being of the rural poor. | Vigorous implementation of afforestation, social and farm forestry and the development of bio-gas and other alternative energy sources. (12) |

| *Original (1975)* | *Revised (1982)* |
|---|---|
| This point was one of the points of the five-point social programme. The plan of action was to cover the total population as part of an integrated package of health, family planning, nutrition and maternal and child health. | Promotion of family planning on a voluntary basis as a people's movement. (13) Substantial augmentation of universal primary health care facilities and control of leprosy. |

| | |
|---|---|
| The Five Year Plans have consistently place special emphasis on providing minimum health facilities integrated with family welfare and nutrition for women and children. | Accelerated welfare programmes for women and children, nutrition programmes for pregnant women, nursing mothers and children, specially in the tribal, hills and backward areas. (15) |
| This point was covered under the five-point social programme. Social education has been made a comprehensive programme of community uplift through community action. | Spread of universal elementary education for children in the 6-14 age group with special emphasis on girls and involvement of student and voluntary agencies in the removal of adult illiteracy. (16) |
| This point has been added with a view to improve the working of the public sector enterprises, so that industrialisation is accelerated. | Improvement in the working of the public sector enterprises. (20) |

## 20-POINT PROGRAMME 1986

The war on poverty is our first priority. In the past five years more than ten crores of our poor have been raised above the poverty line. Our goal is to remove poverty and create fuller employment.

The Twenty Point Programme is the cutting edge of the plan for the poor. The programme has been restructured in the light of our achievements and experience and the objectives of the Seventh Plan. The restructured programme renews our commitment to:

Eradicating poverty

Raising productivity

Removing social and economic disparities, and improving the quality of life.

### 1. Attack of Rural Poverty

We shall:

Ensure that poverty alleviation programmes reach all the poor in every village;

Dovetail wage employment programmes with programmes for area development and human resource development and create national and community assets like school buildings, roads, tanks, and fuel and fodder reserves;

Correlate the various rural development programmes to:

Improve productivity and production

Expand rural employment

Promote handlooms, handicrafts, village and small industries, and improve skills for self-employment;

Revitalise panchayats, co-operatives and local bodies.

### 2. Strategy for Rain-fed Agriculture

We shall:

Improve the technology for conserving moisture and ensure better management of land and water resources;

Develop and distribute appropriate and improved seeds;

Reduce vulnerability to drought through suitable changes in droughtprone area and drought-relief programmes.

### 3. Better Use of Irrigation Water

We shall:

Develop the catchment areas and improve drainage in basins and deltas;

Improve irrigation management in command areas; prevent water logging, salinity and wasteful use; co-ordinate the use of surface and ground water.

**4. Bigger Harvests**

We shall:

Revolutionise rice production in the eastern region and other areas of low productivity.

Achieve self-reliance in edible oils;

Secure greater production of pulses;

Intensify the cultivation of fruits and vegetables;

Augment facilities for modern storage, processing and marketing of agricultural produce;

Help livestock and dairy farmers to increase productivity;

Develop fish farming and sea fishing.

**5. Enforcement of Land Reforms**

We shall:

Complete compilation of land records;

Implement agricultural land ceiling;

Distribute surplus land to the landless.

**6. Special Programmes for Rural Labour**

We shall:

Enforce minimum wages for unorganised labour in agriculture and industry;

Fully implement laws abolishing bonded labour;

Involve voluntary agencies in programmes for the rehabilitation of bonded labour.

**7. Clean Drinking Water**

We shall:

Provide safe water for all villages;

Assist local communities to maintain the sources of such water supply in good condition;

Pay special attention to water supply for scheduled castes and scheduled tribes.

**8. Health for All**

We shall:

Improve the quality of primary health care;

Fight leprosy, TB, malaria, goitre, blindness and other major diseases;

Provide immunization for all infants and children;

Improve sanitation facilities in rural areas, particularly for women;

Pay special attention to programmes for the rehabilitation of the handicapped.

**9. Two-child Norm**

We shall:

Bring about voluntary acceptance of the two-child norm;

Promote responsible parenthood;

Reduce infant mortality;

Expand maternity and child facilities.

**10. Expansion of Education**

We shall:

Universalise elementary education with special emphasis on girls' education;

Improve the content of education at all levels;

Promote non-formal education and functional literacy programmes, including promotion of skills;

Stimulate adult literacy programmes, with the participation of students and voluntary agencies;

Emphasis on national integration and social and moral values and instill pride in our heritage.

**11. Justice to Scheduled Castes and Scheduled Tribes**

We shall:

Ensure compliance with the constitutional provisions and laws for the Scheduled Tribes;

Ensure possession of land allotted to Scheduled Castes and Scheduled Tribes;

Revitalise the land allotment programme;

Organise and assist special coaching programme to improve education standards;

Eradicate scavenging and undertake special programmes for the rehabilitation of Safai Karmacharis;

Provide better direction and adequate funds for the special component programmes;

Pursue programmes for the fuller integration of Scheduled Castes and Tribes with the rest of society,

Ensure the rehabilitation of tribals displaced from their habitat.

**12. Equality for Women**

We shall:

Raise the status of women;

Enhance awareness of the problems of women;

Create mass consciousness about women's right;

Implement a national programme of training and employment for women;

Enable women to participate with equality in socio-economic development and nation-building;

Rouse public opinion against dowry and ensure effective implementation of anti-dowry legislation.

**13. New Opportunities for Youth**

We shall:

Enlarge opportunities for youth in sports, adventure and cultural activities;

Promote physical fitness;

Involve youth on a massive scale in projects of national development such as:

The cleaning of Ganga;

The conservation and enrichment of the environment;

Mass education.

Identify outstanding young persons in all fields to encourage and develop their talents;

Involve youth in promoting national integration; cultural values, secularism and the scientific temper;

Expand the network of Nehru Yuvak Kendras;

Strengthen the National Service Scheme and the National Cadet Corps; Charge voluntary agencies working for the welfare of rural youth.

**14. Housing for the People**

We shall:

Make available house sites to the rural poor;

Expand programmes of house construction;

Lay special emphasis on construction of houses for Scheduled Castes and Scheduled Tribes;

Develop low cost building materials.

**15. Improvement of Slums**

We shall:

Restrict the growth of slums;

Provide basic facilities in existing slum areas;

Encourage planned house building in urban areas.

**16. New Strategy for Forestry**

We shall:

Grow more trees and raise more forest, with the full involvement of the people.

Protect the traditional rights of tribal populations and local communities of access to fuel, wood and forest produce;

Reclaim wastelands for productive use;

Plant appropriate vegetation in hill, desert and coastal areas.

**17. Protection of the Environment**

We shall:

Enhance public awareness of the dangers of environmental degradation;

Mobilise popular support for environment protection;

Promote recognition that enduring development demands preservation of the ecology;

Ensure judicious site selection for projects and proper choice of technology.

**18. Concern for the Consumer**

We shall:

Bring essential consumption goods within easy reach of the poor;

Build a consumer protection movement;

Restructure the distribution system so that subsidies reach the most needy;

Strengthen the Public Distribution System.

**19. Energy for the Villages**

We shall:

Expand the supply of electricity for productive use in the villages;

Develop alternative sources of energy, particularly bio-gas;

Promote integrated area specific programmes for rural energy.

**20. A Responsive Administration**

We shall:

Simplify procedures;

Delegate authority;

Evolve monitoring systems from block to national level;

Attend promptly and sympathetically to public grievances."

A restructured 20-Point Economic Programme which renews government's commitment to eradicate poverty, remove socio-economic disparities, raise productivity, reduce income inequalities and improve the quality of life was placed before Parliament on August 20, 1986.

The introductory note the programmes says 'the war on poverty' is the government's first priority and goes on to reaffirm: "Our goal is to remove poverty and create 'fuller' employment. The main thrust of the restructured 20-Point Programme, which inter alia restates the seventh plan approach, and strategy is heavily tilted towards rural development. The action Programme envisages an attack on rural poverty in a multi-pronged manner."

The special thrust has been placed on eradication of rural poverty by ensuring that poverty alleviation programmes reach all the poor in every village. Other measures include of dovetailing wage employment programmes with programmes for area development and human development. The attack lays stress on education, good health, improving skills and creating entrepreneurship among the rural poor. In the non-farm sectors, the emphasis is on the development of handlooms, handicrafts, village and small industries to provide additional employment to the rural people. The attack on rural poverty is to be spearheaded by the panchayats, co-operative and local bodies. Unless the attack on rural poverty is effectively implemented, there is no remedy. Does the government have the necessary political will to bring in necessary structural changes which may affect 10 per cent elites and bring in relief to the poor?

The Seventh Plan document after reviewing the various Rural Development and Poverty Alleviation Programmes and achievements under them during the Sixth Plan (1980-85) gives the targets during the Seventh Plan period. Integrated Rural Development Programme (IRDP), National Rural Employment Programme (NREP), Rural Landless. Employment Guarantee Programme (RLEGP), Drought Prone Area Programme (DPAP), Training of Rural Youth for Self-Employment (TRYSEM) and so on have all been in operation to augment employment and to accelerate development in rural sector. Many of these programmes make a very interesting reading.

In the new restructured 20-Point Programme the emphasis is placed on administrative reform, youth welfare, environment and consumer protection. Described as the 'cutting edge of the plan for the poor' the programme aims at removal of poverty and creation of fuller employment. Its objectives are spelt out by the government as: 'Eradicating poverty, raising productivity, reducing income inequalities, removing social and economic disparities and improving the quality of life'. It proposes to involve youth in the cleaning of the Ganga and conservation and enrichment of environment projects. Services of educated youth will also be utilised for imparting mass education. Though the main thrust of the new programme is attack on poverty, stress is laid on two-child norm and providing equality for women. Rigorous enforcement of land reforms and new strategy for forestry are other thrust areas of the new programme.

Bringing about better use of irrigation water, special programme for rural labour, providing clean drinking water, new opportunities for youth and a strategy for rain-fed agriculture are among the new thrust areas of the recast programme.

The new responsive administration envisages simplification of procedures, delegating the authority, enforcing accountability, evolving monitoring systems from block to national level and attending promptly and sympathetically to public grievances.

The programme ensures justice to Scheduled Castes and Scheduled Tribes by stipulating possession of land allotted to them as well as revitalisation of the land allotment programme. It is also proposed to organise and assist special coaching programmes to improve their educational standards and ensure rehabilitation of tribals displaced from their habitat.

## Empowering the Rural Poor

Since the poor generally lack economic and physical capital, focusing on strengthening their social capital makes sense, as it is a prerequisite for achieving sustainable collective action and useful for acquiring all other forms of capital. The focus of actions therefore aims at overcoming identified institutional and organisational gaps or weaknesses in order to empower the rural poor. It would imply the strengthening of collective self-help capacities at the local level to enable the poor to plan, manage and monitor their access to assets more in line with their needs and views. Yet, since local-level self-help initiatives often require support from higher decision-making levels, the establishment of a two-way communication system connecting the bottom with the top and the top with the bottom is essential. In this sense, institutional empowerment goes beyond beneficiary participation at the grassroots level, as it has been practised in so many recent externally funded projects.

It is important to emphasize that great care must be taken to ensure that these measures add or modify locally existing institutions and organisations rather than replace them. Problems of acceptance are likely to occur when introducing completely new forms of organisations. It is also problematic simply to transform or modernise "traditional organisations".

*(i)* strengthening the social capital of the poor at the grassroot level.

*(ii)* strengthening horizontal organisational and institutional linkages

*(iii)* strengthening vertical organisational and institutional linkages for poverty alleviation, and

*(iv)* the need for partnerships and coalitions between governments, civil society, the private sector and the poor themselves.

## PRINCIPAL ELEMENTS OF A SMALL GROUP APPROACH

*Focus on the rural poor*. Group approaches aim at promoting disadvantaged groups of the poor.

*Groups and voluntary and self-governing*. Participants decide who joins the group, who leads the group and what rules the group should follow. Ideally groups are built on already existing collaborative links between group members.

*Small and homogeneous groups*. A key element is the formation of small self-help groups. Conflicts are reduced when members live in similar socio-economic conditions.

*Group promoters* assist in group development and in linking groups to governmental and NGO services. The group promoter's role is that of an *adviser*, strengthening the groups' leadership, organisational and planning capacity; a *participatory trainer*, teaching basic problem-solving and technical skills; and a *link*, facilitating communication between the groups and governmental and NGO development services. When a group reaches "maturity", the group promoter withdraws.

*Training*. Organisational and production skills are improved through demand-driven training and workshops.

*Formation of intergroup associations*. Once groups are mature, they link together in intergroup association to tackle bigger community problems and to improve their economies of scale.

The ultimate aim is *self-reliance.* It is stressed through income increases, training, savings mobilisation, consolidation in intergroup associations.

## PARTICIPATORY LEARNING

Participatory learning describes an interactive learning process that enhances the co-operation and problem-solving capacities of the poor. It requires two-way communication, from top-to-bottom and from bottom-to-top and it addresses participants at all levels, from local to national.

By working through groups, the rural poor can link up more easily and more cheaply with services and gain access to productive assets. When group members come from the same socio-economic level and have similar concerns, learning is easier.

The learning focuses on demand-driven skill development in fields of direct relevance to the rural poor, such an organisational management and leadership, group savings and credit and small business management and accounting. Beneficiaries, not outsiders, set the demands.

Participatory learning methods are based on participatory rural appraisal (PRA) techniques as well as small group learning techniques.

❑ ❑ ❑

# SECTION SIX

# RURAL MANAGEMENT

Even after having so many varied programmes for the uplift of the poor for more than three decades, the achievement is far from satisfactory; expected results have not been realised, "The main drawback of these schemes is that they have failed to generate a local multiplier of a required magnitude owing to which rural economy is constrained from take-off. The subsidy or financial assistance provided to the identified persons under these schemes in a majority of cases, has not led to asset formation either due to the fact that the household is not in a position to make it self-sustaining or the scheme itself is ill-conceived.

Employment generation under various employment-oriented schemes has also not been satisfactory. Most of the rural employment were 'ad hoc', in nature with the result that they did not ensure continuity of employment to the army of unemployed or under-employed. These programmes proved to be relief measures rather than solutions to unemployment or poverty. In many cases, because of the existing agrarian structure, the flow of benefits of these programmes has been in favour, of rural rich whereas the benefits are intended to be for rural poor. Misconceptions regarding the programmes have also been responsible for their failure to some extent. For instance, a milch cattle is made available to an agricultural labourer. This can become an asset if and only if he has other complementary inputs like fodder, marketing and medical facilities. Even with these facilities the per unit cost for him will be higher as compared to the large farmer who has complementary resources of his own.

## POVERTY ALLEVIATION: THE ROLE OF RURAL INSTITUTIONS AND PARTICIPATION

Most approaches to poverty alleviation focus on income and subsidy measures; however, there is a growing realization that these measures alone are not sufficient. The growing amount of literature on the important role that "social capital" and institutions play in the development process indicates that there is a social-institutional dimension as well. This article focuses on the institutional dimension of rural poverty alleviation and outlines why institution and capacity-building should be fundamental elements of any strategy aiming at alleviating rural poverty. Analysing some of the main weaknesses of past poverty alleviation strategies, it highlights the potential role and function that rural institutions and grassroots organisations can play in poverty alleviation efforts.

### The Complexity of Rural Poverty

Poverty has various dimensions. The food dimension is the most fundamental, since food accounts for 80 percent of all basic human needs. People who are chronically lacking access to sufficient food are considered to be poor. Malnutrition negatively affects people's working and learning capacity, thus leading to decreased productivity and incomes. Food shortages caused by natural disasters and civil strife also may affect "vulnerable" groups living just above the poverty threshold, thus causing them to enter the ranks of the poor. Malnutrition is mostly measured on the basis of daily nutrient requirements. The number of poor is defined in terms of those people with an income level which does not allow them to access sufficient food. For the eradication of poverty, eliminating hunger and malnutrition is therefore a precondition; however, poverty and hunger, although closely associated are not synonymous.

Poverty cannot be defined simply in terms of lacking access to sufficient food. It is also closely associated with a person's lack of access to productive assets, services and markets. Without access to these, it is unlikely that production and income-earning capacities can be improved on a sustainable basis. Low incomes and purchasing power limit the poor's ability to produce and/or purchase food and other domestically produced products and services. This in turn keeps internal markets from growing, which limits potentials for agricultural and economic growth, thus stimulating outmigration.

There are also socio-psychological and institutional dimensions of poverty. Living so close to the margin, the poor give highest priority to day-to-day survival. Most do not have enough time, energy or security to think about the future or plan on a long term basis. Moreover, owing to their limited resource base and small scale of production, they have little economic bargaining power and consequently are often pushed aside into marginal and low-production areas — which further weakens their access to markets, social services and income-earnings capacities. Partly because of the above factors, the poor's level of socio-political organisation tends to be low and their capacity to make their voice heard in the corridors of power weak, meaning they are often excluded from political participation and rural decision-making processes.

### A Need for New Strategies

As we see, rural poverty is a very complex issue. It is related to food insecurity, access to assets, services and markets; income earning opportunities; and the organisational and institutional means for achieving those ends. It has an urban as well as a rural dimension and impacts on a large variety of different groups in different ways. In view of this complexity, there are no global blueprints or solutions to eradicate poverty. It logically follows that strategies to reduce poverty should be specifically tailored to reach each desired group, yet at the same time be comprehensive and flexible. New strategies will have to be more cost effective in view of the constant decline in development assistance. Approaches must therefore be found that reduce costs at both ends; the service delivery costs of governments, non-governmental organisations (NGOs) and the private sector, and the access costs faced by the poor for obtaining these services.

### What was wrong with previous approaches to Alleviating Poverty?

Some of the reasons for failures in the past were:

A low level of participation by the poor: even though the ultimate stakeholders in the poverty alleviation process are the rural poor, all too often they are denied a voice in the formulation and even the execution of poverty programmes.

Programmes have tended to rely on grants and subsidies as the main tools for serving the poor, but even when the subsidies did arrive, they often ended up undermining the poor's incentives to mobilise their own resources and creative energy.

Too little attention has been given to strengthening the negotiating capacities of the poor, to enhancing their power to participate meaningfully in policy formulation and in the marketplace.

Most poverty alleviation programmes have had a single vector of intervention and have failed to confront the multidimensionality of poverty. Priorities usually have been set from "the outside", thus being supply-driven rather than demand-driven and unable to respond to the particular needs and potentials of the poor.

## Chapter 33

# AGENCIES FOR RURAL DEVELOPMENT

### Introduction

There is no dearth of agencies for rural development. At present, one could list out 45 agencies/institutions including nine international organisations, which have been actively working for the rural development in India. The list is incomplete. Among these, co-operatives, commercial banks, regional rural banks have been working at the grass-root level. Under the multi-agency approach, the commercial banks, re-organised primary agricultural co-operatives are functioning in rural India. In the present context, it is expected that the banking system would be an instrument for bringing about socio-economic change/revolution in rural India through *(i)* reducing regional and sectoral imbalances; *(ii)* promoting growth and distributing justice and *(iii)* harnessing science and technology for improving the productivity of rural assets — land, labour, livestock, water, forests, grassland, etc., and neutralising the liabilities of poverty, unemployment, indebtedness, etc. All these call for crystallizing the role of specialised branches/units set up by banks.

### Agencies

Besides, the financial and other agencies play a catalytic role in rural development. This apart, the corporate sector and the voluntary agencies have also engaged themselves in the task of rural development. In addition, a number of scientific and technical organisation like research stations of the ICAR, Agriculture Universities', Regional Research Laboratories, Krishi Vigyan Kendras, Community Polytechnic, Indian Institutes of Science and Technology etc, are located in various parts of the country. Mobilisation of resources and its development in agricultural, non-farm activities, rural artists, cottage industries, and integrated rural development is a continuous process.

# AGENCIES FOR RURAL DEVELOPMENT

(1) Central Government
(2) State Governments
(3) Village Panchayats, Panchayat Samitis, Mandal Panchayat, Nyaya Panchayat and Zilla Parishad
(4) District Rural Development Agency (DRDA)
(5) District Industries Centres (DIC)
(6) Council for Advancement of Rural Technology (CART)
(7) National Institute Rural Development (NIRD)
(8) National Co-operative Development Corporation (NCDC)
(9) Primary Co-operatives (Agricultural/Non-agricultural)
(10) Primary Land Development Banks (PLDB)
(11) Large-sized Multi-Purpose Societies (LAMPS)
(12) Farmers' Service Societies (FSS)
(13) Scheduled Commercial Banks (Branches in Rural Areas)
(14) Regional Rural Banks (RRB)
(15) National Bank for Agriculture and Rural Development (NABARD)
(16) Rural Electrification Corporation (REC)
(17) Agriculture Finance Corporation (AFC)
(18) Internal Fund for Agricultural Development (IFAD)
(19) Agro-Industries Corporation (AIC)
(20) National Land Resources Conservation & Development Commission (NLRCDC)
(21) National Land Board (NLB)
(22) State Farms Corporation of India (SFCI)
(23) Cotton Corporation of India (CCI)
(24) National Dairy Development Board (NDDB)
(25) National Committee on the Development of Backward Areas (NCDBA)
(26) Khadi and Village Industries Commission (KVIC)
(27) Rural Marketing and Service Centres (RMSC)
(28) District Supply and Marketing Societies (DSMS)
(29) Composite Rural Training Centre (CRTC)
(30) Voluntary Agencies (VA)
(31) Industrial Houses (IH)
(32) Adult Education Centres (AEC)
(33) Indian Dairy Corporation (IDC)
(34) Institute of Rural Management (IRM)
(35) World Bank (WB)
(36) Agro-Industries Corporation (ADC)
(37) Afro-Asian Rural Reconstruction Organisation (AARRO)
(38) Centre oñ Integrated Rural Development for Asia and Pacific (CIRDAP)
(39) Food and Agricultural Organisation (FAO)

(40) United Nations Educational, Scientific and Cultural Organisation (UNESCO)

(41) World Health Organisation (WHO)

(42) United Nations Industrial Development Organisation (UNIDO)

(43) International Development Association (IDA)

(44) Organisation for Economic Co-operation and Development (OECD)

(45) Rural Management Institutions (RMI)

Rural development is a part of the same process of economic development and social change. They have to go on simultaneously. Although, various agencies are working in this direction, the rural development programme lacks co-ordination and cohesion. Moreover, until and unless a strong will for development develops within the rural community the development process would not gather momentum.

The country is poised for growth and the rural environment is conducive for concerted action in improving rural standard. Financial institutions, particularly banks have been helping in multidimensional way in achieving their goals. The need of the hour is a co-ordinate action on the part of the government, corporate bodies, voluntary agencies and the banks. It is also important that efforts and resources deployed by various agencies do not overlap. In fact, each agency should supplement the efforts of others and treat the programme as a joint endeavour with one single purpose. The principal objective of rural development is the development of the rural people, particularly the rural poor. The three crucial inputs in rural development are the motivation of rural people, the relevant technology and management and implementation of the transfer of technology to rural poor.

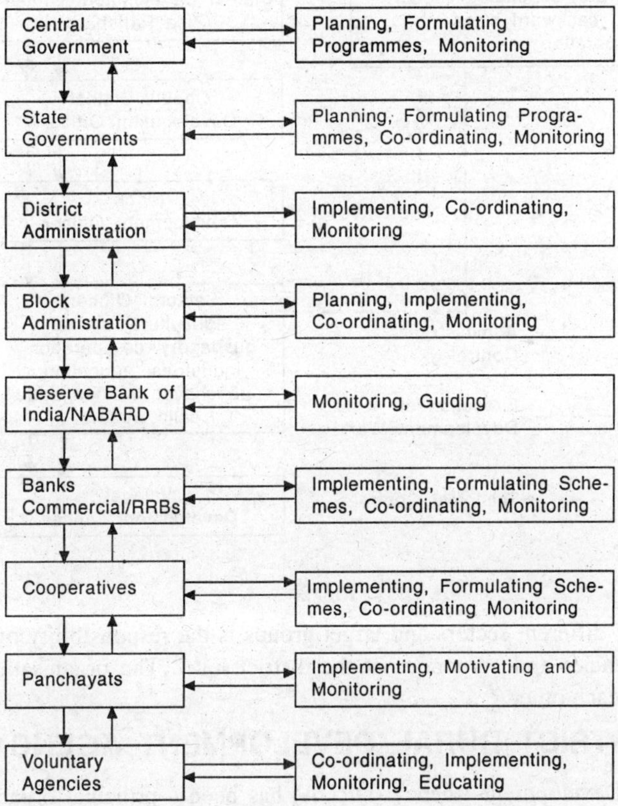


*Fig. 1. Multiple Agencies for Rural Development*

## Agency for Rural Development: District Level

At the district level, the Collector is the head of the development administration and the chief co-ordinator of the work of different development departments, agencies and societies functioning in the district. He is also the chairman of different development institutions. viz., the District Rural Development Agency, the Scheduled Tribes Co-operative Financial Corporation, the District Scheduled Castes Co-operative Service Society and the District Backward Service Co-operatives and others at the district level.

At the district level, the chief executive of the Zilla Parishad, known as District Development Officer (DDO), has, under his control, the BDO and his team of development officers.

At the block level, the BDO is the chief executive officer. He has a team of village development officers (VDOs) and extension officers. The BDO has only day-to-day administrative control over his subordinate staff. The sectoral departments have technical control the staff, with the exception of the VDOs.

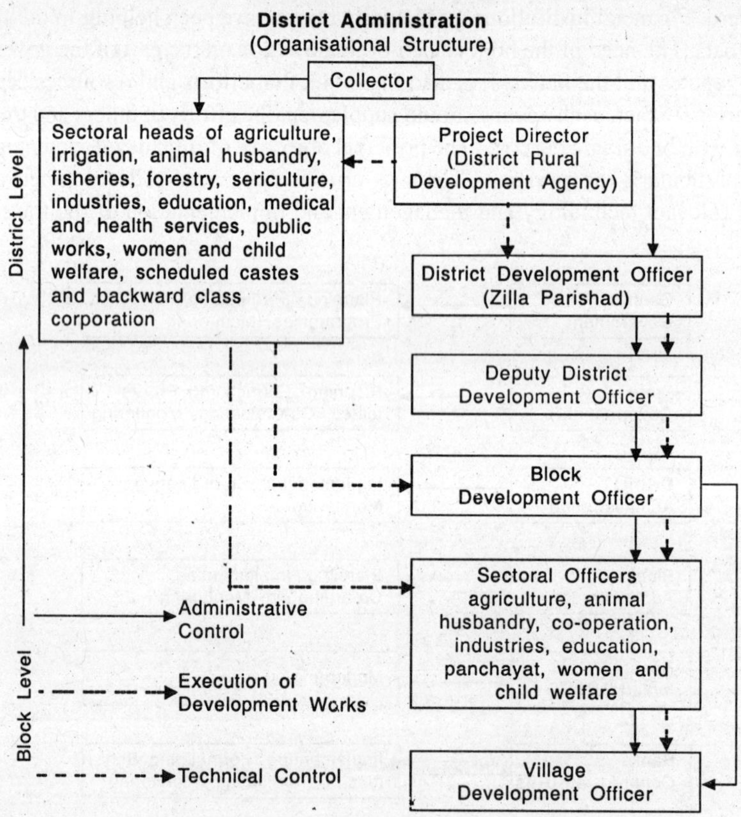


*Fig. 2.*

The development of different sectors and target groups is the responsibility of the heads of different sectoral departments, agencies and corporates at the district level. The organisational structure of these departments differs from each other.

## DISTRICT RURAL DEVELOPMENT AGENCY

The District Rural Development Agency (DRDA) has been a principal organ over the years at the district level to oversee the implementation of various anti-poverty programmes. Since inception, the administrative costs of the DRDAs were met by way of setting apart a certain percentage of the allocation for each programme. Of late, the number of programmes increased and while some programmes provided for administrative cost of DRDAs, others did not. Keeping in view the need for an effective agency at the district level to co-ordinate the Anti-Poverty Programmes, a new centrally sponsored scheme for strengthening the DRDAs has been introduced w.e.f. $1^{st}$ April, 1999.

**Objectives:** The primary objective of the Scheme of DRDA Administration is to professionalise the DRDAs so that they are able to effectively manage the anti-poverty programmes of the Ministry of Rural Development and interact effectively with other agencies. The DRDAs are expected to co-ordinate effectively with the line departments, the Panchayati Raj Institutions, the banks and other financial institutions, the NGOs as well as the technical institutions with a view to gathering the support and resources required for poverty reduction effort in the district. However, under all circumstances, DRDAs will maintain their separate identity and will function under the chairmanship of the Zilla Parishad.

## Salient Features

### Organisational Structure

Each district will have its own DRDA. The DRDA would be headed by a Project Director, who should be of the rank of an Additional District Magistrate. In respect of such States where DRDA does not have a separate identity, a separate cell will be created in the Zilla Parishad to maintain a separate account so that these are capable of being audited separately.

The DRDA must emerge as a specialised agency capable of managing the anti-poverty programmes of the Ministry on the one hand and to effectively relate these to the overall efforts of poverty eradication in the district.

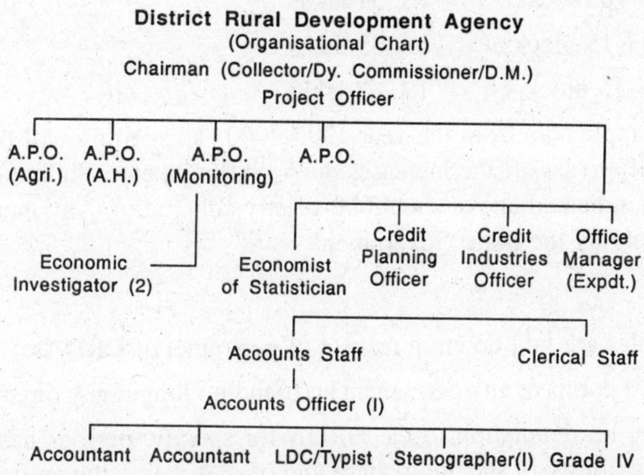


*Fig. 3.*

Actual execution of the programmes will be handled outside the DRDAs and that DRDA's role will be to facilitate the implementation of the programmes, to supervise/oversee and monitor the progress, to receive and send the progress reports as well as to account for the funds.

DRDAs will also need to develop the capacity to build synergies among different agencies involved for the most effective results.

The DRDAs should deal only with the anti-poverty programmes of the Ministry of Rural Development. If DRDAs are to be entrusted with programmes of other ministries or those of the State Governments, it should be ensured that these have a definite anti-poverty focus.

The Chairman Zilla Parishad would be the chairman of the Governing Body of the DRDA. The DRDA shall also have an Executive Committee.

The Project Director should cause the annual accounts of the DRDA to be prepared not later than 30th June. These should be duly audited.

## Staffing Pattern

The staffing pattern is expected to reflect a clear departure from that of a purely administrative organisation. The staffing structure of the DRDAs include positions for Planning for poverty alleviation, project formulation, social organisation and capacity building, gender concerns, engineering supervision and quality control, project monitoring, accountancy and audit functions as well as evaluation and impact studies.

Each DRDA should have the following wings:

*(i)* Self-employment wing;

*(ii)* Women's wing;

*(iii)* Wage employment wing;

*(iv)* Engineering wing;

*(v)* Accounts wing;

*(vi)* Monitoring and Evaluation wing; and

*(vii)* General Administration wing.

## Administrative Cost

The administrative cost per district may be fixed as follows:

| | |
|---|---|
| Category A district (< 6 blocks) | Rs. 46 lakhs |
| Category B district (6-10 blocks) | Rs. 57 lakhs |
| Category C district (11-15 blocks) | Rs. 65 lakhs |
| Category D district (> 15 blocks) | Rs. 67 lakhs |

The above limits are applicable from the year 1999-2000. The ceiling will be raised every year, on a compounding basis, up to 5% to set off the increases due to inflation etc. While the States follow their own salary structure, the ceiling indicated above should be strictly adhered to. Any increase over and above the ceiling should be met entirely by the State Government.

## Personnel Policy

The following principles are laid down in respect of personnel of DRDAs:

The DRDA should not have any permanent staff and no longer any direct recruitment be allowed.

Taking employees on deputation to the DRDA for specific periods has the advantage of better choice of staff, flexibility in staffing pattern and of motivating the staff.

It is most essential that at least the Project Directors, Project Officers, APO and all technical posts are manned by an officer with proven capability and motivation and are selected in an objective manner by specific Selection Committees.

In the selection of Project Directors and APOs, emphasis should be on selecting officers of young age. Indicatively, the PDs and APO should not be more than 40-45 years of age, and in any case not more than 50 years of age.

## Central Allocation and Release of Funds

Being a centrally sponsored scheme, it is funded on a sharing basis between the Centre and the States in the ratio of 75:25. Allocation of funds to the districts is based on the ceiling prescribed in the guidelines depending upon the number of blocks in the districts. Central assistance under the Scheme is released directly to the DRDA/Zilla Parishads, in two instalments as per the Guidelines of the programme; 10% of the total entitlement of the DRDAs in a State is earmarked for the State Headquarter.

## Farmers' Service Societies

The government has been constantly striving to find out a solution to the problem of adequately meeting the credit needs of the rural sector through a proper institutional credit set-up. Since 1951, the central and state governments have been experimenting with varied programmes with the sole objective of eliminating rural poverty and raising the level of living in rural India. The promotion of Farmers' Service Societies (FSS) is one such effort, which was initiated in 1978 to meet the challenge. The need for a new rural credit institution of this type was felt because of the inadequacy of the conventional types of co-operatives and commercial banks, the continued neglect of small and marginal farmers and rural artisans, and the non-availability of package of inputs and customer services along with technical advice and complementary services under one roof to small and marginal farmers. The aim of the Farmers' Service Societies was to provide a national network of integrated credit services for an extensive modernisation of agriculture by fully utilising the talent, experience and resources already available with the co-operatives and commercial banks.

## Objectives

The objectives of the FSS are:

*(i)* To make the contribution of the small farmers, marginal farmers and agricultural labourers in the agricultural development quite meaningful;

*(ii)* To provide credit in the right amount at the right time for credit worthy schemes;

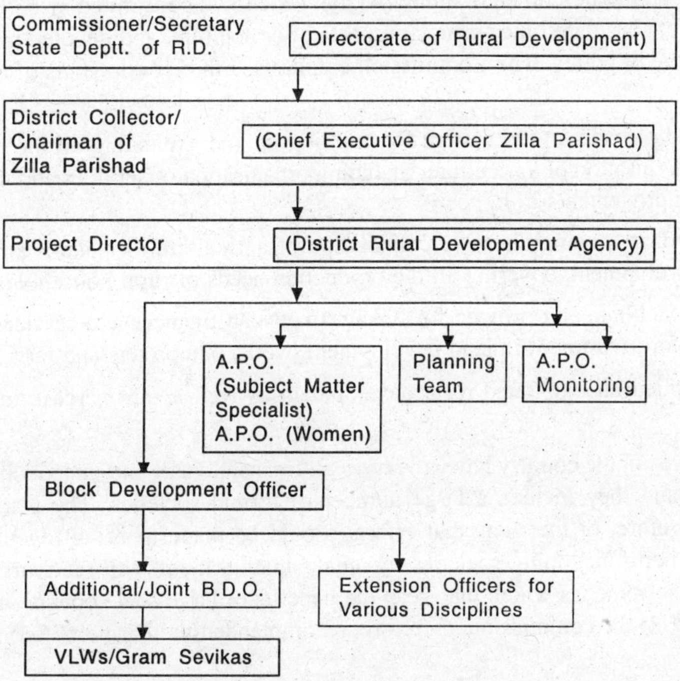


*Fig. 4. Implementing Structure*

*(iii)* To supply inputs and services at reasonable rates at the right time;

(iv) To arrange for a fair market where the small man would get a reasonable surplus; and would be able to buy his requirements of fertilisers, pesticides, seeds, agricultural implements as well as consumer goods at a fair price.

In addition, the Farmers' Service Societies provide a package of inputs and customer service, along with technical advice and supporting services for storage, transportation, processing and marketing at a single contract point.

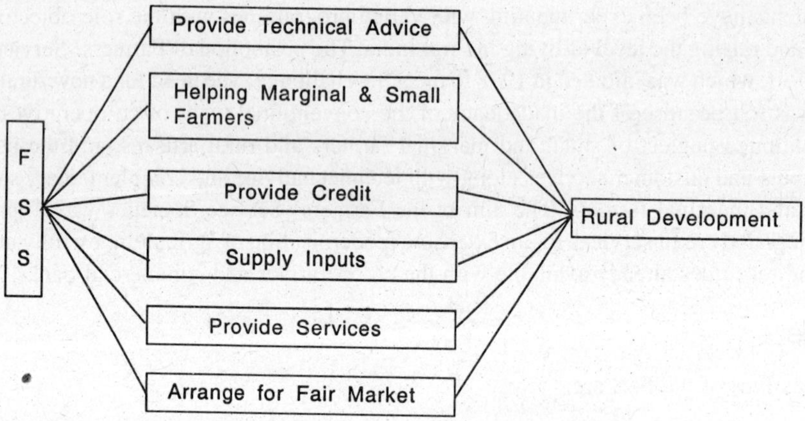


*Fig. 5. Objectives of Farmers' Service Societies*

## Genesis of FSS

The National Commission on Agriculture (NCA), which was constituted in 1970 to go into the various aspects of agriculture, considered the financial aspects of agriculture, and devoted much thought to a satisfactory agricultural credit policy. The Commission emphasised three basic goals of credit policy in respect of agriculture *viz.*

(i) It should provide a total system for building up and expanding all the activities and facilitate the modernisation of agriculture, including organisation of services and marketing and bringing about improvements in it;

(ii) It must have a comprehensive connotation of agriculture to make it almost co-terminus with rural development, covering all the production needs of rural households; and

(iii) It must facilitate and provide for linkages between finances and services for current inputs as well as for investment in land development, wells, pumps sets and farm equipment.

In short, it implied an integrated rural development as well as an increase in rural production and productivity.

The co-operatives in the country have a very weak financial base, and uneconomic scale of operations and poor coverage; and they include a large number of formal societies. The National Commission on Agriculture was, therefore, of the view that efforts should be made to bring together small uneconomic societies and revive non-functioning societies by amalgamating them with the working ones so that they may become large-size societies which may reap the benefits of large-scale operations and offer integrated credit facilities. In 1971, the commission, therefore, recommended the Farmers' Service Societies (FSS).

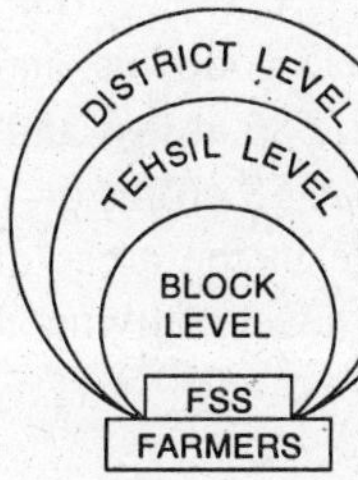


*Fig. 6. Linkages within the District*

## Phased Action Programme

The National Commission on Agriculture (NCA) was of the opinion that the formation of Farmers' Service Societies at the tehsil/block level and the district union of these societies, as also their linkage with the lead bank and other financial institutions might first be tried out in 46 SFDA districts and 41 MFAL districts. It recommended that operation of these arrangements should be carefully studied and that with suitable adaptations as a result of the experience gained in these districts, the schemes might be extended every year to cover more districts at a rapid pace.

A study on the working of the FSS by the Reserve Bank of India revealed that:

(1) In certain states like Gujarat, Bihar Andhra Pradesh and Maharashtra, the primary agriculture credit societies and the FSS have been functioning side by side and there has been an overlapping of area of operation and duplication of work;

(2) Large farmers continued to wield more influence than the weaker sections in getting benefits, quite contrary to the objective of the FSS and representatives of state government and sponsoring banks did not take much interest in correcting this trend;

(3) In many cases, the total amount of loan given to the weaker sections was found to be unsatisfactory;

(4) In many FSS there were no technical personnel and hence no technical guidance was available;

(5) In many states the overdoes of FSS ranged from 20 to 40 per cent of the payments due; and

(6) The non-credit functions, including provision of services like marketing etc., were found to be limited in many FSS.

In the rural credit structure, the FSS have an important part to play at the base level. The sponsoring banks, the NABARD and the state government have a responsibility to activate the FSS so that the weaker sections in the rural society get the benefits of integrated credit delivery system.

During the year 1987-88, the 1,826 FSSs with a paid-up capital of Rs. 52.63 crores mobilised Rs. 12.25 crores, loaned Rs. 212.78 crores to 13.17 lakh borrowers of which, Rs. 187.34 crores was short-term and Rs. 25.44 crores long-term credit. The total outstanding credit stood at Rs. 336.42 crores consisting of Rs. 252.55 crores of short-term credit and Rs.83.98 crores of medium and long-term credit of the total outstanding credit, Rs.115.72 crores or 34.4 per cent was overdue as on 30.6.1988.

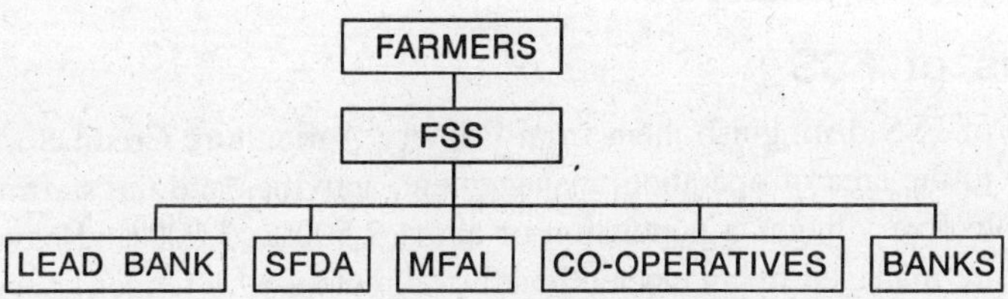


*Fig. 7. Area of Operation of FSS*

The FSS owned 1,825 godowns, hired 675 godowns, and offered storage facilities in 1,562 godowns. Of the total 1,826 FSS 1,042 worked at profit, 686 at loss and 143 just balanced their budgets. The cost of the management of all the FSS aggregated Rs.4.58 crores or, on an average, Rs. 24,500 per FSS. The FSS have brought about a socio-economic change in the areas of their operation, and helped the small and marginal farmers and rural artisans raise their level of living above the subsistence level.

## Organisational Structure

The organisational set-up of the FSS is a grand synthesis of all that is good in the co-operatives and commercial banks.

The FSS has threefold objectives:

*(i)* To have a sound capital base,

*(ii)* To have a paid management with effective control of the government, the financing institutions and the members, and

*(iii)* To extend a variety of services required by farmers under one roof.

In order to have a sound capital base the Reserve Bank of India now NABARD gives loans to state government from its National Agriculture Credit (long-term operation) fund towards their share capital contribution is restricted to Rs. 50,000 to a FSS operating in an area covering a population of 10,000 and to Rs. one lakh for block level societies. In order that the FSS may avail themselves of the share capital contribution, they have to fulfil certain conditions, such as viability, financial linkage with central co-operative banks or commercial banks appointment of full time managing directors and technical staff, adoption of model bye-laws etc.

The activities of the FSS are managed by Board of Directors, which consist of representatives of farmer-members, financing institutions which may be commercial banks or central co-operative banks or regional rural banks, and the state governments. There may be nine or eleven or thirteen members on the Board of Directors. In a set-up where there are eleven directors, one full-time paid director manages the day-to-day activities of the FSS. Of the remaining ten directors, five come from the farmer-members of the FSS, of whom three are small and marginal farmers and two are farmers of other category. The remaining five directors are: a representative of the financing institutions, a block development officer, an assistant director of agriculture, an assistant director of veterinary services and an assistant registrar of co-operative societies. However, the designation of the directors coming from the various departments of the state governments may vary from state to state. From the composition of the Board of Directors it is evident that an effort has been made to protect the interests of all concerned with the activities of FSS.

The staffing pattern of the FSS, consists of a managing director, three extension officers with appropriate support. The staffing pattern, however, may vary from FSS to FSS, depending upon it coverage, the composition of its credit and the area of its operation. Managing directors and extension officers are initially deputed by the state government. While the salary of managing directors is borne by the financing institutions for an initial period of three years, the state governments subsidies the salaries of the technical staff. The FSS also have cashiers-cum-salesmen to look after their dealings in such agricultural inputs as fertilisers, seeds, pesticides, agricultural implements etc.

## Salient Features of FSS

Certain features of FSS distinguish them from Primary Agriculture Credit Societies (PACS). These features relate mainly to the area of operation, management, activities and the staffing pattern. The PACS generally cover three to five villages a population of about 2,500 to 3,000 and having about 250 to 300 members. The PACS are managed by an elected board of directors who render honorary service and have paid secretaries to look after the daily accounting work. In many cases, even the secretaries are honorary.

The PACS are linked to district central co-operative banks and ordinarily meet only the short-term requirements of agriculture. There is generally no supervision of the end-use of credit except for the disbursement of the component of the credit. As against this, the structure of the FSS envisages a wider coverage. There can be two types of FSS viz., a small-size FSS covering a population of about 10,000 and comprising 20 to 30 villages, and block-level big-size FSS covering a population of about one lakh. However, the difference between the two types of FSS is only of the area of operation and not of function.

## Administration

**Table 1**

**ECONOMIC FEATURES AND BUSINESS POTENTIAL OF THE FARMERS' SERVICE SOCIETIES**

| *Item* | *Block size FSS* | *Small size FSS* |
|---|---|---|
| Area of operation | 100 Villages or a block | 10 Villages |
| Population | 1,00,000 | 10,000 |
| Number of cultivating households (50%) | 10,000 | 1,000 |
| Number of agricultural labourers household (30%) | 5,000 | 600 |
| Average holding size | 3 acres (1.2 ha) | 3 acres (1.2 ha) |
| Assume 50% coverage of agricultural holdings in 5 years representing small farmers | 15,000 acres (6,070 ha) | 1,500 acres (607 ha) |
| Cropping pattern | 2 crops | 2 crops |
| Major crop | paddy | paddy |
| Average area to be covered per year | 3,000 acres (1,214 ha) | 1,500 areas (607 ha) in the first year itself |
| Scale of finance for HYV* | Rs. 350/- in kind | kind component + Rs. 100/- cash component |

* The credit requirement is calculated taking only short-term financing into consideration. However, medium and short-term mix depending on the need of the individual farm will be required in which case this would roughly equal to Rs. 1,350/- per holding participating in the programme. Calculations are made on this conservative assessment.

The affairs of the FSS are managed by a board of directors, of whom some are nominated by the various departments of the state government and others are elected by the members. Besides, they have paid managing director and technical staff to look after the disbursement, supervision and end-use of funds. The FSS render short, medium and long-term financial assistance and deal in agricultural inputs and implements. They also assist in the marketing of farm produce and extend loans against agricultural commodities whenever required. They offer a variety of other services, such as the collection of milk, the maintenance of chilling centres, the cultivation of demonstration plots, the maintenance of artificial insemination centres, the sale of articles of food and other rationed commodities, etc. Apart from these activities, the FSS accept current, savings and other deposits, and extend deposits, banking facilities to their members. The amalgamation of societies is one of the important aspect of FSS which, from the point of view of achieving the required level of business, is quite significant because the main objective of the scheme is to establish an institution which will ultimately have an economic size and reap the benefits of paid management.

## Advantages to Financing Institutions

The FSS offer distinct advantages to financing institutions, particularly to commercial banks. While extending credit through FSS commercial banks have only to supervise the activities of the FSS. The FSS take the responsibility of preparing the seasonal credit-limit statements on the principles of co-operative finance and submit them to financing institutions. Separate credit limit statements are prepared for the kharif and rabi seasons and for term loans. The credit-limit statement furnish the required data about the borrowers, such as total holdings, proposed cropping pattern, area to be benefitted by the proposed loan, scale of finance for meeting cultivation expenses, the amount of loan asked for, the amount of loan which borrowers are eligible, the amount of loan recommended, security offered, the repayment schedule etc. The preparation of these statements is important, and the officials of financing institutions may make a preliminary scrutiny of these statement before they are processed by the Board of Directors of the FSS. Since these statements are passed by their Board of Directors, the managers of financing institutions should normally have no difficulty in approving the credit-limit statements. In this way, the maintenance of individual loan accounts and follow-up and supervision of credit on the part of financing institutions are avoided. That is why even small branches of commercial banks can easily manage five to ten societies and have far more coverage than would have been possible through direct lending.

Apart from the advantage of larger coverage through the FSS, commercial banks can also reduce the operational cost of agricultural lending. The FSS have a better feel of the area of operation, for they have farmer members on their board who can give them a better feedback about individual borrowers and also assist them in the recovery performance. More over, the FSS, being co-operative institutions are vested with effective summary power which can be utilised, if necessary to recover dues from recalcitrant borrowers.

Apart from the advantages the FSS offer to the financing institutions the FSS have the potential to develop themselves into community based organisation which, after meeting the financial requirements of the community, can develop the required infrastructural facilities which are the prerequisites of the integrated development of the rural economy. In this way, they offer a unique opportunity to financing institutions for their effective participation in the rural development of the regions which are served by farmers service societies.

## Marginal Farmer and the Rural Development

One of the common features of the agrarian economy of the less developed countries is the preponderance of small and marginal farmers. A large number of factors, economic, geographic and sociological, contribute to the proliferation of the problems of small farmers who subsist in precarious living conditions in most of these countries. It is a historical fact that over the years their problems have been aggravated with the rapid growth in population and the sluggish rate of growth in agricultural productivity. The sub-division and fragmentation of holdings and very little improvement in irrigation facilities have perpetuated the poverty of these people. The pathological symptoms of peasant farming are too well known now to be enumerated here. Quite a few research studies have been published in recent years, analyzing the problems of "subsistence farming"; "peasant farming" and other types of farm living in different parts of the world.

In most of the policy formulations adopted for agricultural development in developing countries, the emphasis has been on huge investments in multipurpose irrigation projects and on land legislation aimed at changing man and land relation. In the capital-starved agricultural economics there are instances which show that the investment made by the state in these highly capital-intensive projects have not yielded the desired results, because the farmers, who are expected to make use of these irrigation facilities do not have credit facilities, it is only the bigger farmers who have taken advantage of the new situation. Those who made use of the new farm inputs prospered. The big cultivators themselves became exploiters of the smaller and weaker section farmers. Next to the village money lender, the big cultivators and landlords were the major source of credit in the rural areas. The inevitable consequence of this financial dependence was that the differences between the big farmers and the small farmers, in terms of their economic prosperity widened considerably.

With use of hybrid varieties particularly in irrigated areas, the total agricultural production as well as farm income had almost doubled within a short span of time. Such a rapid transformation was possible only with the aid of the necessary farm inputs. The total cost of cultivation under modern farming is being fairly high, and the credit requirements of the farmers taking to modern farming have also increased. The availability of credit and other farm inputs became a bottleneck for small farmers. Most of them could not reap the benefit of the green revolution, which was ushered in large parts of the country. The green revolution no doubt created an additional demand for farm labour, for farming became a commercial proposition. A number of studies have been made on the benefits accruing to the rural society because of the green revolution. Some of the studies have no doubt shown that the benefits have percolated down to the agricultural labourer in the form of higher wage rates and additional employment. Some other studies have revealed that, on the sociological plane also, there have been some changes.

The government has introduced various schemes to boosting agricultural production during the last three decades. The Intensive Area Development Programme which has been introduced in some of the selected districts aimed at intensifying the agricultural operation through the extension of farm technology and the disseminating of knowledge of modern farming. The results obtained, at least in some selected pockets, are quite tangible. However, the beneficiaries are usually the big and medium farmers.

Credit was one of the major bottlenecks in the developmental process. As organised banking was reluctant venture into agricultural financing, much hope was pinned on the co-operatives. The co-operative credit movement has been given all the necessary incentives because it was behind idea that if the farmers were to be rescued from the clutches of village money lenders, the institutionalisation of credit was an imperative need.

The co-operative movement, which has been in existence in the country for over eight decades, has done very little to ameliorate the economic conditions of small farmers. The problem of these farmers was one of competing with those big farmers who had the capacity and influence to secure co-operative credit and other benefits. Ever since these issues were categorically highlighted by the Report of all India Rural Credit Survey, efforts were made to rectify the short comings of the co-operative credit institutions. Yet the problem remained. The power structure in rural areas being what it is, the small farmers were helpless. The study team on agriculture credit constituted by the National Commission on Agriculture categorised them as the neglected partners in agricultural growth and recommended the establishment of Farmers' Service Societies. It may be noted here that the formation of Farmers' Service Societies, which offer him credit and supply all the inputs, is a step in the right direction — it revitalises co-operative societies and makes them a powerful instrument for the development of the farming community.

The data published by the National Sample Survey through their various rounds have been one of the major sources of information on the concentration of land holdings on the one hand and the preponderance of the small farmers on the other. Recently for the first, time an attempt was made to conduct an agricultural census in the country. The report contains data relating to the number of operational holdings, tenurial relationships and many other useful details. Of the reported 70.5 million operational holdings in the country, 50 per cent classified as "marginal farms" of less than one hectare. These holdings, however, account for only 9 per cent of the total area of 161 million hectares. It has been reported that the marginal and sub-marginal holdings have on an average, only 0.3 hectare of irrigated land. Another very important feature of the Indian farming situation revealed by the Agricultural Census is that, in the cropping pattern of the marginal and sub-marginal farmers, such food crops as paddy and jowar predominate. This is perhaps an infallible indicator of the subsistence character of small farming.

Apart from small farmers and marginal farmers, the agricultural labourers form a substantial part of the rural population. They occupy the lowest rung of the rural pyramid. Their living conditions are no better than those of marginal farmers. With the increase in the population in rural areas, the size of the agricultural labour force has increased almost proportionately or more than proportionately, whereas the rate of growth of employment opportunities in non-farm activities in the villages are lower than the rate of growth of the rural population. It is normally assumed that economic development would bring about a shift in the occupational pattern in favour of non-farming activities. But it is perplexing to observe that the available decennial demographic data indicate a trend which is quite countrary to this notion.

A comparison of the number of persons classified as agricultural labourers in the 1961 census and 1971 census reveals that there has been an increase of nearly 80 per cent in their number during the decade. Even if we make allowances for definitional differences it may be observed that there has been a remarkable increase in the number of agricultural labourers during the census period. Where rural unemployment manifests itself in many forms, any increase in the labour force is likely to aggrieve the situation rather than ease it.

The problems of marginal farmers and agricultural labourers are so deep-rooted in our rural economy that it is so believed that they are beyond economic measures. They are considered as welfare problems and not as an economic proposition under the available technology. This is basically due to the reasoning that the size of a holding is considered to be an obstacle to the development of small farmers. However, the latest development in the field crop genetics has belied this assumption. The new technological possibilities thrown open by the hybrid varieties have proved that the total yield per acre can be boosted up even on small farms by applying the optimum package of farm inputs. This possibility has led the farm economists to think that the small size of a farm holding is not necessarily a limiting factor in the improvement of the economic status of marginal and potentially viable farmers.

## An Agency for Development

The plight of small farmers and marginal farmers attracted the attention of the planners and others during the Fourth Five Year Plan period In the "Approach to the Fourth Five Year Plan" (November 1968) emphasis was laid on the necessity of improving the small farmer and his economy in the overall framework of objective for the development of agriculture. It was said that, in the agricultural sector, besides providing the conditions necessary for increasing agricultural output by 5 per cent per annum, steps should be taken to enable a large section of the rural population, including the small cultivators, the farmers in dry areas and landless labourers, to participate in the development and to share its benefits. It was thought advisable to promote separate agencies for accelerating the process of the development of small and marginal farmers because the existing schemes, aiming at overall agricultural development, would not, per se, improve their conditions. The all-India Rural Credit Review Committee, after making a review of the farm situation in the country with special reference to co-operative credit, recommended the formation of the Small Farmers Development Agency. The report said: The marginal and sub-marginal cultivators have to be healed to raise themselves on the basis of the land, equipment and skills which constitute the resources available to them. The problem is, therefore, to make their farm business more efficient in technology and surplus in economic terms and to supplement their resources and knowledge for this purpose. This effort is obviously restricted to those cultivators who can be developed into surplus farmers if they adopt improved techniques on the basis of the support in terms of supplies, irrigation services, machinery, etc. Appropriate schemes have to be drawn up by technical experts with reference to the local resources and requirements, so that such cultivators can undertake specified lines of investment, adopt a suitable crop pattern, use modern inputs, and so on. It is to deal with this limited problem that we propose an institutional set-up in the form of a small farmers' development agency. This agency was expected to co-ordinate the activities of the developmental departments and credit agencies in order to ensure that the requirements of the small farmers were adequately met. The task of the agency included that of identifying the special problems of the small farmers and devising programmes by which the farm economy might be made viable. Another major task of the agency was to arrange for credit either from the co-operative or from commercial banks, by providing the necessary incentives by way of subsidies. This proposal was accepted by the Government of India and the schemes was interdicted in 1970. It was extend to 46 districts, where small farmers were found in large numbers. The central government made a provision of about Rs. 1.5 crores for each district over a period of 5 years.

Simultaneously with the implementation of the scheme for the development of small farmers, a separate scheme for the development of marginal farmers, and agricultural labourers was introduced. It was felt that the problems of the latter category of peasants were more acute and deep-rooted than those of the former and that they, therefore, required a separate treatment. The Marginal Farmers and Agricultural Labourers Development Agency was charged with the responsibility of enabling marginal farmers to maximize the productive use of their holding by suitable changes in the crop pattern, barely taking to horticulture, animal husbandry, bee-keeping etc. the necessary credit for productive investment was provided by co-operative and commercial banking institutions, which were given the incentive of subsidies. The marginal farmers, and agricultural labourers' development agency was set up 41 districts in the country, where the marginal farmers and agricultural labourers resided in large numbers. Besides the districts selected by the central government for the execution of this scheme, state governments also selected some districts for its implementation. The year 1971-72 was the first full year of the working of this scheme in most districts. In the initial stages, efforts were directed at the identification and enumeration of marginal farmers and districts after the formation of the development agency. The schemes formulated for implementation in were put through in most of the districts with the active support of co-operative bank.

## DIC — Instrument of Rural Development

Very often, banks are criticized for going slow in fulfilling socio-economic objectives to the desired extent. The assumption is that finance is the only constraint in uplifting the lot of the neglected sections of society and the backward areas. It is the common experience of banks that, in spite of sincere efforts, they cannot do what they are supposed to do, for either the required infrastructure is lacking or the projects are not viable. The District Industries Centres, therefore, provided the right type of set-up for the promotion of the development of rural industries and crafts. More such specially devised institutional arrangements are necessary if the flow of bank credit to rural areas and the rural poor is to increase. The problems of these areas are so many and complex that unless the various agencies come together and evolve a common strategy, banks alone would not be in a position to achieve much.

The advantage of promotion of cottage and small units are too well known to be repeated. In fact, for a developing country like India, with large population, there is no choice other than the promotion of rural cottage small units. Considering that poverty and unemployment are the most pressing problems facing our country, even after five decades of planned economic development the promotion of the small and cottage sectors. If planned systematically, can work wonders. Japan has shown the way.

No single factor can be advocated as the most important determinant of the success of a small unit. there has to be a blend of entrepreneurship, managerial abilities, the period of work experience, technical know-how and educational background, among others. With the passage of time, small-scale industries are entering highly sophisticated areas of production. A single individual cannot normally be expected to possess all the abilities required for the successful running of the unit. For the self-sustained growth of small industries, it is essential they should be as self-reliant as possible. The inner strength, can come to small units only from combined approach to their development, involving the grouping of entrepreneurs from various disciplines to set up a given unit.

Against this background, the setting up of a District Industries Centre (DIC) in every district, eventually, has a good promise of transforming the rural scene by promoting small, village and cottage industries. The major aim of making the district headquarters a focal point of decentralised development is that it can serve as a link chain between large cities and remote villages. it has also the advantage of checking the migration of the skilled rural population to cities. Under the DIC programme, each credit is manned by a General

Manager of the rank of Joint Director of Industries. He is supported by a team of seven functional managers who are specialists in credit, raw materials, machinery and equipment, economic investigation, research extension and training, marketing, handloom, khadi and village industries. The idea is to provide prospective entrepreneurs a package assistance under one roof so that it may be easier for them to set-up new units. The centres are given the necessary powers and statutory support for the regulation of the development of rural industries and the provision of infrastructure for new ventures.

The policy change, emphasising the need for the rapid development of cottage and small-scale industries in rural and semi-urban areas aimed at generating larger employment opportunities. Obviously, small scale industries, sustained by locally available resources, have to be encouraged. It is only by the establishment of such industrial units which absorb raw materials and other resources available in the local and adjacent areas and which reduce commodities generally consumed by the local people that economic activity can be accelerated. The industrial policy hitherto followed had led to the growth of a few industrial pockets without creating any impact on the surrounding hinterland.

The DIC programme continues as a centrally sponsored scheme during the 7th plan period and Government of India shares its expenditure with the state government on 50:50 basis. As end March 1989, the total number of approved DICs stood at 422 covering 431 districts in the country. Over the years, the scale and scope of their operations have undergone substantial changes, in response to the changes that have been taking place in the social, political and economic environments. During the year 1987-88 the 422 DIC identified 3,85,286 entrepreneurs, established 4,40,568 new units comprising of 3,28,316 artisan based and 1,12,252 small scale units, arranged for credit of Rs. 1,371.50 crores from financial institutions and generated additional employment for 14.11 lakh persons. In order to make DICs more effective, more particularly as an agent of rural development, the organisational pattern of the DICs is being restructured keeping its conceptual base intact. DICs have been playing a pivotal role in providing opportunities for self-employment.

## Co-ordinated Endeavour

The process of the generation of employment opportunities was a co-ordinated endeavour in which such financial institutions as commercial banks, voluntary agencies, such as business houses government agencies and local bodies participated simultaneously. Now that the commercial banks have been in the field for quite some time, it has been recognised that the non-availability of financial assistance is not the only reason for the non-exploitation of local resources.

In fact, the outstanding credit extended by commercial banks for the small-scale industrial sector amounted to Rs. 12,290 crores or 14.9 per cent of the total credit extend by the banking industry covering about 24.15 lakh SSI accounts as at end June, 1989, as compared to this, in June 1969 (on the event of bank nationalisation) outstanding credit to small-scale industries stood at Rs. 251 crores, which constituted about 7 per cent of the total banks have channelised a substantial portion of their incremental resources into this vital sector. The outstanding credit of the state financial corporation stood at Rs. 5,725 crores at the end of March 1989 showing a rise of Rs. 168 crores over the year.

The lead bank scheme is deeply involved in district development throughout the country, and banks have gained sufficient knowledge of the district economy, their expertise and knowledge can be beneficially harnessed to make a success of the District Industries Centre. While preparing Land Bank Survey reports and District Credit plans, banks have identified growth centres as well as economic activities having a potential for growth and expansion in each district. Based on the readily available data with banks the task of the DIC is to facilitate in identifying prospective entrepreneurs, bankable projects and their locations. What is more important now is that the DIC should undertake promotional activities and motivate local manpower to come forward and take advantage of the facilities offered. For this propose, the active involvement of voluntary agencies already working in the area is necessary. In other words, the target group should be clearly identified; and, obviously, such a group would mainly comprise the weaker sections of the population. Care, however, should be taken to weed out entrepreneurs whose main objective is to make quick money.

An overview of the DICs and their operations generally shows a poor picture. In most cases, the DICs had become an information centre and did not achieve the objective of providing a complete package of services and support to prospective entrepreneurs from the one office. The major reason for this was the lack of various allied facilities which were outside the purview of the DICs. Entrepreneurs has to visit State Financial Corporations raw material depots and sometimes even markets in distant towns or cities. The reluctance of officers to camp in rural areas which lacked the minimum physical comforts was another factor adversely affecting their performance. These could have been provided at a small cost while taking care to ensure that they did not smell of conspicuous consumption and was generally within the larger cultural landscape of the rural areas.

## PEOPLE'S ACTION FOR DEVELOPMENT (IN INDIA) (PADI)

This is a voluntary organisation registered under Societies Registration Act 1860 under the administrative control of the Department of Rural Development. the Minister of Agriculture is the President of the Society, Minister of State for Rural Development, the vice-president and the Secretary of this Department, the chairman of its governing council. It is responsible for promoting voluntary action as a supplement to government efforts in rural development. To this end, it assists a large number of voluntary organisations to implement viable projects for economic and social development of the weaker sections in the rural areas.

PADI has been canalising funds from foreign donor agencies for financing projects of voluntary organisations. From 1984-85 funds under central sector schemes of promotion of voluntary schemes and social action programmes have also been made available to PADI for giving financial assistance to voluntary agencies. From 1985-86, PADI has started assisting voluntary organisations in implementing the following additional schemes with government funds:

(1) Development of Women and Children in Rural Areas (DWCRA)

(2) Accelerated Rural Water Supply (ARWS)

(3) Low Cost Sanitating in Rural Areas

(4) Rural Landless Employment Guarantee Programme

(5) Organisation of Beneficiaries.

During the year 1987, 383 project proposals were received and PADI approved 101 projects worth Rs. 1,131.71 lakhs involving PADI assistance of 394.82 lakhs. During the year PADI has released Rs. 193.07 lakhs including foreign contributions.

During the year Rs. 10.5 lakhs were received from foreign donors and Rs. 42.86 lakhs were released for financing projects out of foreign funds.

PADI organised five conferences during the year 1985. The conference of co-ordinating voluntary organisation was organised in New Delhi in April 1985 and the conference of Voluntary Organisations on Development of Women and Children in Rural Areas was organised in New Delhi in June 1985. Regional conferences of voluntary organisations were organised at Pune in August 1985 at Tripat in September, 1985 and at Indore in November, 1985.

### Role of Industry

Although the involvement of business houses in rural development goes back to many years, it gathered some momentum in the seventies. The industrial houses have managerial skills and organisational competence which could be deployed in a co-operative endeavour with the government and voluntary organisations to improve the consumption levels of the poorest in the rural areas. Aware of the technical and managerial resources available with the industrial houses, the Sivaraman Committee in the report submitted to the government in 1978, recommended the participation of the non-government organisation, especially industrial houses, in rural development. To encourage the industry to participate in rural development union government started giving them tax incentives. Accordingly the expenditure incurred by business houses on approved programmes of rural development became deductable expenses items while computing their taxable profits.

Even before the announcement of tax incentives, many industrial houses, including Tatas, Mafaltlals, and Hindustan Lever were engaged in rural development work. Some big business houses adopted villages near their factories and undertook welfare and other service activities in these adopted villages. Fertiliser manufacturers, as part of their promotion strategy, provide extension services, free of cost or sold fertilisers at subsidised rate and supplemented it with the input to farmers in adopted villages. Some business houses engaged in the manufacture of consumer goods based on agricultural raw materials, put up pilot projects, the benefits of which are reaped by many farmers in the adopted villages.

Companies which have set up their own organisation to undertake rural development work go about it more systematically than others. These companies carry out village surveys to identity the economic activities and assess the scope for development. On the basis of these surveys, eligible target groups of beneficiaries and economic activities are identified and specific schemes formulated, financial allocation is then made according to the priority assigned to various activities and availability of funds. So far, the response of private sector industry to rural development has not been overwhelming and the impact on the rural poor has been negligible. There are many medium sized industries which can be encouraged to participate in this work through appropriate incentives. The participation of industry and voluntary organisations can only supplement the efforts of the government towards alleviating rural poverty.

Industry can play an important role in the upliftment of rural areas. With the organisational and managerial expertise at its command, the industry can involve itself in the following areas:

Programmes which directly improve the economic well-being of the people, such as, propagation of cottage and village industries, improvement of agriculture, etc.

Programmes aimed at transfer of appropriate technologies, revitalisation of village crafts and traditional technologies, etc.

Programmes directed at improving the quality of life, such as health programmes, sanitation, educational programmes, recreational, etc.

The programme adopted shall be acceptable to the rural people and should not disturb the rural environment. It should be based on the utilisation of local raw materials, with minimum energy per unit consumption of production and, at the same time, fall within guidelines set by government. In other words, the industry should undertake only those programmes in rural areas which are simple enough to be adopted by the people who have limited education, skills and resources. The projects and processes feasible at the village level are totally new to organised industry. Establishment of rural development cells by different industries may be a step in the right direction to cope up with rural problems. These cells should have sufficient managerial input and financial soundness to pack up the developmental programmes on a continuous basis. Admittedly, in several industrial units, there are such cells and they are functioning well. But there is a need to revitalise their functioning.

## Role of Banks in Rural Development

Banks play a key role in rural development. Wealth is created as a result of the application of human efforts. Human effort compromises of the passive one and the active one. The banks, or more specially, the bankers who conceive rural development, plan it in all its detail, mobilise the material and human resources for the project and benefit by the integrated development of the common area of its operation. The characteristics of banking, therefore, are knowledge, vision, meticulous (micro level) planning and drive, dynamism and translation of the plan into reality. A good banker is one who is capable of inspiring confidence in people, and has the ability to motivate them to work with him in fulfilling the socio-economic goals set by him. In other words, a good banker ought to be a good, progressive and dynamic leader of men.

Banks can give the right lead for rural development, as they are the repositories of resources to accelerate the process of rural development. Beside making available the finance for development, banks can play a catalytic role in developing infrastructure, transfer of technology and know-how, guidance and above all education of the rural people of varied target groups.

Government has assigned a pivotal role to the banking system in developing the village economy. In the sphere of credit the major thrust of government's policy has been on ensuring availability of credit to all classes of rural borrowers, especially those belonging to the weaker sections, on terms better than the usurious rates charged by village money lenders. With this end in view, government's endeavour has been to strengthen, through the Reserve Bank of India (RBI), the multi-tier co-operative credit structure, which primarily serves the credit needs of the rural areas. The RBI has, in addition, played an important role in co-ordinating the efforts of commercial banks and co-operative credit agencies in rural development. The accent of government policy in regard to banks has been on ensuring their penetration into rural area. Emphasis has also been laid by the banking sector on evolving programmes for an all-round development of the village economy by providing credit to agriculture and village industries. In the endeavour to develop the rural economy, the efforts of commercial banks, State Land Development Banks and State Cooperative Banks, are complemented by those of the NABARD.

The Bank's role perhaps is in terms of taking up those programmes which could provide employment to the rural labour. Generation of additional employment opportunities in the rural sector is somewhat difficult to achieve in a short period. Considering the magnitude of the growth in rural labour force, it is also necessary to find employment opportunities for at least a major portion of them in the non-agricultural sector. How exactly the banks can play their role in this process of employment generation depends upon their ingenuity in adopting suitable schemes for financing. For the development of skills among the rural youth for self-employment, the Government of India has introduced the programme of Training Rural Youth for Self-employment (TRYSEM) By co-ordinating their lending programmes, banks can contribute substantially in this sphere, if they have the conviction to implement their own programmes effectively.

Towards this end, banks which are involving themselves deeply in the formulation of credit plans for rural development, evolving strategies for development, visualising the growth process in the rural economy and planning for the development of credit facilities in accordance with the requirements of growth in addition to providing credit to agriculture and other rural activities on an increasing scale. Banks are, therefore, more suited to take up the challenging task of rural development. And, the activities of all other agencies have to be co-ordinated with the banks in the true spirit of integrated area development for eradication of mass poverty in rural India. Above all, rural people should rise above the present state of affair and strive hard to develop with the assistance and guidance offered to them. They should accept that rural developments is aimed at improving the living conditions of the people living in rural area.

The commercial banks which are now actively engaged in rural credit have on their rolls technical persons (agricultural graduates) trained in different ways as Agricultural Officers, Rural Credit Officers, Agricultural Finance Officers, etc. They are supposed to guide the farmer in all technical matters and supervise the credit. But it appears that these technical persons have to spend more time in processing the loan applications, disbursing of the loan amount and preparing periodical reports to be sent to the central office. In the process, considerable time is not devoted for technical service and supervision. Further, the technical staff is quite inadequate. Loan amounts reach the rural community without adequate technical assistance and proper supervision. Even though it cannot be concluded that all borrowers need technical assistance and all misuse the loan amount, yet credit with necessary follow-up action is bound to yield better returns.

Provision of adequate and timely institutional credit is an important condition for rural development. But credit should not become a "hangman's noose" for the borrower. Nor should it jeopardise the interests of the banking institutions. To have an adequate impact on agricultural production the provision of credit should be accompanied by, and co-ordinate with, extension services and supervision. Co-operatives are better suited to exercise supervision, and effective supervision should be invariably traced as a legitimate function of the apex banks and central banks. As financiers of societies, they should take the necessary steps to ensure sound working of the primary credit societies and primary land development banks. Through proper supervision, the mounting co-operative overdues can be minimised. The government with necessary support should help the co-operatives to introduce suitably modified and supervised credit programme. To start with, such scheme may be introduced in places where co-operatives are functioning well and gradually extend the scheme to other places. The commercial banks may be insisted upon to have adequate technical staff on their rolls. It is paradoxical that agricultural graduates remain unemployed in some states, in a situation of inadequate technical staff, including extension personnel.

The Regional Rural Banks sponsored by the commercial banks maybe utilised for introducing the supervised credit scheme. For effective implementation of the programme, well-trained persons should be employed as local supervisors. Young persons with high school education preferably from agricultural families with practical farm experience maybe chosen for training to serve as credit supervisor. One-year's specialised training in agricultural economics with emphasis on farm credit, co-operative organisation, farm management, techniques of supervised credit, etc., is necessary. The technical aspects of farm operation such as crop choice, use of fertilisers, control of insects and plant diseases should be included in training courses. The Reserve Bank of India has to necessarily play a crucial role in helping co-operative and commercial banks to introduce supervised credit schemes.

The credit-giving institution, while providing short-term credit to weaker sections should take into consideration the normal credit requirements for consumption purposes. However, a greater proportion of the credit should be in kind. Further, it should examine carefully the technical feasibility and productive capacity of the proposed farming operation with the help of credit. Technical advise, if required, should be provided to the loan applicant at this stage to evolve a suitable plan. Follow-up action must begin with the release of the first instalment of the loan. The credit supervisor must work closely with the borrowers. He has to supervise and control the use of the loan amount throughout the crop year. The subsequent instalment of the loan amount should be released after the bank is fully satisfied with the proper utilisation of the loan, other weaker sections should be made credit worthy by helping them to take to certain gainful occupations through supervised credit programme. Attention should also be given to marketing and it should be made obligatory on the part of the borrower to sell his produce with the knowledge of the concerned bank. The credit supervisors have to assist the borrowers in marketing their products. Even an element of effective supervision over credit will go a long way in using the credit for productive purposes and reap the benefits. A well thought out supervised credit system with organisational efficiency aiming at the benefit of the weaker sections in immediately called for.

## KHADI AND VILLAGE INDUSTRIES COMMISSION (KVIC)

With an ever-increasing population and a fixed stock of land, rural landlessness in India is rising. Disguised unemployment in the rural agricultural sector is widely held to be true in the sense that more people are actually associated with a given piece of land than is required. The result is that the productivity of land may actually fall.

In this situation, the development of rural industries is essential and consequently, khadi and other village industries become crucial. They not only generate employment in rural areas but contribute to the process of rural demand creation and capital formation as well.

If we look at the current euphoria over the state of the economy, much of it has to do with the fact that rural demand has picked up, buoyed by the rebound in agricultural growth. The dependence of the economy on the monsoons cannot be done away with any time soon but by developing village industries, the extent of dependence can be reduced.

Village industries such as the khadi industry typically utilise local resources and skills, and provide employment to the local youth. The employment potential of these industries is huge. By the end of the tenth plan, it is expected that khadi and other village industries will provide employment for up to 9m people. Of these, 2m new jobs are to be created during the tenth plan period, from '02-07. In fact, the Khadi and Village Industries Commission (KVIC) is the nodal implementing agency for the Rural Employment Generation Programme (REGP).

| | *FY99* | *FY00* | *FY01* | *FY02** | *'06-07*** |
|---|---|---|---|---|---|
| Production (Rs Cr) | | | | | |
| Khadi Cloth | 636 | 552 | 432 | 444 | 750 |
| Other Village Industries | 4,477 | 5,613 | 5,914 | 7,141 | 12,500 |
| Employment | | | | | |
| (Million people) | 5.8 | 5.9 | 6 | 6.6 | 8.9 |

* Estimates.

** Tenth Plan Target.

*Source:* Tenth Plan Data.

The production of khadi has however, been declining over the years. One of the major reasons that have been put forward is the uncertainty regarding the continuation of the rebate policy for khadi, which has upset production schedules and consequently, khadi output to some extent. Another reason has been the shortfall in funds from the banks, which has affected the marketing of these products. Though marketing efforts for khadi and village industry products focus more on the domestic front, they have performed well in the export market too. Exports of village industry products are expected to touch Rs 35 crore by '07.

The government has taken policy measures to support and revamp the workings of KVIC. For marketing, funds have been provided for the renovation and expansion of existing outlets, as well as the purchase of mobile vans and the organisation of exhibitions to raise awareness about KVIC products. Apart from this, KVIC is participating in international exhibitions organised by the India Trade Promotion Organisation. Khadi Gramodyog Bhawans have also been proposed in the US, UK Germany and South Africa.

In order to extent quality control for KVIC products, 17 national laboratories have been selected. Anti-crease treatment for khadi is expected to be achieved, by tying up with one of the laboratories. The National Institute of Design, Ahmedabad has been engaged to introduce new and trendy designs for khadi.

Under the National Programme for Rural Industrialisation (NRPI), 50 clusters have already been identified by KVIC for cluster development. The clusters will provide the necessary infrastructure and support services to the village industries.

## Micro-Level Planning

One of the solutions suggested by economists is to adopt bottom up macro-level planning to achieve the positive result in the field of rural development. The micro level planning is based on the socio-economic, political and administrative needs, problems and aspirations of the people, potentialities of the area, local skills and entrepreneurship and possibilities of development with the active involvement of banks to achieve the goals set at macro level through an integrated process.

The major objectives of micro planning are:

(1) To cater to the basic needs of specific areas people and develop harness rural skills and entrepreneurship.

(2) To solve problems of areas and regions of extreme backwardness through active participation in the rural development programme.

(3) To share the benefits of planned development to the optimum extent.

(4) To work towards removing inter and intra-regional socio-economic imbalances.

(5) To create greater employment opportunities and strive to improve the quality of life of the rural poor.

(6) To remove rural poverty and inequality in income and wealth.

(7) To achieve goals of integrated rural development.

In this type of planning there is scope to integrate the varied schemes, programmes, sectors and policies at the local level on fixed priorities.

## Conclusion

We would like to reiterate that rural development is a part of the same process of economic and social change. There are a number of programmes formulated by the government and the industry, voluntary agencies, etc. Banks have been implementing them by providing necessary financial assistance. There are multi-disciplined institutions for rural development. What is wanting at the present moment is the co-ordinated and sustained effort. What is more, it is necessary to bridge the gaps of inequalities in rural areas. This could be attempted by well organised service co-operative to give support to farming.

Towards this end, the corporate sector, banks and other financial institutions should invest sizeable portion of their profits towards increasing basic infrastructure like schools, hospitals, health centres and take up the onerous task of propagating family panning, planned parenthood and motivating rural people to achieve a higher living standard. Rural development is a human development programme and, therefore, it should be above party politics. The motto should be to help with all the might the down-trodden irrespective of caste, creed, sex, etc.

Rural development should be looked upon not merely as ameliorating the socio-economic conditions of the rural people but also as motivating rural people to take up the integrated development of rural areas. In this direction, the process of development should ordinate at the individual level then linking it to family and then to a group of families and the village. It should develop from bottom to top. The people's active participation will bring in a sea-change in the scale and scope of operation. The results are in terms of change rather than the sum of crores of rupees spent on a project without bringing any benefit to the concerned people. The experiments in rural development have remained more or less at the top. It is, therefore, necessary the emphasis should be laid on 'Planning' from the bottom and that the exclusive reliance, so far placed on the 'pyramid structure' approach, be given up.

At the district level, the Collector, who is the Chairman of District Rural Development Agency (DRDA), acts as a catalytic agent. At the block level, it is the Block Development Officer (BDO) who is entrusted with the responsibility of relating to rural development. The village level worker is the person who acts as a liaison between the different agencies and the target. Since all these personnel are over-burdened with their other administrative work, they have little time to attend to the principal task of rural development. In this context, two alternative organisational patterns are available. First, to entrust the responsibility of rural development to the banking sector by providing all the necessary growth inputs for it. Second, all the related sectoral activities of rural development should be brought under one or two ministries/agencies.

Experience indicates that the planning and implementation of rural development calls for a substantial measure of decentralisation, involving the strengthening of village/block level development agencies and institutions. An institutional arrangement — perhaps in the form of regional planning units or co-ordinating committees — must be found to resolve issues and, in the last resort, to provide adjudication machinery. Where national investment priorities are concerned, provision has to be made to ensure that the central planning authority is brought into the picture. Decentralisation may mean decentralisation of authority:

*(i)* To formulate projects:

*(ii)* To administer projects and run enterprises;

*(iii)* To allocate expenditure; and

*(iv)* To raise revenue.

If three major levels of government are considered—the Central or federal, the State or provincial, and the district — it will be seen that the responsibility for planning, budgeting and executing rural development schemes usually resides at the provincial level. But, almost everywhere, central planning agencies and ministers have been playing an increasingly dominant role in directing and providing funds for rural development. In some countries, special ministerial or presidential units have been established to plan, co-ordinate and accelerate the rural development activities of the central as well as regional agencies.

In the ultimate analysis the desire for development, the direction this process takes and the momentum it gathers, depends upon the will of the people. Various institutions for rural development can help in harnessing the energies of the people, especially of the rural people as well as the student community and in providing institutional and organisational channels for their efforts. The environment in the country today is conducive for concerted action in improving rural conditions and rebuild rural civilisation.

Until and unless organisational and institutional arrangements are reoriented towards integrated rural development, the achievements, if any, will not be as satisfactory as visualised. Further, these organisations and institutions in the villages should be manned by trained and educated personnel, and they should provide dedicated and committed leadership to the target groups without submitting to the pressures brought to bear upon them by the vested interests in rural areas. Local institutions have potential advantages for coping with administrative difficulties. They provide some measure of participation and impetus in rural development programmes. The need of the hour is streamlining the organisational machinery and channelising the work relating to rural development through one single agency, which will serve as a model for development.

**Annexure – I**

# LIST OF SUBJECTS ALLOCATED AND PROGRAMMES IMPLEMENTED BY THE MINISTRY OF RURAL DEVELOPMENT

## Department of Rural Employment and Poverty Alleviation

1. (a) All matters pertaining to rural employment such as working out strategies and programmes for rural employment including special works, wage or income generation and training related thereto.

   (b) Implementation of the specific programmes of rural employment such as Jawahar Rozgar Yojana, (JRY), Employment Assurance Scheme (EAS) and other programmes evolved from time to time.

   (c) Micro-level planning related to rural employment or unemployment and administrative infrastructure therefor.

2. Integrated rural development including Ganga Kalyan Yojana, Small Farmers' Development Agency, Marginal Farmers and Agricultural Labourers Agency.
3. Desert Development Programmes and Drought Prone Areas Programme.
4. Rural housing including Rural Housing Policy and all matters germane and incidental thereto under country or rural planning, in so far as it relates to rural areas.

## Department of Rural Development

1. All matters relating to panchayati raj and panchayati raj institutions.
2. Land reforms, and tenures, land records, consolidation of holdings and other related matters.
3. Administration of the Land Acquisition Act, 1984 (1 of 1984) and matters relating to acquisition of land for purposes of the Union.
4. Recovery of claims in a state in respect of taxes and other public demands, including areas of land revenue and sums recoverable such as arrears, arising outside that State.
5. Land, that is to say, collection of rents, transfer and alienation of land, land improvement and agricultural loans excluding acquisition of non-agricultural land or buildings, town planning improvements.
6. Land revenue, including the assessment and collection of revenue, survey for revenue purposes, alienation of revenues.
7. Duties in respect of succession to agricultural land.
8. Nodal responsibility for all matters relating to the Minimum Needs Programme in rural areas in the field of elementary education, adult education, rural health, rural electrification and the nutrition programmes.
9. Water supply (subject to overall national perspective of water planning and co-ordination assigned to the Ministry of Water Resources), sewage, drainage and sanitation relating to rural areas. International co-operation and technical assistance in this field.
10. Public co-operation, including all matters relating to voluntary agencies for rural development and National Fund for Rural Development.
11. Warehousing in rural areas, including rural godowns.
12. Setting up of agricultural markets in rural areas and the Agricultural Produce (Grading and Marking) Act, 1937 (1 of 1937) (This item has since been deleted from the Department of Agriculture and Co-operation with effect from December, 1988).
13. Co-operatives relatable to the items in this list.
14. All attached or subordinate offices or other organisations concerned which any of the subjects specified in this list.
15. All matters relating to rural roads including those under the Minimum Needs Programme in the Rural Areas.
16. Road works financed in whole or in part by the Central Government in tribal areas of Assam specified in part I and part II of the table appended to paragraph 20 of the Sixth Schedule to the Constitution.

17. National Social Assistance Programme incorporating National Old Age Pension Scheme, National Family Benefit Scheme and National Maternity Benefit Scheme.
18. All matters relating to co-operation with the Centre for Integrated Rural Development for Asia and Pacific (CIRDAP) and the Afro-Asian Rural Reconstruction Organisation (AARRO).

## Department of Wastelands Development

1. National Wastelands Development Board.
2. National Land Use and Wastelands Development Council.
3. Promotion of rural employment through Wastelands Development.
4. Promotion of production of fuelwood, fodder and timber on non-forest lands, including private wastelands.
5. Research and development of appropriate low cost technologies for increasing productivity of wastelands in sustainable ways.
6. Inter-departmental and inter-disciplinary co-ordination in programme planning and implementation of the Wastelands Development Programme, including training.
7. Promotion of people's participation and public co-operation and co-ordination of efforts of Panchayats and other voluntary and non-governmental agencies for Wastelands Development.

❑ ❑ ❑

# Chapter 34

# ROLE OF VOLUNTARY AGENCIES

## Introduction

Intervention of business in rural development has gained momentum in the recent years. Presently, there are more than 600 business houses which are engaged in development activities in rural areas, either directly or indirectly. Some theoretical underpinning is necessary to substantiate the rationale of intervention of business. Of interest here is backward and forward linkages of rural development. For most of the raw materials to industry, the supply point is rural areas. Inadequate and intermittent supply of raw materials would affect the working and profit margin of industry, Rural development, in its wake, brings about an increased supply of raw materials at a stabilised price to the industry. This is termed as the backward linkage of rural development to industry.

On similar lines the forwarding linkage can also be established. The products of industries, whether it is agro-based like fertilisers, pesticides or of consumer industry like soap, toilet, oil or of engineering industries like pumps, motors, agricultural appliances, etc have to penetrate into rural markets.

Rural development brings about increased purchasing power to the peöple which would enable them to place a higher demand for more goods and services.

Undoubtedly, involvement of business in rural development has to achieve a new dimension. The managerial and organisational capabilities with the corporate sector can be deployed to find solutions to many rural problems. Importantly, greater stress has to be laid on solving crucial and immediate problems, but, at the same time, not loosing sight of the integrated nature of the development process to be initiated. Fox example, a programme on immunisation of children can pick up only if the income of the people increases. So care has to be taken to see that the programmes are properly linked and co-ordinated.

There are certain programmes which requires special and concerted action. Sometimes a piecemeal approach has to be adopted to implement the programmes, for they are very basic. Mention has to be made about drinking water supply programme which is being accorded top priority by the Government of India. There are 78,876 villages in India which do not have a single source of drinking water supply. For more than half of the total villages, there is only one source of water supply. To supply adequate and safe water to the problem villages, involvement of business houses is necessary. The implicit reasoning is that businessmen penetrate deeper into village near their factory sites. This will give them a leverage for implementing rural water supply programme more effectively and speedily, of course, with the support of other agencies, such as, government functionaries, UNICEF voluntary organisations, etc.

Closely linked up with this, is the sanitation problem. The present status of rural environmental sanitation is deplorably poor. Construction of sanitary latrines and disposal of waste water, garbage, cattle dung, etc. have to pick up in rural areas. Moreover, programmes on drinking water, immunisation, nutrition, etc., can be effective only if basic sanitation is ensured. The point is, how business can dovetail drinking water supply and sanitation programmes into their general development programmes in rural areas. This does not mean that their contribution in water supply and sanitation lag behind, in fact, there are more than 200 business houses which have specific programmes in these areas. The idea is to explore how their involvement can be augmented in a scientific and systematic manner.

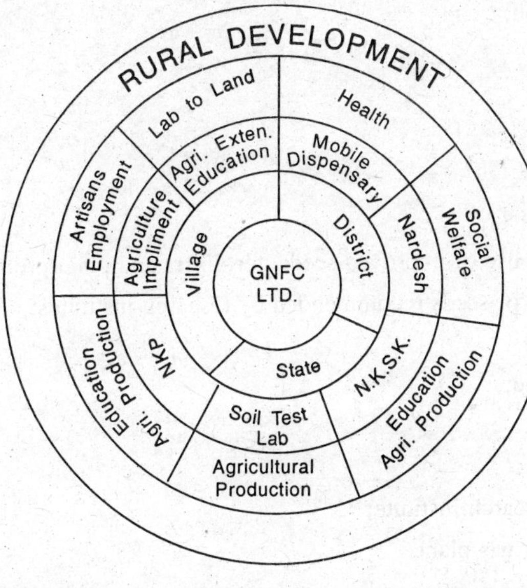


*Fig. 1. Rural Development Programmes Growth Nucleus for the Country*

Understandably, the problems is an gigantic one and has to be tackled in a multi-disciplinary way. Government, UNICEF and business houses should come together, to chalk out programmes for their implementation.

## Involvement of Business — An Overview

The priorities in rural areas suggest a natural sequence for beginning multi-sectoral activities. They have to be planned in relation to each other and implemented as an integrated whole. These essential services include, nutrition, education, safe supply of water, waste disposal, simplified health care, introduction of simple technologies to increase productivity and income generating activities. Intervention of business in rural development is generally of an integrated nature and is mainly to promote the following.

(*a*) Income generating activities;

(*b*) Development of small scale and village industry;

(*c*) Health;

(d) Education;

(e) Infrastructure; and

(f) Recreation.

Varied activities are clubbed under each category and the break-up is given below:

## A. Agriculture:

Under this head, the following activities are clubbed:

Providing cross breeding services to cows, sheep etc. of rural people;

Extending credit to farmers for agricultural purposes;

Periodical checking up of animals by a veterinary doctor;

Circulating pamphlets and booklets explaining profitability of modern agriculture;

Reclamation of waste/salty land;

Minor irrigation;

Artificial insemination;

Tree plantation;

Poultry farming;

Calf breeding;

Shed for cows;

Setting up compost pits;

Demonstration of the use of improved seeds, fertilisers and plant protection;

Testing new varieties of seeds recommended by research institutes;

Vaccination of birds;

Social forestry scheme;

Tractorisation;

Pest control;

Setting up of land research institute;

Construction of gobar gas plant;

Fisheries;

Agricultural extension works;

Free soil testing service;

Promotion of balanced fertiliser application;

Distribution of free literature regarding modern techniques of agriculture;

Setting up handpumps and motors for pumping in water for agricultural uses;

Crop insurance.

## B. Village and Cottage Industry:

The following are listed under this head

Assistance in setting up rural industries for self-employed people;

Training for unemployed youths like blacksmiths, carpenters, etc, and also extending assistance to buy equipments;

Setting up basket and mat-knitting centres;

Tailoring equipments and training in this field;

Assisting unemployed to set up printing trade;

Providing khadi spinning wheels;

Assistance to set up bangle works;

Upgrading skills of leather work and imparting training on motor winding, welding, carpentry, sheet metal; etc.

Energisation of village crafts and also extending adequate market facilities.

**C. Health and Medical:**

The following activities are listed under this head:

Immunisation of children against communicable disease;

Setting up sanitation facilities;

Assistance in constructing convenient houses, conducive to health;

Provision for adequate and safe drinking water;

Supply of preventive and curative medicines;

Conducting health survey;

Sight conservation camps;

Hearing conservation camps;

Assisting to set up blood banks;

Hygiene exhibitions;

Setting up allopathic and homeopathic dispensaries and clinics;

Digging up soak pits;

Provision for public conveniences;

Free medical treatment;

Family planning schemes;

Free milk for children;

Diagonistic centres;

Assistance for setting up X-ray clinics, pathological centres;

Mobile medical care unit;

Maternity hospitals.

**D. Infrastructure:**

Various activities undertaken under this head are:

Rural electrification;

Food for work scheme for constructing roads and pavements;

Construction and maintenance of rural link roads, village street, drainage, etc;

Construction of culverts;

Yuvak and mahila mandals in villages;

Setting up of Gram Vikas Kendras;

Promotion of women's organisation;

Plantation of trees along road side;

Organisation of co-operative society;

Improving transport facilities;

Construction of wells and canals.

### E. Educational:

The main activities under this head are:

Establishment and running of educational institutions;

Adult education;

Aid to educational institutions including degree colleges;

Setting up social and cultural organisations;

Aid to orphanges;

Setting up balwadis;

Training women volunteers to organise women's group in villages;

Providing uniforms to primary school children;

Social education through film shows, exhibitions; etc

Stipend for college and school children;

Setting up libraries;

Giving aid for buying books.

### F. Recreational:

Some units have undertaken the work of extending recreational facilities to rural areas. The following activities are done:

Playground and provision for nets and balls for players;

Gifting transistor radios to the elementary schools;

Cattle shows;

Cultural programmes;

Prizes to individuals for talents in social service as well as Gaon Sabhas for Community Work.

## VOLUNTARY AGENCIES IN RURAL DEVELOPMENT

The voluntary agencies working for the uplift of rural people have had a long history in this country. The earliest to take up this work were missionaries and religious organisations. The impact of their work may be seen in the fields of education and health and the general uplift of the people is backward and remote areas of the country.

It has been recognised that voluntary agencies can play a very creative role motivating the people and supervising the distribution of the resources with a view to ensuring their proper utilisation. They can also play a very useful role in matching projects to the local conditions and supplying local know-how about the various factors affecting productivity and marketing.

The term voluntary agencies has been used in a broader sense here. While it covers organisations registered under the various trusts and charitable Acts, it includes unregistered groups and organisation willing to accept the responsibility for some aspect of rural development with or without the aid of a government agency. It covers various youth organisations, mahila mandals, civic organisations (like the Lion's

Clubs, Rotarians etc.), organisations of beneficiaries such as farmers organisations, workers' union, religious organisations, professional bodies, whether they have registered or are informal.

The experience of some of the voluntary agencies shows that where they have sought to tackle the social problems related to traditions and religious values, they have had to face problems of acceptance by the villagers. This factor has been recognised by the new voluntary organisations which plan their programmes specifically for the purpose of raising productivity and providing employment. They feel that other social changes and changes in outlook and attitudes will follow, however slowly.

Voluntary agencies have generally been started by an individual or a group of individuals often motivated by the spirit of charity or social work. Some of these agencies have had people working on a part-time, honorary basis. But the situation appears to be changing now, as evidence by such agencies as the Maliwada Human Development Project (Aurangabad, Maharashtra), Kishore Bharati (Hoshangabad, Madhya Pradesh), Social Work and Research Centre (Tilonia, Rajasthan), Land Research Institute (Shedgewadi, Maharashtra), and Rural University (Jawaja, Rajasthan). These organisations have been formed by professional people, and they have been able to attract others like themselves.

Although voluntary agencies have, by and large, adopted the integrated development approach, they initially concentrated on the provision of such basic services as medicine, education, etc. The rapport with local leadership and the acceptance by the local community are easier to establish in this manner. It is only after this has been achieved—and it may sometimes take as long as five to six years—that they have sought to take up more comprehensive programmes of village improvement covering such aspects as agricultural extension, construction of roads and minor irrigation projects and, at times, even social problems. The emphasis given to each of these activities depends on the needs of the particular area and the specialisation of the agencies. For example, the Yusuf Meherally Centre, (Bombay) places emphasis on medical services; Kishore Bharati on agricultural extension and education; and the Social Work and Research Centre on groundwater surveys and the promotion of handicrafts.

The specific fields in which voluntary agencies may participate with advantage are quite numerous. In addition to disaster relief operations—famine, floods, fire riots etc., where the contribution of voluntary organisations in bringing succour to the victims of calamities in the form of food, doles, rehabilitation housing and sanitation has been most conspicuous—the voluntary agencies often participate in programmes for the development of social services and income improvement programmes for the poor. Health, general education and social welfare institutions for the handicapped, destitute and deserted ones, pre-school education and nutrition have attracted very sizeable donations from philanthropic citizens and organisations. It is now the income development programme for the poor which is engaging the attention of voluntary agencies. Social forestry, water management (Warabandi for example), soil conservation (on area basis), implementation of various minimum needs programmes might provide fitting challenges for voluntary initiative in the field.

## Important Role

Voluntary agencies have an important role in informing and motivating people and in carrying out supplemental action for improving incomes by promoting self-employment activity, helping in the identification of eligible households, organising them for group action, informing them about schemes and official procedures, preparing application, and offering follow-up and liaison services etc. The main responsibility for resources transfer has to remain with official financial institutions. They can help in guiding and project formulation process. Universities and professional institutions, for example, can help in block and village planning exercise. The voluntary agencies may bring supplementary funds to oil and lubricate the movement of projects which often get blocked because of the rigidities inherent in official programmes and procedures.

## Resources Problem

One of the major problems that faces voluntary agencies is lack of resources, both financial and human. Since most of the activities under taken by them are in the nature of extension work, they cannot become self-supporting. They are dependent for funds on the government, whose procedures are often slow and time-consuming, on foreign donor agencies and industries whose grants may not be available on regular basis. Often, voluntary agencies do not have information about the government resources earmarked for the development of the area in which they operate, nor about the methods and procedures to be adopted to avail themselves of these resources. It is, therefore, not unusual to come across a situation where, on the one hand, the voluntary agency complains of lack of funds and, on the other, the government provisions lapse for lack of suitable projects to utilise them.

Some voluntary agencies levy a charge, generally fixed on a no-profit no-loss basis, for such services as medicine, groundwater, surveys and land development, which have been provided by them. This is done partly with a view to covering some part of their expenditure. Their primary objective, however, is to inculcate the spirit of self-help among villagers by making them pay, albeit partially, for their social consumption.

When it comes to replicability the constraint of human resources for rural development is equally difficult to overcome for voluntary agencies, as it is for government agencies and the corporate sector. Lack of trained and dedicated people has been a major stumbling block to the multiplication of voluntary agencies. Paradoxically, it is in this area that they have a significant contribution to make to their role as catalysts for change.

## Conclusions

The advantages of voluntary agencies, like flexibility in operations, rapport with local community and their commitment to planned social changes, are sometimes set off by the fact that they generally become personality oriented. They are build around the leadership qualities and dedication of an individual; and it is therefore, difficult to replicate the experiment.

Second, dependence on personality characteristics has sometimes proved to be detrimental to professionalism, partly because the involvement and dedication of the leaders makes up for their lack of training. Voluntary agencies, though they have been able to attract professionals, have not been able to retain them on a permanent basis; their turnover is very high.

Voluntary agencies can contribute to human resource development in two ways. They already provide a training ground for rural development workers who may, with the experience gained, venture out to start new centres of work on their own. The existing voluntary agencies may thus help create a core of workers, capable of providing leadership and organisation for rural development programmes. Some of the field workers of the voluntary agencies may, as is already happening, join the government, and thereby improve the implementation of government programme.

Voluntary agencies may also consciously attempt to become dispensable by training villagers to carry on the task initiated by them. A cadre of village level workers from among the beneficiaries would come up in due course, and would help the process of the withdrawal of voluntary agencies.

❑ ❑ ❑

## Chapter 35

# VIKAS VOLUNTEER VAHINI

### Introduction

The preamble to the National Bank for Agriculture and Rural Development Act, 1981, states that NABARD has been established for providing credit for the promotion of agriculture, small industry, cottage and village industries, handicrafts and other rural crafts, and other allied agriculture activities in rural areas with a view to promoting integrated rural development and securing their prosperity. The mandate of NABARD is therefore much larger than that of an institution for providing refinance to banks. To secure an integrated development of rural areas and the economic prosperity of the rural people, NABARD naturally is closely linked with the entire operations aimed at development through credit.

The National Bank for Agriculture and Rural Development has developed a code of ethics for rural borrowers which is embodied in the five principles of development through credit. These are:

*(i)* Credit must be used in accordance with the most suitable methods of science and technology.

*(ii)* The terms and conditions of credit (or techno-economic parameters) must be fully respected.

*(iii)* Work must be done with skill so as to increase productivity and income.

*(iv)* A part of the additional income created by credit must be saved.

*(v)* Loan instalments must be repaid in time and regularly so as to recycle credit.

Good banking systems would automatically lend strength to NABARD and any frailties or problems faced by banks would naturally worry it. The problem of increasing overdue has, therefore, caused anxiety to NABARD. Accordingly, it postulated the five principles of development through credit and started the innovative programme of Vikas Volunteer Vahini (VVV) which aimed at securing proper credit use and its timely repayment.

## WHAT IS VVV?

The Vikas Volunteer Vahini, as conceived by NABARD, comprise a body of ordinary men and women, who have successfully put into practice the five principles of development through credit and have volunteered to disseminate these principles amongst the rural people. Two important elements of the VVV programme are:

*(i)* An institution called "Friends of Banks" Club established in the village covered under the programme. This Club normally consists of borrowers who have not defaulted in the repayment of their loans. In the village, the Club serves as the nerve centre for the promotion of the ethics of repayment and a bridge between the borrowers on the one hand and the banks and development agencies on the other.

*(ii)* Area specialist volunteers chosen from amongst the borrowers themselves. The area volunteer will act as an extension worker (agent) for the banking system in the villages under his jurisdiction where the Clubs have been set up. He offers technical guidance to rural borrowers in the proper maintenance and up keep of the assets acquired through credit.

The flow of institutional credit for rural development has increased rapidly over the last decade or so. However, as far as the recovery of loans is concerned, the performance has been dismal. In fact, the problem of overdue has assumed serious proportions in recent years. The high level of overdue restrict the capacity of lending institutions to recycle funds, besides threatening the prospects of continued flow of external aid for agricultural and rural development. There is, therefore, an urgent need for reversing the increasing trend in overdue. The increasing level of overdue was the primary reason which promoted NABARD to start the VVV Programmes. The consequences of such a large proportion of overdue are likely to be very serious. The VVV programme is NABARD's remedy for correcting the situation.

## Coverage

The VVV programme was first launched in the two districts of Tamil Nadu, namely, Madurai and Tiruchi, in two phases in May and September 1983. In each district, 50 villages, at the rate of five villages per development block, were covered. It was hoped that, through a ripple effect an impact would be made on the neighbouring village as well. The programme strategy included a proposal to shift to a new cluster of five villages in the block after a period of about three years so that in a few years, the entire block might be covered, partly as an impact zone.

The second state covered was Gujarat where Sabarkaṇtha and Rajkot districts were selected and the programme was launched in January 1984 and May 1984 respectively. In these districts too five villages each were selected. The third state was Orissa, where Ganjam and Dhenkanal district was covered under the programme. It was launched in Ganjam district in May 1984, covering 55 villages, in a cluster of five villages in each of the 10 selected blocks with an additional cluster in one block. The programme in Dhenkanal district was launched in April 1985, when a new approach was adopted by which instead of about 50 villages spread out in clusters in 5 to 10 blocks, a compact area of 28 villages in one block was taken up. the advantages of this approach were expected to be in the form of effective monitoring and a systematic development of infrastructure. This type of sample would also be appropriate for evaluating the tangible and intangible gains of the programme.

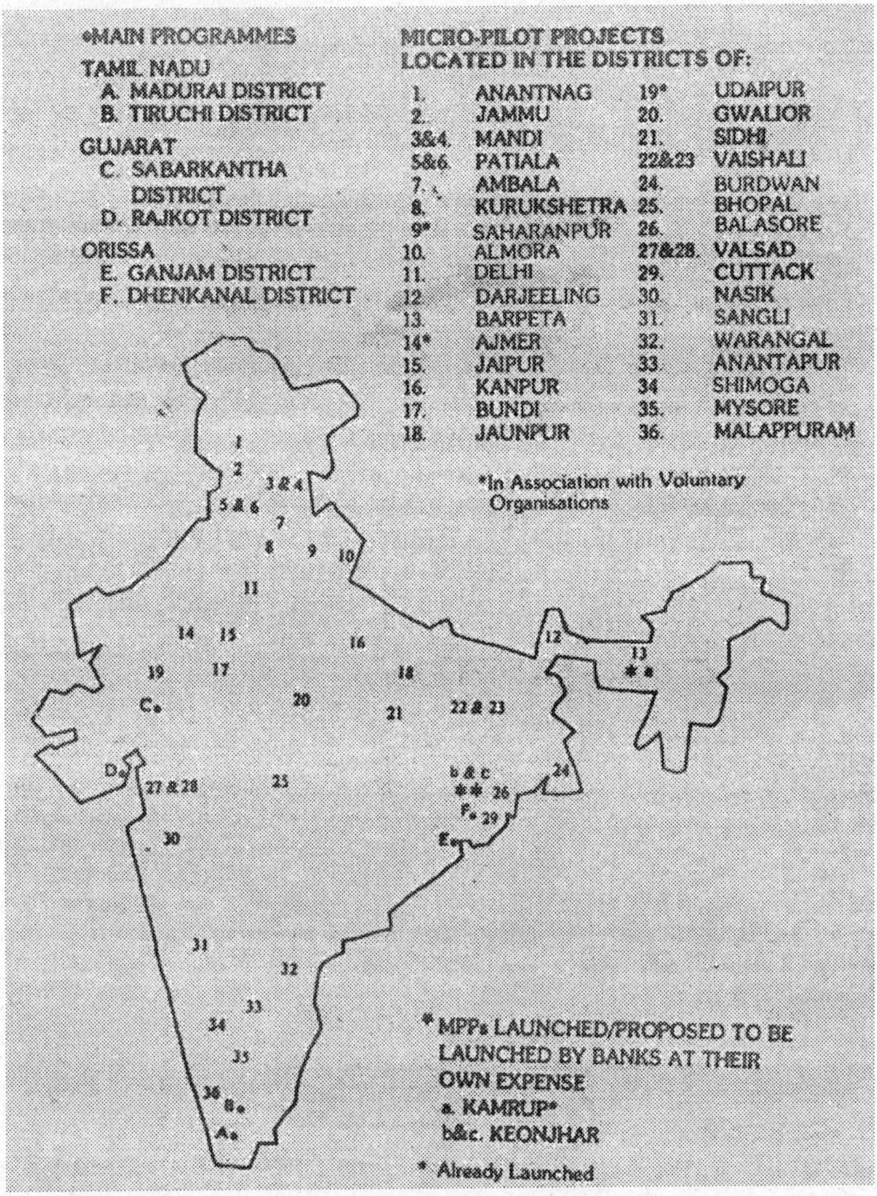


*Fig. 1. VVV Programmes — Coverage*

Besides the Main Programme in these three states, 36 Micro Pilot Projects (MPPs) were started in 17 states, usually in clusters of five villages each. Twenty-nine of these MPPs had been launched by June 1984 in clusters proximate to the villages of the residence of the first batch of volunteers. During 1984-85, seven more MPPs were launched, three of them in association with voluntary organisation. So far, 183 villages have been covered under these MPPs.

In all, 468 villages had been covered under the programme financed by NABARD by the end of the co-operative year 1984-85. The programme has been also started in Bamundi block, Kamrup district, Assam by the Prajyotish Gaonlia Bank in a cluster of five villages at its own expense, and is proposed to be started by the State Bank of India and the Bank of India in two clusters of five villages each of Keonjhar District, Orissa.

## Activities

The objectives of the programme were:

*(i)* To prepare feasible comprehensive Village Development Plans for each of the villages covered under the programme. These plans would be financed by the banks operating in the area, and efforts would be made to satisfy the credit needs of all the villagers on a time-bound basis;

*(ii)* To disburse loans to cover beneficiaries for various developmental activities in the programme area;

*(iii)* To motivate borrowers in the programme area to clear their dues partially or fully;

*(iv)* At the base village in each cluster, to arrange demonstration for the rectification of defective installation of pumpsets, cattle fairs and extension activities, such as exhibition for the benefit of the villagers;

*(v)* To improve the existing infrastructure and make an effort to create forward and backward linkages. These activities would help to establish a direct linkage between repayment on the one hand and credit delivery on the other. It would create in the minds of the village people a feeling that the programme was aimed not only at recovering the bank's dues but was essentially meant to ensure the overall, development of the programme villages.

**Box 1**
**VVV SATELLITE CLUB**

The VVV Satellite Club programme of the National Bank is an indigenous way to achieve 'Development through Credit'. The purpose of conceiving need based, location specific, borrower/gender-specific clubs such as women's clubs, artisans' clubs, small/marginal farmers' clubs is to identify and assess the credit requirement of these sub-groups of the community and also to address to their specific problems. Besides credit, other support services/special inputs required by them for productive use of credit and human development are also identified and made available through the Satellite Clubs with the help of corporation /agencies concerned. The Satellite Clubs in turn are required to promote Self Help Groups and other informal groups in their respective areas.

All the Satellite Clubs launched are operating under a federal set up within the boundaries of respective Services Areas. Voluntary Agency/Non-Governmental Organisations' support would also be made available with financial assistance for liaison, follow up work and documentation.

## Flexible Approach

An in-built element of flexibility has been provided in the programme so that it may suit local requirements. That is why the pattern adopted varies from one state to another, and even from one district to another in the same state. During the first phase launched in May 1983 in Tamil Nadu, the stress was primarily on repayment. Subsequently, several other activities were undertaken to broaden the appeal of the programme. It was soon discovered that because of inter-linkages, the issues related to local planning, need-based schemes and the requirements of infrastructure had become relevant. The programme, therefore become an exercise in participative local planning based on the felt needs of the community. The voluntary agencies associated with the programme have been left largely free to marshall their resources and talents to achieve the objectives of the programme in the manner they think fit.

The intangible results are, however, more important. These do not lend themselves easily to exact quantification as they do for all programmes of social engineering. For the first time, villagers were shown the success models of good borrowers. They witnessed the public disapproval of defaulters led by people from amongst themselves.

Secondly, they understood the direct link between credit disbursement and recovery. the message of the success stories of repayment of earlier loans and taking another loan which led to economic betterment, conveyed effectively the benefits to be derived from the repayment of the loans. The holding of credit disbursement and recovery camps simultaneously, brought this aspect into sharper focus.

Thirdly, the people discovered that banks did not lay stress on recovery alone but were concerned as much with developmental schemes for the villages. There was a conscious effort on the part of the banks to give loans to those who were needy and eligible.

Another substantial indirect gain was the training of the bankers themselves. From traditional bankers they become development bankers. Instead of formulating schemes merely on paper, they moved out into the field, sat with the villagers, determined their felt needs, and then proceeded to see how they could help in financing them. A healthy communication link was thus established between the rural banker and the rural borrowers. For the district and block authorities and the banker, the programme also become an important means of undertaking decentralised participative planning.

In addition, some banks offered to finance the programme in one of their lead districts on a pilot basis. In all, seven commercial banks and nine regional rural banks agreed in principle to adopt the programme. The Governments of Madhya Pradesh, Rajasthan, and U.P. also requested NABARD to start the VVV Main Programme in their states. The Tamil Nadu Government requested NABARD to extend the programme to all the development blocks in the state at the state government's expense. Some banks have already taken a lead in starting the programme at their own cost.

An evaluation of the programme was carried out during July-Sept 1984. In view of the short period in which the programme had been operative the evaluation was confined to the main programme in Tamil Nadu, where it was first launched, and in 11 out of 29 MPPs launched by June 1984. The findings of the study reports have been briefly enumerated below:

The study covered all the 100 Clubs in the States. It was observed that the Clubs functioned fairly satisfactorily and that about 25 percent of these Clubs performed very well. Only about 15 per cent performed unsatisfactorily. A common feature of these weak Clubs was that the leaders elected to run them did not devote enough time to their affairs. Efforts are under way to tone up these Clubs, and wherever necessary, to replace the leader. Regarding the convening of and participation in, club meetings, the performance was satisfactory. In the initial stages government departments extended the maximum support to the programme. Later however, their interest could not be sustained to the desired extent. This was so because they considered the programme to be the responsibility of NABARD. Following the transfer of maintenance work relating to the Clubs to bankers and the orders issued by the Rural Development Department of the state governments, their participation showed significant improvement.

The follow-up of Club decisions with appropriate authorities was also satisfactory. As for the issue of loans, there was evidence of greater lending in the villages covered by the programme in both the districts by co-operative banks as well as commercial banks, though the Primary Land Development Bank (PLDB) in Tiruchi district showed low lending because of reduced eligibility. This was in the context of the overall decline in lending in the two districts.

An attempt was made to compare changes in the percentage of overdue to demand between the years 1982-83 and 1983-84 with reference to the block-district level position. This revealed an uneven impact on recoveries in the villages covered by the Clubs. It may be mentioned, however, that these Clubs had been functioning only for a few months at that time; and it was probably too early to expect a radical change during this period. Besides, the situation in these district had been aggravated by drought, floods, farmers agitation and the state government directive restraining the co-operative from invoking the provisions of the Reserve Recovery Act. The climate for the repayment of overdue was therefore congenial for initiating steps for recoveries. The study, however suggested that the Club had become a bridge between the villagers on the one hand and the bankers and government officials on the other. All Club villages in the two districts have been brought under the Integrated Rural Development Programme (IRDP) through the co-ordinated efforts of the agencies involved. This has refurbished the image of the Clubs.

Banks have been persuaded to lend to the Industry Services and Business (ISB) sector on a larger scale than before. The Clubs have also been able to get speedy remedial action in regard to the revival of defunct societies and the formation of new milk societies. They have convinced the villagers that viable development activities can be undertaken with financial assistance from the banks even without subsidy. Some Clubs come forward to monitor the end-use of bank loans, and are assisting bankers in the collection of deposits and the promotion of the savings habit among the villagers. All this has contributed to the attainment of the objectives of development through credit.

A similar exercise was carried out in 11 MPPs established in November 1983. To gain first-hand knowledge of their performance. It was revealed that, in the villages where the programme had been launched, both the recovery and the disbursement of loans had invariable been greater than in previous years. Most of the Clubs held the stipulated number of meetings, which were well attended by Club members and bank officials. The attendance of government officials, however, with a few exceptions, was unsatisfactory. A majority of the volunteers were found to be working effectively. Even in areas where the performance of the volunteers was unsatisfactory, it had been offset by the good performance of the Club leaders. As a result, even in the MPPs which have not been performing well, there was a follow-up of Club decision at the appropriate level. The most heartening feature of the exercise was that, almost without exception, financing agencies in the villages covered by the MPPs showed an improvement in their recovery position. This was revealed by the data on the percentage of overdue to demand of village borrowers, which registered a decline in most MPPs. It has been generally agreed by the bankers that the Club and its members have been generally of great assistance to them in their recovery efforts. The formulation of Village Development Plans was carried out in several MPPs and five village development plans have already been prepared. In the short span of their existence, the interest taken by banks has resulted in the decentralisation of the maintenance of the Clubs. So far 22 Clubs established under 15 MPPs, have been taken up for maintenance by various banks.

## Organisation Structure

The organisational set-up of the VVV Programme consists of two types for Clubs maintained by banks and voluntary agencies. At the apex level, the Department of VVV, NABARD, Head Office, has an overall responsibility for policy strategy, implementation, administration, monitoring of the programme, control, review and training. At the district level, in the case of VVV Clubs maintained by banks, the designated officer, with the guidance of the Regional Officer of NABARD and the Collector of the district, implements and monitors the rural development programmes in co-operation with other participating banks/co-operative societies and district/block administration and extension agencies, through the Club Volunteers. In the case of Clubs maintained by voluntary agencies, the project co-ordination committee plays a distinctive role. For the successful implementation of the VVV Programme, the regional offices of NABARD play a pivotal role by maintaining a close rapport with the state/district government officials as well as with the controlling offices of the banks. From time to time, they monitor the impact of the programme in given areas. At the village level, the Club is the nerve centre of VVV activities. Although the basic objectives are to ensure the right use of credit and timely repayment, it is the fountain head inspiration for developmental activities in the villages. It is an effective tool of rural development.

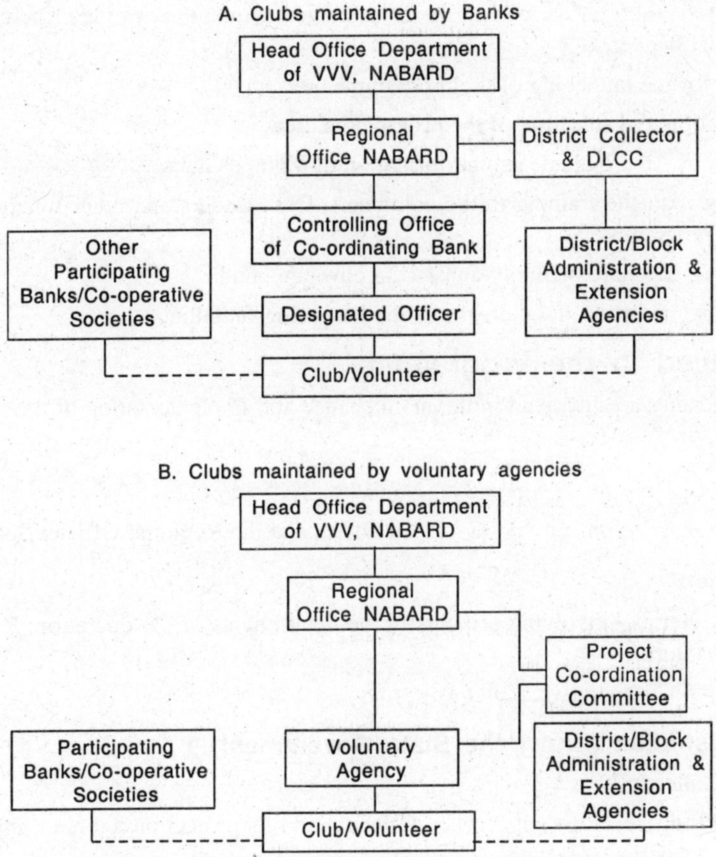


*Fig. 2. Organisational Set-up of the VVV Programme*

The development authorities and bankers, wherever feasible draw up bankable development schemes in consultation with the people. The development authorities and the banks join hands with the Club to promote the camp approach for the preparation of credit application, their sanction and disbursements. The block authorities and the banks organise small exhibitions and cattle fairs/melas to effect local purchase of the assets. The volunteers and the Club leader enlist the services of other public-spirited farmers and artisans, who, in turn disseminate the principles of development through credit and promote repayment ethics in every village. The idea is that the Club, duly assisted by the banks, the district local authorities and NABARD, supports and enlarges the band of volunteers who promote the correct use of loans and repayment ethics. The performance and working of the Club is a subject of discussion at the district level consultative committee, set up under the Lead Bank Scheme. Block level, and at times district level, interaction and feedback sessions are held to evaluate the impact of the programme.

The success of the programme as an extension approach depends, among other things, on the following considerations:

*(i)* Social recognition of volunteers, Club leaders and members by banker and Government extension departments.

*(ii)* A close and purposeful co-ordination among the different functionaries associated with the working of Clubs in respect of improving the overall rural economy in the area specified.

*(iii)* Proper motivation on the part of the change agents/functionaries the principal amongst whom is the local banker.

The basic tasks for the launching of the programme are:

*(i)* Identification and selection of the programme area;

*(ii)* Selection of Area Volunteers and formation of Village Clubs;

*(iii)* Imparting requisite training to the volunteers, Club leaders and other functionaries associated with the programme;

*(iv)* Organising adequate publicity and media coverage; and

*(v)* Operational and procedural details of the launching function.

## Agencies Involved in the Programme

A number of agencies are involved in the maintenance and implementation of the programme. These are:

### A. NABARD

Department of Vikas Volunteer Vahini—Head Office and the Regional Offices.

### B. State Government

*(i)* State Secretariat—involving principally the departments of Co-operation, Rural Development and Agriculture.

*(ii)* Registrar of Co-operative Societies.

### C. District Administration (Under the State Government)

*(i)* District Collector

*(ii)* District Rural Development Agency (DRDA) and its project directors or any other officer assisting the District Collector.

### D. Block Administration

*(i)* Block Development Officer (BDO)

*(ii)* Concerned Extension Officers

*(iii)* Village Level Worker

### E. Commercial/Regional Rural Banks

*(i)* Head Office/Policy Decision

*(ii)* Regional Set-up/Co-ordinating and Monitoring

*(iii)* Branch Manager at the branch level implementation

### F. Co-operation Credit Institutions

*(i)* The State Co-operative Bank and the State Land Development Bank

*(ii)* District Central Co-operative Banks and Primary Land Development Banks

*(iii)* Primary Agricultural Credit Societies.

### G. Other Agencies

These agencies may be the departments of irrigation, lift irrigation, roads, electricity boards, etc. Their role is important in the context of the development of infrastructure for the village development of infrastructure for the village development plan and schemes suggested by the Club.

## H. Voluntary Agencies

In line with the national policy, NABARD has laid emphasis on involving non-governmental organisation in implementing the rural development programmes and VVV Programme. These voluntary agencies (Sewa Mandir in Udaipur, Social Work and Research Centre (SWRC) in Ajmer and DISHA in Saharanpur) have already been entrusted with the implementation of the MPPs established in these district. Their role as Chief Local Co-ordinators of the programme is important whenever it is entrusted to them.

Each and all the above agencies have an important role in the management of the VVV Programme. The various stages of consultation and/or co-ordination have been indicated below.

First the State Government is consulted by NABARD for the launching of the VVV Programme in selected villages under the guidance of the district administration. Generally, a state level committee is set up (formally or informally) by which operational decisions are taken on programme implementation. In Orissa, a formal committee under the chairmanship of the Chief Secretary has been set up. In Tamil Nadu and Gujarat, specific meetings of all concerned are convinced by the Additional Secretary or Secretary, Rural Development, to consider operational problems and programme implementation. In the state-level meeting, invariably convened at the State secretariat, all the connected department of the state governments, state level co-operative banks and state level representatives of the commercial banks participate. The outline of the programme is decided and instructions are issued to the district and block level authorities by the concerned departments of the state government. As a sequel to the decisions at the meetings, the state level representatives of commercial banks and co-operative banks issue comprehensive instructions to their regional offices, branch managers etc launching the programme and later for its maintenance.

## Role of District Administration

The role of the District Collector has been considered crucial in the implementation of the VVV Programme. He provides the leadership to the extension agencies operating in the block and in the village, and heads the District Co-ordination Committee (DCC) of the banks. His intimate involvement in the programme has lent strength to its proper implementation. Generally, the District Co-ordination Committee is set up under the chairmanship of the Collector to monitor the programme. In some states, the committees are headed by the PA to the Collector (in Tamil Nadu), the Chairman of the DRDA (in Gujarat) and the Collector himself (in Orissa).

The block administration's involvement is crucial because it allocates the subsidy for loaning, prepare application for loans, and provides the basic extension services at the village level. That is why a representative of block administration has been included as a member of the Bank's Club. The BDO also attends the District Co-ordination Committee meetings.

## Role of Banks

The role of banks is direct and crucial. It is the branch of the bank operating in the village that takes charge of the programme right from the beginning. After the Head Office of the bank has taken the policy decision of participating in the programme, the main role is assigned to the local Branch Manager, who is called the Designated Officer, for its implementation. Equity important is the role of the Regional Officer of the bank. The Regional/Area Officer has to oversee the role of the programme implemented by various branches of the banks, which are expected to furnish periodical reports to NABARD.

Similarly, the role of the Secretary, Central Co-operative Bank (CCB) and the Secretary, PLDB, is important insofar co-operative banks are concerned. About 25 per cent of the Clubs have entrusted to the care of the CCB or the PLDB and its branches. The Chief Executives are expected to oversee and the monitor the programme and ensure periodical reporting to the Regional Office, NABARD, by their branches.

## Co-ordination at District Level for Banking Institutions

Although the implementation of the programme is a team effort, past experience shows that a common leadership for the banking institutions needs to be entrusted to one of the banks involved in the implementation of the programme in a particular area. This can either be Lead Bank in the district, but not necessarily so. For example, in Madurai district, the Central Co-operative Bank is informally performing this responsibility. In Ganjam district the Andhra Bank, which is also the lead bank, has undertaken this responsibility. In Dhenkanal, the State Bank of India has assumed this role. In the main programme districts, a chief co-ordinator is necessary for the banking institutions. The sorting out of inter-bank problems will be end of the tasks of the chief co-ordinator.

## Identification and Selection of Programme Area

As the programme is at an experimental stage and is undertaken on a pilot basis, it is all the more essential that proper care is taken to select the right type of areas for its introduction.

The emphasis should however, to be on identifying areas where normal banking facilities are available; where a potential or bringing about integrated rural development supporting infrastructural facilities either exists or can be provided; and where the people of the area could benefit by the adoption of banking ethics etc. Another important factor is the availability of persons with a progressive outlook who would offer their service for this voluntary work for their fellow villagers. Special consideration is given to weaker sections and to belts inhabited by backward and tribal communities. The practice followed is to select the villages in a meeting of the DCC or a special meeting convened by the Collector, where the bankers and the block administration arrive at a consensus about the villages to be selected. These proposals are then ratified at the states level. Of course, the districts where the programme is undertaken are first identified by the state government at a discussion with NABARD and lending State level bankers.

## Concept of Village Development Plan

The concept of the village development plan is not a new one. Village development plans have been undertaken by various institutions and agencies on model lines quite often in the past. Banks, too, have prepared such plans as part of villages adoption and Gram Vikas Schemes. Though planning at the village level cannot be a substitute for block or district level planning and cannot be the basis on which to build the entire planning structure, it is an essential requirement for rural development. This is so because it is only at the grass-root level that a comprehensive exercise, based on the felt needs of the population, can be carried out. This can further help to develop forward and backward linkages for integrated rural development — a factor which has not been given adequate importance in the past.

The village development plans have a two-fold thrust. First, given the infrastructural facilities, to create avenues for generating additional incomes in the target villages. Secondly, where the necessary infrastructure does not exist, to identify the infrastructural requirement for making various types of activities viable which, in turn, are incorporated in block and district levels plans.

Village development plans can help to give direction to anti-poverty programmes, such as the IRD Programme to ensure that they are not implemented in a haphazard manner without taking into consideration the limitations of the existing infrastructure in the programme areas. The formulation of such plans may form the basis for co-operation and community effort at the village level, which at present is badly lacking.

Similarly, loaning by banks may be stepped up. As far as banks are concerned, the monitoring of loans and their recovery would become easier with the help of Club leadership—a fact which yields considerable saving.

Finally, village development plan, as an exercise undertaken by the bank's Club with the assistance of bankers and extension worker ensures their involvement in the planning process. This involvement would also make possible the flow of information of banking norms at repayment ethics among the rural population.

## VVV Programme and Village Development Plans

When the VVV Programme was first launched in Madurai and Trichy districts of Tamil Nadu, the predominant objective was the recovery of overdue of village borrowers. Thereafter, the MPPs set up in November 1983, and the main programmes launched subsequently, the recovery of overdue was placed in the larger context of the development of the target areas. The other components of the programme such as extension services, circulation of banking norms and literature, identification, infrastructural constraints and promotion of the camp approach for preparation of credit applications, their sanction and disbursements and the holding of exhibitions and cultural activities were integrated into the programme.

The village development plan has emerged as a key element of this broad-based approach of the VVV Programme. This is so because of the need to relate the recovery of loans to the process of the overall development of the villages economy. Though this type of approach may not be necessary in some areas covered by VVV Programme because of the high availability of credit facilities and knowledge of banking ethics, in most areas it is felt to be worthwhile. This is specially true of the MPPs where the target area of experimentation is small and it is desirable to have a high degree of impact in the surrounding areas. So far, five village development plans have already been prepared for villages covered by MPP clusters, in various parts of the country, and several others are under preparation. In the context of the decentralised maintenance of the programme, the village development plans should involve financing by more than one banking agency to bring about a better cohesion in their development efforts. Equally important is the involvement of extension officials in the preparation of the plan. They should be associated with the household survey on which the plan is based and address themselves to the problems of infrastructural constraints for different types of activities. Apart from the involvement of the villagers themselves, the planning exercise would help to bring about a co-ordinated approach in the functioning of various types of banking and extension agencies. The overall benefit of this rural development cannot be underestimated.

## Preparation of Village Development Plan

The first task in the preparation of the village development plan is to prepare an exhaustive profile of the village where the plan is to be implemented indicating clearly the infrastructure facilities available in and around that village. Data on the village economy may be collected during a brief field visit by the Designated Officer of the co-ordinating bank and his associates. Thereafter, a comprehensive household survey should be conducted to ascertain the credit status and the expressed requirements of the entire set of households in the village. The feedback received is processed and cast in the form of a plan for finance by banks, after taking into account technical factors and infrastructural facilities, and specifying additional requirements for successful implementation. The plan is then subdivided into IRDP/Non-IRDP, farm/non-farm activities, production credit/medium and long-term credit, programme for non-defaulters/defaulters (conditional on their repaying the overdue) as well as the breakdown of financing to be undertaken by different participating banks. The plan should clearly indicate the unit cost of each activity, the subsidy available, the loan component and the refinance required from NABARD. A copy of the plan should be submitted by the Designated Officer to the NABARD's Regional Office. An attempt should be made to introduce innovative schemes and to ensure adequate coverage of the ISB sector. The eligibility status of various financing branches may also be indicated so that it may be consistent with the share of the programme allotted to them.

The plan, as formulated, may involve financing over a period of two years, with year wise targets specified therein. It is imperative that once the plan has been put into effect, a close monitoring of progress should be carried out. The coverage of household under the plan should be available to the Club for its review and record, and even displayed at a prominent place in the village. The monitoring and evaluation exercise is of the utmost importance, for it is a means of learning from past experience and increasing the scope and impact of village development plans under the VVV Programme.

The VVV Programme is primarily a programme of the banks. It is only with their active involvement and support that the movement can be sustained. Since the stake of the banks and of NABARD is direct, it is desirable for them to undertake the financial responsibility for running the programme. NABARD has explored with the nationalised banks, which have a sound financial base, the possibility of their undertaking to meet 50 per cent of the maintenance expenses of the Clubs which have been set up under the programme. Some banks have already agreed to share these maintenance expenses. They have also been asked to consider the starting of the programme at their own expense in some of the districts where they have lead responsibility. Towards this end, banks, might include development through credit and the VVV Programme in the curricula of their in-house training, both at the cutting-edge and the supervisory level. NABARD would, however, continue to provide, where called for, other training and infrastructural support to the activities of the banks when these activities bear directly on the programme.

❑ ❑ ❑

*"Technology has benefited the poor. It is truly technology for its masses. Mass technology functions best with mass markets. Technology is a problem-solving process."*

*"The main thrust of advancement of rural technology is to promote innovative technologies in the villages, upgradation of technical and production skills of village youth, artisans, women and strengthening of existing technological institutes."*

Chapter 36

# COUNCIL FOR ADVANCEMENT OF PEOPLE'S ACTION AND RURAL TECHNOLOGY

## Introduction

The voluntary sector plays an important role in the development particularly with reference to the programme aimed at the rural poor and for improving the quality of life of rural poor in rural areas. The Ministry of Rural Development has been earmarking funds for the voluntary sector not only in the nationally planned programmes but also for mobilizing and motivating people's participation. With a view to encouraging, promoting and assisting voluntary action in rural development and with focus on injecting new technological inputs for the enhancement of rural prosperity, the Government of India, in September 1986, set up the Council for Advancement of People's Action and Rural Technology (CAPART), a registered society of under the aegies of the Ministry of Rural Areas and Employment by merging two autonomous bodies; People's Action for Development India (PADI) and Council for Advancement of Rural Technology (CART). The Cabinet Minister/Minister of State (IC) Incharge of

*Fig. 1. CAPART helps the rural poor to become self-employed through assistance to voluntary agencies*

the Ministry of Rural Areas and Employment is the President of the General Body which comprises officials of the Ministry of Rural Areas and Employment, eminent social activists, experts in different fields in rural development and representatives of voluntary agencies. The General Body lays down the broad policy framework within which projects under various schemes are sanctioned. The Executive Committee, which is also headed by the Cabinet Minister/Minister of State (IC) incharge of the Ministry of Rural Areas and Employment, formulates the policy parameters and guidelines for the functioning of CAPART. The Secretary, Department of Rural Development is the vice-chairman of the Executive Committee of CAPART, The Secretary, Department of Rural Employment and Poverty Alleviation has been appointed as second vice-chairman in the year 1998-99. The Director General, who is in the rank of Additional Secretary, is the Chief Executive of CAPART.

## Objectives

The main objectives of the Council:

*(i)* to act as the national nodal point for co-ordination of all efforts at development and dissemination of technology relevant for rural areas for sectors other than those covered by ICAR and its sister bodies;

*(ii)* to act as a catalyst for development of technology appropriate for the rural areas by identifying and fund research and development effort by different organisations;

*(iii)* to strengthen existing institutions of research and develop or set up institutions so that national level institutions on matters of purely or largely rural interest are built up;

*(iv)* to act as a clearing house of information and a data bank;

*(v)* to disseminate knowledge on rural technology to manufacturers of machinery, tools, equipment and spare parts so that large scale production of technically improved machinery etc. is carried out in the private, co-operative and public sector;

*(vi)* to act as conduit for transfer of appropriate technology to government departments public sector undertakings and members of the public;

*(vii)* to conduct or sponsor training programmes for trainers so that improved technology is passed on to the beneficiaries in the rural areas;

*(viii)* to carry out research studies, surveys, evaluation etc. on the use of appropriate technology;

*(ix)* to do all other such things as the society may consider necessary incidental or conducive to the attainment of the above objectives.

In developing and transmitting appropriate rural technologies, priority sectors in rural development with emphasis on poverty alleviation and the policy objectives appropriate to rural area contained in the 1983 Technology Policy Statement of the Government of India have been kept in view. Transfer of technology to scheduled castes, scheduled tribes and other weaker sections of rural society like landless labourers and artisans who require special assistance which is not immediately available now in the existing schemes, is given special attention.

## Advancement of Rural Technology

The broad mandate was to co-ordinate all efforts for advancement of technology relevant for rural areas. The thrust under this programme is to promote and support efforts for transfer of technology to the rural areas. The technologies which benefits a larger spectrum of people in rural areas are supported and the major fields are as follows:

Construction/Housing technologies

Village Industries

Primary sector fields

Food Processing

Herbal medicine

Energy

Bio-mass utilisation

Handicrafts.

Regional Resource Centres are created to test technologies feasible for specific geographical area, make modifications where necessary and initiate the process of transfer of viable technologies through demonstration, training and manufacture.

As for special group, particular importance is given to rural women and youth. The later group would be of two categories viz, rural youth with little formal education and young professionals.

To begin with, some related technologies have been selected and steps taken to disseminate them. So far 19,265 projects for technology transfer have been assisted by the Council as a means to field test and disseminate suitable technologies. The projects are mostly aimed at the improvement of the rural people living below the poverty line. The projects are designed to achieve the following objectives:

Opportunity to upgrade one's skills.

Utilisation of these skills in better rewarding activities.

Humanisation of toil.

As may be evident from the list of projects, the life of a project ranges from six month to three years, the former being very few. Further as the projects were sanctioned only in 1984-85, it is premature to assess the results yet. The real impact can be evaluated only after the projects are either completed or have run for a sufficient time.

Under Advancement of Rural Technology, the broad mandate of CAPART is to coordinate all efforts towards advancement of technology relevant to rural areas except for sectors being dealt with by ICAR, CSIR and their sister organisations. The main objective of the Council under this Scheme is development, demonstration and dissemination of innovative rural technologies for the transfer to the target groups. Projects aimed at conducting need-based study, survey, skill upgradation, adaptive Research and Development, dissemination of appropriate technologies amongst rural poor and capacity building of the VOs are funded under this Scheme. A programme of setting up of Technology Resource Centres (TRCs) was initiated by CAPART under this Scheme. Under this programme, voluntary agencies with proven track record of adaptive R&D and technologies transfer are supported with one time grant for creation of necessary infrastructure and some recurring expenses for development and dissemination of appropriate technologies through a network of small VOs within their area of operation. CAPART has provided support to 19 VOs for Technology Resource Centres. Several TRC proposals are in pipeline. CAPART's objective is to set up at least one TRC in every state and eventually about 100 TRCs to cover all districts in India.

In addition to project assistance CAPART is taking stock of technologies already generated to upgrade the technological content of the ongoing rural development programme. A publication entitled Rural Technology Guide is being brought out by CAPART in English and in major regional languages and has been circulated to all DRDAs and blocks as part of its task of information dissemination. In addition, publication of clippings from newspaper and journals relevant to rural technology are brought out once in two months. A journal is also being brought out by the Council.

## Decentralisation

As a prelude to the preparation of the Ninth plan, the government had initiated a dialogue with the Voluntary Organisation (VOs) by forming a working group to formulate a viable strategy to involve them in a big way, CAPART has taken the initiative of mobilising the efforts of VOs by decentralising its activities for a more purposeful functioning. In order to be close to the VO in the field, CAPART had decentralised its functioning by constituting six, regional committees in 1994 at Jaipur, Lucknow, Bhubaneswar, Guwahati, Ahmedabad and Hyderabad. During the financial year 1997-98, two more regional committee offices were opened at Patna and Chandigarh. Thus, CAPART has at present 8 Regional Committee offices. They cater to the different regions in the country. They are headed by eminent persons from the Voluntary Sector. The regional committees sanctions all projects up to Rs 10 lakhs.

## People's Participation

For ensuring the success of water supply schemes or rehabilitation of degraded lands or any capacity building project, strong people's groups with enhanced management capacities are required. Hence, the Government has issued guidelines on people's participation, stressing inter alia that the participation should include the notions of contributing, influencing sharing or redistributing power and of controlling resources, benefits, knowledge and skills to be gained through beneficiary involvement in decision making. Participation is a voluntary process by which people, including the disadvantaged (in income gender, caste or education) influence or control the decisions that affect them. It has also been emphasized that the three outcomes of participation—learning, empowerment and a vibrant organisation, need to be measured through observable indicators, which will vary from project to project. Each project must develop clearly observable indicators on people's participation, so as to judge whether they are on track or not. Such indicators should then be given to monitors and evaluators, who have to do mid-course evaluation and impact assessment. Accordingly, CAPART has constituted National Standing Committees on different subject matters for sanction of projects including one on Monitoring and Evaluation at the Headquarters. These committees predominantly comprise eminent subject matter specialists and representatives drawn from the voluntary sector. In this manner, CAPART is trying to make its functioning more participatory and transparent.

## Transparency in CAPART's Working

Regional and National Standing Committees on different subject matter formed with a larger participation of VOs to sanction projects.

VOs are involved in monitoring process.

Particulars of project sanctioned to be exhibited at the projects site made mandatory.

Community resources network formed for dissemination of information among VOs.

CAPART news incorporates project sanctions.

## CAPART's Assistance

While CAPART seeks to associate the voluntary sector in several schemes that are part of planned development and are being implemented on national basis, it also supports several innovative projects keeping in view the needs of specific areas. The main thrust of these programmes is on employment generation, houses for shelterless, conservation of water, enhancement of income and development of community assets. While CAPART receives most of its funds from the Ministry of Rural Area and Employment, it also channelises some funds to VOs areas and employment, it also channelises some funds to VOs from funding agencies like DANIDA, SDC, etc. Efforts are also being made to mobilise international donors. A beginning has been made in this direction.

CAPART provides assistance to VOs under different programmes like Indira Awaas Yojana, Watershed Management, Social Forestry, Link Road in Hilly Areas, Promotion of Voluntary Action in Rural Development of Women and Children in Rural Areas, Organisation of Beneficiaries, Central Rural Sanitation Programme, Drinking water under the Technology Mission on Accelerated Rural Water Supply Programme and Advancement of Rural Technology. Since 1995, CAPART is also providing assistance for taking up capacity building and rehabilitation programme for persons with disability. Three percent of the allocations made under different programmes to CAPART are being set aside to fund this programme. It has been decided to give preference in the coverage to disabled beneficiaries under all the programmes.

## Policy Guidelines

A revised set of guidelines on the functioning of CAPART has been issued on 20.01.99 so that genuine and committed Voluntary Organisations are brought into the fold of CAPART in its efforts towards rural development. The guiding principle "fund every VO, if there is nothing against it," for funding by CAPART has been sought to be changed to "fund only those carefully selected ones who have done or have the potential of doing outstanding work in empowerment and welfare of the disadvantaged."

Collaboration between the government and the Voluntary Organisations, whenever it works always yields both qualitative and quantitative results. It is the endeavour of the Government that CAPART should make all-out efforts to help growth of collaboration between the Government and the VOs.

*Policy Guidelines*

CAPART will add the following qualifications to the existing eligibility criteria:

The VO must have proven experience in social mobilisation of the rural community for development projects and in improving the capability of the rural people in ensuring that development funds from Government and other sources are well spent without leakage;

Generation of awareness among them regarding social and economic development;

Project by the VO must have been implemented through people's participation preferably through their role in control over funds; and

The VO's projects in the past must have led to empowerment of any of the following: *viz.*, SC, ST, people below the poverty line, women, people living in remote areas, involuntarily displaced due to development projects, people who are suffering because of any particular policy of Government, people with physical disability and bonded labourers, etc.

*Fig. 2. CAPART Plays a vital role in Promoting rural art and craft through NGOs for rural properity*

With the new emphasis on innovation and participation, the quality of outcomes and impact is required to be judged objectively and regularly. CAPART shall therefore, develop verifiable indicators for effectiveness of these additional eligibility criteria.

CAPART will work out a system for continuous monitoring and grading as well as upgrading/downgrading of VOs based on their performance after completion of each project along with grading of VOs on the basis of organizational profiles. This would enable VOs constantly to strive to improve their performance.

Towards acting as a think tank, CAPART would provide a forum for experts/VOs and others associated with rural development to present concepts, discuss issues and even review CAPART's policies at the regional, national and/or international level.

From April 1999 CAPART has been providing assistance to VOs under three main schemes, namely Promotion of Voluntary Action in Rural Development (PVARD) Organisation of Beneficiaries (OB) and Advancement of Rural Technologies (ARTS).

The scheme of Young Professionals (YPs) started in 1988 continued with some modification with a view to strengthen the VOs and the DRDAs in which their services were made available. Since the inception of the scheme, CAPART has so far selected about 205 YPs and out of which about 65 are women. The scheme evoked positive response from the selected professionals and several of them evinced interest in continuing to work in rural areas after the tenure of two years with CAPART. The organisations floated by them gets a preferential treatment in the sanction of projects. In this way, CAPART could also reach underserved and unrecalled areas of this country.

## Promotional Role

CAPART has a significant role in promoting a variety of activities of transfer of technology, people's participation, development of marketing for products of rural enterprises, generating awareness among rural masses for bringing about attitudinal changes towards persons with disability to contribute in the field of rural development activities and delivery systems in non-governmental sector.

## Examples of such Activities are

- Establishment of regional resources centres for training and propagation of appropriate technologies through out the country.
- Facilitating large-scale production and marketing of proven technologies by the voluntary sector by propagation and dissemination of proven technologies appropriate of the rural areas.
- Provision of marketing support and services to the beneficiaries of the IRDP/DWCRA programmes. This effort has resulted in the organisation of popular "Gram Shree Melas" throughout the country. Till 31st December 1998, CAPART has organised 127 Gram Shree Melas throughout the country involving a sales turnover of Rs 20 crores.
- Organisations of seminars/workshops to provide an opportunity for direct interaction between beneficiaries and professionals; providing support for establishing marketing outlets; creating linkages with established outlets/institutions, buyer for continuous marketing facilities, etc.
- Funding training programmes for grassroots level VOs.
- Dissemination of information through communication resources network. The network is in the business of distribution of material and information in their area of specialisation.
- Production of audiovisual material and broadcasting through All India Radio in local languages.
- Information technology is being upgraded with the help of National Informatics Centre both to deal with the decentralisation set up and disseminate information to the VOs on various aspects of rural development.

## Initiatives in Disaster Mitigation and Disaster Preparedness

CAPART has been playing a pro-active role wherever natural disaster has struck and adversely affected the rural population across the country. Some of the areas where CAPART has recently taken initiatives to provide assistance to the affected people through voluntary organisations, are the earthquake affected areas of Uttarakhand and super cyclone affected areas in Orissa, the severe drought affected areas of Rajasthan, Gujarat, Madhya Pradesh and Andhra Pradesh and the earthquake hit areas of Gujarat. CAPART has not only been providing relief assistance but has initiated long-term strategies to deal with this recurring natural phenomenon by people's action through the voluntary sector.

## Organisation of Beneficiaries

CAPART gives organisation of beneficiaries of anti-poverty programmes due importance through this scheme. The objectives of this scheme are to create awareness among the rural poor, organise them into groups and strengthen their bargaining capabilities.

Under this scheme CAPART has so far supported 3703 projects at a cost of Rs. 26.74 crores.

## Disability Programme

The Disability Action Division was set up in 1995 in CAPART. CAPART views disability as a development issue rather than as a problem of health or welfare. The aim of this division is to change the development paradigm from one of charity to that of empowerment. It attempts to provide equal opportunity in rural development to people with disabilities and promote their full participation in all initiatives by supporting Community Based Rehabilitation (CBR) programmes for the differently disabled.

## Marketing Development — A Gateway towards Rural Industrialisation "We bring better livelihood to Rural India"

CAPART introduced its Marketing Division in 1989 with a view to provide opportunities, exposure and sustainable market linkages to rural producers covered under various income generation schemes of the Council.

The first step towards extending an overall Marketing Development was the organisation of Gram Shree Melas, Gram Shree meaning 'The Wealth of Villages'. Gram Shree Mela is a gateway through which rural producers come together to market their products, providing an opportunity to rural producers to sell their products directly in major markets, to interact with the buyers, to study and comprehend the latter's tastes, preferences and choices. Thus it helps them to upgrade and adjust their products and marketing skills and provide a better service to consumer while benefiting from a larger marketing opportunity.

NSC approved a total of 14 Melas for the year 2002-03, out of which 5 Melas were held in 2002 at Hyderabad, Chennai, Ahmedabad, Mumbai and Bhubneswar respectively. The next scheduled Melas up to March will be at Lucknow, Ranchi, Chandigarh, Jaipur and Trivandrum.

Apart from organising/participating in regional/national level melas, exhibitions, the Marketing Division is also organising a large exhibition under the banner 'SARAS' during the India International Trade held from 14$^{th}$ to 27$^{th}$ November every year. SARAS promotes the rural products manufactured by producers under the income generation schemes of the Ministry of Rural Development and CAPART ensuring a participation of over 1500 participants. SARAS 2002 bagged gold medal for the best display from India Trade Promotion Organisation (ITPO) carrying forward the previous year's tradition. SARAS 2002 resulted in direct sales of more than Rs. 4.50 crores and firm orders worth Rs. 2.00 crores.

**Table 1**

**SCHEME-WISE NUMBER OF PROJECTS SANCTIONED BY CAPART**
**(since inception till 30.11.2000)**

| Year | JRY** | Housing | CRSP | OB/SAT | DWCRA | ARWSP* | ARTS | PC | IRDP | PR | SF | WSD | DA | Media | Total |
|---|---|---|---|---|---|---|---|---|---|---|---|---|---|---|---|
| Since inception up to 1987 | 35 | – | – | 229 | 48 | 30 | 151 | 128 | – | – | – | – | – | – | 621 |
| 1987-88 | 86 | – | 48 | 160 | 97 | 89 | 27 | 40 | 2 | – | – | – | – | – | 549 |
| 1988-89 | 150 | – | 260 | 230 | 194 | 89 | 35 | 50 | 64 | – | – | – | – | – | 1072 |
| 1989-90 | 144 | – | 123 | 202 | 145 | 362 | 42 | 99 | 51 | – | – | – | – | – | 1168 |
| 1990-91 | 103 | – | – | 224 | 111 | 541 | 46 | 99 | 22 | – | – | – | – | – | 1146 |
| 1991-92 | 237 | – | 325 | 278 | 177 | 1122 | 122 | 217 | 62 | – | – | – | – | – | 2540 |
| 1992-93 | 207 | – | 302 | 390 | 147 | 934 | 99 | 192 | 70 | – | – | – | – | – | 2341 |
| 1993-94 | 176 | – | 484 | 498 | 300 | 433 | 107 | 244 | 85 | – | – | – | – | – | 2327 |
| 1994-95 | 144 | – | 374 | 247 | 125 | 514 | 80 | 227 | 103 | – | – | – | – | – | 1814 |
| 1995-96 | 496 | – | 277 | 142 | 89 | 104 | 73 | 135 | 50 | 4 | – | – | – | – | 1370 |
| 1996-97 | 140 | 289 | 412 | 339 | 89 | 51 | 69 | 165 | 44 | 7 | – | – | – | – | 1605 |
| 1997-98 | 45 | 1 | 436 | 241 | 62 | 118 | 59 | 136 | 22 | 4 | – | – | – | – | 1124 |
| 1998-99 | – | – | 122 | 55 | 62 | 125 | 56 | 109 | 12 | 3 | 6 | 80 | 28 | 17 | 675 |
| 1999-2000 | – | – | 2 | 71 | 16 | 12 | 80 | 186 | 2 | 2 | – | 65 | 15 | – | 451 |
| 2000-2001 | – | – | – | 92 | – | – | 70 | 225 | – | – | – | 36 | 9 | – | 462 |
| Total | 1963 | 290 | 3165 | 3398 | 1662 | 4524 | 1116 | 2282 | 589 | 20 | 6 | 181 | 52 | 171 | 19265 |

*Note** ARWSP also include Drinking Water & Awareness Camp projects

** JRY include Housing & other than Housing up to 1995-96.

1996-97 includes Social Forestry & Watershed Development.

**Table 2**
**SCHEME-WISE AMOUNT SANCTIONED BY CAPART**
**(since inception till 30.11.2000)**

*(Rs. in Crores)*

| *Year* | *JRY** | *Housing* | *CRSP* | *OB/SAT* | *DWCRA* | *ARWSP* | *ARTS* | *PC* | *IRDP* | *PR* | *SF* | *WSD* | *DA* | *Media* | *Total* |
|---|---|---|---|---|---|---|---|---|---|---|---|---|---|---|---|
| Since inception up to 19 87 | 1.31 | – | – | 1.09 | 1.44 | 1.37 | 8.89 | 3.48 | – | – | – | – | – | – | – |
| 1987-88 | 3.16 | – | 1.37 | 0.58 | 1.89 | 3.57 | 0.91 | 1.16 | 0.04 | – | – | – | – | – | 12.68 |
| 1988-89 | 7.04 | – | 5.62 | 0.64 | 3.23 | 3.41 | 1.96 | 5.19 | 0.92 | – | – | – | – | – | 28.01 |
| 1989-90 | 5.52 | – | 1.85 | 0.89 | 1.91 | 3.83 | 0.66 | 7.92 | 0.70 | – | – | – | – | – | 23.28 |
| 1990-91 | 4.60 | – | – | 1.07 | 1.51 | 5.90 | 0.87 | 2.66 | 0.66 | – | – | – | – | – | 17.27 |
| 1991-92 | 10.46 | – | 8.24 | 0.93 | 2.46 | 10.11 | 3.24 | 10.64 | 1.21 | – | – | – | – | – | 47.29 |
| 1992-93 | 8.60 | – | 8.35 | 2.58 | 2.01 | 13.16 | 3.20 | 6.34 | 1.25 | – | – | – | – | – | 45.49 |
| 1993-94 | 8.87 | – | 10.45 | 2.38 | 5.55 | 15.32 | 2.49 | 10.82 | 1.95 | – | – | – | – | – | 57.83 |
| 1994-95 | 9.70 | – | 8.09 | 1.85 | 2.84 | 18.02 | 2.54 | 9.54 | 2.38 | – | – | – | – | – | 54.96 |
| 1995-96 | 50.97 | – | 7.50 | 0.72 | 2.24 | 3.37 | 3.13 | 5.50 | 1.08 | 0.15 | – | – | – | – | 74.66 |
| 1996-97 | 5.98 | 25.26 | 12.37 | 1.34 | 2.27 | 1.95 | 5.09 | 6.45 | 1.08 | 0.19 | – | – | – | – | 61.98 |
| 1997-98 | 5.71 | – | 9.76 | 1.06 | 1.47 | 4.88 | 4.04 | 6.50 | 0.49 | 0.10 | – | – | – | – | 34.01 |
| 1998-99 | – | – | 3.15 | 0.47 | 1.62 | 5.70 | 4.62 | 5.79 | 0.31 | 0.03 | 0.16 | 9.16 | 1.47 | 0.65 | 33.13 |
| 1999-2000 | – | – | 0.12 | 0.57 | 0.51 | 0.41 | 3.98 | 8.63 | 0.07 | 0.09 | – | 4.00 | 0.35 | – | 18.73 |
| 2000-2001 | – | – | – | 1.08 | – |  | 4.81 | 13.60 | – | – | – | 5.04 | 0.48 | – | 25.01 |
| Total | 121.92 | 25.26 | 76.87 | 17.25 | 30.95 | 91.00 | 50.43 | 104.22 | 12.14 | 0.56 | 0.16 | 18.20 | 2.30 | 0.65 | 551.91 |

**Table 3**

**SCHEME-WISE FUNDS RELEASED BY CAPART TO SANCTIONED PROJECTS**

**(since inception till 30.11.2000)**

*(Rs. in Crores)*

| *Year* | *JRY** | *Housing* | *CRSP* | *OB/SAT* | *DWCRA* | *ARWSP* | *ARTS* | *PC* | *IRDP* | *PR* | *SF* | *WSD* | *DA* | *Media* | *IITF* | *Total* |
|---|---|---|---|---|---|---|---|---|---|---|---|---|---|---|---|---|
| Since inceptich up to 1987 | 0.23 | – | 0.29 | 1.02 | 0.10 | 0.32 | 1.44 | 0.45 | – | – | – | – | – | – | – | 3.85 |
| 1987-88 | 1.03 | – | 0.39 | 0.31 | 0.73 | 1.80 | 1.60 | 0.70 | – | – | – | – | – | – | – | 6.56 |
| 1988-89 | 3.74 | – | 3.22 | 0.53 | 2.36 | 2.89 | 2.02 | 1.20 | 0.31 | – | – | – | – | – | – | 16.27 |
| 1989-90 | 4.05 | – | 2.58 | 0.52 | 1.26 | 3.72 | 1.44 | 1.80 | 0.46 | – | – | – | – | – | – | 15.83 |
| 1990-91 | 4.34 | – | 1.62 | 0.72 | 1.01 | 4.39 | 1.04 | 2.80 | 0.24 | – | – | – | – | – | – | 16.16 |
| 1991-92 | 7.47 | – | 2.60 | 0.93 | 1.98 | 8.04 | 1.73 | 5.04 | 0.68 | – | – | – | – | – | – | 28.47 |
| 1992-93 | 8.30 | – | 4.52 | 1.77 | 2.24 | 9.72 | 2.79 | 5.94 | 0.76 | – | – | – | – | – | – | 36.04 |
| 1993-94 | 10.76 | – | 9.54 | 2.44 | 4.32 | 12.58 | 2.56 | 11.32 | 1.23 | – | – | – | – | – | – | 54.75 |
| 1994-95 | 7.49 | – | 6.65 | 1.81 | 2.33 | 13.84 | 2.26 | 7.78 | 1.74 | – | – | – | – | – | – | 43.90 |
| 1995-96 | 27.59 | – | 6.17 | 0.82 | 1.70 | 6.23 | 2.55 | 4.89 | 0.98 | 0.22 | – | – | – | – | – | 51.15 |
| 1996-97 | 2.97 | 8.79 | 8.27 | 2.36 | 2.80 | 3.27 | 2.63 | 5.63 | 0.86 | 0.15 | – | – | – | – | – | 37.73 |
| 1997-98 | 3.87 | 10.37 | 7.56 | 1.51 | 2.72 | 3.42 | 3.53 | 5.43 | 0.55 | 0.08 | – | – | – | – | – | 39.04 |
| 1998-99 | – | 1.13 | 3.42 | 1.34 | 1.98 | 3.67 | 2.17 | 3.16 | 0.40 | 0.09 | 0.91 | 3.43 | 1.00 | 0.43 | – | 23.13 |
| 1999-2000 | – | 0.80 | 3.50 | 2.20 | 1.92 | 3.93 | 4.68 | 10.05 | 0.13 | 0.09 | 0.41 | 1.06 | – | – | – | 28.77 |
| 2000-2001(till Nov. 2000) | – | 0.45 | – | 1.80 | – | 0.65 | 4.76 | 11.19 | 0.04 | 0.05 | 0.31 | 1.29 | 0.23 | – | 0.86 | 21.63 |
| Total | 81.84 | 21.54 | 60.33 | 20.08 | 27.45 | 78.47 | 37.20 | 77.38 | 8.38 | 0.68 | 1.63 | 5.78 | 1.23 | 0.43 | 0.86 | 423.28 |

* JRY includes Social Forestry projects also.

## Recommendation on Future Role of CAPART

Reduction of poverty through skill development, income generation and providing livelihood options.

Creation of cadre of Rural Young Professionals in the villages who can be a friend, facilitator and guide to the village community.

Promotion of voluntary action and projects in the most backward underserved and unreached areas.

Creation of Nodal NGO in each District/Block to ensure that need based programmes for development are implemented in the most backward areas and also to create sound data base of grass root NGOs in the area.

Support Primary Processing Units of fruits and vegetables which are cost effective, hygienic and simple, both for consumption as well as for commercial purpose.

Working out innovative model projects for dissemination & implementation by NGOs to achieve the above stated objectives.

## Recommendation on Future Role of Rural Technology Promotion & Dissemination

Dissemination of innovative rural technologies relevant for rural areas.

Focusing on gap areas in the life cycle of a rural household by drawing up model schemes.

Establishment of a Centre for Rural Technology and Poverty Alleviation.

Use of Information Technology for dissemination, awareness generation and skill development in the rural areas.

## Conclusion

The CAPART has been playing a significant role in creating employment and income generation among the rural poor, through its schemes like, Promotion of Voluntary Action in Rural Development through its various programmes structured to provide permanent source of income to target beneficiaries.

Technology transfer and development involve teaching rural people the process of living and somehow linking him/her to that activity as it is carried on elsewhere. Self-reliance is a worthy goal, but it does not have to mean autarky or local, inward-looking policies of using technology. The choice of technology provides essentially more or better of something they want. Thus, promotion of technology and its use accelerate the process of rural development. CAPART as a promoter of different models of development has undertaken in developing rural technology, watershed development programmes, drought proofing, disaster mitigation, disability programme and marketing.

The financial assistance is provided by CAPART for building infrastructure, training, assets creation, production and marketing. Under Promotion of Voluntary Action Scheme, innovative projects are encouraged as per the needs and requirements of the area. For landless labourers and persons with no employment, thus CAPART is playing a pivotal role to integrate rural development activities through experimental and innovative efforts.

❑ ❑ ❑

*The training of our youth in mind and body is a subject of the highest importance for us. We must get rid of the extraordinary notion that manual work is something degrading. There is nothing more ennobling than manual work and nothing better for physical and mental health.*

— ***Jawaharlal Nehru***

# Chapter 37

# RURAL MANAGEMENT

## Introduction

The rural development programme calls for a concerted effort and a fusion of will and of skills in the political, administrative, professional and executive fields. Rural management, therefore, is an important aspect of integrated rural development. The managerial component of the task of improving the living standards of the rural poor is a very complex one and calls for gigantic efforts. The key to success lies in building up teams of trusted, dedicated and motivated people. An effort has been made by the Institute of Rural Management. Anand, to fill the managerial gaps in rural management. In a note, it briefly analyses its objectives and its utility in the implementation of the Integrated Rural Development Programme (IRDP) in India.

In economic terms, it signifies a low propensity to consume rather then to save and less productive agriculture is the dominant occupation of the majority of the rural poor. In a typical rural family, insufficient resources arise from the fact that:

*(i)* The number of individual consumers in the household is large relative to the production services the household is able to supply;

*(ii)* Lack of skills or educational attainments result in low quality as well as quantity of services relative to its own requirement;

*(iii)* Poor health and low productivity leads to a vicious circle of poverty, low income, poor, health, low productivity and poverty;

*(iv)* Disability exists on an extensive scale.

The problem of poverty in the rural environment stems from the fact that the supply of labour competes for employment on an inadequate agricultural base, resulting in vast differentials in income—from skilled and unskilled urban labour to unskilled rural labour. Unfortunately, poverty leads to a higher number of births and to increased poverty. The ability of a family to plan its size optimally is crucial from the long-run point of view of eradicating poverty. This apart, the structure of rural society, the land-man relationship the social relation between different classes, the inequitable flow of resources and benefits to and by the various socio-economic groups and individuals call for an integrated area approach for the rapid development of rural India.

## RURAL DEVELOPMENT

In fact, rural development is often confused with agricultural development. No doubt, agriculture development is the basis of the development of the rural areas and of the industrial sector; but it is not an end in itself. Agriculture development, or, to be more specific, agricultural productivity, is closely related to rural development. The health of the rural community and the quality of life deteriorates in proportion to the decline in agricultural and other allied activities. The term *rural development* is much wider than the term *agricultural development*. There are other sectors in rural areas, *viz* infrastructural development like roads, drinking water, housing, fuel cottage and small scale industries, processing and marketing of goods, which play an important role in the overall economic development. Moreover, improvement in health, education, housing, communication, etc., call for a planned approach.

### Experiment in Rural Development

The concept of development is not a new one. Several pioneering experiments have been attempted by many eminent people in India. Although, poet Rabindranath Tagore sowed the seeds of a planned programme of development for the villages it is Mahatma Gandhi who is responsible for the beginning of an integrated development of rural India. It was he who reminded us again and again that the soul of India lives in her villages and that in rural reconstruction alone lies the salvation of this country. That is why, the government since independence, has been experimenting with the concept of rural development.

The strategies for rural development have changed over the years. In the fifties, community development and national extension service block were started with the object of taking integrated development to rural areas. At that time, the development of agriculture and allied sectors was emphasized as the most important function of the national extension service. It was, however, soon realized that the machinery devised for the purpose was not equal to the task of the programme of regenerating the rural economy, nor were the funds sufficient for this purpose. The achievements of the community development blocks, however, cannot be minimised. They represent the first organised attempt at lifting the centuries-old stagnant rural economy from the morass and inertia of a fatalistic outlook.

They brought about visible changes in the social and cultural modes of the people and generated some hope in the masses living in the rural areas.

The major programmes for rural development under execution are:

*(i)* Community Development Programme

*(ii)* Panchayati Raj

*(iii)* Applied Nutrition Programme

*(iv)* Extension Education and Training Schemes

*(v)* Small Farmers' Development Agency/Marginal Farmers' and Agriculture Labour Scheme

*(vi)* Drought-Prone Area Programme

*(vii)* Tribal Development Agency

(viii) National Rural Employment Programme

(ix) Hill Area Development Programme

(x) Desert Development Programme

(xi) Food for work Programme

(xii) Command Area Development

(xiii) Jawahar Rozgar Yojana

## Integrated Rural Development

Conceptually, integrated rural development refers to the multifaceted, multi-direction development of the rural economy by the fullest exploitation of local resources in men, material, land and water. The idea was first proposed in the central budget of 1976-77, and a beginning was made on the basis of local initiative and drive. The government acted as a catalyst to bring about a change, but it was the intrinsic strength of the economy itself which supported the service, and rising standards of living and sectoral economic activities. Environmental and infrastructure improvements can only be supported by outside help; it is the local population which has to pay for their economic activities of a village for any length of time. Hence, the importance of integrating all the economic activities on the basis of the local resources. The vast untapped rural labour force is a liability which has to be turned into an asset by harnessing it in fruitful and gainful employment. Full rural employment is the goal of integrated rural development. In a rural situation, the following are likely to be the main elements:

(i) In the agricultural sector, the emphasis has to be on land reforms, the supply of inputs, soil conversation, water management, fisheries, poultry, dairy-farming, post-harvest technology, augmentation and harnessing of new sources, conservation of energy.

(ii) cottage and small industries including agro-industries management and marketing of the products.

(iii) Health and Family Welfare, including environmental improvements.

(iv) Education, social education and cultural activities.

(v) Social Welfare Programmes, including programmes for children, women and other weaker sections.

An integrated development plan, however, should be in consonance with resources, local enterprise, and should be based on an intimate knowledge and understanding of local conditions, local needs and local possibilities.

The alleviation of rural poverty is the prime objective of Indian Plans. An increase in the productive potential of the rural economy is an essential condition for the solution of the problems of rural poverty. At the same time, recognising the constraints which limit the scope for higher growth rate in the medium-term, a more direct means of reducing the incidence of poverty and destitution would have to be employed. It is well known that the hard core of poverty is to be found in rural areas. The poorest sections belong to the families of landless labourers, small and marginal farmers, rural artisans, scheduled castes, scheduled tribes and socially and economically backward classes. Households living below the poverty line have to be assisted with an appropriate package of the technologies, service and asset transfer programme.

The strategy and methodology for accelerated rural development relate to:

(a) Increasing production and productivity in agriculture and allied sectors;

(b) Resources and income development of the vulnerable sections of the rural population by development of primary, secondary, and tertiary sectors;

(c) Skill formation and skill upgrading programmes to promote self and wage-employment amongst the rural poor;

(d) Facilitating and adequate availability of credit to support the programme taken up for the rural poor;

(e) Promoting marketing, support to ensure the viability of production programmes and to insulate the rural poor from exploitation in the marketing of their products;

(f) The provision of additional employment opportunities for the rural poor for gainful employment during the lean agriculture season under the National Rural Employment Programme (NREP);

(g) The provision of essential minimum needs; and

(h) The involvement of universities, research and technical institutions in preparing a shelf of projects, both for self-employment and NREP, and in preparing strategies for the scientific utilisation of local resources.

## Need for Professional Rural Managers

Increasing investments have been made in the rural sector to combat the massive problems of unemployment and poverty. A large number of rural development projects, addressed to the needs of specific groups of people, geographic areas and commodities, have been implemented. Besides, the number of rural enterprises in the co-operative and public sectors have increased rapidly in the past few years. Professional rural managers are urgently needed in all these projects and enterprises.

Operation Flood II—with an envisaged total investment of nearly Rs. 485 crores over a period of seven years—will need around 400 fresh graduates in rural managerial cadres each year. This programme aims at helping some 10 million rural milk-producing families to set-up co-operatives in 150 districts in the country. Similarly, the setting up of oilseeds producers' co-operatives, with an investment of over Rs 2,000 million will call for another 200 managers each year, at least until the mid-1980s. Programmes further envisaged include co-operativisation of fruits and vegetables, cotton and fisheries.

The present supply of graduates from the management institutions in India is inadequate to meet the demand for them. Moreover, almost all these management graduates are absorbed by the industrial sector. The rural sector, which so desperately needs professional managers, continues to suffer from acute shortage. Besides, the rural areas, whose development has such an important place in our Five-Year Plans, face diverse socio-culture and institutional problems which require specialised managerial resources.

## The Institute: IRMA

The Institute of Rural Management Anand (IRMA), was established in 1979 in Kaira District of Gujarat, with the active support of the Government of India, the Government of Gujarat, the National Dairy Development Board and the Indian Dairy Corporation.

IRMA is an autonomous body registered under the Societies' Registration Act, 1860, and is the first in India to undertake the professional education of young graduates in rural management.

IRMA is born out of a conviction that an all-round and sustained development requires specialised managerial manpower for the producers' organisations—and these are crucial for the development of the rural economy in India. IRMA seeks to generate appropriate management resources under management education and training, research and consultancy activities.

## Objectives of the IRMA

(i) To impart education and training to young men and women so that they may manage income-generating and development activities for and on behalf of rural producers;

(ii) To offer training courses for policy-makers, directors, general managers and those in charge of specific managerial functions in rural enterprises and projects;

(iii) To conduct research in operating problems in order to help improve the management of rural enterprises and projects;

(iv) To undertake basic research into the processes of rural management to augment the existing body of knowledge; and

(v) To provide consultancy services to rural enterprises and organisations in the co-operative and other sectors in order to improve their organisational efficiency and effectiveness.

## Programme in Rural Management

The institute offers a two-year residential post-graduate Programme in Rural Management (PRM). The programme aims at preparing outstanding young men and women for careers leading to management responsibilities in farmer's organisation. It will equip its participants with those professional managerial skills and abilities which are essential for the management of rural enterprises and institution that endeavour to bring about a change.

The distinctive features of IRMA's post-graduate programme in Rural Management is that it effectively blends education at Anand with field based training in village situation as well as in rural producers' organisation. Its aims is to build up practical, professional rural managers is reflected, on the one hand, in the strong application bias built into the courses, and on the other in the emphasis placed on the two segments of field-based training to which nearly one half of the programme period is devoted.

The design of the PRM is based on the premise that it is as important for students of rural management to learn about the contextual realities in which they will have to work as it is for them to learn about management theories and concept. Hence, in the Field-Study Section, which forms one part of field-based training, Students have opportunities to study the conditions of village life and the functioning of rural institutions in their setting. In the Management Traineeship section, forming the second part of the field-based training, students are given an opportunity to appreciate the problems and conditions of rural enterprises and their functioning as organised systems working to bring about a change in rural India.

Two field-work modules of five weeks each are conducted under the faculty guidance at sites spread all over India. For instance, for their first field-work module, PRM 80-82 students were formed into eight groups and attached to the NDDB Spearhead Teams operating in Ahmedabad, Kolhapur, Guntur, Erode, Batinda, Rohtak, Maraud and Varanasi. Similarly, PRM 81-83 students were located in four groups in villages in Banaskantha, Ujjain, Nalgonda and Madurai districts.

**Table 1**
**PROFILE OF MANAGEMENT PROCESS**

| *Function* | *American* | *Indian* |
|---|---|---|
| ***Planning*** | | |
| Major objectives | Highly profit-oriented | Somewhat profit-oriented |
| Documentation of Objectives | Fully/partially documented | Partial/no documentation |
| Orientation | Medium term (2-5 years) | Short term/no planning (1-2 yrs) |
| Nature | Systematic, comprehensive | Limited/not detailed |
| Participation | Top and middle managers | Top managers, usually |
| Frequency of Review | Monthly | Monthly/ad hoc |
| ***Organising*** | | |
| Layers of Hierarchy | 4-7 | 5-8 |
| Organisation Charts | Yes | Some/None |

| | | |
|---|---|---|
| Authority Definition | Clear | Vague and ambiguous |
| Committee Usage | High | Low to none |
| Policy Decisions | Top and middle management usually formally stated | Top management — not formally stated |
| ***Staffing*** | | |
| Policy Formulation | Top managers—parent company —formally stated—documented | Top managers—not usually formally stated—no documentation |
| Job Description | Detailed comprehensive and basis | Ad hoc little need basis |
| Recruitment | | |
| Managers | Advertisement, feelers, and campus interviews | Advertisements |
| Non-Managerial Cadres | Word of mouth, files and consultants | Word of mouth, files and consultants |
| Training and Development | Some in—company, job rotation, on-the-job, external management programmes, parent company plants | Job rotation, on-the-job, external management programmes |
| Compensation Systems Managers | Surveys, comparable managers in multi-national corporations | Ad hoc |
| Non-Managers | Collective bargaining | Collective bargaining |
| Promotion Criteria | Competence, training, education, experience | Seniority and experience |
| ***Directing*** | | |
| Leadership Style | Authoritarian/Democratic | Authoritarian/paternalistic |
| Middle Managers | Authoritarian | Authoritarian |
| Trust and Confidence in Subordinates | | |
| Top Managers | Some | Some |
| Middle Managers | Some | Some |
| Trust and Confidence in Superiors | | |
| Top Managers | High | Low |
| Middle Managers | High | Low |
| Interpersonal Relations | Somewhat co-operative | Somewhat co-operative |
| Decision-making | Low | Low |
| ***Controlling*** | | |
| Quality Control | Extensive parent company quality audits | Extensive |
| Budgetary Control | All Departments | Most Departments |
| Cost Accounting | Professional personnel | Professional personnel |
| Time/Motion Studies | Some | None/Some |
| Production-Setting Decisions | Committee/Production manager | Top manager |
| Sales-Setting Decisions | Committee/sales manager | Top manager/sales manager |

The format of this profile chart has been adapted from Boseman, G.F. & Phatak A "Management Practices of Industrial Enterprises in Mexico: A Comparative Study," *Management International Review*, 1978, 18(1), 43-48.

## Management Information System

The combination of status and timely access to accurate and relevant information enables the programmer to function well in those roles of decision-making. Information is of great significance because the quality of managerial decisions is directly related to the information available to the decision maker. The better the information, the more conclusive it becomes in guiding decisions, whether confirming the existing choices or suggesting a search for new ones. This in turn emphasises the need for developing formal management information system' (MIS)

Stated simply an MIS is a communication process in which information is recorded, stored and retrieved for decision-making in regard to planning, operating and controlling. In its simplest form, MIS, in the context of decision-making can be represented schematically. The basic transformation underlying MIS is to proceed from "data to information". The term data may be defined as any bit of information, from the dust in the air to the flecks in the carpet to the latest inventory list. Information, on the other hand, is considered to be data processed to affect choice.

The organisational problem is to convert data into information. Only a proportion of data available in an organisation is of real management importance; much of it may be relatively valueless some may even tend to create confusion. The rise of modern electronic data processing (EDP) has both alleviated and aggravated the organisational dilemma inherent in having too much random data and too little ordered information. The chance that data will be missed has gone down, but that data will be lost or misinterpreted has gone up. It is therefore, important that the information system identify the information needs of different levels of management (top, middle and operating), the form in which it should be made available, the time and frequency at which it should be supplied, and the method of processing information to suite the requirements of each level. These aspects have been briefly discussed here. Moreover, some basic considerations in designing and implementing an MIS have been delineated.

Decision-making is an iterative process involving:

*(i)* The recognition of the opportunity or the problems;

*(ii)* Obtaining data;

*(iii)* Understanding the information content;

*(iv)* Seeking alternatives;

*(v)* Evaluating them; and

*(vi)* Choice and implementation.

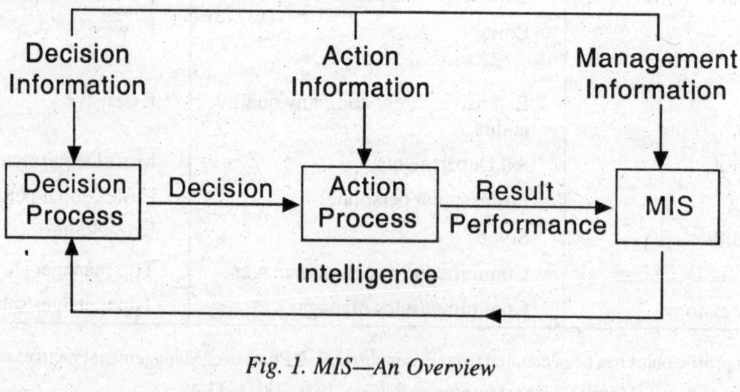


*Fig. 1. MIS—An Overview*

Table 2 summarises the distinguishing features of three levels of management and the decision categories identified. Table 1(b) elaborates the information characteristic by the decision category.

**Table 2**
**MANAGEMENT LEVELS, DECISION AND INFORMATION**

| | *Characteristic* | *Top Management* | *Middle Management* | *Operating Management* |
|---|---|---|---|---|
| 1. | Planning | Heavy | Moderate | Minimum |
| 2. | Control | Moderate | Heavy | Heavy |
| 3. | Time frame | Long-term | Short-term | Day-to-day |
| 4. | Scope of activity | Extremely broad | Entire functional area | Single sub-function or sub-task |
| 5. | Nature of activity | Relatively unstructured, complex, many variables | Moderately structured, less complex, better defined variables | Highly structured ·straightforward |
| 6. | Type of decision making | Strategic non-programmed | Tactical, mainly non-programmed | Technical, mainly programmed |
| 7. | Decision environment | Uncertainty | Risk | Almost certainty |
| 8. | Type of information utilised | *(a)* External information<br>—Competitive actions<br>—Customer actions—availability of resources<br>—Demographic studies<br>—Government actions etc.<br>*(b)* Predictive information (long-term trends)<br>—"what if" information | *(a)* Descriptive<br>—Historical information<br>*(b)* Performance—Current information<br>*(c)* Predictive—future information (short-term)<br>*(d)* Stimulated "what if" information | *(a)* Descriptive<br>—Historical information<br>*(b)* Performance—current information |
| 9. | Mental attributes | Creative, innovative | Responsible, persuasive, administrative | Efficient, effective |
| 10. | Departmental/divisional interaction | Intra-division | Intra-department | Inter-department |

At the strategic level, decision-making is largely a planning activity, and decisions are characterized by a great deal or uncertainty and are future-oriented. Strategic decisions include establishing objectives, policy making, organising and attaining an overall effectiveness of the organisation. The decision-making process is non-programmed—that is, it deals with ill-defined problems, usually complex and involving many variables, relies heavily on external information.

Tactical decision-making pertains to short-term activities and the allocation of resources for the attainment of objectives. This kind of decision-making relates to such areas as the formulation of budgets, funds flow analysis, decisions on plant layout, personnel problems, product improvement and research and development. Tactical decision-making process has little potential for programmed decision-making. The decision rules are mostly ill-structured and not amenable to routine and self-regulation. Tactical decision-making relies to a greater extent on internal information.

Table 3
INFORMATION CHARACTERISTICS BY DECISION CATEGORY

| Characteristics of Information | Levels of Decision-making | | |
|---|---|---|---|
| | Strategic | Tactical | Technical |
| Source | External | – | Largely internal |
| Scope | Very wide | – | Well defined |
| Level of aggregation | Aggregate | – | Detailed |
| Time horizon | Future | – | Historical |
| Required accuracy | Low | – | High |
| Frequency of occurrence of information change | Low | – | High |
| Frequency of uses of information | Infrequent | – | Very frequent |

*Note:* From strategic to technical, the scale is a continuum.

## Rural Development Activities

The Project Director, DRDA sends one monthly, five quarterly and one annual progress reports to the Secretary, Department of Forests and Rural Development. The Assistant Project Officer (Monitoring and Evaluation) compiles the information received from various banks and other officials in the department and fills up the prescribed pro forma. The selection of eligible beneficiaries under IRD Programme will be done by the DRDA officials, bankers and block officials in the presence of village officials and leaders. The APO (M&E) used to monitor and evaluate the different schemes with the available data and also by meeting the beneficiaries personally. A separate cell was established in the Secretariat under the guidance of a Director exclusively for IRD Programmes. The Deputy Director also monitors the IRD Schemes at state level and gives suggestions to the DRDA officials.

The District Co-operative Officer sends six monthly, eight quarterly and one-yearly reports to the Registrar of Co-operatives. The three Divisional Co-operative Officers collect the data from Taluk Co-operative Officers working under their jurisdiction. They consolidate the information and send it to the District Co-operative Officer who in turn consolidates the figures and submits the progress report of the Registrar of Co-operatives. The monthly and quarterly pro forma deal with targets and achievements of Co-operative Bank's activities, recovery of loans, sanction of loans, etc.

The District Lead Bank Officer sends three quarterly, two half-yearly and two annual reports to the Development Manager, Lead Bank Department, Hyderabad. He also sends credit reports to the Reserve Bank of India. A consolidated report will be presented in the District Consultative Committee meeting to be held quarterly. In this meeting the progress of different banks and various schemes will be reviewed which helps to plan the financial activities in the district.

The qualitative aspects of data primarily depend upon the skills needed for data collection and analysis and also on inter-personal interaction within the organisation and rapport with the personnel in the other organisations supplying data. Though training is a part of the activities in most of the departments, imparting of adequate skills for effective collection and analysis of data to those associated with these tasks, has not drawn the attention of trainers/department to the extent desired. The nature and duration of training should be identified based on the tasks assigned to a person and the level of functioning in the organisation. So accordingly, it is suggested that for field-level functionaries (who are) responsible for data collection and reporting, periodical training meant for improving working knowledge—purpose of a scheme and its objectives, concepts used, field supervision, cross-checking of data supplied, etc. will suffice. The officials/persons at the higher level who are generally associated with survey designs, data analysis and supervising the work of field personnel, should be trained on design of surveys, statistical methods and also management practices (orientation courses) in order to discharge the functions/tasks more effectively.

Besides training, the inter-personnel interaction in the organisation (to a desirable extent) and also with the concerned departments/agencies is expected to improve the reliability of the data to some extent. In fact, such interaction provides an opportunity to the field staff about the current use or data (collected) and also make them appreciate the need for and utility of the data. Further, the officials at the higher level will be in close contact with the field situation (including problems of data collection) and thus may plan for their data needs more precisely. The training programmes are expected to facilitate such interaction of personnel (for mutual benefit) and this in a way helps in strengthening the organisation. The interdepartmental interaction will help in understanding the limitations of data and thus interpreting data accurately by the data-user department(s).

## MANAGEMENT BY OBJECTIVES

The basic lack of motivation cannot be cured without scientific management effort. Motivation is that intrinsic power that makes things happen. We cannot merely create a programme with its apparatus of targets and statistical feedback proformas, and then sit back and wait for great things to happen. On the other hand, we cannot coax and cajole the extension staff to achieve the results, both quantitatively and qualitatively.

A call has been given in some quarters for the creation of a cadre of "rural managers". The answer lies in adopting the Management by Objective (MBO) approach. It is a test of managerial competence to visualise and plan, and of executive skill to implement and achieve. It is perhaps the most effective means of integrating motivated individual effort into a composite and wholesome contribution to the overall objectives of the programme. It seeks to convert resources into results by planning, organising, directing, co-ordinating and controlling activities and functionaries in any programme. It seeks to quantify and integrate objectives down to the individual engaged in any programme. In other words, the first requisite is that the programme must have specific goals or objectives which it must achieve. An objective is a managerial tool which sets the direction and pace of an activity to utilise resources optimally in order to produce results. It has to be distinguished from purpose, which is in the nature of the *raison d'etre* to the programme. In simple language, "objective" would mean a specific goal to be achieved in a given period of time in pursuance of the purpose of the programme. But objectives are not to be handed down in a spirit of authoritarianism. Instead, they should be fixed after discussion and mutual consultation at all levels, taking into account the long-term and short-term priorities at all levels.

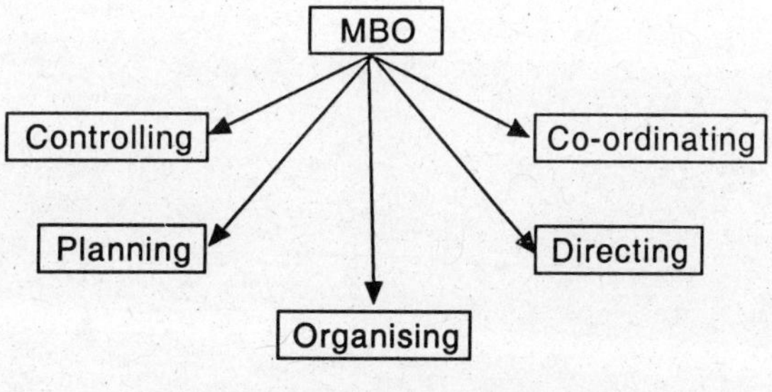


*Fig. 2. Management by Objectives*

Performance review is an integral part of the MBO process, for periodic performance review help in identifying the reasons for success or failure and in developing a definite plan of future action. These reviews can also throw up the inadequacies of the structure and provide guidelines for the modification of policies and practices. The focus in performance review in MBO is on the future; and an evaluation of past performance is important only as a source for ideas and the direction of future planning. Focus on performance, emphasis on improvement, future orientation and self-appraisal are essential features of this review. Self-appraisal not only increases such functionary's influence in the review process, but enhances the credibility of review results. An information system, designed to facilitate frequent reviews, has also to be developed.

## Conclusion

Planning for an accelerated growth of rural areas requires planning for flexibility; both in respect of the human and non-human resources in a rural organisation and in the scope for a revision of plans. Organisation should be explicit in recognising the personal values and aspirations of its beneficiaries as well as its workers and administrators. A careful consideration should be given to the ethical aspects and to the organisation's obligations to society.

Progressive rural organisations/institutions that plan ahead provide promising job opportunities, set fair prices for their products, plan for a reasonable development of the rural environment in an integrated manner, and have a healthy regard for the interests of the community. It must be evident that however skilled the planner-executives are, the most important requirement of all is that of men who are wise enough not only to plan for others but to plan in a manner that would encourage others to plan for themselves. In the final analysis, this might well prove to be a very important guide to strategic management.

❑ ❑ ❑

*"Just as the whole universe is the self, so is India contained in the villages."*

***— Mahatma Gandhi***

# Chapter 38

# TRAINING FOR RURAL PEOPLE

## Introduction

The implementation of the various poverty alleviation and rural development programmes which call for an efficient and motivated stream of Government as well as non-government functionaries, is a very challenging task. Further, to strengthen the Panchayati Raj Institutions, it is pertinent to empower the elected representatives at all levels with necessary knowledge and skills, so that they can discharge their constitutional obligations.

Training is one of the tested tools for performance improvement as well as upgradation of knowledge and skills of the personnel. Organisational motivation and moral, as reflected in the attitudes and administrative culture, are rendered relevant and sharply focused through effective training programmes. Training has thus constantly gained an important position in rural development activities in the various poverty alleviation programmes which calls for an efficient and motivated stream of government as well as non-government functionaries. This is a very challenging task. As training, research and development are inextricably linked, continuing education of both policy makers and programme implementers is imperative. Towards facilitating this, the National Institute of Rural Development (NIRD), an apex Training and Research Institute was set up in 1965 to impart training to the rural development functionaries as well as Panchayati Raj Institutions through classroom interaction and field work. Thereafter, 25 State Institute of Rural Development (SIRD) and 88 Extension Training Centres (ETCs) were set up in the country for intensifying training related activities.

In consonance with the National Training Policy (1996) these Training Institutes have made a variety of programmes including participatory methods of training with a view to not only imparting skills to the trainees but also enlisting participation of people, action groups and local institutions like the panchayats.

In addition, extensive support has been provided to a number of training and research institutions dealing with issues related to rural development.

## TRAINING

The term training refers to the act of increasing the knowledge, aptitude and skill of a rural manager to do a particular job related to rural development. It is concerned with imparting specific skills for particular purposes. That is why training forms a part of the management development programmes in rural India. With the required shift in emphasis, the rural managers develop from *technical* to *human* and *conceptual* and *finally* to *conceptual skills.*

Trained personnel, led by a good leader, are essential prerequisites of a rapid development of rural areas. To manage the change we not only require managers, but those who would make a constant endeavour to improve—to improve themselves, to improve the effectiveness of their team and to improve the range and quality of rural services, so that their impact is felt by the teeming millions living in the rural environment.

**Chart 1**
**THE CROSS-CULTURAL MODEL**

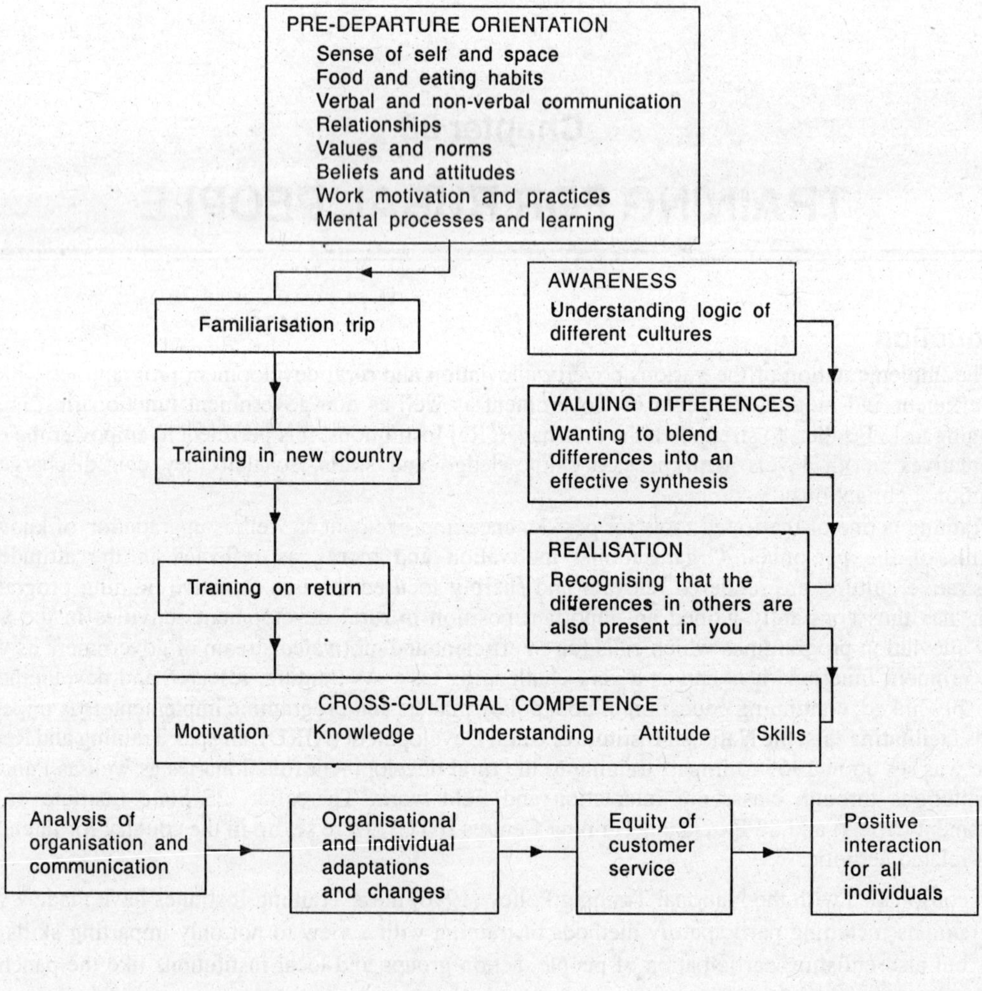

## Objectives of Training

The main objectives of training is to bridge the gap between the existing performance ability and the desired performance. The following are the main objectives of training.

*(i)* To impart to new entrants the basic knowledge and skills they need for the performance of definite tasks in a better way;

*(ii)* To assist the employees to function more effectively and efficiently in their present position by providing them the latest information and techniques and developing their skills in their particular field;

*(iii)* To build up a second line of competent officers and prepare them to occupy more responsible positions; and

*(iv)* To broaden the minds of senior managers so that they may correct the narrowness of the outlook that may arise from over specialisation.

The Integrated Rural Development Programme is basically an attempt to launch a frontal attack on the problems of poverty and unemployment in the rural areas. Without the objectives of enabling the rural population to get maximum benefit out of the various schemes being implemented under the IRDP, it would be necessary to acquaint the beneficiaries with the latest technology in the relevant fields by evolving suitable training programmes. Keeping this objective in view, training of the beneficiaries, who are introduced to new schemes, new occupations, or modern technology is an important component of the IRD Programme. The full cost of training of beneficiaries may be provided out of this programme. Training is envisaged both in the agricultural and allied activities as well as in industrial activities. Training in the agriculture and allied activities should, however, be conducted only in courses organised in Gram Sevak Training Centres, Farmers' Training Centres, Krishi Vigyan Kendras and Agricultural Universities. Training for setting up rural industries/artisan activities etc. may be imparted in the ITIs, polytechnic, training schools run by the KVIC, All India Handicrafts Boards or any other similar organisation of the Government of India or any other institution/organisation recognised by the concerned state governments. as capable of conferring, the necessary skills on the participant.

Our main problem in fact, is training of personnel for rural development especially, the village level workers, the supervisor and others. Trained band of workers will bring a new direction to rural development, since these programmes call for a great deal of organisational ability, skills of planning, efficiency for execution and consistency in monitoring the implementation. The infrastructure for imparting training comprises a network of institutions, namely the National Institute of Rural Development (NIRD), State Institutes of Rural Development (SIRD), the Extension Training Centres (ETCs), and other institutions of management development and rural management.

Training of the functionaries involved in the implementation of rural development programmes surveys several purposes and its important has been recognised at all levels. It helps in upgrading the professional competence of the functionaries, changing their attitudes and provides feedback from the field. Training of functionaries of both official and non-official agencies is essential for improving the performance in the field and accelerating the pace of rural development.

Accordingly, the training needs of various types of functionaries have been identified which are as under:

*(a)* Familiarisation with the broad objectives, strategy and targets etc, of special programmes like IRDP/DPAP/DDP/NREP/TRYSEM. The role of each programme has to be explained to the functionaries as well as the role of each functionary in the programme;

(b) A special course on IRDP for the implementing agencies. This would convey operational details on identification of beneficiaries, credit mobilisation, block level planning, rural industries, component, monitoring and evaluation etc.

(c) A course on rural industrialisation and TRYSEM for functionaries of the industries and rural development departments, special programme agencies, organisation in the decentralised industrial sectors and credit institutions. This would help in developing a co-ordinated perspective for all implementing agencies;

(d) Different training programmes on institutional financing intended for various levels. Special accent has to be provided on orientation courses for branch managers and agents of banks. District level workshops to which collectors, project officers, district officials and bank managers are jointly called, need to be organised;

(e) Processing and marketing of agricultural produce;

(f) Marketing of products of rural industrial units;

(g) Management of rural enterprises;

(h) Financial management for project officer of special programmes agencies;

(i) Accounts management for account staff of special programme agencies;

(j) Course on organisation of the rural poor;

(k) Project formulation, appraisal implementation, monitoring and evaluation of rural development projects;

(l) Rural employment including NREP and others;

(m) Block-level planning. This would be a detailed course on how exactly such a plan is to be drawn up;

(n) Management of rural development projects;

(o) Courses in training methodology and programme content for trainers of state and district-level institutions. Orientation courses also need to be organised;

(p) Sectoral courses in sheep and pasture development, piggery development, dairy development, poultry development, irrigation management, watershed management, dry land technology, etc

(q) Joint course for revenue and development functionaries and police officials with focus on the socio-economic development of the rural poor;

(r) Basic services, minimum needs programme;

(s) Voluntary action and people's participation;

(t) Drought/emergency relief and their integration with on-going development programmes;

(u) Women, child and youth welfare;

(v) Welfare programmes for scheduled castes and scheduled tribes.

**Chart 2**
**THE EXPERIENTIAL LEARNING MODEL**

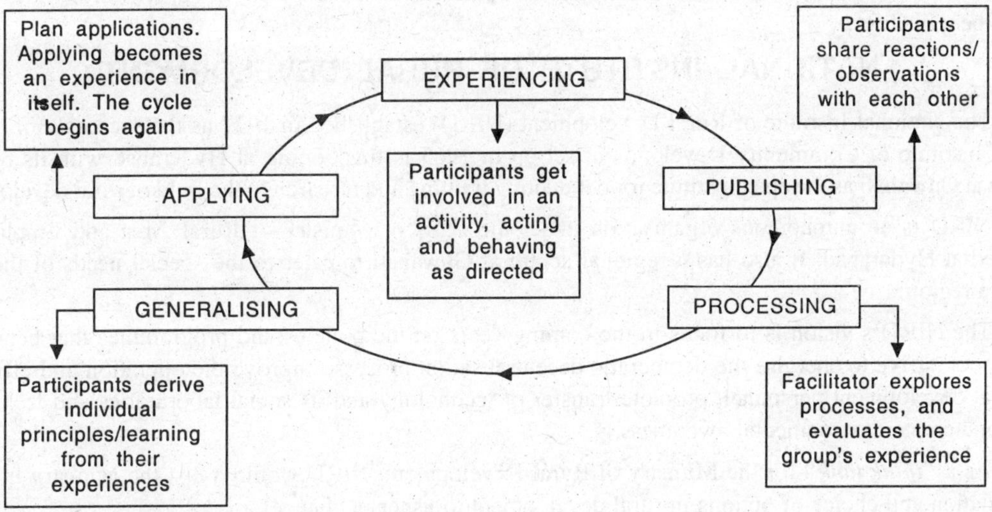


## Institutions at Work

With the task in view various training centres, institutes in various sectors have been functioning in India. A state-wise and sector-wise detail of training institutions is presented elsewhere in this book. In all, there are 1,485 training institutions in India which are fighting with this gigantic task of imbibing skills in rural development personnel as well as target groups to make the rural development programme a success.

Hundreds and thousands of personnel from various levels are being trained from time to time by these institutes. With this, the task of implementation of schemes and programmes is being simplified day by day. Simultaneously the beneficiaries are being trained at various local-level institutions with the help of group discussions, demonstrations etc. At state level, State Institutes of Community (Rural) Development and Panchayati Raj are imparting training to the lower and middle-level personnel involved in implementation of Rural Development Programmes.

## Training of Beneficiaries

Besides the education of the families participating in the programmes about the objective of the programme and their responsibility towards the programme, they also need training to equip them with the skills and knowledge relevant to the economic activities selected by them. As most of the IRDP families live at the subsistence level, they are unlikely to be acquainted with better methods of production and management. Also, not having produced much for the market, they lack these skills. The attention paid to the training needs of the beneficiaries at present is grossly inadequate. It is often assumed, though very erroneously, that they do not need any training for carrying on the economic activities on such a small scale. There is no wonder many of the families flounder at the very beginning on account of lapses in management which would appear to others to betray the absence of simple common sense.

The viability of the programme will be greatly enhanced if the training aspect is diligently taken care of. The training needs of the beneficiaries should be identified at the stages of identification of the families and formulation of schemes. Schemes which require a greater training input than the implementing agencies are able to cater to are better shelved than implemented. The content of training should be carefully worked out, keeping its relevance and practicability and the level of the participants in view. Tips for efficiently managing the units and proper use of credit and other facilities should form an important part of training. Implementing personnel in various organisations should be developed as trainers of the IRDP beneficiaries. Simple manuals may be produced for the use of these personnel to enable them to impart worthwhile training to the beneficiaries.

## NATIONAL INSTITUTE OF RURAL DEVELOPMENT

The National Institute of Rural Development (NIRD) established in 1977 as the successor of the National Institute of Community Development set up in 1965 is functioning at Hyderabad with its regional centre at Guwahati as the apex institute for conducting training and research in the field of rural development.

NIRD is an autonomous organisation under the aegis of Ministry of Rural Area and Employment situated at Hyderabad. It also has a regional centre at Guwahati to cater to the special needs of the north eastern region.

The NIRD's vision is to focus in the coming years on the policies and programmes that benefit the rural poor, strive to energise the democratic decentralisation process, improve the operation and efficiency of rural development personnel, promote transfer of technology and its social laboratories and technology park and create environmental awareness.

As a *"think tank"* for the Ministry of Rural Development, NIRD would assist the Ministry in policy formulation and choice of options in rural development to usher in change.

The Mission of the Institute is as follows:

To examine and analyse the factors contributing to the improvement of economic and social well-being of people in rural areas on a sustainable basis with focus on the rural poor and the other disadvantaged groups through research, action research and consultancy efforts;

To facilitate the rural development efforts with particular emphasis and focus on the rural poor by improving the knowledge, skill and attitudes of rural development officials and non-officials through organising training, workshops and seminars.

Training is a major activity of NIRD. The training efforts of the institute are intended to create knowledge-based development of skills and understanding of the various dimensions of rural development. Consultancy is another activity of the NIRD.

The broad areas of its activity are:

Social and economic well-being of rural communities.

Institution building for rural development with particular reference to the evolving needs of rural development administration and management.

Formulation of area-level plans for generation of employment and higher incomes for rural people.

Promotion of human resources development and training.

Transfer of technology appropriate to rural development.

Dissemination through publication, of rural development information and knowledge.

Strive to energise the democratic decentralisation process.

Improve the operation and efficiency of Rural Development Personnel.

Promote transfer of technology through its social laboratories and technology park.

Create environmental awareness.

Issues relating to evolution of an egalitarian agro-industrial society.

New strategies and policy formulation with regard to rural development.

NIRD's mandate is to organise training programmes, conferences, seminars and workshops for senior level development managers; elected representatives of Panchayati Raj Institutions (PRIs), State Legislatures and Parliament; Bankers, NGOs and others; undertake, aid, promote and co-ordinate research on its own and through other agencies; study various aspects of the Panchayati Raj Institutions and Rural Development Programmes across the States; analyse and propose solutions to problems in planning and implementation of the programmes of rural development and disseminate information through periodicals, reports and other publications.

The Institute attempts to translate into action the strategies and programmes of rural development in the national socio-economic growth process. Within each area, not only specific research studies are developed but training programmes, seminars and workshops with focus on specific topics are also organised. The research studies are action-oriented and are formulated in a pragmatic way so that they not only constitute a vital input for the various training programmes, but are also useful for policy formulation and programme implementation.

## Research

The objectives of conducting the research studies are three-fold – *(i)* to enhance the understanding of the changing rural socio-economic scenario; *(ii)* to identify major constraints of proper implementation of various developmental schemes; and *(iii)* to suggest suitable policy interventions for improving the quality of life of the rural people. The research studies are of three types – *(a)* programme-based; *(b)* thrust area-based; and *(c)* individual-based. Research studies are also undertaken with a view to provide regular feedback to the ministry on the programmes implemented by it. The Institute also takes up action research which is location-specific and is a specialised field-interventional methodology for understanding and sustaining rural development. At present, two Action Research projects are in progress. While the first project being undertaken in one of the backward districts of Andhra Pradesh, *i.e.*, Mehaboobnagar, the second project aims at enabling the gram panchayats to prepare integrated plans in accordance with the provisions of the 73$^{rd}$ constitutional amendment.

## State Institutes of Rural Development

The centrally sponsored scheme for strengthening/establishment of State Institutes of Rural Development (SIRD) was considered vital for human resources development. This scheme was taken up for implementation during the Sixth Five Year Plan. The Scheme was continued during Seventh and Eighth Plan to revitalise training infrastructure so as to train the rural development functionaries and implement the programme more effectively. With this in view, it was decided to set up/strengthen one apex training institution at state level in each State.

There are 25 SIRDs set up under this scheme in 25 States which include 8 Composite Institutes in Gujarat, Himachal Pradesh, Jammu and Kashmir, Karnataka, Maharashtra, Manipur, Rajasthan and Tripura. Out of the 25 SIRDs, 24 SIRDs have become operational either in their own building or in rented buildings. The SIRDs in Goa and Mizoram are yet to be operationalised.

The SIRDs have the requisite linkages with NIRD and ETCs so as to function in a hierarchy to serve the vital role of imparting training to the rural development functionaries. The scheme is being monitored constantly at the various levels in order to chalk out requisite strategy/plan for further strengthening and removing constraints in the functioning of the SIRDs. A system of regional consultations has been introduced between the Ministry, the NIRD and the State Governments. In these consultations, emphasis is laid on improving the content and quality of training programmes.

After the enactment of the 73rd Constitutional Amendment Act, it has been decided to strengthen the existing training infrastructure both at the state level as well as district level to meet the training requirements of elected members of Panchayati Raj as well as officials in the near future. The financial assistance by

Government of India to SIRDs is 100% for non-recurring expenditure and 50% for recurring expenditure. The Scheme is, however, demand-driven in nature. Special emphasis is being laid for recruitment of core faculty members in SIRDs. 100% funding support from the Centre is available to cover expenditure on procuring the services of five core faculty members for each SIRD.

## Extension Training Centres

The scheme of strengthening/establishment of Extension Training Centres (ETCs) for imparting training to village/block level development functionaries was taken up since the Seventh Five Year Plan for implementation.

The ETCs are expected to provide necessary training inputs for raising the professional competence of the villages and block level functionaries. So far, 87 ETCs have been established/upgraded with central assistance. Considering the increase in the number of development functionaries and rural organisation and the rejuvenation of the Panchayati Raj systems the role of ETCs has acquired added importance. With the enactment of the constitutional 73rd Amendment Act, 1992 relating to the setting up of the Panchayat Raj Institutions, the need for training for Rural Development/Panchayati Raj functionaries has increased tremendously. The Extension Training Centres are the only training set up to reach down to the village level. Keeping all these in view, it has been decided to strengthen training infrastructure in the existing Extension Training Centres. For this purpose, central assistance is 100% for non-recurring expenditure and the recurring expenditure is provided to a maximum ceiling of Rs. 5.00 lakhs per annum per ETC. However, the Scheme is demand-driven in nature.

The Extension Training Centres are required to design training modules in consultation with NIRD and SIRD, and thereafter compulsorily conduct courses for:

*(i)* Rural artisans

*(ii)* Rural entrepreneurs

*(iii)* Self Help groups under SGSY

*(iv)* Gram Sevaks/Gram Sevikas/VLWs

*(v)* Secretaries of Panchayats and Co-operatives

*(vi)* Sarpanch and Panch of Gram Panchayats

*(vii)* Facilitates/NGOs used under SGSY programme

*(viii)* Grass-root level functionaries of all other development departments

*(ix)* Office bearers of social service organisations dealing in rural development programmes

*(x)* Orientation to sustainable Development themes like Watershed Development

*(xi)* Convergence of important social sectorial themes at the field level.

## Organisation of Training Courses, Seminars and Workshops (OTC)

Organisation of Training Courses, Seminars and Workshops (OTC) Scheme is a central sector plan scheme for providing financial assistance for organising training courses, seminars, workshops etc on subjects related to such ongoing programmes as the SGSY, Rural Housing, Panchayati Raj, Rural sanitation and Drinking Water Supply.

The objective of the Scheme is to train the functionaries involved in the implementation of Rural Development Programmes by upgrading their professional competence. Training Programmes, Seminars and Workshops under the Scheme are conducted through the SIRDs/ ETCs/ Regional Institutes of Rural Development and other Institutes, including university departments. Under the scheme, proposals having bearing on Rural Development received and are examined and approved by a Departmental Screening Committee

(DSC) headed by the Additional Secretary & Financial Advisor (AS&FA), Ministry of Rural Development. The central assistance is generally about Rs. 2.00 Lakhs per programme.

The financial assistance under the OTC scheme is provided for conducting courses/seminars on the various subjects such as:

(*a*) Rural Development (both self-employment and wage-employment)

(*b*) Rural water supply and sanitation

(*c*) Land Reforms

(*d*) Development of special problem areas like drought prone areas, desert prone areas etc.

(*e*) Training of rural functionaries

(*f*) Rural Housing

(*g*) Training and Employment of rural women and youth belonging to BPL families.

(*h*) Panchayati Raj

(*i*) Problems of SCs/STs in the context of PAPs.

The Plan outlay for this scheme for the year 2002-03 is Rs.1.25 crore.

## Panchayat Development and Training (PD&T)

The scheme of Panchayat Development and Training (PD&T) is centrally sponsored scheme under which central assistance is provided to the States, NGOs and other institutions for their efforts to impart training to the elected and official functionaries of the Panchayati Raj Institutions. The funding pattern under the scheme is as follows:

(*a*) 20% funding is provided for lodging and boarding and 50% for other items to State Governments;

(*b*) 100% Central assistance is provided to NGOs and other institutions.

Proposals received under the scheme are considered by the Training Research and Advisory Committee (TRAC) headed by the Secretary (RD).

The elements of support by Ministry of Rural Development under this scheme include the following:

Expenditure on participation for training of elected representatives of Panchayati Raj Institutions including awareness generation programmes.

Cost of expenditure on accommodation/hiring of rooms.

Audio/Video training equipment expenditure.

Workshops/Seminars, awareness generation campaigns on Panchayati Raj.

Support for mobile training facilities for training in Panchayati Raj.

The success of the Panchayati Raj system hinges largely on the extent to which their capabilities are built to perform these functions and responsibilities. Thus, a time bound and systematic training programme to provide orientation of the elected representatives on a very large scale is considered to be the most important pre-requisite for the success of the PRIs. The States/UT governments are required to work out systematic strategy for training of representatives of PRIs and to generate awareness among the masses at the grassroots level and to strengthen the Gram Sabha.

# TRAINING OF RURAL YOUTH FOR SELF-EMPLOYMENT (TRYSEM)

The National Scheme of Training of Rural Youth for Self-employment (TRYSEM) was initiated with effect from 15th August, 1979. The main thrust of the scheme is on equipping rural youth with necessary skills and technology to enable them to take to vocations of self employment.

It is felt that the launching of various special programmes like DPAP/DDP/SFDA/MFAL/TRYSEM, etc., have created a need for continuous training of officials and non-officials who are involved in the policy planning and implementation of these programmes. It is sometimes possible to invite all the state level officers to national seminars, workshops, training courses etc. at the NIRD. But very often, the various constraints prevent officers from attending such programmes at Hyderabad/Delhi. To some extent, this difficulty has been obviated by conducting regional meetings. But this is no substitute for a regular training infrastructure at the state level, which could continuously organise training and research in the programmes and problems of a particular state/region.

This ministry has also launched upon an ambitious programme of preparing block level plans in selected blocks of the country. Ultimately, such plans have to be formulated for the entire country. In order to work out the methodology for the preparation of such plans and to give suitable training to state and district level officers, state centres proved valuable.

The dispersal of training facilities also removes the difficulty of communication as it is possible to organise programmes in the local languages and the training programmes are directly related to the situations prevailing in the states served by the training centres.

## Functions

The main functions of the states centres will be:

*(i)* To conduct short-term training courses for the officials and the non-officials engaged in rural development and administration in the states;

*(ii)* To organised seminars, conferences and workshops for experts, academicians, administrators, researchers and non-officials on various problems of rural development and administration;

*(iii)* To undertake action-oriented researches on various problems of rural development and administration, so as to prepare case studies as inputs for the training programmes;

*(iv)* To serve as centres for the collection and dissemination of information regarding rural development and administration; and

*(v)* To provide consultancy service on problems of rural development and administration.

## Training and Extension Support by NABARD

NABARD's basic objective to assist in bringing about integrated rural development calls for investment in human capital besides that in tangible assets in the farm and non-farm sectors. This necessitates simultaneous action and the demand and the supply sides of credit. Firstly, to make credit delivery system more responsive to the needs of borrowers, it is necessary to upgrade the professional skills of officials working in the credit institutions through training. Next, the borrowers from rural areas have to be enlightened through a specially designed extension service on how to make efficient use of credit, a scarce resource, to rise their output and income and to repay the loans from incremental income.

## Vikas Volunteer Vahini (VVV)

NABARD constituted VVV as an extension service for disseminating the five principles of 'Development through Credit' among rural masses. The five principles briefly are: *(i)* Credit must be used in accordance with suitable methods of science and technology; *(ii)* The terms and conditions of credit (techno-economic parameters) must be fully respected; *(iii)* Work must be carried out with the desired skill so as to release optimum increase in the productivity and income; *(iv)* A part of the additional income created by credit must be saved; and *(v)* Loan instalments must be repaid in time and regularly to facilitate recycling to credit.

The VVV consists essentially of small farmers, rural artisans and other persons of small means who have successfully put into practice the five principles of 'Development through Credit'.

The volunteers chosen, duly assisted by specialists or technocrats and a representative each from NABARD and commercial/co-operative banks, visit villages according to a programme drawn up by NABARD in close co-ordination with state government. During such visits the volunteers share with the village folk their own experience and propagate the message of 'Development through Credit' and repayment ethic. In each village visited by the volunteers, a NABARD Club is established with membership restricted to those who have repaid their loans regularly and practiced the principles of 'Development through Credit'.

The VVV was inaugurated by the Prime Minister on 5 November, 1982 at New Delhi. A beginning was made by launching the programme in May 1983 in two districts of Tamil Nadu, *viz.*, Madurai and Tiruchirapalli, which are now experiencing a scarcity of institutional credit due to increased defaults in repayment of earlier loans. In each selected district, 10 blocks and a cluster of 5 villages in each block. Apart from organising a NABARD Club in each selected village, 12 volunteers were selected from each district to propagate the principle of 'Development through Credit'. The banks and the state government evinced keen interest in the programme, with some of the banks offering to launch the programme, at their own cost in other districts where they had lead bank responsibilities.

With the experience gained and success achieved in Tamil Nadu, the programme was extended to the states of Gujarat and Orissa during the year. In Gujarat, 50 villages in five blocks of Sabarkantha district and 51 villages in 5 blocks of Rajkot district were covered. The programme evoked anchoring response on the part of the local population and officials of banks and state governments; it also motivated many defaulters to repay their old overdue loans. In Orissa, 55 villages in ten selected blocks of Ganjam district were brought under the programme.

For effective utilisation of the services of the selected volunteers, who were presented badges by the Prime Minister in November 1982, 29 Micro Pilot Projects (MPP) were launched in 18 states including the union territory of Delhi. Under these projects, volunteers were to operate in a cluster of 5 to 6 villages to help villagers in obtaining institutional credit for development purposes with a commitment to timely repayment. NABARD Clubs were also to be established for each cluster. Following the launching of MPP, a maintenance phase was ushered in by monitoring the activities of volunteers and holding regular meetings of members of NABARD Clubs. The focus of the VVV Programme was extended to include preparation of village development plans and credit facilities for various economic activities, besides timely repayment. The main thrust was to bring about attitudinal changes in the users of institutional credit and propagating repayment ethic.

The launching of the main programme in three states and MPP and 18 states has created a favourable climate for institutional credit. Several banks operating in the projects areas were prepared to take over the responsibility for the maintenance phase of the programme of the 332 clubs functioning in 18 states and one Union Territory in the country, 324 (97%) clubs are under decentralised maintenance by CBs, CCBs or RRBs having major loaning operations in the area.

## The World Bank and the Training and Visit System

The training and visit system of agricultural extension, initially developed as a systematic programme by Daniel Benor, was first used extensively by the Bank of India in the early 1970s.

Agricultural extension, a system of supporting services aimed at making farmers particularly small-scale and subsistence farmers more productive, is being increasingly affected by the philosophy and methods of this approach. The experience with traditional extension work was quite disappointing. The reasons were varied—research did not take account of local conditions; extension was biased toward men, when women played an important role; support services were inadequate; and so on. The key improvement offered by the training and visit system are the development of better links between farmers and extension workers, and between both of these and research; and the increased effectiveness of the extension worker.

The essence of the system is that it should be sufficiently flexible to be used effectively in any type of farming, under any conditions. Its aim is to improve the use of existing resources, concentrating initially on key improvements in major crops. In some areas, where farming practices are already efficient and appropriate, this has meant giving farmers technical advice on more productive crops or more appropriate types of fertilisers or seed. In other words, advice on better farming methods—when to sow, how to weed—can produce dramatically better yields fairly quickly without much cash being paid out by the farmer. Quick and successful results are an important way of demonstrating the use of the system and in persuading more farmers to adopt it.

"System" is an appropriate name for the approach. Centered on providing farmers with relevant, clear, and sensible advice, which depends on close two-way contacts between farm families, extension workers, researchers, and administrators, it functions by allocating precise responsibilities and by timing activities carefully. The Chart I shows the line of command: not shown are all the links with research and time table of extension and extensional research activities, which are equally important. Village extension workers visit small group of "contact" and other farmers at least once a fortnight, to teach them three or four carefully chosen recommendations about what to do over the next two weeks. Since farmers attending the sessions also pass the advice on to other farm families, one extension workers—who generally spend eight days out of every two weeks on these visits—spend one day at a training session where subject matter specialists teach them the recommendations of the next two weeks and discuss farmers' problems from the previous fortnight. When appropriate, these sessions are attended by representatives from supply and credit agencies who collect information on the support the farmers will be needing.

The subject matter specialists divide their time, according to an equally structured programme, between these training sessions, research, and field work—an important element of the latter involving adaptive trials on farmers' field work to improve recommendations. The supervisors of extension field-workers also attend training sessions, in addition to spending at least eight days every two weeks in the field. At every level, contact in maintained between field work and research, concentrating the system on making the extension work deal effectively with farmers' problems. The system embodies few new ideas, by emphasizing key principles that are frequently neglected and by providing a resilient implementation system, it can have a significant impact.

Adopting the system for reforming the existing extension services is a major organisational effort. The key changes were to make the extension staff responsible only for extension work in a unified service and to put pressure on researchers to concentrate on the practical problems of the average farmer. As a result, technical recommendations are now available that can substantially increase farmers' incomes. The success of these recommendations for farming—both under irrigation and rainfed conditions—is well known and proven; a number of them are also available for improving the productivity of small farmers in the rainfed areas with minimal investment on their past, as well as for raising productivity of larger farmers.

To make its greatest impact, the system depends on all elements functioning well: extension staff need to be dedicated, capable of learning on the job, and respected; contact farmers need to be representative; research needs to provide the advice and improvements in technology and practices that are capable of increasing yields; supervisors need to monitor extension and research in the field; separate support facilities—to supply credit and inputs—must be available; and the distribution service and infrastructure must be in place to market the crops and provide the boreholes or the irrigation needed. In many areas, there are simply not the resources, either human or physical, to establish such a concentrated, inter-locking system. In these cases, it has to operate with more limited horizons to avoid the extension service losing its credibility.

**Chart 3**

**ORGANISATION PATTERN OF THE TRAINING AND VISIT SYSTEM OF AGRICULTURAL EXTENSION IN INDIA**

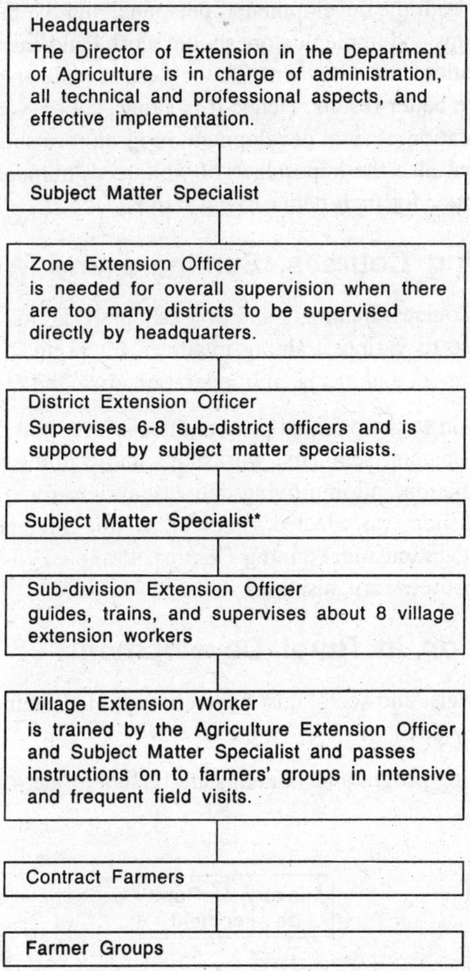


* *Subject Matter Specialists*— the link between extension work and research. They sit on technical committees at headquarters and district levels, visit research stations, and organise field trials with and train Agricultural Extension Officers and Village Extension Workers.

The difficulties shows that it had seemed perhaps deceptively simple to implement in the early days. While its main ideas are straightforward, its concentrated approach requires a radical change for extension work in most areas—in its focus on fieldwork, its procedures, and in the attitudes of staff at all levels. Once a system has been reorganized it has to be monitored and support continuously for improvements to be maintained. This can only be done by field supervision of extension work and farmers' responses by monitoring the relevance of research work, and by training sessions—all of which require substantial commitment. Nevertheless, once established, the system has tremendous scope for self-sustained improvement. Given the needs of modern agriculture, suitably adapted to each set of circumstances, it seems a logical way to ensure long-term progress.

Even though several institutes have been in operation for fulfilling the training needs of the rural development personnel and target people, there is every need to inculcate among the development officials a sort of responsibility and interest in implementing the programmes for the best of the target groups. In turn there is a dire necessity to educate the rural masses about various schemes and programmes, their utility and motivate them to accept and adopt such schemes for improving their standard of living. Even though the training to improve the skills of both the developmental personnel and the target people is a must, it is also essential that both the target groups and implementors should work hand-in-hand and with an understanding of personnel development and national development. The selfless attitude among the development personnel at field level will be sure to give better results. Hence it is suggested by various eminent scholars that the personnel involved in implementation of rural development programmes should be imparted not only technical and administrative skills but also the importance of welfare of humanity so that they could consider the human values and help the poor for their better living standard.

## Organisation of Training Courses, Seminars and Workshops (OTC)

Organisation of Training Courses, Seminars and Workshops (OTC) is a Central Sector Plan Scheme for providing financial assistance to various training institutes for organizing training courses, seminars, workshops, etc. on rural development and has been in operation since the 6th Five Year Plan.

With the increasing thrust on target-oriented programmes in the rural development and identification of specific issues in rural development, seminars, workshops and training programmes on various topics became critical for policy formulation and improving delivery system for rural development. The training programmes, seminars and workshops on selected topics under this Scheme are conducted through State Institutes of Rural Development, Extension Training Centres, Regional Institutes of Rural Development, Universities and other reputed institutes/organisations.

## Importance of Motivation in Rural Development

Through the ages, psychologist and sociologist have concentrated their attention on the question, why do people behave in the way they do?

It is expected that the training programme contents are related to the job chart of trainees to make the training meaningful and effective.

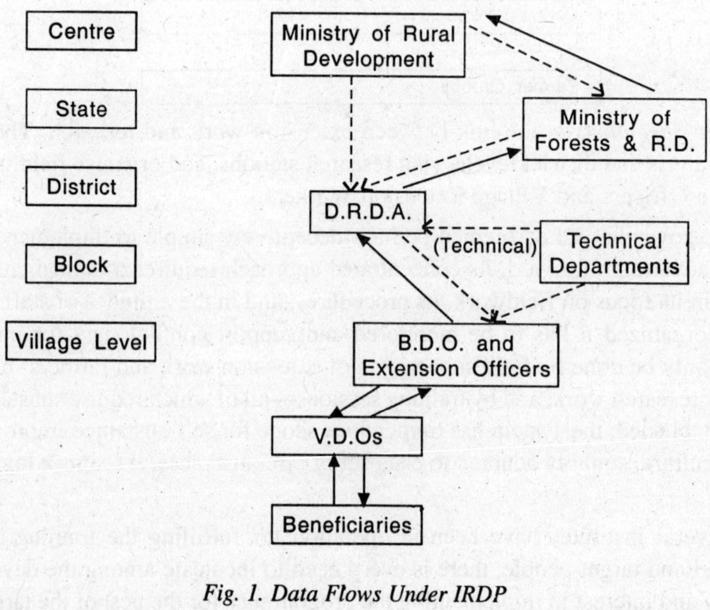


*Fig. 1. Data Flows Under IRDP*

The rural people should be motivated to participate in the development programme. They should be made to act in a certain way so that they may have the *motive* to do better for their own advancement.

## What is Motivation?

The word *motivate* means to move, to activate. Literally speaking, therefore, the motivational function of the rural worker should refer to the creation in the individual of a mental predisposition to perform the required activity and, thereafter, make him persist in it for the desired duration. Motivation, however, is internal to human beings—people are motivated by their own needs and not by others.

The programmer's function of motivation is, as such, concerned with working on these needs so as to influence behaviour in a desired or predetermined way. The findings of subsequent researches of Elton Mayo and Roethlisberger conclusively proved that work efficiency and output depended on the individual, as well as on the employees as a whole; and not wholly on the work itself or on the environment, but on several other psychological and motivational forces influenced by informal groups and by group cohesion. Later researches have further established that the employee's behaviour may not conform to the expectation of the work study forecasters mainly because the work has to be done by a human being, and the output of human energy is influenced by innumerable complex factors operating simultaneously on the system.

If a person's work *per se* adds to his or her happiness, then the job itself becomes the ultimate motivator. But for this to be so, the work must be valued and recognised as such. For the programmer/workers, this implies a continuing effort to underscore the importance of what the subordinate is doing in the overall context of the organisation. Motivation is a matter of human understanding—of the superior understanding subordinate. If and when that state is achieved, it becomes a process of encouraging people to go, as far as possible, towards meeting their aspirations—their hopes and dreams. This requires giving them an opportunity to show what they can do. Their effort must then be recognised and rewarded to the extent that this is possible within that system. This can be done by bringing home to them an awareness of the fact that their efforts do contribute to the organisation as a whole.

Motivation is not much different from friendship. A friend attempts to understand you and to help you, as far as possible, to achieve your aims. A friend is concerned about your happiness, and tries within the limits of his or her abilities to make you happy. A friend is someone who supports you and knows that he or she can count on your support in return. Above all, a friend is someone who will go out of his or her way to do things for you. The motive for this nothing more then the knowledge that you would do the same for him or her. And so it is with mutual motivation in an organisation.

There are various ways to build motivation into a job which may be found in the voluminous literature on this subject. Writings on motivation tend to suffer from professional jargon, which psychologists and management experts employ in their attempt to be explicit.

## Conclusion

Training refers to the process of increasing knowledge and skill of an employee for doing a particular job. Soon after a worker is selected and inducted into a job we may not expect full contribution from him in attaining the objective of the factory, as he is just a "raw" human resource. For ensuring satisfactory job performance, training is essential at all levels of development. Training serves not only the purpose of motivation but also as a means of developing various methods of work. The terms "training" and often synonymously used. But there is difference between the two. While training is viewed as a process by means of which the aptitudes, skills, and capabilities of an individual employee to perform a specific job are enhanced, development implies the nature and training. Several factors have contributed to the increased adoption of training and development schemes of rural development.

The vision is to focus in the coming years on training in the policies and programmes that benefit the rural poor, strive to energise the democratic decentralisation process, improve the operation and efficiency of rural development personnel, promote transfer of technology through its social laboratories and technology park and create environmental awareness.

It is obvious from the foregoing that the achievement in rural areas is contingent upon the evaluation of a national training policy, the creation of a national training infrastructure, the formulation of suitable co-ordinative mechanisms at all levels, the acceptance of manpower planning and budgeting as the basis for training programmes, the development of multiple skill courses, the acceptance of area planning approach for training institutions at district and block levels, and the participation of the people through their own organisations, especially at the cutting edge level. Unless a massive training programmes is launched at full throttle, the goal of full employment may not be achieved within the stipulated period of time.

More importantly, the government and the specialised institutions and agricultural universities are in the forefront in imparting training in varied facets of rural development. The focus of training is to improve the ability of the rural people and potential of rural areas, both land-based and otherwise, for a sustainable income generation. In doing so, effective linkages are being established between the various components such as capacity building of the poor, skill development, credit, training, technology, marketing and infrastructure. In particular, the rural areas be on sustainable development on an ongoing basis.

❑ ❑ ❑

# ANNEXURE - 1

## Important Programmes Conducted during 2007-07
## Sponsored Programmes by NIRD and NERC

Estimation of Poverty and Evaluation of Poverty Alleviation Programmes (sponsored by Central Statistical Organization, Ministry of Statistic and Programme Implementation);

Monitoring and Evaluation of the officers of the Ministries/Departments of GOI, State Govt. and UTs (sponsored by Planning Commission);

Orientation programme for Young Professionals of CAPART, Sponsored by CAPART, New Delhi;

Cultivation and Processing of Medicinal and Aromatic Plants (sponsored by National Medicinal Plant Board (Ayush) Ministry of Health and Family Welfare);

Training-cum-Exposure visits on PESA and Local Governance (sponsored by Govt. of Chattisgarh); and

Course on Holistic Approach to Watershed Management through People's Participation (sponsored by Ministry of Environment & Forest).

## Few Important National Level Training Programmes :

Management of Agriculture in Drought Prone Areas;

Training cum Exposure visits to SGSY Units;

Innovative strategies for marketing of rural products under SGSY;

Good Governance and Rural Development;

Information Technology for Management of Rural Development programmes;

Community Mobilization for Community Driven Development;

Good Governance and Social Audit;

Community Based Disaster Management;

GIS Applications in Watershed Development;

Development of Livestock enterprises under SGSY;

Implementation of NREGA through PRIs;

Planning and Management of Rural DW & S programmes;

Participatory Planning and Management of Watershed Projects;

Community Based Management of Natural Resources for poverty alleviation;

Planning and Implementation of IAY; Social Security Programmes in Rural Areas;

Planning and Implementation of Wage Employment programmes;

Computer Applications and e-Governance;

Schedule Caste Development Approaches, Strategies and Programmes; and

Integrated Planning and Management of RD programmes for District level officials.

## Few Important Sponsored International Programmes

(A) **Sponsored by Ministry of Rural Development, Government of India**

The NIRD has successfully conducted the following six NIRD-CIRDAP Collaborative Training Programmes.

Planning, Management, Monitoring and Evaluation of RD Projects in Asia-Pacific Region (PMME), organized at NIRD;

Women Empowerment and Development through Enterprise Promotion, organized at Indonesia;

Knowledge Management for Decentralization and Role of Local Government in Service Delivery and Poverty Reduction, organized at NIRD-NERC, Guwahati; and

Advocacy and Facilitation for Good NGOs in SAARC Region, organized at Nepal.

(B) Sponsored by Ministry of External Affairs, Government of India.

The NIRD has successfully conducted the following two International Training Programmes under ITEC and SCAAP of MEA, Government of India, up to December 2007 in India as against the planned seven programmes for the year 2007-08.

Rural Micro Enterprises Development.

Management of Natural Resources for Sustainable Rural Livelihoods.

## Some Important Workshops and Seminars

Gender Sensitive Policies and Programmes in Rural Development;

Planning and Sustainable Settlements for HIV/AIDS affected people;

Policy Dialogue on Functioning of SIRDs;

Women's participation in NREGA;

Development of Training Modules on Rural Drinking Water and Sanitation;

Development of Training Modules for Management of Watershed Projects (Hariyali);

Preparation of Training Modules of IAY;

One day consultation on Areas of Co-operation and Collaboration for RD policy formulation and training;

Panchayat Finances and Fiscal Decentralization to Panchayats; and

Minor Forest Produce based Forest Management for Socio-economic Development.

# ANNEXURE - 2

## Extension Activities by Banks in Rural Areas

Rural development is not only a function of economic factors but socio-psycho cultural factors, knowledge factors and physical input factors also play a dominant role in it supported by strong extension services.

Though credit is a *sine qua non* for rural development, banks should not be treated as mere lending institutions. The efforts of the bankers should also concentrate around building up awareness in the rural people to bring in the desirable changes in the attitude, knowledge and skill.

Change is a process that occurs over a period of time and consists of a series of stages like communication, knowledge, persuasion, decision and confirmation. These stages are largely influenced by a host of factors, such as personality, socio-cultural communication, extension service, etc. At any stage, the suggestion can be thrown off. Thus, an extension agent should realise that extension is a continuous process of transmitting knowledge apart from lending to a section of community and the feedback on the problems arising therefrom for further improvement.

### Objectives of extension activities

The objectives of banks' extension programmes in rural areas should depend upon the socio-economic conditions of the people in the area and need to transmit the latest developments supported by adequate credit. The main objectives should be:

*(i)* to assist people in identifying their problems and needs for the development of the individual;
*(ii)* to develop leadership among the various sectors of the rural community;
*(iii)* to keep abreast of the latest developments in technology for agriculture;
*(iv)* to change the outlook and attitude of the farming community and to educate them.

### Basic efforts

To fulfil these objectives, the extension agent should:

*(i)* develop personal contacts with local leaders and inform them of banks' myriad programmes for the rural development;
*(ii)* develop personal contacts with a group of farmers;
*(iii)* conduct group meetings and general meetings in the rural areas on the felt needs of the farmers. These meetings can be made more effective by involving scientists, etc.
*(iv)* visit farms and homes and spread banking information;
*(v)* go around the farm, after office hours when the farmers are free from farms to facilitate meetings for providing solutions to their problems;
*(vi)* casually visit the dwellings of farmers to help in identifying the needs of people like, whether aged persons are getting old age pensions or not, if not by contacting village accountant the matter may be referred to higher authorities;
*(vii)* involve in religious functions to enhance the image of the bank;
*(viii)* keep continuous contact with the village accountant, school teachers, religious heads, etc., and help in identifying the problems of the village in general;
*(ix)* look after the essentials for the villages like road construction work, health camps, etc. during off-seasons with the help of the people;
*(x)* conduct adult education programmes and educate the people about modern technology to bring about desirable changes in the behaviour of the people.

### For success

Bankers could use the following simple methods to fulfil the objectives of extension activities.

### Training and visit system

The essence of this programme can be utilised by the field level staff of banks by identifying a specific group of farmers before the season and educating them about the agricultural practices to be adopted. This should be followed up by making persistent visits to the fields.

Since this programme is already in vogue, assistance can be obtained from the extension staff of the department of agriculture in educating the farmers through film shows, demonstrations, etc. This also helps in effective supervision of agricultural credit.

### Whole farm demonstration approach

This is essentially an individual approach where on the farm of a single farmer several crop enterprises and other enterprises in an approved manner are demonstrated over a period of time by giving adequate finance. This particular approach helps in influencing other farmers.

### Problem solving approach

Designed by an Australian social scientist, under this project, a small group of farmers identify a relevant problem on their own and get motivated for urgent follow-up action which is facilitated by the extension agency. In other words, this is a technique of pre-conditioning of the farmer for action.

### Media method

The banker can approach other departments concerned like health, agriculture, horticulture and animal husbandry to exhibit some films/slides in a village to educate the farmers. This is a very easy method for good publicity of the bank among the villagers. The development departments are too willing to do this as it is a part of their extension work.

### Through opinion leaders

The programmes cannot succeed fully, unless responsible and responsive leadership emerges at the local level. The importance of non-professional leaders to reach larger number of farmers has been increasingly felt with growing demands for extension services in the agriculture sector.

Communication of the innovations to the farmers is greatly facilitated by these opinion leaders which in turn greatly influences its adoption among the farmers. Reaching every individual farming families through the professional extension workers is an uphill task as the number of extension workers is comparatively lower than the farming families. The opinion leaders, in this, context, have an important role to play.

### Extension agency vs. Opinion leaders

*(i)* Extension agency should have different communication strategies while selecting the opinion leaders and working with them to enhance diffusion of agricultural innovations.

*(ii)* Extension agency, which may prefer to use opinion leaders as their informal change agents, should look for some common characteristics of these individuals since the norms and the degree of progressiveness which prevail in the community have a certain say on the pattern of opinion leadership in the respective communities.

*(iii)* Wherever possible, the extension agency should select the opinion leaders and train them on improved agricultural technology and other spheres of rural development so that they can speedily diffuse technology information.

*(iv)* Extension agency should try to decrease the status differences between the farmers and the change agents themselves to bring about the desired changes.

*(v)* The contacts established with opinion leaders should also be used for recovery.

*(vi)* Opinion leaders could be used as a publicity tool to project various programmes of the banks in rural areas.

These methods are only illustrative. Bankers can devise their own programmes that are best suited to them and their areas. The ultimate aim of an extension worker is to reach the heterogeneous masses of farmers. As such, no single method of communication is effective for all people and in all situation. A judicious combination of various methods depending upon the local resources has to be used to get desired maximum results.

With the introduction of service area approach from the year 1989, extension agencies have a vital role to play. The success of the service area approach depends on the right tools and approach that commercial banks as an extension agent will use with the coordination of developmental departments of the government.

# ANNEXURE - 3

**List of State Technical Agencies (SATs)**

| *S.No.* | *State* | *STAs* | | |
|---|---|---|---|---|
| 1 | Andhra Pradesh | (i) | National Institute of Technology | Warrangal-506004 |
| | | (ii) | J.N.T. University, Kukatpalli | Hyderabad-500072 |
| | | (iii) | College of Engineering, Andhra University | Visakhapatnam |
| | | (iv) | University College of Engineering, Osmania University | Hyderabad-500007 |
| 2 | Arunachal Pradesh | (ii) | North-Eastern Regional Inst. of Science & Technology | Nirjuli-791109 |
| | | (ii) | Jorhat Engineering College | Jorhat-785007 |
| 3 | Assam | (i) | Indian Institute of Technology | Guwahati |
| | | (ii) | Assam Engineering College, Jalukbari | Guwahati-781013 |
| 4 | Bihar | (i) | National Institute of Technology | Patna University, Patna-800005 |
| | | (ii) | Muzaffarpur Institute of Technology | Muzaffarpur-842003 |
| | | (iii) | Bhagalpur College of Engineering | Bhagalpur-813210 |
| 5 | Chattisgarh | | National Institute of Technology, GE Road | Raipur-492010 |
| 6 | Goa | | College of Engg. | Farmagudi-403401 |
| 7 | Gujarat | | National Institute of Technology | Ichcharath, Surat-395007 |
| 8 | Haryana | | National Institute of Technology | Kurukshetra-136119 |
| 9 | Himachal Pradesh | | National Institute of Technology | Hamirpur-177005 |
| 10 | Jammu & Kashmir | (i) | NIT Srinagar-190006 | Srinagar, J & K |
| | | (ii) | Govt. College of Engineering & Technology | Jammu, Jammu-Tawai-180001 |
| 11 | Jharkhand | (i) | Birla Institute of Technology | Mesra-835215 (Ranchi) |
| | | (ii) | National Institute of Technology, Jamshedpur | P.O.-R.T.I. Jamshedpur Pin Code-831014 |
| 12 | Karnataka | (i) | Bangalore University | Bangalore-560056 |
| | | (ii) | National Institute of Technology, Surathkal | P.O. Srinvasnagar, Mangalore-575025 |
| | | (iii) | P.D.A. College of Engineering, Gulbarga | Aiwan-E-Shahi, Station Area, Gulbarga |
| | | (iv) | IR Rasta, Road Institute | Bangalore-560058, Karnataka |
| 13 | Kerala | (i) | College of Engineering | Trivandrum-695016 |
| | | (ii) | National Institute of Technology, Calicut | Kerala. |
| 14 | Madhya Pradesh | (i) | Maulana Azad National Institute of Technology | Bhopal-462007 |
| | | (ii) | Govt. Engineering College | Jabalpur-482011 |
| | | (iii) | SGS Institute of Technology & Sciences | Indore |

| | | | | |
|---|---|---|---|---|
| 15 | Maharashtra | (i) | Visvesvaraya National Institute of Technology | South Ambazariwad, Nagpur-440011 |
| | | (ii) | Indian Institute of Technology | Powai, Mumbai |
| | | (iii) | Govt. College of Engineering, Aurangabad | Aurangabad-431005 |
| | | (iv) | Govt. College of Engineering, Shivajinagar | Pune-05 |
| 16 | Manipur | | National Institute of Technology | Silchar-788010 |
| 17 | Meghalaya | | Indian Institute of Technology | Guwahati |
| 18 | Mizoram | | Indian Institute of Technology | Kharagpur-721303 |
| 19 | Nagaland | | Jorhat Engineering College | Jorhat-785007 |
| 20 | Orissa | (i) | National Institute of Technology | Rourkela-769008 |
| | | (ii) | College of Engg. & Technology | Bhubaneshwar Burla |
| | | (iii) | University College of Engineering | Sarang-759146 |
| | | (iv) | Indira Gandhi Institute of Technology, Sarang | Dist-Dhenkanal (Orissa) |
| 21 | Punjab | (i) | Punjab Engineering College | Sector-12, Chandigarh-160012 |
| | | (ii) | Giani Zail Singh College of Engg. & Tech. | Dabwali Road, Bhatinda-151001 |
| | | (iii) | Thapar Institute of Engineering & Tech. | Patiala-147004 |
| 22 | Rajasthan | (i) | Malaviya National Institute of Technology | Jaipur-302017 |
| | | (ii) | MBM Engineering College | Jodhpur-342011 |
| | | (iii) | University College of Engineering, Rajasthan Technical University | Kota-324010 |
| 23 | Sikkim | | Govt. Engineering College | Jalpaiguri-735102 |
| 24 | Tamil Nadu | | National Institute of Technology | Tiruchirapalli-620015 |
| 25 | Tripura | | National Institute of Technology | Agartala-799055 |
| 26 | Uttar Pradesh | (i) | MNNIT Engineering College | Allahabad-211004 |
| | | (ii) | Indian Institute of Technology | Roorkee-247667 |
| | | (iii) | Kamla Nehru Institute of Technology | Sultanpur-228118 |
| | | (iv) | Hurcourt Butler Technological Institute | Kanpur Sitapur Road, Lucknow-226021 |
| | | (v) | Institute of Engineering & Technology | Varanasi-221005 |
| | | (vi) | Institute of Technology, Banaras Hindu University | |
| 27 | Uttaranchal | | Indian Institute of Technology | Roorkee-247667 |
| 28 | West Bengal | (i) | Indian Institute of Technology | Kharagpur-721302 |
| | | (ii) | Govt. Engineering College | Jalpaiguri-735102 |
| | | (iii) | Bengal Engineering and Science University, Shibpur | Howrah-711103 |
| | | (iv) | Jadavpur University | S.C. Mallik Road, Kolkata-700032 |

# ANNEXURE - 4

**List of Principal Technical Agencies (PTAs) & States allotted to them**

| *Sl.No.* | *Name of the PTA* | *States Covered* |
|---|---|---|
| 1. | Central Road Research Institute (CRRI), New Delhi | Union Territories |
| 2. | Indian Institute of Technology, Roorkee | Uttranchal, Uttar Pradesh, Bihar and Jharkhand |
| 3. | Indian Institute of Technology, Mumbai | Maharashtra, Gujarat and Madhya Pradesh |
| 4. | National Institute of Technology, Warangal | Andhra Pradesh, Orissa and Chhattisgarh |
| 5. | Birla Institute of Technology and Science, Pilani | Rajasthan, Punjab, Haryana, Jammu & Kashmir & Himachal Pradesh |
| 6. | College of Engineering, Bangalore University, Bangalore | Karnataka, Tamil Nadu, Kerala and Goa |
| 7. | Indian Institute of Technology, Kharagpur | North Eastern States of Assam, Arunachal Pradesh, Manipur, Mizoram, Meghalaya, Nagaland, Sikkim, Tripura and West Bengal. |

❑ ❑ ❑

*"Over 70 per cent of our people live in villages. India is poor because the villages of India are poor. India will be rich if the villages of India are rich. Therefore the basic problem of India is to remove the poverty from the Indian villages. Some years ago we abolished the zamindari and the jagirdari systems in various parts of India, because the villages of India could not prosper under a semi-feudal system of land ownership. This is not enough. We have to go ahead further... Panchayats should be given greater power. For we want the villager to have a measure of real swaraj in his own village. He should have power and not have to refer everything to big officials. We do not want the officials to interfere too much in the life of the village. We want to build swaraj right from the village up."*

***— Jawaharlal Nehru***

*"The Panchayat is the executive body of Gram Sabha to provide civic facilities to the people in its jurisdiction. Indian independence must begin at the bottom. Thus, every village will be a republic or Panchayat having full powers."*

***— Mahatma Gandhi***

# Chapter 39

# PANCHAYATS FOR RURAL DEVELOPMENT

## Introduction

Panchayats have been the backbone of the Indian villages since the beginning of recorded history. Gandhiji, the father of the nation, in 1946 had aptly remarked that the Indian Independence must begin at the bottom and every village ought to be a Republic or Panchayat having powers. Gandhiji's dream has been translated into reality with the introduction of the three-tier Panchayati Raj system to enlist people's participation in rural reconstruction. In the 21st century village panchayats in India will be in the forefront of rural development. Towards this end, panchayats are to be given more powers, finance and training. Panchayats will strive for pro-poor sustainable economic growth, social development, and facilitate good governance as well as sound macro-economic management.

## Grass-root Unit

Village is a basic unit of our Indian society. Crores of people live in 5,79,132 villages. The concept of rural development emphasises on development of these villages, people living in these villages. The process of development should, therefore, originate in villages. Instead for the last three hundred years the administration has been concentrated. The cry for decentralisation appears to respond both to organisational needs within the district and the demands of emerging linkages with the dynamics of the development.

The "panchayat" or the institution of the village council is as old as India's history and is a part of her tradition. The ancient panchayats, serving as units of local government, discharged most of the functions that affected the life of the village community. These institutions flourished in relative isolation and were unaffected by the social and political changes that took place in the urban India up to the 18th century. Dr. Altekar gives us a detailed account of village communities in India and of the working of rural communities. He states: "Since early times, the villages has been the pivot of administration in India.... There is no doubt that villages were the real centres of social life and important units of the country's economy. They sustained the edifice of national culture, prosperity and administration." Rural development will be more meaningful when the village agency assumes responsibility and initiative for developing the resources of the village. Only a village organisation representing the community as a whole can provide the necessary leadership.

*An all-woman panchayat meeting*

## The Concept

The concept of panchayats was a part of the philosophy of 'Purna Swaraj' and 'Gram Swaraj'. Mahatma Gandhi and Jawaharlal Nehru breathed into those concepts an inexorable and practical patriotic impetus during the era of India's struggle for independence. Indeed, at the time of framing our Constitution, the concept of village panchayats was not a remote and hoary historical concept. It was a part of the legacy of India's struggle for freedom and its quest for its own traditions and identity.

The Constitution of India was enacted, adopted and proclaimed in the name of the people of India as an organic document of democratic self-government as a rule of law. It enshrines for democratic faith and resolve of the resurgent people of India committed to the philosophy of "Swaraj" not only in the sense of emancipation from the colonial yoke of an alien imperial power but in the sense of self-government and the protection of the fundamental rights and dignity of the individual as a way of life and social habit. The fabric of our constitutional philosophy is woven with the warp and weft of democracy and rule of law.

The Constitution of India provides for republican democracy at the national level in the form of its bicameral Parliament and by making the Council of Ministers collectively responsible to the House of the People. The same basic pattern of parliamentary institutions is replicated at the level of states which form the Union of India. The quasi-federal framework of India's parliamentary democracy, the creation o Panchayati Raj institutions and their organisation was, however left to a general directive embodied in Articl 40 of the Constitution in the following terms:

## Objective

The primary objective of Panchayati Raj is to strengthen the base of democracy at the grassroots, o one hand, and hand over the powers as well as responsibilities to the people, on the other, so as to allov them to manage their affairs in the best possible manner. And, also to enable the people of each village t achieve intensive and continuous development in the interests of the entire population, irrespective of caste class, creed or religion. The Panchayati Raj, basically, different from all other facets of government, is process that involves the Government as a whole. It is not an administrative arm of the government but part of the whole government. Its great potentialities lie in the fact that, under the guidance and supervisio of the State Governments, the final responsibility for carrying out rural development will fall more and mor on the people themselves through their elected local representatives. The greatest stress and attention must therefore, be put on the village panchayats and gram sabhas, periodic elections, evaluation and proper loca planning.

Democratic decentralisation is not merely a devolution of powers. It must also comprise a devolutio of responsibility. The first is financial discipline. The second is of protecting and safeguarding the interest of the weaker sections of the society: the Scheduled Castes and Scheduled Tribes, the minorities, the poor women and other disadvantaged or potentially disadvantaged sections of society.

## Organisation of Village Panchayats

"The states shall take steps to organised village panchayats and endow them with such powers an authority as may be necessary to enable them to function as units of self government."

The true potential of Article 40 lies not merely in its directive to the Indian State at all levels as a par of constitutionally formulated Principles of State Policy to organise village panchayats but in its significan concomitant mandate that panchayats should be endowed with "such powers and authority as may b necessary to enable them to function as units of self-government." The message of that mandate is clear an the tryst of the founding fathers of the Constitution would remain incomplete unless village panchayats begi to function as units of self-government as a part of our democratic policy. An attempt to conceptualise th framework of panchayat institutions is to take its inspiration from the constitutional mandate to complet that unfinished task. The theological emphasis of that constitutional mandate is structural, operational an functional with its implicit ramifications for our democracy and development, for freedom and welfare, an for justice, liberty, equality, individual dignity, national unity and Indian people's fraternity as integrall correlated concepts.

*Objective*

## Participatory Development

Participation is a powerful tool for building capacity and creating ownership of projects. Respect, patience, and perseverance can lead to more effective, equitable, and sustainable impacts. Participatory development is a unique process for rebuilding rural areas as well as reducing poverty. It is committed to engaging stakeholders—both citizens and institutions—in participatory decision-making processes so they can influence and share control over development initiatives and the resources involved in these. This requires time, resources, appropriate incentives, and careful, respectful listening. It supports poverty reduction by creating more effective, equitable, and sustainable activities.

People develop a sense of ownership, pride, and commitment to an activity when they work together to assess their resources and problems, reflect on possible solutions, select criteria for evaluating various options, choose the best course of action, and then formulate and act on plans for initiating, managing, monitoring, and evaluating a shared project, program, or policy change.

Poor and vulnerable citizens discover hope and feel empowered when they are given a voice in decisions that affect their lives. Members of government, civil society, and private sector organisations build trust and gain capacity as they learn through shared experience. Donors and other international organisations co-ordinate better when they discuss planned activities openly.

By building and enriching social networks, participatory development enhances social capital, the most fundamental resource on which the poor, like everyone, rely for survival and mobility in the face of adversity or limited opportunity.

Inclusion of diverse stakeholder groups supports human rights, promotes gender equity, and helps with equalizing opportunity for indigenous peoples and members of minority groups.

Participation thus enhances the quality and effectiveness of development efforts, improves operation and maintenance, and promotes sustainability of outputs and impacts. In the long run, it also reduces delays during project implementation and averts legal problems by facilitating communication and addressing potential conflict before misunderstanding becomes counterproductive.

As an approach to the process of public decision making, participation requires planning for each specific situation. Involvement of key stakeholders in these preparatory steps may significantly increase learning and country ownership. Stakeholder interests and capacities, the national and institutional context, social conditions, the extent and quality of networks, and features of the relevant sector must all be analyzed in each case. This will help in determining an appropriate strategy for disseminating information about the proposed activities, eliciting views of relevant groups, and engaging stakeholders more deeply in analysis and planning, and later in implementation and monitoring of activities.

## Integrated Vision of Democracy

The National Parliament and the Central Government, the State Legislatures and the State Governments and the whole pyramid of our judicial system are important to the working of democracy and the maintenance of the rule of law. In their own respective spheres, these legislative infrastructure play a complementary role in upholding democratic process and form the core of integrated vision of democracy. However, to the common India villager, they do not represent a preoccupying part of his daily life. The revolution in communication technology does often enough lift and transport him audio-visually to the ambiance of these institutions but he cannot quite relate to them in terms of his daily needs and everyday concern.

"Our democracy cannot be strong unless democracy in the villages is strong. We cannot have real development in the country unless the panchayats are made responsible for development in the villages, and the people who live in the villages are involved in their own development."

Self government may mean to him only the spectacular occasion when he exercises his franchise; but his participation in the electoral process for the Lok Sabha and the Vidhan Sabha cannot give him a sense of full and meaningful participation in the democratic responsibility for being a citizen in the democratic republic of India. There are gaps and anomalies in the democratic experience of the Indian citizen, particularly in the countryside. Panchayati Raj institutions in our rural areas and municipal bodies in our urban areas represent, first and foremost the possibility of a truly dependable and durable institutional assurance of overcoming those distances and gaps. Without local units of self-government, we cannot hope to establish a viable and vibrant democracy. It is in its perspective that rural and urban development are, in effect, two sides of the same coin and are parts of a composite continuum of what may be called democratic urbanisation. Self-government necessarily subsumes and supplements developments in all its ramifications in rural as well as urban contexts. It is with an integrated vision that they have to be reviewed, restructured, reclaimed, renewed and revitalised.

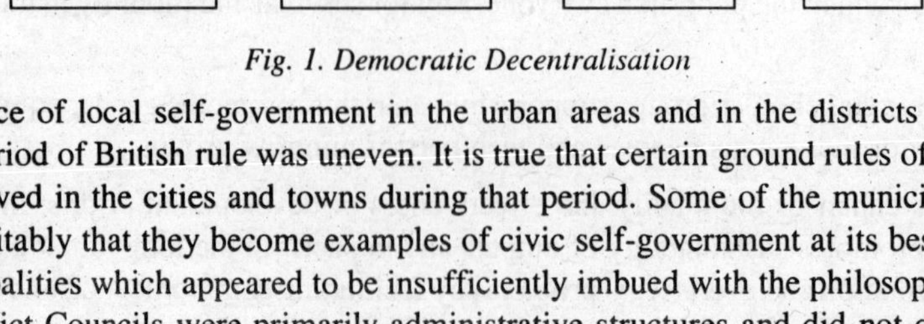


*Fig. 1. Democratic Decentralisation*

The experience of local self-government in the urban areas and in the districts in different parts of India during the period of British rule was uneven. It is true that certain ground rules of municipal self-government were evolved in the cities and towns during that period. Some of the municipal bodies acquitted themselves so creditably that they become examples of civic self-government at its best. There were, however, other municipalities which appeared to be insufficiently imbued with the philosophy of local self-government. The District Councils were primarily administrative structures and did not quite come into their own. One of the obvious reasons was that the country was dominated by colonial administration and its pre-emotive imperatives. In the countryside, panchayats were quite often caste institutions with a pivotal social role but they did not function as institutions of State and instruments of self-government and social change.

The constitutional vision of republican self-government at the village level enshrined in Article 40 came to be unfolded a few years after the commencement of our Constitution when it become increasingly self-evident that community development and socio-economic transformation could not be achieved without democratic participation. This compelling and inescapable realisation of the limitations of the bureaucratic models led to an enthusiastic interest in Panchayati Raj institutions which was enlivened by generous impulses.

The Community Development Programme was launched in 1952. The blocks came to be established as units of development administration. The National Extension Service was established soon thereafter with a view to reinforce the administrative network to tackle the problems of growth and development at different local and functional levels. At that stage there was, relatively speaking, only nominal public interest. Soon, lack of public involvement and participation began to be perceived as an impediment in the successful implementation of the Community Development and National Extension Service Programmes. Based on that perception, the Second Plan document recognised the necessity for speeding up the development of democratic institutions and concluded that "unless there is a comprehensive village planning, which takes into account the needs of the entire community, weaker sections like tenant-cultivators, landless workers and artisans may not benefit sufficiently from assistance provided by the Government." Referring to the aim of the National Extension Movement to reach every family in the village, the Second Five Year Plan reported that in order to fulfil that aim it was necessary to have "an agency in the village which represents the community as a whole and can assume responsibility and initiative for developing the resources of the village and providing the necessary leadership. Indeed, rural progress depends entirely on the existence of an active organisation of the weaker sections mentioned above into common programmes to be carried out with the assistance of the administration." The thinking underlying the Second Plan was that village panchayats along with co-operatives could play a considerable part in bringing about a more just and integrated social structure in rural areas. The thrust of the Second Five Year Plan was to establish statutory panchayats in all the villages though more as vehicles for national extension and community development projects and not so much as units of self-government. It was primarily from this angle that the number of panchayats was to be more than doubled by 1960-61.

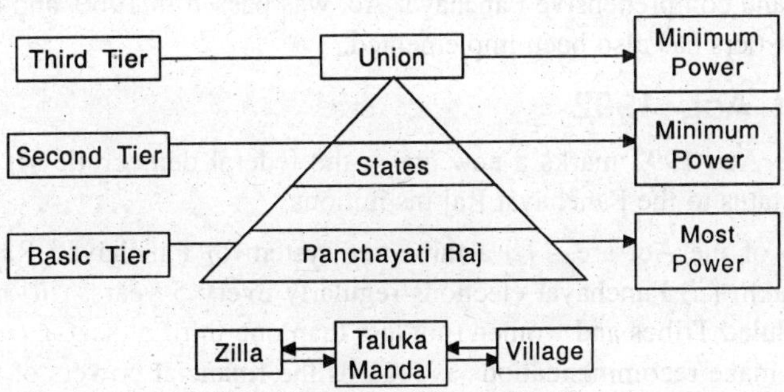


*Fig. 2. Ties of Administration*

## Ascent on Panchayati Raj Momentum

The Balwantray Mehta Team was appointed in January, 1957 to study and report on the Community Development Projects and National Extension Service with a view to "economy and efficiency" and, among others "for the assessment of the extent to which the movement has succeeded in utilising local initiative and in creating institutions to ensure continuity in the process of improving economic and social conditions in rural areas." Once again the approach was primarily to achieve economy and efficiency. The Balwantray Mehta Team, however, found that "Development cannot progress without responsibility and power. Community development can be real only when the community understands its problems realises its responsibilities, exercise the necessary powers through its chosen representatives and maintains a constant and intelligent vigilance on local administration." It was with this objective that the team recommended an early establishment of statutory elective local bodies and devolution to them of the necessary resources, powers and authority.

The recommendations of the Balwantray Mehta Study Team came as a fresh breeze and gave a new lease to community development and extension service projects. It paved the way for a new era of Panchayati Raj institutions which was inaugurated by Pandit Jawaharlal Nehru on 2nd October, 1959 at a national rally at Nagpur.

Pandit Jawaharlal Nehru described the new beginning as "the most revolutionary and historical step in the context of new India." In a sense, it was an act of faith in republican democracy and was as important an event as the establishment of the parliamentary system itself for the people of India and by the people of India. The idea rode on the crest of the new wave of public enthusiasm which had found a sense of direction and an institutional habitat. The spirited launching of Panchayat Raj institutions at Nagpur seemed to capture the public imagination. That memorable rally aroused high hopes and great expectations. The idea was not meant to be a mere counsel of convenience or as a design of an auxiliary system of development administration. Indeed, the momentum of that momentous change was lost and the Panchayati Raj institutions began to decline when their status and role as units of self-government were eclipsed by a combination of several factors of decadence and disarray. When the base premise of Panchayati Raj institutions as units of self-government was lost, these institutions also lost their capability to fulfil the promise of development.

## Panchayati Raj Legislation

All the states have accordingly established Panchayati Raj. The necessary legislation has been passed an implemented in the States of Andhra Pradesh, Assam, Tamil Nadu, Maharashtra, Karnataka, Orissa, Punjab, Rajasthan and Uttar Pradesh. Legislation for this purpose has also been passed in the states of Bihar, Gujarat and Madhya Pradesh and has been implemented. In West Bengal, the West Bengal Panchayat Act, 1956, is in force, and legislation for the setting up of bodies at the block and district levels has been undertaken. In Kerala, a new and comprehensive Panchayat Act was passed in 1960, and has been implemented. Legislation for the upper tiers has also been implemented.

## 73rd Amendment Act, 1992

The passage of the Act, 1992 marks a new era in the federal democratic set up of the country and provides constitutional status to the Panchayat Raj institutions.

The main features of the Act are – *(i)* a three-tier system of Panchayati Raj for all States having population of over 20 lakh; *(ii)* Panchayat elections regularly every 5 years; *(iii)* reservation of seats for Scheduled Castes, Scheduled Tribes and women (not less than one-third of seats); *(iv)* appointment of State Finance Commission to make recommendations as regards the financial powers of the Panchayats and *(v)* constitution of District Planning Committees to prepare development plans for the district as a whole. As per the Constitution (73rd Amendment) Act, the Panchayati Raj Institutions have been endowed with such powers and authority as may be necessary to function as institutions of self-government and contains provisions of devolution of powers and responsibilities upon Panchayats at the appropriate level with reference to *(a)* the preparation of plans for economic development and social justice; and *(b)* the implementation of such schemes for economic development and social justice as may be entrusted to them.

## Origin and Coverage

Panchayati Raj was introduced in 1959 as a three-tier structure of self-government at the village, block and district levels.

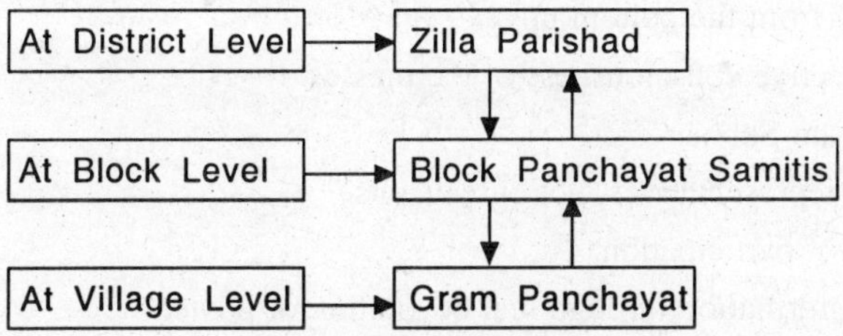


*Fig. 3. Structure of Panchayats*

There are today 2,32,278 village panchayats in the country covering over 96% of about 5.79 lakhs inhabited villages and 92% of the rural population of our country. There are about 6,022 panchayat samitis of different nomenclature at the block, taluka or tahsil level; each panchayati samiti or mandal panchayat has on a average 60 village panchayats covering an average population of about 65,000. There are 535 Zilla Parishads in the country; each Zilla Parishad has on an average 13 to 14 Panchayati Samitis and about 826 Gram Panchayats covering population of 9-10 lakhs on an average. These Panchayats are being manned by about 29.2 lakh elected representatives of Panchayats at all levels.

**Box 1**

Towards realizing the vision of Mahatma Gandhi of every village being a republic through three-tier system of Panchayati Raj.

2,32,278 Panchayats at village level; 6,022 Panchayats at intermediate level and 535 Panchayats at district level manned by about 29.2 lakh elected representatives, the broadest representative base that exists in any country.

Panchayati Raj Institutions (PRIs) empowered to function as institutions of self government and to prepare plans for economic development and social justice and their empowerment. Panchayati Raj Institutions constitute the bedrock for the implementation of most of Rural Development Programmes.

Strengthening of Gram Sabha as a vibrant forum of decentralized democracy and effective instrument for ensuring social audit.

## THE PHILOSOPHY OF PANCHAYATI RAJ

Panchayati Raj philosophy is based on the conviction that the paramount need of the rural people is real power devolution, when the elected representatives of the people, not the bureaucrats, administer (control the government) at the grassroots level, *i.e.*, the district level and below. The way to develop them is through Panchayati Raj by releasing their potential powers for personal, economic, social and civic growth and ensure social justice. Towards this end, all aspects of administration, including law and order, should be entrusted to panchayats, the real elected representatives. It is of the utmost importance to actually bring all the subjects, including revenue and resources, under the district, block and village level governments, with a view to bringing about a real change in rural India. The guiding principles of Panchayati Raj are embodied in the credo of Panchayati Raj.

## Credo of Panchayati Raj

- Give Power to the People.
- Power is about people's participation.
- Build democracy from the bottom up.
- Awaken the collective consciousness of the masses.
- Start with the Gram Sabha.
- Through elected representatives, not bureaucrats.
- Give the feeling of participation.
- Bring about transformation through real devolution of power.
- Teach by showing, learn by doing.
- Plan with the people's consensus.
- Work with the people in co-operation.
- Motivate people to strive for their own good.
- Approach with humility and a measure of faith.
- Lead the people to achieve their goals.
- Not a showcase but a pattern.
- Not coercion but consensus.
- Not order but participation.
- Not rule but representation.
- Not relief but realising their potential power.
- Not to conform but to transform.
- Not a piecemeal but integrated approach.

**Table 1**
**PANCHAYATI RAJ : ADVANTAGES AND DISADVANTAGES**

| *Advantages* | *Disadvantages* |
|---|---|
| **A. POLITICAL** | |
| 1. Hands over power and responsibility to the people. | 1. In the present context, the powerful misuse of power. |
| 2. Ensures furthering of democratic institutions at the district, block and village levels. | 2. Since the panchayats are dominated by economically and socially privileged sections of society, they have facilitated the emergence of oligarchic forces which do not carry benefits to the weaker sections. |
| 3. Facilitates people's participation in all the activities of the village. | 3. Has become a seed bed for political factionalism and disputes. |
| 4. Ushers in democracy in villages. | 4. Criminalisation of politics diminishes the utility of democracy. |
| 5. The Gram Sabha of a village or a group of villages, Block/Mandal becomes a fundamental unit of democracy. | 5. They make an average villager more conscious of his rights rather than of his duties. |
| 6. The distribution of power enables the villagers to plan for their own development. | 6. Political immaturity of the people dilutes political advantages. |
| 7. Develops political consciousness at the grassroot level and fosters real democracy in the country. | 7. Though the elections to the panchayats are held regularly, they may be accompanied by tension and violence. |

| B. ADMINISTRATIVELY | |
|---|---|
| 1. Village panchayats as units of, self-government can impart speed and substance to the planning process. | 1. A village is no longer the basic unit of administration. There is a shift towards a larger size for effective services. |
| 2. Makes micro level planning more meaningful. | 2. Further, to be viable economically, it should cover a larger number of families. |
| 3. Ensures the most effective use of the country's resources for development | 3. Inter-village planning will be more meaningful with a bigger unit. |
| 4. Bridges the gulf between the bureaucratic elite and the people. | 4. Non-availability of trained persons hampers administration. |
| 5. Enables elected representatives to control the government and ensures people's participation in all rural activities. | 5. The administration cannot be effective. |
| 6. Brings in administrative autonomy and rebuilds an adequate administrative structure. | 6. It increases the influence of manipulation and power-brokers. |
| **C. SOCIO-CULTURALLY** | |
| 1. Generates a new leadership, which is relatively young in age, modernistic and pro-social change in outlook. | 1. It creates division in the villages either caste-wise or class-wise or both. |
| 2. Youths, women and others get greater opportunity to participate in the village programmes. | 2. Corruption erupts and covers various segments of society. |
| 3. It will be a good training programme for the youth. | 3. Exploitation and favourtism increase. |
| 4. Fillip to art, stage and other cultural activities. | 4. The value systems get diluted. |
| 5. More opportunities to widen their vision with the increase in literacy and health programmes. | 5. Criminal activity and rule-of-the-thumb take a front seat. |
| 6. Brings in greater awareness of collective consciousness and will. | 6. The oppressed people get disillusioned. |
| 7. Brings about the necessary social change in the people. | 7. Centralisation of power with the elite does not bring about any change. |
| **D. DEVELOPMENTAL** | |
| 1. It helps rural people to cultivate a developmental psyche. | 1. The nexus of middlemen, corrupt officials and politicians blocks the implementation of development programmes. |
| 2. Micro level planning will be more meaningful. | 2. It results in widespread disparity in rural areas. |
| 3. In planned programmes, people's participation with increase. | 3. Malfunctioning of administration inhibits people's participation. |
| 4. People's participation will control population growth, increase productivity and promote family welfare. | 4. Planning will result in chaos. Everyone shows higher expenses and lower resources. |
| 5. Integrated development will reduce poverty and unemployment. | 5. Exploitation of scarce resources for private enrichment by a few increases. |
| 6. Panchayati Raj will be in a better position to tap local resources. | 6. There may be greater wastage of scarce resources for lack of better co-ordination. |
| 7. The schemes executed by panchayats cost significantly less than technically similar schemes executed by following conventional procedures. | 7. Panchayats are riven by caste and class antagonisms and the rural gentry will resist any equitable sharing of forest or grazing land and thus rendering the management of resources difficult. |

## Structure

A review of the present position of Panchayati Raj in the states shows a similarity in the basic institutional structure. In many States, there is the Gram Sabha, consisting of all adult residents. It discusses the annual budget of the panchayat, the administration report and the development works to be undertaken in its area. But, in all the states, panchayat is the basic unit of local government. The structure of Panchayati Raj institutions varies from state to state. In 14 states/UTs, the three tier system exists while 4 states have two-tier and 9 states/UT one tier. In Nagaland, Meghalaya, Mizoram, and Lakshadweep, Panchayati Raj institutions are established in accordance with the traditions and customs of their villages.

A Gram or Village Panchayat is a statutory body covering one or more villages with an average population varying between 1,000 to 3,000 people, and an average area of about six square miles. It is a body of elected representatives. The number of members varies from 5 to 31, but is 15 on the average. The Village Panchayat area is generally divided into wards, each ward returning its representative to the panchayat. In Assam and the Punjab, the entire village electorate elects all its members at one time. Reservation for women and for scheduled castes and scheduled tribes is provided for in most states. The members of panchayats are elected by a secret ballot in most states, while election by show of hands obtains in Assam, Jammu & Kashmir, parts of Madhya Pradesh, Uttar Pradesh and Himachal Pradesh. The Sarpanch {President} and Upasarpanch (Vice President) are generally chosen by the panchas (members) from among themselves. The direct election of the Sarpanch is prescribed in Assam, Bihar, parts of Madhya Pradesh, the Punjab. Rajasthan, Uttar Pradesh and Himachal Pradesh. His term of office is five years in Kerala, Tamil Nadu and Uttar Pradesh, four years in Gujarat, Jammu & Kashmir, Maharashtra, Karnataka, Orissa and West Bengal. and three years in others states.

**Table 2**
**VARIOUS TIERS OF PANCHAYATI RAJ SYSTEM (STATE-WISE)**

| States/UTs having Traditional Councils of Village Elders | State/UTs/having Only one Tier System | States/UTs having Two Tier System | States/UTs having Three Tier System |
|---|---|---|---|
| 1 | 2 | 3 | 4 |
| 1. Meghalaya | 1. Jammu & Kashmir | 1. Assam | 1. Andhra Pradesh |
| 2. Nagaland | 2. Kerala | 2. Haryana | 2. Bihar |
| 3. Lakshadweep | 3. Tripura | 3. Orissa | 3. Gujarat |
| 4. Mizoram | 4. Andaman & Nicobar | 4. Manipur | 4. Himachal Pradesh |
| | 5. Sikkim | | 5. Karnataka |
| | 6. Goa, Daman & Diu | | 6. Madhya Pradesh |
| | 7. Dadra & Nagar Haveli | | 7. Maharashtra |
| | 8. Pondicherry (Only at block level) | | 8. Punjab |
| | | | 9. Rajasthan |
| | 9. Delhi | | 10. Tamil Nadu |
| | | | 11. Uttar Pradesh |
| | | | 12. West Bengal |
| | | | 13. Chandigarh |
| | | | 14. Arunachal Pradesh |

## Panchayat Samiti

The next tier in Panchayati Raj is the Panchayat Samiti. It is called Anchalik Panchayat in Assam, Panchayat Union Council in Tamil Nadu, Taluka Development Board in Karnataka, Kshetra Samiti in Uttar

Pradesh, and Anchalik Parishad in West Bengal. The Panchayat Samiti is normally co-terminus with a community development block. In Karnataka, it comprises the taluka; in Maharashtra, some samitis cover two or three blocks. In West Bengal, there is an intermediary stage, called Anchal Panchayat, between the Panchayat and the Anchalik Parishad. The Anchal Panchayat corresponds to the former Union Board and has been allowed to continue in view of its historical associations. It is the Anchal and not the Village Panchayat that has taxation powers. The Anchal Panchayat takes care of the safety and protection of the area by appointing Dafedars and Chowkidars, while the development and civic activities are assigned to the Gram Panchayat.

Panchayat Samitis in most cases are indirectly elected bodies, the Sarpanchs of the constituent panchayats being its member. In Karnataka, the members are directly elected; and in the new Act of Madhya Pradesh, electoral colleges of panchas are provided to elect members of Janpanda Sabhas. There is a provision for co-option of, or reservation for, women, scheduled castes and scheduled tribes and for special interests, such as co-operative societies and banks. The MLAs and MPs representing the constituencies, of which the Panchayat Samitis form part, are ex-officio members, generally without voting rights. The term of the Panchayat Samiti is concurrent with that of the Panchayat. Its President and Vice-President are selected from among the elected members. There are, however, slight variations in Assam, Madras, Maharashtra and the Punjab. In Assam, the election of the Anchalik Panchayats is direct; but an organic link with the Panchayat is established by making the elected members ex-officio members of the panchayats. In Tamil Nadu and the Punjab, every panchayat has to elect from among its members it representatives on the Panchayat Samiti. Orissa provides for one of the panchas to be elected to serve on the Panchayat Samiti in addition to the Sarpanch. In Maharashtra, the councillors of the Zilla Parishad directly elected from the division in a block area become ex-officio members of the Panchayat Samiti.

## Zilla Parishad

The highest tier is the Zilla Parishad, the jurisdiction of which generally extends over a district. In Assam, however, this generally corresponds to a sub-division, while, in Tamil Nadu, 13 districts have been demarcated into 21 development districts for this purpose. As in the case of the Panchayat Samiti, the members of the Zilla Parishad are generally in directly elected, with the Presidents of Panchayat Samitis, local MLAs and MPs as members. Provision is made for the co-option of women, scheduled castes and scheduled tribes and special interests, such as co-operative banks and societies and persons interested in rural development. MLA and MPs have no voting rights in Orissa and the Punjab. In Gujarat, the Punjab and Uttar Pradesh, additional members of the Panchayat Samiti are elected to serve on the Zilla Parishad. The only exception is Maharashtra, where a pre-determined number of councillors is directly elected from the electoral divisions in the district; but an organic link is established with the Panchayat Samiti by making the councillors members of the corresponding Panchayat Samitis. The term of office of the Zilla Parishad and that of the Panchayat Samitis is the same.

Though there are variations from state to state, the functions entrusted to panchayats include: (1) Village roads, (2) Community wells, (3) Maintenance of Public Parks, (4) Construction and maintenance of tanks and small irrigation works, public hygiene, drainage and other civic amenities.

In some states, PRIs have also been responsible for: (1) Primary education, (2) Rural industries, (3) Primary health care and medical relief, (4) Women and child welfare, (5) Maintenance of common grazing grounds and other community lands and properties, (6) Providing of inputs for agricultural production etc.

## Eleventh Schedule

The functions included in the Eleventh Schedule (Article 243 E) are as follows:

(1) Agriculture, including agricultural extension. (2) Land improvement and soil conservation. (3) Minor irrigation, water management and watershed development. (4) Animal husbandry, dairying and

poultry. (5) Fisheries. (6) Social forestry and farm forestry. (7) Minor forest produce. (8) Small-scale industries, including food processing industries. (9) Khadi, village and cottage industries. (10) Rural housing. (11) Drinking water. (12) Fuel and fodder. (13) Roads, culverts, bridges, ferries, waterways and other means of communication. (14) Rural electrification, including distribution of electricity. (15) Non-conventional energy sources. (16) Poverty-alleviation programmes. (17) Education, including primary and secondary schools. (18) Technical training and vocational education. (19) Adult and non-formal education. (20) Libraries. (21) Cultural activities. (22) Markets and fairs. (23) Health and sanitation, including hospitals, primary health centres and dispensaries. (24) Family welfare. (25) Women and child development. (26) Social welfare, including welfare of the handicapped and mentally retarded. (27) Welfare of the weaker sections, and in particular, of the Scheduled Castes and the Scheduled Tribes. (28) Public distribution system. (29) Maintenance of community assets.

## Functions

The functions of the panchayat may be classified under the following categories:

*(i)* Civic amenities,

*(ii)* Social welfare activities; and

*(iii)* Development work.

## Civic Amenities

Sanitation, conservancy, public health, street lightening, the supply of safe drinking water and the maintenance of villages roads, culverts, school, etc., come under civic amenities which are generally obligatory, while the other activities, which are optional, include the setting-up and maintenance of a library, a reading-room, a community hall, a playground and recreation centre, maternity and child welfare centres, cart and bus stands, and a burial ground. In regard to development works, the panchayats function generally as agents of the Samitis or Zilla Parishads.

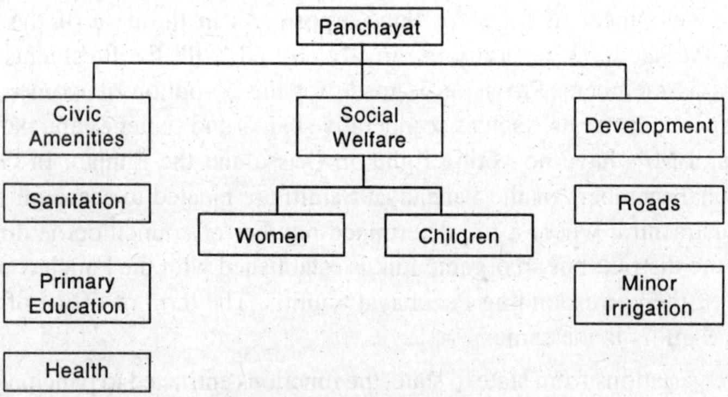


*Fig. 4. Functions of Panchayats*

## Social Welfare Activities

The social welfare activities of the panchayats encompass the development of women and children, inparticular of people who are backward and live below the poverty line. In fact, they form the vary core of rural development.

Women's Empowerment is critical to the socio-economic progress of the community and to bring women into the mainstream of national development has, therefore, been a major concern of the Government.

The Ministry of Rural Development has special components for Women in its programmes and funds are earmarked as 'Women's Component' to ensure flow of adequate resources for the same.

The major schemes, having women's Component (implemented by the Ministry of Rural Development during the year) include the Swarnjayanti Gram Swarozgar Yojana (SGSY), Sampoorna Grameen Rozgar Yojana (SGRY), Indira Awas Yojana (IAY), the Restructured Centrally Rural Sanitation Programme and the Accelerated Rural Water Supply Programme.

*Capacity building through self-help group*

**Box 2**
**TOWARDS EMPOWERMENT**

| SCHEME | PROVISIONS |
|---|---|
| 1. SGSY | 50% of SHGs in each block to be exclusively reserved for women |
| 2. SGRY | 30% of employment opportunities reserved for women |
| 3. IAY | Dwelling houses to be allotted in the name of women or joint names of husband and wife. |
| 4. Restructured centrally rural sanitation programme (CRSP) | Special Toilet Complexes for women. |
| 5. Accelerated Rural Water Supply Programme (ARWSP) | Training for women in using and maintaining hand pumps.<br>Representation of women in village level committees.<br>Active involvement of women in selection of sites for hand pump and other sources. |

**BOX 3**
**WOMEN'S PARTICIPATION IN RURAL WORKFORCE ON THE WANE**

THE labour force participation rate (LFPR) in rural India has gradually declined, falling to 66% in 1999-2000, from 69% in 1993-94. Women workers in the rural areas have been affected more than the rural male. While LFPR for rural males has declined by two percentage points to 85.4% from 87.6%, it is three percentage points for the rural female (down to 45.6% from 48.8%). While this is a result of a decline in the LFPR for rural females, the extent of overall decline has been curtailed by a rise for some states.

At the all-India level, 45.6% of females were part of the labour force for 1999-2000, a slight decline from the 49% it was in 1993-94. The LFPR or the number of persons in the labour force, is defined as the proportion of persons in the age group 15 years and above, who are either working or seeking work. Since the all-India LFPR is derived from data from individual states, it's evident that most states in the country would show a declining participation of rural women in work. The states of Arunachal Pradesh, Goa, Haryana and Jammu and Kashmir have shown the largest decline in female participation.

Each of these states report a decline of about 12 percentage points, which is far higher than the three percentage point decline at the all-India level. A number of other states such as Tamil Nadu, Tripura, Rajasthan, Karnataka and Maharashtra have also reported a decline of more than 5 percentage points in female participation. So what keeps the all-India decline low?

Firstly, some of the larger states such as Madhya Pradesh and Uttar Pradesh, which by virtue of their size, contribute a significant quantum of the labour force, have seen a low decline in rural women's availability to the workforce. For instance, Madhya Pradesh has seen a decline of 1.7 points, while UP has shown a 1.5 point decline.

Also, some states have reported an increase in the participation of rural women. The eastern states of Nagaland and Mizoram, for instance, have shown a rise of as much as 33 points and 16 points respectively. States such as Bihar, which again contribute significantly to the overall workforce, have in fact, seen a rise in their participation. While the increase is small, it amounts to large absolute numbers, given the state's size.

## Development

The Panchayat Samiti intended to take over the development functions which were performed by the community development block. Besides, it performs such civic functions as the administration of primary education, health and sanitation, including rural dispensaries, the maintenance of villages roads and minor irrigation sources. In many states, Panchayat Samitis have been entrusted with the supervision and control of panchayats, including the scrutiny and passing of their budgets. Tamil Nadu is a notable exception, for it may be the responsibility of the Panchayat Samiti, the execution of such works as the construction of school buildings, roads, etc., is generally entrusted to panchayats, the latter making some contribution to the cost.

The function of panchayats in different states are more or less similar, though their enumeration and classification vary considerable. In some states, they are divided into two categories, *viz.*, obligatory and discretionary. For instance, in Tamil Nadu, they have been divided into eight obligatory and ten discretionary heads, and in Andhra Pradesh, twelve obligatory and twenty-seven discretionary. In the Punjab, 27 functions have been made obligatory, and the State Government has power to direct that seven discretionary functions should be treated as obligatory. In Maharashtra, Kerala, Karnataka and some other states, a large number of functions under each head, such as agriculture, animal husbandry, education, health, etc have been listed. It has generally been enjoined that, subject to their financial limitations the panchayats should make provision for safe drinking water supply, sanitation and conservancy, the maintenance of village roads, school buildings, street lighting and some other amenities, such as the radio, a community hall and a children's park.

## What is Needed

The Panchayati Raj is crucial for rural development. If rural development is to be really meaningful and if we are sincere in our approach to make it a reality, we need not only basic structural changes but also bring about the decentralisation of administration, including planning. The long overdue reforms that are necessary include land reforms, a committed administrative service, removal of corrupt officials and politicians, taking stern action against oppressive and criminal elements, stoppage of illegal activities like toddy (liquor) shops, gambling dens, undertaking of education of rural people, organisation of agricultural labourers and other weaker sections, removal of middlemen in trade and other activities and revitalising the rural credit delivery system. In addition, development awareness has also to be instilled among the people through proper motivation, so that they participate in all the development activities of the village.

First and foremost, decentralisation of planning is a must. Then, agriculture and allied activities, rural artisans and rural industries have to be given their fair share in preference to industrial activities. The marketing net work has to be strengthened to market all the goods produced in rural India and give a fair return to the farmer and farmhands. The poverty alleviation programme should originate from villages. It is these wide structural reforms which go beyond the concept of merely giving constitutional sanctity for strengthening the institution of panchayat that may prove to be more important for the success of Panchayati Raj in India.

Panchayati Raj, devolution of power, decentralisation of administration and popular participation in the development process may appear to be very appealing concepts and ideas. The country should march ahead in the spirit of unity and brotherhood. There should be no distinction between man and woman and there should be faith in our work and ourselves. But the conflict of interest in society and tension in polity tend to sharpen differences and threaten the stability of the established order. In fact, decentralisation of power should be preceded by a series of measures to implement with determination to effect land reforms, consolidation of land, reduction in the concentration of income, wealth and economic power and removal of inequality, discrimination and exploitation in social, cultural and economic life. These are also interlinked with the existing family structure, property laws, caste system, religion, land tenurial arrangement, agrarian relations etc.

The villagers are neither incompetent nor inefficient producers. Given the state of art, the villagers can be competent administrators and efficient producers. What the villagers lack is the organisation, the like of which we find in urban society. The organisation of the villagers is necessary for any sustainable development.

The dominant impulse is always in favour of greater and greater concentration of power and centralisation of the administrative and economic apparatus of the state. This calls for a number of basic changes whose scope in many cases goes beyond the village. More importantly, in the absence of structural reform, of property laws, election reforms and socio-economic reforms, Panchayati Raj will not be an effective administrative apparatus. Yet, a fresh start for Panchayati Raj must be made if villages are to achieve basic development and not remain cesspools of poverty, with no light, water, roads, schools or medical care.

However, care should be taken in not transferring powers to the sarpanch, who may become all powerful and rule ruthlessly. It may lead towards concentration of power. All the developmental and other powers should be transferred to the Gram Sabha to which the Panchayat is accountable. The Gram Sabha should also approve the projects, their costs and as well as monitor them at every quarter. This apart, the Gram Sabha will have adequate powers to call back their representatives, if their performance is found inadequate and is clouded with doubts. This will ensure people's participation, weakening of the power politics and speedy development. The transformation of villages in India depends primarily upon proper leadership, conservation of resources, optimum use of all available natural resources, co-operation and an urge to work for the community as whole. If development is viewed as a process by which natural resources are conserved, developed and used to improve living standards, this can be brought about by increasing the availability of biomass *per capita* on a sustainable basis. Development Programme, to be effective, should be conceptually sound, and clear in its objectives. There should be a committed cadre who have conceived its spirit to implement it with a missionary zeal in inculcating social awareness. Such cadre should actively work with the people, involving them in decision-making, implementation and monitoring process. Education and training are the essence of development. The key is to enable communities to manage their own resource base equitably, profitably. Power to people also emphasises on laying down an elaborate land use plan and also strictly enforce it. This enables the land to sustain livelihood.

As a unit of development, each one will contribute his might, sacrifice personal gains in the larger interest of the village, help the weaker sections and bring them within the mainstream. In the long run, it is the social mobilisation of people which produces results on an ongoing basis. Power to villages will mark an important step towards a more equitable pattern of development. The government should not set examples of writing off of loans for political purpose, but inculcate credit discipline and build public confidence in the financial system. The panchayats should be encouraged to mobilise resources and credit discipline. All village people must be assured of a congenial environment for developing all the creative, innovative efforts which shall be sustained only through conscious efforts on the part of the panchayats and the state. The fulfilment of panchayat's duties in this regard is certainly a pre-requisite for the meaningful exercise of rural development.

Given the necessary inputs such as proper training and effective participation in the democratic set-up, people can play a pivotal role in the running of the Panchayati Raj system. But, to be successful, rural people have to be enlightened about the meaning of democratic decentralisation, equality, co-operation, social justice. They should realise that development can be achieved only with their participation in community development programmes. Each village will have its own plan, strategy and committed leadership in bringing a sea change in the village economy.

The Panchayati Raj will be a nodal agency in fostering this transformation. Thus, power to villages/people means safeguarding their rights and duties towards the community/village, both individually and collectively. The success of the Panchayati Raj depends on a stable government and progressive policies of vision and able leadership of an unwavering purpose and promises the country even a better future. The crucial need is to build up local leadership and make people feel that they can become responsible to themselves. Peace, prosperity and development come from the people's commitment, active participation and the steadfast spirit that lives in the people. Power to the people will see the dawn of a brighter future to rural areas and crores of people living in nearly six lakh villages in India. The last decade of the 20th century will see the young nation grow into one of the most vibrant democracies in the world and also make Panchayati Raj as one of the most enduring vibrant institutions at the grassroot level in the country. The Panchayati Raj will be a leader in integrated rural development and also an edifice of democracy at the grassroot level—*i.e.* the villages.

## Resources of Panchayat

Panchayati Raj institutions have their own powers of taxation. They levy taxes on houses and certain types of lands, fairs and festivals, and sale of goods, and impose octroi duties. They also build up remunerative community assets.

The powers and responsibilities of Panchayat Raj institutions are derived not only from state legislation but from the procedures—administrative and financial—laid down by state governments. Gujarat, Maharashtra and Tamil Nadu have entrusted these institutions with responsibilities for a wide range of activities.

## Resources

The resources of the panchayats may be classified into:

*(a)* Proceeds from taxes levied by them;

*(b)* Fees and charges imposed;

*(c)* Income from property, investments and remunerative undertaking;

*(d)* Assistance received from State Governments; and

*(e)* Public contributions.

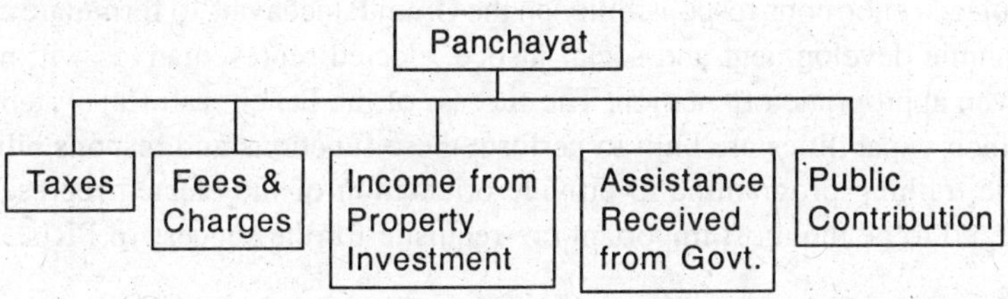


*Fig. 5. Resources of Panchayats*

As per Article 243-H of the Constitution, State Legislature have been empowered to enact laws:

to authorise a Panchayat to levy, collect and appropriate some taxes, duties, tolls and fees;

to assign the Panchayat, some taxes, duties and tolls levied, and collected by the State Government;

to provide for making grants-in-aid to the Panchayats from the Consolidated Fund of the State; and

to provide for constitution of such funds for Panchayats for crediting all money received by or on behalf of Panchayats and also the withdrawal of such money therefrom.

It is in the constitution and functions of the Zilla Parishads that the greatest difference are to be found in the states. In Tamil Nadu, Rajasthan and the Punjab, the Zilla Parishad is purely advisory and co-ordinating arise in connection with Panchayati Raj and the development schemes of this State is the most important self-governing body with large executive functions, which cover primary and secondary education, district roads, hospitals and dispensaries, health and sanitation, etc. The Panchayat Samiti is mainly the implementing agency. The head of the Zilla Parishad is of the rank of the District Collector and the Zilla Parishad has powers of supervision over Panchayat Samitis and Panchayats. Between these two extremes are Andhra Pradesh and some other states, where the Zilla Parishad has some executive functions, such as those of the administration of public secondary schools and the distribution of the grants received from the state for social welfare.

There were, of course, instances where the Panchayats were not discharging even the minimum obligatory functions, largely because of the paucity of funds. Even the basic civic amenities—safe drinking water supply, sanitation and conservancy—were not provided to the community. They had shown greater initiative and enthusiasm in constructing school buildings, community halls, panchayat ghats and village approach roads, through local contributions and government matching grants; but they had been unable to maintain them in good repair.

The Panchayat Samitis, too, are unable to exercise any initiative in instituting special programmes of development projects on their own, because they do not have independent sources of revenue. Most of the grants they receive are tied to specific projects, and.they act merely as agents for their implementation. The schematic pattern of the community development programme is not sufficiently elastic to provide much scope for their initiative.

The Zilla Parishads, where they are advisory bodies, do not experience any particular difficulty; but they feel that procedures for consultation with them are not satisfactory, and their advice is not given sufficient weight by the state government. Where they have executive functions, the scarcity of resources has the same limiting effect on their activities as it has on those of the Samitis.

## Training of PRI Members

As a result of the elections of Panchayats in all the States, there are about 29.2 lakh elected representatives at all levels of Panchayats. Out of this an overwhelming majority is new entrants, particularly from the weaker sections of the society, *i.e.,* Scheduled Castes, Scheduled Tribes and women (33%). The Constitution having placed enormous responsibility on the Gram Panchayats to formulate and execute various programmes of economic development and social justice, elected representatives will have to acquire the required skill and given appropriate orientation. The success of the Panchayati Raj system hinges largely on the extent to which their capabilities are built to perform these functions and responsibilities. Thus, a time-bound and systematic training programme to provide orientation of the elected representatives on a very large scale is considered to be the most important pre-requisite for the success of PRIs.

## Control and Supervision

The Acts in many states provide for the control, supervision and assistance of the lower tiers of Panchayati Raj institutions by higher tiers. Except in Madhya Pradesh, Madras and the Punjab, Panchayat Samitis have power of scrutiny and approval of the budgets of the Panchayats. In all the states except Tamil Nadu, the Zilla Parishad scrutinises and passes the budgets of Panchayat Samitis. One of the functions of the Zilla Parishads is the co-ordination of the activities of Panchayat Samitis.

In the Third Five Year Plan, Panchayati Raj has been described as a part of inter-connected democratic institutions at the village, block and district levels, the primary object of which was to enable the poor in each area to achieve intensive and continuous development in the interest of the entire population. The Plan emphasised that it was of the utmost importance that there should be a clear recognition of the distinct role of federal co-operative organisation functioning at the state and district levels in the field of banking, marketing, processing, distribution, education and training. It laid down that Panchayati Raj institutions should promote the development of co-operatives and should endeavour to create a climate for community effort and their social functioning at all levels. At the Conference of State Ministers of Panchayats held in six districts in 1961, it was points of the success of Panchayati Raj. Panchayats therefore play an important role in the promotion and development of co-operative institutions within their areas.

## Problems of Panchayats

Initially, the dominant classes had control of the Panchayati Raj institutions; but over a period, the dormant middle class and backward classes, realising the strength of their numbers, have changed the profit from what it was in the beginning. This is all well; but party politics and factionalism at the state level percolate to Panchayati Raj, defeating the partyless character of the Panchayati Raj institutions as they were originally envisaged.

At the Panchayat level, caste and class constraints are the hampering factors. Many panchayats, particularly in Saurashtra, helplessly watch the bullies disregard the Panchayat. Such violations become difficult to check because candidates manipulate caste loyalties for their election and even indulge in terrorism.

In the circumstances, the effective functioning of the Panchayati Raj institutions is vitiated by wide economic disparities, social disabilities and caste loyalties. This is evident from the fact that there is too much politicisation of issues to the detriment of real development work.

There is one more drag on the smooth functioning of the Panchayati Raj institutions—the relationship between the non-official and the official.

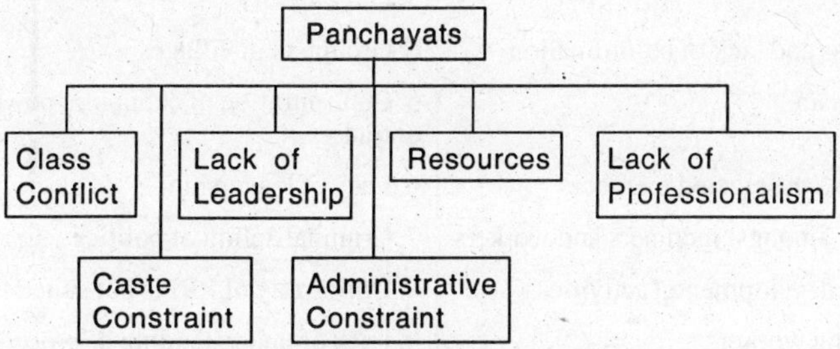


*Fig. 6. Problems of Panchayats*

The Panchayati Raj institutions have to undertake and carry out development work within their jurisdiction. Their sources of income for this purpose include local cess, matching grants, plan grants, deficit adjustment grant and their own sources of revenue, such as professional tax, pilgrim tax, property tax, enterprises tax, etc. Because of planning at the national level and the rigid administrative framework that implements it, Panchayat Raj institutions are neither autonomous nor innovative in character. There is hardly any Zilla Parishad which, by its own efforts, had added to its revenue, apart from the conventional sources mentioned above. Though Zilla Parishad and panchayats are empowered to raise their own resources by way of taxation on professions and trades, there is always an unwillingness on their part to impose any such levies because they have always an eye on their re-election. As a result, the developmental activities of the panchayats are hampered.

The Ashok Mehta Committee has thrown adequate light on the developments which have undermined the Panchayati Raj structures and made them ineffective. They are:

(1) Expect in Maharashtra and Gujarat, the PRIs were rarely given and opportunity to take up planning or implementational work on a sizeable scale.

(2) Planning was entrusted to a body outside Zilla Parishad under the chairmanship of a minister.

(3) Adequate and proper staff was not provided to the districts and blocks.

(4) The plan allocation resources were tapered off.

(5) PRIs were wilfully kept out of developmental work so that it never become stronger.

(6) Bureaucracy's role in dissociating the PRIs from the development process for its own benefits is equally great.

(7) There was a lack of clarity in regard to the concept of Panchayati Raj itself and the objectives for which it should stand.

(8) PRIs were dominated by economically or socially privileged sections of society and have as such facilitated the emergence of oligarchic forces yielding no benefits to weaker sections.

(9) Corruption inefficiency, scant regard for procedures and rules political interference in day-to-day administration, parochial loyalties, motivated actions, concentration of power and lack of services inflicted a large number of panchayats.

(10) In sum, the activities of PRIs were meagre, their resources base weak and the overall attention given to them niggardly. There was a lack of political will to the PRIs.

**Table 3**

**PROBLEMS OF PANCHAYATS**

| *Administrative* | *Non-administrative* |
|---|---|
| 1. Lack of bureaucratic response to PRI | 1. Widening economic disparity in the villages |
| 2. Poor and inadequate staff at grassroot level | 2. Illiteracy of the elected members |
| 3. Lack of technical support | 3. Party loyalty |
| 4. Unscientific plan process and lack of co-ordination | 4. Groupism in villages |
| 5. Corruption and favouritism | 5. Concentration of economic power with the rich farmers or traders |
| 6. Lack of proper training to the elected members | 6. Lack of leadership |
| 7. Lack of missionary zeal amongst members and workers | 7. Criminalisation of politics |
| 8. Scant attention given to developmental activities | 8. Uniformity of PRI is not suited to the country |
| 9. Lack of awareness among workers | 9. Lack of understanding of procedures and scant respect for rules |
| 10. Lack of resources | 10. Members work for their self interest |
| 11. Inadequate provisions of funds | 11. Proper awareness is not there among villagers |
| 12. Elections are not being held on one pretext or the other | 12. Vested interests have seized the democratic process |
| 13. Lack of clarity about PRI's concept | 13. Decline in value system |
| 14. Lack of dedication for work | 14. People have lost faith in PRIs. |
| 15. No career path has been drawn for PRI workers. | |

Initially, the dominant classes had exercised control of the Panchayati Raj institutions, but over a period, the dormant middle class and backward classes, realising the strength of their number, have changed the profile from what it was in the beginning. This is all well; but party politics and factionalism at state level percolate to Panchayati Raj, defeating the partyless character of the Panchayati Raj institutions as they were originally envisaged.

The other reasons attributed to its dismal performance are:

*(i)* The election system introduced in the Panchayati Raj system has divided the villagers into parties/groups with conflicting interest.

*(ii)* Non-co-operation and non-participation of villagers in the development work.

*(iii)* There is lack of will, determination, dedication and missionary zeal amongst the members to take up development work.

*(iv)* Invariably funds are misappropriated.

*(v)* There is a problem of uniformity of PRI system.

*(vi)* The debatable issue is the unit of administration at the grass root level. While over 60 percent of inhabited villages have less than 1000 people. The question is whether a panchayat will be a viable unit of administration?

*(vii)* There is no co-ordination between the elected representatives and bureaucracy.

*(viii)* Widening economic disparities in rural India have belittled the Panchayats.

## Findings of the Administrative Reforms Commission

According to the Administrative Reforms Commission's findings, nearly 80 per cent of the villagers are dissatisfied with the Panchayat Raj because the "undesirable and unhealthy tendencies have the upper hand," in rural affairs, with "considerations of religion and caste taking the first place and qualification and sincerity taking almost the last place."

Another major reason is the restricted authority and paucity of funds, The state government have not been very equitable in their relationship with the infant Panchayati Raj institutions. The financial resources granted to them have been meagre and inadequate. Adequate financial support has generally been denied to these institutions in most states, often even in respect of the "transferred" schemes and performances. Moreover, these institutions have shown little inclination to raise their own resources locally.

Apart from the paucity of funds, there has been a general apathy at the administrative and political level towards a strengthening of these bodies. Elections to those bodies have been repeatedly postponed; there is a state having the dubious reputation of postponing panchayat elections over a hundred times! Supersession of local bodies are too common. According to an able commentator: "Not much power can be exercised, holders of real power, at the central and state levels, have been reluctant to delegate authority." In fact, all the development programmes such as the IADP, CADP, DPAP, and so on—financed and operated by the central government—have no relation with Panchayati Raj Institutions. In short, the higher level government in India have been rather allergic to the concept of sharing the power with the lower level ones.

A review committee (Committee to Review the Existing Administrative Arrangements for Rural Development and Poverty, CAARD) was constituted on 25th March, 1985 under the chairmanship of Dr. G.V.K.Rao, Ex-Member, Planning Commission, to review the existing administrative arrangements for rural development and poverty alleviation programmes and to recommend appropriate structural mechanism to ensure that they are planned in an integrated manner and effectively implemented.

The committee's important recommendations relating to Panchayati Raj are as follows:

(1) Panchayati Raj institutions (PRIs) have to be activised and given all the needed support so that they can become effective organisations for handling people's problems.

(2) PRIs at the district level and below should be assigned the work of planning, implementation and monitoring of rural development programmes.

(3) The block development office should be the sheet anchor of the entire rural development process.

## A Plea for Integrated Administrative Structure

The L.M. Singhvi Committee (1986) concurs broadly with recommendations made in the Report of the Committee to Review the Existing Administrative Arrangements for Rural Development and Poverty Alleviation Programmes (CAARD) in respect of integrated administrative structures for planning and development. The Committee considered it appropriate to underline that these administrative structures for planning and development should be dynamic and independent and should at the same time be integrated with institutions of local self-government losing their dynamism and independence.

The principal technical and administrative officers of various specialised departments along with their line formations should be part of the organisational and administrative structure of the Zilla Parishad. The District Development Commissioner would have to be the chief executive officer of Zilla Parishad. The District Development Commissioner should be entrusted with the task of assisting in co-ordinating, the planning and implementation activities of various departments, agencies and institutions at the district level.

Officers of high calibre, proven competence and with sympathy for Panchayati Raj institutions should be detailed to function as Panchayati Raj officials.

The Committee recommends that newer officials in the administration should be made to work in Panchayati Raj and rural development settings so as to sensitise our public administration to the problems of rural India.

The Committee is strongly of the view that substantial training, research and public education inputs should be provided to strengthen the Panchayati Raj institutions and the performance capabilities of those who are called upon to function as voters, elected representatives, administrative officials and voluntary workers in relation to Panchayati Raj institutions. Voluntarily institutions should be given the pride of place in providing these inputs. The Committee feels that this would be the most productive and profitable investment in democratic institution building.

A model legislation within the framework of the proposed new chapter in the Constitution should be prepared with sufficient scope for appropriate local adaptations.

The Committee recommends the national and state level local self-government institutes, and centres for training at the district level, should be established and entrusted with training, evaluation and research responsibilities particularly in relation to Panchayati Raj and urban local institutions. The institutes and centres should also be clearing houses of information relating to local self-government and should monitor and report development in that field.

The Committee is of the view that the proposed National Institute of Local Self Government should, in respect of its research and evaluation functions, utilise universities, research bodies and voluntary organisation such as All India Panchayats Parishad which should have consultative nexus with it and which would be an invaluable resource for dissemination of information as well as for proper motivation.

## Revitalisation of Panchayati Raj Institutions for Democracy and Development

Accepting the recommendations of the L.M.Singhvi Committee (1986) of giving constitutional sanctity to PRI as the third tier of government, the government introduced the Sixty-fourth Constitutional Amendment (1986) on May 15, 1989.

The objective of setting up local self-government for the rural areas is to break the bottlenecks and to straighten the links which were the outcome of the perpetuation of certain sordid vested interests. People to become partakers in the process of development is the aim of the new Panchayati Raj legislation. The salient features of the Act are:

As the Panchayati Raj institutions became weak and ineffective due to a variety of reasons, there was an urgent need to revamp the system. It is common knowledge that elections were not held regularly. Suppressions were a regular feature. Weaker sections did not have any say in its manning and running. The financial resources were grossly inadequate to take up any meaningful development work. The meagre devolution of powers made the system a mockery.

In order to eliminate these inadequacies and to enable them to function as units of effective self-government, the recent bill was introduced in the Parliament. It is now obligatory for all states to establish a three-tier system of Panchayats at the village, intermediate and district levels. For those states having a population of less than 20 lakhs, it is not obligatory to establish the intermediate level.

All seats in Panchayats, at all levels, will be filled by direct election. There will be reservations to ensure due representation in the Panchayats of the SC, ST and women categories. The tenure of office will be five years. In case of dissolution, there is provision to conduct election within a period of six months or reconstitute Panchayat for the remainder of the term. It also provides for the devolution by the states legislature of powers and responsibilities upon Panchayats with respect to the preparation of plans for economic development and social justice for the implementation of development schemes. It ensures sound finance for the Panchayats by securing grants-in-aid from the consolidated fund of the state as well as appropriating the revenues of designated taxes, duties, tolls, fees, etc. Finance Commissions may be set up in the states every five year to review the finance of Panchayats and recommend principles to apportion the taxes and assign grants-in-aid to the Panchayats from the consolidated fund of the state.

The ratio between the population of the Panchayat area and the number of seats should be the same throughout the state. Panchayats will be divided into territorial constituencies based on, almost equal ratio between population and the seats. Only those directly elected members alone have voting powers in the meeting. The chairperson of the panchayat elected from amongst the elected member can be removed by two-thirds of such members present and voting. The number of reserved seats will be decided depending upon the size of their population, subject to a minimum of one seat for SC/ST. Thirty per cent of the total seats to be filled by direct election in every panchayat shall be reserved for women and allotted by rotation to different constituencies.

It would prepare and implement plans for socio-economic development. Social justice will be the major guiding principle. The accounts shall be kept in such forms as desired by Comptroller and Auditor General (CAG) of India. The CAG shall cause the accounts to be audited and be submitted to the State Governor, who shall cause them to be laid before the state legislature. However, both the CAG and Election Commission have indicated that it would be difficult for them to estimate the likely additional work involved. There will be no other recurring or non-recurring expenditure.

The Important recommendations of the committee of Chief Ministers are:

- Leave selection of beneficiaries to Gram Sabha.
- Waive requirement of technical sanction for works up to Rs. 10,000.
- Innovate to provide adequate manpower support to the Gram Panchayats.
- Delegate total control over such manpower to Gram Panchayats.
- Zilla Parishad chairpersons be made the chairpersons of DRDAs.
- Provide reasonable opportunity of hearing to the PRIs before suspension/dismissal.
- Gram Panchayat President to be accountable solely to Gram Sabha.
- Expeditious constitution of District Planning Committees.

In order to ensure that Panchayati Raj Institutions function as instruments of local government, it is important that their functional and financial autonomy is guaranteed and transparency in their functioning is ensured. This has to be accomplished in most of the States. The role of the Gram Sabha is, perhaps, the most important in ensuring the success of Panchayati Raj Institutions at the village level. The role of local people in conducting social audit and fixing responsibility on panchayat functionaries will be effectively ensured with Gram Sabha becoming active. It is essential that the village community perceives meetings of the Gram Sabha as useful. The most important factor for that is the empowerment of the Gram Sabha.

Another important factor for the success of the Panchayati Raj system is the need for transparency in the functioning of these bodies. Panchayats being closer to the people, their right to information and accessibility to the panchayats must be ensured.

Declaration adopted by the Sammelan held in April, 2002 indicate, inter-alia that the States and Union Territories would initiate, by the end of December, 2002, the necessary measures:

- to hold regular and timely Panchayat elections,
- to devote funds, functions and functionaries to Panchayats,
- to constitute District Planning Committees and make them functional,

- to set up Ombudsman (to be headed by a retired judge) to look into the complaints against the Panchayats,
- to ensure parallel bodies function under the guidance of the Panchayats,
- to amend the State Legislations to provide Panchayats adequate control over natural resources like, land, water, minor forest produce and minerals,
- to make legal provisions for accountability and transparency in the functioning of Panchayats in accordance with the 4-Point strategy – Awareness, Participation, Transparency and Social Audit, and
- to strengthen the Gram Sabhas and Gram Panchayats.
- to devise an appropriate mechanism to provide significant non-budgetary resources in the form of loans with adequate maturities to PRIs, specifically to be used for such developmental projects as are planned and executed by PRIs themselves.
- to put in place an appropriate structure of incentives to recognise and encourage the Panchayats for outstanding performance, especially in respect of improvements effected in accepted Social Development Indicators.
- to discuss the need for an appropriate new Amendment to the Constitution to bring about speedy and effective devolution of financial and administrative powers to PRIs and to quickly initiate the process of bringing in the much needed new Constitution Amendment. The Sammelan also urges all the Political Parties and Members of Parliament to pass the Amendments and thus usher in the era of Second Generation of Panchayati Raj Reforms.

## Conclusion

The organisation of the village as a social and political unit finds reference in Vedic literature and Jataka stories. Old inscriptions tells us how the village councils or assemblies were constituted, who were eligible to serve thereon and how they functioned. The village gramanee (headman) carried on the village government and the council or sabha of the village decided questions relating to village administration. The headman was always from the village and was not an officer appointed from outside. Panchayats have been an integral part of the rural cultural heritage of India. The term "panchayat" literally means an assembly of five (Panchi), elected by villagers.

These village organisations were not only self-sufficient economically but also were self-governed. Village panchayats in ancient times were developed, nurtured out of a necessity of protection from raids and economic survival in absence of adequate infrastructural facilities and development. It was in their unity and co-operation that their sustenance was possible.

Since then, the rural scene has seen a sea change. The scale and scope of their activities diversified. Rural population has increased from little less than 100 million in 1901 to 615 million in 1989. Agriculture strategy has undergone a sea change. Rural industries and service sector has eclipsed the ranks of agricultural labourers, marginal and small farmers has swelled. Joint family has also been eclipsed. The villager and the villages are being increasingly drawn into ever-widening market economy. Administration innovations have also undergone changes with the implicit needs of the power structure. Today, villages are dependent on the cities for their supply of inputs and other basic needs, even for food. With the development of infrastructure and communication, villages have come under closer contact and demonstrative effect of urban areas.

In the changed context, the sole concept of village panchayat is not only feasible but also viable. What is needed is redesign of decentralisation. Moreover, India is a country of diversity and hence no one model suits the requirement of villages in India. So instead of one model, each state should evolve a pattern of village administration. What is needed is a positive approach appropriate strategy, co-ordinated efforts co-operative approach and hard work to achieve the objectives.

If the villages are to achieve rapid social and economic development and not remain in the cess pool of poverty, with no lights, no water, no roads, no schools, no medical care and no gainful employment, Panchayat Raj should be strengthened. The only answer is that we must, therefore, decentralise democracy and bring it to the grassroot level. In a democracy, the people are sovereign and therefore, distribution of power should be from the base upwards. The gram sabha should determine what powers it should keep for itself for the purpose of administration and development. The residuary powers will be delegated to the other levels. Similarly, the district (Zilla) and the state should decide likewise. The resources have to be distributed correspondingly. This is exactly to be the process of devolution of power from village to mandal, to district, to state and the centre. A strong panchayat, with plenty of power, a strong school with vision and innovation, a strong cooperative and a strong innovative and committed branch of a bank for each village or a group of villages are necessary to look after the integrated development of the village. Panchayati Raj should contribute to the philosophy as well as practice of a rich, rewarding life in rural India. Its success depends upon the continued political will, committed administration, dedicated leadership and above all, the full participation of the people.

Development work in future needs intricate designing and greater co-ordination at the state level. The entire rural development programme needs co-ordination at village or group of villages level. Panchayati Raj, a new system of local government came in as the logical answer to the new situation that emerged. Panchayati Raj meant the creation of the Gram Sabha as the crucial base of our growing democracy. The Gram Sabha consisted of the entire adult village population, the body men and women. Gram Sabha was to elect its executive, the Village Panchayat, to look after the day-to-day administration of the village. The Village Panchayat cannot go far in matters of inter-village development. Thus came the block Panchayat Samiti at the block level consisting of representatives of the Panchayats. The Panchayat Samiti was to take over the administration of all programmes of development at the Block level using the block administration as its instrument of action. Subjects which went beyond the scope of the Block Panchayat Samiti and matters connected with the co-ordination of the activities of the blocks were vested in the Zilla Parishad. Above the Zilla Parishad stood the state government. The State Government received its support and guidance from the Centre. Thus the Gram Sabha got linked with Lok Sabha in a single chain. The individual village could thus have the touch of the nation as a whole in every facet of its life and the nation could receive the echo back of the achievements, hopes and frustrations of the people in the process of development.

Politically speaking, it is a process of democratic awareness, making effort to improve the living standard of the people as well as improving the conditions of the villages.

Administratively speaking. it bridged the gulf between the bureaucratic elite and the people. Socio-culturally speaking, it generated a new leadership with pro-social change in outlook. It also helped rural people to cultivate and harness a development psyche. It is hoped that the Panchayati Raj will accelerate the developmental process in rural communities.

The success of the Panchayati Raj system hinges largely on the extent to which their capabilities are built to perform these functions and responsibilities. Thus, a time-bound and systematic training programme to provide orientation of the elected representatives on a very large scale is considered to be the most important pre-requisite for the success of the PRIs. The States/UT governments are required to work out systematic and comprehensive training programmes to train the representatives of PRIs and to generate awareness among the masses at the grass-roots level and to strengthen the Gram Sabha.

The Panchayati Raj is both an end and a means. As an end, it is an inevitable extension of democracy; as a means, it would continue to be responsible for discharging obligations entrusted to it by the people. Altogether, Panchayati Raj should contribute to a rich, rewarding harmonious and fully vibrant live in rural

India. It is a useful object lesson, for we all can learn to take unexpected difficulties and mistakes and weave them advantageously into greater pattern of our lives. There is an inherent good in most difficulties. Thus, Panchayati Raj has a bright future, if properly guided.

The primary object of a village panchayat is to strengthen the base of democracy at the grassroots on the one hand and hand over the powers as well as responsibility to the people on the other hand so as to allow them to manage their affairs in the best possible manner.

The Panchayati Raj, like democracy at the national and state levels, is both an end and a means. As an end, it is an inevitable extension of democracy; as a means it would continue to be responsible for discharging obligations entrusted to it by the people. As an edifice of democracy, it makes the base of the democratic pyramid in the country. Altogether, both as an end and a means, Panchayati Raj contributes to the philosophy as well as practice of a rich, rewarding life in rural India. Jawaharlal Nehru emphasises that, "Panchayats should be given greater power, for we want the villager to have a measure of real swaraj in his own village. He should have power and does not have to refer everything to big officials. We do not want the officials to interfere too much in the life of the village. We want to build swaraj right from the village up."

The future of the country really depends upon effective Panchayati Raj and people's co-operation. It is the only effective instrument which can put speed and substance in our planning process and also ensure the most effective use of the country's resources productively. In that lies the future both of democracy and real development of the economy as well as of the people in the country. In the years to come, Panchayati Raj will be a catalytic agent of integrated development of rural India.

All in all, Panchayati Raj—power to the people is a comprehensive, promising and idealistic proposition. But to fulfil it, the political leadership—both in and outside the government—has back-breaking work to do. Along with this the people should be aware of their rights and duties and involve in development with boldness. One hopes that those responsible—both leaders and people—will show the necessary determination and commitment.

## What Panchayats should be...

*"Independence must begin at the bottom. Thus every village will be a republic or panchayat having full powers. It follows, therefore, that every village has to be self-sustained and capable of managing its affairs. This does not exclude dependence on, and willing help from neighbours or from the world. It will be free and voluntary play of mutual forces... In this structure, composed of innumerable villages, there will be ever-widening, never ascending circles. Life will not be a pyramid with the apex sustained by the bottom. But it will be an oceanic circle whose centre will be the individual always ready to perish for the village, the latter ready to perish for the circle of villages, till at last the whose becomes one life composed of individuals, never aggressive in their arrogance but ever humble, sharing the majesty of the economic circle of which they are integral units. Therefore the outer most circumference will not wield power to crush the inner circle but will give strength to all within and derive its own strength from it."*

***—Mahatma Gandhi***

- Panchayat Raj Institutions constitute the bedrock for the implementation of Rural Development Programmes:
- Panchayat have been given a key role in identification of beneficiaries, project selection, monitoring, supervision of various programmes of the ministry.
- The success of the Panchayati Raj System hinges on the extent to which the capability of elected representatives are developed to discharge their functions and responsibilities effectively.

❑ ❑ ❑

**Table 4**
**PANCHAYATI RAJ STRUCTURE IN DIFFERENT STATES**

| State | Bottom Tier | | Intermediate Tier | | Top Tier | |
|---|---|---|---|---|---|---|
| | *Level* | *Body* | *Level* | *Body* | *Level* | *Body* |
| Andhra Pradesh | Village or Group of Villages | Gram Panchayat | Block | Panchayat Samiti | Revenue District | Zilla Parishad |
| Assam | Do | Gram Panchayat | | (Abolished) | Sub-Division | Mokhuma Parishad |
| Bihar | Do | Executive Committee of Gram Panchayat | Block | Panchayat Samiti | Revenue-District | Zilla Parishad (in 8 districts only) |
| Gujarat | Do | Gram/Nager | Taluk | Taluk Panchayat | Do | District Panchayat |
| Haryana | Do | Gram Panchayat | Block Panchayat Samiti | | | |
| Himachal Pradesh | Do | Gram Panchayat | Block | Revenue District | Zilla Parishad | |
| Jammu & Kashmir | Do | Gram Panchayat | Block Panchayat Board | | | |
| Karnataka | Do | Village/Town Panchayat | Taluk Mandal | Taluk/Development Board | Revenue District | District Development Council |
| Kerala | Do | Panchayat | | | | |
| Madhya Pradesh | Do | Gram Panchayat | Block | Janapada Panchayat | | |
| Maharashtra | Do | Gram Panchayat | Taluk/Block | Panchayat Samiti | Revenue District | Zilla Parishad |
| Manipur | Do | Gram Panchayat | | | | |
| Orissa | Do | Gram Panchayat | Block | Panchayat Samiti | (Abolished in Nov. 1968), | |
| Punjab | Do | Gram Panchayat | Block | Panchayat Samiti | Revenue District | Zilla Parishad |
| Rajasthan | Do | Panchayat | Block | Panchayat Samiti | Do | Zilla Parishad |
| Tamil Nadu | Do | Village/Town Panchayat | Block | Panchayat Union/Council | District | District Development Council |
| Tripura | Do | Gaon Panchayat | | | | |
| Uttar Pradesh | Do | Gram Panchayat | Block Kshetra Samiti | Revenue District | Zilla Parishad | |
| West Bengal | Do | Gram Panchayat | Block | Panchayat Samiti | Do | Zilla Parishad |

**Table 5**

**ILLUSTRATIVE FUNCTIONS OF THE THREE TIERS OF PANCHAYATI RAJ STRUCTURE**

| | *Zilla Parishad* | | *Panchayat Samitis Taluka Board* | | *Mandal Panchayat* |
|---|---|---|---|---|---|
| I. | Programme implementation of transferred functions as indicated below: | I. | Function assigned by Zilla Parishad in the decentralised sector, e.g., Rabi Kharif, Pig farms, Minor Irrigation, Health, Dispensaries, Water Supply, Rural Roads, Tubewells, Subplans. | I. | Implementational (illustrative only): |
| | (*a*) Agriculture except research in universities | | | | (*a*) Fodder development activities with subsidies fodder cultivation |
| | (*b*) Animal Husbandry and Veterinary Services | | | | (*b*) Land-shapping in the command area or water arrangement demonstrations |
| | | II. | Preparation of Block Plans | | |
| | | III. | Co-ordination or Dovetailing of Panchayat Works where the programmes cover more than one panchayat or taking up directly till they develop capacities. Administrative | | |
| | (*c*) Fisheries | | | | (*c*) Field channels demonstrations |
| | (*d*) Forestry | | | | (*d*) Farmers' training |
| | (*e*) Marketing | | | | (*e*) Multiple cropping pattern demonstration |
| | (*f*) Irrigation | | | | (f) Demonstration of drainage-cum-recycling |
| | (*g*) Health; Family Welfare | | | | (*g*) Minikit distribution |
| | (*h*) Education | | | | (h) Pisciculture demonstration |
| | (*i*) Public Health Engineering | | | | (*i*) Fisheries propaganda and fairs |
| | (*j*) Communication | | | | (*j*) Facilities for creation of coastal brackish water fishery development |
| | (*k*) Industries | | | | (*k*) Farm forestry |
| | (*l*) Urban Development | | | | (*l*) Soil conservation schemes |
| | (*m*) Welfare of Backward Classes | | | | (*m*) Rural housing and allotment of house sites for landless |
| | (*n*) Social Welfare | | | | (*n*) Assistance to handloom weavers |
| | | | | | (*o*) Establishment of mulberry farms or gardens |

| | | | | | |
|---|---|---|---|---|---|
| | | | | (*p*) | Tassar collection or rearing projects |
| | | | | (*q*) | Assistance to handicrafts with improved tools or collection for marketing |
| | | | | (*r*) | Health sub-centre construction |
| | | | | (*s*) | Recruitment and looking after health workers |
| | | | | (*t*) | Running adult literacy classes |
| | | | | (*u*) | Rural and link roads and culverts construction etc. |
| | | | | (*v*) | SFDA-identification and payment of subsidies |
| | | | | (*w*) | Family welfare projects |
| II. | Planning Review, Monitoring and Evaluation | | | II. | *Promotional (illustrative only):* |
| III. | Co-ordination | | | (*a*) | Organisation of literacy centres |
| IV. | Administrative and those flowing from organic linkages | | | (*b*) | Co-operation |
| | | | | III. | *Procedural (illustrative only):* |
| | | | | (*a*) | Control of fairs and festivals |
| | | | | (*b*) | Registration of deaths and births |
| | | | | (*c*) | Construction and maintenance of Dharmashalas and Sarais |
| | | | | (*d*) | Opening and maintenance of public markets and slaughter |
| | | | | IV | *Municipal and Civic functions at village level:* |
| | | | | (*a*) | Water supply |
| | | | | (*b*) | Health and hygiene |
| | | | | (*c*) | Lighting |

# SECTION SEVEN

# FUTURE OF RURAL DEVELOPMENT

## TASKS AHEAD

Self-reliance has been our major objective ever since we attained Independence. There is no denying the fact the significant progress has been made since then in various sectors including agriculture, industry, education, health, telecommunications, transport, energy, science and technology. However, if we reflect and look back, would be satisfied with what we have achieved so far especially in the field of rural development? The answer, unfortunately, would be in the negative.

It is said that India lives in its villages. But have we been able to improve the lot of our brethren living in the villages? The answer could be in affirmative as well as in negative. On one hand, it claimed that a lot has been done to uplift the rural poor and there are facts and figures to support this, on the other, we are still struggling to provide even safe drinking water to a sizeable number of villages. Poverty alleviation is still the most important aspect of our rural development programme. We have been unable to generate adequate gainful employment for unemployed rural youth.

Unfortunately, during the last 56 years, Only 15 percent of the real value of the schemes reached the genuine beneficiaries and the rest was lost due to red tapism. Added to this those administering these programmes were not responsive to the urges and aspirations of the teeming millions who were for centuries lingering in abject poverty, deprivation and destitution. The majority of them belong to the elite class and have no or inadequate rural orientation and as such they implemented the programmes in a half hearted manner. More importantly, something appears to be amiss in the utilisation of funds allocated for rural development. However, there is no need for despondency as the Government has rededicated itself to make the Rural Development programme a real success.

## NEW INITIATIVES

- **Paradigm shift in the strategy for Rural Development:** Emphasis towards participation of people through Panchayati Raj Institutions (PRIs), Self Help Groups in the planning, formulation and execution of the Programmes.
- **Enhanced allocation of funds:** To ensure adequate budgetary support, allocations for Rural Development Programmes enhanced to Rs.13670 crore in 2002-2003 from Rs.12265 crore in 2001-2002. Allocations further increased to Rs.14070 crore for the year 2003-2004.
- **Promoting decentralisation to ensure participatory development:** Ministry is striving to make Panchayati Raj Institutions an effective and vibrant forum for decentralised planning and implementation of rural development programmes in consonance with the people's hopes and aspirations.
  - On 25th December, 2002, a new initiative **'Swajal Dhara'** launched to empower Panchayats to formulate, implement, operate and maintain Drinking Water Projects.
  - In order to further involve PRIs in development process, a new initiative **'Hariyali'** launched on 27th January, 2003 to strengthen and involve Panchayati Raj Institutions in the implementation of Watershed Development Programmes.
- **Capacity Building of Rural Poor through Strengthening of Infrastructure:** The incidence of poverty is not only because of absence of requisite economic development, but also due to absence of opportunities to the poor for their capacity building such as lack of avenues for employment and access to basic amenities like drinking water, housing, education and roads. Various Programmes of the Ministry strive to address these issues.
- **Rejuvenating Wastelands/degraded lands:** through Area Development Programmes such as Integrated Wastelands Development Programme, Drought Prone Areas Programme and Desert Development Programme being implemented on Watershed Development basis.
- **Facilitating participatory development through awareness generation:** Communication Planning is an integral part of planning for development. Concerted efforts made to disseminate information to people in rural areas about nature and content of Rural Development Programmes.

*Water harvesting through Area Development Programmes*

*Water conservation under DPAP*

*Harvesting of water through a stop dam*

*Our work lies in visualising the future of our country not by looking to the stars and basing our calculations on their movements but by assessing our strength, resources and means and knowing how best to use them.*

***— Jawaharlal Nehru***

# Chapter 40

# Future of Rural Development

## Introduction

Rural India is real India. Seventy-six percent of the population lives in rural India. It produces about 165-170 million tonnes of food as well as agricultural raw materials like sugarcane, cotton, tobacco, groundnut etc., to feed the agro-industries. The contribution of village industries, too, is equally significant. Above all, rural India offers a vast domestic market for the goods produced in urban India. However, over the years, the quality of village life has deteriorated and poverty in all spheres has afflicted over 35 crores of people.

Development as a concept, when applied in the specific context of rural India, acquires a new meaning. Fundamentally, rural development signifies not only the aggregate development of the area but the development of the people living there. The objectives of development includes sustained increases in per capita output and incomes, expansion of productive employment, greater equity in the distribution of the benefits of growth, and adequate provision of infrastructure and other amenities which promote socio-economic growth. It also includes upgradation of the cultural level as well as value systems of the people living in rural areas.

## Rural Development

Over the years, rural development has emerged as "a strategy designed to improve the economic, social and cultural life of a specific group of people living in rural areas." The objectives of rural development are multi-directional as well as multi-dimensional. It aims at increased employment, higher productivity, higher income, minimum acceptable levels of food, clothing, shelter, education, health, as well as a sound value in other words, the term "rural development" refers to all aspects of human development. It is a major part of the development strategy which is designed to serve the rural population.

Over the years, the village socio-economic fabric has undergone a profound change. More than 31 crore of our rural people do not have an adequate income. Employment opportunities fall short of demand. Illiteracy and ignorance are rampant. Under-cultivation of land and its fragmentation have created new problems. Ecology has been degraded, and infrastructural facilities have not kept pace with the growth of the rural population which, moreover, is unorganised. A large number of marginal farmers and agricultural labourers are without any skill. More than 75 per cent are illiterate; 80 per cent live in unhygienic houses; nearly 30 per cent go hungry everyday; many villages do not have all-weather roads or safe drinking water. Rural India is divided into the rich and the poor. Only 22 lakh rich families in rural India have grabbed all wealth and rule over 60 crores of rural people. The apathy of the villagers have been accentuated by the prevalence of social and deep-rooted caste hierarchy. Village politics has deteriorated following the dilution of the spiritual value system. To lift the people from this near-stagnant milieu of life, integrated rural development has acquired a new urgency. It is now the core of development, and is a continuous process.

In order to alleviate the lot of the rural poor—the small and marginal farmers, landless labourers, rural artisans, women, tribals, etc.—the government at the Centre and in the States have implemented a variety of programmes. Broadly speaking, these programmes are either beneficiary-oriented or promote the development of infrastructure. The former directly benefit individuals and their families, while the latter are directed at strengthening those infrastructural activities which have an indirect long-term impact on the socio-economic milieu of the rural population. There are, moreover, some time-bound programmes which are limited to small geographical areas. In a way, these programmes are economically-oriented, and touch only one aspect of rural development—improvement in the income generation of the beneficiaries. But the dilemma is still there: how to make life better of the rural poor without encouraging their migration to urban areas and, at the same time, enlarge their opportunities for work and for a better standard of life.

Rural development has assumed greater significance, particularly since the beginning of the Fifth Five-Year Plan. During the last 40 years, the Government has done more to alleviate rural poverty than to promote rural development. New programmes were introduced as and when the older ones lost their appeal or validity.

Numerous evaluation studies have referred to identical areas of weakness and shortcoming in the sphere of implementation. It has been stated that "the comprehensive strategy of rural development not only dovetails the schemes for provision of minimum needs (food, clothing, house) but envisages a far-reaching transformation of the socio-economic structure including redistributive land reforms and the promotion of Panchayati Raj institutions."

The Seventh Plan document identified the weaknesses in the implementation of the poverty-alleviation programmes so far and outlined the strategy that would be followed in the Seventh Plan to make the anti-poverty programmes more effective and useful to the rural people.

## Poverty Alleviation Programme

Poverty alleviation programmes have to be viewed in the wider perspective of socio-economic transformation in the country. While the present strategy of direct attack on poverty through specific poverty alleviation programmes is justified on account of insufficient percolation of benefits to the poor from overall economic growth, it should be appreciated that the strategy of direct attack on poverty cannot be sustained and would not yield the desired results, if the overall growth of the economy itself is slow and the benefits of such growth are inequitably distributed. For one thing, the resources and the capabilities needed for running such programmes cannot be generated in the system unless the economy itself is buoyant and there is a sustained increase in output. Secondly, the demand for goods and services produced by the poorer household enterprises rises significantly in response to the overall increase in incomes in the country so that the viability of these household enterprises depends critically on the sustained increase in national income. Further, it is necessary to ensure that the pattern of overall economic growth itself is such as to generate adequate incomes for the poor sections through its greater impact on employment generation and on the development of the less developed regions. The programmes for poverty alleviation should thus be regarded as supplementing the basic plan for overall economic growth, in terms of generating productive assets and skills as well as incomes for the poor.

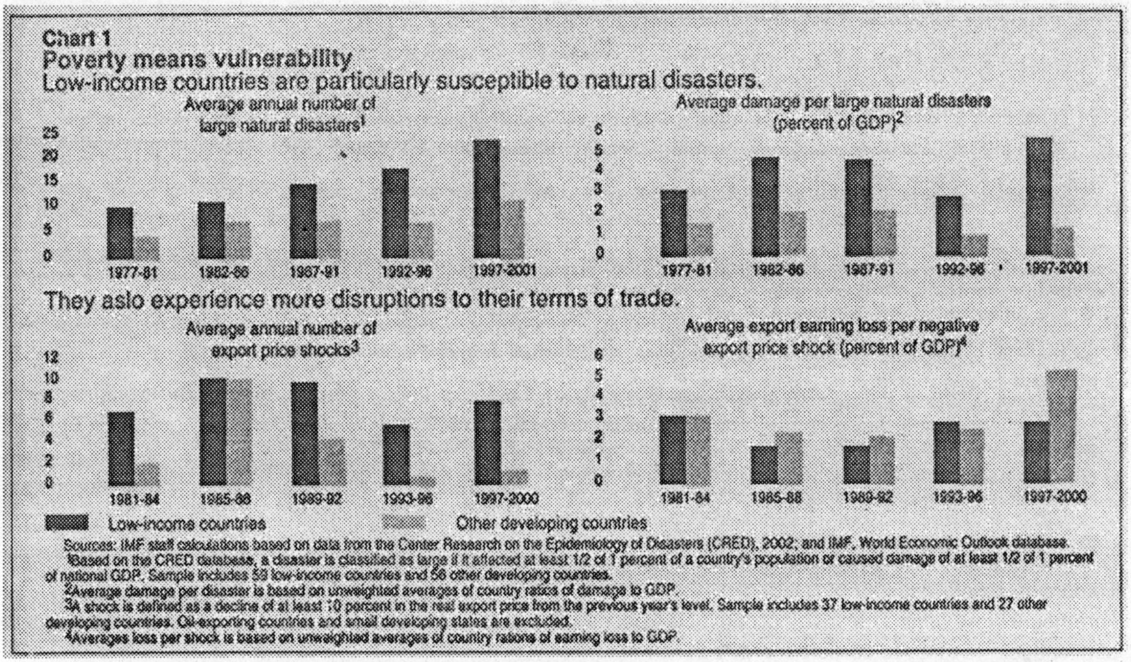


The economic betterment of the poorer sections cannot be achieved without social transformation involving structural changes, educational development, growth in awareness and change in outlook, motivation and attitudes. The social framework should be such as to provide opportunities for the poorer sections to display initiative and to stand on their legs. Moreover, such a framework can ensure that the benefits of poverty alleviation programmes really reach the poor and are not frittered away through various leakages. Strict enforcement of land reforms and revamping of credit institutions can provide the necessary access to assets and resources for the poor as well as promote a more equitable social structure. Greater participation of the poor through the elected institutions is another means to achieve social change. Improvement of literacy and education, both through formal and non-formal means, and the imaginative use of various mass media for communicating useful information and knowledge as well as for changing the outlook of the people by instilling in them the egalitarian spirit, the urge for and confidence in achieving self-betterment through co-operative endeavour, are essential for speeding up the process of socio-economic transformation.

**Box 1**
**NATIONAL GOALS**

For the next five years, with certain progress behind us, the challenge is to launch a major thrust for attaining national prosperity. We should convert the present opportunity and work towards giving our future generations, a competitive nation that has the following characteristics :

A Nation that is prosperous, healthy, secure, peaceful and happy.

A Nation where the rural and urban divide has reduced to a thin line.

A Nation where there is an equitable distribution of energy and quality water.

A Nation where agriculture, industry and service sectors work together in symphony, absorbing technology thereby resulting in sustained wealth generation leading to higher employment potential.

A Nation where education is not denied to any meritorious candidates because of societal or economic discrimination.

A Nation which is the best destination for the most talented scholars and scientists all over the world.

A Nation where the best of health care is available to all the billion population and the diseases like AIDS/TB, water borne diseases, cardiac diseases and cancer are extinct.

A Nation where the governance uses the best of the technologies to be responsive, transparent, easily accessible and simple in rules, thereby corruption free.

A Nation where poverty has been totally alleviated, illiteracy and crime against women are eradicated and the society is unalienated.

A Nation that is one of the best places to live in, on the earth and brings smiles on a billion faces.

To continuing our mission of national development and economic growth in our sub-continent, peace is a paramount ingredient. The development of the society also weans away its people from destructive activities of alienation, leading to celebration of peace-makers.

Certain challenges before the nation are to be addressed collectively in the immediate future to facilitate faster pace of national development.

## Beneficiaries

Admittedly, there have been various deficiencies in the implementation of the poverty-alleviation programmes. However, there has been a distinct improvement in the actual implementation of these programmes over the Sixth Plan. The approach to the Seventh Plan reiterates the goal of bringing down the percentage of population below the poverty line to less than 10 by 1994-95. Therefore, the special programmes for income generation for the poor through assets endowment and wage employment for them will be continued at an accelerated pace during the Seventh Five Year Plan.

In view of the deficiencies noticed in the implementation of the Integrated Rural Development Programme (IRDP), it has been suggested that greater priority should be assigned to rural employment programmes by shifting resources away from IRDP. The argument is two fold. First, the household enterprises of the type visualised are inherently uneconomic and are in any case handicapped for lack of necessary infrastructure. Secondly, owing to the illiteracy and weak economic position of the beneficiaries and the existence of a chain of intermediaries, only a small portion of the intended outlay reaches the actual beneficiaries. Employment programmes on the other hand, it is argued, can provide/secure wage-income to the poor, through the creation of durable community assets.

However, the experience of the working of the poverty-alleviation programmes is by no means uniform in the country. In general, the performance of IRDP has been better in the relatively developed regions which are well provided with infrastructure and where level of awareness among the beneficiaries is high. Even in the less developed areas, performance has been satisfactory wherever special efforts have been made for undertaking the necessary follow-up measures and for greater involvement of people through their representatives.

As to the economic viability of the household enterprises, it should be noted that such enterprises are already in existence on a wide scale in the developed as well as the less developed regions. In fact, they are a major source of employment and income for the poor in rural areas—next only to land. But they suffer from various handicaps in regard to the supply of raw materials, access to credit, facilities for marketing etc. As a result, there is considerable exploitation of these households by the middlemen. Public intervention to provide the necessary services to these already existing enterprises would contribute to a substantial increase in their income. Government-sponsored programmes for the poor, such as dairy and poultry, account for only a small proportion of the total market for such products now, sometimes even less than one per cent.

The demand for such products, and for a number of other rural crafts, is highly responsive to increase in income and, therefore, there is no reason for pessimism about the prospects for income generation for the poor from such activities so long as overall economic growth is satisfactory, besides, the possession of productive assets and skills confers other advantages such as economic security, social status and credit worthiness. Such activities are labour-intensive and not land-intensive and, therefore, typically suit the marginal holdings and the landless. Even though the capital-output ratios (investment per unit of output) for some of these activities are higher than that for crop production, they are still very much lower than for many of the small-scale industrial enterprises. In many cases, where traditional skills are available and remain underutilised for want of resources, the capital-output ratio turns out to be much lower than even for crop production. These activities, in general, required government support for resources, training in skills and marketing.

IRDP and employment programmes are not mutually exclusive. As it is, most of the IRDP beneficiaries supplement their incomes through wage earnings in agriculture as well as from projects under National Rural Employment Programme (NREP) and Rural Landless Employment Guarantee Programme (RLEGP). These activities supplement one another and together ensure a more stable flow of income to the poor throughout the year. The problem of ensuring maximum benefits to the target groups by minimising leakages is common for all the poverty-alleviation programmes and indeed for the rural development programmes in general. Apart from the necessary restructuring of the administrative set-up, there is no alternative to raising the awareness of the rural poor and involving representative institutions from below in the formulation as well as implementation of such programmes

## Cost Effectiveness

Cost-effectiveness of the programmes and minimisation of leakages should be the two guiding principles in the implementation of poverty-alleviation programmes. Economic viability should be understood primarily in terms of cost effectiveness, *i.e.* maximum income generation per unit of total expenditure incurred. This is to be distinguished from economic viability defined as level of investment sufficient to enable a family to cross the poverty line. The ability of a poorer household to cross the poverty line depends on its overall income *i.e.*, income from the poverty-alleviation programmes and other wage and non-wage incomes accruing to them.

Cost-effectiveness or efficiency of programmes depends to a considerable extent, on the nature of activities chosen. In view of the significant regional diversities in the country in regard to resource endowments, availability of infrastructure, administrative arrangement, etc there needs to be sufficient flexibility in the choice of activities in different regions in keeping with the specific circumstances of the area concerned. One should thus expect considerable diversity in the mix of activities from region to region.

The total impact of the programme depends on the degree to which the different poverty-alleviation programmes, including the Minimum Needs Programme (MNP), are integrated with one another and with the overall development of the area. For example, endowment of land under land reform measures can enable a family to grow fodder for the animals given under the IRDP; development of house sites under MNP can be integrated with the construction of houses under NREP or RLEGP can also be used extensively for raising productivity in agriculture through construction of fields channels for irrigation and for drainage.

To achieve the above objectives of cost-effectiveness and minimisation of leakages by imparting the necessary flexibility in the choice of activities and by achieving integration in the programmes, a three-pronged strategy is envisaged in the Tenth Plan.

*(a)* Poverty-alleviation programmes would be formulated and implemented in a decentralised manner with the participation of people at the grassroots level through village panchayat, panchayat samitis, zilla parishads, etc. Such an approach will contribute to the selection of projects suited to local conditions and to the integration of poverty-alleviation programmes with area development. This framework will also help in the timely provision of services in their appropriate sequence and in ensuring that the benefits of such programmes really reach those for whom they are intended. The Working Group on District Planning constituted by the Planning Commission had recommended a gradual approach towards decentralisation for achieving the objectives of effective implementation of poverty-alleviation programmes and balanced regional development. During the Tenth Plan, decentralisation of the planning process and full public participation in development will be pursued on the lines suggested by the Working Group.

*(b)* The launching of a large number of programmes both through the normal sectoral efforts and other steps designed to cater to target-group household has resulted in multiplicity of organisation, leading to duplication of management efforts. Further, the delivery system at various levels has proved to be inadequate. The effective implementation of poverty alleviation programmes would call for better planning at the district level involving various disciplines or department, tighter organisational set-up to ensure optimal use of resources and closer monitoring. A high-level committee has been set up by the Planning Commission to review the existing administrative arrangement for rural development and poverty-alleviation programmes and to recommend an appropriate structural mechanism to ensure that they are planned in an integrated manner and effectively implemented. Measures will be taken during the Seventh Plan for strengthening proper training and orientation of the local administrative machinery. within the framework of an integrated administrative organisation.

*(c)* Keeping in view the limited absorptive capacity of the poorest households, the approach to the Seventh Plan has also emphasised the need for taking up group oriented activities for beneficiaries to the extent possible, through the promotion of co-operatives, registered societies, informal groups, etc. so that the economics of scale, inherent in some of these activities, especially in the provision of services, are fully realized while, at the same time, group initiative and effort of the poor are promoted. This is necessary to protect the beneficiaries from the adverse operation of market forces whether on supply on inputs or on the sale of their products. The mass media will have to be geared for increasing awareness among the rural poor and for dissementing information, non-formal education and functional skills and knowledge required by them. For purpose of bringing about a greater degree of awareness among, and participation of beneficiaries, a central scheme is proposed to be launched for the organisation of the beneficiaries, both in terms of group-oriented economic activities and increased conscientisation. Further, voluntary agencies would be increasingly involved in the formulation as well as implementation of poverty-alleviation programmes during the Seventh Plan, especially for ensuring greater participation of the people.

Given proper project planning for the development of local infrastructure, the Panchayat make a positive contribution to increased agricultural productivity and improving the quality of rural living. Wage employment can create an effective demand for the wage goods produced can lead to the avowed goal of higher employment, increased production, alleviation of poverty, and rural development.

**Box 2**

**WHY BETTER INFRASTRUCTURE IS CRUCIAL**

There is growing recognition that improving infrastructure is crucial to achieving the MDGs. Yet most country strategies do not factor in infrastructure in an integrated manner because of lack of clarity at the country level as to how reliable and affordable provision of infrastructure services can help in reducing poverty through faster growth and better service delivery. Below are two examples of how infrastructure affects progress on MDG-related outcomes:

***Through growth:*** In Uganda, a survey of 243 firms conducted in 1998 showed that inadequate electricity sources were the most important constraint to investment. Firms did not receive electricity from the public grid for 89 operating days a year, on average, with the result that 77 percent of large firms (in addition to 44 percent of medium and 16 percent of small firms) purchased generators, representing 25 percent of their total investment in equipment and machinery. Provision of reliable electricity services would likely attract more firms to invest in Uganda—improving the outlook for growth and poverty reduction.

***Through service delivery:*** In rural India, a study found the prevalence and duration of diarrhea among children under five are significantly lower, on average, for families with piped water than for those without piped water. However, the results also show that the health gains largely bypass children in poor families, particularly when the mother is poorly educated. This points to the importance of combining infrastructure investment with effective public action to promote health knowledge and income poverty reduction

## Some Observations

The experience of rural development programmes and projects initiated and implemented by the Central and State Governments, voluntary agencies, industrial houses and individuals, both at the macro and micro levels over the years, appears to confirm that:

*(i)* It is possible to develop rural areas under local leadership with a dedicated approach by awakening the rural people, by the exploitation of environmental resources and the development of infrastructural facilities, and by removing the cultural barriers to rural development, which is best achieved through education. A package of programmes aimed at the all round development of the target groups with enforced discipline and value systems would go a long way in sustaining development in rural areas.

*(ii)* Rural development is a continuous process, and a dedicated local worker or leader can bring about drastic change in the living conditions of the rural poor.

*(iii)* Whenever the strident Kulak lobby develops some political clout, it uses it largely to garner benefits for the Kulaks in the form of cheaper credit, subsidised power, cheaper fertilisers and pesticides, high prices for their products, and so on. So, in the name of justice to rural India, the top 10 per cent of the rural rich grab the maximum benefits. In the process, rural India continues to suffer. Rural development programmes should guard against the strident Kulak lobby in rural areas.

*(iv)* It is possible to reach a large number of rural poor as well as target groups at a moderate cost and with reasonable expections of acceptable economic returns. Towards this end, stress should be on the rapid development of agriculture and allied activities in the tertiary sector.

(v) If this is done, it would involved political commitment to a strategy for rural development and to the general policies necessary to support such a dynamic strategy. Political commitment is to be translated into reality by the target groups with the co-operation of others, particularly the well-to-do people in rural areas.

(vi) Low cost delivery systems for the supply of inputs on credit terms, for providing extension and marketing services, and for organising communal activities are of crucial importance if large number of the rural poor are to be reached. A greater use of special financial intermediaries, cooperatives, community groups and farmers' associations should be explored. In particular, regional rural banks, supported by other commercial banks, should play a catalytic role in the development of rural areas.

(vii) It is important to balance overall central control with decentralised regional and sectoral project planning. Rural development programmes require a degree of flexibility in design and in responding to the lessons of experience; but the flexibility must be within the limits of minimum national, regional or village standards and financial resources. Though village level, sector-wise and target group-wise planning is essential, block level planning should be given a good trail by improving the techniques of local planning.

(viii) Greater efforts should be made to integrate project management into existing and, if necessary, reformed central and local government organisations and procedures for providing the necessary momentum to rural development.

(ix) It is important to involve the rural poor and particularly the target groups in the planning and implementation of rural programmes. With their active co-operation, various productive and economically viable programmes can be successfully started and implemented in rural areas. This will go a long way in creating tangible assets as well in improving the living conditions of rural people.

(x) Increased training is necessary at the local level, particularly for development managers, regional and project planners, branch managers and the staff of bank branches co-operative societies and extension agents. These people should lead the rural people and, in particular, the target groups, and motivate them for a united effort at rural development.

(xi) An equitable and adequate provision should be made for the recovery of costs so that funds for additional rural development programmes may flow back into the villages. This will provide the necessary momentum to rural development.

(xii) Technical packages have to be devised which are appropriate to the requirements of small farmers, rural artisans any tiny industries based on adaptive national research. Adaptive technology is a forerunner of development.

(xiii) It is necessary to improve knowledge of local natural resources and provide an improved flow of information as a basis for a realistic national, regional, district and village planning.

(xiv) Although increases in output can be achieved with existing technology, increases in productivity will require new technology which is suitable for use by small farmers, tiny entrepreneurs and rural artisans. In particular, educated rural youth need appropriate guidance in channelling their energy productively for the betterment of the rural community; in this way they would contribute to national development. Educated rural youth will provide the necessary leadership for rural development.

(xv) The pricing of agricultural and other rural products has always been biased in favour of the urban consumer. In pricing agriculture and other rural products, the same considerations as are prevalent in industry should be made applicable. The prices of agricultural products should not only cover the cost and margin but serve as a cushion for possible crop failures, which are quite frequent in the rural setting in India.

*(xvi)* The principle of treating agricultural labourers on par with industrial workers in the matter of reasonable wages and social security benefits must be accepted.

*(xvii)* A crash programme of adult literacy must be mounted to educate agriculture labourers, so that they may organise themselves to protect their own interests.

*(xviii)* An integrated approach to rural development has proved very beneficial in uplifting the rural areas from the existing apathy and at the same time, improving the living conditions of the rural poor. In this effort, the co-operation of the rural rich and upper castes is most essential. The target groups should be educated so that they may adhere to the principle of a small family norm and realise the importance of development.

The major premise of the anti-poverty programmes or rural development programmes is that benefits will flow to the weaker sections or the target groups. In the absence of comprehensive studies of the impact of the varied programmes on the weaker sections, it is rather difficult to judge whether the intended beneficiaries have, in fact, gained from these significant public interventions across the country. Partial studies present a mixed picture. The weaker sections did benefit under some of the programmes and not under others.

The progress of rural development in India is marked by instances of achievements on one side and marred by disturbing shortcomings on the other. While blooming fields and highly productive livestock reflect the prosperity of the farmers in some areas, the scenes of conspicuously low-productive farms, ill-fed animals and farmers struggling hard to make both ends meet are not rare either. The instability of output and income and the disparities in sharing the benefits of growth may still be broadly described as the chronic maladies of the Indian rural scene. The frequent incidents of drought and scarcity are still accepted as a part of life in most rural areas. Disparities exit between different geographical areas and even within areas between different economic classes of people. While the success of the green revolution and the strategies of dairy development have raised the productivity of farms and have reduced the intensity of instability in some, they have widened disparities both among regions and within region among different segments of the rural society.

It has been found that funds are sometimes allocated on considerations other than the prescribed ones. Worse still, funds are not released on time, which makes it impossible to spend the allotted money, besides promoting spending in a hurry, leading to waste and infructuous expenditure. Above all, the bureaucracy is still dominated by the upper caste and the relatively well off members of society, brought up in urban environment and with urban orientation, who are unmoved by, and are indifferent to, rural poverty. And they seldom feel the urgency of the need for fighting the abysmal poverty of the rural poor, who include most members of the scheduled castes and tribes. More importantly, it is difficult to have the right type of men who are in sympathy with the poor in the villages and who recognised the imperative necessity of fighting the scourge of poverty. The anti-poverty programmes are not, to be sure, exercises in gratuitous benevolence. They are generally connected with productive work. Even when they are not and are in the nature of welfare work, they make for social peace, without which no orderly progress is possible particularly in developing countries which require social peace for faster growth and where, paradoxically enough, social peace in hard to maintain. The anti-poverty programmes have to be continued with a clear-cut reorientation and stress on production and productivity to create a suitable climate for development in rural areas.

## A Pragmatic Approach — the need of the hour

A pragmatic approach to rural development can be made only if the Central Governments and State Governments concentrate on strengthening the rural infrastructure, on regulating land laws, providing marketing avenues for goods, fixing fair prices for both inputs and outputs, and creating a proper climate for the growth of labour-intensive works in rural areas. The main responsibility for rural development—mobilising resources, supplying inputs, opening up marketing avenues, deployment of funds—should be entrusted to rural regional banks, rural branches of commercial banks, and co-operatives. Voluntary organisations, industrial houses and others should take the responsibility of education, health care, motivation, training and other disciplines. All funds have to be channalised through banks/co-operatives, and they should be given the necessary support by other institutions. The government should discontinue all welfare fringe benefits for the people. The same money should be utilised to create productive as well as protective tangible assets. Though rural development is an continuous process, the initial development effort may be phased and planned. During the first phase, the most backward villages should be taken for micro-level development. In the second phase, medium level villages should be taken up for development. Finally, the well-to-do villages. In this way, rural development will gather momentum. Once it reaches the take-off stage, the strategy of development has to be suitably modified to fit it into the requirements that may then emerge.

This programme of rural development will open up increasing employment opportunities in rural areas rather than create a hierarchy of employment opportunities in urban areas. Second, villager's participation will be forthcoming in a large measure. Third, new marketing opportunities will be created for consumer goods. Fourth, the awareness so generated would be conducive to rapid growth. Finally, this will reduce non-development expenditure considerably.

Today, rural development has been done more by urban and middle class people with the concurrence of rural vested interests. Trickle down scheme has failed, failed miserably. As such, rural India, paradoxically became poorer, while a small segments amassed wealth. In the result, the rank and file of rural poor swelled to well over 41 crores, there is an exponential growth of unemployment, prices are soaring and poverty is growing, matched by growth of corruption in the administration, criminalisation of politics and debasing of value systems. Over the years, terrorism, corruption, communalism are spreading with ease. The growth achieved in some segments has pushsed the country into a debt trap.

In such a grim situation, the administration, design and strategy of rural development should be entrusted to village panchayats. Let the Gram Sabha raise the resources and with the co-operation of the people and the state achieve rural development on an ongoing basis. Panchayats, co-operatives, banks and schools should be the corner stones of rural development.

Each sector should give top priority to growth, productivity, stability, awareness, motivation, participation and population reduction. This should be followed by education, health care, character building, value system, consolidation and unity. The third priority would be the eradication of social evils such as drinking, smoking, drugs etc., which are now constraints on growth and are injurious to health. At the socio-cultural levels, the right type of education will be effective in giving the necessary push to the rural development movement. But much depends upon organisational resources and political and entrepreneur skills.

A national debate has been initiated on the question of strengthening the Panchayati Raj Institutions to enable them to function as vibrant instruments of democracy and local self-government at the villages. Necessary legislative measures are under consideration for the purpose.

The present strategy of direct attack on rural poverty through the existing major programmes of self-employment and wage-employment will be continued and diversified.

NREP and RLEGP will be merged into the new Jawahar Rojgar Yojana to make a single programme. The implementation will be decentralised on the basis of revised guidelines. Government of India will fund 75 per cent of the cost of the scheme and the states will contribute 25 per cent from their resources.

The new Rojgar Yojana introduced for the first time and named after Jawaharlal Nehru is to be launched in 120 backward districts. The guidelines for the selection of the districts have been worked out. This will allow fuller employment opportunities to at least one member of each family living below the poverty line in these districts. A special provision of Rs 2,100 crores has been made in the Budget of this scheme in addition to allocation under the existing employment programmes.

Efforts are being made to strengthen the professional competence of DRDAs. Young professionals from reputed management institutions are being deputed to selected DRDAs on a pilot basis to prepare resources survey of the area and take readily implementable projects. At the state level, Planning Cells are being strengthened to effectively co-ordinate activities of various departments with programmes of IRDP. Special programmes like development of sericulture, fisheries, fruit and vegetable growing, garment making, assembly of electrical and electronic goods etc. are being promoted on project basis.

Rural industrialisation will be the key to greater diversification of IRDP. With the shift in emphasis to the secondary sector, the major concern under the programme has to be on marketing the products of the IRDP beneficiaries. State governments have been advised to review and strengthen the infrastructure for marketing. A Marketing Cell has also been set up in CAPART and it will be taking up the consultancy and advisory functions not only for voluntary organisations but also to various other IRDP groups set up through DRDAs.

In order to strengthen the Computerised Rural Information System Programme (CRISP) which has become operational during the year, it is proposed to develop a technical support organisation at the state level. The main functions of this support system will be to take over on-going process of software enhancement, training of staff and general technical support to DRDAs. States have been advised to identify a state level electronic corporation or a computer directorate which can be the nodal agency for this purpose.

In the field of land reforms, one of the major tasks in the coming years will be to concentrate on speeding up disposal of pending litigation cases on ceiling surplus lands by setting up special tribunals and complete the distribution of all available surplus lands to the rural poor. The other items of work relate to ensuring possession of land to the allottees of surplus land, restoration of alienated tribal lands to the tribals and updating of land records.

## Concurrent Evaluation

Besides monitoring the performance of the various programmes through periodical returns and field visits by senior officers, concurrent evaluation studies in respect of the major programmes are being under taken by the department with the help of reputed research institutions. The aim is to ascertain the areas of concern and to improve/streamline implementation of the programme.

## Plan Policy Perspectives

The development strategies in the Five Year Plan place emphasis on creation of productive work on a large scale in agriculture and related activities and in villages and small industries, through massive efforts at skill formation and technological upgradation on farms and industries. In the field to agriculture, more diversification in terms of activities and regions will be aimed at and with the help of scientific research, efforts will be made to cross the humps in crops where significant productivity gains have already been achieved.

Inter-regional productivity differentials will be sought to be overcome, with emphasis on improved land and water management strategies and formulation of regional agriculture plans, on the basis of agro-climatic regions. Emphasis on agro-climatic, regional planning will also entail detailed attention to non-crop based agriculture including dairying, horticulture, poultry, fishery and forestry. Rural development programmes will have to be more closely integrated with related sectors on an area-wise basis. Agro-climatic regional programmes will have to organise land-use as between crop-production and other agriculture activities, on the basis of regional specialisation of agriculture crops. Agro-climatic regional projects will provide planning back-up but the details will have to be integrated with the district and state level plans.

## Looking Ahead

The experiences of government programmes, voluntary agencies industry and the financial intermediaries, particularly banks, in the task of rural development bring important issues and problems into focus. In fact, these hurdles have been responsible for none-too-impressive performance of rural development. Many explanations are offered for the failure of special programmes for the weaker sections—IRDP, NREP, 20-Point Programme, etc.—to make any significant impact on the magnitude of poverty and unemployment. The failure is attributed to the technocratic approach, administrative inefficiency, lack of motivation and urban bias of political leadership and bureaucracy, organisational weakness, non-application of refined management techniques and faulty delivery system. Hesitant approach to decentratisation of planning and decision-making and the consequent absence of people's participation, ad hoc and piece meal approach, inadequate attention to forward and backward linkages and lack of co-ordination amongst implementing agencies at the local (district) level are also emphasised as being responsible for poor results. Several case studies have established the validity of one or all of the above explanations. Although, some programmes have resulted into significant progress but resulted into inequality and gave birth to a neorich culture on the basis of western culture in Indian ways. As a result, poor in rural India continue to multiply and remain poor. Even though rural development has failed, it must succeed and rural development programmes should be taken up with enthusiasm, there should be no illusions about the inherent difficulties and complexities of rural development. The need of the hour is to implement policies effectively with courage and sincerity.

## Economic Outlook

The Indian economy is in shambles. To rejenuvate it, a careful planning of imports is necessary so as to contain the trade deficit. Liberalisation policy has to be reversed, determined action is required to check prices. The continuous current account deficits over years have added to India's external indebtedness. However, India's external liabilities and debt service payments in relation to Gross Domestic Product have remained so far at reasonable levels. They call for drastic actions to keep them in manageable proportion. While estimating the net inflow of resources from abroad for the Ninth Plan, which aims at a higher rate of growth than was envisaged in the previous Plans, the policy of keeping external liabilities within the prudent limits should be maintained. With a contemplated target of 6 per cent rate of growth in GDP, it seems appropriate to plan for not more than 1.5 to 1.6 per cent of GDP as net inflow of resources from abroad during the next plan.

Broadly, the three major objectives of economic policy are growth, social justice which implies a more equitable distribution of income, and price stability. While all of these objectives are relevant for development policy, price stability has to be its chief focus. This does not, however, mean that it cannot contribute to the attainment of other major objectives. Credit and banking policy, particularly during the past two decades, through the various schemes of direct credit allocation and interest rate change, has helped to promote such objectives as the promotion of the weaker sections of society and balanced regional development. Nevertheless, monetary policy is able to make a more effective contribution towards the objective of price stability than to the other objectives. The importance of price stability as an objective of economic and monetary policy is not, always, well appreciated. In some situations there is perhaps a trade-off between growth and inflation in the very short run. Over a longer time period growth cannot however be bought with the aid of higher prices and there is no evidence to show that a higher growth rate is associated with a higher inflation rate. In India, quite the contrary is the case. In fact, it is price stability which provides the appropriate environment in which healthy and sustainable growth can occur. In an economy where a predominant proportion of the population operates in the unorganised sector with little protection against inflation, maintenance of price stability is intimately linked with social justice.

## Population

Rapid population growth slows down development. It restricts investment in development. It also slows down the continued effort in raising the quality of life of the rural population. It not only enlarges unemployment, underemployment, but also affects productivity and ultimately production. During the eight decades, rural population rose by 315 million from 210 million in 1901 to 525 million in 1981. The growth was highest at 87 million in 1971-81 decades as against 78 million in the previous decade. At this rate, the level of population is likely to be around 620 million in 1991 and 725 million in 2001. As a result, the land resources available for agriculture and allied activities will be shrinking during the next two decades. Two serious consequences will be rapid for deforestation of land under forests. It means that about 200 million more people within the age group of 20 will be added during the next two decades. On the present reckoning, the population below poverty line in rural areas is expected to be around 410 million in 1989 as against 271 million in 1984-85. Growth of rural population will, therefore, have to be checked drastically so that the impact of rural development becomes meaningful and effective. The growing pressure of population will on land will indeed lead to a deterioration in the rural employment situation. Increase in population during the next two decades makes additional demand for about 65-70 million tonnes of food, 180-200 lakh tonnes of milk, 8,500 million eggs, 16-20 lakhs tonnes of fish, 250-300 lakhs tonnes of tea as well as social demands like health—6,800-7,500 additional hospitals, doctors, health, workers and lakhs of health centres, particular in rural areas and 15 lakhs of educational institutions with particular stress on technical education in rural areas over, 60,000-75,000 bank offices and additional recreational and cultural facilities, additional open space for play grounds, gardens and zoos etc., and more employment opportunities have also to be created to the teeming millions, who are likely to be thrown out of land or surplus labour. The net increase of 192 million in rural areas during the next decades means more divisions in land, the main supporter of rural living. The pressure on land is going to be quite tremendous. Efforts should be made to slow down the population growth by all religions, castes and the poor. The country has to adopt one child policy for survival.

## Structure

The causes of rural poverty are structural in nature. Between 1964-65 and 1974-75, the number of rural households has increased by 11.7 million or 17 per cent from 70.4 million to 82.1 million, and further to 90.87 million in 1981. On this reckoning, it is likely to increase to over 120 million by 1990. They do not stem from what its people have done or not done but from the social and economic relations that prevail in rural India. The National Commission on Agriculture (1976) has pinpointed the need for reordering of the agriculture structure for the establishment of a prosperous and egalitarian rural society. On the one hand, only 11.5 percent of farmers own over 52.5 per cent of land, another 32 per cent cultivators own 35.7 per cent of land, and 56.5 per cent own only 12 per cent of cultivated land. Small and medium cultivators account for over 84.5 per cent of total cultivators. A far more important structural hurdle is the excessive and growing fragmentation of land holdings. Consolidation operation should be given high priority in irrigated areas and in the command areas of irrigation projects.

According to the 1981 census, there were 5.55 crores agriculture labourers constituting 24.9 per cent of total working force and 37.5 per cent of total agriculture workers. There were 10.48 crores of scheduled castes and 5.16 crores of scheduled tribes in India. They formed 23.6 per cent of the population. Class and caste barriers have suppressed the people from improving their living conditions. This can be interpreted as growing proletarianisation within the rural economy. The need of the hour is rural integration.

## Land

The most valuable assets in the rural economy is land. However, land is limited. The total land area is 328.8 million hectares, of which, 55.4 per cent available for cultivation. It is estimated that the land available for cultivation may increase by 7.1 million hectares to 158.0 million hectares by 2000 A.D. Of which 78 per cent is likely to be under foodgrains and 22 per cent under non-foodgrains. On account of soil erosion, waterlogging and salinisation at least two-third of the cultivated land is in poor health. Further one-third has become unproductive. While, soil erosion is caused by deforestation, waterlogging and salinisation is due to the absence of adequate drainage. With the steady erosion in the land not available for cultivation, the pressure on land for human settlement will increase in coming decades pushing the land prices higher and higher. Additional demand for land will be forthcoming for strengthening rural infrastructure, building additional houses, recreational centres, locating new agro-based industries and for schools, storehouses, dispensaries, etc.

## Land Holdings

With the increase in rural population during the next two decades, it is estimated that the marginal and small holders are expected to increase by 24.70 million households from 62.13 million households (74.4 per cent of total farm households) to 86.83 million households (80.4 percent). With further division in land holdings, there will be a sharp increase in the population growth of agricultural labourers. The average holding is likely to decline to less than 0.5 hectare as against 1.7 hectares in 1982. With a view to check this from further deterioration inheritance laws have to be suitably amended so that there is no further sub-division in land holding in particular at its earliest and at the same time, fragmented holdings be consolidated into economically viable units for better farming and increased production of food as well as non-food, particularly cash crops.

## Land Reforms

If land reforms is to serve as an effective instrument of planned social change—*i.e.*, eliminate constraints on growth of agricultural production and secure social justice—it is necessary to have a fresh look at its theory and practice in the country. Land in rural India has already undergone minute sub-division and fragmentation as a result of partition and population pressure. There has been an increasing struggle for living space leave alone land for cultivation. In the process, the land prices are shooting up from one year to another. With a view to create an improved and equitable system of agriculture, land reform must be followed by appropriate institutional and organisational arrangements that will help to organise the rural population for each successive stage of rural development. The economic balance can and should be shifted in favour of the small and marginal farmers mainly by helping them increase their productivity and by other concomitant measures. To realize the objectives of the land reform measures which ensure access to land to all farm households who are depending on agriculture for their sustenance, there is need for effective land reform policy backed by political and administrative commitment to fulfill the unfinished task in a time bound manner.

## Agriculture

Although, food production has gone up, it has, however, been neutralised by population growth. The average per capita availability for consumption has stagnated at 460-470 grams per day. This average consumption conceals a severe mal-distribution of available foodgrains. A large segment of rural people are not only affected by under nourishment but also by malnutrition. This calls for increasing food production and also augment the purchasing power of the rural poor to avail nutritious food.

Extension of minor irrigation, application of modern technology are the means to increase yields of all crops and thereby substantially increase agricultural production. Marginal and small farmers' lands should be consolidated into viable agriculture units and cultivated and managed on the principle of co-operative and collective farms—irrigation land 10-15 hectares, dry land 150-200 hectares. Supplementary jobs in village crafts, forestry, animal husbandry, piggery, fisheries, etc. should be encouraged and developed. Productivity of food and non-food crops should be almost doubled with the application of scientific methods and technology in order to be self-reliant in food production and produce adequate surplus for exports. From the point of view of exports, there is a special need to set up production of plantation products by extending their area as well as improving their yield per hectare. Co-operative or commercial banks shall guide the farmers in their production efforts, storage and marketability. Village panchayats will have to play a lead role in regard to development of agriculture, village industry, forestry, animal husbandry, horticulture, sericulture and other allied activities.

**Box 3**
**TIME FOR NEW ORIENTATION**

Five basic principles which should shape the future development programmes in agriculture can be set out. First, the pattern of production advance should be "land saving crop husbandry and grain saving animal husbandry."

Secondly, ecological sustainability and equity in the use of national resources should constitute the basic norm of all agricultural and rural development programmes. Protecting the livelihood of the poor is essential for enduring ecological security.

Thirdly, explicit attention should be given to promoting beneficial growth linkages among the primary, secondary and tertiary sectors of economic activity. At least 200 million persons in the rural areas should be found skilled jobs in the off-farm sectors by the year 2000.

Fourthly, agricultural technology should be intellectually satisfying and economically rewarding to attract and retain youth in farming and related activities in villages. Over 50 per cent of the population is below the age of 21 and the agricultural future is in its hands.

Finally, the comparative strengths in agriculture with regard to exports should be carefully identified and nurtured. For this purpose, coastal and mountain area planning and post-harvest technologies require particular attention.

These ground rules should constitute the fundamental basis of the development of packages of technologies, services and policies. Progress in agrarian reform has been patchy. Unless the tiller has a long term stake in the land, there will be little interest in making the investments on land essential for sustained high yields. A few of these aspects are worth discussing at length along with indications of what can be done.

## Irrigation

As at end 1987-88 74.29 million hectares was under gross irrigation (net being 61.5 million hectares). However, a recent study by Administrative Staff College of India has estimated that around 10 million hectares of canal irrigated land has become water-logged and therefore, is no longer fit for cultivation. Another 25 million hectares is threatened with salinity. It means that 68.8 per cent of the irrigated area is in danger. In view of this imminent danger, proper scientific and technical methods be applied and the managerial problems be sorted out before embarking on fresh investment in irrigation. Every efforts should be made to reclaim the water logged and saline land with the adoption of new technology. Further, irrigation should not be considered in terms of short-term gains but planned for long-term and lasting benefits. It calls for judicious water management. Plans are in operation to provide irrigation facility to 45 per cent of net sown area by 2000 A.D. If available techniques of minimising the loss of water through evaporation, sewage and over watering are fully used, the irrigated area can be easily increased by 50 per cent to 100 per cent. To introduce new plastic technology to cover the village tank beds for storage and rivulets to store water for irrigation purpose. These measures go a long way in managing water for productive purposes.

*Rejuvenating wastelands through Watershed Development*

## Modern Technology

However, mere adoption of optimum crop pattern is not enough. The key to raising productivity and production of crops lies in the technology that is applied to crop cultivation. The HYV seed-fertilisers technology, that has proved successful since its introduction in the mid-sixties, is supposed to be scale-neutral in theory, but, in practice, it favours those farms and areas which are well endowed with irrigation resources or have assured rainfall or access to irrigation facility. The technology succeeds to the degree that this critical condition is fulfilled. This has meant that the technology, from the very start, contained seeds of causing or exacerbating inequalities among farmers and among regions. These variations in growth and development have to be corrected through appropriate area-specific strategies. Otherwise, a large segment of the country will continue to be poor. the need of the hour is to reassess the feasibility of modern technology to rural development.

## Forestry

Forests have multifarious uses. They meet the basic needs of the poor people in many ways. Development of forests will accelerate the momentum of rural development. With proper linkages forests will foster development. As at end 1986-87, only 10.7 per cent of land was under forest cover. In order to ensure balance in the eco-system, the land under forest must be raised. It is envisaged that additional 65.70 million hectare is expected to be brought under forest raising its share to 28.0 per cent by 2000 A.D. Reforestation is a must. Besides extended farms and social forests to meet the increased requirements of fuel, fodder, wood and other raw materials, Panchayats should be entrusted with the task of reforestation work within rural areas. The development of protected forests should be the responsibility of forest divisions.

**Box 4**

**LOOKING AHEAD**

The Global Vision for Forests 2050 project—an initiative that brought together leading experts, non-governmental organisations, industry, and donor institutions—yielded the following scenario for a global closed forest area of 3 billion hectares in 2050 (see Chart 4): an increase in community-owned and –managed forests (from 380 million hectares in 2000), and a significant increase in protected areas as defined under the World Conservation Union categories I-VI. The area of state and private production forests under intensive management would remain roughly the same as at present, and industrial plantation forests would increase slightly from 95 million hectares to 100 million hectares.

**Chart 2**

**A Possible global forest situation, 2050**
**(million hectares)**

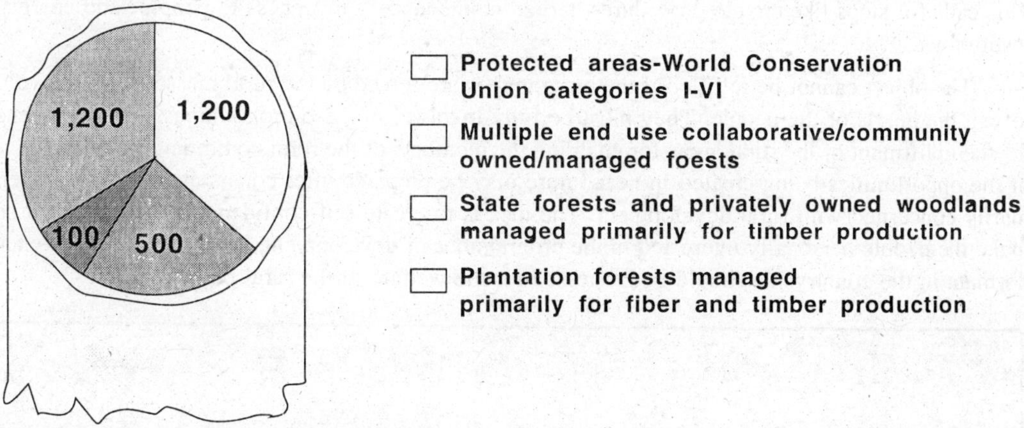


***Source :*** Gobal Vision for Forests 2050 project.

## Long-Term Planning

In the wake of massive growth of rural development programmes and the stress on rapid development of rural areas, in the post-Independence period, certain stresses and strains have developed. It is in this context that we would like to submit the need for formulation of a well-defined long-term rural development. The long-term plan will cover all facets of rural activities, production and conversion of the available resources to meaningful wealth and their equitable distribution to the community, while protecting as well as enriching the eco-system. Towards this end, India would do well to borrow more and invest the funds in carefully selected projects for generation of new wealth in rural areas. Until and unless rural area produce a surplus to sell in the urban market, their economy will not improve. Further, the long-term planning should emphasise on launching non-farming projects in rural environment to absorb the surplus labour productively. If need be a reversal of economic activities has to be enforced. The ultimate objective of long-term planning should be to identify priorities for action concerning social and economic policy interventions, appropriate investments, and institutional changes. Thus, it would be enough to take care of debt servicing burden and for providing surpluses for re-investment. What is needed is the prompt implementation of selected projects.

## Integrated Development Programme

Integrated programme for rural development should be formulated so that the living standards of people in rural and urban areas are continuously improved and the eco-system is enriched. This should be also linked with industrial development. Integrated development assessments calls for an understanding of the proximate and under lying physical and economic linkages between different levels and manners of resource use, and their socio-economic consequences. The extent to which the management skills, the knowledge and know-how the scientific and technological resources could be harnessed should ultimately be left to the choice of the local people rather than to the manipulative coterie. Gunnar Myrdal has already given a timely warning, "In the absence of more discipline—which will not appear without regulations backed by compulsions—all measures for rural uplift will be largely ineffective."

## Awareness

The Khadi and Village Industries Commission (KVIC) is a potential instrument of change. It was conceived to play and it has to play a transforming role, not merely a change in economic status, but creation of a new man with a yearning for self-reliance is the inspiring ideal of the Commission. What we need today is a result oriented approach, which puts a special responsibility on the implementing agency or individual. This calls for steps like simple procedures, target maintenance, "awareness to people" and energising rural institutions.

The object cannot be fulfilled if the programmes are forced on the rural masses from above. We have to win the hearts of the people. They must be fully involved in these programmes. A comprehensive plan for the upliftment of the rural areas for enabling the members of the rural community to take full advantage of the opportunities being created in near future may be prepared after consultation with the agencies primarily concerned with rural development. The idea is to create self-confidence in the rural masses and to make the people personally interested in the programmes of development. The vast unutilised energy lying dormant in the countryside should be harnessed for the welfare of the rural poor.

*Generating wage employment under SGRY*

## Group Effort

There is a need for promoting group co-operation among families living in a village. Promoting group effort without affecting the basic structure of land ownership can be achieved by an intelligent deployment of public policy instruments, involvement of Panchayati Raj institutions and community orientation to administrative co-ordination. At the same time, through minimum productivity and soil health care guidelines, it should be made clear that the right of land ownership does not include the right to abuse it and destroy or diminish its biological potential.

A mission mode of organisation which involves mechanisms for effective co-ordination and monitoring and for adoption of a system approach may be good for tackling a multi-dimensional problem with uni-dimensional administrative structure. It is a method by which the return from investment from the available resources and the existing infrastructure can be optimised.

For example, irrigation water will increasingly become the most important limiting factor in several parts of the country. Water conservation and use can be organised at the state and village levels in a mission mode. A micro-level and location-specific approach is what is needed.

At the same time, better co-operation and co-ordination among the agencies working in the field of agriculture, industry and rural development is necessary. Group efforts compelled with trusteeship will not doubt change the rural scene. In this respect, the village panchayat has to play a pivotal role.

*A view of the houses constructed under IAY*

## Leadership

The need of the hour is a benevolent leader like Chandragupta Maurya aided by able administration like Kautilya for speedy uplift of rural people. There has to be more human touch, an approach closer to the people than to the insipid institutions that have enslaved them throughout the past. The leaders should not be allowed to float trusts in the name of the rural poor but for their acquiring additional power. All such trusts must be taken over by the government in the larger interest of people. The leadership at all levels should be enlightened, self-less benevolent, concerned for the rural poor, innovative, not interested in power or position. And at the same time, firm and innovative. More important task to get dedicated, able men at helm. The leaders should be exemplary to one and all.

## Political Stability

Political instability hinders economic development in various ways. In short phase, food prices shoot up, garbage clearance affects, raw materials do not reach industries, finished goods do not reach consumers. In fact, working of trade and industries stand paralysed. There will be transport bottlenecks. On the other hand, not only it wipes out the infrastructure facilities built up over the years, but also the gains of economic development. Political instability increases crimes and destroys property—public as well as private created over the years. It throws people on the streets who should be given the basis necessities like food, clothing and housing. Above all, to rehabilitate the affected people from scratch. In a way, political instability means burning both ends at the same time. Political stability depends on matured leadership, communal harmony and patriotism. The people living in India should live like Indians as a one nation. Feudalism and fanatism should cease to exit and people should be aware of their rights and duties to the community and the country. People should give up the narrow mindedness and broaden their vision and attitude to mankind.

## Democratic Decentralisation

Democracy means equal opportunities, discipline, tolerance and mutual regard. In a democracy changes are made by mutual discussion and persuasion and not by violent and/or unfair means. It goes without saying that for real rural development, decentralisation is must, be it in the area of economy, structural changes, institutional network and their reorientation, planning process, industrial strategy etc.

Decentralisation in true sense envisages a devolution of decision making authority both at the levels of the formulation and the implementation of plan and programmes within the framework of given political, social, and economic structure. It encompasses a field wider than mere administrative devolution which is pragmatic, bureaucratic in nature. In its wider sense, decentralisation has to adopt to local conditions fully and respond to the local environment, local level activities suiting the needs, resources endowments and potential of a particular region, coupled with democratic process, the process of development is made much easier.

When we say, democratic decentralisation, we admit that there is centralisation of power. We start from the wrong end. In a democracy, the distribution of power, planning, discussion and development should be from the base upwards. The Gram Sabha is the fundamental unit of democracy and not the Lok Sabha as it is today. The very expression of democratic decentralisation carries an odour of condescension.

The prerequisite of successful democratic decentralisation is, therefore, to create a proper environment to bring a kind of attitudinal change among the people toward democratic development; to make them conscious about their rights and duties through various audio-visual aids at the grassroot level. Thus the rural development covers from village to village, town to town. On the whole, democratic decentralisation for rural development would mean working for a number of basic changes in the rural society, the basic concept of democracy as well as in the approaches being adopted for its development.

The Balwant Rai Mehta Committee emphasised the importance of local bodies from the development point of view aptly observe that:

"So long as we do not discover or create a representative democratic institution which will supply the local inter-supervision and care necessary to ensure that expansion of money upon local object conforms with the needs and wishes of the locality, invest it with adequate power and assign to it appropriate finances, we will never be able to evoke local interest and excite local initiative in the field of development."

## Panchayati Raj

The network of Panchayati Raj institutions covers the length and breadth of the country today but not in the sense and manner they were meant to. Numerically and quantitatively there are myriads of these institutions dotting the entire landscape of our country. Powers and functions have been conferred on them by legislative enactments. There is, however, a feeling that these institutions have become moribund and that they have been denuded of their promise and vitality. There is a legitimate question mark against these institutions, not because the constitutional promise has been abandoned nor because self-government is no longer an article of faith with us, not because we have lost faith in ourselves; but because we have allowed these institutions to be neglected, because we have failed to nurture them with the inputs and material and human resources necessary for them and because the operational claims and quest of political power have taken a heavy toll on the fundamental concept of self-government and public service.

The Panchayati Raj should be entrusted with the task of village administration, community development from decision, strategy to implementation.

**Box 5**
**WOMAN POWER**

In December 1992, when Parliament passed the 73rd and 74th amendments to the Constitution, making the panchayats and municipalities "institutions of self-government" and reserving not less than one-third seats for women in these bodies, it was hailed as the beginning of a silent revolution.

In 1994, all Indian states passed the Conformity Act reshaping their Panchayati Raj (PR) system according to the new amendments. Today, out of 3,200,000 members elected every five years to panchayats and municipalities, more than 1 million are women. Women head one-third of all local bodies.

Stories of empowerment can be found in many states. Geeta Rathore (44) belongs to Jamonia Talab gram panchayat in Sehore district of Madhya Pradesh. She was elected sarpanch in 1995 from a reserved seat; but in 2000, the people rewarded her for her admirable work by way of re-election — this time from a non-reserved seat. From a humble housewife, Geeta has grown into a leader displaying political farsightedness — she was harnessed the collective energy of her panchayat to renovate water tanks, build a school building, construct village roads, fight against domestic violence and create environmental awareness.

But Sukhiya Bai, tribal sarpanch of Gubrail panchayat in Betul district of the same state, died a year ago of 80 per cent burns in a Bhopal hospital. Sukhiya was trying to fight against corrupt officials, who were demanding a cut for releasing money for development work. She was also under pressure from villagers who wanted to be paid for their labour. As a result, she was forced to borrow Rs. 4,000 from a relative to pay the panchayat secretary so that he'd release the money for the well, which was constructed by the villagers. Unable to bear the constant tension, she set fire to herself.

In Tamil Nadu, Leelavathi contested the Madurai municipal elections in 1996, promising to bring water to the ward. Within six months of her election, water came to the area. This threatened the mafia of water tanker owners, who had a flourishing business in the area. Soon after, Leelavathi was murdered.

Ten years is a short time. Even if the representatives have not worked wonders, they have made significant beginnings, although they have often had to pay a huge price for them.

Times of India, 29-04-2004.

Striking a balance between techno-economic viability and village identity in an optimum mix of demographic and geographical size should be a policy goal and practical endeavour keeping in mind that each village must be viewed as a unit of self-government. Optimisation of economic growth and social justice is bound to follow in the wake of village panchayats operating as units of self-government and as cradles of civic culture, social ethos, public education, poverty alleviation programmes, voluntary citizens' action and constructive work. It will require considerable patience but it will pay handsome dividends.

The strengthening of the Panchayati Raj provides an opportunity for dealing with the management of local resources and local commons in a more meaningful and sustainable manner. The Panchayati Raj institutions should be organised as a part of the process of democratic decentralisation for building up the institutional edifice from the grassroots upwards and not as gift of devolutionary process. Thus, the Indian villages and the Gram Sabhas becomes the base of our democratic nation.

In fact, the Gram Sabha is the embodiment of direct democracy. It is time to restructure and redefine democracy from Gram Sabha upward to Lok Sabha and not vice versa, In the process the real representatives of the people and not the dummies head the nation.

The implementation of the programmes has of necessity to devolve on the "associate" organisations of people. The social programmes under Panchayati Raj can be handled by the chain of social organisations that can be set up such as Yuvak Mandals, Mahila Mandals, Bal Mandals and other functional groups of people. Economic activity has necessarily to be conducted as part of Sahakari Samaj through different specialised co-operatives inter-acting and cross fertilizing mutually. Panchayati Raj and Sahakari Samaj are twin instruments for a common consummation. They can play their part only if they blossom in freedom and achieve mutual interdependence. A working group was appointed by the Ministry a short while ago which has recommended how co-ordination should be achieved between these two vital institutions so as to avoid conflicts and overlapping in effort. These recommendations will soon be put in operation. But ultimately their implementation will depend on the wisdom of the people themselves whose organs these are, whether they function as inter-dependent institutions for promoting the larger interest of the people or as feudal organs to battle against each other at the expense of the people.

## Test of Health in Co-operative Society

The co-operative society must progress in sound health if it is to discharge the role assigned to it in the economy of the country. This calls for clear criteria. For the present these may consist broadly of whether or not there is:

(1) Broad-based membership in the villages;

(2) Linking of credit, supplies and services with concrete production plans;

(3) Development of marketing and processing services;

(4) Spontaneous spread of the movement in the direction of the other sector of the economy, more particularly industries;

(5) Pooling of savings by the community in co-operative institutions;

(6) Evolution of the federal organisation of co-operatives to guide and regulate institution;

(7) Help offered by the strong in the co-operative sector to the weaker members;

(8) Inter-relationship and cross fertilisation between different sectors of the co-operative movement;

(9) Progressive growth of competence in non-official leadership in the movement;

(10) Cohesion, mutual aid and co-operative self-help in the community and participation by members in formulation of policies and review of action.

## Co-operative Society and Integrated Development

The socialistic pattern in India visualises a strong public sector controlling the basic means of production. There will also be a strong private sector whether or not government wills it; for the private sector depends on private initiative. In a democracy growing from a feudal and colonial base, private sector cannot but have a major pressure of its own to exert for its own survival and promotion. The public sector as has already been mentioned earlier, can tend in certain context to foster totalitarian trends to the extreme left. The private sector left to itself cannot but have feudal trends to the extreme right. The two sectors are vital as they are for national existence in the context of the fast advancing sputnik age, cannot be left free to become a menace to freedom and initiative. A growing co-operative sector as an active balancing force between the two groups thus seems to be an inevitable must. To play this strategic role, the co-operative sector must develop the requisite organisational strength and technical competence to provide services at economic cost. It should not grow to a monopoly at the cost of the community. Co-operation between members of a community can act like magic.

The socialist pattern demands reduction in inequality between citizen. It calls for an egalitarian economy. It demands reduction in the wide disparities of income and wealth that now rule. Co-operation which literally means operation by equals, grows thus to be the yardstick for the growth of our people in the democracy we have set as our goal. The essence of Community Development is the extension of the concept of the joint family till it encompasses the nation as a whole. Joint family means co-existence of the genius and the moron, the artist and the buffoon with all the ramifications in between. Joint family cannot permit starvation, physical or spiritual for any member of the family however weak or unfit. Co-operative society means mutual aid between members of the joint family. It means aid by the strong to the weak so that the latter can rise to the level of the strong as equal members of the community. Co-operative Society and Panchayati Raj are but the means to the building of the joint family — the community. The development of the community will depend on the development in freedom of co-operative society and Panchayati Raj as the twin instruments of integrated development of the rural community. The goal is co-operation, unity, discipline, dedication and hardwork.

## Other Measures

The most important aspects of rural development are the education of rural people, improving the health standards, bringing in new awareness towards benefits of small family and sanitation and motivating them towards whole-hearted participation in all developmental activities.

All ameliorative and welfare measures should be abolished and the said amount of money be invested in projects generating additional employment opportunities as well as in increasing production. Maximise the output per labour, capital to meet the crisis of tomorrow. This could be done by building up character, identity, better utilisation of resources and adequacy of administration and leadership. Totally eradicate the permissive atmosphere prevailing everywhere in the society. This is an uphill task.

Politics should be an effective tool of development rather than seat of power. This calls for various changes in the structure and organisation of rural society. The foremost aspect is rejuvenating values system governing life. Particularly, inculcating 'discipline', 'truthfulness', 'perseverance', 'honesty', 'dedication', 'patriotism', and 'service'. The dominating feature of demographic development is the sharp rise in the number of persons in the working age group.

To accelerate the rate of productive employment, productive work opportunities will have to be generated on a very large scale in agriculture and related activities and in village and small industries. This will require a massive effort at skill formation, technological upgradation in rural areas and small towns, in farms, artisan households and small manufacturing units. Hence, it is now an economic necessity to promote quality improvements in education, vocationalisation, training and re-training programmes for workers and the orientation of the scientific and technological infrastructure to serve the needs of rural areas and the unorganised sector.

The real task is to ensure that no person anywhere in the country is held back from improving his lot because of the lack of education or appropriate technical skills. This aim must be translated into specific programmes for education, training technology development and scientific research.

Elimination of poverty on a durable basis and rural development on ongoing basis can be achieved only by ensuring that all rural households, especially those currently below the poverty line, (Rs. 9,800 per annum per family of 5) have an entitlement to productive viable assets and skills which provide them gainful employment and adequate earnings to enable them to live above subsistence level. Hence, all the avenues which would facilitate removal of poverty or arrest the process of poverty in rural areas need to be explored. The attack on rural poverty and emphasis on rural development calls for a multi-pronged approach administered through a nodal agency which is really committed to the important task of rural development.

## Strategies for the Future

1. A multi-agency approach in agriculture and rural development is crucial for its development. Public, private, NGOs, Farmers' organisations must act with better co-operation and co-ordination.
2. People's participation in decision-making regarding planning development process and technology choice is very important to adopt appropriate technology and to improve the development process.
3. Capacity building in the poorer sections of the society by skill training and upgradation.
4. Promote private sector participation in agriculture through contract farming.
5. Priority should be given to evolve location specific and economically viable technologies, for example, region specific improved varieties of agricultural and horticultural crops, and local knowledge based technologies for rural development.
6. Initiation of a farming system research which integrates all the factors of production, viz., land, water, labour, capital, and all farm activities such as crop production, livestock rising, dairying, sericulture, fisheries, social forestry etc. together to development a whole farm production system.

## End Results

Otherwise, more and more power will be monopolised by a select few, cutting at the roots of social justice to the majority of rural poor. And, what is more, the percentage of rural poor may increase to over 60 per cent as against 50.8 per cent in 1989. In absolute terms, over 440 million rural people will continue to remain poor, in spite of huge investments. Poverty is however still the No.1 problem. Rural people may continue to live lacking bare essentials, face grim, ordeal of hunger, malnutrition, disease, illiteracy and wise noble living conditions. Rural isolation, unemployment and poverty are closely linked. If not checked, the country may disintegrate, lose national identity and character, development of more and more permissive society, loss of rural heritage, spread of corruption, scarcity of food, ecological imbalance and disruptions, natural calamities, spread of disease, spread of violence and agitations, (as it is erupting in the various parts of the country and the world) and crisis of civilised culture and mankind, like bad money drives away good money, bad elements may drive away good things from the rural society and cultural heritage.

In the ultimate analysis, all efforts towards improving the standard of living in rural areas through varied rural development programmes may result in inequality and millions of rural poor knocking at urban centres for food, cloth and work. This may give rise to law and order problems too. What is more, all efforts of rural development and planning will be washed away. Frustration looms large and the rural India stands disintegrated.

The principle components of rural development are coined in 20 words forming ***I promise rural welfare*** which is in consonance with the process of rural development. It means as follows:

| | | | | | |
|---|---|---|---|---|---|
| I | Increase in irrigation potential | (1) | R | Rural Electrification | (11) |
| P | Pulses Oilseeds Development | (2) | A | Afforestation | (12) |
| R | Rural Development | (3) | L | Lever for Family Welfare | (13) |
| O | Observe Equitable distribution of Land | (4) | W | Wealth Through Health | (14) |
| M | Minimum Wage Payment | (5) | E | Eradicating Malnutrition | (15) |
| I | Independence to Bonded Labour | (6) | L | Literacy Promotion | (16) |
| S | Scheduled Castes Welfare | (7) | F | Fair Price Shops | (17) |
| E | Essential Water Supply | (8) | A | Accelerate rural Industrial Growth | (18) |
| R | Rural Housing | (9) | R | Restrain Anti-Social Elements | (19) |
| U | Urban Housing | (10) | E | Efficiency in rural sector | (20) |

This is as it should be, as our progress to be rapid and enduring has to be based on the development of rural resources.

If rural poverty and degradation of the environment is not tackled properly, it will push urban areas also into a poverty trap. So, a corrective step is necessary right now.

We may conclude by quoting Pandit Jawaharlal Nehru, "whatever plan we might make, the test of its success is how far it brings relief to the millions of our people who live on a bare subsistence level, that is, the good and advancement of the masses of our people," and pledging to put this test to whatever development plans we make for rural upliftment.

## Conclusion

Rural India needs a new social contract in which there will be a reliable infrastructure supplied at commercial prices rather than given for free. The Government's commitment, both at the national and State levels should be that every village will be assured clean water, a road to the regional market and reliable power and minimal telephone services but the village will be responsible for covering the commercial costs on a normal user-fee basis. Recent technological changes in each of the areas (telephone, water, road building and maintenance, and power) allow these key sectors to be organised, at least in part, on the basis of competitive, private sector producers, who will provide the initial financing of the investments in return for a reliable stream of user charges overtime.

❑ ❑ ❑

*"Economic growth can reduce poverty by generating employment and incomes; labour-intensive growth can reduce it even faster. Promoting inclusive, more equitable, pro-poor, sustainable economic growth relies on the successful pursuit of the other pillars of poverty reduction strategy: social development and good governance."*

Chapter 41

# RURAL DEVELOPMENT IN THE 21ST CENTURY

## Introduction

In the new millennium, the world is certainly a much smaller place than it was at the beginning of the last one. Technological advances in transportation and communication have seemingly obliterated many of the obstacles between peoples. Even some major political borders have been dismantled, with, for instance, the demolition of the Berlin Wall. Europe, which began the current millennium warring over borders, will enter the next as a virtual land-without-border, where ordinary citizens are able to connect and transact as freely as their leaders have for the past few decades.

While physical borders remain armed and guarded in India and throughout much of the world, integration is nevertheless proceeding on a global scale.

## Rural Development

Rural development does not just mean growth of rural income, it encompasses a spectrum of activities and human mobilisation to make people stand on their own feet. It includes the following:

| *Agriculture* | *Rural Development* | *Rural Industries* | *Holistic Self Supporting Development* |
|---|---|---|---|
| Agriculture, Horticulture, Forestry, Sericulture, Animal Husbandry, Fisheries, etc. | Health, Small Savings, Pollution, Environment, Ecology, Drinking Water, Education, Roads, Housing, Tourism, Sanitation, Science and Technology and many other programmes. | Rural industrialisation means value addition on local raw material like agriculture, forest, horticulture, chemical etc. or demand based industries — thus making marketable products and marketing either in villages and/or cities or export etc. | This pre-suppose the development of closely related systems and linkages where exploitation less, holistically developed systems becomes acceptable and possible. This should be the ultimate aim of not only rural employment generation but in planning for quality of life. |

## Since Independence

Over the last five decades of Indian Independence, attempts have been made by various governments — Central and State — industrial houses, voluntary agencies and other social workers to lift the rural poor from the vicious circle of poverty, hunger, ignorance and ill-health. The State and Central Governments have attempted to take the economy to new heights of development and to promote social justice through a series of five-year plans, and have formulated various strategies and policy programmes for the purpose. In spite of these efforts and a huge investment, plan after plan has failed to lift the poor and, more particularly, the rural poor, to a richer and more varied life. Their levels of living remain abysmally low. Poverty, hunger, deprivation, ill-health, high fertility, unemployment, underemployment—all these continue to haunt the rural folk. Statistically, the percentage of rural poverty has slid down; but it has been conditioned by an en masse migration of the rural poor in search of green pastures to urban and metropolitan centres. Planned development during the last four decades has, therefore, not made a significant dent on unemployment, underemployment, hunger poverty and exploitation of the rural masses.

## Dimension of Poverty

Poverty has often been divided into food poverty, health poverty, education poverty, energy poverty, character poverty, income poverty and poverty in respect of the consumption of industrial goods. The link between household poverty and high fertility is reinforced by high rates of infant and child mortality; in poor families, many births and the high probability of infant deaths go hand-in-hand. The life of the poor is conditioned by religion, culture and social norms. Economic poverty, low education, poor health, high death rates lead to the emergence of large families and the spread of poverty. The industrial world has shown that, with improvements in their opportunities for education, for developing and using skills, for leisure, and for earning money, their horizons would expands and the size of the family would become smaller.

**Box 1**

**THE FACE OF POVERTY IN INDIA**

Being poor in India means lacking the good health and skills to make the most of the economic opportunities growth can open. Over half of India's children under five years of age still suffer from malnutrition and, later in life, from the illnesses to which an ill-nourished childhood exposes those who survive it. Being poor in rural India means, as well, a higher than 50 percent likelihood of being illiterate. In the state of Andhra Pradesh, Bihar, and Rajasthan, barely half the rural men (poor or not) can read; in Rajasthan and Bihar barely a quarter of *all* the women are literate, a percentage that drops to 17 percent in rural Rajasthan and 22 in rural Bihar.

The incidence of poverty and the poor's access to social services varies considerably from state to state and even within states. Poverty in rural Bihar, for instance, was almost twice as widespread (a 58 percent rate of incidence) in 1993-94 as in rural Kerala (31 percent). Even within a single state, the variance can be striking, for example, between rural poverty incidence in southern (68.8) and northern (45.5) Orissa, and inequality is higher within wealthier regions. Similarly, living in Kerala rather than in Bihar made an average child 25 percent more likely to attend school. And the better health status of the poor in Kerala is largely explained by Kerala's better education, water, and sanitation and basic infrastructure services.

Even more noticeable than geographic differences in poverty, social indicators, and regional inequality are the inequalities that persist across gender, caste, and ethnic groups. The size of the gender gap in schooling varies widely across states, but works out to a significant average disadvantage for girls wherever they live and however affluent or disadvantaged their families. Boys all over India are about 20 percent more likely than girls to have finished the 8 years of basic education. Being a poor, pregnant woman means risking death. India's maternal mortality is so high (437 per 100,000) that the nation accounts for one in every four maternal deaths worldwide.

Similarly, members of scheduled castes, particularly their children, are more likely to die prematurely.

## The Process of Rural Development

The process of rural development includes the development of the rural poor. In spite of concerted efforts, the programmes had limited success for they touched only a fringe of rural problems and rural areas. In this context, the observations of Gunnar Myrdal in his book, Asian Drama, are worthy of recollection. His focus on the failure of several measures intended to promote egalitarianism in Indian society, and implement land and tenancy reforms, which were intended to cut away the roots of the inegalitarian structure of Indian villages, is not only important but also a cause of great concern. More important are his findings that rural upliftment measures have themselves tended to benefit primarily those who are already better off than most. This tendency has been a natural, indeed a necessary, consequence of the application of uplift policies in an inegalitarian society without prior or simultaneous effort to break down the existing institutional barriers to greater equality.

Douglas Ensminger of Ford Foundation, who played a leading role in community development in India, had earlier warned against the caste system. He firmly believed that caste attitude were a deterrent to the success of the community development programme. The late V.T. Krishnamachari, the then Deputy Chairman of the Planning Commission, had focused on the growing distance between the educated and uneducated. Rural development is, therefore, interwoven with various other socio-cultural components.

## Human Development

A study of economic growth in the post-Independence period clearly indicates that human development—better education, health, nutrition and family planning at local levels—promotes economic growth as effectively as capital investment in plants. The highest social returns is as high as 27 per cent. Educated farmers tend to produce up to 15 per cent more than the uneducated. This makes all the difference between a decent diet and malnutrition, and distinguishes the poor from the non-poor. Poverty, economic growth and the level of education are correlated. In this connection, Theodore Schultz says: "It is not possible to have the fruits of modern agriculture and an abundance of modern industry without making large investments in human resources. Social returns on such investments are very high in the long run." The gains arising out of mass education outweigh its negative aspects, such as educated unemployed or social tensions. The strains and tensions produced by a widening of the base of education in a way are signs of vitality and of the process of change. In such a situation, demand will call forth its own supply, and economic progress will be more rapid.

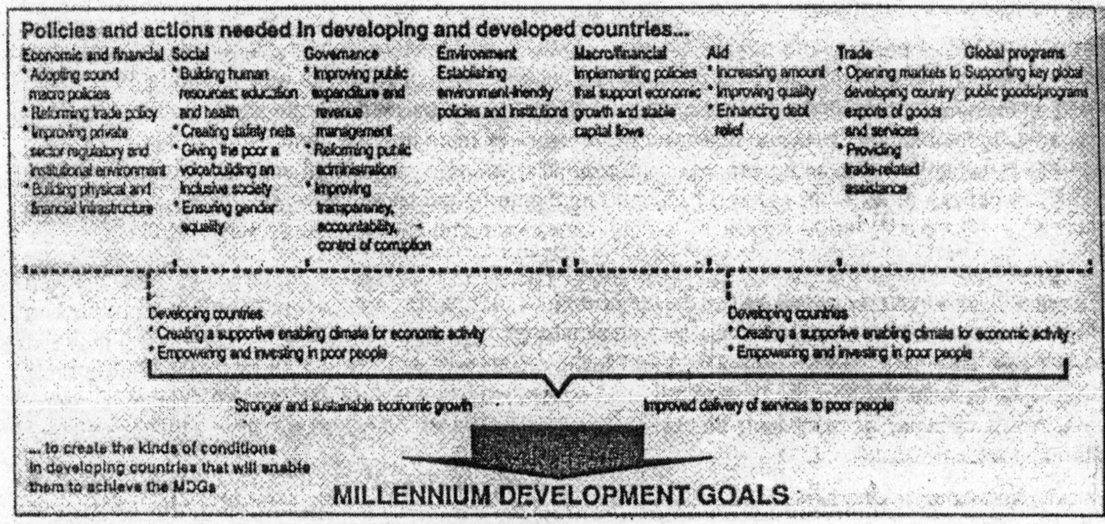

**Box 2**
**THE MILLENNIUM DEVELOPMENT GOALS**

1. Eradicate extreme poverty and hunger

   Halve, between 1990 and 2015, the proportion of people whose income is less than one dollar a day.

   Halve, between 1990 and 2015, the proportion of people who suffer from hunger.

2. Achieve universal primary education

   Ensure that, by 2015, children everywhere, boys and girls alike, will be able to complete a full course of primary schooling.

   Although the focus on education is justified in light of the evidence that investing in girls' education yields high returns, education alone is insufficient for eliminating the range of gender inequalities or for empowering women to participate in society. Gender equality and the empowerment of women can remain elusive goals—without the opportunity to fully use education to obtain decent employment or to participate fully in decision making in the political arena.

3. Promote gender equality and empower women

   Eliminate gender disparity in primary and secondary education, preferably by 2005, and in all levels of education no later than 2015.

4. Reduce child mortality

   Reduce by two-thirds, between 1990 and 2015, the under-5 mortality rate.

5. Improve maternal health

   Reduce by three-fourths, between 1990 and 2015, the maternal mortality ratio.

6. Combat HIV/AIDS, malaria, and other diseases

   Have halted by 2015, and begun to reverse, the spread of HIV/AIDS.

   Have halted by 2015, and begun to reverse, the incidence of malaria and other major diseases.

7. Ensure environmental sustainability

   Integrate the principles of sustainable development into country policies and programs and reverse the loss of environmental resources.

   Halve, by 2015, the proportion of people without sustainable access to safe drinking water.

   Have achieved, by 2020, a significant improvement in the lives of at least 100 million slum dwellers.

8. Develop a global partnership for development

   Develop further an open, rule-based, predictable, nondiscriminatory trading and financial system.

   Address the special needs of the least developed countries.

   Address the special needs of landlocked countries and small island developing states.

   Deal comprehensively with debt problems of developing countries through national and international measures to make debt sustainable in the long term.

   In cooperation with developing countries, develop and implement strategies for decent and productive work for youth.

   In cooperation with pharmaceutical companies, provide access to affordable, essential drugs in developing countries.

   In cooperation with the private sector, make available the benefits of new technologies, especially information and communications.

## Education

Education is the most effective instrument for moulding the responses of the agents of production to a common goal. It can generate potent forces helpful in the transformation of a traditional society. The need to develop such human resources as skill, functional literacy, health care and hygiene, environmental knowledge, nutrition, education, social behaviour, attitudinal change, home science, self-confidence and decision-making power, political structure, distribution and value systems — all these are all related to the life-style of the rural people and should form part of their educational curricula. A formidable barrier to development in rural areas has been the almost total absence of educational opportunities. Education has to deal with their problems, enlighten them about the support and succour available to them within the system, and stimulate solidarity among them in their efforts for change, growth and programmes, schemes, resources, organisations and activities. To do so, exposure to the following subjects relevant to their life-style may be useful:

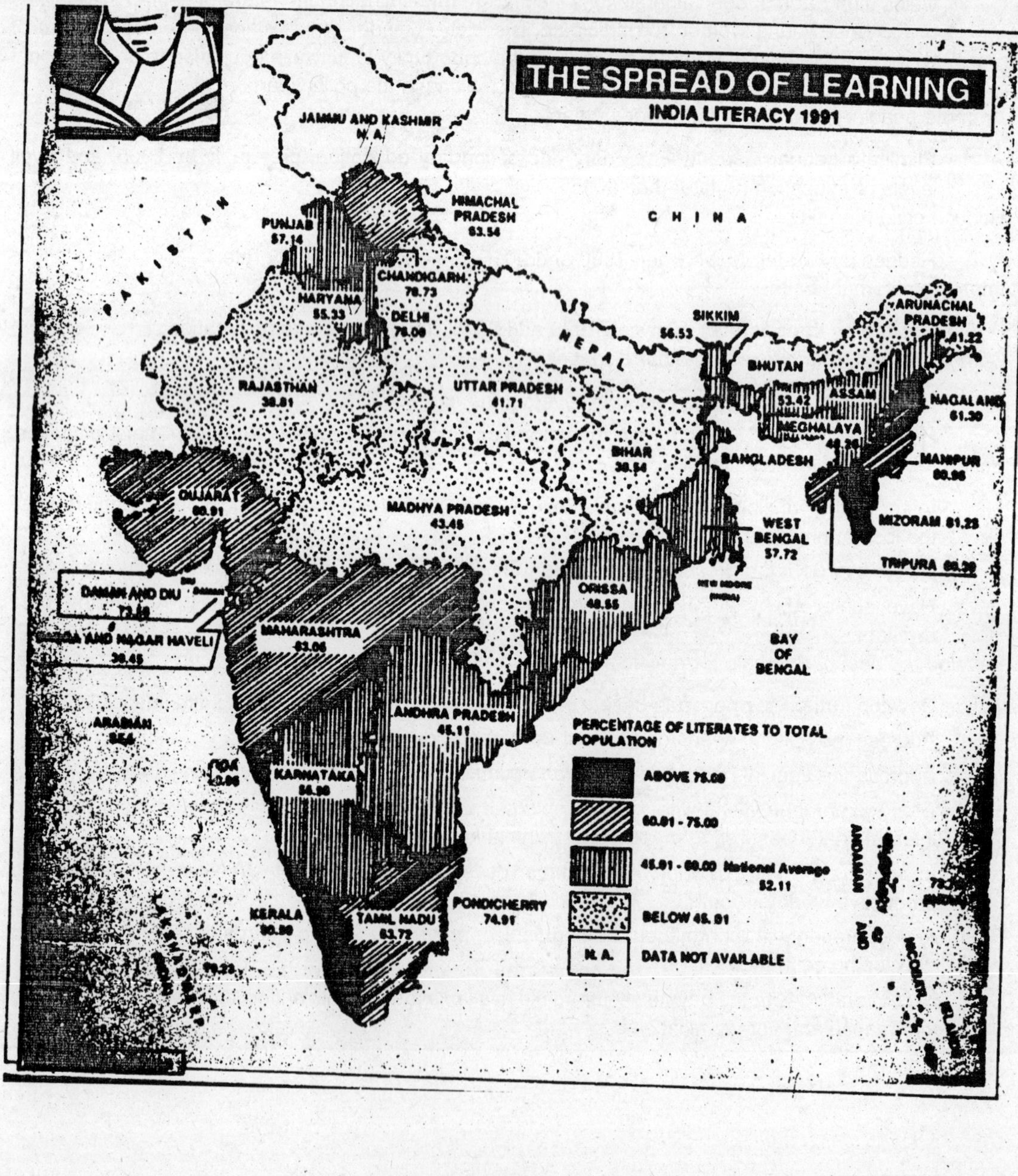

(i) Rural Society and barriers for development;

(ii) People's organisation and its importance;

(iii) Motivation;

(iv) Health and Hygiene;

  (a) Mother child care;

  (b) Food values — vitamins, proteins, minerals, etc., and food intake for the prevention of diseases and malnutrition;

  (c) Water — drinking, bathing, etc.;

  (d) Elementary home science;

  (e) Development of physical and mental faculties through sports and cultural activities;

(v) Management of domestic livestock;

(vi) Value system;

(vii) Literacy and relevant vocational training;

(viii) Democracy, rights and responsibilities as a voter, the political set-up and the delivery and distribution system within the district;

(ix) Planning, implementation, monitoring and evaluation of all developmental activities at the micro level, communication and participation and modification/alternatives.

The success of the non-formal educational system depends largely on how the system is effectively operated or implemented by the operators, i.e., change agents (block officials, panchayat members, field workers, teachers, etc). To make it result-oriented, the operators themselves have to be exposed to a knowledge of:

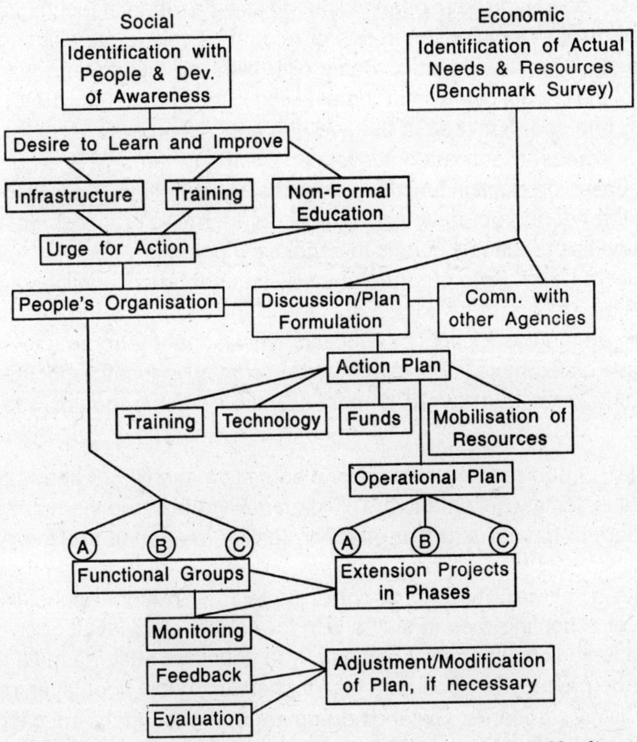


*Fig. 1. Attainment of Objectives and Targets towards Self-reliance*

(a) The concept and planning process from below, including implementation, monitoring and evaluation;

(b) Basic human needs and philosophy of human resources development (social work);

(c) Individual and group dynamics, with special reference to social interaction;

(d) The subjects of the suggested syllabus;

(e) The method of teaching and the use of aids and media — participatory communication method.

**Box 3**

**THE CENTRALITY OF EDUCATION TO GROWTH AND INDIVIDUAL AND SOCIETY'S WELFARE**

Two overall conclusions can be drawn from the survey of the economic and social outcomes of education. ***First,*** the economic and social benefits of education are greatest when a critical minimum level of educational attainment has been achieved across the population. Mass expansion of primary education that raises India's currently low educational attainment (averaging about 1.9 years for workers in 1981), to a threshold of about 4 to 5 years of completed primary education per worker, would have high payoffs in economic and social benefits. ***Second,*** the benefits of education extend beyond individuals who receive schooling directly. Other members of society also gain. The resulting improvements in economic efficiency provide continuing justification for public sector involvement in education. Primary schooling offers the greatest economic and social returns, followed by secondary schooling.

The economic outcomes of education have been estimated using a range of techniques, including aggregate and enterprise-based production functions, and rate of return analysis (a survey is the World Bank 1997a). All show positive returns to education in India. Some even showed higher returns in the 1980s compared with the 1970s, a result of the impact of the timid liberalization in the 1980s (Loh, 1995). Aggregate production functions suggest that a one-year increase in the average education of the work force can raise output by 13 percent and that the increased educational level can contribute around one-quarter of the increase in economic output. Farm-based production functions show that in agriculture, education helps increase output, primarily by increasing the adoption of new technologies and farming practices. In areas where schooling across the farm population has reached a certain threshold, the potential effects of an advance in agricultural technology are more fully realized. Rate of return analysis and earnings' functions suggest that private and social returns to education are around 8 to 9 percent with the highest returns registered for lower-caste graduates. The literature on the cost-benefit of education shows that the returns to schooling are very high in developing countries. For example, one extra year of primary education increases a person's future productivity (that is, hourly wage rate) by 20 percent in India (Psacharopoulos 1994, as cited in van der Gaag 1997).

With respect to the social (or non-market) outcomes of education, the NFHS shows strong overall relations between educational levels, fertility and infant and child mortality rates, and the nutritional status of children. Primary schooling appears to have a stronger effect on fertility rates than previously thought. Two effects are discernible. ***First,*** within each state, there is a clear inverse relation between the level of schooling and both the desired and the actual fertility rate. ***Second,*** in states with higher schooling levels, fertility rates are lower at each level of schooling than in states with lower schooling levels. Lower levels of fertility are also generally judged to have social benefits, particularly in countries such as India that have high rates of population growth. A demographic transition from high to medium or low population growth is widely viewed as important in raising living standards. Expanding primary and secondary education could bring such a demographic transition in India.

> The mother's education reduces infant and child mortality, and even a few years of schooling have a positive effect. Here again, there appears to be a wider societal effect that is dependent on a critical threshold of schooling across the population.
>
> These social outcomes have many spill-over efforts. Lower population growth rates substantially reduce the financing required to achieve and maintain universal primary education. Lower child mortality rates reduce suffering, increase female labour force participation rates, and probably play a part in the process through which parents come to desire fewer but healthier children. Healthier, better-fed children tend to achieve more while in school and to become more productive adults. All these outcomes appear to be closely linked to the level of mothers' education.
>
> *Source:* World Bank 1997a.

Initiating and sustaining the process of development in rural areas is an enormous task. At the same time, it is a continuous process, calling for a sound organisation, committed management and active people's participation. The role of the village level worker, teacher, village panchayat and co-operative worker/banker is quite vital. Some of the very poorest people in rural areas are chronically sick, handicapped and will always need help from society as a whole. In the changed context, in which social values have suffered a sea-change, and the climate is not favourable to the sick, unemployed, underemployed, poor, handicapped, old and crippled, the State has to look after them on a continuing basis. The rural poor are the weakest lot and need the support of the State in a good measure. By and large, experience has confirmed that the goals of economic growth and poverty reduction can be and often are, complementary.

For poor people, financial and economic stability are vital. They need multi-directional approach to recover and regain economic viability. With the implementation of sectoral programmes to improve education, health, agricultural productivity, sanitation, ecology and environment, abject poverty can be eliminated. With redoubled efforts on their part, with continued assistance from the Government, voluntary agencies, industrial houses and the industrial countries, the elimination of absolute poverty is a feasible proposition. Rural development is not confined to merely higher material consumption but include a more decent standard of living with better health, hygiene and sanitation. Moreover, a reorientation of higher social value system is essential among the rural people, particularly among the rural poor — landless agricultural labourers, marginal and small farmers, poor rural artisans and other rural destitutes.

The urge to economic and social change in the present conditions comes from the fact of poverty and of inequalities in income, wealth and opportunity. The elimination of poverty cannot, obviously, be achieved merely by redistributing existing wealth. Nor can a programme aiming only at raising production remove existing inequalities. The two have to be considered together, only a simultaneous advance along both these lines can.create the conditions in which the community can put forth its best efforts to promote development. The problem, therefore, is not one of merely re-chancelling economic activity within the existing socio-economic framework; that framework has itself to be remoulded so that it may accommodate progressively those fundamental urges which express themselves in the demands for the right to work, the right to adequate income, the right to education and to a measure of insurance against old age, sickness and other disabilities. The Directive Principles of State Policy enunciated in Articles 36 to 51 of the Constitution make it clear that, for the attainment of these ends, the ownership and control of the material resources of the country should be so distributed as best to subserve the common good, and that the operation of the economic system should not result in the concentration of wealth and economic power in the hands of a few. It is in this larger context that the task of planning has to be envisaged.

## Planned Approach

A planned economy aiming at the realisation of larger social objectives necessitates a vast increase in governmental functions. For these to be discharged efficiently, appropriate local, regional and functional organisations have to be built up and strengthened. Each of these must have a defined sphere of action and responsibility, and must function with a measure of autonomy. Arrangements for the necessary co-ordination between them must be made at various levels from the village upwards. The activities of all developmental institutions in the country, official and non-official, will have to be reorientated in terms of the requirements of the plan; and, in this process, due stress must be laid on the appropriate role of various local and functional organisations. The function of the Central Government is to evolve a national plan, to work out a co-ordinated policy for its implementation, to watch and assess the progress of major development schemes in different parts of the country, and initiate and promote action in furtherance of the objectives and targets defined.

The central objective of planned development in India has been the promotion of rapid and balanced economic development. The successive plans were designed to ensure that the benefits of development should accrue in an increasing measure to the relatively less privileged classes of the society, and bring about a progressive reduction in the concentration of income, wealth and economic power. The purpose of the distribution of the fruits of development to the weaker sections was to create a milieu in which the poor man, who has so far had little opportunity of perceiving and participating in growth and social mobility to improve his social and economic status, is able to function effectively. Secondly, such distribution creates purchasing power which in turn, becomes an effective tool for the development of other sectors of the economy. In the beginning of the planning process in India, one assumption was that a high rate of economic growth itself would take care of the poverty of the masses.

The economic performance of our country during the last forty years does not compare well with that of many developing countries which were seething with discontent. The poor will have to be organised at the grassroot level for self-help and group action so that they may bring effective pressure to bear on the politicians and the bureaucrats for a Rama Rajya of their dreams. As Swami Vivekananda said: "The poor, the illiterate, the ignored and the afflicted are our gods." With time-bound planning and a fuller involvement of the people at large, the uninspiring record of the past, which has been dominated by half-baked ideologies of the propertied class, can lead to a dynamic era of simple and honest living which is free from political corruption.

The agencies of rural development should be in a position to create:

*(i)* An awareness among the rural poor about the availability of assistance through the Government and banks under various development programmes;

*(ii)* An urge for development in the agencies instead of tempting the rural poor to avail themselves of subsidy and bank loans simply because both the Government and banks have to fulfil their targets;

*(iii)* A climate for growth, upliftment, production, distributive justice and recycling of funds in close collaboration with the banks, the Government and other agencies.

The evaluation studies indicate that the administrative and organisational set-up at various levels required to be strengthened. Greater attention needed to be given to the placing of competent personnel in various positions, to the continuity of tenure of programme functionaries, and to training programmes and better supervision and monitoring. Regarding the planning process, the study emphasised the need for the preparation of perspective plans for each block and district as envisaged in the guidelines, and for the integration of these plans with the local plans of the blocks and districts. Regarding the selection of beneficiaries, the Study found that as many as 25.8 per cent were ineligible, for they already belonged to the income group of Rs. 3,500 and above and stressed the need for proper identification of beneficiary families. It was also found that only 15.2 per cent of the beneficiaries belonged to the income group of Rs. 1,500 and less. Some anomalies in the functioning of financial institutions, in matters such as the adjustment of the subsidy amount, security from beneficiaries and the norms of repayment, were also observed; and the Report stated that it was necessary to introduce suitable procedures to eliminate them. Another finding of the Report was the over emphasis on assistance for schemes in the primary sector. As many as 75 per cent of the sample beneficiaries were from the primary sector; only 8 per cent from the secondary sector and 17 per cent from the tertiary sector. The need was stressed for having a shelf of bankable schemes suitable for different areas and conditions, taking into account variations in infrastructure, marketing facilities, etc.

The plan lays emphasis on adequate growth of fertilisers, pesticides and essential agricultural machinery to sustain the growth in agricultural production, and on sizable increases in the production of wage goods and essential mass consumption goods, such as sugar, vegetables, oil, drugs, textiles, and paper and consumer durables.

One way in which agriculture can contribute to poverty reduction is indirect. A growth that provides new, more productive, non-agricultural employment opportunities is essential for the long-term alleviation of poverty. Judicious policies to improve agricultural production and incomes may create more non-farm employment and higher incomes. Skills for non-farm activities are almost always acquired on the job, either informally or via the more formal apprentice systems. Strong agricultural performance can stimulate the process of economy-wide structural transformation. Combined agricultural and economy-wide growth simultaneously generate more employment in urban and rural sectors. If the momentum of growth is maintained, earnings and productivity in agriculture itself should accelerate. And if the lagging growth of other States is stimulated, many more States will have this option.

But agriculture can also make a direct contribution to the alleviation of poverty. Programmes emphasizing production by small farmers are a major means of extending the reach of agriculture to affect the rural poor. The plan lays stress on the capacity of the small family centered production unit to use its labour and management abilities to overcome the presumed advantages of larger farms, and achieve a better access to capital, new technology, and inputs, Higher incomes accrued because of higher productivity in agriculture, and non-farm activities will go a long way in improving the living conditions of marginal and small framers.

Agrarian reforms—meaning, in the broadest context, the establishment of clear ownership and use, and rights to land (whether private or communal) as well as land consolidation and distribution in some cases—are a critical element in stimulating the incentive to invest in land and are a contributing factor to the reduction of poverty through improved rural income distribution. They are also a means of improving the capacity of Governments to tax efficiency and redistribute the benefits of agricultural growth.

Planning, provides a framework of time and space which binds sectors, regions, and States together, and relates each year's effort to the effort in succeeding years. By strengthening the social and economic fabric of the country as a whole and of the different regions and States, it makes a powerful contribution to the goal of national integration. The planning process has contributed a great deal to the evolution of a broad development polices and growth. This has helped to generate a broad mass support for national economic policies and has added greatly to the cohesion and stability enjoyed by our polity.

**Box 4**

## HIGH WATER MARK

**Barren acres become lush oases as an engineer shows an ingenious way to harvest rainwater**

Aurangabad is the epicentre of Maharashtra's torrid zone. Here temperatures soar to a scorching 45 degree Celsius, turning the earth into a dust bowl. But you wouldn't know it from the Kedia farm, a bumpy half-hour ride to the south of the city. The 15-ft-high teak saplngs which sway in the undulating terrain at the foot of a small clump of hills tell the inspirational story of innovation and self-help which transformed a once-barren land into a lush oasis.

Eight years ago, Vijay Kedia, 48, a prosperous industrial contractor in the throes of a midlife crisis, switched tracks to become an agriculturist. He bought 47 acres of hilly land to grow teak and fruit trees. Reality soon hit hard. When it rained, the rocky terrain failed to hold the slurry torrents that rushed down the hills and took the precious topsoil with it. When it didn't rain (and that was more often), Kedia spent lakhs of rupees to extract water from wells as the water-table plummeted lower with each passing month. Yet for all his efforts, the saplings did not survive the blazing heat. In 1998, the entire papaya crop worth Rs. 14 lakh withered away.

So Kedia shopped around for technology. First he tried drip irrigation but gave it up when it proved to be expensive. Then the BITS Pilani-trained mechanical engineer racked his brains and came up with a simple solution. In 2000, he made a series of check dams and trenches that were 5-10 ft deep. He lined the walls with PVC sheets and filled the dugouts with mud. With the next rains, Kedia knew the plan was a success. The water falling on the trenches percolated into the 45 reservoirs built beneath them. While the PVC sheets prevented water from flowing out, the trenches checked evaporation.

Now over 80 per cent of the rainwater which falls on Kedia's farm trickles to the underground reservoirs. The project cost of each acre worked out to Rs. 2,000, plus the labour for digging pits and ditches. A week's rainfall is enough to keep the reservoirs full, equipped for a year's supply. The soil remains like a moist brown sponge, the wells are brimful all year. Kedia hasn't wasted even the long pipes he bought for his drip-irrigation project. A tailor's measuring tape stuck on them, they form ingenious devices to gauge the water level.

The motor-mouth proponent of Maharashtra Government's rainwater harvesting programme and its "Jal Mitra" (Water Friend), Kedia is carrying forth his mission: "To make rainwater harvesting affordable to all and raise the groundwater table." With a jeep-load of audio-visual aids, he has conducted about 500 meetings across the country. To the doubters, he points to the dozens of villages in Maharashtra where people are enjoying the fruits of his labour.

*High Water Mark - Son of The Soil : Kedia at his farm*

Land, water and biodiversity—the basic natural resources for sustainable agricultural development—are deteriorating and shrinking. Recognising that agricultural development cannot subsist on a deteriorating natural resources base, the issue of conservation and judicious utilisation of the resources occupies centre stage for the sustainable development of agriculture. it is essential to improve the inventory of the natural resources and develop strategies for increased and sustainable use of such resources. Recognising that the country encompasses distinct agro-eco regions with specific characteristics, research and technology development efforts should be geared to address the capabilities, problems and prospects of these agro-eco regions. Moreover, there are several common issues across the agro-eco regions such as analysis and deline-action of land use capability, appraisal and management of soil and water resources and the need for an integrated farming system approach through a programme and partnership mode.

The nature of poverty is shifting. About 30 years ago, 48.4 per cent of those living in rural areas were poor and 20 per cent of those living in urban areas were classified as poor. Recent studies show that the number of poor in urban areas has been increasing at a relatively higher rate compared to the rural areas but still the total poor in the country towards the year 2020 will be sizeable. Therefore, in the context of poverty alleviation, equal emphasis will have to be placed on production of food by the poor as well as on the availability of food to the urban poor. It must also be recognised that a large proportion of the rural poor are located in regions with low potential for food production (mountain and hilly areas, coastal areas, degraded land and forest areas and arid and semi-arid areas).

The contribution of the agricultural sector to total national exports has been increasing steadily. The diversity of India's agro-ecological settings, abundant natural resources including high biodiversity and relatively low-cost of labour provide potential for great agricultural competitiveness in a globalised economy. It is expected that with the globalisation of market over the years, there will be a demand for agricultural intensification. This will also be favoured because of the greater backward and forward linkages between food and agricultural industry and income and employment multipliers that are found in the rest of the economy. Therefore, increases in production and productivity are bound to be strategically important to the national economy. Intensification will not only favour alleviation of rural poverty but also improve resources conservation, particularly in the small farming sector where farmers can be encouraged to take up organized production of high value crops such as fruits, speciality vegetables, spices, flowers, medicinal herbs, etc, Stronger demand for the crops of the small farmers will not only improve incomes and welfare but will also make investment in technology and resources conservation more attractive.

## Removal of Poverty

The removal of poverty, the building up of a modern society, making the maximum possible use of science and technology, and the attainment of self-reliance are the basic objectives of planning in India. The previous plans had made a valuable contribution to the achievement of these national goals. The ninth Plan constitutes yet another important milestone in the nation's quest to rid this country of the ancient scourge of poverty, ignorance and disease. Effective planning must be based on a vision of the future. It must have a long-term perspective to translate the vision into reality and to make it operational.

We have, therefore, to sustain and accelerate the momentum of economic growth. Agriculture, industry, infrastructure and social services have to function at progressively higher levels of efficiency and productivity. Full advantage must be taken of advances in science and technology to bring about the required structural transformation of our economy. Simultaneously, measures designed to raise the productivity and incomes of the poorer sections of society and of the poorer regions must be pursued with greater vigour.

Chart 1

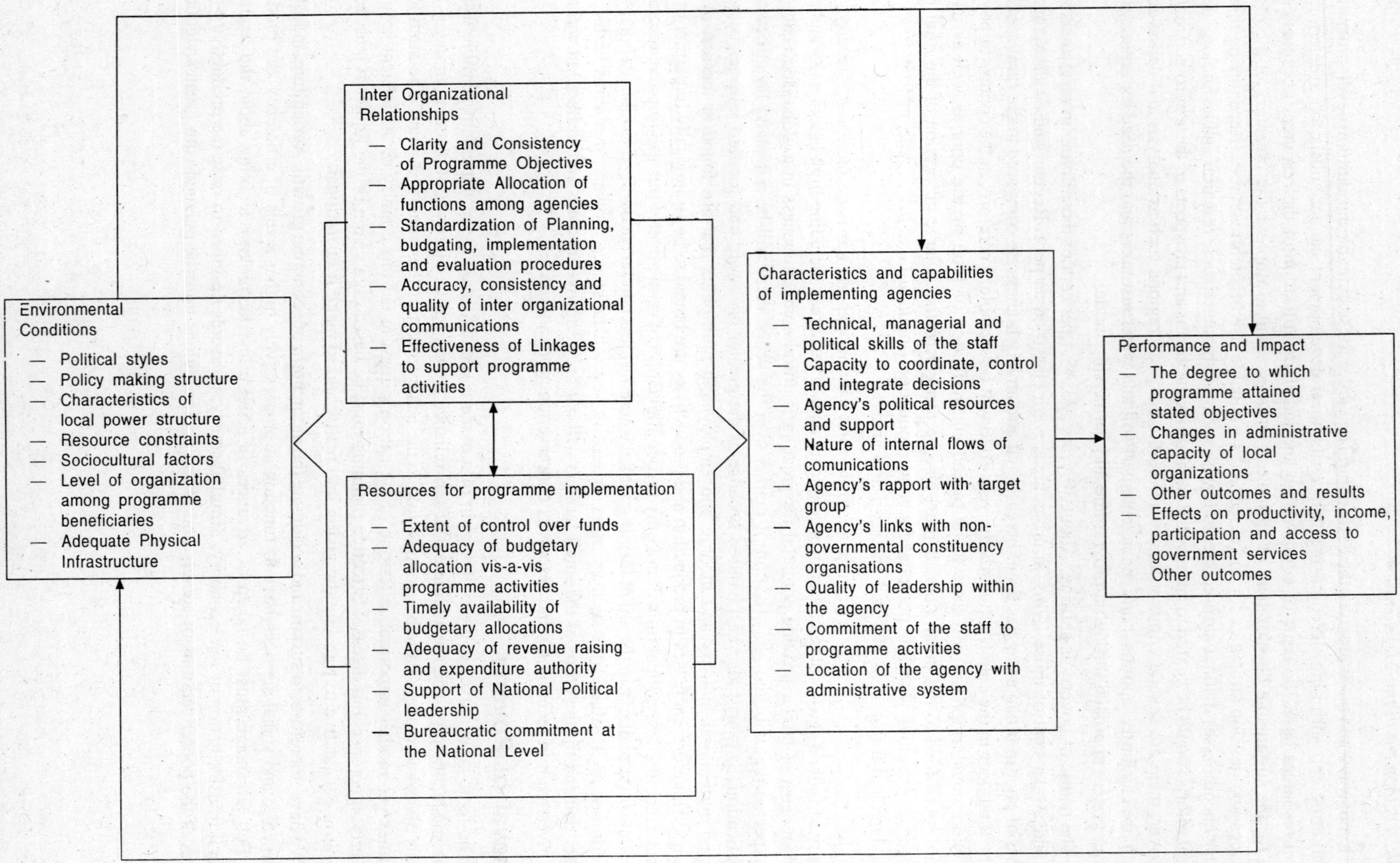


*Fig. 2. Factors affecting implementation of Rural Development Programmes.*

The central element in the development strategy of the Seventh Plan is the generation of productive employment. This will be achieved by an increase in cropping intensity made possible by increased availability of irrigation facilities, the extension of new agricultural technologies to low productivity regions and to small farmers; by measures to make the rural development programmes more effective in the creation of productive assets by the expansion of labour intensive construction activities for providing housing, urban amenities, roads and rural infrastructure; and by changes in the pattern of industrial growth. With the emphasis on the generation of productive employment, the Ninth Plan aims at a significant reduction in the indicence of poverty and an improvement in quality of life the poor in villages and towns. There is also a need for generating employment opportunities for educated youth in rural areas. The expansion of education and health facilities will open up job opportunities, and the spread of credit institutions and other development activities will create opportunities for self-employment.

The increase in the spending power of poor households will lead to a more rapid expansion in the demands for mass consumption of goods, particularly foodgrains, clothing and shelter.

Efficiency and employment generation are closely linked with measures for human resources development. The attention paid to education and manpower development in the previous plans had ensured the availability of a substantial infrastructure for education and technical training. Skill formation had also been provided for in various beneficiary-oriented programmes. The primary task now is qualitative improvements in curricula and teaching methods to ensure relevance and impart to students, workers and artisans the values, knowledge and skills required for emerging development tasks. Besides this, human resources development includes measures to improve health status and steps to improve the participation of vulnerable groups of the scheduled castes, scheduled tribes, women and disabled persons in the development process. The development strategy for the Seventh Plan involves an accelerated effort at human resources development in this wide sense. Given the twin emphasis on employment and productivity in the Ninth Plan, the objective is to expand employment opportunities consistent with increases in productivity.

The development strategy of the Ninth Plan aims at a direct attack on the problems of poverty, unemployment and regional imbalances. It requires for its success substantial improvements and economy in resource use. These improvements will be achieved by accelerating the development of human resources, by greater selectivity in the development and use of domestic technological capabilities, by the widespread induction of new technologies in our farms, factories and offices, by a stronger emphasis on capacity utilisation and better project implementation, and by the pursuit of policies that would cut down the costs of production, particularly in the industrial sector.

Specific sector programmes — for example, those concerned with the provision of feeder roads, village electrification, water supplies, health facilities, promotion of education, proper houses and the promotion of rural industry — may be the important means of conveying benefits to the rural poor. The major issues involved are the need to integrate these programmes with programmes of rural development and with particular projects, and choosing appropriate design standards suited to rural conditions. The latter is a serious problem for a number of these services. In some cases, pending further technical development, the extension of facilities to villages will remain prohibitively expensive. One reason for the neglect of the small-scale system suitable for rural areas is the convenience and lower unit cost of preparing and appraising projects for larger undertakings that are better suited to urban environment or, in the case of transport, for inter-urban connections. Here, too, however, recent research indicates some promising new approaches calculated to reduce difficulties in the future.

The promotion of rural industry in the context of rural development merits special attention. In many countries, existing village crafts are disappearing rapidly, while the modernisation of agriculture creates a demand for new inputs and consumer goods which could often be produced locally. If these two trends can be combined with relevant planning and support measures, the outcome might be modernised local industrial structures, geared to serving the rural areas, but having linkages with the national industry as well. These rural industries could provide employment, increase incomes, slow down rural-urban migration, increase the supply of goods and services to farmers at lower prices and generally stimulate rural and regional development.

The expansion of rural industry at an early stage of agricultural development, may, in the long run, facilitate a more rational spatial distribution of industrial and economic activity than might otherwise occur. Much of rural industry is likely to be located in market towns. That would generally be a more desirable form of urbanisation than the expansion of the already large urban centres. The modernisation of agriculture creates a demand which has a great potential for pulling certain categories of industries into rural towns. These industries, are, in general, small; and their interaction with medium and large enterprises is, in the long run, essential. Consequently, some urban-based industries achieve a better interaction and a more balanced distribution of industrial activity. At the same time, with an industrial base to provide for continuing expansion and development, such regional centres can attract and retain professional and technical skills that otherwise tend to be concentrated in the major cities.

Apart from the linkages with agriculture itself, there are other important cross-sectoral requirements for rural industry. At some stage, the village must have access to electricity for productive purposes. It is equally essential to develop the capacity to design and manufacture simple producer goods—appropriate for small-scale village industry. The reservoir of potential skills—technical and entrepreneurial—in rural areas is often large. Without special efforts, however, to upgrade the skills, to improve tools, to diversify production, to open up markets and to change the outlook of the artisans, this important asset would threaten to disappear. In many circumstances, the mechanisation of agriculture requires small pumps and motors (up to 20 or 25 horsepower), as well as the services of tractor drivers, tubewell operators, tractor and small motor mechanics, and people skilled in maintaining and repairing mechanical equipment. Rural homes need basic furniture and improved kitchen utensils. Such requirements are either not fulfilled or are met by the cities. It would seem, natural to upgrade the skills and organisation of village blacksmiths, carpenters, shoemakers, weavers and potters, so that they may assume new manufacturing and service roles in modernising rural communities. This kind of support should be part of an integrated plan to modernise and develop rural communities.

Agricultural extension services are considered essential for the introduction of new technology and development of agriculture. In the same way, industrial extension should be seen as a necessary element in developing rural industry. The essential characteristics of such an extension service are mobility and relevance to rural industries in meeting local demands. An important aspect of any such programme must be the development and support of the existing industrial structure in order to capitalise on the base of technical and entrepreneurial skills which already exit in villages, market towns and urban centres. The development of rural industries requires a nationally supported programme to provide inputs like credit, raw materials and equipment, electricity, training for technical and managerial skills, and efforts for research, development and engineering. The provision of such a package is, in principle, facilitated by linking efforts with a rural development programme. Indeed, the general lack of rural development planning cannot be more clearly illustrated than by the weakness of current efforts to promote it. The variety of programmes and approaches that have been examined confirms that no single package or formula is likely to be either necessary or sufficient for effective rural development.

Community involvement in the selection, design, construction and implementation of rural development programmes has often been the first step in the acceptance of change leading to the adoption of new techniques of production. The manner in which early participation is to be achieved, and balanced with the need for overall guidance and control from the centre, is a problem which can only be resolved within each country. There is some evidence, however, such as at Comilla in Bangladesh, that a strengthened local authority is better able to secure effective participation than are officials answerable to far-away central governments. It appears that Tanzania has gone further in its attempts to deal with these problems than most other countries. For example, the preparation of regional development budgets now begins with proposals by local committees, composed of villagers and low-level officials. The proposals are then filtered through higher-level district and regional committees, again composed of a mixed group of officials and party members, before being presented to the central government. Agreement must be reached at each level before the proposals are passed on to the next higher level. A somewhat similar system of decentralised planning and decision making is practised in Malaysia, and one is being developed in Indonesia. Several countries have found that rural people have perceptions of needs and possibilities which are generally different from those of "national" officials. The "right" balance in this relationship is hard to strike. At one extreme, local politicians may completely dominate local officials, with the possibility of perverse results. At the other extreme, also common, officials may make the final decisions and recommendations.

Local institutions, such as farmers' associations, panchayats and co-operatives, have obvious potential advantages for coping with administrative difficulties in reaching the rural poor. On the one side, they provide some measure of participation through the involvement of their members. On the other, they perform intermediary functions which make it possible for them to provide credit to larger numbers than can be done through official agencies.

The implementation of the rural development programme requires, among other things, a planned programme, a strong organisation, a number of agencies involved in the task of rural development on an ongoing basis. The programme envisaged:

*(i)* A national plan or programme of action for rural development, together with supporting national, regional block level policies and adequate central financing arrangements.

*(ii)* A strong organisation at the national level to co-ordinate vertically organised, Central Government sectoral departments and other interlinked programmes;

*(iii)* Greater decentralisation with effective machinery at the regional and local level to co-ordinate the sectoral activities of national departments operating in the region and regional and local departments;

*(iv)* Participation by the rural poor in the planning and implementation process through village panchayat project advisory committees, village level committees, co-operative and other forms of group organisations.

The Tenth Plan aims at activising Panchayati Raj institutions particularly at the village and block levels, with a view to ensuring their active involvement in the planning and implementation of programmes of rural development, particularly those concerned with poverty alleviation and the provision of minimum needs. In the Seventh Plan period (1985-90), a Central scheme has been started for the establishment of a computerised District Rural Information System (DRIS) in each district with the ultimate objective of providing a data base for planning, for the selection of beneficiaries and schemes, and for monitoring their performance. Steps have been taken to strengthen the data collection and monitoring machinery at the block and district levels.

The scheme for strengthening the block level machinery, with the objective of restoring the full complement of the administrative staff, has been continued. Besides this, steps have been taken to strengthen and upgrade the position of the BDO, rationalise and increase the strength of implementation and supervisory staff for the efficient implementation of rural development and poverty alleviation programmes.

To achieve the objectives of cost-effectiveness and minimisation of leakages by imparting the necessary flexibility in the choice of activities and by achieving integration in the programmes, a three-pronged strategy has been envisaged in the Seventh Plan:

(*a*) Poverty alleviation programmes have been formulated and implemented in a decentralised manner with the participation of people at the grassroots level through village panchayats, panchayat samitis, zilla parishads, etc. This approach is expected to contribute to the selection of projects suited to local conditions, and to the integration of poverty alleviation programmes with area development. This framework is also expected to help in the timely provision of services in their appropriate sequence and in ensuring that the benefits of such programmes really reach those for whom they are intended. The Working Group on District Planning constituted by the Planning Commission had recommended a gradual approach to decentralisation for the attainment of the objectives of effective implementation of poverty alleviation programmes and balanced regional development. During the Seventh Plan, decentralisation of the planning process and full public participation in development will be pursued on the lines suggested by the Working Group.

(*b*) The launching of a large number of programmes, through the normal sectoral efforts and other steps taken to cater to target-group households, has resulted in a multiplicity of organisations, leading to duplication of management efforts. Further, the delivery system at various levels has proved to be inadequate. An effective implementation of poverty alleviation programmes calls for better planning at the district level, involving various disciplines or departments, a tighter organisational set-up to ensure optimal use of resources, and a closer monitoring. A high level committee was set up by the Planning Commission to review the then existing administrative arrangements for rural development and poverty alleviation programmes and to recommend an appropriate structural mechanism to ensure that they were planned in an integrated manner and effectively implemented. Measures will be taken during the Seventh Plan to strengthen, train and orient local administrative machinery within the framework of an integrated administrative organisation.

(*c*) Keeping in view the limited absorptive capacity of the poorest households, the Approach to the Seventh Plan has also laid emphasis on the need for taking up group-oriented activities for the beneficiaries to the extent possible with the promotion of co-operatives, registered societies, informal groups, etc., so that the economies of scale, inherent in some of these activities, especially in the provision of services, may be fully realised while, at the same time, group initiative and efforts on the part of the poor are promoted. This is necessary to protect the beneficiaries from the adverse operation of market forces, whether on the supply of inputs or on the sale of their produce. The mass media will have to be geared to bring about an increasing awareness among the rural poor and to disseminate information bearing on non-formal education and functional skills and knowledge. For purposes of bringing about a greater degree of the participation of, and awareness among the beneficiaries, a Central scheme was launched for the organisation of the latter, both in terms of group-oriented economic activities and increased conscious efforts. Further, voluntary agencies would be increasingly involved in the formulation as well as implementation of poverty alleviation programmes during the Seventh Plan, especially for ensuring greater participation of the people.

Rural development has acquired prime importance in the development policy of the Government. The central objective is to bring about a social change and a desire to attain a higher living standard. So, one of the pre-requisites of this should be to create a desire among the people to change rather than encouraging outsiders to desire them to change. This is a long process. In a country where a majority of the people have been poor for centuries and a bulk of them are illiterate, ignorant and exploited, a lead has to be given. This is the responsibility of governments and governmental agencies. But these are outsiders, and urbanites; and they do not have any feel of rural India, the real India. In the circumstances, local institutions like the village panchayat, the school, the co-operative society and/or the bank and other voluntary organisations have to co-ordinate their activities, foster the necessary awareness, and bring about a social change in the village community. But the village community is not a homogeneous unit. This call for varied protections to the poor.

The experience of the working of the poverty alleviation programmes is by no means uniform. It differs widely from one State to another; and within a State, it varies from district to district, within a district from one block to another, and within a block it differs from village to village, depending upon the various exogenous factors that are so essential for development.

The main reasons for the failure of these programmes may be attributed to the fact that almost all of them were or are sectoral in character, covering specific aspects, isolated from each other and imposed from outside without the concerned people being involved in decision-making at any stage. So it has created a culture of dependence. To start any work, people have to be consulted and involved at each stage, right from the conception of planning for implementation and the actual implementation itself. The outside agency and governmental organisation should work only as a starter and catalyst, and intervene only for purposes of monitoring, correction and support wherever and whenever required. There should be technology validation before its application in any programme. There should be linkages of each activity with other, the interaction of which yields a higher productivity and income than the individual activities taken in isolation. There can be one primary rural market, one bank, one demonstration-cum-training centre, and one high school for every five villages. Greater emphasis may be laid on minor irrigation, such as bore wells and open wells.

The other shortcomings of the rural development programmes have been indicated below:

*(i)* The project formulation under these programmes is weak. It neglects micro-level details and creates obstacles in the smooth working of the projects.

*(ii)* Though the programmes are launched with great fanfare, the spirit wanes in a short time. And there is no follow-up action.

*(iii)* The infrastructural support for these programmes is weak. Any deficiency of basic inputs affects the programmes very badly.

*(iv)* There are some problems bearing on the identification and implementation of appropriate technology relating to some of the programmes. Science, technology, skills, etc., have to be made simple, so that the target groups may understand and implement them with ease.

*(v)* Co-ordination among the various agencies providing the necessary inputs is found to be weak.

*(vi)* There is a multiplicity of institutions providing assistance and implementing the programmes. In some cases, there is too much duplication of work. The result is that the target group is not benefited.

*(vii)* There are serious managerial and administrative weaknesses in the working of the programmes.

*(viii)* The village panchayat, the school, the co-operatives do not play an effective role in the implementation of these programmes.

*(ix)* There is also the problem of misuse of power by the elite. The rural rich use their power to strengthen their own position at the cost of the poor. As a result, the poor do not profit from the programmes in an adequate measure. In many cases, the benefits of the varied programmes have been reaped by the rich.

*(x)* These programmes have not achieved their full potential either in terms of employment generation or in terms of asset creation.

One thing is of great importance. Millions of people will continue to live in rural areas for several decades to come. Rural development, therefore, has to be multi-disciplined, multi-purpose, multi-functional, fully designed to increase and improve food production and protect village industries, rural artisans and other skilled persons, power generation, drinking water supply, sanitation, wealth, employment generation, societal adoption of technology and overall rural ecological management. There have been numerous deficiencies in the implementation phase. These programmes have achieved some success in the relatively developed regions which are well provided with infrastructure, where the level of awareness among the beneficiaries is high, where the necessary follow-up measures have been taken and the involvement of people through their representatives has been ensured. This indicated that the impact of the programme depends on the degree to which the different rural development programmes, including the Minimum Needs Programme, are integrated with one another and with the overall development of the area.

Rural development administration is a composite of several elements. These include:

*(a)* The technical and extension services of the State Government at the district and block level;

*(b)* Panchayati Raj institutions at the villages, blocks and district levels;

*(c)* Co-operative institutions at various levels; and

*(d)* Voluntary organisations.

In view of the role which credit institutions, and specially banks, are now required to play in rural development, employment and agricultural production programmes, they should be considered an integral part of the machinery for rural development. The various components of rural administration have to function together in the given context of each region and area in so far as planning and implementation are concerned.

Over the years, in many States, Panchayati Raj institutions, especially at the block and district levels, have treated as marginal to the development process, and have failed to receive adequate support at the higher political levels. Co-operatives have come in for increasing criticism for failing to serve the weaker groups. By and large, voluntary organisations have remained on the fringes of poverty alleviation and rural development programmes. The Planning Commission's Expert Group on Poverty Alleviation Programmes had urged the following:

"It should be emphasised that, in the very nature of rural development, in each field, there are activities of which some aspects or components could be assigned with advantage for implementation to competent voluntary agencies which might be already at work, or whose formation and development should be encouraged. In designing each programme, therefore, the Planning Commission and the concerned Central Ministries and Departments in the States should make a special effort to mark out those components and areas of action which can be 'passed on,' with the necessary administrative and technical guidance and financial support, for implementation by appropriate voluntary organisations."

The Expert Group had also proposed that universities, colleges and research institutions should be drawn into rural development and antipoverty programmes in each region and assist in monitoring, action research, and planned experimentation. It is crucial to the success of all action against poverty in the Seventh Plan period that rural development administration as a whole be thoroughly overhauled and all its components raised to a level of effective functioning as a well-knit system of institutions and services which are capable of responding to local conditions and harnessing local resources and potentials for a comprehensive development with a special focus on the weakest socio-economic groups and on poverty concentration areas.

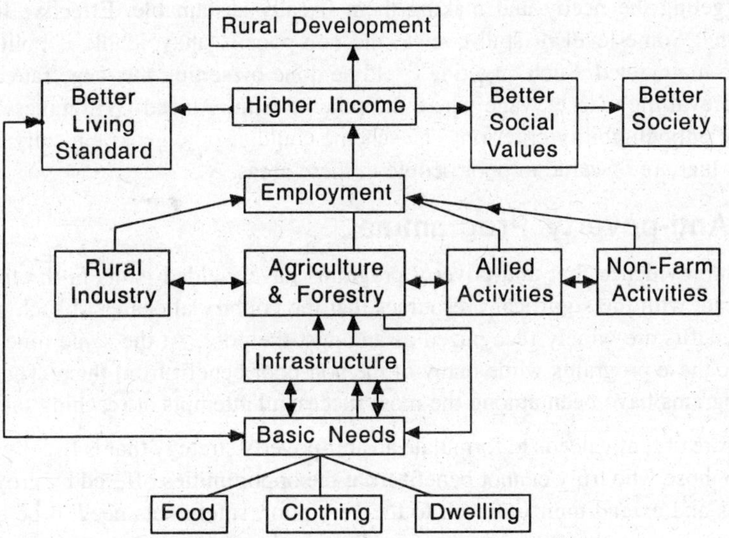


*Fig. 3. Conceptual Framework of Rural Development*

In the final analysis, the process of rural development should wage a war against multi-dimensional problems in a multi-directional way. The multi-pronged attack on economic poverty, social attitude and basic needs is the need of the hour. Unless this is done, all the programmes will end up with little effect on the rural poor. What is most needed is the will to strengthen the rural poor and give them ample opportunities to better their rural environment and standard of living. It is important to design these programmes so that they are efficient and complementarily productive. On the one hand, the productivity of small farmers should be increased, more non-farm activities should be encouraged, forestry should be integrated with agriculture and rural industry, and positive action should be taken to achieve rapid rural industrialisation. On the other hand, more and more basic needs are taken care of, together with better education, better health facilities. More importantly, social cohesion has to be brought about within a period of time. The task is gigantic. But with the political will, determined and organised efforts, selfless work and dedication, rural development can be made a reality. And this is a vitally important element, for rural development accelerates the process of economic growth and strengthens socio-cultural heritage.

In the half century its independence, India has made many notable social and economic achievements in a democratic political setting: among them, the eradication of famine, the reduction in population growth and the creation of a large pool of technical and scientific talent. It also managed to reduce poverty over that period, but only since about 1975 has the decline become fairly steady, albert slow. And, although the incidence of poverty has declined from 45 to 36 percent between 1950 and 1998-99 population growth caused the numbers of the poor almost to double in the same period, from 164 million 372 million. Of that total, more than three out of four (76 percent) live in rural areas.

Where policies have increased growth, particularly agricultural growth, and improved human development (as measured by various indicators), poverty has fallen faster, as indicated in the World Bank's 1997 Poverty Assessment. In contrast, where growth was slow or where human development policies were lacking, ineffective, or misdirected to the politically or economically more advantaged, poverty reduction has been relatively slow. Policies that sustain and accelerate labour-intensive economic growth and raise the poor's health status and education provide them with the skills to take advantage of opportunities for better paying jobs while avoiding the ravages of ill-health. In the prevailing environment, the priority would therefore appear to focus on improving the effectiveness of public works through effective ill-health. In the prevailing environment; targeting the needy and making them fiscally sustainable. Effective targeting need not be exclusive targeting. Some level of spill over to the non-poor is unavoidable if political support for such programmes is to maintained. Such targeting could be done by setting the wage rate at a level which is no higher than the prevailing market wage where the scheme is introduced. Willingness to work at this wage rate would be the only eligibility criterion. The scheme could also be geographically targeted to poor areas and create assets that are of value to poor people in these areas.

## Reforming Anti-poverty Programme

There is little evidence that anti-poverty programs have yielded gains in the living standards of the poor commensurate with the significant resources that the country allocates to such programs. Many recipients of their benefits are widely recognized as amongst the poor. At the same time, many of the poorest people do not use these programs while many of the non-poor benefit from them. There is a consensus that public works programs have been among the most successful attempts at reaching the poor.

India therefore urgently needs to formulate an anti-poverty strategy that is fiscally sustainable and more finely targeted to those who truly cannot benefit from the opportunities offered by growth. To increase their cost effectiveness and extend their outreach to the very poor, safety nets need to be targeted to those who either cannot participate in the growth process or face continuing exposure to risks, which are outside of their control. Rural households are largely uninsured against agricultural yield shocks, for example. Effective safety nets that insure rural poor against income fluctuations—such as public works programs—are essential in overcoming an important market failure.

The challenge that India faces in reducing poverty in the future faster and more effectively than it has in the past is an enormous one. India has met the mastered other major challenges and is laying the foundation for higher growth with the continued liberalization of the economy. Building on this foundation for faster growth would require that the challenge of poverty reduction remains at the forefront of the official concern and becomes the subject of the same imaginative, thorough, change-minded actions as the country's experiments in stabilization and structural adjustment. In particular, the liberalization of the economy needs to focus on deregulating sectors on which depends the livelihood of many of the poor (agriculture, particularly agro-industry, small scale industries), and on improving the provision of infrastructure and social services to the underprivileged. Resources can be generated by reducing subsidies and by reevaluating existing anti-poverty programmes.

## Long-term Strategic Frameworks

It is well recognised that pro-poor growth is essential for sustained poverty reduction and enhancement of the equality of life for all.

The strategic goals are :

To reduce poverty by improving the health, living standards and livelihood of people, by strengthening institutions; building capacity; reforming policy; and providing loans and technical assistance in the education, health and nutrition, water supply and sanitation, and urban development sectors.

Education helps empower the poor, enhances their income-earning potential, and improves the quality of their lives. People with basic education are more productive and more likely to earn higher incomes.

Investments in health are key to improving people's welfare and enhancing economic and social development. Improving human capital enables citizens to participate fully in civil society and thereby contribute to a nation's development.

- The water supply and sanitation subsector helped reduce pollution, protect water resources, and enhance rural water supply and sanitation coverage, thus contributing to improved health and living conditions.
- The main objectives in urban development and housing are to reduce urban poverty; lift living standards in urban areas; enhance the quality of life, including promoting human development, raising public health awareness and standards, and improving the status of women; and achieve sustainable urban development by protecting the environment development projects.
- Sound environmental management is vital to sustain development and reducing poverty.
- Small and medium enterprises (SMEs) and major generators of the employment and income needed to help reduce poverty. The Governments helps create the enabling policy environment for SMEs by promoting the establishment and provision of business advisory services, encouraging credit extension to SMEs from commercial sources, and encouraging the investment of equity funds that can cater directly to the needs of SMEs.
- Law and policy reform is at the heart of good governance, supporting the legal and institutional framework for predict-ability, transparency, accountability, and participation and thereby empowering the socially disadvantaged.
- Participation empowers people to influence decisions regarding development that affects them and their resources. A sense of ownership over development activities often motivates their sustained involvement in projects and helps ensure the effectiveness and long-term success of development investments. Participation also relates to institutions at local, regional, and national levels, and civil society, government, and the private sector—all partners in development. As participation in shared decision making expends, the basis for increased competency, integrity, and accountability in public and corporate governance also expands. Social capital—the diverse, trust-based, and normatively reinforced networks in society—is fostered through participation, contributing to effective social safety nets for the poor and other vulnerable groups.
- Cooperation with non-government organisations (NGO's) strengthens the effectiveness, sustainability and quality of life with increased importance on consultation and dialogue in project and technical assistance activities, country programming, and policy development.

## Biotechnology

Biotechnology has been rightly called the *Technology of the new Millennium* – the best thing to happen to this globe after the Information Technology Revolution. It is being presented as a panacea, a cure to solve all the problems of twenty first century – food scarcity, controlling pests, increasing yields and so on. Biotechnology increases agricultural productivity with guaranteed yields and innovative products. It is an environmentally sound approach with depleting natural resources such as land and water reduces erosion of topsoil and obliterates the need for harmful chemicals. It produces better quality and healthier foods with improved nutritional value, appropriate calorie content and reduced allergens. As a farming technology, it does not discriminate between the small and big farmers, provides inbuilt crop protection against insect and pests and increases farmer income and reduces risks. The increasing world population, depleting natural resources, call for alternatives to chemical pesticides and a host of other problems are troubling the agricultural community. The rate of increase of world population has surpassed the world food production. If this trend continues there might be a food crisis in the next century with all the accompanying socio-political instabilities and dangers. This is where the transgenic chip in to fill the hiatus created by the rising demand and the depleting natural resources. Transgenic may come as a boon in disguise because genetic engineering can offer solutions which conventional methods cannot. Besides increasing the productivity and growth of crops, it leads to the development of crops with better ability to fix up atmospheric nitrogen and better tolerance in extreme conditions like cold, drought and salt where plants could not grow otherwise. The genetic engineering through gene manipulations also increase the nutritional value of fruits and vegetables in terms of carbohydrates, starch and proteins besides extending the shelf life and making them more appealing with respect to colour, shape and size.

## Conclusion

The challenge that India faces in reducing poverty faster and more effectively than it has in the past in enormous. Later year's poverty report concluded that growth accounted for most of the reduction in poverty incidence over 1951-93. Improvements in redistribution (which occurred either through deliberate government policies or independently) achieved greatest impact by the mid-1960s, but even that was minimal. As shown in last year's report, the gains to the rural poor since 1970 have been due almost entirely to growth. That report also documented the ineffectiveness of the direct poverty alleviation programmes in raising the living standards of the poor. The benefit incidence analysis in this report confirms that finding. It is clear that there is a need to phase out a number of the anti-poverty programmes, as suggested in the Approach Paper to the Ninth Plan, and direct some of the savings to ensure quality education, which the analysis has shown is more effective in reducing poverty over the long-term than various poverty programs. For the poor to take advantage of the new educational opportunities, however, their health status needs to improve and this calls for allocating public spending where it is expected to deliver the highest gains to the poor: attacking communicable diseases and increasing access of the poor to good-quality water and sanitation facilities. Improved access to basic services will not only make the poor healthier and better educated persons, it will also allow them to contribute to growth through the higher productivity that education and good health bring and raise their level of welfare through higher earnings that both higher productivity and growth would offer. The message for India is therefore clear: fundamental reforms are needed in the way in which the public sector delivers health and education services to the poor, in order to allow them to take advantage of opportunities for raising their living standards that will come with rapid labour-intensive growth.

Sustainability of high future economic growth could critically depend upon expansion and upgradation of infrastructure on the one hand, and accelerated pace of reforms on the other, leading to a climate that would make investment in India productive and internationally competitive in a scenario of globalising markets. The explosive expansion in the use of information technology the world over by almost all segments of society including producers and consumers, is unleashing new challenges and opportunities. Proactive and progressive policy initiatives in this area can multiply foreign exchange earnings, expand employment and provide India with a source of sustainable competitive advantage. Appropriate application of information technology can bring direct benefit to rural India and accelerate economic growth.

❑ ❑ ❑

## SECTION EIGHT

# EXPERIMENT IN RURAL DEVELOPMENT

Traditional anti-poverty programmes are not compensating for the shortcomings in the fields of education and health. Indeed, they are funneling many of their benefits to the non-poor. According to data from the 1993-94 National Sample Survey (NSS), 76 percent of the wealthiest rural households, for instance, are likely to take advantage of the subsidized prices for food under the Public Distribution System while, at the opposite and of the wealth scale, fewer than 70 percent of the poorest households benefit from food subsidies. The poor do participate in rural public works and to a lesser extent in credit programmes.

Since the bulk of the required investments to build human capital comes from public rather than private sources in India, and yields many externalities, it is important that poverty-reduction strategies focus increased public spending on expanding the poor's access to ***quality*** education and health care. To avoid increasing the already large fiscal deficit, the funding for these needed increases could come from reducing the costly and integrated subsidies that are currently the source of large fiscal imbalances and micro-economic distortions.

### Priority for Human Capital

The returns on primary education are huge: better family health, smaller family size, and healthier children for educated women, for instance. A mother's primary education may do even more than food subsidies to improve child nutrition. Educated workers can take advantage of growth in demand for labour to raise their productivity and earnings. And because educated parents are more likely to send their children to school, education (even if limited to the primary level) perpetuates the benefits from one generation to the next. It is no coincidence that Kerala has enjoyed the highest levels of both male and female literacy and the fastest decline in the incidence of poverty over the past 40 years.

If India is to meet its objectives of sustaining high rates of economic growth with equity, then schooling must reach the economically and socially disadvantaged. This would require policies that can expand both the quantity and quality of schooling and that work to eliminate social exclusion based on income, gender or caste. The problems are concentrated in UP, Bihar, Madhya Pradesh, Orissa, Rajasthan, Uttar Pradesh and West Bengal. Notwithstanding the remarkable accomplishments of the District Primary Education Project (DPEP) in increasing enrollment in lower primary education, three-quarters of the 33 million 6- to 10-year-olds in these seven states are still not in school.

The policy prescriptions for bringing the poor children into school are not obvious. Success will depend on much stronger political commitment to educate the children of the poor. There is no question that spending levels on education inputs (teachers, classrooms, textbooks and instructional material) need to increase. The empirical findings and those of other research in India produce a consistent picture that ***increased spending alone will not be enough to improve enrollment and attainment of the poor.*** Improvement in quality of schooling is crucial to attract poor children to school and retain them there. Because the opportunity cost is high for them and their families, poor children would not go to school if they perceive it as a waste of their time.

Improving quality of education needs fundamental reforms to change the incentive framework within which teachers, school officials, bureaucrats, and politicians operate. The accumulated experience under the DPEP, the Lok Jumbish, and the experiences of states such as Kerala and Himachal Pradesh should be analyzed to help provide the information necessary to underpin such deeper educational reforms, particularly in the seven states with the highest incidence of school dropouts or non-enrollment. Interesting findings from recent theoretical and empirical research provide some guidance to reforms that are likely to improve outcomes. Some of these reforms are already underway in many states in India. These include decentralization of control over the provision of schooling to the local areas themselves, direct parental involvement, competition through school choice, and community involvement. Madhya Pradesh, for example, is by far the most advanced in decentralizing school management to local institutions such as the Panchayati Raj Institutions, with a consequent increase in enrollment and retention among children of underprivileged groups.

The process and the potential for bringing education closer to its users and beneficiaries through decentralization has generated significant optimism but also considerable caution. The chief fears reflect concern that decentralization could perpetuate, and quite possibly increase, regional disparities in school quality, and social and economic inequities in access to good schooling. Lowered funding levels for education also might be a problem if local control serves as a pretext for diminishing central responsibility.

Guidance on the choice between the various options and the likelihood of success requires further analysis, however, to understand better what changes would be required to the underlying incentives framework for teachers and officials to perform better. Gradually expanding the DPEP model and collecting appropriate information to assess its impact on educational attainment is essential. Raising quality is not as easy as increasing spending, and therefore a stock-taking exercise of what has worked elsewhere in the world and within India is also needed to inform public policy about the design of an effective educational system.

Effective health programmes must complement education in raising the potential productivity of labour to reduce poverty. Yet the research carried out for this report found that the public sector has failed to deliver some of the promised care to India's poor. This raises important issues, and more research is needed to understand fully the factors behind the poor performance. This should constitute a priority research area, because the policy implications would be different if the main reason is poor quality than if it is because of the availability of an easily accessible and large private sector, or both.

Public expenditure on health as currently constituted is likely to have only a limited redistributive impact. Despite its relatively equitable distribution, it is small relative to overall health use and its effects on health outcomes appear to differ greatly from one intervention to another and place to place, especially in its impact on the poor.

Four priority areas have been identifies for increasing the impacts of public spending on the health of the poor, and indeed on the economy in general.

***First,*** combating communicable disease and expanding public health interventions (see below) would deliver substantial gains from public health spending, particularly for the poor.

***Second,*** improving access to safe water sources and sanitation facilities and vaccinations would help reduce infant and child mortality and thus reduce fertility and improve maternal health. Because these are activities in which the poor are vastly underserved relative to the non-poor, public interventions in these areas will achieve their biggest impact on the poor. The net cost to the government of extending water and sanitation facilities to poor areas may not be very large, since willingness to pay for these goods is usually quite high and could cover the extension of the system.

***Third,*** analyses have shown that health education concerning basic hygiene, the value of better nutrition, and preventive care such as public campaigns against tobacco use and for the use of appropriate measures to avoid contracting HIV-AIDS and other sexually transmitted diseases, is an important part of encouraging behavioural changes needed for long-term improvement in health outcomes.

***Fourth,*** because the rural poor must often meet the financial burden of medical emergencies through debt, distress sale of real assets, or reductions in food or other important consumption items, there is merit in subsidizing hospital treatment. The benefit of providing this "in effect" social insurance—on top of the value of the service itself—is in the range of 40 to 70 percent of the costs of providing the service to patients in the lowest 40 percent of the population, people for whom insurance is not a realistic option. Public subsidies to hospital care can thus play an important redistributive role as long as referral systems are reformed to ensure that access is based on need rather than income and social status.

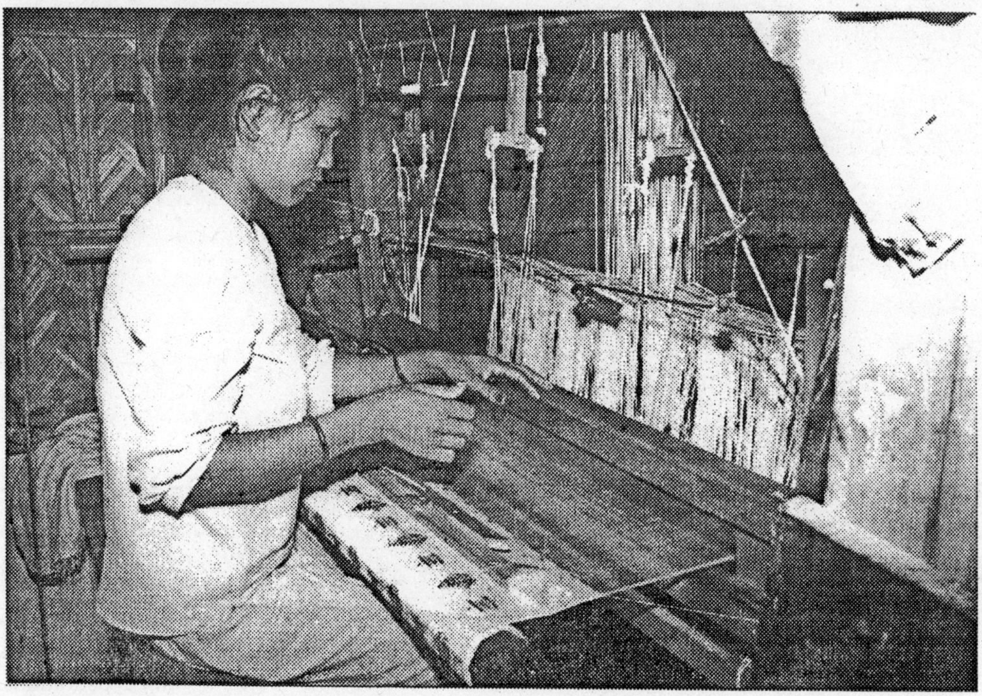

*A woman artisan realising her dream of self-reliance*

*To make good plans is not easy, but far more difficult is to implement them. The implementation demands the joint efforts of all our people. More particularly it demands the efforts of the vast Government administrative machinery.*

*— Jawaharlal Nehru*

*"We have the resolve. We have a road map—the poverty reduction strategy. We can begin to make good of a brighter tomorrow for every poor."*

# Chapter 42

# CASE STUDIES

## Introduction

Village studies in India have analysed the varied facets of the rural economy. Case studies of eleven village resurveys focus attention on village communities in India. These case studies throw ample light on the distribution of holdings, agrarian structure, concentration of power, changes in village institutions, shifts in occupational patterns, employment, standard of living, and the impact of various development programmes implemented in the course of six five-year plans.

It is evident now that, in several villages, growth has taken place, and the village scene has undergone tremendous changes. Irrigation is the most significant factor in the growth of agriculture. In this connection, Prof. M.L. Dantwala aptly observes: "Its modernizing influence can be seen in the diversification of crops, greater use of fertilizers, larger marketed surplus, changes in the composition of consumption expenditure." According to one study, rapid agricultural growth (in the green revolution belt) in Punjab and Haryana was not rapid enough to stimulate rapid employment growth or to maintain rural real wages. On the other hand, agricultural prosperity has given rise to the drinking habit, both as a relaxation and as a symbol of social prestige. In some villages, the are radios, TV sets, bicycles, scooters, and motor cycles. Every village in Punjab has become a place of working factories.

In many villages, unanimity was achieved by threats by the use of the weapon of fear. This is one of the fruits of growth and development. Another phenomenon, which is of considerable social and political significance, is that a large number of young people in their twenties and thirties contest elections for the post of sarpanch, or for a position of influence in co-operative societies, or for a seat in the state assembly. A new generation of young men, particularly those belonging to the relatively well-off sections of land-owning peasantry, has got politicized during the last two decades or so. As a result, and this is symbolic of the change of the times, some leading cadres in villages are under threat of physical annihilation. This phenomenon deserves special attention. It is expected that this will arouse the interest of research workers, as also of agro-economic research centres. Further, village studies relating to the structure of its economy will help the various institutions and the government to draw up appropriate plants for integrated rural development.

In working to create an environment conductive to pro-poor sustainable economic growth—the first pillar of our poverty reduction strategy—and recognizing that the private sector is an indispensable partner for poverty reduction.

---

## BALAMPUR (Madhya Pradesh)

Balampur which is only 22 kms from Bhopal, the capital of Madhya Pradesh, is probably the most celebrated village in the state. Heaven was supposed to be round the corner for the village's 1,100 inhabitants. A health unit, a veterinary centre and gobar gas plants were promised. There would be assistance in improving agricultural practices, loans to 30 people for goats, to 50 for poultry and 60 for cows and buffaloes. Twenty-six cottage industry units would be set up. And, most important, 50 wells with 50 electric pumps as well as nine tube wells would be provided for irrigation and all within five years (1980-85)

A vet visits the village every day now and a doctor once a week; but Balampur's most tangible gain is undoubtedly the construction of 52 huts for the homeless. But that is about all. Electricity poles, rise up a few yards away; but the homes are unlit. A villager, who worked on their construction because he was promoted one for himself, says, with sorrow and apathy. "An investigation will show that about a dozen are occupied by people who don't belong to this village at all. But they are in because they know the landlords, and people like me are out."

**Unfulfilled Promises:** But that is a small disappointment compared to the others: not one of the dozens of wells, pumps and tubewells promised has materialised so far. In 26 months, only two loan applications for electric pumps have been cleared, and even those were pending from the time before the village was adopted.

Balampur provides a living contradiction of the fallacy that poverty can be banished by pouring money liberally under the Integrated Rural Development Programme (IRDP). About 60 goats, provided under the programme, have died due to illness, a fact confirmed by the young local vet.

Another villager gets furious when the subject turns to the supply of a buffalo each to 40 beneficiaries under the IRDP. "Ever heard of a Rs. 3,200-buffalo that gives a negligible trickle of milk?" he asks disgustedly. "I've got one. Yes, it is true that I was present along with officials when we bought them in Kosi (Haryana), but the whole purchase works in such a way that the dalals crowd you and push you into making a bad choice." The local 20-point programme committee, say the villagers, is now inquiring into the widespread complaints against the poor quality of animals.

## Dashed Hopes

It is close to a year since a dozen gobar gas plants were set up. They are still lying idle. Idle, like the 25 women who make up the dormant Mahila Mandal. A gram sewika came a year ago, and made them fill up forms for a dozen sewing and a few wool knitting machines. One of the women, who applied for a wool knitting machine, hasn't so much as seen one, but says she asked for one because the gram sewika told her to. Says another: "It is many months since she took the forms. We haven't heard from her since then. Nobody tells us what is happening."

Summing up to two years' experience in this area, a villager said: "It is like being adopted only to become an orphan soon again."

## DISPUR (Assam)

## Impact of Industrialisation

Industrialisation and urbanisation open up new avenues of employment for the villages in their vicinity. In this respect, a study of Dispur, district Kamrup, in Assam is instructive. It underscores the impact of the growing city of Gauhati on the village between the years 1955 and 1961, when a re-survey was undertaken. The Noonmati Oil Refinery is only three miles from the village.

Dispur has a total number of 108 households. In 1955, it had only 81 households, a fact which underscores the point that there has been an influx of immigrants into the village. There was no industrial establishment in 1955; in 1961, there were six major industrial establishments. By 1964, another five were added.

The industrialisation and urban growth round the village have had a profound impact on the villagers, especially with regard to their occupational pattern, sources of income, standards of expenditure, investment patterns, social habits, cultural patterns and value system etc. The pace of industrialisation of the village has been so rapid that it might lose its rural character in the near future.

Although the proportion of households dependent on non-agricultural occupations has increased since the first point survey, agriculture is still the main occupation for the majority of family members. People belonging to the "kacheri" and "koch" communities have not benefitted from it. Land is sold to outsiders. The proportion of tenant farmers in the village has increased in recent years. There has been a greater concentration of land ownership and of operational holdings since the first survey was completed in 1955.

Mr. P.C. Goswami observes: "Inspite of the increased opportunities for employment in trade and commerce, the economic condition of the villagers has not improved." Many households showed a deficit in their family budgets; but its magnitude was higher in the re-survey year. The benefits of industrialisation are thus mixed in character.

## HASTEDA (Rajasthan)

Hasteda in Rajasthan is an example of the village which has been isolated by heavy floods and soil erosion. It has a total population of 356 households. A majority of the villagers are engaged in non-agricultural activities. Only 27 per cent of the total number of households pursue cultivation as a primary occupation; the remaining 63 per cent are employed in the secondary and tertiary sectors.

The agricultural sector contributes only 39 per cent of the total village income. Nearly 43 per cent of the income is generated by the non-agricultural sector. Another 15 per cent is contributed by remittances from outside.

The fact that every household in the village has to follow more than two occupations highlights the unremunerative character of most of their occupations. The agricultural economy of the village is subsistence oriented, inferior cereals constituting nearly 96 per cent of the gross cropped area.

The distribution of land holding in Hasteda is skewed, for only 3 per cent of the households in the village own as much as 37 per cent of the land; while 63 per cent of the household do not own any land.

The rural problem of Hasteda is how to shift the village economy from its stagnation towards modernisation. Soil erosion is a major problem. A full and efficient utilisation of all the resources in the village is called for. The introduction of Panchayat Raj and the establishment of institutions like Gram Nirman Sangh are hopeful pointers to the future.

## IRUVELPATTU (Tamil Nadu)

Iruvelpattu is a village in south Arcot district of Tamil Nadu, 12 kms south of Villupuram on the Grand Southern Road from Madras to Tiruchirapalli and further south to Madurai and Kanyakumari. It is a medium sized village with a population of 1,544 and an area of about 1,131 acres.

It is one of the South Indian villages surveyed originally by Gilbert Slater in 1916. Two further surveys took place-one in 1937 by A.K. Veeranghavan (AKV) and the other in 1961 by M.R. Haswell (MRH). It was relisted after 65 years in 1982. The main purpose of the re-survey was to assess the change or continuity in living conditions, technology, land ownership and the village power structure.

### Two Civilisations

Speaking of the caste village and the "cheri", Slater wrote nearly 70 years ago: "Even in this small, almost self-contained Dravidian community, we find two civilizations, but apparently of vast antiquity, existing side by side; and though each for innumerable generations has acted upon the other, they still remain distinct." In other words, in Iruvelpattu as well, East (Harijan Colony) was East and West (caste village) was West. The dualism that Slater noticed in 1915 between the two has persisted to a remarkable degree. The combined effects of economic inequality, social discrimination and physical segregation on the Harijans are vividly visible. As a result, a number of Harijan families left 15 years ago for work in the coffee plantations in Karnataka; and their relatives and friends continue to follow them in trickles. Young men from the Harijan colony have also gone as coolies to Madras and Bangalore, returning to their village only for short periods.

**Table 1**
**IRUVELPATTU, EAST AND WEST**

| | *(Percentages, unless otherwise indicated)* | |
|---|---|---|
| | *(East) Harijans* | *(West) Harijans* |
| Population proportion | 30 | 70 |
| Schooling proportion : Male | 13.7 | 54.7 |
| Female | 6.7 | 26.7 |
| Total | 10.2 | 42.1 |
| Post-middle level school | 7.1 | 17.3 |
| Dropouts at primary level | 77 | 52 |
| Proportion of terraced and tiled houses | Nil | 15.6 |
| Proportion of electrified houses | Nil | 27.6 |
| Water connection (public & private) in Nos. | Nil | 49 |
| Share in land ownership | 3 | 97 |
| Pumpset ownership (in numbers) | Nil | 78 |
| Share in cattle ownership | 78 | 92.2 |
| Bank deposits (in numbers) | Nil | 60 |
| Savings accounts (in numbers) | 5 | 97 |
| Proportion of agricultural labour households | 82.2 | 15.2 |
| Poverty (%) | 100.0 | 47 |

## Landlord

The "plutocrat" (big landlord) of Iruvelpattu, whom Slater encountered and whom MRH rediscovered in 1961, has survived successive stages of land reforms with little damage to him. All that can be said is that the ceiling legislation has divested him of about 10 per cent of this holdings; it has put a brake on further acquisition by him, and, in future, it might lead to a reduction in ownership if benamidars assert themselves in the course of time. He owns 400 acres of land in the village (out of 665 acres) and another 200 acres in the adjoining village. The plutocrat's economic power has given him effective control over the village and the lower-level bureaucracy, the village institutions and over the village commons. He is in a position to promote or prevent anything happening in or to the village. The big landlords (BL's) influence extends over the village institutions and the state. His support has been forthcoming for primary education, health care, veterinary services, and temple renovation and maintenance in the caste village. But he has stood in the way of anything that would make the Harijans more self-reliant *e.g.*, in the grant of housesites and purchase of milch cattle; and he has shown no interest in securing even the simple welfare needs for them, *e.g.*, drinking water and street lighting. He has tried to promote temperance; even now, there is no arrack shop or illicit distillation plant in Iruvelpattu.

## Economic Power of the Plutocrat

At the same time, BL has actively come in the way of the grant of house sites to Harijans, has prevented the nationalized banks from lending money to them for the purchase of milch cows in the colony; and none of the good works of the Panchayat have extended to the colony. He has maintained his control over house sites, fuel and thatching materials. He has taken the fullest advantage of the new technology. As a dominant employer in the labour market, he has been able to keep wages down. His position, however, it is not free from tension and threat. The kind of control that was exercised in Slater's times by the senior BL is no longer possible, and tyranny has come to be considerably tempered with tact. Resentment is openly expressed in the colony, and also in the caste village. Higher wage demands are becoming more insistent and the Harijans are beginning to stir on many fronts.

## Irrigation

The use of pumpsets had led to the spread of the new technology of high yielding seeds and chemical inputs. The fixed and operating costs of pumpsets, and the cost of purchased inputs in the new technology, are such that its spread has been limited to the larger and more affluent landholders. the productivity of small and petty farmers does not seem to have increased much beyond the levels noticed nearly four decades ago. The scope for further extending the new technology is fraught with constraints that are institutional (credit), structural (fragmentation of ownership and operational holdings), and ecological (ground water depletion)

## New Technology

The new technology has helped to create more employment in the village as well as outside it because of the extension of sugar-cane cultivation. Additional employment has been created in non-agricultural occupations to which the use of pumpsets, the growth in public services, and a general increase in trade and services activities have contributed. However, real wages seem to show a stubborn tendency to continue at about the same levels as they did decades ago. Even with more days of employment, the wage levels of agricultural households remain such that their real earnings are below the minimal subsistence norms. The enforcement of legal minimum wages would be a significant step towards poverty reduction. Marginal cultivators, who are not in a position to adopt the new technology, are a sizable component of the poor.

## Welfare Measures

Many more public services have been extended to the village than in the past. They have created a useful avenue of employment. However, for various reasons, the access of Harijans and other poor to education, health, water supply, electricity, veterinary services and the distribution of essential commodities has been limited. The provision of these basic minimum needs is not marked by either efficiency of equity.

## Poverty

The estimate of the poverty line at Rs. 51 is well below the official estimate of Rs. 76 for rural India at 1979-80 prices. Even so, all the agricultural labour households in Iruvelpattu are below the poverty line. A detailed survey of 11 landless labour households indicates that the income of a family is of the order of Rs. 1,645. Even this higher estimate is well below the poverty line of Rs. 2,738 per family per annum.

Cultivators operating less than 2 acres of land without access to pumpsets are not likely to achieve any significant economic success even if they cultivate two crops, and may be taken as falling below the poverty line. Altogether some 200 agricultural-labour and marginal-cultivator households, or 62 per cent of the total number of 323 households in Iruvelpattu, may be considered to be absolutely poor. They include all the Harijan households and about 47 per cent of caste Hindu households, divided about equally between agricultural labourers and marginal cultivators. the high incidence of poverty in Iruvelpattu, despite the "low" poverty line indicated above (Rs. 51), is the effect of an extreme concentration and ownership in this village and of particularly low wages.

---

## KANTHAN TERANG (Assam)

Kanthan Terang is a small village of 22 households situated in the United Mikir and North Cachar Hills district, Assam. The study, changes in Mikir society, is a study of a traditional village under the impact of urbanisation in a hill society. The village was first studied in 1961 and was resurveyed in 1965.

Shifting cultivation remains the primary occupation of the households. Villagers do not hold any land privately because they belong to their semi-nomadic tribes. Their secondary sources of income are negligible. Paddy is the main crop grown.

The present resurvey report gives a clear picture of the changes which have occurred within a short period of five years in a tribal society which is experiencing the impact of urban growth. Dipu, the nearby town, provides a ready market for the sale and purchase of goods by the people of Kanthan Terang.

The urban growth in the neighbourhood has facilitated the expansion of such commercial crops as cotton, gourd and castor seeds. The importance of fishing and hunting has declined; but the sales of firewood and thatch have increased. The per capita income in the village rose from Rs. 233 in 1960 to Rs. 454 in 1965. The expenditure of the villagers also went up. The changes in the attitude of the tribal people to the acceptance of urban employment are worth noting.

In spite of the village being near a growing town, the villagers could not avail themselves of any direct benefits of the developmental programmes covering electricity, water supply, etc. The village inhabitants have remained apathetic to educational and medical facilities.

There are signs of a gradual transformation of the village economy from the traditional self-sufficiency type to a market-oriented type. There is nothing in the finding of the study that can be interpreted to mean that the people of Kanthan Terang in a hill society are inherently averse to change or slow in adjustment any more than the ordinary village folk in India.

---

## KASHIPUR (West Bengal)

Kashipur in West Bengal was surveyed in 1956 and was resurveyed in 1960. The economy advanced during this period. The improvement was small but not negligible. The data showed a rise in production and real income, a fall in debt and an increase in investment. The intensity of cropping increased from 99.51 to 113.72. The total crop production in 1960 at 1956 prices increased by 36 per cent over the level of 1956.

The total value of output, too, went up. Higher prices of produce enabled the cultivators to plough back their investments. The value of sale of assets per household during 1956-60 was Rs. 216.25; the value of the purchase of assets per household was Rs. 551.91, that is, more than double.

Nearly half the cultivating households participated in investment of some type or the other. But it was house construction which dominated the new investment scene. Most of the new investment activities reported to have taken place in the village were self-financed. Institutional credit was nearly absent.

The expansion of irrigation facilities was the main factor contributing to the progress of the village. There was a growing demand for fertilizers. The extension of communication facilities promises a more ready contact with markets. But the river girding the village on three sides presented a problem of communication in the absence of a bridge, and restricted to a large extent the working of the economy and development of the social relation of Kashipur with the neighbouring area, including the city of Durgapur, a potential market.

New institutions emerged as a result of the implementation of various programmes, such as the setting up of a social education centre, a Mahila Samiti, a health centre and the agricultural extension agency.

The occupational structure of the village did not exhibit any steady change in a definite direction. Caste traditions did not lessen their grip on the occupational pattern, particularly for the upper caste people. About half the number of inhabitants in the village belonged to the depressed castes category who were without either land or education. Their occupational mobility was of an oscillating type of movement within the manual labour sector.

---

## KHAMARIYA (Madhya Pradesh)

If Balampur's proximity (22 kms from the capital city of Bhopal) did not do it any good, it is hardly surprising that further away things were still more dismal. Khamariya is 115 kms from the district headquarters of Raisen district; and it takes a jeep nearly three hours to travel the last 35 kms. The list of achievements is dismal. "I hope you have noted that we installed two hand-pumps in Khamariya," says a district official of Raisen. "Hope you have noted that last year we held adult literacy classes." They don't appear to have done much good; in Khamariya, inhabited by 250 tribals and Harijans nobody knows what a newspapers is. Villagers haven't seen one and find it hard to comprehend when it is described to them.

---

## HONNAPURA (Karnataka)

The rural development not only means building up of some infrastructure in village like roads, health centres, schools, panchayat offices, etc., but also developing socio-economical, political and cultural environment along with enriching the eco-system. Rural development thus encompasses area development on the one hand and human resources development on the other.

Under the village adoption scheme, Honnapura was adopted by a Grameena Bank. The concept behind the adoption of a village is to provide a supportive local organisation which would co-ordinator between the various governmental, financial and country agencies to ensure that benefits flow in the right direction towards the real target group without any seepage. The parent organisation is also supposed to act as the conscience-keeper of the people and promote social development in the level village.

As an exception to this general trend, the Malaprabha Grameena Bank has been endeavouring to bring about a total socio-economic transformation in one of its adopted villages called Honnapura in Karnataka. Honnapura is 18 kilometres away from Dharwar, the district headquarter, on the Pannage-Dharwar Highway. The village is attached to the Mugadha branch of the Grameena Bank, which is situated only 6 kilometres away from Honnapura. It is located in very idyllic surroundings amidst the hills. There is a big tank in the village, from which a small stream flows, which is used for irrigation purposes.

## Origin and Growth

Honnapura village has been newly created for the purpose of rehabilitating the people of the village known as Majali-Sidlivadi, when the latter was submerged in 1975 following the construction of Hidkal Dam. Before 1975, the area of Honnapura was covered by forests. About 800 acres of forest area were cleared to create this village.

Following the submersion, the government took three years to distribute the land to the people who lost their landed property. The process of distribution of land has not yet been completed. There are 20 families which have yet to receive land, and 300 acres of land have yet to be distributed. Even while distributing the new land, the government appears to have done little justice to them. Every family has been given land of 2 to 4 acres. People are very sore about the difference between the quality of the land they had lost and the land that was allotted to them. The submerged village was on the river bank and was therefore very fertile. The villagers used to grow a minimum of two crops per year. The land which was allotted to them at Honnapura is dry; and there is no water facility worth the name.

## Features of the Village

There are 350 households in Honnapura. Out of these, 25 households are Harijans, ten Muslims, and six Brahmins. Only 50 houses out of 350 have a tiled roof. All the houses in the village were constructed by the inhabitants themselves. The government has given only financial assistance to them.

The total population of the village is around 2,000 about 80 per cent of whom are Lingayats. Harijans, the Vokkaligas, Muslims, Brahmins and other sub-sects constitute the remaining chunk of 20 per cent of the population.

Honnapura does not have a panchayat. There is a non-political leader among them, who looks after the needs of the village. He is the school master. People have accepted him as their spokesman.

Honnapura has a primary school, a post-office and a branch of a rural bank. The nearest primary health centre is situated at Alnavar, 17 kilometres away from the village. The Malaprabha Grameena Bank has been trying to get a primary health centre for the village. Again, the Grameena Bank acted as a liaison officer between the simple villagers and the colossal Kamataka Electricity Board, and managed to get the village electrified. This has certainly changed the quality of agricultural operation in the area. The passenger transport facility is very weak in the village. There is only one government bus running between Honnapura and Dharwar; and this, too not regularly. People, therefore, use trucks for their movement.

## Main Occupation — Agriculture

The main crops grown in the village are paddy and sugarcane. Groundnut, horse gram, tomato and other vegetables are the subsidiary crops grown in the area. People have been encouraged by the Grameena Bank to diversify their crop pattern to optimise production. Farmers have been encouraged and given financial assistance by the bank to go in for irrigation. They have been goaded into taking their surplus produce to Dharwar market themselves, and sell it there. Sugar factories lift the sugarcane directly, at the point of production. As there is no exploitation by middlemen, farmers have been getting a reasonable price for their produce.

But they complain that the wild animals from the nearby forest frequently enter their fields and destroy their crops. Moreover, following the planting of eucalyptus around the paddy fields by the Agriculture University of Dharwar, the crops do not grow in a 20 feet strip in the bordering areas, resulting in loss of income for them. The officials of the Malaprabha Grameena Bank intend to take up the matter with the Agriculture University about this problem. In fact, a debate is going on at the national level on the question of the effect of eucalyptus plants on food crops.

## Participation of Grameena Bank

The Malaprabha Garameena Bank has been participating in a big way in the socio-economic development of the village. With the exception of four households, all the households have been financed by the bank for one economic activity or the other. Even these four houses have been provided with crop loans. In the last three years, as many as 60 crop loans were distributed in the village. They were disbursed for the purchase of as many as 200 buffaloes and 50 pairs of bullocks. Out of 50 loans given for the purchase of bullocks, 30 were advanced for the purchase of carts as well as pairs of bullocks, because the bullock-cart is the major mode of transportation for the villagers. Ten farmers were given loans for land development, and other six for digging wells and installing pumpsets. Four were financed for growing and selling vegetables, five for retail trade, two each for beedi shops, tile manufacturing and flour mills, and one for a bangle shop. In addition to these, a large number of farmers were given loans for the purchase of organic manure. To ensure a proper utilisation of loan amount, the bank has been taking sufficient care to give the loan amount directly to the shops which supply the inputs to the farmers. One community sprinkler irrigation project, having 21 members, has been financed by the bank. A loan has been advanced for digging a big tank for the purpose of irrigation. Since there is scarcity of drinking water in the village, three bore-wells have been financed by the bank. With the objective of taking sufficient care to see that all the requirements of the village are met, the bank has given loans for diversified activities in the primary sector, cottage and small-scale industrial sector and the tertiary sector, instead of concentrating only on limited economic activities.

## Customs and Traditions—No Caste Factor

There are two temples in the village—one, Allamaprabhu Temple, and the other, Lakshmi Temple. The Archak of the Allamaprabhu Temple belongs to the Lingayat community and of the Lakshmi Temple, to the Valmiki Community. The Brahmins of the village appear to have no dispute over this, and participate in all the activities of the village. For instance, every year, in the month of Shravana, Brahmins perform abhisekha in Lakshmi temple. People of all communities join together to celebrate festivals in the temples on auspicious and holy days. Once in a year, there is a mass feeding without consideration of caste or creed. This is a very pleasant feature of this village society.

## Communal Harmony

The villagers have a common fund for the expenditure incurred on these festivals. Donations are collected from all the communities. The expenditure incurred on Muslim festivals is also met from the same common fund.

There is a mosque in the village. The Hindus participate in all the Muslim celebrations held at the mosque. They entertain the audience gathered in the mosque during the festival with their fancy dress competition. The Hindus offer pooja in the Mosque. The Muslims, too, participate in all the Hindu festivals and offer pooja in the temple. Muslim-Hindu unity appears to be a feature of village life.

Even among the caste Hindus and scheduled caste Hindus, a cordial relationship exists. For instance, Brahmin ladies bring drinking water from the tubewells without any hesitation, situated in a Harijan hamlet.

## Why Harmony?

One of the main factors responsible for the great degree of communal harmony in the village appears to be the essence of a village panchayat. The entry of the panchayat brings with it elections. With elections, as we, knowing India, start unhealthy group politics, which ultimately lead to communal disharmony. Then, should we say that the panchayat and elections, by encouraging groupism among the people, destroy the peace of village? This is a very serious matter to be considered by all the social scientists interested in rural development.

## Social Awareness

The people of Honnapura do not seem to be attracted to city life. They go to Dharwar only to purchase the cattle, and to sell the vegetables and other surplus food products grown by them. The youth of the village have no particular partiality for the cinema. Instead, they spend their idle time working in the forest maintained by the Agricultural University. About 50 of them have already joined as watchmen in these protected forests.

The people of the village are well aware of the need for family planning. After their shift to Honnapura, all those who had two children or more went in for surgical intervention to limit the size of the family. The Alnavar primary health centre has conducted three family planning camps here so far.

The villagers send their children to school. But there is a heavy percentage of drop-outs because there is no proper atmosphere for education in this agriculturally dominant village.

## Drinking Habit—Minimum

There is no liquor shop in Honnapura. When enquiries were made with the people, they said that when they were in Majali-Sidlivadi, most of them used to consume liquor everyday. But when they were shifted to Honnapura, a majority of them, because of the absence of liquor shop, stopped drinking. Now they are habituated to non-drinking. Only three, according to them, go out of the village for a drink.

The liquor contractor in Dharwar wanted to open a liquor shop in the village. But people protested against this and did not allow him to open it. The contractor complained to the police against the people for, as the contractor of the area, he had every right to open a liquor shop in the village. The police, on the basis of the complains, asked the head of the village to come to the police station and explain why the contractor should not be allowed to open the liquor shop. But the people of the village refused to go to police station, asked the police to come to the village and hold the enquiry. At last, the police, respecting the sentiments of the people, went to the village. At the time of the enquiry, a memorandum, signed by 60 villagers against the opening of a liquor shop in the village, was submitted to the police. When the contractor despite this protest, tried to open a temporary shed for liquor sales, the villagers pulled down the shed. The social awareness of the people, and the unity among them are really astounding.

## Summary

Honnapura village has been newly created to rehabilitate the people who were evacuated from the Hidkal Dam Project Area. The socio-economic development of this newly-created village is really heartening. After the adoption of this village by the Malaprabha Grameena Bank, the latter has made strenuous efforts to develop the village. The sociological features of the village reveal that there is a great degree of communal harmony between the Hindus and the Muslims, and between caste Hindus and scheduled caste Hindus. This may be so because the village society has not been corrupted so far by politics since there is no panchayat in the village.

---

## RALEGAON SHINDI (Maharashtra)

With the active participation of villagers under dedicated leadership, the tiny village of Ralegaon-Shindi is now pulsating with new life. There is a sea-change in the scale and scope of village activities. The result are both in terms of monetary benefits and social reforms. What is more, the value system in the village has scaled a new high. As a result, the village culture has been revived and reoriented. Within the short span of a decade, a significant transformation has taken place. New community assets have been created. The irrigated area has increased nearly six-fold; and the per capita income almost trebled. Modern amenities and technologies are in the offing. The village has a model school and a bank. The social reforms that have taken place in this village are remarkable. What is more, prohibition is complete. The village is neat and clean.

There is no unemployment, no indebtedness, no hunger, no poverty. Ralegaon-Shindi is an ideal village of integrated rural development.

## The Village Then

Ralegaon-Shindi is a small village in the Parner Taluka, Ahmednagar district in Maharashtra. According to the 1981 census, the population of the village was 1,800. Ten years ago, this village was an impoverished den of illicit liquor, with no less than 40 distilleries. Liquor was supplied to Parner, Ghodnadi, Shirur and Ahmednagar. This was a notorious village in Parner taluka. Villagers took to manufacturing and selling illicit liquor as their chief source of livelihood. The main reason for this was continual drought, and no facilities of irrigated water for agriculture; and there was inadequate supply of food. In seven years, the village became the most outstanding example of participatory village development. It has become a model village in the district. The transformation is quite astonishing. Today, not a single distillery operates in the village. Not only has liquor been banished but indulgence in smoking, singing of film songs, tamashas is frowned upon. The Tarun Mandal is engaged in constructive work.

## The Village Now

The main architect of this transformation of Ralegaon-Shindi is Shri Anna Hazare—an ex-serviceman. Anna Hazare a Khadi clad Gandhian—is neither interested in politics nor in himself. He is devoted to the integrated development of the community as a whole. On seeing the tattered conditions of this village, he vowed to eradicate the evils of illicit liquor, drinking, etc. In the initial stages, he had to face a number of problems. He started his work with education and persuasion. First of all, he impressed upon the village folk the evil effects of illicit liquor and drinking. Some of the villagers were convinced and stopped the illicit liquor business; but in some cases, he had to use force to get rid of anti-social activities in the village. He formed Tarun Mandals (Youth Clubs) to tackle the liquor menace. Tarun Mandals smashed brewing vessels wherever they found them, and those caught distilling were tied up and publicly beaten.

## Social Reforms

Thereafter, he devoted his energies to the development of the community, both economically and socially. The social reforms that have taken place here are remarkable. Nobody is found loitering without a job. The school-going children are fully engaged in their studies, even on holidays. They wear simple clothes but they are always clean and neat. Anna first applied his basic principles of development to school-going children. Principally, children should have love their homes, their village, district, province (state) and their country. Initially, there was only one school up to fourth standard in Ralegaon-Shindi. A spacious school building and a hostel for school children were then built by the villagers. Around the school building, a vast playground has been provided. In school education, due importance is given to physical education, and the development of the personalities of the children. Children are taught to clean their village once a week, to keep it clean and beautiful.

## Social Change

Anna brought all the villagers together. With their united effort (shramadan), they built a temple and a big public hall, where group marriages of people belonging to all the castes are celebrated. As a result, the cost of a wedding has come down to Rs. 500/- against Rs. 4,000/- earlier. This has helped the villagers significantly to reduce their indebtedness.

## Economic Development

Occasionally, villagers assemble in the public hall to discuss their main problems of development. In 1972, there was a terrible drought. The villagers constructed three nulla bundings and one pazar talao. They also constructed a very big public well with the finance made available by a nationalised bank. Agriculture, which was solely dependent on rains, has been assured a regular supply of water. There has been a six-fold increase in the irrigated area. The rainfed subsistence agriculture has been replaced by vegetable and seed farming, both for home consumption and export. Farmers grow cauliflower at the cost of Rs. 6,000/- per acre, and the returns are around Rs. 50,000 per acre—a net profit of Rs. 44,000 per acre. The bore wells are community assets, and people have ration cards for irrigation water. Afforestation has also been attempted. Three hundred and fifty fruit trees have been planted in orchards, which are looked after by the school children. The barren hill slopes have been planted with sisal so that the fibre extraction industry may be started in a couple of years. More than 80,000 subabuls have been planted to tackle the fodder problem. Ralegaon-Shindi has its own nursery and it sells subabul seeds to nearby villages.

## Towards Prosperity

On the education front, there has been tremendous progress. More than 100 students are studying in 10th standard. Literacy is over 75 per cent. A nationalised bank opened its branch in Ralegaon-Shindi in 1981 with a business of about Rs. 5 lakhs. Within two years, the volume of the bank's business was valued at more than Rs.55 lakhs. In the initial stage, the bank gave a loan of Rs. 12 lakhs to 250 farmers. They cultivated vegetables on co-operative lines, and earned about Rs. 20 lakhs. They repaid the entire bank loan within a short period. presently, the bank has invested about Rs. 16 lakhs in public bio-gas plants—gobar-gas plants for three Harijan families and twenty for others. Another outstanding feature of this village is that there are no open drains anywhere. (Every house has a soak pit). The villagers are confident of getting the advantage of the water from Kukadi canal. They are planning to have lift irrigation to bring a larger area under irrigation and double cropping. They have very systematic crop planning on the basis of co-operative farming, where the separate plots are earmarked to grow high grade seeds. With the increase in the area under irrigation, the availability of better seeds and a planned cropping pattern, the village has embarked upon a green revolution.

## A Selfless Leadership

The village economy is expected to receive a big push in the ensuing years.

The entire community in Ralegaon-Shindi is devoted to Anna Hazare. But Anna takes it as his moral duty to serve the entire community. He has nothing of his own. He lives in a temple that the villagers have built with shramadan. Though his family owns land and his parents live in the same village, he does not stay with them. They come to the temple to meet him. He has vowed to change the face of Ralegaon-Shindi methodically by attending to one problem after another. His constructive approach acts as a beacon light and leads the villagers to prosperity.

## Crux of Rural Development

The crux of the integrated development of a village depends on the implementation of a constructive programme of prohibition, bringing dry land under irrigation, rotation of crops, taking up subsidiary occupations, co-operation, community feeling, villagers' participation, social integration, application of new technology, sanitation, literacy, methodical and planned development, planned family and parenthood, youth's involvement in constructive work, untouchability and, above all, dedicated and selfless leadership. The three basic principles successfully adopted and strictly implemented are family planning, prohibition and ecological development (cutting of trees has been socially banned). Along with this, the village has built its own reservoir, taken up social forestry, windmills are erected, canals are constructed, reoriented education. More importantly aroused a greater awareness about a rich and healthy life. People are co-operative, open to new innovations, aware of their rights and duties. They are well organised. The Ralegaon-Shindi experiment is a eye-opener to others. It is one of the best rural development strategy, worth emulation.

## SAHAJAPUR (West Bengal)

The objective of the socio-economic study of Sahajapur, a West Bengal village, was to analyse the social and economic system and to undertake a study of changes in the village. Rural change has been interpreted as the economic and social change that takes place as a result of the dynamic forces operating within the country. This village had a total number of 128 households.

The village was included in the National Extension Service (NES), and many changes took place in many directions. All the changes, observed in 1956, were initiated by forces outside the village and solely through the activities and programmes undertaken by the government. The abolition of zamindari and the introduction of canal irrigation in 1955 are by any means far-reaching in their impact on the economic system. Other changes include the expansion of primary education, the eradication of malaria and the consequent reduction in the death rate, the improvement in public health and repairs of major roads, etc.

In this village of 128 households, eighty per cent of the households were engaged in agricultural occupations—43 per cent were farmers, 31 per cent agricultural labourers, and 6 per cent agricultural rent receivers. Mobility was noticed in respect of secondary occupations.

Comprehensive land reform legislation has been enacted, though not yet enforced in the village. The abolition of zamindari has been welcomed by all sections of the village people; but it has not affected their economic resources or pursuits. The pattern of the distribution of land has not really changed. There have been large-scale transfers of land title among fictitious owners because of the threatened ceiling on agricultural holdings.

The landless share croppers, agricultural labourers and some sections of the non-agricultural producers form the bulk of the population. The benefits of improvements in the field of education, recreation, medical and public health have not been shared equally by the different classes of people. These are availed of mostly by big and medium farmers belonging to the higher castes. There are no social barriers; but the economic position of the lower classes does not permit them to avail of the these gains of development.

There have yet been no major dents in the rural social structure. The caste structure is as strong as ever. The leadership and hierarchial structure has not changed in spite of the abolition of zamindari. No significant improvements are noticeable in respect of livestock and implements either.

There does not seem to have taken place any fundamental change in the organisation of production. There are, however, signs of the village economy progressing towards market-price orientation. The construction of residential houses certainly shows a tremendous improvement during the last ten years in 1970-1980, and this investment is largely self-financed.

## SHAMASPUR (Uttar Pradesh)

Shamaspur in Saharanpur district of Uttar Pradesh is a small village of 67 households. It is a village with backward agriculture and suffers from heavy rainfall and floods. It was surveyed during the year 1955-56. The focus of the study was on the structural change in the village economy, the pattern of land holdings, the cultivation of crops, the disposal of produce, the distribution of occupations and of resources.

Land holding in the village was skewed. One single household owned one-third of the entire owned land. In spite of the land reform measures introduced in Uttar Pradesh since 1952, the practice of crop sharing was prevalent to a significant extent in the village. Trading and money lending were concentrated in the hands of a single household. This implied non-availability of adequate employment opportunities for a large section of the population. A majority of the households followed multiple occupations; only 31 households had a single occupation. In fact, the number of households having more than one occupation increased within a generation. Tenants with small holdings and artisans having very little scope for widening the scale of their business worked as agricultural labourers to supplement their meagre earnings.

Food crops constituted a major item of agricultural production both in terms of area and value. Small holdings raised inferior cereals like millets; big holdings cultivated superior crops like paddy and wheat.

It is interesting to note that even though agriculture in this village was in a backward stage, its economy was linked to a significant extent with that of the neighbouring village. The value of sales of crops was 28 per cent of the gross production Another 24 per cent of the produce was disposed off in kind in contractual obligation, wage payments, etc.

The crux of Shamaspur village problem was the need for a major redistribution of economic resources, including land, so as to open up employment opportunities for its inhabitants and improve the productivity of their fields.

## SIDDIQGANJ (M.P.)

Siddiqganj, an adopted village 76 kms from Sehore is marginally better off. About Rs. 2.5 lakhs have been spent on a waiting room for bus travellers, a building for a panchayat, two school buildings, a dozen houses and a paving of almost one kilometre of village paths. But if it is to be a model village, much more obviously needs to be done. "Work has ground to a halt after the panchayat elections six months ago," says the sarpanch, a mild mannered man. "Since I took over, absolutely nothing has been done." One rather serious problem is a stream some kilometres away, which cuts the village off in the rains. "We've got Rs. 50,000 from the collector's fund," he says, "but I suspect that since this isn't enough and the Public Works Department has no money to spare, the bridge will remain incomplete." Also incomplete is the paving, with two-third of the village still to be covered. Even in winter, the narrow streets are dirty. During the rains, the slush is terrible.

Siddiqganj has a mini-primary health centre; but the nearest doctor is available at Ashta, 33 kms away. "It is common for people to die on the way to the hospital. A government doctor is supposed to come twice a week; but there are times when he doesn't appear for weeks."

A government booklet says that five bio-gas plants are to be set up, of which work on two has already started. But there has been no real beginning so far. More than 92 people have so far applied for loans under the IRDP; but only 20 have actually received them. Most of the applications have been pending for more than two years now.

### Follow-up Action

"These schemes of giving goats and poultry and buffaloes will never change the situation," says a Harijan and the village sarpanch. "What we need is a cottage industry and we wish someone would train us, someone who knows these things,"

Some attempts have been made in this direction, but as usual there has been no follow-up action. Three young boys were taught motor winding, but they have not been given loans and so their recently acquired skills, therefore, are being wasted away. Some 30 women were trained in the use of the charkha for over three months; but since then, there has been no action, and so the women continue to sit at home.

The sarpanch points out that many promises have yet to be fulfilled. Apart from the bridge and improvements to the road—a bone-rattling 12 kms stretch that links it to the main road—the construction of a building for the high school, the upgrading of the existing water supply scheme, and the establishment of a primary health centre continue to be a far-off dream.

## TERAI (Uttar Pradesh)

The Terai region along the Himalayan range, facing the foot-hills bordering Nepal in Uttar Pradesh and cut off from the world for centuries is a fine example of the Green Revolution in the country. It has large farms, which have achieved a degree of prosperity during the last thirty years, which has spread to the district of Shahjahanpur and Lakhimpur in Uttar Pradesh. It is their prosperity which the Terai neo-rich farmers flaunt.

Thirty years ago, the Terai was sparsely inhabited by Thari and Buxha tribals, who knew nothing about farming. They were unaware of the value of their lands. The new settlers dispossessed them after paying them ridiculously low prices—for example, a bottle of liquor for an acre.

The settlers are broadly classified into three distinctive groups of non-agriculturists; the Punjab refugees, who came from the west following the partition and were offered lands in Terai and others incentives; the Kumaon ex-servicemen, who were settled on small pieces of land; freedom fighters of eastern Uttar Pradesh who were gifted lands; and hordes of other people.

The new settlers cleared the forest, levelled the virgin land and laid the foundation of an agricultural revolution. Today, the Terai region hums with prosperous activity. This is a region unlike any other, a different world in itself. What is more – Terai yields (wheat: 20 quintals per acre, sugarcane: 400 quintals) are easily comparable to those of Punjab's at lower investments in inputs. Better water-management, mechanised farming and other allied activities have brought prosperity to the region.

Beginning with Kashipur at the western tip of Nainital district in Uttar Pradesh, the road eastward meanders through the lushest of Green Revolution country, all covered with tall sugarcane interspersed with patches of blooming mustard. Surprisingly, there are not many villages along the road—only a few typically Bengali huts by the roadside and small towns predominantly populated by Sikhs. In fact, if the region differs in any ways from the most prosperous areas in Punjab, it is in having a much larger number of tractors in the country side—in fact, the majority of road side filling stations sell only diesel.

Instead of villages what appear intermittently on the horizon breaking the non-unpleasant monotony of farms are massive farmhouses, their TV antenna gleaming symbols of the bounty these farmers harvest in the Terai. The signboards along the road read: Cheema Farm House, Garewal Farms, Bhatia Farms; and so on.

## Large Holdings

It shows in the life-style of the farmers. The bigger ones have got around the ceiling laws by using the simple expedient of co-operative farming to retain farms that often sprawl over a thousand acres. This enables them to go in for mechanisation in a big way. The large farmers consider that land ceiling is the death of good farming. They have avoided the ceiling laws by dividing land among their family members, friends and absolutely imaginary partners in the co-operatives. A scrutiny of the records of a number of co-operative societies shows names such as Majh Kaur, Khupri Ram, Tamatar Singh, as partners in societies owning some of the biggest farms. Majh, Khurpi and Tamatar in Punjab means buffaloes, hoe and tomato. The so-called co-operatives of big farmers are in fact family associations controlled and managed by one person.

## High Living

Their massive farmhouse displays TV antennae, air-conditioners projecting from every room and carpets, chandeliers and fine furniture. The house itself is a pre-fabricated one, imported from Switzerland. Mehta lives here with his four young sons and their wives and children in a modern 20th century world of the farmer's joint family. While the Mehtas live in a world of beer parties on the lawns and shikar in the Kumaon foothills, the more traditional families let their prosperity show in different ways. Churamani Singh, who owns a large farm near Bahedi in Bareilly district, has an elephant for a pet, besides his massive pair of Great Danes, an Alsatian and a number of smaller dogs. Outside him farmhouse, on the edge of the road, lies his tiger cage, with signboards warming passers-by to keep away from the bars. Smaller farmers go in for different status symbols—bigger tractor, guns and colour TVs.

People who owned the lands originally now pick cow-dungs from the farms of the new owners. Obviously, the rather sudden colonisation of a region cut off from the world for centuries has resulted in social tensions; and government officials have been placed in an unenviable situation. Pressures are brought to bear on them to stop tribal land alienation as well as guard the interests of the settlers who have done hard work and have a political clout outside the state.

## KAKKADAMPOYIL: A Remote Village Develops Rapidly

Kakkadampoyil, a village in Calicut district in Kerala, is an example of what a bank can do to transform it with an integrated rural development approach. There is now a better utilisation of local resources and skills. With the development of infrastructural facilities for socio-economic development, the banks aim at improving the quality of life of the rural population, particularly of the rural poor, by creating employment opportunities for them. Above all, the economic level of the village has been raised. Remotely perched on the Western Ghats at an elevation of over 2,000 ft., Kakkadampoyil presented an impoverished appearance. It provided shelter to 600 and odd families of settlers and adivasis. Almost all of these people lived below the poverty line before the banks drew up an integrated development plan and implemented it. It was a very backward and under developed area which had been untouched by all development agencies. Dusty winding roads made access to the village very difficult. There was no clinic, no upper primary school, not even a tiled house, except small huts thatched with dry grass. The only house in the area to speak about was the one in which a priest lived. The village did not have a provision store and the people had to walk seven kilometres downhill to buy their daily provisions.

There was no post office in the village. The plight of the people in the absence of this facility was pitiable. The nearest post office at Koompara was about eight kilometres from the village. Many farmers had applied to the land tribunal at Kukkam for their rights, since they had migrated there about 25 years ago from central Travancore, with a lot of hope grounded on the virgin soil of the village. They were never able to appear before the tribunal to plead their case, for the notice of hearing never reached them, or was received too late. As a result, records were not available to the farmers. They were not able to secure loans from banks to improve the land, raise crops and engage in allied activities.

The families which settled in Kakkadampoyil felled trees and planted the area with pepper, rubber and other crops. But once the green canopy was removed, nature's fury fell on the fertile land. Incessant rains lashed the region during the monsoon and washed away its rich top soil. Slow wilt destroyed it gradually. Rubber and other plantation crops did not grow well. Food crops like tapioca were destroyed by wild boars. The people were pushed below the poverty line.

There was a lower primary school in the village. The children had to walk about 14 kms and 24 kms up and down the steep path to attend the upper primary school at Koompara and the high school at Koodaranhi respectively.

Within a few years, the inhabitants found life very difficult. Furious winds and wild animals destroyed whatever they cultivated. their hopes slumped further when news reached them that the much awaited Dairy Development Project, proposed for the Western Ghats Development Programme, would be shelved. Many people started leaving the place.

## Bank's Efforts

It was at this critical juncture that the Canara Bank's branch at Mukkam, 18 kms from the village, involved itself in shaping the destiny of Kakkadampoyil. It was felt that the most urgent need of the people of this village was something which yielded quick returns. Dairying was the right solution. An abundance of natural grass provided an excellent scope for it. Loans of Rs. 7,500 were granted to each of more than 100 families to enable them to acquire three buffaloes each to supplement their income; but many hurdles had yet to be overcome. Milk had to be transported to Mukkam downhill over rough and winding roads. People joined hands to lay a few kilometres of road and made the remaining portion traversable by jeep. The bank extended aid for the purchase of a jeep to transport milk and people. Since dairying was new to the villagers, training was arranged with the Dairy Development Board.

Milk began to flow, and arrangements had to be made to market it. The bank helped the villagers to form a Milk Producers' Co-operative Society. The society, which began by supplying 20 litres of milk, was, before long, supplying 400 litres. The milk contained quite a high percentage of fat—more than the normal percentage—and yielded very good returns to the farmers.

A comprehensive report was prepared by the bank in its capacity of the lead bank for the development of infrastructure, and submitted to the Government. On the basis of this report, the Government sanctioned a pucca road to Kakkadampoyil under the Hill Tract Development Programme. This road linked its destiny with the rest of the country. The bank granted a loan to the Co-operative Milk Supply Society for the construction of a building which houses several shops as well. The bank played a pivotal role in conferring on farmers proper titles to lands by pursuing the matter with the Government. It provided a drinking water facility for students. The employees of the bank contributed dress materials for poor tribal students. A one day medical camp was also organised.

## Government Aid

Under the dairy development scheme, 200 families were provided financial assistance for the purchase of 204 milch buffaloes and 187 cross-bred milch cows. Also five stud bulls were financed to inseminate the buffaloes. On an experimental basis, ten farmers were financed to form a Community Cow Rearing Centre with veterinary facilities. A veterinary hospital sanctioned for the village by the Government was recently commissioned. The sight of buffaloes or cows in almost every house is an indication of the prosperity of the village. Each family earns an extra income of Rs. 125 per month after fulfilling production and repayment commitment.

Since it was essential to keep the route open all through the year to facilitate an uninterrupted supply of milk, protective walls and culverts were constructed as part of Government schemes. The laying of the first 3.5 kms was already in progress; and the Government is expected to sanction funds for the remaining distance next year.

The existence of about 70 acres of Robust a coffee plantation on the slopes induced a desire for coffee cultivation. A feasibility study was conducted in collaboration with the Coffee Board. The Bank formulated a pilot project for the planting of coffee in about 500 acres, with banana plants offering shade during the initial years. A group of 150 families was organised, and a training programme was initiated, for the cultivation of coffee plants.

## Facilities

The absence of any educational facility beyond the lower primary stage in the village resulted in many drop outs. The Government responded to the representation of the people and the bank, and an upper primary school was sanctioned. A building was constructed with the people's contribution. Over 150 students are studying there now. The absence of a post office posed many difficulties. Repeated requests were made to the P & T Department by the bank and the people to open a post office. The authorities have agreed to do so.

## Assistance from Rural Development Trust

Encouraged by the developments at Kakkadampoyil, the bank's Rural Development Trust has agreed to pay Rs. 40,000 for the construction of a rural dispensary in the village at a total cost of Rs. 50,000/-.

**Table 2**
**DETAILS OF LOANS GRANTED IN THE LAST FOUR YEARS TO THE VILLAGE**

| *Purpose* | *No. of Loans Granted* | *Amount Granted (Rs. in lakhs)* | *Amount Outstanding (Rs. in lakhs)* |
|---|---|---|---|
| Crop loans | 534 | 9.34 | 431 |
| Dairy loans | 214 | 10.19 | 6.05 |
| Breeding bulls | 5 | 0.13 | 0.05 |
| Sprayers' loans | 28 | 0.17 | 0.18 |
| Coffee development | 170 | 30.59 | 15.98 |
| Cashew project | 7 | 0.26 | 0.06 |
| Pepper rehabilitation | 40 | 6.63 | 1.44 |
| Cocoa development | 2 | 1.11 | 1.46 |
| Others | 13 | 0.62 | 0.35 |
| | 1013 | 59.04 | 29.88 |

The progress in the village has made such visible impact that the cost of an acre of land has shot up from Rs. 3,000 to Rs. 20,000/- Effective co-ordination by the bank has facilitated the work of various development agencies. The bank is justly proud of having been the means by which a village awakened to new life. Kakkadampoyil is poised for faster development, and bears ample testimony to what the will to serve can achieve, despite heavy odds.

**Table 3**
**IMPACT OF ADOPTION IN A NUTSHELL**

| | *At the Time of Adoption* | *As on 30-9-1982* |
|---|---|---|
| Banana (in acres) | 100 | 250 |
| Coffee (in acres) | 50 | 500 |
| Pepper (in acres) | 100 | 500 |
| Vegetables (in acres) | 20 | 50 |
| Cocoa (in acres) | — | 200 |
| Arecanut (in acres) | — | 200 |
| Buffaloes (No.) | 30 | 204 |
| Exotic cows (No.) | — | 186 |
| Grocery shops | — | 10 |
| No. of children attending school | 100 | 300 |

## Disappointments

Electricity did come to Khamariya about a year ago and now 15 houses have connection; but recently it went off abruptly for four months. There are seven electricity poles but none fulfil its function. On the credit side, there is now a two-room school building, whereas earlier classes were held in the open air.

"We are terribly disappointed," say the villagers, "We had told of so much but so little has happened. The road to Begamganj (35 kms away) would be fixed, we were promised. But we continue to be cut off from the world four months in a year." Another villager adds that there are no irrigation facilities and that loan applications for electric pumps—the village has only one—have been pending for months.

Khamariya presents a classic example of the attitude of superiority that government officials adopt when dealing with villagers; a neo-colonial attitude of we-know-what-is-good-for-you that has never done anyone any good. Few explanations are given by officials, and few are sought by the villagers. The gulf between the ruler and ruled is wide, and the absence of dialogue total. It is easy to see why villagers are so alienated from the process of their own development.

A community centre lies incomplete. No work has been done on it for several months. Even the better-off in Khamariya have no idea of what purpose the centre will serve, when it is completed if at all it is completed.

More than a year ago, officials gave 550 chickens to 20 villagers to start a small poultry farm. But the beneficiaries were not educated on how to care for the birds. There was no follow-up, and now nearly all of them are dead. Many have succumbed to disease, others have been destroyed by predatory birds and animals. A young boy has lost all his chickens: "We never asked for them; but these officials told us to fill in forms and so I did. I never wanted them, but took them only because they were free." He shrugs and adds: "Anyway, now they are all gone."

## Unsatisfactory Gifts

Take the case of an agricultural labourer. He say: "I wanted a bull but the sahib said: Why do you want one if you don't have land? I told him if I had one, I could cultivate the landowners' fields (under the system of share-cropping). He turned that down and said that I would be given goats. But I don't want goats. What should I do with them?"

## Summing-Up

From a study of the selected villages situated in different parts of the country, some conclusions may be drawn of the broad socio-economic conditions of life in rural India. By and large, life in each village in India corresponds to the existing environment with minor variations.

The villages in India continue to be in a bad shape, in spite of the Green Revolution and the implementation of Operation Flood.

Although their economic conditions have improved the benefits are enjoyed only by a few.

There is a greater inequality.

Two civilizations continue in every village. Caste Hindus have kept Harijans at a distance.

Social discrimination and physical segregation of the Harijans are very much in evidence.

Big landlords (farmers) have survived the successive stages of land reforms.

They have acquired enormous economic power in the village as well as in the state. They continue to exploit their brethren in the village for their own benefit. In some villages, there are small cohesive groups within castes which are the focus of power and decision making and contribute to the compartmentalised and segmented nature of the social organisation. The younger generation of the well-to-do farmers is in the forefront of village polity.

The local scene is dominated by important landholders and leaders of village factions. They wield enormous influence on village institutions and the bureaucracy.

Recent legislation by state governments, particularly the Zamindari Abolition Act and the Panchayat Raj Act, has brought about some significant changes in the pattern of the exercise of authority; yet the rich land is concentrated in the hands of a few.

Irrigation is the most significant factor in the rapid growth of agriculture in villages in rural India.

Farm mechanisation has also helped in revolutionising agriculture. But this has only helped the big farmers.

In some villages, electricity has come; but generating plants often breakdown or the use of electricity is limited to a few. So also irrigation facilities. In regard to the construction of houses, the picture is quite dismal. There is a wide gap between achievement (statistically) and reality.

Poverty is visible among the agricultural labourers, scheduled castes and tribes and small cultivators.

Rich farmers live in pomp, dignity and isolation. This prosperity of the large farmers in villages building up socio-political tensions.

Invariably, all welfare measures meant for the poor have been grabbed by the well-to-do.

Although it is evident that growth has taken place throughout the country in several villages in India, the benefits of growth have not reached equally to all the sections of the rural population.

The gap between the rich and the poor has widened in rural India.

The educated rural people among new generation do not want to engage in farming. They either want a sophisticated business or service which will bring more money for less work; and they often migrate to urban areas in search of pleasure and employment.

## ANaRDe, PARTNER IN RURAL DEVELOPMENT

Acil-Navasarjan Rural Development Foundation (ANaRDe), is an organisation engaged in Integrated, Rural Development. Set up in 1979, it now operates from about thirty centres and works in more than 2000 villages of Gujarat and Maharashtra. the Foundation's rural development programme is mainly aimed at assisting poor people to help themselves so that their socio-economic level is improved for the better. It comprehends both economic activities and creation of infrastructural facilities. To support its efforts the Foundation garners help from all developmental agencies — official and non-official.

### Agriculture

In agriculture, the Foundation exposed small farmers, agricultural labourers and economically weaker sections to modern agricultural practices and also provided timely inputs to the farmers. This brought about a considerable increase in per hectare production. Foodgrains production increased by 20 to 25 per cent. Besides, irrigation facilities like digging of wells and installation of oil-engines or electric motors to lift water were arranged during both Kharif and Rabi crops. Bullocks, buffaloes and improved implements were provided to beneficiaries by arranging subsidies/loans through banks. Farmers' meetings, training camps and demonstration camps were also arranged to educate the farmers. To help small and marginal farmers get agricultural inputs like seeds and fertilizers regularly, Gram Vikas Sanghs have been set up at the two centres at Vapi and Morvi.

### Animal Husbandry

In animal husbandry, farmers were provided with bank loans to purchase milch cattle, cattle feed and for putting up of cattle sheds. ANaRDe in association with the veterinary departments of the State Governments, arranged veterinary facilities for beneficiaries for better care of the livestock. Veterinary camps were organised for artificial insemination of cattle in villages so that the farmers were not required to take the cattle for long distances. Besides, diagnostic camps for animals were held which provided free animal health services and medicine.

In four centres covering tribal areas, 1000 bio-gas plants were installed by the beneficiaries at the instance of ANaRDe so that the inhabitats could be free from smoke menace and also to curb felling of trees for fuel. Similarly 1100 improved latrines have also been built in the villages to inculcate a sense of health and sanitation among the rural people.

## Social Forestry

Under NREP, about ten lakh trees of different species were planted in 300 hectares of land in 63 villages. These plantations are at present being maintained by ANaRDe Foundation and will be handed over to the Gram Panchayats after three years. This has been done under the Gram Van Programme of the Foundation. In addition, over three lakh seedlings were raised in Kisan Nurseries in seventy villages and distributed to the farmers for planting them in their own fields and long bunds.

## Women's Welfare

To make use of the talents of rural women for their economic development and betterment, Mahila Mandals were formed in the villages. The Mandals organise programmes like savings, house beautification, tailoring, papad-making, etc. More than sixteen thousand women were able to get employment through these programmes which not only helped to augment their income but also improved their standard of living. Besides, a co-operative of exclusively tribal women was set up for Zari Sari work. After getting the necessary training, the co-operative has started production. Very very poor tribal women were benefited by this out-fit. Each one of them earned Rs. 250 per month. Within a year the co-operative hopes to enlist 5000 members.

## Education

Balwadis, construction of balwadi buildings and Uttar Buniyadi schools are the main plans of the Foundation's educational programme. In Vapi and Morvi centres, 125 Balwadis were started where in nearly nine thousand children were given pre-primary education and nutritious diet.

At Vapi, the Foundation along with other philanthropic organisations, constructed seven school buildings at a total cost of Rs. five lakhs. Community hall and Balmandir facilities also exist in these buildings. Uttar Buniyadi schools are being run at four places in Jamnagar district. In all 500 boys and 300 girls attend the schools at a time. The teachers and boys of these schools assist in the implementation of various Rural Development programmes in the nearby villages.

## Rural Health and Sanitation

The Foundation has undertaken programmes for creating awareness by propagating preventive steps needed for combating various diseases among rural people. Such programmes included organising medical camps, eye camps, village cleaning camps, child health competitions and water purification. Other welfare and philanthropic organisations too gave a helping hand to the efforts of the Foundations either in cash or in kind.

ANaRDe has taken up immunisation, inoculation and vaccination programmes in about 500 villages in Junagarh district alone. The Foundation plans to extend the work to another 1500 villages next year.

## Vocational Training

At the instance of the Foundation, young boys and girls are provided training facilities in different trades to enable them to start their own cottage industries. The training is imparted in Gujarat Industrial Development Corporation (GIDC) complex at Vapi. In the project area different vocational training centres are at work and 525 beneficiaries utilise these facilities. Besides, 350 Scheduled Caste, Scheduled Tribe and identified beneficiaries were trained under TRYSEM in the trades of wireman, tailoring, carpentry, typing, radio and T.V. repair.

## Smokeless Ovens

The Gujarat Energy Development Agency provided assistance of about Rs.5 lakh for installing 10,000 smokeless ovens for the beneficiaries identified by ANaRDe Foundation. This not only saved fire-wood but also prevented damage to the eyes of the poor women. Their kitchen too remained soot-free.

## Social and Cultural Activities

Cultural activities are also undertaken to channelise the youth and women power in developmental activities. Recreation and family planning camps are organised and nearly 20,000 people participate in these activities. Other programmes taken up by ANaRDe include construction of rural roads, Balmandirs, additional rooms in schools, houses for landless labourers, drinking water facilities and electrification.

These programmes of ANaRDe have brought about an all-round development in the region. The local rural poor now need not leave their homes to go to cities in search of work. Indeed, ANaRDe is playing a constructive role as partner in Rural Development.

# RURAL PROSPERITY DEVELOPMENT STRATEGY

The Rural Development Programme, should not superficially concentrate upon Rural Amenities Development (as Schools/Roads/Dispensaries/Libraries/Parks etc.), but primarily concentrate upon Rural Prosperity Development i.e. scaling-up the individual prosperity of the destitutes in the targeted village, in the following broad directions :

(1) Commercial Exploitation of the **local resources** of Plants, Animals, Skills, Minerals, Environment, Water, Soil etc., through harnessing external Capital & Expertise.

(2) **New Introduction** of Plants, Animals, Skills, Tools etc. into the targeted Village;

(3) **Industrial Farming** of the Raw Material Crops of Agro-based Industries as Sugar/Paper/Fibre/Rayon/Match/Pharmaceutical/Phyto-Chemical/Food processing industries (20,000–50,000 Acres of Captive Factory Plantations on Farmers' Holdings in the Factory-Neighbourhood 100 Villages of each Factory all-over India)

(4) Large-scale sponsoring of **Service-Oriented Self-Employment schemes** as Motorised Rickshaws, Tea Shops, Repair shops, Craft Centres, Rural Produce Collection for urban marketing, Rural Waste utilisation, Health Care etc.

(5) Establishment of **Village Work Cum Food Centres** in each and even Panchayat Village, where in destitutes who cannot find the day's work elsewhere for survival will report for duty at 10.00 A.M. daily, to be productively engaged for at least 2 hours in Hand-Pounding of Paddy/Brick-making/Well-Sinking/Land Reclamation/Tree Plantations etc. (and then given free food or Rs.2-00 each so that he can continue to be alive till the better tomorrow).

For achieving the above objectives, there should be a high-Tech Panel of high-H.P. firebrand self-propellent Prosperity/Experts as Industrial Agronomists/Industrial Engineers/Industrial Chemists/Animal Experts/Mineralogists/Hydro-Geologists/Craft Experts/Prosperity Economists etc., for instant-identification of the local opportunities all-over India, formulate viable wealth-generating schemes and then monitor the prosperity development schemes through harnessing the local destitutes.

# CORPORATE FARMING

The real panaca for rural poverty eradication in India, will be the emergence of corporate farms all over India (similar to Corporate Industry, Corporate Trade etc.)

All marginal/small farmers of drylands all-over India, should be made join together as share holders in a Joint-Stock Company of 1000-10,000 Acres in each Market Town·all-over India, under Corporate Farming Project (similar to the existing farmers share-holders of the sugar factories all-over India).

Each Corporate Farm will conceive, plan & develop Commercial farming/Industrial Farming/Tree Farming/Expert Farming/Perennial Farming etc., through methodically harnessing Capital, expertise, materials, labour, processing, storage, marketing etc.

Each Corporate farm of 1000 Acres will involve an initial investment of Rs. 5-00 crores which will be suitably mobilised from the investors/banks/consumers etc. (like the corporate Industry/Corporate Trade etc.)

A corporate form of 1000 Acres can annually generate Rs.5-00 crores over the years, benefiting about 1000 farmers/share holders.

About 10,000 Corporate Farms all over India, could be organised (at 20 Corporate Farms per District), embracing about 5 Crore acres of drylands, metamorphosing the prosperity of 1-5 Crore marginal farmers/small farmers (who will be regularly advanced Rs.100/- per Acre per month from the date of enrollment)

Rotary Clubs/Public Trusts/Welfare Foundations/Voluntary organisations Finance Companies etc., all over India, can take up the responsibility of organising such Corporate Farms.

Interested fire-brand organisations any where in India, may harness the project Consultancy services of this Seasoned Expert.

## COMMERCIAL FARMING
## HIGH-POTENTIAL CROPS SPECTRUM

(Crops am enable for generating an Annual income of Rs. 20,000 – Rs. 40,000 over the years, from an Acre of the irrigated plantation).

### (A) TRADING CROPS

| | | | |
|---|---|---|---|
| I. | (1) | Dry Fruits | Coconut / Cocoa / Kajur / Tarmarind / Raisin Grape. |
| | (2) | Fresh Fruits | Banana / Citrus / Pineapple / Jack / Papaya / Grape / Guava. |
| | (3) | Tree Nuts | Cashewnut / Country Almond / Hazel Nut / Pistachia Nut / Pecan Nut / Soap – Nut. |
| | (4) | Food crops | Tapioca / Perennial Redgram. |
| | (5) | Vegetable crops | Vegetable Banana / Drum stick / Karepak / Bush Leafy vegetables. |
| II. | (6) | Fedder crops | Hybrid Napier Grass / Sudan Grass / Mesta / Bush Agathi / Perennial Sunhemp / Asparagu cowpea / Mucuna Bean. |
| | (7) | Fuel crops (Coppicing Trees) | Eucalyptus / Prosopi juliflara / Zizypus molucana / Cassia auriculata. |
| | (8) | Timber crops (Pillar Trees) | Inga dulcis / Indigofera tasmani / Daleergia latifolia / Acacio auriculipmis. |
| | (9) | Flower crops | Jasmine / Rose / Tuberose / Champak / Nerium. |
| | (10) | Tree oilseeds | Oil-palm / Salmalaia malabarica / Schelichera trijuga / Salvodora persica / Simmondsia. |

### (B) PHYTO-CHEMICAL CROPS

| | | |
|---|---|---|
| (1) | Perfumery crops | Palmarosa Grass / Tuberose Lily / Abelmoschus mostachus / Bush camphor / Bush Eucalyptus / Skimmia loureola / Attar Rose |
| (2) | Detergent crops | Acacia Concina / Sapindus emarginate / Sheperdia canadense. |
| (3) | Tannin crops | Rummex hymeno-sepala / Uncaria gambier / Rhus coriara / Caelsalpania diagyna / Cassia auriculate. |

### (C) PHARMACEUTICAL CROPS

| | | |
|---|---|---|
| (1) | Alkaloid crops | Vinca rosea / Atropa belladona / Dature inosia / Hyoscyamus mutica / Colchicum luteum / Centella asiatica. |

| | | |
|---|---|---|
| (2) | Contraceptive crops | Solanum ariculare / kalstromia pubescene / Gloriosa superba / Abrus precotorius / Trillium govania. |
| (3) | Anthelmitic crops | Cassia angustifulia / peganum hamale / psorella ceribolia / Artmesia kurromensis. |

**(D) INDUSTRIAL CROPS**

| | | |
|---|---|---|
| (1) | Rayon pulp crop | Sunhemp / Mesta. |
| (2) | Paper pulp crop | Sesbania exalta / crotalaria anagyroide / Laucena glauca / Indigofera tasmani / cassia auriculata / Ipomea carnea / Mesta / Sabai Grass / Silk cotton / perennial castor. |
| (3) | Fibre crops | Ramie / Sisal / Bauhinia vahli / Decaschistia crotonieflora. |
| (4) | Matchwood crops | Sesbania exalta / crotalaria anagyroide / Erythrina lithosperma / Thespesia populne / Indigoefera tasmani / Mesta / Ipomea carnea / Papaya / Drumstick / silk cotton / Tapioca / Perennial castor |
| (5) | Export crops | Mango / Cashewnut |

# MAKING A DIFFERENCE : SUCCESS STORIES FROM DISTRICTS

## 1. Kisan Credit Card Scheme Showed Path of Development — Osian Block of Jodhpur (Rajasthan)

Mr. Noor Mohd. a resident of Tinwri village in Osian block of Jodhpur who had 54 bighas unirrigated land and 27 bighas irrigated land, used to avail crop loan from Tinwari GSS (Gram Seva Samiti) for undertaking agricultural operations on his farms. But he was not able to meet entire credit requirement from the crop loan available from GSS due to ceiling limit fixed on crop loan amount. So he had to borrow from retailers/money lenders in the Tinwari town, who were charging exorbitant rates of interest, for meeting his balance credit requirements for agriculture operation, repairs of agriculture machinery, payment of wages of labourers, electricity bills, purchase of inputs and domestic needs. One day he came to the office of DDM Jodhpur and inquired about credit card facility. DDM called him to the function organized by SBBJ (State Bank of Bikaner and Jaipur), Tinwari for distribution of KCCs, DDM advised him to approach Branch Manager SBBJ, Tinwari for sanction of KCC limit. Accordingly, he was provided with a card cum pass book. Noor Mohd. found KCC scheme very convenient for meeting his credit requirement for the chain of activities of agriculture operation and depositing income from sale of agriculture produce/allied activities.

Noor Mohd. is now a very progressive farmer who changed the cropping pattern from food crops to cash crops like raida, zeera, chilli, garlic, onion for which he has installed one more tube well. He no more resorts to distress sale of his produce at the time of harvesting for repayment of loans, borrows from retailers/money lenders as he has now learnt to avail of credit facilities from banks under the KCC.

## 2. Area Development Project on Vanilla Cultivation in Areca Plantation as an Inter Crop — Uttara Kanada (Karnataka)

During the last one and half year the arecanut prices have crashed from a peak of Rs. 12000/- to 15000/- per quintal to Rs. 2500/- to 3000/- per quintal due to variety of reasons including banning of Pan Masala. An initiative was taken by AGM(DD) of Uttara Kannada district to encourage farmers to go for an inter-crop in areca plantations. This was done by organising a series of extension programmes highlighting the benefits of vanilla cultivation and processing through VVV club, promoted by NABARD in the district. It was also decided to launch an Area Development Project (ADP) for Vanilla cultivation and processing in Uttar Kannada district which was launched during the year 2002-03 covering 75 acres with a financial outlay of Rs. 47.25 lakh a year for two years.

The first step taken by AGM(DD) was to take all the banks into confidence about financing of vanilla cultivation. The scientists and experts from Spices Board and progressive farmers from adjoining district were invited to explain to areca farmers the agro economic practices of vanilla crop and advantage of vanilla crop over the traditional inter crops. An economic analysis prepared impressed the farmers as they were informed about the good prices the vanilla beans could fetch for them. The DDM also collected data about the potential demand and supply position to market the crop. Syndicate Bank, Varada Gramin Bank and Kanara District Central Co-operative Bank participated actively in the ADP by issuing circulars to their branches and also allocating targets for financing vanilla units. The PCARDB was initially hesitant to finance vanilla units citing the lack of knowledge in appraising the scheme. The AGM(DD) readily came forward to help them in appraising the scheme so that financing activity was undertaken in the right earnest.

The efforts of the AGM paid excellent results as more than 150 units were financed as against target of 75 units for 2002-03. The PCARDBs ended up with highest tally of 61 units, as against allocation of 20 units made to them in ADP.

While Varada Gramin Bank financed 58 units, commercial banks financed 32 units. The total area brought under vanilla cultivation during 2002-03 was 233 acres as against target of mere 75 acres envisaged in ADP. The financial achievement was even more impressive with total loan sanction of Rs. 124.75 lakh against which disbursement of Rs. 66.71 lakh was made during 2003-04.

The Horticulture Growers Society announced the auctioning system for vanilla beans for the year 2002-03. The joy of vanilla farmers knew no bounds, when news reached that the auction by tender system was fetching a high price of Rs. 800 to Rs. 900 per kg as against the assumption of Rs. 150 to Rs. 200. The prices of processed and cured vanilla beans also commanded a rate of Rs. 6000 to Rs. 9000/- kg paving the way for the farmers to take to processing and curing of vanilla beans to add substantial value to their produce.

*Source :* DDM Digest-April-June 2003.

❑ ❑ ❑

# ANNEXURE - I

## List of Rural Development Programmes (1950-2008)

| Sl. No. | Schemes/Projects/Programmes | Year of introduction | Target Area/ Group | Purpose |
|---|---|---|---|---|
| (1) | (2) | (3) | (4) | (5) |
| 1. | The Community Development Programme (CDP) | 1952 | All Blocks | Development of villages through agriculture. |
| 2. | National Extension Service (NES) | 1952 | Block (Lesser coverage than CDP) | To provide scientific and technical assistance for increasing productivity. |
| 3. | Applied Nutrition Programme (ANP) | 1960 | All States Mothers/Children | To improve the health and nutritional status of people, particularly mothers and children in rural areas. |
| 4. | Intensive Agricultural District Programme (IADP) | 1960-61 | Selected (13) Districts | To provide package of inputs including credit to farmers for increasing production through intensive cultivation. |
| 5. | Rural Industries Project (RIP) | 1962-63 | Area covering 3 to 5 Blocks | To provide a package of inputs to the rural artisans. |
| 6. | Intensive Agricultural Area Programme (IAAP) | 1964-65 | Selected Districts in all States—Farmers | To increase agricultural production and induce the farmers to apply improved techniques. |
| 7. | High yielding variety programme (HYVP) | 1965 | All states | To increase agriculture production and induce farmers to use high yielding variety seeds and apply improved techniques. |
| 8. | Multiple Cropping Programme (MCP) | 1965 | Selected districts | Special programme for development of selected crops. |
| 9. | Lead Bank Scheme (LBS) | 1969 | All Districts (Expect metropolitan cities and urban centres) | Banking development through branch expansion and development banking through implementation of district credit plans, Blockwise, scheme-wise credit estimation, being implemented by public sector banks. |
| 10. | Small Farmers Development Agency (SFDA) | 1969-70 | All States (in selected districts) small farmers | To enable small farmers to participate in the process of development and share its benefits. |
| 11. | Marginal Farmers and Agricultural Labourers (MFAL) Programme | 1969-70 | All States (in selected districts marginal farmers) | To enable Marginal Farmers & Agricultural Labourers to participate in the process of development and share its benefits. |

| | | | | |
|---|---|---|---|---|
| 12. | Crash Rural Employment Programme (CREP) | 1969-70 | All States-landless labourers and other rural un-employed. | To provide employment opportunities in cultivable barren lands and other public works projects which do not require skilled labour. |
| 13. | Export Oriented Programme (EOP) | 1970 | Selected crops | Special Programme for the development of selected crops. |
| 14. | Drought Prone Area Programme (DPAP) | 1970-71 | 554 Blocks in 73 districts of 13 states. | To ensure that rural works taken up under the programme are of a lasting nature and to provide employment through construction work. |
| 15. | Backward Area Development | 1971 | Backward Districts | 1. Special Scheme with Central outright grant/subsidy for setting up industrial units in such areas. 2. Concessional Finance Scheme for the projects in less developed areas. |
| 16. | Rural Artisans Programme (RAP) | 1971-72 | 41 RIP Districts | To provide all-round training to villages artisans in different trades. |
| 17. | Differential Interest Rate Scheme (DIR) | 1972 | Weaker sections (Family income not exceeding Rs. 7,200 in urban areas in Rural Areas Rs. 6,400) | To provide Concessional Credit at 4% Rate of Interest to weaker sections for their upliftment. |
| 18. | Employment Guarantee Scheme (EGS) | 1972 | Rural unemployment and landless labourers. | To guarantee employment to all able bodied persons in the rural areas, willing to work in manual and unskilled jobs. |
| 19. | Tribal Development Projects (TDP) | 1972-93 | Andhra Pradesh, Bihar, U.P. & Orissa, Tribal and Semi-Tribals. | Integrated development of tribes and the areas occupied by them. |
| 20. | Intensive Rural Employment Projects | 1972-73 | All states rural un-employed and landless labourers. | To provide employment in public work project which do not require skill of a high order. |
| 21. | Half-a-Million Job Programme/Employment Promotion Programme (HMJP/EPP) | 1973-74 | Educated unemployed | To assist educated unemployed in self-employment ventures. |
| 22. | Hill Area Development Project (HADP) | 1973-74 | Kangra in Himachal Pradesh, Nilgiris in Tamil Nadu Tribals and Semi-Tribals, Agricultural labourers and farmers. | To maximize agricultural production through multiple cropping, HYV, horticulture etc. |
| 23. | Command Area Development Agency (CAD) | 1974-75 | Selected area farmers falling under the command area of selected irrigation projects. | To realise optimum utilisation of irrigation potential created by major irrigation projects. |
| 24. | Special Live Stock Programme | 1974-75 | 21 States & 4 Union territories (weaker sections of the rural population). | To provide employment opportunities to the weaker sections of the rural population. |

| | | | | |
|---|---|---|---|---|
| 25. | Integrated Rural Development Programme (IRDP) (Revised in VI Five Year Plan (1978-83)) | 1976-77 | Selected Blocks Rural poor (Subsequently covered in all Blocks). | SFDA and MFAL were merged into District Rural Development Agency (DRDA) to implement IRDP. To cover 600 families in every Block. |
| 26. | Minimum Needs Programme (MNP) | 1976-77 | All States Landless labourers. | To improve rural health, water supply etc. |
| 27. | Food for Work Programme (FWP) | 1977 | All States un-employed and under-employed in rural areas. | To provide employment opportunities for the target group in rural areas. |
| 28. | Village Adoption (VAS) Schemes | 1977 | Selected villages in the command area of the Bank Branches. | To meet the credit needs of the villages adopted, by the commercial banks. |
| 29. | Antyodya | 1977 | Jaipur, Jodhpur, Kota & Chittor Districts of Rajasthan SC/ST people. | To provide employment opportunities to the poorest of the poor in rural areas. |
| 30. | Rural Health: People's hand | 1977 | 5000 Administrative Blocks in the entire country-Rural people. | Imparting training to the community health workers. |
| 31. | Village Health Scheme | 1977 | All States/Rural poor. | To strengthen health care and family welfare services in rural areas. |
| 32. | Desert Development Programme | 1977-78 | Desert areas in Rajasthan, Gujarat, Kashmir, Himachal Pradesh people in desert areas. | To check further desertification of the desert areas and to raise the productivity of local resources of these areas. |
| 33. | Fish Farmer's Development Agency (FFDA) | 1977-78 | All States Fish Farmers | To assist fish farmers for promoting inland fishing. |
| 34. | Preventive Voluntary Health Organisation Programme | 1977 | All States | To provide community based health service in Tribal and Rural areas and to expand and improve basic and preventive health services. |
| 35. | Environmental Slums Scheme | 1977 | All States-poor in slums | To improve the living conditions of the people living in slums. |
| 36. | Integrated Child Development Services (ICDS) Programme. | 1977-78 | Union Territories/Children | To provide improved living conditions in slums. |
| 37. | Rehabilitation of the Bonded Labour Programme | 1977-78 | Selected states, Karnataka, M.P., Orissa, Tamil Nadu, U.P., Bonded labourers. | To improve the living condition for children. |
| 38. | National Adult Education Programme | 1978 | All States Adults in Rural areas. | To extend educational facilities to adults in rural areas. |
| 39. | District Industries Centre Programme (DIC) | 1978 | All States | To give a thrust for Industrial Development in rural areas. |
| 40. | Training for Rural Youth for Self-Employment (TRYSEM) | 1979 | Rural Youth | To assist Rural Youth in Self-Employment. |

| | | | | |
|---|---|---|---|---|
| 41. | Self Sufficiency Scheme (SSS) | 1979-80 | Tamil Nadu—rural poor | To provide basic infrastructure in rural areas. |
| 42. | Special Animal Husbandry Programme (SAHP) | 1980 | Selected Districts/Blocks | To develop supplementary sources of income for the rural people and to increase milk production. |
| 43. | National Rural Employment Programme (NREP) | 1980 | Rural and Semi-urban areas | To provide short term relief through employment to uneducated in rural and semi-urban areas. |
| 44. | Rural Labour Employment Guarantee Programme (RLEGP) | 1980 | Rural areas—Landless Labour household | To assure guaranteed employment to atleast one person for every landless labour household in rural areas. |
| 45. | Development of Women and Children in Rural Areas (DWCRA) | 1982-83 | Women and Children | Assistance for the uupliftment of women and children in rural areas. |
| 46. | Self-Employment Scheme for Educated Youth (SEEUY) | 1983 | Un-Employed Youth in all areas except cities with a population of more than 10 lakhs. | To assist educated un-employed youth in self-employment ventures. |
| 47. | Massive Assistance for increasing Agricultural Production Programme (MAPP) | 1983-84 | Small and Marginal Farmers | To assist Small and Marginal Farmers through minor irrigation schemes |
| 48. | Self-Employment Programme for Urban Poor (SEPUP) | 1986 | Urban Poor | To provide self-employment opportunity for urban poor. |
| 49. | Service Area Approach (SAA) | 1989 | All the villages in India | To prepare a credit plan and implement the same for the development of allotted villages by the commercial banks. |
| 50. | Nehru Rojgar Yojana (NRY) | 1989 | Urban Poor | To provide wage-employment to urban poor. |
| 51. | Jawahar Rojgar Yojana (JRY) | 1989 | Rural Poor | To provide wage employment to rural poor |
| 52. | Scheme of Urban Micro Enterprises (SUME) | 1990 | Urban Poor | To provide support for urban poor for setting up the urban micro-enterprises to augment self-employment opportunities. |
| 53. | Prime Minister's Rozgar Yojana (PMRY) (subsuming SEEUY) | 1993 | Educated unemployed youth | To provide assistance to educated unemployed to start self-employment ventures. |
| 54. | Swarna Jayanti Shahari Rozgar Yojana (STSRY) | Dec. 1997 | Urban Poor | Self-employment & wage employment. |
| 55. | Swaranjayanti Gram Swarozgar Yojana (SGSY) | 01-04-1999 | Poor Families | Self-employment. |
| 56. | India Awaas Yojana (IAY) | 1985-86<br>1999-2000 | People living below the Poverty Level | Shelter to people. |

| | | | | |
|---|---|---|---|---|
| 57. | Pradhan Mantri Gram Sadak Yojana (PMGSY) | 25-12-2000 | Rural Roads | Roads in rural areas |
| 58. | Sampoorna Grameen Rozgar Yojana (SGRY) | 25-09-2001 | Rural Areas | Wage employment |
| 59. | Provision of Urban Amenities in Rural Areas | 15-08-2003 | Rural India | Social upliftment |
| 60. | National Food for Work Programme (NFWP) | 14-11-2004 | Rural Poor | Wage employment |
| 61. | National Rural Employment Guarantee Scheme (NREGS) | 07-09-2005 | All India rural areas | Better livelihood security, Guaranteed 100 days employment. |

## INSURANCE SCHEMES

Credit insurance, crop insurance and life insurance are the main schemes under this category.

* *Credit Insurance*

The Deposit Insurance and Credit Guarantee Corporation of India offers a measure of protection to banks and other financial institutions which extend credit to borrowers of small means and to small scale industries. The insurance premia for limits up to Rs.25,000 is borne by the credit institutions. Various priority sector advances are covered under the scheme.

* *Crop Insurance*

The Comprehensive Crop Insurance Scheme, introduced on 1st April 1985, is an area based credit linked voluntary scheme, covering wheat, paddy, millet, oil seeds and pulses.

All farmers availing crop loans for these crops from cooperative credit societies, RRBs and commercial banks are eligible for insurance coverage under the scheme.

Barring a few states, other states had implemented the scheme.

The scheme was kept voluntary to make it more popular and beneficial to the farmers so that they evince interest in the scheme on their own.

The mounting losses under the scheme led the government to suspend the scheme in January, 1988 and the states were advised not to notify any crop for Kharif 1988.

However, it has been reintroduced from the coming rabi season by limiting the sun insured per farmer to Rs. 10,000 irrespective of the amount of loan taken and also reducing the insurance coverage from 150 per cent to 100 per cent of the loan amount. A high level committee is set up to conduct an indepth study and critically review the functioning of the scheme.

* *Life Insurance*

The organised workforce in India were provided a good measure of social security by various schemes such as Employees' State Insurance Scheme (1948). Employees' Provident Fund Scheme (1952), Family Pension Scheme, Deposit-linked Life Insurance Scheme, Gratuity, etc. However, only 10 per cent of the total workforce in the country is organised. There was thus a felt need for low-cost social welfare schemes, especially for workers below the poverty line and agricultural labourers, who could not bear any part of the cost of social welfare scheme.

A pioneering scheme was first introduced by the Gujarat Government, by which all landless agricultural labourers between the ages of 18 and 60 were covered for a sum assured of Rs.1,000 with the cost entirely borne by the Gujarat Government.

Inspired by this, was born the world's largest group insurance scheme known as the Landless Agricultural Labourers' Group Insurance (LALGI) Scheme. Introduced in August 1987, the scheme covers all landless agricultural labourers between the ages of 18 and 60 for a sum assured of Rs.1,000, at a premium of Rs.10 per head per annum, which is borne by the central government. Approximately, over three crore landless labourers are covered under the scheme. The scheme is to be run as a pilot measure for three years after which it will be reviewed.

* *Insurance for IRDP Loanees*

A similar scheme for IRDP loanees, who are granted loans on or after 1st April 1988 has been launched on that date. The scheme provides life cover for Rs.3,000 for natural death and Rs.6,000 for death by accident. The loanee should be aged between 18 and 60. Approximately, 40 lakh beneficiaries are covered by the scheme. The cost is borne by the central government.

* *Social Security Fund*

In the latest Union Budget, a social security fund with a corpus of Rs.100 crores has been created. The fund is to be utilised towards payment of 50 per cent cost of group schemes for groups of workers sustaining themselves on a day-to-day basis. So far, handloom weavers and rickshaw pullers/drivers are covered under the scheme.

Apart from these, a number of low cost group insurance schemes to cover productive rural assets are in operation. The cost, however, is borne by the beneficiaries, either individually or through their associations.

Almost each and every aspect of rural development is thus, sought to be covered by specific schemes. And yet, the impact on rural development is not notable. Multiplicity in programmes and implementing agencies is probably the bane for effective development. Consolidation of the various programmes could perhaps be a solution for their effective implementation.

❑ ❑ ❑

## SECTION NINE

# SELECT BIBLIOGRAPHY

### BOOKS


Agarwala, A.N. — The Economics of Underdevelopment, Oxford University Press, Bombay, 1969.

Arora, R.C. — 'Integrated Rural Development', S. Chand & Co. Ltd., New Delhi, 1979.

— 'Industry and Rural Development', S. Chand & Co. Ltd., New Delhi, 1985.

Bandyopdhaya, T. — 'The Poverty of Nations: A Global Perspective of Mass Poverty in the Third World', Allied Publication Pvt. Ltd., Calcutta, 1988.

Balakrishna, S. — 'Some Demographic Features of Rural India, Rural Development of India, Some Facets', National Institute of Rural Development, Hyderabad, 1979.

Basu, A.S. — 'Tribal Development Programme in Himachal Pradesh: A Study of Bharmaur': A Doctoral Thesis, Punjab University, Chandigarh, 1981.

Behari Bipin — 'Rural Industrialisation in India', Vikas Publication, New Delhi, 1976.

Bhatia, B.M. — Poverty, Agriculture and Economic Growth, Vikas Publishing House, New Delhi, 1977.

Bhattachary, B.N. — 'Indian Rural Economics', Metropolitan Book Co., New Delhi, 1984.

Bhattachary, S.N. — 'Rural Development in India and other Developing Countries', Metropolitan Books Co., New Delhi, 1983.

Bhattachary, S.N. — 'Community Development: An Analysis of the Programme in India', Academic Publishers, Calcutta, 1970

Bhattachary Sibnath — 'Rural Industrialisation in India: Its Nature & Problems', B.R. Publishing Corporation, Delhi, 1980.

Bruce R. Crouch & Shankariah Chamala — 'Extension Education & Rural Development', John Wiley & Sons Ltd., New York, 1981.

Chambers, Longhurst & Pacey — 'Seasonal Dimensions to Rural Poverty', S. Chand & Co. Ltd., New Delhi, 1985.

Dakshinamurthi C., Michael, A.M. & Shri Mohan — 'Water Resources of India and their Utilisation in Agriculture', Water Technology Centre, IARI, 1973.

Dak, T.M. — 'Management in Rural Development', Oxford and IBH, New Delhi 1983.

Dandekar, V.M. & Rath, N. — 'Poverty in India', Indian School of Political Economy, Poona, 1971.

Das Gupta, P.K. — 'The Impact of Industrilisation on a Tribe in South Bihar', Anthropological Survey of India, Calcutta, 1978.

Deogaonkar, S.G. — 'Administration for Rural Development in India', Concept, New Delhi, 1980.

Desai, A.R. — 'Rural Sociology in India', Popular Prakashan, Bombay, 1983.

Desai D.K. — 'Management in Rural Development', Oxford and IBH, New Delhi, 1983.

Desai S.S.M. — 'Rural Banking in India', Himalaya Publishing House, Bombay 1983.

Desai Vasant — — 'Rural Development'.

— Vol. I-Issues and Problems.
Vol. II-Programmes and Strategies.
Vol. III-Organisation and Management.
Vol. IV-Experiments in Rural Development
Vol. V-Rural Development in the Seventh Plan, Himalaya Publishing House Bombay, 1988.

— A Study of Rural Economics, Himalaya Publishing House, Bombay.

— Rural Banking in India, HPH, Bombay.

— Financing Rural Development, HPH, Bombay.

— Fundamentals of Rural Development.

— Issues in Agriculture & Forestry.

— Indian Agriculture: Its Nature & Problems.

— Forestry Management in India.

— Agricultural Economics.

Dholakia & Iyengar — 'Planning for Rural Development—Issues and Case Studies', Himalaya Publishing House, Bombay, 1989.

Dube and Murdia (ed.) — 'Land Alienation and Restoration in Tribal Communities in India', Himalaya Publishing House, Bombay, 1982.

D. Vasudeva Rao — 'Rural Development Through Irrigation', Ashish Publishing House, New Delhi, 1988.

— 'Facets of Rural Development', Ashish Publishing House, New Delhi, 1972.

E.M. Sminger, Douglas — 'Rural India in Transition', All India Panchayat Parishad, New Delhi, 1972.

Elic, A.N. — 'Operational Problems of Rural Banking', Vora & Co., Bombay, 1967.

Elliot, Charles — 'Problems of Poverty in the Third World: A Study of Social Economic Stratification', Praeger, New York, 1975.

Fonseca, A.J. (ed.) — 'Challenge of Poverty in India', Vikas Publishing House, New Delhi, 1971.

Franda, M. — 'Small is Politics: Organisational Alternatives in India's Rural Development', Wiley Eastern Ltd., New Delhi, 1987.

Gadgil, D.R. — 'District Development Planning', USO Publishing House, Bombay, 1967.

Gaikwad, V.R. — 'Panchayati Raj and Bureaucracy', National Institute of Community Development, Hyderabad, 1969.

Gandhi, Rajee & Singh, Rao Birendra — 'Agricultural Development and the Small Farmer', S. Chand & Co. Ltd., New Delhi, 1984.

Garg, Usha & Jagdish Vibhakar — 'Poverty of Nations and Third World', UDH Publishers, New Delhi, 1985.

Gedam, R.M. — 'Poverty, Economic Development and Industrialisation', Deep & Deep Publications, New Delhi, 1988.

Ghate, Prabhu — 'Direct Attack on Rural Poverty: Policy Programmes and Implications', Concept, New Delhi 1984.

Giriappa. S. 'Income Saving and Investment Pattern in Rural India', Ashish Publishing House. Bombay, 1988.

— 'Rural Energy Crisis', Himalaya Publishing House, Bombay, 1988.

Grewal. P.S. 'Rural Banking In India'. Kalyani Publishers Ludhiana, 1985.

— 'Rural Economics', Kalyani Publishers, Ludhiana, 1983.

Gupta & Gupta 'Rural Development in India – Poverty and Development', Himalaya Publishing House, Bombay, 1988.

G. Morley Mohan Lal 'Poverty Alleviation—Indian Experience', Himalaya Publishing House, Bombay, 1988.

Hague, M.L. 'The Poverty Curtain', National, New Delhi, 1988.

Hanumappa, H.G. (ed) 'Sericulture for Rural Development', Himalaya Publishing House, Bombay, 1986.

Haariharn, C. 'Panchayati Raj and Rural Development—A Study of Tamil Nadu', Concept, New Delhi, 1983.

Harison. Paul 'Inside Third World: The Anatomy of Poverty', Second Edition Penguin, 1981.

Jain L.C., Krishnamurthy, & Tripathi P.M. 'Grass Without Roots—Rural Development under Government Auspices', Sage Publication Pvt. Ltd., Delhi, 1985.

Jain S.C. 'Community Development and Panchayati Raj in India', Allied Publishers, Bombay 1975.

Johnston, Bruce F. and William, C. Clark 'Redesigning Rural Development: A Strategic Perspective', the John Hopkins University Press, Baltimore, 1982.

Joshi, Navin Chandra 'Indian Rural Economy', Young Asia Publications, New Delhi, 1980.

Kashyap, C.L. 'Management and Planning of Rural Development in India', Ashish Publishing House, New Delhi, 1989.

Kaur, Santnam 'Women in Rural Development', Mittal Publication, New Delhi, 1988.

K. Manu. 'Tribal Women in a Changing Society', Mittal Publications, New Delhi, 1988.

Kocher, E. James 'Rural Development, Income Distribution and Fertility Decline', The Population Council, 1970.

Laxman & Narayan (ed.) 'Rural Development in India—A Multi-dimensional Analysis', Himalaya Publishing House, Bombay, 1988.

Lal A.K. 'Politics of Poverty: A Study of Bonded Labour', Chetana Publications, New Delhi, 1977.

Lal, Mohan. 'Rural Industrialisation & Regional Development', Deep & Deep Publications, New Delhi, 1987.

Lele; Uma. 'Design of Rural Development – Lessons from Africa', John Hopkins University Press, London, 1975.

Long, N. 'An Introduction to the Sociology of Rural Development', Tavistock Publications Ltd., London, 1982.

Madan, G.R. 'India's Developing Villages', National, New Delhi, 1986.

Mahajan, V.S. — 'Studies in Indian Agriculture & Rural Development', Deep & Deep Publications, New Delhi, 1988.

Maheshwari, S.R. — 'Rural Development in India—A Public Policy Approach', Sage Publications (India) Pvt. Ltd., New Delhi, 1985.

Mardal, R.B. — 'Planned Development of Rural Settlements', Concept, New Delhi, 1981.

Marriott, McKim. — 'Village India', The University of Chicago Press, USA, 1963.

Mathew, T. (ed.) — 'Rural Development in India', Publishers Academy, New Delhi, 1986.

Mehta B.C. Awadh Prasad. — 'Agrarian Relations and Rural Exploitation', Ashish Publishing House, New Delhi, 1988.

Mehta N.C., Panandikar, and V.A. Pai. — 'Rural Banking', National Institute of Bank Management, Pune, 1974.

Mehta, S.R. — 'Rural Development Policies and Programmes', Sage Publications, New Delhi, 1984.

Mehta V.D. — 'Growth in Agriculture Employment in Rural India', Prateeksha Publications, Jaipur, 1988.

Mellor, John W. — 'The Economics of Agricultural Development', 1964.

Minhas, B.S. — 'Planning and the Poor', S. Chand & Co. Ltd., New Delhi, 1988.

Mishra, G.P., Rai, R.P. and Bajpai, B.K. — 'Village Industries and Agriculture in Changing Agrarian Situation', Ashish Publishing House, New Delhi, 1989.

Mishra R.P. and Sundaram, K.V. — 'Rural Area Development—Perspective and Approaches', Sterling Publishers (P) Ltd., New Delhi, 1979.

Mishra R.P. — 'Rural Development – Capitalist and Socialist Paths,' Vols. 1-5, Concept Publishing Co., New Delhi, 1985.

Mishra S.N. — 'Rural Development & Panchayati Raj', Concept Publications, New Delhi, 1981.

Mohapatra, P.C. — 'Economic Development of Tribal India', Ashish Publishing House, New Delhi, 1988.

Mohsin, Nadeem. — 'Rural Development through Governmental Programmes', Concept, New Delhi, 1985.

Moris, Jone. — 'Managing Induced Rural Development', International Development Institute, Indiana University, Bloomington, 1981.

Mosher, A.T. — 'Thinking About Rural Development', Agricultural Development Council, New York, 1976.

Moynihan Daniel P. — 'On Understanding Poverty: Perspective from the Social Sciences', Basic Books, New York, 1969.

Myrdal, Gunnar. — 'Asian Drama: An Enquiry into the Poverty of Nations' (3 vol.) Penguin., New York, 1968.

'The Challenge of World Poverty', Penguin, 1970.

NABARD — 'Vikas Volunteer Vahini – Genesis and Methodology', Bombay 1984.

Naidu, L.K. — 'Bank Finance for Rural Artisans', Ashish Publishing House, New Delhi, 1988.

Nanavati, B and Anjaria, J.J. 'The Indian Rural Problems', Indian Society of Agricultural Economics, Bombay, 1970.

Naoroji, Dadabhai, 'Poverty and Un-British Rule in India', Swan Sonnenschein, London, 1901.

N.I.R.D. 'Rural Development in India: Some Facets', (Revised Ed.) National Institute of Rural Development, Hyderabad, 1986.

Pais, H. & Singh, C.S.K. 'Poverty Alleviation Programmes: Feedback from Jhahna (M.P.)', National Labour Institute, New Delhi, 1986.

Pandey, B.N. (ed.) 'Role of Science and Technology in Rural and Economic Development in India', S. Chand & Co. Ltd., New Delhi, 1986.

Pareek, Udai 'Education and Rural Development in Asia', Oxford and IBH Publications, New Delhi, 1982.

Patel, K.V., Shah, A.C., and D'Mello L. 'Rural Economics', Himalaya Publishing House, Bombay, 1987.

Radhy, Kishore C. 'Commercial Banks and Rural Development', Asian Publication Services, New Delhi, 1980.

Rao, R.V. 'Rural Industrilisation in India: The Changing Profile', (2nd ed), Concept, New Delhi, 1987.

Rao, V.K.R.V. 'Food Nutrition & Poverty in India', Vikas Publishing House, New Delhi, 1982.

Rao, Vasudeva D. 'Rural Development Through Irrigation', Ashish Publishing House, New Delhi, 1987.

Rao, Vasudeva D. 'Facets of Rural Development', Concept, New Delhi, 1986.

Robert, Chambers. 'Rural Development', Longman, London, 1983.

Sharma, S.K. (ed.) 'Dynamics of Rural Development', Concept, New Delhi, 1977.

Sharma, S.K. and Malhotra, S.L. 'Integrated Rural Development: Approach, Strategy and Perspectives' Abhinav Publications, New Delhi, 1977.

Shah, S.M. 'Rural Development Planning and Reforms', Abhinav Publications, New Delhi, 1977.

Shah, Ajit 'Rural Development & Banking in India', Deep & Deep Publications, New Delhi, 1985.

Singh Mohinder. 'Rural Development Administration & Anti-Poverty Programme', Deep & Deep Publications New Delhi, 1988.

Singh Katar, 'Rural Development—Principles, Policies and Management', Sage Publications (India) Pvt. Ltd. New Delhi, 1986.

Sinha, A.K. 'Mass Media and Rural Development—A Study Village Communication in Bihar', Concept, New Delhi, 1985.

Singh G.S. 'Rural Modernisation, Contradiction and Change', Intellectual Publishing House, New Delhi, 1982.

Singh A.K. 'Agricultural Development and Rural Poverty', Ashish Publishing House, New Delhi, 1987.

Singh Pramod 'Ecology of Rural India', Ashish Publishing House, New Delhi, 1986.

Sirisikar, V.M. 'The Rural Elite in Developing Society', Orient Longmans Ltd., Bombay, 1976.

Singh R.Y. & Singh A.K. 'Planning in Integrated Rural Environment', Deep & Deep Publications, New Delhi, 1980.

Srinivas, M.N. 'India's Villages', Media' Promoters and Publishers, Bombay, 1978.

— 'India : Social Structure', Hindustan Publishing Corpn. Delhi, 1982.

Srivastav, M and Singh A.K. 'Rural Development in India', Deep & Deep Publications, New Delhi, 1988.

Subramanian, C. 'Integrated Rural Development', Abhinav Publications, New Delhi, 1976.

Sudha. V. Rao. 'Education & Rural Development', Sage Publications (India) Pvt. Ltd., New Delhi, 1985.

Swaminathan, M.S. 'Science & Integrated Rural Development', Concept, New Delhi, 1982.

Tiwari T.T. & Sinha R.C. 'Rural Development and Planning in India', Deep & Deep Publications, New Delhi, 1986.

Thakur, Devendra. 'Rural Development and Planning in India', Deep & Deep Publications, New Delhi, 1986.

Townesend, Peter. 'The Concept of Poverty', Heinemann, London, 1970.

Tripathi, P.C. 'Rural Transport and Economic Development', S. Chand & Co. Ltd., New Delhi, 1972.

U.N.A.P.D.I. 'Local Level Planning & Rural Development: Alternative Strategies', United Nations Asian & Pacific Development Institute (U.N.A.P.D.I.) Bangkok, Concept, New Delhi.

Upadhyaya. Rakesh. 'Integrated Rural Development Programmes: A Policy Approach', Himalaya Publishing House, Bombay, 1989.

Venkaiah, V. 'Impact of Agro-Based Industries on Rural Economy', Himalaya Publishing House, Bombay, 1987.

Venkatappiah, B. 'Recent Trends in Rural Development Objectives and Programmes', Andhra University Press, Waltair, 1974.

Venkata Reddy, K. 'Rural Development in India (Poverty & Development)', Himalaya Publishing House, Bombay, 1988.

Vidyarthi, P.L. 'Rural Development in South Asia' Concept, New Delhi, 1982.

Vivekanand, M. 'Planning Unit Areas for Integrated Rural Development', Ashish Publishing House, New Delhi, 1986.

Wadhava, Charan D. 'Rural Banks for Rural Development: An Analysis of the Working of Regional Banks in India, With Two Case Studies', MacMilan, New Delhi, 1980.

Wedderburn, Dorothy (ed.) 'Poverty, Inequality and Class Structure', Cambridge University Press, London. 1974.

Whitey M.C. 'Rural Resource Development', Mathuen and Co. Ltd., London, 1974.

Yerram Raju B. 'Agricultural Finance: Commercial Banks and Rural Development—Issues and Trends', A Data News Features Publications, New Delhi, 1982.

Yujiro, Hayani. and Ruttan, Vernon W. 'Agricultural Development: An International Perspective', The Johns Hopkins University Press, Baltimore, 1971.

Zaidi, Sayed, Sajid Husain, 'Rural India and Malnutrition: Implications, Problems & Prospects', Concepts, New Delhi, 1982.

## Reports

Adm. D.W. "Policy Issues in Rural Finance and Development" Report of the Conference of Rural Finance Research, San Diego, California, 1977.

All India Rural Debt and Investment Survey (1971-72) "Indebtedness of Rural Households and Availability of Institutional Finance, " R.B.I Bombay, 1977.

All India Rural Credit Review Committee Report, R.B.I. 1969.

Annual Reports, Ministry of Rural Development, New Delhi.

Bank of India, "Farm Business Finance-Background Paper" for Workshop on Financing Agriculture Organised at Orissa University of Agriculture and Technology, Bhubaneshwar, 1986.

Evaluation Report on the Administrative Arrangements for Rural Development PEOs Study, 1983.

Financing Agriculture by Commercial Banks—Report of a Seminar held on December 6-8, 1968, Bombay, 1968.

India, Government of, Ministry of Agriculture and Irrigation, *Reports of the National Commission on Agriculture*, 1976.

Part II, Policy and Strategy.

Part V, Resource Development.

Part VI, Crop Production, Sericulture and Agriculture.

Part VII, Animal Husbandry.

Part VIII, Fisheries.

Part IX, Forestry.

Part X, Inputs

Part XI, Research, Education and Extension.

Part XII, Supporting Services and Incentives.

Part XIII, Rural Employment and Special Area Programmes.

Part XIV.

Part XV, Agrarian Reforms.

India, Government of, Directorate of Economics and Statistics, Ministry of Agriculture and Rural Development, *Indian Agriculture in Brief*, 1985.

India, Government of, Different Five Year Plan Reports.

India, Government of, Ministry of Education, *Challenges of Education*, New Delhi, 1985.

India, Government of, *Royal Commission on Agriculture in India*, Report, Calcutta, Central Publications Bureau, 1928.

India, Government of, *India* 1987.

India, Government of, *Report on India's Food Crisis and Steps to Meet It by the Agriculture Production Team sponsored by Ford Foundation, April 1959.*

India, Government of, *Report on High-Yielding Varieties Programme* (Studies in eight districts, Kharif, 1966-67).

India, Government of, *Report of the Expert Committee on Assessment and Evaluation on the Intensive Agriculture District Programme.* (1960-68).

India, Government of, *Report of the Irrigation Commission,* 1972.

India, Government of, *The Advisory Board on Energy – Recommendations,* Sept. 1983 and Feb.1984.

Govt. of India, Planning Commission, 6th and 7th Five Year Plans, Yojna Bhawan, New Delhi, 1989.

Govt. of India, Planning Commission, "Evaluation Report on Integrated Rural Development Programme". Yojna Bhawan, New Delhi, May, 1985.

Govt. of India, Planning Commission, Report on Evaluation Study of Small Farmers, Marginal Farmers and Agricultural Labourers, Yojna Bhawan, New Delhi, 1979.

Govt. of India, Planning Commission, "Report of Working Group on District Planning", Vol. I & II, Yojna Bhawan, New Delhi, 1984.

Govt. of India, Ministry of Rural Development, "Important Circulars on IRDP (issued since 2.10.1980) Krishi Bhawan, New Delhi, July, 1982.

Govt. of India, Ministry of Rural Reconstruction, Manual on IRDP, Krishi Bhawan, New Delhi, 1980.

Institute of Financial Management & Research, "An Economic Assessment of Poverty Eradication & Rural Unemployment Programme and their Prospects," Mimeo, Madras, April, 1984.

International Communication Agency, "Proceedings of Seminar on Dynamics of Rural Development," Missourie-U.S.A., May. 23-25, 1980.

International Labour Organisation, "Human Resource Development, Objectives, Programmes and Policies," Geneva, 1968.

Management Development Institute, "Backward Area Development: Strategies and Policies," Proceedings of a Seminar, New Delhi, 1977.

National Institute of Rural Development, "Rural Development Statistics," Hyderabad, 1984.

National Bank for Agriculture & Rural Development, "Study of the Implementation of IRDP", Mimeo, NABARD, Bombay, 1985.

Rath, N., "Re-orientation of the Rural Anti-Poverty Programme: A Note—On Rural Development Vol. II, Deptt. of Rural Development, Ministry of Agriculture, New Delhi, 1985.

Report of the Expert Group on "Alleviation of Poverty", Planning Commission, Yojna Bhawan, New Delhi, 1982.

Report of the Committee to Review the "Existing Administrative Arrangements for Rural Development and Poverty Alleviation Programmes", CAARD, 1985.

Report of the working Group on the "Role of Banks in Implementation of New 20-point Programme" (Ghosh Committee), Bombay, 1981.

Report of the Committee to Review Arrangement for Institutional Credit for Agricultural and Rural Development, CRAFICARD, 1981.

Report of the Public Accounts Committee for the year 1987-88 on IRDP, Ministry of Agriculture, New Delhi 1988.

R.B.I. Report on "Guidelines for Advances to Priority Sector," Bombay, 1984.

R.B.I.'s Important Ciculars for IRDP", Bombay, 1984.

R.B.I., Report on "Marginal farmers and Agricultural Labourers Development Agencies," 1973 (Field Study) Bombay, 1976.

R.B.I. Report on "Priority Sector Lending and the 20-Point Economic Programme—Role of Banks," Bombay, 1981.

UNCTAD, "The Least Developed Countries: 1984 Report," U.N.O., New York, 1984 Annex. 1985.

World Bank, "Demography and Poverty", World Bank Staff Working Paper No. 623 by Michael Lipton, Washington D.C., 1983.

World Bank, "Poverty and Hunger: Issues and Options for Food Security in Developing Countries." Washington D.C., 1986.

World Bank, "Poverty Undernutrition and Hunger," World Bank, Staff Working Paper No. 597 by Michael Lipton, Washington D.C., 1988.

World Bank, "Rural Development: Sector Policy Paper," Washington D.C., 1975.

World Bank, "Agricultural Credit Sector Policy Paper," Washington D.C., 1975.

World Bank, "The Assault on World Poverty," Baltimore, John Hopkins University Press, USA, 1975.

Y. Venugopal Reddy, "Multilevel Planning with Special Reference to District Planning: Some Issues," Seminar on District Planning Lal Bahadur Shastri Academy of Administration, Mussoorie, 1973.

❑ ❑ ❑